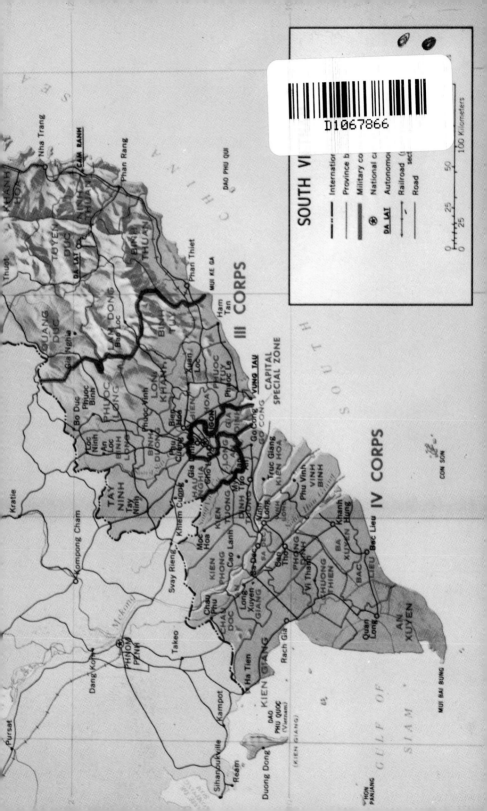

SOUTH VI...

International ...
Province b...
Military co...
National c...
DA LAT Autonomo...
Railroad (...
           sect
Road

0   25   50   100 Kilometers
0   25

D1067866

III CORPS

IV CORPS

CAPITAL
SPECIAL ZONE

S O U T H

G U L F   O F

S I A M

VIETNAM FOLLY

by

U. S. SENATOR ERNEST GRUENING

and

HERBERT WILTON BEASER

THE NATIONAL PRESS INC., 128 C STREET, N. E.
WASHINGTON, D. C. 20002

Library of Congress Catalogue Card No. 67-29093

DEDICATED

to the courageous men and women of the

ARMED FORCES OF THE UNITED STATES IN VIETNAM

"Theirs not to reason why..."

Permissions to Quote

TABLE OF CONTENTS

Preface i

I. The Dilemma. 1

II. Vietnam to its Colonialization. 29

III. French Indochina. 38

IV. Vietnam During World War II. 45

V. Vietnam: Hostage to the Cold War. 56

VI. Korea and Vietnam: 1950-1954. 62

VII. The French-Indochina War. 75

VIII. Brinkmanship - 1954 Style. 82

IX. Failure of the "Mission of Peace Through
     Strength." 96

X. Four Days that Almost Shook the World. 105

XI. The 1954 Geneva Conference. 111

XII. The Geneva Accords. 118

XIII. The Seato Treaty and What it Really Means. 128

XIV. Dgo Dinh Diem Takes Over In South Vietnam. 135

XV. Ngo Dinh Diem Consolidates His Position - And
     His Power 146

XVI. Why The Vietnam Elections Were Not Held
     In 1956. 158

XVII. Cease-Fire, Regroupment, Exodus and Repression. .. 169

XVIII. The Origins and Character of the Civil War
     In Vietnam. 179

XIX. Beginning of United States Military Escalation. 189

XX. Kennedy and Vietnam - Year of Decision - 1961. .. 198

XXI. Kennedy and Vietnam - The Later Years. 213

XXII.   Growing Disenchantment and Increasing
           Involvement In Vietnam. _____ 228

XXIII.   The Gulf of Tonkin Incident and Resolution. _____ 236

XXIV.   Building The Image, A "Man of Peace". _____ 251

XXV.   Open Ended Escalation. _____ 262

XXVI.   Congress Abdicates. _____ 285

XXVII.   United States "Peace Offensives." _____ 293

XXVIII.   The Congress Dissents. _____ 301

XXIX.   The Congress Dissents-But Consents. _____ 312

XXX.   Vietnam Folly-Its Effects at Home. _____ 327

XXXI.   Vietnam Folly-Its Effects On South Vietnam. _____ 345

XXXII.   Toward Peace In Vietnam. _____ 370

Chapter Notes. _____ 387

Appendix. _____ 406

Selected Bibliography _____ 650

Index. _____ 653

PREFACE

This book was written to set forth—as simply as possible—the authors' reasons for opposing, since early in 1964, the escalating United States military involvement in Vietnam.

While the book is thoroughly documented, it is not intended as the definitive history either of that involvement or of Vietnam. Others have done that. Neither is it intended as a detailed record of the military engagements between the Vietnamese and the Chinese, the French, the Japanese or the Americans. Military tacticians and historians have recorded and will record and evaluate the battles of all the armies which have crisscrossed the terrain of Vietnam for over two thousand years.

A number of crucial episodes in the tragic involvement of the United States militarily in Vietnam will be examined in detail.

Some of those are:

• the decision to support—with money and material—the efforts of the French after World War II to reestablish control over Indochina;

• the assumption of responsibility by the United States in Vietnam after the defeat of the French forces in 1954;

• the causes underlying the refusal of South Vietnam to hold the reunifying elections in 1956 called for by the Geneva Accords;

- the circumstances surrounding the Gulf of Tonkin incident;
- the many instances in which the Congress abdicted its responsibilities;
- the military escalation of the war in 1965 as the United States sought to achieve a military solution to a civil war.

As the feeling has grown in the country that the United States is mired in a war in which no end is in sight, it has become fashionable to say: "Never mind how we got into this mess in the first place—the fact remains that we are THERE!"

The authors have a contrary conviction.

An informed opinion on the course of action which the United States should now pursue with respect to Vietnam can only be reached by a thorough understanding of the events which brought about the present impasse.

On October 12, 1967, Secretary of State Dean Rusk stated that he could not understand how those who supported United States military intervention in 1964, when the Congress voted in favor of the Tonkin Gulf resolution, could now reverse themselves. However, many already have. And this book is written with the conviction that if more of the American people became aware of the basic mis-calculations which have brought the United States, step by step, to its present dilemma, the greater would be the number opposing its present course.

In the preparation of this volume, the persons who have assisted have been too numerous to thank individually, not to mention the thousands upon thousands who have written. We are grateful for their assistance.

The opinions, observations and recommendations are solely those of the authors.

The Authors

Washington, D.C.

CHAPTER I

THE DILEMMA

The "dirty little war" in Vietnam has now escalated into a "dirty BIG war," involving hundreds of thousands of United States fighting men—with the end nowhere in sight.

How did the United States become involved in a land war ten thousand miles from its shores—a land war which General MacArthur and General Ridgway had warned against and in which President Johnson in 1964 had promised not to engage?

It would have been comparatively easy to describe and assess United States foreign policy in November of 1964. Intervening events have drastically altered any such assessment. At that time, President Johnson had overwhelmingly defeated Barry Goldwater on issues that seemed clear to the great majority of Americans.

On the domestic front the major issue was civil rights, a cause which President Johnson had strongly supported. His presidential opponent, Senator Goldwater, had opposed and voted against civil rights legislation.

In the foreign field, Goldwater had supported and preached a belligerent foreign policy, giving the impression that he supported any military efforts needed to "win" the war in Vietnam—whatever that meant. President Johnson's campaign utterances conveyed the impression to millions of Americans that he would achieve peaceful solutions to U.S. entanglements in Southeast Asia.

Most Americans hoped that, with President Johnson's election, the United States would be able to extricate itself from its limited military involvement in Southeast Asia. The United States was represented there only by military "advisers." This widespread hope was clearly responsible for the magnitude of President Johnson's electoral victory.

As far as foreign policy was concerned the American verdict was virtually unanimous. Five States—South Carolina, Georgia, Mississippi, Alabama and Louisiana—were carried by Goldwater wholly on the race issue, and Arizona by a small margin because of its peoples' affection for their native son.

No presidential election in recent times, perhaps ever, was so clearly based on such simplified and accepted convictions. To the majority of voters, Barry Goldwater represented a trigger-happy jingo; Johnson a mature statesman, experienced in government and aware of the solemn responsibilities of his high office. One would get the United States into war; the other would keep it out.

Since the 1964 election, however, the Johnson Administration has steadily—hour by hour, day by day, month by month—escalated the war in Vietnam. Bombing raids against North Vietnam have increased in scope and intensity while the number of United States troops committed to ground action in South Vietnam has steadily increased so that by November, 1967 it was reported that they numbered more than 500,000, with more on the way.

Since November of 1964 the Johnson Administration has committed itself, and thereby the United States, by executive action alone, to a vast military venture in Southeast Asia, the ends and grave consequences of which cannot be foreseen. It violates the long-standing assumption of Americans, who consider themselves a people cherishing the rule of law, firm in their adherence to treaty commitments, seeking to practice what they preach, and striving to exemplify in their international conduct rectitude and good faith for all mankind to see, to admire, and to use as an example.

In the fall of 1964, Americans had much to be proud of. The United States in the preceding decades had come close to achieving a generally accepted image of high purpose and deeds.

The United States had foresworn the pursuit of "manifest destiny" which took it into the war with Mexico in the 1840's; had aban-

Mauldin in The Chicago Sun-Times

*The "dirty little war" in Vietnam has now escalated into a
"dirty BIG war."*

doned the imperialism of half a century later in its war with Spain and the subsequent "gunboat diplomacy" which led to the Marine occupations of the Dominican Republic, Haiti and Nicaragua; and had reversed its policy of armed interventions in Mexico in 1914 and 1916, and of subsequent non-recognition of Mexican regimes to seek to compel them to abandon their revolution-born land reform policies when they affected American properties.

After the election of 1964—after President Johnson was sworn in in his own right as the elected President of the United States—events moved swiftly to an acceleration of United States military involvement in Vietnam. Because the facts concerning United States involvement in this undeclared war differ so widely from the repeatedly proclaimed and generally accepted Administration position, it will be necessary to present these facts in some detail and make clear that there is ample, unbiased documentation to confirm them. And in presenting them it is necessary to go back to their beginnings.

Of late a new "line" has emerged from the seats of power in Washington.

This "line" is that the past should be forgotten. In effect this "line" says that there is no use crying over spilled milk—or perhaps we should say spilled blood—that the United States is in Vietnam in strength now and must face that reality and proceed from there.

But any possible solution to this grave predicament cannot be disentangled from the origins and subsequent course of American involvement. It is impossible to know where the United States can and should go unless it knows where it has been.

How did it all begin?

In the middle and later decades of the 19th century the European powers—Britain, France, Germany, Spain, Portugal, Belgium, the Netherlands, and Italy—extended their colonial rule by invading and occupying all of Africa and much of Asia and Oceania—the Monroe Doctrine precluding most of Latin America from similar incursions.

In Southeast Asia the French carved out a colony called Indochina. It was not one indigenous nation. It was composed of three nations—Laos, Cambodia, and Vietnam—each with its own historical, independent background. During World War II, Indochina was overrun by the Japanese. Fighting to liberate this area were the Vietnamese and the Allied Forces at war with Japan. The Vietnamese forces were led by a man named Ho Chi Minh who desired to establish the independence of one part of this colony— Vietnam. He was considered a hero by his people. He has been referred to as their George Washington, although it must be left to future historians to assess the appropriateness of this ascription. He was, however, Moscow-trained and a Communist. Whether he was more nationalist than Communist also must be left for future determination.

These native aspirations were part of the world-wide revolt against colonialism which has given birth to 77 countries since World War II, not including two Koreas, two Germanys and two Vietnams.

But in 1945 the French wanted to regain their Southeast Asian colonial possessions, which they called Indochina.[1]

Because of the fear that China, which shortly before had been taken over by Communists, might also take over this area, the Eisenhower Administration was urged to assist the French militarily in restoring their former colony. Certain voices in the United States, notably those of Vice President Richard Nixon and Admiral Arthur Radford, urged all-out assistance. Others, such as General Matthew Ridgway, advised against it. After exploring the situation in Congress, whose support he deemed necessary for such military action, President Eisenhower declined to send our troops into combat.

Nevertheless, the United States continued to give the French substantial financial assistance (over $2 billion) and cooperation through a military mission established in Saigon.

But lacking this all-out support the French were defeated by the local forces, the Viet Minh, suffered staggering losses, and surrendered at Dien Bien Phu on May 7, 1954.

The day before, a meeting had convened at Geneva of representatives of ten nations.* Accords were ultimately drawn up which provided that three new nations should be created from the former

---

*The nations were: Cambodia, the Democratic Government of Vietnam (North Vietnam), France, Laos, the People's Republic of China, the State of Vietnam (South Vietnam), the Union of Soviet Socialist Republics, the United Kingdom, and the United States of America.

French colony—namely Laos, Cambodia, and Vietnam. The Accords provided that Vietnam was to be temporarily—but only temporarily—divided into North and South Vietnam for reasons of demobilization, and with the stipulation that within two years an election would be held to choose the officials who would govern the re-united Vietnamese.

The United States was in South Vietnam with its small military mission at Saigon and, upon the military and political demise of the French after Dien Bien Phu, took charge. It was the United States that brought Ngo Dinh Diem back from monastic life in the United States, installed him as President of the Council of Ministers and, in a subsequent rigged plebiscite, backed him successfully against the playboy Emperor Bao Dai.

The United States did not sign the Geneva Accords of 1954 but pledged support of them in a unilateral statement.

The statement by Under Secretary of State, Walter Bedell Smith, dated July 21, 1954, and confirmed the same day by a statement issued by President Eisenhower, was declared by the Under Secretary to be a unilateral declaration of United States position on these points:

(1) The United States would refrain from the threat or the use of force to disturb the Accords;

(2) The United States would view renewed aggression with "grave concern" and as "seriously threatening international peace and security";

(3) The United States, with respect to "nations divided against their will," would continue to seek to achieve their unity through free elections supervised by the United Nations.

It is interesting to note that in the unilateral declaration issued by the United States mention is made only of Vietnam, not South Vietnam or North Vietnam, but Vietnam, and the United States reiterated its traditional position that the peoples of Vietnam were entitled "to determine their own future."

The official justification for the United States ever-increasing involvement in an undeclared land war in Southeast Asia varied over the years.

It was set forth by President Johnson in his State of the Union message in January 1965 in these words:

"We are there, first, because a friendly nation has asked us for help against Communist aggression. Ten years ago we pledged our help. Three Presidents have supported that pledge. We will not break it."

He elaborated on this statement in his Johns Hopkins speech on April 4, 1965, saying:

"Why are we in South Vietnam?

"We are there because we have a promise to keep. Since 1954 every American President has offered support to the people of South Vietnam. We have helped to build, and we have helped to defend. Thus, over many years, we have made a national pledge to help South Vietnam defend its independence.

"I intend to keep that promise. To dishonor that pledge . . . would be an unforgivable wrong."

But a careful analysis of the promises of support made by "every American President" since 1954—President Eisenhower and President Kennedy—clearly indicates that neither President promised to send American forces into South Vietnam to fight.

President Eisenhower's proffer—not promise—is admittedly contained in his letter of October 23, 1954 to President Diem, as President of the Council of Ministers of Vietnam. (See Appendix)

After telling Diem about the concern that had been caused about the future of Vietnam—"a country temporarily divided by an artificial military grouping, weakened by a long and exhausting war and faced with enemies without and by their subversive collaborators within"—President Eisenhower went on to discuss the request for aid which had been received from Diem. The request for "aid to assist . . . in the movement of several hundred thousand loyal Vietnamese "who wanted to move South of the 17th parallel." He expressed pleasure that the United States was able to assist in this humanitarian effort.

The letter says nothing about a further request by President Diem for assistance. The only request of record was limited to assistance in moving the refugees from the north to the south. There was nothing to indicate that Diem was asking and President Eisenhower was responding to a request for "help against Communist aggression."

The letter then went on to tell Diem that we—the United States—had been "exploring ways and means to permit our aid to Vietnam to make a greater contribution to the welfare and stability of the Government of Vietnam." President Eisenhower then told Diem that he had instructed the United States Ambassador to Vietnam to "examine" with Diem how aid given directly to Vietnam could assist it "in its present hour of trial."

But President Eisenhower conditioned the proffer of direct aid. It would be given "provided your Government is prepared to give assurances as to the standards of performance it would be able to maintain in the event such aid were supplied."

Then another condition was added to the offer:

"The Government of the United States expects that this aid will be *met by performance on the part of the Government of Vietnam in undertaking needed reforms.*" (Emphasis supplied)

The needed reforms which were a condition of United States aid were never undertaken.

President Eisenhower's letter contained a third condition. Such aid—"combined with your own continuing efforts"—the United States Government hoped, would contribute "toward an independent Vietnam endowed with a strong government." President Eisenhower said he hoped that such a government would be "responsive to the nationalist aspirations of its people," that it would be "enlightened in its purpose", and that it would be "effective in its performance" so that it would be "respected at home and abroad."

The Government of Vietnam was none of these.

It was so little respected at home that a widely supported civil war broke out against it.

It was so little respected abroad that United States Ambassador Henry Cabot Lodge supported the removal of Diem and his relatives.

But in any event there was nothing in President Eisenhower's letter about sending in United States troops. There was no promise or pledge of United States military involvement.

This is further confirmed by a White House statement of November 3, 1954, in which President Eisenhower instructed General J. Lawton Collins, as his special representative, "to explore" with

President Diem and his government how "to help them with their critical problems and to supplement measures adopted by the Vietnamese themslves." Again, no mention of any request by Diem for or offer by President Eisenhower of United States military aid. Had there been, it is hardly likely that such a request or assent thereto would not have been mentioned. That is why it seems clear that the United States asked itself in.

If further confirmation is needed to show that only economic aid was intended to be given to Vietnam by President Eisenhower, there is his own statement of August 17, 1965, in which he said: "We said we would help that country. We were not talking about military programs, but foreign aid."

During the remaining six years of the Eisenhower administration, the United States had a military mission in Vietnam which did not exceed some 600 officers and men; none engaged in combat.

No American lives were lost in combat during that period!

President John F. Kennedy was persuaded by his Secretary of Defense, Robert McNamara, to escalate the United States commitment to the extent of sending additional military advisors. Their number rose, before the end of his presidency, to some 16,500, due to the deteriorating military and political situation in South Vietnam.

But as late as September 2, 1963, less than three months before his death, in an interview with CBS newscaster, Walter Cronkite, President Kennedy said:

"I don't think that unless a greater effort is made by that Government to win popular support that the war can be won out there."

President Kennedy had reached the conclusion that Diem had not fulfilled Eisenhower's conditions although he had had nine years, from 1954 to 1963, to do so.

And then President Kennedy went on to say during the interview:

"In the final analysis it is their war. They are the ones who have to win it or lose it. We can give them equipment, we can send our men out there as advisers, but they have to win it— the people of Vietnam—against the Communists. We are prepared to continue to assist them, but I don't think that the war can be won unless the people support the effort, and in my opinion, in the last two months the Government has gotten out of touch with the people."

This record clearly proves that neither under President Eisenhower nor under President Kennedy was "a national pledge" made to support the Government of South Vietnam by sending in American troops to fight the Vietcong.

Almost two months to the day after President Kennedy's interview, in which he uttered the prophetic words that "the Government (of South Vietnam) has gotten out of touch with the people," Diem was overthrown and killed. From the very inception of his administration, President Diem had been out of touch with the people. He had little popular support among the Vietnamese people, being widely viewed throughout Vietnam as the puppet of the United States. Instead of seeking popular support by carrying out the economic and social reforms President Eisenhower had made conditional in return for aid, Diem sought to rule by repression. He jailed thousands of people without trial; built up, with United States assistance, a ruthless secret police force; and generally terrorized the populace.

But there were other reasons for the outbreak of civil war in South Vietnam. Diem, with U.S. concurrence, or as some have put it, at United States urging, repudiated the provision in the Geneva Accords to hold general elections for the reunification of Vietnam in July 1956. This was one of the most basic items in the Geneva Accords. The United States unilateral commitment to it was made by Walter Bedel Smith, Under Secretary of State, when he stated that:

"In the case of nations now divided against their will, we shall continue to seek to achieve unity through free elections . . . ."

Yet, the United States, which dominated the situation in South Vietnam, which filled the vacuum left by the French withdrawal, approved and ratified the Diem government's refusal to hold the elections. Both Administrations refused to hold them for the reason, frankly stated, that Ho Chi Minh would be elected President.

What principles does the United States espouse when after agreeing to the holding of an election calls it off because it feels its side is going to lose? That is the unquestionable record on this issue. How can the United States square that with its national conscience and its tradition that free elections should be inviolate under its standards?

One of the partial myths on which the Administration bases its actions is that the whole trouble—not just part of it—stems from agression from Hanoi. To make this theory plausible the Administration has had to deny that there is a civil war going on in South Vietnam. No one could have been better informed on this issue than John F. Kennedy, who was elected to the House of Representatives in 1946, was in the Senate from 1954 to 1960, was a member of its Foreign Relations Committee and who, in his news conference of July 18, 1963, referred to "the civil war which has gone on (in South Vietnam) for 10 years."

Returning from a three-week visit to South Vietnam in the winter of 1965, Senator Stephen Young (D. Ohio), a combat veteran in World War II and a member of the Senate Armed Services Committee, reported on the floor of the Senate on February 6th, 1966, about what he had found:

"This is a civil war going on in Vietnam. Before I visited Southeast Asia, it had been my belief that the Vietcong fighting in South Vietnam were communists and infiltrators from the North. But I had not been in Vietnam for more than 4 days— and during that period of time, I was in every area of Vietnam —when almost immeditately I observed very definitely that we were involved in a miserable civil war in the steaming jungles and rice paddies of South Vietnam. I learned from General Westmoreland that the bulk of the Vietcong fighting in South Vietnam were born and reared in South Vietnam. I learned from General Stillwell and other Generals that 80 percent of the Vietcong fighting the Americans and the South Vietnamese in the Mekong Delta . . . were born and reared in that . . . area."

The newspaper columnist, Clayton Fritchey, stated in "The Other Civil War in South Vietnam," a dispatch from Saigon in December, 1966:

"Secretary of State Dean Rusk says 'we are trying to see that North Vietnam doesn't seize South Vietnam by force, and we'll accomplish that.' Yet it is all too clear that North Vietnamese have already seized South Vietnam, and are running it by undisguised force.

"The secretary would be on better ground if he admitted the fighting here is not only a civil war between north and south, but in addition is a civil war between two rival northern groups for control of the south."[2]

Fritchey went on to point out that most of the ruling generals in South Vietnam were from the North and had fought with the French in their recolonialization attempt—just as the Tories sided with the British in the American Revolutionary War—so that there was deep resentment on the part of those who did not collaborate with the French, many of whom have been replaced in government jobs by northerners.

When interviewed on television on August 1, 1966, four veteran reporters discussed United States news policies in Saigon. They were Dean Brelis of the National Broadcasting Company; Malcolm Browne, formerly of the Associated Press and a Pulitzer Prize winner, who had been in Vietnam for four years; Charles Mohr, of *The New York Times,* who had also been in Saigon a considerable time; and Jack Foisie, a star correspondent for *The Los Angeles Times,* also an old Asia hand. As reported in *The New York Times* for August 2, 1966:

"He (Malcolm Browne) said the Administration, and particularly Secretary (of Defense Robert S.) McNamara have deliberately misled American public opinion.' An example of this, he said, is 'the continual harping on the North Vietnamese aggression.' Mr. Browne said the war in Vietnam was basically a civil war. The three other correspondents agreed."

The reason for the consistent denial by the Administration of the basic character of the conflict in South Vietnam was made clear by Under Secretary of State George W. Ball in February 1966 in a speech to the Northwestern Alumni Association at Evanston, Illinois. He said then: "If the Vietnam war were merely what the Communists say it is—an indigenous rebellion—then the United States would have no business taking sides in the conflict and helping one side to defeat the other by force of arms."

There are other commitments more binding on the United States and mitigating against its military involvement in Vietnam than the one most frequently cited by President Johnson: "We have a promise to keep. Since 1954 every American President has offered support to the people of South Vietnam." (See Appendix)

Chapter 3, Article 16, of the agreement on the cessation of hostilities in Vietnam—the Geneva Accords an agreement which the United States by unilateral declaration agreed to adhere to— forbids the introduction into Vietnam of any troop reinforcements . . . additional military personnel . . . (and) all types of arms, munitions and other war material." (See Appendix)

The Geneva Accords provided for an International Commission to supervise the carrying of their provisions in Vietnam. The Commission consisted of three representatives: one from Canada, one from India, and one from Poland. Over the years it made various reports which indicated increasing violations of the agreements by **both** parties. A careful, objective reading of these reports from the very beginning shows clearly that the violations by the South Vietnamese under United States tutelage and with United States military assistance were far more serious and far more extensive.

Thus, for example, in its special report on June 2, 1962, the Commission complained of the fact that South Vietnam had persistently denied the Commission's inspectors "the right to control and inspect" and for that reason the Commission could not report precisely how many military personnel and how much war material had been brought into South Vietnam. Even so the Commission reported that in the five month period from December 3, 1961 to May 5, 1962 the Commission observed, but did not control, coming into South Vietnam, "173 military personnel, 62 helicopters, . . . 57 fighters/fighter bombers, 25 transport aircraft . . . 102 jeeps . . . 29 armoured fighting vehicle trailers, 404 other trailers . . . 5 visiting aircraft carriers and spares of various kinds . . ." (See Appendix)

In the same report the Commission found, with respect to North Vietnam, "that there was evidence to show that armed and unarmed personnel, arms and other supplies had been sent from the North to the South with the purpose of supporting, organizing and carrying out hostile activities including armed attacks . . ." (See Appendix)

These violations on both sides were charged by the Canadian and Indian Representatives who may well be credited with impartiality. The Polish delegate, whose report may not be accepted as unbiased, refused to join in the indictment of the charges against North Vietnam but joined with his colleagues in those against the South.

There are other treaty violations as well. The United States is a signatory to the United Nations Charter. In fact, the United States was largely instrumental in creating the United Nations.

In Paragraph 4 of Chapter 1 of Article 2 of the Charter the Members agreed to refrain from the "threat or use of force against the territorial integrity or political independence" of any nation or to act in any other manner inconsistent with the purposes of the Charter.

Under Chapter 6 of Article 33 the Members agreed that parties to any dispute likely to endanger the maintenance of international peace and security "SHALL FIRST OF ALL" try to arrive at a solution by (1) negotiation, (2) inquiry, (3) mediation, (4) conciliation, (5) arbitration, (6) judicial settlement, (7) resort to regional agencies or arrangements, or (8) other peaceful means of their own choice.

The latter Article does not say that the parties to a dispute MAY utilize the eight negotiating methods enumerated specifically in the Article. The Article uses the term *"shall,"* making those methods mandatory upon the signatories to the United Nations Charter.

When there were violations of the Geneva Accords, the answer of the United States was to speed the military buildup in South Vietnam. Did the United States seek a solution by arbitration? It did not. Did it seek a solution by judicial settlement? It did not. Did it seek a solution by resorting to regional agencies or arrangements? It did not. Nor did it seek a solution by "other peaceful means" of its own choice. All these specified requirements under Article 33 of the Charter of the United Nations were ignored—and hence violated—by the United States.

One of the "regional agencies or arrangements" whose aid the United States might have invoked for a peaceful solution was the Southeast Asia Treaty Organization which was created under the leadership of Secretary of State John Foster Dulles and whose signatories were the United States, Australia, France, New Zealand, Pakistan, the Philippines, Thailand, and the United Kingdom. The parties, in Article I, reaffirmed the agreement:

"as set forth in the Charter of the United Nations, to settle any international disputes by peaceful means so that international peace, security and justice are not endangered, and to refrain from the threat or use of force in any manner inconsistent with the purposes of the United Nations."

Thus having used force, the United States was also violating the SEATO treaty. (See Appendix)

The violation of Article 2, paragraph 4, Chapter 1 of the Geneva Accords of 1954 (which was specifically mentioned by Under Secretary Walter Bedell Smith's declaration of United States policy which it would adhere to) and the violation of Article 33, Chapter 6, of the United Nations Charter, which provides for the settlement of disputes by peaceful means, have already been mentioned. Another violation was that of Article 37 which provides that if parties to a dispute of the matters referred to in Article 33 fail to settle it by the means indicated in that Article they shall refer it to the Security Council. The word used again is "shall" and not "may." The United States has not done that. (See Appendix)

So when those in authority in Washington speak of "a national pledge" as a justification for our course of action in Vietnam, it is difficult not to contrast that dubious, conditional, qualified, tentative proffer of aid to a now vanished South Vietnamese chief of state—who did not fulfill the requested conditions for such aid—with the United States violations of its unqualified treaty commitments, of which there could be no more solemn category—the United Nations charter, the Southeast Asia treaty, the violation of the unilateral statement by Under Secretary Walter Bedell Smith, reiterated on the same day by President Eisenhower, and the pledge of the United States that it would support supervised Vietnam elections in 1956.

When the dubiousness of relying upon the claim that the United States was asked in by a friendly government to protect it from aggression from without was pointed out, Administration spokesmen began relying upon the provisions of the SEATO treaty.

Thus, testifying before the Senate Committee on Foreign Relations on February 18, 1966, Secretary of State Dean Rusk stated:

"... in joining SEATO the United States took a solemn treaty engagement of far-reaching effect. Article IV, paragraph 1, provides that—'each party recognizes that aggression by means of armed attack ... would endanger its own peace and safety, and agrees that it will in that event act to meet the common danger in accordance with its constitutional processes.'

"It is this fundamental SEATO obligation that has from the outset guided our actions in South Vietnam.

"If the United States determines that an armed attack has occurred ... then it is obliged 'to act to meet the common danger' without regard to the views or actions of any other treaty member."[3]

Secretary of State Rusk quoted only one portion of Article IV of the SEATO Treaty.

This article covers two possible situations.

The first is where there is "aggression by means of armed attack." The obligation of a signatory to the SEATO treaty, in these circumstances, would be to "act to meet the common danger in accordance with its constitutional processes" and to report such action immediately to the Security Council of the United Nations.

For the United States, "in accordance with its constitutional processes" would mean a declaration of war by the Congress under the provisions of Article I, Section 8, of the United States Constitution, which provides:

"The Congress shall have power ... To declare War ..." This is what the United States Senate was told this provision meant when it was asked to ratify the SEATO treaty.

Congress has not declared war against any nation in Southeast Asia. Neither has the Administration asked it to do so.

In addition, the United States did not fulfill the requirement for an immediate notification to the Security Council of the United Nations.

If, as the Administration has claimed, it is not a civil war that is going on in South Vietnam but rather "aggression from the north," then it should have been reported to the Security Council, under the provisions of the SEATO Treaty, long before Ambassador Stevenson's report after the Gulf of Tonkin incident.

The second situation covered by Article IV of the SEATO Treaty is where the "inviolability or the integrity of the territory or the sovereignty or political independence" of a Party is "threatened in any way other than by armed attack or is affected or threatened by any fact or situation which might endanger the peace of the area." In such a situation, the only obligation on the parties is to consult with each other. The "parties [did not] consult immediately" as required nor, indeed, did they "consult" at all.

In either situation, any action had to be taken at the invitation or with the consent of the government concerned.

It was therefore important, to enable the United States to justify its position, that it have in South Vietnam a government which would invite it in and to deny—because there had been no consultation with the other signatories to the SEATO Treaty—that it was a civil war.

Secretary of State John Foster Dulles issued a statement right after the signing of the SEATO Treaty which explained his theory of massive retaliation in support of the Treaty rather than committing the United States military to fighting a land war in Southeast Asia. Secretary of State Dulles said:

"We considered at Manila how to implement the treaty. One possibility was to create a joint military force. However, I explained that the U. S. responsibilities were so vast and so far flung that we believed that we would serve best, not by earmarking forces for particular areas of the Far East, but by developing the deterrent of mobile striking power, plus strategically placed reserves."

While we are puncturing some of the myths of why the United States is in Vietnam with more than 500,000 ground troops, and some 50,000 troops in Thailand, in addition to the men of the Seventh fleet offshore, let us puncture the major myth that the aggressor is North Vietnam. Of course, it is necessary for the Administration to assert this as a collary to a denial that the United States is interfering in a civil war. It is true that there has been and is increasing infiltration from the North but this infiltration began considerably after the United States escalation in arms, in violation of the Geneva Accords.

When one reads the various books written by objective observers —David Halberstam, of *The New York Times, The Makings of a*

Quagmire; Malcolm Browne, of the Associated Press, *The New Face of War,* both Pulitzer prize winners; and others—it is clear that up through the middle of 1963 virtually all the arms used by the Vietcong were either captured weapons of American make or were French weapons left over after France's unsuccessful attempt to recolonialize Vietnam. After military escalation by the United States, substantial and increasing help began flowing from the North, bringing to the Vietcong sophisticated and improved weapons.

It is painful to admit this, but we can come to no other conclusion but that it is the United States that is the aggressor in Vietnam. The United States is the intruder, the outsider who barged into a quarrel between Vietnamese and was largely responsible, because of the actions of its man Diem and its denial of promised elections, for that quarrel. The United States came half way 'round the globe to enter into that quarrel, violating solemn treaty commitments in the process. South Vietnam is a political entity only by United States say-so. It was continued in existence in violation of treaty commitments, and hence has no valid legal or juridical existence.

South Vietnam is sustained only by United States arms and funds. Its ephemeral regimes are self-imposed and respond to no popular desire. There have been eight coups since the fall of Diem in 1963. One of the "white hopes" of the United States is Nguyen Cao Ky, a school dropout who, when asked by a London newspaper who his heroes were, replied: "I have only one, Adolph Hitler."

The shabbiness of the Thieu-Ky regime is a reflection on the whole character of United States involvement in Vietnam. As pointed out in the October 2, 1967 issue of *Newsweek,* more Americans were drafted in August, 1967, than were drafted by South Vietnam in the preceding 6 months. In 1965, there were 96,000 deserters from the South Vietnamese Army; in 1966 this number rose to 110,000. And yet the United States is sending its boys, regulars and draftees, to fight and die in a cause that has such doubtful support from those whose cause it should be. Or is it? Can one blame those South Vietnamese deserters for not supporting corrupt and malodorous coup-imposed juntas?

Now to review briefly what has happened in Congress: In August of 1964 it was reported that two, or possibly three, PT boats had attacked the United States Seventh Fleet in international waters in the Tonkin Gulf, off the coast of North Vietnam. It is questionable whether the full facts have yet been revealed to the American people. If the incident happened as reported, then it was an unprovoked act of aggression. As an unprovoked aggressive act against the United States, the President was wholly within his rights and powers to order a retaliatory attack by airplanes from the fleet on the PT boats. We may have to find out what the facts really were. One version that has filtered through is that South Vietnamese vessels and troops were raiding the North Vietnamese coast, that American warships were standing by and were in line of the fire of the North Vietnamese vessels in their repelling of the South Vietnamese attack. Actually not a single United States vessel was hit or a United States serviceman injured.

Be that as it may, the next day a resolution, drafted in the White House, was submitted to the Congress that not merely approved everything that had been done before in Southeast Asia, but gave the President unlimited power in his own discretion to use the armed forces of the United States anywhere in Southeast Asia.

The Resolution passed the House unanimously, and in the Senate there were two opposing votes—those of Senator Wayne Morse (D, Ore.) and Senator Ernest Gruening (D, Alaska), although a handful of Senators did express doubts about giving the President this unlimited, unrestricted power out of which the steadily escalating United States military involvement stems. For one thing, as already noted, the Constitution of the United States is specific that only Congress can declare war. The United States is now at war, and in the judgment of Senator Wayne Morse, a constitutional lawyer, and numerous other legal scholars, it is thereby in violation of the Constitution of the United States.[4]

In February of 1965, the United States started bombing North Vietnam. The justification for this drastic change of policy was that there had been an attack on one of the United States outposts at Pleiku. Pleiku is about 200 miles south of the 17th parallel, the boundary between North and South Vietnam. At night a group of Viet Cong passed through the lines of the South Vietnamese troops who were either too inert or uninterested to alert the United States soldiers in the barracks. The Viet Cong opened fire with a mortar of American make, which they had apparently secured from the South

Vietnamese forces, and killed 8 American soldiers. There was no direct relation between this incident and North Vietnamese infiltration.

Pulitzer prize winner Malcolm Browne, then the Associated Press chief correspondent in that area, arrived on the scene of the Pleiku incident shortly after the attack and described what he saw in these words:

"The enemy force consisted of several infantry assault squads and several mortar crews, its total strength being probably fewer than 50 men. Their 'sophisticated weapons' (several of which were defective and left behind) were wire cutters to get through the perimeter fence, American hand grenades, and a large number of TNT blocks wrapped into pole bombs made from palm leaves, vine thongs, and bamboo. These charges, which were placed on or under aircraft by the raiders, did most of the damage at Pleiku. In addition, several mortar crews (whose location was kept secret by the local population) fired many shells into the base from a supposedly secure hamlet a few hundred yards away. All this weaponry was more sophisticated than spears, but not much advanced over 18th century devices. And the explosives appeared to have been extracted from captured American shells."[5]

Senator Mike Mansfield, Senate majority leader, has made the uncontroverted statement that: "When the sharp increase in the American military effort began in early 1965, it was estimated that only 400 North Vietnamese soldiers were among the enemy [indigenous South Vietnamese] forces in the south which totaled 140,000 at that time."[6] Regardless of the uncontroverted fact that North Vietnamese infiltration had been so low compared to the number of indigenous troops, the Pleiku incident was made the justification for the bombings of North Vietnam which, except for short suspensions, have continued in mounting numbers with no appreciable result, These bombings appear rather to have hardened the determination of the North Vietnamese to continue what they have been doing and to increase their aid to the South Vietnamese National Army of Liberation.

As Pultizer Prize-winning historian Arthur Schlesinger, Jr. pointed out in a major address in Washington, D. C. on October 8, 1967, after 32 months of increased bombing of North Vietnam, "the statistics show that more than half the Americans killed in the Vietnam war . . . were killed since the beginning of this (1967) year . . . during the period of the most intense escalation . . . the number of American deaths declined during the bombing pause of last February. The statistics . . . strongly suggest that the way to increase casualties is to escalate the war — the way to reduce casualties is to slow down the war."

In May 1965, the President sent to Congress an appropriation request of $700 million to conduct this undeclared war in Vietnam. President Johnson frankly stated that this request was being made not because monies were needed to supply U. S. armed forces in Vietnam (he could have transferred the money needed from other sources) but rather was being used as a vehicle to secure additional Congressional approval of his carrying on the war in Vietnam and anywhere else in Southeast Asia that he saw fit. This the President made clear at the onset of his message, when he stated:

"This is not a routine appropriation. For each Member of Congress who supports this request is also voting to persist in our effort to halt Communist aggression in South Vietnam. Each is saying that the Congress and the President stand united before the world in joint determination that the independence of South Vietnam shall be preserved and Communist attack will not succeed."

Since this money was not needed and the appropriation was to be used merely as a symbol of support, Senators Morse, Gaylord Nelson (D., Wis.) and Gruening voted against it. In the House, seven members voted against it: Representatives George E. Brown, Jr. (D., Calif.), Philip Burton (D., Calif.), John J. Conyers (D., Mich.), John G. Dow (D., N.Y.), Don Edwards (D., Calif.), Edith Green (D., Ore.), and William Fitts Ryan (D., N.Y.).

When a similar supplemental military authorization bill came before the Senate on March 7, 1967, Senator Morse and Senator Nelson voted against it. Senator Gruening had a live pair against the bill.*

---

*"Live pair" means that where a Senator who is absent would, for example, vote "No" he is paired with a Senator who is present and would otherwise vote "Yes". The Senator who is present withholds his vote.

When the same measure had been before the House of Representatives on March 2, 1967, it had been passed by a voice vote. On the question of inserting a provision prohibiting the use of any funds to carry out military operations in or over North Vietnam, 18 members voted for the restriction.*

The United States, in the writers' view, has made a serious mistake in getting involved militarily in Vietnam because not only was the United States not attacked, but furthermore nothing that happens in South Vietnam threatens or jeopardizes the security of the United States. And even if it did, there is a question of whether that would justify its invading Vietnam and bombing it any more than one can justify the seizure by Stalin of the formerly independent countries surrounding Russia—Latvia, Lithuania, Esthonia, Poland, Czechoslovakia, Hungary—on the grounds that their control was essential to the security of Soviet Russia, even though those countries were geographically adjacent to Soviet Russia and not half way round the world from it.

Nor can the writers subscribe to the domino theory which is that had the United States not gone in, these nations of Southeast Asia would have fallen, one by one, into the hands of the Communist Chinese. And then we are told in subsequent flights of fancy that after Southeast Asia, the Philippines, Australia, and New Zealand would fall and the United States would have to fight the Communists on the beaches of Hawaii or California! That is arrant nonsense. Certainly United States control of the Pacific by sea and air renders that absurd.

The writers are not pacifists and do not like and are utterly opposed to the advance of totalitarianism of the right or of the left—anywhere. United States' entry into World Wars I and II as well as in Korea were entirely justifiable legally, morally, and militarily. If a situation should arise whereby a free government, such as that of

---

*Representatives Jonathan Bingham (D.-N.Y.), George E. Brown, Jr. (D.-Calif.), Philip Burton (D.-Calif.), John J. Conyers (D.-Mich.), Charles C. Diggs, Jr. (D.-Mich.), Don Edwards (D.-Calif.), Leonard Farbstein (D.-N.Y.), Robert Fraser (D.-Minn.), Edith Green (D.-Ore.), Henry Helstoski (D.-N.J.), Robert Kastenmeier (D.-Wis.), Patsy Mink (D.-Hawaii), Thomas M. Rees (D.-Calif.), Benjamin Rosenthal (D.-N. Y.), Edward R. Roybal (D.-Calif.), William Fitts Ryan (D.-N.Y.), James H. Scheuer (D.-N.Y.), and Sidney R. Yates (D.-Ill.).

Australia or New Zealand, were threatened by attack and invasion by the forces of imperial communism and those governments requested United States' aid, the writers would favor giving that aid without stint or limit. But such aid should be preceded by Congressional hearings and buttressed by a Treaty, unless the emergency was so great that time permitted no delay.

The situation is South Vietnam is quite different.

The writers are confident that, and this is further in the realm of opinion, had the United States stayed out of Vietnam entirely there would be three independent countries formed out of French Indochina, they would have installed their own social and political ideology which they would have had every right to do, and a united Vietnam would probably have adopted Communism as its social and economic system. But it would have been a Communist regime independent of Peking.

Evidence is plentiful that nationalism—the nation's independence—is the strongest element in the Vietnamese people's aspirations rather than the political and social ideology they might adopt. There is considerable evidence that many non-Communists are enlisted in the civil war against the South Vietnam Government. The history of Vietnam shows conclusively its people's dislike and fear of the Chinese—who conquered and ruled them for 1000 years—and their war is largely motivated by a desire to get rid of all foreign rule. They want independence, and that should be a cause that ought to appeal to Americans. They did not want the French, and drove them out. They did not want the Japanese, and helped drive them out. They did not want the Chinese, and we doubt whether a majority want the United States there now. In Europe, to achieve a corresponding situation, namely in Yugoslavia, the United States invested $2 billion in aid for Tito. This was possible because, although he was a Communist with all that implied of tyranny and the suppression of basic freedoms, he made Yugoslavian Communism independent of Moscow. United States policy-makers, under both Democratic and Republican Administrations, considered that a sound and profitable investment.

Such a result could have been achieved without the loss of American lives in Vietnam, and at no other cost.

The United States bombing of North Vietnam in our view, is totally without justification morally, legally, militarily, or otherwise. It is the sort of performance American public opinion condemned scathingly when done by totalitarian powers in past years. As we have seen now after years of such bombing, it has merely stiffened the resistance of those whom the United States is fighting. Our nation is getting in deeper and deeper; not only are its casualty lists growing, but the toll of not merely those fighting but of civilian non-combatants mounts daily.

In its effort to stop the advance of imperialist communism, the United States is actually aiding it. The situation must be to the liking of the Communist rulers of China and Russia, for to date neither China nor Russia has committed a single soldier to fight alongside the Vietcong in this war. And yet the United States—a great Western power, the greatest in the world—is bogged down in a desperate, bitter and horrible struggle on the continent of Asia with a small Asian nation, largely a primitive peasant people, sacrificing the lives of American youth and spending billions of dollars. The current estimate is $3 billion dollars a month. Think of it! Think what one month's war expenditure would buy in needed schools, hospitals, resource development, slum clearance, and in meeting other pressing needs at home. The Mansfield Report of January 3, 1966, by the member of Congress most expert in Far Eastern Affairs concurred in by Senators Muskie (D., Me.) and Inouye (D,. Hawaii) and Senators Aiken (R., Vt.) and Boggs (R., Del.) after an intensive study on the ground came to the gloomy conclusion that there will be indefinite expansion and escalation on both sides with no end in sight in the near future. They called it an open-ended war! (See Appendix.)

The situation is different from that of Korea.

First, in Korea there was overt aggression from the North.

Second, the United States was in Korea under a United Nations mandate. Americans fought there under a United Nations flag as the United Nations' executive agent for aims prescribed by United Nations resolutions and the forces of 16 other nations fought side by side with Americans.

Third, the South Koreans wanted to fight.

And yet it will be recalled that a cheer went up from the American people when Dwight Eisenhower said in the course of his campaign: "I will go to Korea" indicating that he would stop the conflict. That promise was an important factor in his election.

Those factors, which justified United States action in Korea, are not present, at least not in the same degree in Vietnam. There was no overt initial aggression from the North at the start. There had been infiltration, but following and paralleling U.S. support of South Vietnam, and not appreciable until the United States supported Diem's refusal to hold elections and Diem's oppression of his own people. The United States went in unilaterally. Until very recently, and then only in response to great pressure from the United States, it had little support from its SEATO allies—none from Pakistan, none from Britain, none from France. When administration spokesmen cite the total number of nations that are allegedly supporting the United States—in a kind of numbers game—one finds that they have come in lately and largely with only token assistance. *Newsweek* magazine had this little item in its *Periscope* column entitled "Spain Lends a Hand":

"Spain is the latest country to lend a hand in Vietnam. After much prodding from LBJ, the Franco Government hopes to ship 4 ambulances with medical crews. Actually the ambulances will have little significance (the helicopters do their work now) but the medics are wanted and the Spanish contingent will be welcomed as evidence of support for the U.S. and Saigon."

Senator Fulbright (D., Ark.), Chairman of the Senate Foreign Relations Committee, pointed out in the Senate on October 10, 1967 many countries were not giving assistance in Vietnam on a continuing basis.

"I find," he said, "that there has been no change in the description of the assistance given by Denmark, Ecuador, Greece, Guatamala, Honduras, Luxembourg, Malaysia, the Philippines, Spain, Turkey, Uruguay, Ireland, Israel, Norway, Pakistan, and Switzerland. In other words, there has apparently been no new material assistance given by these countries since December 1966 at the latest. And in some cases it is obvious that the assistance was given well before the end of 1966."

When the writers were in South America, in January of 1965, they found that every American ambassador to a Latin American country had received orders to go to the President of the country to which he was accredited to request support for United States efforts in Vietnam. Some of them were reluctant to do this. In some cases, their pleas were unheeded, while in others there was the same kind of token compliance that has been coming from Spain. These countries are all recipients of lavish American aid and the United States is, in effect, paying for these tokens and is in a position to apply pressure. Brazil, for example, is sending—coffee!

It is worth noting that the United States Ambassadors were the ones asking the Latin American countries to send troops to the supposedly independent country of South Vietnam. It is indeed most strange for one country to ask a second country to send troops to enter upon the territory of a third country!

Korea is a dependent. The United States occupies that country militarily with over 50,000 troops, supports its army and, in large part, its economy. The troops which it has sent to Vietnam the United States pays for at specially exacted high rates of pay. We do not question that the Koreans' own experience makes them willing and able combatants.

But the United States' course evokes no support or enthusiasm from the leading Asian nations that are anti-Communist such as Japan, India, Burma, Afghanistan, or Iran.

Australia, although far nearer the scene and presumably or at least, allegedly, imperiled by an Asian Communist take-over, in response to much pleading and prodding from our administration has sent combat units of 4500 men. That nation's dilemma and true feelings were expressed in an editorial in its leading newspaper, *The Australian* on April 16, 1965. It says in part:

"The United States went into South Vietnam in the first place with the most honorable of intentions, even though its presence there was against the spirit and the text of the 1954 Geneva agreements and its accompanying declaration.

"But, by going into South Vietnam, America got itself involved in a conflict with which it had nothing to do. Its presence there has always been indefensible, for civil war has always been going on in Vietnam, and America and her allies have turned this into a full-scale campaign against Chinese communism.

"It is time the Australian Government was honest with us. It must admit openly that we are not in South Vietnam to help a friendly government fight aggression from the north.

"We are there because . . . the Americans want us to and need our moral support.

". . . we have got ourselves into an untenable position in Asia. The consequences of withdrawal from South Vietnam will be horrifying. The consequences of staying will be even more tragic . . . Our Government must tell the United States that we are its ally — but the time has come to stop the bitterness of Vietnam."

Unfortunately, there is no ready and quick answer to or a way out of the tragic dilemma in which the President, his advisers, and the people of the United States find themselves. A part of this dilemma arises from ignorance. Perhaps a kinder word would be "misinformation." We Americans, basing our belief on our national success story — and it has been one of the world's great epics — are inclined to assume that we have all the answers. Coupled with this built-in confidence is a collateral assumption that the President of the United States must have information which the rest of us less important mortals do not have, which leads to the support of his foreign policy, unquestioningly.

But how misled a President can be was tragically illustrated in the Bay of Pigs fiasco. In that instance, President Kennedy had all the most expert advice that a President could be expected to have. He had the advice of the Joint Chiefs of Staff. He had the advice of the Central Intelligence Agency which had been preparing the Cuban invasion. He had the advice of his various staff assistants. And all of it was wrong. The President was badly mis-advised.

The situation in Vietnam is similar. President Johnson's chief advisers on Vietnam were among the chief advisers of President Kennedy on the Bay of Pigs disaster, namely Secretary of State Dean Rusk, and Secretary of Defense Robert McNamara. Here are just a few of the latter's optimistic forecasts:

May 1962. "Progress in the last eight to ten weeks has been great . . . . The government has asked only for logistical support."

May 1963.. "The corner has been definitely turned toward victory in South Vietnam."

October 1963. "The major part of the U. S. military task can be completed by the end of 1965, although there may be a continuing requirement for a limited number of U. S. military personnel . . ."

February 19, 1964. "Secretary of Defense Robert S. McNamara has told members of Congress that the U. S. hopes to withdraw most of its troops from South Vietnam before the end of 1965."

One may wonder why one whose forecasts have proved so dismally wrong is retained in the position of policy maker on an issue of such vital importance.

It might be added at this point that some of the best advice that has been given the United States in regard to engaging on the ground on the continent of Asia has not been accepted by our present policy makers. General Douglas MacArthur, undoubtedly one of the greatest soldiers of our time, warned repeatedly against engaging in a ground war on the continent of Asia; so did General Matthew Ridgway. But their advice was not taken.

More recently, on Memorial Day, 1967, Brigadier General Robert L. Hughes, who had served with distinction on General MacArthur's staff in World War II stated:

"We are losing the flower of American youth in a war that could stretch into perpetuity . . . They died in support of an unstable foreign government that is maintained only on the strength of the United States . . . We are prosecuting a war in support of a Government that is a dictatorship by design. It . . . is composed of morally-corrupt leaders who adhere to a warload philosophy . . . We must disengage from this tragic war."

General David Shoup, former Commandant of the Marine Corps, in stating that "I don't think the whole of Southeast Asia . . . is worth the life or limb of a single American," continued:

"I believe that if we had and would keep our dirty, bloody, dollar crooked fingers out of the business of these nations so full of depressed, exploited people, they will arrive at a solution of their own."

Meanwhile, behind an almost impenetrable veil of secrecy, the United States has committed itself to another Vietnam-type military involvement in Thailand.

Coming to the rescue of the corrupt, tyrannical, oppressive Military Junta which rules Thailand, the United States is pouring hundreds of millions of dollars into that country to suppress by military force all opposition to military rule and the desires of the people for economic, social and political reforms.

When one of the authors of this volume was in Bangkok in May of 1967 he was given a briefing by the officials of the Agency for International Development. More than 85% of the aid program was devoted to a military effort to support the Military Junta and to repress the people. The officials admitted that there were only 1400 "Communist trained" rebels in the hills. To hold them in check, the United States was pouring into that country in economic and military aid over one hundred million dollars a year. When it was pointed out that the AID program was identical to that in South Vietnam to support Diem's efforts to suppress all dissent in the late 1950's and in the early 1960's, he was assured that this time, in Thailand, it would be different!

It was obvious that the United States was repeating in Thailand the same blunders it had made in South Vietnam.

United States military forces, by the end of 1967, had increased to 50,000 in Thailand. Already the "dry rot" now plaguing South Vietnam had begun to set in in Bangkok. The overpowering American presence was all too evident.

"The Johnson Administration", author Louis E. Lomax stated in his perceptive volume entitled *"Thailand: The War That Is, the War That Will Be,* has committed the American people to another Vietnam type war without seeking the advice or consent of either the people or the Congress."

And this senseless war goes on, getting steadily more diastrous.

How and why did the United States become so tragically involved?

Between a policy of "cut and run" and a policy of unlimited military escalation, what is the "third alternative" which the United States could adopt to extricate itself from the Vietnam morass?

The "third alternative" is discussed in detail in Chapter 32.

CHAPTER II

VIETNAM, TO ITS COLONIALIZATION BY FRANCE

More than two thousand years before Columbus discovered America, the peoples inhabiting that part of the world known as Southeast Asia[1] were exploring and colonizing lands beyond their borders and attempting to conquer and rule the lands of their neighbors — even as today! The struggle now going on in Vietnam can only be understood within the context of the millenia-long history of the peoples of that area — their customs — their cultural and religious heritage — their economic development — their political experiences and aspirations — the geographical location and character of their lands.

The term Vietnam refers to the long, narrow, "S" shaped area, 1,000 miles long, on the Indochinese peninsula in Southeast Asia. It lies between 8°33′ and 23°22′ north latitude and is bounded on the north by China, on the west by Cambodia and Laos, and on the east by the South China Sea and the Gulf of Tonkin.

Today's Vietnam contains approximately 127,000 square miles, with about 62,000 square miles lying north of the 17th parallel and 65,000 square miles lying south of the 17th parallel. The total area of Vietnam can be compared to the State of California, 158,000 square miles.

Vietnam's people today number 31 million, with approximately 17 million north of the 17th parallel and 14 million south of the 17th parallel. For its size Vietnam is underpopulated in relation to other Asian nations, having a density of population one fourth that of Japan, which has approximately the same geographical area. This sparcity of population is due in large measure to its rugged topographical features.

In the mountainous areas of Vietnam the land is covered with deep forests and dense jungles. Even if cleared, the land is not very fertile. In contrast, the alluvial plains running north and south along the South China Sea and the Gulf of Tonkin, in a fairly narrow strip, contain rich, rice-growing deltas — the largest of which are the Red River Delta in the north and the Mekong River Delta in the south. These large deltas, together with the many other smaller deltas in the lowlands, make up — or made up — the so-called breadbasket of Southeast Asia. Even so, the delta areas north of the 17th parallel never have produced enough food to satisfy the needs of the population densely crowded into that area even in early times. However, that food, together with the food produced in the lowlands south of the 17th parallel, were, in normal times sufficient to feed the people of all the united Vietnam well, leaving a surplus for trade.

A large part of Vietnam is hilly or mountainous and covered with thick jungles. These areas are sparsely populated. South of the 17th parallel, the mountains are occupied by minority groups, usually nomadic either by nature or because of the poor quality of the soil.

After driving their Chinese conquerers out of their land in about 939 A.D., the Vietnamese began their long drive south in search of land into which they could expand and on which they could settle to carry on their agricultural pursuits. It was but natural for them to settle on the coastal lowlands, driving the minority groups[2] living there into the mountainous lands where the living was not as good.

As with many ancient lands, early Vietnamese history, reaching back thousands of years, is largely unrecorded. Some of it is only now coming to light. Much of it remains shrouded in mystery or is based on folklore touched with mythology. Some of it was apparently even made up out of whole cloth in an effort to resist Chinese attempts at assimilation during Vietnam's 1000 year occupation by the Chinese.[3]

The independent kingdom of Van Lang, later known as Au Lac, is said to have existed between 500-207 B.C.[4] It reputedly consisted of what is now the southernmost Chinese province of Kwang-tung and Vietnam, extending south to the 17th parallel. During the early years of the Han dynasty in China (206 B.C. — 221 A.D.). the Viets were pushed out of Kwang-Tung province so that at the time of their conquest by the Chinese in 111 B.C. they occupied what we would refer to today as North Vietnam to the 17th parallel.

In about 207 B.C., Au Lac was conquered by a Chinese General who had broken with the Chinese Emperor. It then became known as Nam (South) — Viet.[5]

Thus, from about 500 B.C. to 111 B.C. — a period of about 400 years — whether under the name of Van Lang or Au Lac or Nam Viet, the people occupying the country north of the 17th parallel to the Chinese border were free of foreign domination. True, they were influenced greatly by Chinese customs, literature, and culture during that period. But they were similarly influenced by the people coming to Vietnam from India by sea.

"The era before 939 was marked by the gradual imposition of Chinese economic, social, and political institutions. Chinese governors brought in their political and economic organization, instituted a mandarin type bureaucracy, and introduced Confucian ethics and the Chinese writing system. It is unclear however, to what extent Chinese culture and institutions, channeled to the upper levels of society, actually modified the political condition of the peasantry."[6]

However, despite these Chinese and Indian influences, the Vietnamese were able to retain and develop their own Vietnamese customs and traditions in such a deep-rooted fashion that they were able to withstand 1000 years of Chinese attempts, often by force, to make them Chinese.

Part of the "staying power" may be traced to their homogeneity.

"The Vietnamese . . . show a remarkable cultural unity, possess a high degree of civilization, speak the same language . . .

are of an almost identical physical constitution all over the country . . . the minority groups . . . constitute the chaos of races, civilizations, and languages . . ."[7]

In 111 B.C. the Chinese Emperor crushed and conquered the independent kingdom of Nam Viet and kept it under its rule and domination for the next 1000 years. The inverted name of Nam Viet was used until it was changed by royal decree in 1802 — well after the Chinese yoke had been thrown off — to Viet Nam. (For ease in reference, it will henceforth be referred to as Vietnam, even for the period before 1802.)

After the conquest of Vietnam, and all through its rule from and by China, strenuous efforts were made to sinicize the Vietnamese people and assimilate them into the Chinese culture. Those attempts failed completely and when Vietnam finally threw off China's rule in 939 A.D. Vietnam emerged a free nation more Vietnamese, more nationalistic, than ever.

". . . the Vietnamese who were under Chinese rule from 111 B.C. to A.D. 939 . . . were subjected to intensive sinization, developed a culture which, while owing an immense amount to China, nevertheless preserved its own identity, with its roots going back to pre-Chinese past."[8]

Many reasons have been put forward for this persistent resistence on the part of the Vietnamese to their assimilation by the Chinese. One of the basic reasons is that when China conquered Vietnam, the latter was not a recently independent nation. It had been independent for more than 400 years — a period of time sufficient for the Vietnamese to become imbued with a nationalistic spirit and to build up their own traditions, religion, customs, national pride, and national heroes.

All attempts at sinization failed because China sought to make of Vietnam a colony ruled by, dependent upon, and exploited for the benefit of the Chinese empire.

At the beginning the rulers, sent to Vietnam from China, passed on to the Vietnamese, China's vastly advanced knowledge of agricultural methods, brought about the building of an intricate system of dikes and canals to increase agricultural yields, and governed mostly through the indigenous population. However, after the short-lived Vietnamese revolution in A.D. 40, Chinese repressive measures became ever harsher and there was less and less interest on the part of the Chinese rulers, and of the subordinate officials they set up to govern, in improving and developing the country and more and more emphasis on their own enrichment and on exacting greater tribute for the Chinese Empire.

The Vietnamese believed that their history and traditions went back at least as far as China's and were as noble, and so saw no reason to substitute China's for their own. Basically this was what sinization would have amounted to.[9]

All during the period of Chinese rule over Vietnam from 111 B.C. to 939 A.D. the desire for independence from Chinese rule continued to burn fiercely in the Vietnamese. Three briefly successful revolutions took place in 40 A.D., 249 A.D. and 544 A.D. and many unsuccessful revolutions as well.[10] But it was not until 939 A.D. that the Vietnamese overthrew their Chinese conquerors and remained free of foreign domination for 900 years, until colonialized by the French, except for a brief period from 1406 to 1431 of reconquest by China.

Following the achievement of its independence in 939 A.D. the Vietnamese began to move south conquering and settling bit by bit as they went, driving the inhabitants they encountered into the hills and mountains or killing them. Thus they settled the lowlands and began their agricultural existence.

The drive south was motivated as much by imperialist feelings as by a need for more food to feed the expanding population beginning to feel itself hemmed in within the original borders of Vietnam. To the east was water; to the north was China, weak enough to have been driven out of Vietnam but still too powerful to be challenged by the Vietnamese in any move to enlarge their territory; to the west lay the rugged, infertile jungle clad hills and mountains; but to the south lay rich, fertile lowlands — the type of land which the Vietnamese had learned to till.

Within 160 years of achieving its independence, Vietnam had conquered and settled upon the lands of the Champs, lying in the lowlands on the South China Sea, as far south as Hue, which, through the marriage of the sister of the King of Vietnam to the King of Champs, became Vietnamese in the fifteenth century.

By 1471 all of Champs was in Vietnamese hands. Then Vietnamese war veterans were given permission to expand to the west into Cambodia, to seize lands and set up what amounted to fortified villages. By 1658 all South Vietnam north of Saigon was in Vietnamese hands. In 1672 Saigon fell and by 1799 Vietnam had expanded to its present — pre-Geneva, 1954 — size.

The Vietnamese came to make the lands they conquered truly Vietnamese, driving those they found living there completely out. Thus wherever they settled became identical with the place they had left, undistinguishable in any way from the villages to the north of the 17th parallel and inhabited to a vast extent by Vietnamese, not, for example by a mixture of Vietnamese and Champs, with the Vietnamese having political and military supremacy.[11]

In many ways the settlement of the south by Vietnam can be compared to the settlement of the West in the United States. The easterners and mid-westerners who crossed the Mississippi to open up and settle the west were not a different ethnic group from their fellow countrymen who elected to remain in the east. They carried with them their heritage as Americans and, when they founded the towns, the villages, and the great cities in the west, they put into these towns and villages and cities the background of their way of life in the east.

A vying for political power took place — in a bloody sort of way — in Vietnam in the 860 years of expansion to the south.

"Between 940 and 1400, Vietnam, after a painful beginning marred by civil wars and conditions close to chaos, developed a stable and efficient political regime. The central power of the state, built around a hereditary monarchy, was normally supreme, and medieval Vietnam, even in times of crisis, always was united under one government."[12]

Then for centuries the country was racked with civil wars with power shifting from factions in the north to factions in the south, and back again.

The people of Vietnam wanted unity, not to become two separate, independent countries. But the question which brought on the squabbles and the fighting and dying was which faction should control the entire country. The southern part of the country had been colonized by people from the north but their descendants resented the seat of power being in the north and sought for hundreds of years to wrest that power away from the north and establish it in the south.

There is the tendency on the part of some Americans, because of the implications of our own North-South war, to equate any North-South struggle anywhere as a struggle of the South to attain independence from the North. In Vietnam's history, nothing could be further from the truth. The South fought the North not to get out from under the control of the North but to conrol both North and South. During the fifteenth century, Vietnam was divided in two for fifty years, reunited in 1590, and split again in 1620.[13]

All during these years of bloody strife for power between the kings and the feudal lords and mandarins for power in the north and the south of Vietnam, what of the people? They continued to live a poor, miserable existence paying for the wars not only with what they could produce from the land but, as always, with their blood, sweat and tears.

The peasants had no protection from the lords who were under pressures from the Trinh rulers in the North and the Nguyen rulers in the South to furnish more men and arms so that the oppression of the peasants increased.[14]

But with all the scrambling for national power by this faction and that faction, the life of the peasant revolved around his little village and when things became too difficult and the conditions of life became unendurable there were peasant revolts (during the 18th century) that were quickly put down.

But, as the historian, Buttinger points out, the "unity of the country, which as a oneness of language, culture and national feelings had existed even during long periods of political separation, was one of the most striking features of nineteenth century pre-colonial Vietnam."[15]

In the light of this historical background, it is indeed incredible for the Legal Adviser of the Department of State on December 13, 1966 to make the following statement during the course of a lecture at the University of Pittsburgh Law School:

"Viet-Nam has a very short political history under that name — one that does not go back even twenty years. Viet-

Nam is made up of three areas that were included in what France called, for purposes of colonial administration, Indochina. Those areas were: Tonkin in the Red River delta of the North, Annam along the central coast, and Cochin China in the South around Saigon. In the 19th Century, France ruled these areas as protectorates and colonies, along with Laos and Cambodia; all together, they made up Indochina." (Emphasis supplied)

CHAPTER III

FRENCH INDOCHINA

The military conquest of Laos, Cambodia, and Vietnam by France was completed in 1893.[1] They were made into colonies or protectorates of France under the name of French Indochina. The road to French military success in that area of the world had been long, hard and extremely bloody.

The conquest of Vietnam began in a purely peaceful way in 1662-1663 with the dispatch of Catholic missionaries from France to the central portion of Vietnam, which the French were later to call Annam. The sending of the missionaries had been inspired by the French Jesuit, Alexander of Rhodes, who, after spending many years in the Far East, returned to France to promote the sending of more French Catholic missionaries there. He was instrumental in the founding of the Société des Missions Estrangeres organized in Paris in 1663 and which was based at the University of Paris.

This was but part of the larger struggle then going on between the French and Portuguese clergy for dominance in China and the Far East. The history of the missionary movement in Vietnam reveals intense struggles by Portuguese and Italian missionaries, already on the scene, to keep French missionaries out of the country. The French clergy with the assistance of the French government, which they were in a position to influence, ultimately played a vital role in the colonialization of Vietnam.

The Dutch, who controlled the Straits of Malacca, successfully resisted efforts by the French East India Company to establish a trading post in southern Vietnam in 1664-5. Other French commercial ventures in Vietnam in 1682 and 1684 were similarly thwarted by the Dutch. Finally in 1749-50, a treaty was concluded with Annam granting trading concessions to the French East India Company. The years following found the French missionaries and traders suffering a series of ups and downs in their relationships with the Vietnamese rulers.

The beginning of France's real penetration of Vietnam centers around the figure of the French missionary Pigneau de Behaine who was sent by the Société des Missions Estrangeres to Cambodia in 1765 and was consecrated in 1774 as "Bishop of Adran and designated vicar apostolic to Cochin-China, Cambodia, and Tong-king."[2]

Pigneau became friendly with Nguyen Anh, a Vietnamese prince in exile, who was seeking to regain the Vietnamese throne. With the assistance of Pigneau, a treaty of alliance was entered into with the French in 1787 at Versailles and some material aid was given Nguyen Anh by France. Pigneau organized a group of French adventurers living in the Far East and went to Cochin-China, where he found that Nguyen Anh had already taken Saigon and installed himself under the name of Emperor Gia Long. By 1800, Gia Long succeeded in conquering the rest of Annam.

Pigneau and his French followers remained in Saigon where they "established a mint, organized a navy, built fortifications."

However, with the coming of the French Revolution, which curtailed French interest in foreign affairs, and the subsequent misadventures of Napoleon, French influence in Vietnam declined.

It began to be revived in 1819, because Gia Long was willing to trade. However, he died and was succeeded by King Minh Mang, a man of Confuscist training who hated the French. In 1832, Minh Mang commanded all missionaries to come to his court at Hue where he kept them as virtual prisoners. From then on the missionaries were banished and killed in increasing numbers. Minh Mang also turned on native Christian converts.

At about that time two changes occurred which altered the course of French activities in Vietnam. First, religious revival swept Catholic Europe. Second, the rulers of France decided that French international prestige should be regained. As a result, French missionary activities in the Far East increased, with the support and encouragement of the French Government.

In 1841, Minh Mang was succeeded by the anti-foreign King Thieu-Tri and the persecutions of the missionaries continued. Missionaries, however, continued to enter, especially in the north, and urged French intervention in support of the pretender to the throne, Le.

In April 1847, two French naval vessels appeared in the harbor of Tourane in northern Vietnam (the port of Hue) to rescue a missionary, demanding a promise that the persecution of the missionaries would stop. The French vessels destroyed the Vietnamese fleet and the forts in the harbor.

Tu-Duc succeeded Thieu Tri shortly thereafter, but his attitude toward the French and toward the missionaries did not differ from that of his predecessors.

While the severe persecutions were going on, the missionaries in Vietnam, through the Societe des Missions Estrangeres, tried to get the French Government to intervene militarily on a sustained basis.[3]

For his coup d'etat of December 2, 1851, Louis Napoleon actively courted Catholic support. Therefore, when he was safely installed, he was "vulnerable to clerical pressure on behalf of missionary interests in the Far East."[4] The entire French policy for the Far East was intensively reviewed.

This and the following decade were the periods when Britain was making inroads and obtaining and asserting privileges in China.

To raise French prestige, an expedition was sent to Vietnam, entering Tourane on August 31, 1857. The troops immediately suffered severely from heat prostration and dysentery, followed by scurvy and cholera.[5]

Acting without orders from Paris, the Admiral who headed the expedition turned south to Saigon where no resistance was encountered and Saigon was taken by the French in February 1858. When the Admiral returned to Tourane in April 1859, his force was again ravaged by disease, so that the death rate from typhus by August was a hundred men a month.

Meanwhile the French and British forces were having a hard time seeking to subdue China — French troops were needed there. The Toulane expedition was disbanded.

The area adjacent to Saigon was secured by June 1861.

Two events in early 1862 caused King Tu-Duc to make peace with the French. The first was that, with the Mekong Delta under their control, the French denied Hue the rice it needed to feed its people. The second was that a pretender from the Le dynasty — a pro-Christian — led a revolt in Tongking.

One June 5, 1861, the Treaty of Saigon was signed between King Tu-Duc and the French. French territorial holdings were limited to the three provinces adjacent to Saigon and the French were given some trading concessions in Tourane.[6]

In 1863, a secret treaty was negotiated with King Norodom of Cambodia giving France exclusive control over Cambodia's foreign affairs and the right to place consulates in the country. In return, France agreed to protect Cambodia against Siam's claim to rule Cambodia.

In 1867, France announced that it would thenceforth consider the remainder of Cochin-China as a French protectorate. After invasions, skirmishes and battles, Hue acknowledged French sovereignty over Cochin China in 1874 .

By July 1893, through various stratagems and military adventures, France was in possession of all of Vietnam, Laos, and Cambodia.

Under the French colonial rule of Indochina, power seeped down from the top — from the Colonial Office in Paris through the Governor General down to the provinces.[7]

In addition, the French followed the practice of importing governmental officials from France rather than training and placing Vietnamese in positions of responsibility.

It has been stated that French colonial policy in Indochina was a policy of exploiting the country for the benefit of France and that "the economy was dominated by a combination of private investors and the Bank of Indochina . . . [which became] . . . the instrument of channeling metropolitan capital into the

colony and directing its investment at highly profitable rates."[8]
This view of the exploitation of Vietnam by the French has been
disputed by Fall, who says that the period of so-called exploitation
can be said to have come only at the beginning and at the end
of the colonialization of Vietnam by the French and that, in between, there was steady development of the country.

Whether exploited or not, the lot of the peasant did not improve
much. With the importation of Frenchmen to man many governmental jobs, a dual rate of compensation was established, even
though a Frenchman and a Vietnamese worked at similar jobs.
The filling of jobs with Frenchmen was also a cause of frustration
to those Vietnamese intellectuals who went to French universities
and came home to find the jobs for which they were trained filled
by Frenchmen.

In contrast, because of the British policy of training the
indigenous population in governmental administration, "the Vice-
roy of India governed in 1925 a total of 325 million Indians
with 4,898 European civil servants, while the [French] Governor
General administrated 30 million Indochinese with 5,000 French
civil servants."[9]

Under French colonialism, the essentially agrarian nature of
Indochina remained unchanged. Before the French came, the custom of individual landholdings in Tongking and Annam prevailed.
This was not changed by the French, although through increased
population the landholdings fragmented and each farmer had a
difficult time earning more than a subsistence living. The biggest
change came about in Cochinchina (in the south) where large
tracts of land were developed through reclamation and were swept
up by wealthy Vietnamese and French absentee landowners.
Tenant farming became the vogue. On the large rubber plantations,
there was a shortage of labor and people had to be brought down
from Tongking, in the north, to operate the plantations under
working conditions tantamount to peonage.

High taxes caused many peasants to sell their holdings and
go to work as tenant farmers. Village life was disrupted when the
villagers' secondary sources of income were taken away when
the French colonial rulers established governmental monopolies
over the purchase and sale of alcohol, opium, and salt. Village

communal life was also disrupted by the authority given to the French Government officials imported from France, thus diminishing the authority of the local officials who had been a cohesive force in the villages before the advent of French rule.[10]

One fact of French colonial rule of Vietnam, Laos, and Cambodia is worthy of note in connection with present day activities in that area. Until 1893, when it was colonialized by France by force of arms, there had been a country known as Nam-Viet or Vietnam, which had been in existence since at least 500 B.C. That country had been conquered and had remained conquered by China for a thousand years during that period but had not been known as other than Nam-Viet or Vietnam. Even after it obtained its freedom from China in 939 A.D. and began to expand southward, the new lands conquered were absorbed into and became known as part of the country of Nam-Viet or, later, Vietnam. Through the Tay-son rebellion in the 18th century and the fall of the Trinh and Nguyen dynasties, and even when it was ruled by three brothers operating out of Saigon, Hue, and Hanoi, it was still known as the country of Vietnam.

After its conquest by France in 1893, however, things changed. In an effort to wipe out history and national pride and nationalistic aspirations, the French renamed the area. It lumped Laos, Cambodia, and Vietnam under one all inclusive term "French Indochina" and then proceded, not only by separate colonial governments of each part but also by renaming the three parts of Vietnam, Annam, Tongking, and Cochinchina, to act as though there had never been a unified Vietnam.

During the thousand years of their colonialization by China, the Vietnamese people tried repeatedly to throw off the Chinese yoke and regain their freedom as they succeeded in doing in 939 A.D. The Vietnamese reacted similarly to French colonialization. Unsuccessful armed revolts against the French were carried out by the Vietnamese, led by the mandarins and the ruling houses, until 1920. Whatever their personal motives, they acted under the rallying cry of independence for all Vietnam.

The more intellectual Vietnamese in the 1920's sought to convince the French colonial rulers that social and economic reforms were needed. They failed.

"When their programs were flatly rejected, they turned once again to violent methods and to clandestine organizations."[11]

Some of the underground organizations which came into being after the outright rejection of the reforms requested by the intellectuals in 1920 were Marxist oriented.

Some were not. Among these one of the strongest was the Viet Nam Quoc Dang (VNQDD—Vietnamese Nationalist Party). This organization wanted to get out from under French rule and establish a form of government modeled after the nationalist, non-communist party, the Kuomintang Party, in China. This party, founded by Sun Yat Sen, was later taken over by Chiang Kai-shek, and later defeated by the Communist Mao Tse-Tung. However, after the French crushed a revolt by the VNQDD near the Chinese border in February, 1930, the organization disappeared, only to resurface again in the 1940s with Chinese support.

In 1927, in China, the Kuomintang split with the Moscow dominated Communist Party. Chiang Kai-shek ruled the former; Mao Tse-Tung controlled the latter. It was at that time that Mao decided to break with the "Party Line" laid down by the Comintern in 1920 for a united front in making revolutions and decided that the Communist revolution in China had to be a Chinese Communist revolution and not one dominated or controlled by Moscow.

Three years later, in 1930, in Vietnam, a Comintern agent named Nguyen Ai Quoc—who later took the name of Ho Chi Minh—succeeded in fusing three splinter Communist organizations into the Indochinese Communist Party."[12]

The Indochinese Communist Party (ICP) stirred up the peasants into demonstrations and strikes. French reaction was quick and by 1932 about 10,000 political prisoners were in jail.[14] The Indochinese Communist Party's ties to the Comintern were ruptured when Ho Chi Minh was thrown into jail by the British in Hong Kong in 1931. The Indochinese Communist Party in the 1930's made common cause with the Popular Front in France and when that Front fell in 1938, the Indochinese Communist Party was forced underground. "However, by its activities and organizational skill, the ICP had come to dominate the revolutionary scene in Vietnam and had laid the foundation for its subsequent claims to historic leadership of the Vietnamese nationalist movement."[13]

CHAPTER IV

VIETNAM DURING WORLD WAR II

France was overrun by Germany in World War II and signed an armistice on June 25, 1940. The French military forces in Indochina were prevented from receiving reinforcements from France. Those were perilous days for England, too, which had suffered great losses in evacuating its troops from Dunkirk and was busy preparing to repel an invasion. Thus, help from Britain was also precluded.

Just prior to French capitulation, the Japanese Government had sent a note on June 19, 1940 to the French Governor General, General Catroux, demanding joint control of the Tonkonese border through which China, which Japan was trying to conquer, was being supplied. General Catroux, having previously tried without success to obtain weapons from the United States, had no choice but to accede. He was replaced by Admiral Jean Decoux.

A few months later the Vichy Government in France agreed that the Japanese position in the Far East should be predominant. After some fighting between the French and the Japanese, Admiral Decoux was instructed to enter into an agreement with the Japanese. During the remainder of the war Japan ruled Indochina through the French who were there, with Decoux remaining as figurehead. "Despite the relative merits of the Decoux regime, it was in most respects a carbon copy of its Vichy masters. It was anti-Semitic, anti-Masonic, anti-Gaullist, and pro-Axis."[1]

In March 1945, toward the close of World War II, with VJ Day fast approaching, the Japanese armed forces brutally attacked the French military rulers of Vietnam and their Vietnamese supporters.

"Of the approximately 13,000 French troops who were not immediately overwhelmed by the Japanese attack, 200 officers and 4,000 soldiers were, according to de Gaulle's *Memoires,* killed or massacred in the course of the fighting retreat to China. A total of 320 officers, both French and Vietnamese, and 2,150 European and 3,300 Vietnamese soldiers survived the 800-mile trek to Yunnan."[2]

All during World War II, while the Japanese still occupied Indochina, the Allied Powers met from time to time to discuss the shape of the world which would lie ahead after the Axis powers had been defeated.

President Roosevelt held firmly to the view that France had badly exploited Indochina all during the years she had ruled that colony. President Roosevelt held that view as a black and white proposition, with no room for shadings or for according France any credit for some of the improvements she had brought to the colony.

As Elliott Roosevelt reports his father's opinions during the Casablanca Conference (January 14-21, 1943):

". . . or take Indo-China. The Japanese control that colony now. Why was it a cinch for the Japanese to conquer that land? The native Indo-Chinese have been so flagrantly downtrodden that they thought to themselves: Anything must be better than to live under French colonial rule! Should the land belong to France? By what logic and by what custom and by what historical rule?"

"Yes, but . . ."

"I'm talking about another war, Elliott," Father cried, his voice suddenly sharp. "I'm talking about what will happen to our world, if after *this* war we allow millions of people to slide back into the same semi-slavery!"

"And besides," I suggested, "we *should* have some say. We're the ones that are freeing France."

"Don't think for a moment, Elliott, that Americans would be dying in the Pacific tonight, if it hadn't been for the shortsighted greed of the French and the British and the Dutch.

Shall we allow them to do it all, all over again? *Your* son will be about the right age, fifteen or twenty years from now."

". . . When we've won the war, I will work with all my might and main to see to it that the United States is not wheedled into the position of accepting any plan that will further France's imperialistic ambitions, or that will aid or abet the British Empire in *its* imperial ambitions."[3]

While Roosevelt was clear that France should not be permitted to come into control of Indochina after World War II, he was not clear how it should be governed until accorded independence. He was vague as to whether some sort of an international agency would exercise those powers or some country chosen to act as trustee by some international organization.

President Roosevelt's statement to his son was made almost two and one half years after the adoption of the Atlantic Charter on August 14, 1941, by President Roosevelt and Prime Minister Churchill. That Charter had pledged:

". . . their respective countries . . . respect the right of all peoples to choose the form of government under which they will live; and they wish to see sovereign rights and self-government restored to those who have been forcibly deprived of them . . ."

During the course of the Cairo Conference between Roosevelt, Churchill, and Generalissimo Chiang Kai-shek of China, at a dinner party at Roosevelt's villa on November 23, 1943, the following discussion took place:

"President Roosevelt advanced the opinion that China and the United States should reach a mutual understanding on the future status of Korea, Indo-China and other colonial areas as well as Thailand. Concurring, Generalissimo Chiang stressed the necessity of granting independence to Korea. It was also his view that China and the United States should endeavor together to help Indo-China achieve independence after the war and that independent status should be restored to Thailand. The President expressed his agreement."[4]

Later at the Teheran Conference (November 28-December 1, 1943) Stalin agreed in principle with Roosevelt's view.

Churchill took a more realistic view of the situation as it would exist after the war were won and did not think that France's interests in Indochina could be disposed of as summarily as Roosevelt and Stalin hoped. On the day before President Roosevelt died (April 12, 1945) Churchill wrote him as follows:

"Now that the Japanese have taken over Indo-China and that substantial resistance is being offered by French patriots, it is essential not only that we should support the French by all the means in our power, but also that we should associate them with our operations in their country. It would look very bad in history if we failed to support isolated French forces in their resistance to the Japanese to the best of our ability, or, if we excluded the French from participation in our councils as regards Indo-China."[5]

On June 6, 1944, the Allied landings in France took place and on October 23, 1944, the United States, Britain, and Russia recognized the provisional regime of General Charles de Gaulle.

Earlier that year meetings had been held at Bretton Woods in July, August, September, and October, 1944, laying the foundation for the peace-keeping organization to be established after the fighting had ended.

At the Potsdam Conference (July 17-August 2, 1945), held after the death of President Roosevelt, it was agreed that, after the defeat of Japan, China would occupy Vietnam to the 15th parallel and Britain would occupy the Southern part of the peninsula.[6]

While it is true that General Widemeyer was serving as Chief of Staff to Generalissimo Chiang Kai-shek at the time so that the extension of the area of his command to include the northern portion of Vietnam appeared logical, it does seem peculiar that no thought was given to the historical reasons for Vietnamese aversion to being conquered by China again, nine hundred years after it had thrown off China's yoke.

President Roosevelt died on April 12, 1945. Mussolini was killed on April 28, 1945, Hitler committed suicide two days later, Germany surrendered on May 6, 1945, and Japan surrendered on August 14, 1945.

However, events in Indochina were moving forward without regard to these high-level happenings on who would do what to, for, or about Indochina.

Nominal French sovereignty over Vietnam had been retained by the French until the Japanese military forces took over control of the country on March 9, 1945, in a last dying gasp. Japan's ships were being battered on the high seas and its land forces were being crushed. The end was clearly in sight. Nevertheless, the Japanese rounded up the French soldiers and imprisoned them at great loss of French lives.

In keeping with President Roosevelt's views as to what should happen to French Indo-China after the war, at that time the United States refused to send help to those French forces who were still fighting the Japanese, together with the resistance fighters.[7]

Who were the resistance fighters?

When the Popular Front collapsed in France in 1939, the Indo-Chinese Communist Party went underground with many of its members going to the southern part of China.

"The eve of the Second World War found the leadership of the ICP [Indochinese Communist Party] forced to reorganize in exile in southern China. However, by its activities and organizational skill, the ICP had come to dominate the revolutionary scene in Vietnam and had laid the foundation for its subsequent claims to historic leadership of the Vietnamese nationalist movement."[8]

The non-Communist VNQDD leaders had also fled to Southern China after their attempted revolt was crushed by the French in 1930.

Many different accounts have been written about the founding of the Viet Minh, differing in emphasis and viewpoint.

The movement started in Southern China in May of 1941. It was but natural that it began there because the resistance leaders—both Communist and non-Communist nationalists—who had been fighting against French occupation of that country before and after the fall of France, had fled there to avoid imprisonment either by the French or the Japanese.

It also began in China because China was engaged in a struggle for survival with Japan which held Vietnam, using it as a gateway for supplies to its forces in China. Chiang Kai-shek could see advantages in encouraging the formation of a resistance movement in

Vietnam to harass the Japanese and Vichy French troops. Also involved was China's age-old desire for the domination of Vietnam.

In May 1941 a "Congress" was held in the southern part of Nationalist China with the blessing of the Nationalist Chinese war lord who governed that area. The avowed purpose of the meeting was to establish a common front against both the Japanese and the French for the liberation of Vietnam.

At that Congress, representatives of all resistance groups, including the Indochinese Communist Party led by Ho Chi Minh, and the non-communist VNQDD gathered and formed the League for the Independence of Vietnam (Viet-Nam Doc Lap Dong Minh Hoi) which came to be known as the Viet Minh.

The tight discipline of the Indochinese Communist Party, under the leadership of Moscow-trained Ho Chi Minh, and the bickering among the non-Communist groups soon led to the Communist playing a prominent but not a dominant part in Viet Minh affairs.

In October 1942, in an effort to cut out or water down this increasing Communist prominence, another meeting was held in Nationalist China, again with the approval of the same Nationalist Chinese war lord general, this time excluding the representatives of the Indochinese Communist Party, but including representatives of the Viet Minh. At that meeting they established the Vietnam Revolutionary League controlled by the VNQDD. At the head of this League was placed a Vietnamese, Nguyen Hai. He was also a general in the Nationalist Chinese army and had lived in China since 1908.

However, they could not agree among themselves. Nguyen Hai did not have the necessary leadership abilities to bring about cohesion. In an attempt to bring the groups together, the Nationalist Chinese jailed Ho Chi Minh until the spring of 1943.

Upon Ho Chi Minh's release the Nationalist Chinese General who ruled the province realized that the Vietnam Revolutionary League could not compete with the Viet Minh and placed Ho Chi Minh in charge of the Viet Minh.

In March 1944, the Provisional Republican Government of Vietnam was established with two objectives: To get rid of the French and Japanese, and to gain independence for Vietnam. This they hoped to attain with the help of Nationalist China. Representatives of the Viet Minh were in a minority in this new "Government" although Ho Chi Minh did hold a ministerial post.

While the non-communist groups represented within the new government were complacently hoping that Nationalist China would succeed in helping the new government attain its objectives, the Viet Minh were aggressive in increasing the strength of their mass support in Vietnam.

When, in March 1945, the Japanese military supplanted French military in nominal political control of Vietnam, what they took over was primarily communications lines, leaving the surrounding countryside alone. The Viet Minh did not hesitate to step into this vacuum and were quickly in control of Northern Vietnam.

By agreement between Great Britain and the United States, responsibility for fighting the Japanese in Indo-China in the closing days of World War II was placed in the hands of General Wedemeyer, the commander in chief in the China Theater, and nominally Chief of Staff to Chiang Kai-shek.

By the end of the war a small number of American forces, consisting primarily of five teams from the U.S. Office of Strategic Services (OSS), had been deployed in Vietnam. With the surrender of Japan, large numbers of Chinese Nationalist forces entered Vietnam. Elements of the U.S. Combat Section, South China Command, under Major General Philip E. Gallagher, also came to Vietnam and established cordial relations with the Viet Minh.[9]

"On October 17, 1945, a 'Viet Nam—American Friendship Association' (VAFA) was created in Hanoi. In the course of its inaugural meeting, attended by high Viet Minh officials, General Gallagher even consented to sing over the Viet Minh controlled broadcasting station."

The Viet Minh had received large quantities of military supplies from the United States during the Japanese occupation.

"Early in the (Indo-China) war, a considerable amount of equipment was shipped from Thailand to the Viet Minh ... Nationalist China sent aid by land and sea ... and some material came from the Philippines."[10]

All this equipment "from Thailand, China, and the Philippines was American equipment, brought in on American aircraft by American pilots."[11]

Ho Chi Minh also seized arms from the French and, after Japan's surrender, Japanese weapons. Ho Chi Minh thus became strong enough to defeat any of the other nationalist parties in his struggle for leadership.

In August 1945, Ho Chi Minh openly discarded the Provisional Republican Government of Vietnam and established a "Vietnam People's Liberation Committee," dominated by the Indochinese Communist Party. However, pursuant to the Potsdam agreement, the Nationalist Chinese were about to take possession of the Northern portion of Vietnam to the 15th parallel. Ho Chi Minh, knowing that the Chinese would support non-Communist liberation leaders, quickly backtracked, even though by that time the "Committee" controlled all of northern Vietnam. He abandoned the Vietnam People's Liberation Committee and on August 29, 1945, established the "Provisional Government of the Democratic Republic of Vietnam" at Hanoi which was more representative of other groups than the "Committee." However, Ho Chi Minh was president and the foreign ministry and other key ministries were in the hands of members of the Indochinese Communist Party or Viet Minh.

"Among the non-Communists were members of the Indochina branch of the French Socialist Party, one brother-in-law of a French Communist member of parliament, one Catholic, one doctor 'known for his extremist opinions,' one member of the VNQDD, one jurist, one engineer, and one man-of-letters."[12]

Just before the defeat of Japan, the Japanese had persuaded Vietnamese Emperor Bao Dai, who had been France's figurehead Emperor of Vietnam at Hue, to proclaim an independent Vietnam—including all of Vietnam in his declaration.

But Bao Dai proved as ineffectual in his new role as he had been as a figurehead of the French. In August, 1945, Bao Dai abdicated in favor of the Provisional Government of the Democratic Republic of Vietnam. The Viet Minh appointed Bao Dai to the post of Supreme Advisor to the new government, thus attempting to cloak itself with whatever legal base Bao Dai had.

The Declaration of Independence issued by Ho Chi Minh a week later—September 2, 1945—attempted to trade on United States sympathies for the independence of former colonies.[13]

With the arrival of the Nationalist Chinese occupation troops, later in September 1945, came representatives of Nationalist Chinese sponsored Vietnam liberation groups, such as the VNQDD and others. As they went south from the Chinese borders, these groups established committees to govern the towns they entered ignoring the "Provisional Government of the Democratic Republic of Vietnam." Soon, Ho Chi Minh and the Viet Minh controlled only Hanoi and some of the area to the south. The area to the North was controlled by the Nationalist Chinese sponsored liberation groups.

In an effort to woo members of these groups, the Indochinese Communist Party was publicly dissolved in November 1945 in the interests of "National Unity." This is to say, it went underground because if the name were kept "a certain number of landowners, progressive intellectuals and members of religious sects would not want to follow us."[14]

On January 6, 1946, general elections were held to select members of a General Assembly. There is considerable question as to how far these elections were "rigged." But even so, the Viet Minh did not receive an overwhelming majority of members of the General Assembly. However, with the departure of the Chinese troops early in 1946 (Chiang Kai-shek was having mounting difficulties in China with the Communists led by Mao Tse Tung), Ho Chi Minh began to consolidate the Viet Minh hold on Northern Vietnam. And because of the hatred of the other Chinese sponsored nationalistic opposition parties for the French, the Viet Minh had no hope of obtaining aid from the French. In March of 1946 Ho Chi Minh began the liquidation of those parties. The opposition leaders either fled to China or went underground. Those who went underground stayed there until July 11, 1946, when No Nguyen Giap, acting Minister of Interior, engaged in a campaign to arrest all opposition leaders and to purge the VNQDD newspaper *Viet-Nam*.

The new government, approved by the General Assembly, was dominated by the Viet Minh. It was definitely a government controlled absolutely by the Moscow-trained Communist Ho Chi Minh.

Open hostilities between the forces of the Republican Government of Vietnam against the French forces, still not yet up to full strength, broke out in earnest on December 19, 1946, in Hanoi, having been preceded by a number of skirmishes.

Thus began the war of the Viet Minh against the French which was to last until their defeat at Dien Bien Phu and the signing of the Geneva Accords in 1954.

During this war the French received massive economic and military assistance from the United States.

After VJ Day France tried to reassert its colonial control over Indo-China. Jean Sainteny headed the French mission and was greatly impeded by the United States in his efforts to get to Hanoi. The United States was at that time actively supplying the Viet Minh with arms and supplies through the Office of Strategic Services Mission in Hanoi.

With British help, French reinforcements finally arrived in Southern Vietnam.

On February 28, 1946, Ho Chi Minh and Sainteny signed an agreement in which France recognized "the Republic of Viet-Nam as a Free State having its own government, parliament, army, and treasury, and belonging to the Indochinese Federation and the French Union."

On May 31, 1946, Ho Chi Minh went to Paris to negotiate the final agreements. The day before he left, Admiral Thierry d'Argenlieu, who had earlier been appointed High Commissioner to Indochina, "recognized the Republic of Cochinchina as a free state" with its own army, finances, and so forth, in exactly the same terms as the Republic of Viet-Nam had been recognized on March 6th. Bernard Fall claims that d'Argenlieu acted without orders from Paris.

Whether he acted with or without orders, to Ho Chi Minh, arriving in Paris to work out final terms for the recognition of the Republic of Vietnam, it looked as though he had been tricked.

"The talks finally began at Fontainebleau . . . on July 6 [1946]. But both sides continued to make serious mistakes: Ho Chi Minh, overconfident of the strength of his Communist friends in Paris, took an inflexible position. In Indochina, d'Argenlieu arranged a 'Federal conference' in Dalat for August 1 and invited the governments of Cambodia, Cochinchina, and Laos— but not the Viet-Minh."[15]

Even though at Fontainebleau Ho Chi Minh had arrived at an agreement recognizing the March 6, 1946, agreement signed at Hanoi, fighting broke out in all of Vietnam.

The Viet Minh felt that they could defeat the French militarily before reinforcements could arrive, especially in view of the political turmoil in France. On the other hand, many of the French military personnel in Vietnam had served there in colonial days and believed that they could again colonialize that land.

CHAPTER V

VIETNAM: HOSTAGE TO THE COLD WAR

The world of sweetness and light envisioned by President Roosevelt in which China, Russia, Great Britain and the United States would mold the world as they saw fit was coming apart. Even before the end of World War II hostilities, the Soviet Union under Stalin began acting with increased intransigence. It began laying plans for spheres of influence and domination around its borders not only in Eastern Europe but in the Far East as well.

The death of President Roosevelt, on April 12, 1945, removed from the scene one of the strongest exponents of the theory that the British, the French, and the Dutch should be denied assistance in their efforts to retain or regain their former colonies.

While President Truman, during his first weeks and months in office, professed to follow the policies of President Roosevelt, the fast moving and momentous events of his first years in office brought about a change in his policies. On VJ Day, August 14, 1945, President Truman looked out over a bleak world. Economically and physically, Western Europe was a shambles. Government after government faced the threat of Communist take-overs. Russia was actively seeking to dominate all the countries on all its borders.

In a briefing paper prepared for President Truman the day after President Roosevelt died, the State Department noted the firm and uncompromising position on nearly every major question that had arisen in United States' relations with the Soviet Union. These were the Polish question, the application of the Crimea agreement on liberated areas, the agreement on the exchange of librated prisoners of war and civilians, and the San Francisco Conference. In the liberated areas under Soviet control, the Soviet Government was proceeding largely on a unilateral basis.

As President Truman saw it victory had turned a difficult ally in war into an even more troublesome peacetime partner. Russia seemed determined to take advantage of war-weakened neighbors.

However, the successful explosion of the first atomic bomb at Alamogordo, New Mexico, on July 16, 1945—slightly more than two months after VE Day and almost three months after the death of President Roosevelt—brought a revolutionary change in thinking on the part of the United States and its foreign policy makers. In dealing with Stalin it seemed to place in the hands of the United States negotiators what they thought was a weapon of enormous strength.

Gar Alperovitz, of the Harvard Institute of Politics, has stated in his analysis of this period entitled "Atomic Diplomacy: Hiroshima and Potsdam:"

"Contrary to a commonly held view, it is abundantly clear that the atomic bomb profoundly influenced the way American policy makers viewed political problems. Or, as Admiral Leahy has neatly summarized the point: 'One factor that was to change a lot of ideas, including my own, was the atom bomb . . . There is both truth and precision in Truman's statement to Stimson that the weapon 'gave him an entirely new feeling of confidence.'

"Before the atomic bomb was tested . . . Western policy makers harbored very grave doubts that Britain and America could challenge Soviet predominance in Eastern Europe."

Truman, Churchill, and Stalin met at Potsdam on July 17, 1945. The results were discouraging for the future peace of the world. President Truman, after having expected Russian cooperation for the peaceful rebuilding of Europe, found the contrary to be the case. He therefore determined not to allow the Russians to have any part in the rebuilding of Japan.

It was during the Potsdam Conference that the Senate ratified the Charter of the United Nations, and it was only a few days after that—on August 6, 1945—that an atomic bomb—the first in history—was dropped on Hiroshima heralding the end of war in the Pacific. The following month, the Council of Foreign Ministers, created at Potsdam, met in London and again made no progress. Secretary of State Byrnes stated that at that Conference was born the United States policy against appeasement of the Soviet Union.[1]

On January 17, 1946, the first meeting of the United Nations Security Council was held. By February 16, 1946, the Soviet Union had cast its first of a long series of vetoes. On March 5, 1946, former Prime Minister Winston Churchill, in his famous speech at Fulton, Missouri, said in part:

"From Stettin in the Baltic to Trieste in the Adriatic, an iron curtain has descended across the continent."

With the Soviet Union thrusting out beyond its borders, Truman adopted a policy which was to have sweeping repercussions not only for Europe but also for the Indochina Peninsula. This policy, which was to become known as the "Truman Doctrine," is best summed up by its author George Kennan, former United States Ambassador to the Soviet Union, as follows:

". . . the main element of any United States policy toward the Soviet Union must be that of a long-term, patient but firm and vigilant containment of Russian expansive tendencies . . . it will be clearly seen that the Soviet pressure against the free institutions of the western world is something that can be contained by the adroit and vigilant application of counter-force at a series of constantly shifting geographical and political points, corresponding to the shifts and maneuvers of Soviet policy, but which cannot be charmed or talked out of existence. The Russians look forward to a duel of infinite duration . . ."[2]

This doctrine was proclaimed to the world at a joint session of the Congress on March 12, 1947, in which President Truman said, in part:

". . . it must be the policy of the United States to support free peoples who are resisting attempted subjugation by armed minorities or by outside pressures.

". . . our help should be primarily through economic and financial aid . . .

"One way of life is based upon the will of the majority, and is distinguished by free institutions, representative government, free elections, guarantees of individual liberty, freedom of speech and religion and freedom from political oppression.

"The second way of life is based upon the will of a minority forcibly imposed upon the majority. It relies upon terror and oppression, a controlled press and radio, fixed elections, and the suppression of personal freedoms . . ."[3]

Previously, on October 27, 1946, Bulgaria went behind the Iron Curtain when it elected a Communist controlled government.

Great Britain and the Netherlands had recognized the handwriting on the wall—the fact that a policy of colonialism would not be successful in the latter part of the 20th Century. On March 15, 1946, Great Britain granted independence to India within the British Commonwealth. On November 12, 1946, the Dutch granted independence to Indonesia. On January 29, 1947, the United States Marines were withdrawn from China in a situation where the chances of Chiang Kai-shek's winning looked hopeless.

When President Truman made his containment speech on March 12, 1947, which became known as the "Truman Doctrine," international Communism seemed to be on the march throughout the world. To thwart the Communist-supported guerillas in Greece and Turkey, President Truman, on May 22, 1947, signed a $400 million aid authorization bill for those two countries.

Meanwhile, the economic situation in the devastated countries of Western Europe was deteriorating rapidly. Six days after Hungary went behind the iron curtain, Secretary of State George C. Marshall, in a commencement address at Harvard on June 5, 1947, proposed the Marshall plan for the economic rehabilitation of Europe.

In his address, Secretary of State Marshall said, in part:

"The breakdown of the business structure of Europe during the war was complete . . .

". . . the consequences to the economy of the United States should be apparent to all. It is logical that the United States should . . . assist in the return of normal economic health in the world, without which there can be no political stability and no assured peace.

"Any assistance that this Government may render in the future should provide a cure rather than a mere palliative . . ."[4] (Emphasis supplied)

When the Committee for European Economic Cooperation met on July 12, 1947, to plan, in accordance within the proposals announced by Secretary of State Marshall at Harvard the preceding month, for their own economic recovery, the meetings were boycotted by he Eastern European "Iron Curtain" countries.

President Truman's message to Congress on December 19, 1947, to implement the Marshall Plan called for a program of $1 billion for European Economic Recovery. From the standpoint of United States policy toward the struggle in Vietnam, this program is significant, for it was through this program that billions were funneled to France for use in fighting to recolonialize Vietnam. Although more than a year before, Vietnam, under Bao Dai had become an independent State within the French Union, conditions had continued to deteriorate there.

Meanwhile the cold war continued with a mixture of successes and setbacks for the Soviet Union. Czechoslovakia fell behind the iron curtain on February 25, 1948. The blockade of Berlin began on April 1, 1948. The United States airlift into Berlin began on June 21, 1948, and ended successfully on May 12, 1949. On October 30, 1948, the Chinese Nationalist Government admitted that all of Manchuria had been lost to the Communists; on January 22, 1949, the Chinese Nationalists surrendered Peiping; and, finally on December 7, 1949, they fled to Formosa.

On April 4, 1949, the North Atlantic Treaty was agreed to in Washington by Belgium, Canada, Denmark, France, Iceland, Italy, Luxembourg, the Netherlands, Norway, Portugal, the United Kingdom and the United States. In this treaty the parties agreed that an armed attack against one or more of them either in Europe or North America would be considered an "attack against them all" and that each party would "forthwith" take such action as was necessary "including the use of armed force."[5]

Korea had all during this time continued to be a trouble spot on the world scene. During World War II it had been occupied by Japan. Under the terms of the Cairo agreement, it was to be occupied in the North to the 38th parallel by the Chinese; below that by the United States troops. A pawn in the Cold War, if it were ever to be a unified country, who would control it? The United States-Soviet Joint Commission for Korea, after innumerable meetings, could come to no agreement.

On November 14, 1947, the General Assembly of the United Nations adopted a resolution with respect to the unification of Korea and the elections there. This resolution called for the establishment of a United Nations Temporary Commission on Korea, consisting of representatives of Australia, Canada, China, El Salvador, France, India, the Philippines, Syria, and the Ukranian Soviet Socialist Republic, and for nationwide elections to be held by March 31, 1948.

Despite this resolution and subsequent actions by the United Nations to secure its compliance, the Soviet Union went ahead to organize its half of Korea. On February 16, 1948, the Soviet Union established a People's Republic in Korea and on September 19, 1948, announced all its troops would be withdrawn from Korea by January 1, 1949.

On August 15, 1948, following United Nations supervised elections in South Korea, the Republic of Korea was declared autonomous.

On January 29, 1950, France recognized Vietnam under Bao Dai and the Soviet Union recognized the Viet Minh under Ho Chi Minh.

On Sunday, June 24, 1950, North Korea invaded South Korea.

CHAPTER VI

KOREA AND VIETNAM: 1950-1954

When North Korea invaded South Korea on June 24, 1950 the Berlin airlift had ended only slightly more than a year before. To President Truman, therefore, the invasion of South Korea appeared to be a continuation of communist attempts at expansion. The next day the United States asked the Secretary General of the United Nations, Trygve Lie, to call an urgent and immediate meeting of the Security Council.

The United Nations had assumed jurisdiction over the Korean problem on November 14, 1947, when the General Assembly had passed a resolution providing for a program for Korean Independence.[1] In accordance with the Moscow agreement of December 1945, the surrender of Japanese troops in Korea had been to Russian troops north of the 38th parallel and to United States forces south of that parallel. At the time of the consideration of the Korean question by the United Nations General Assembly, therefore, there was a Russian Military Government in the north and a United States Military Government in the south.

The 1947 General Assembly resolution established a United Nations Temporary Commission on Korea consisting of representatives of Australia, Canada, China, El Salvador, France, India, Phillippines, Syria, and the Ukranian Soviet Socialist Republic. This Commission, by the terms of the General Assembly Resolution, was to supervise the holding of free elections for representatives in a National Assembly which would meet to form a National Government. These elections were to be held no later than March 31, 1948. The National Government of Korea, thus formed, was to establish its own security forces and arrange for the withdrawal of foreign troops from the north and from the south "as early as practicable and if possible within ninety days."

The military forces of the Soviet Union in northern Korea refused to give members of the United Nations Commission on Korea access to that part of the country.[2]

Supervised elections were held in the southern portion of Korea on May 10, 1948. The United Nations Temporary Commission certified on June 25, 1948, that "in its opinion . . . the results of the ballot . . . are a valid expression of the will of the electorate of those parts of Korea which were accessible to the Commission and in which the inhabitants constituted approximately two-thirds of the people of all Korea."[3]

On December 12, 1948, by Resolution, the United Nations General Assembly had recognized that a lawful government had been established in South Korea. That resolution also established a "Commission on Korea consisting of Australia, China, El Salvador, France, India, the Phillippines and Syria . . . to continue the work of the Temporary Commission" to work for the unification of Korea and the "integration of all Korean security forces."[4]

On January 1, 1949, President Truman issued a statement recognizing the Republic of Korea and promising that the United States Government would "endeavor to afford every aassistance and facility to the new United Nations Commission on Korea established thereunder in its efforts to help the Korean people and their lawful Government to achieve the goal of a free and united Korea."[5]

In a message to Congress on June 7, 1949, President Truman asked for funds for an economic recovery program for Korea in the amount of $150 million for the next fiscal year.[6]

On June 8, 1949, the Department of State announced that United States withdrawal of occupation forces from South Korea had already begun and would be completed shortly. At the same time it was announced that economic assistance to the Republic of Korea would continue and that military assistance to that country had been formalized through the establishment of a United States Military Advisory Group to the Republic of Korea.[7]

Thus, United States and United Nations involvement in Korea was already deep when word was brought to President Truman and to Secretary General Trygve Lie that North Korea had invaded South Korea.

The Resolution adopted by the Security Council on June 25, 1950, called for a cease fire and called "upon the authorities of North Korea to withdraw forthwith their armed forces to the thirty-eighth parallel."[8]

No cease-fire resulted from the passage of the Resolution by the Security Council. President Syngman Rhee, in the face of the advancing North Korean army, was forced to flee from his nation's capital, Seoul.

On June 27, 1950 President Truman issued a statement reading in part as follows:

"The attack upon Korea makes it plain beyond all doubt that communism has passed beyond the use of subversion to conquer independent nations and will now use armed invasion and war. It has defied the orders of the Security Council of the United Nations . . .

"Accordingly, I have ordered the Seventh Fleet to prevent attack on Formosa. . . .

"I have directed that United States forces in the Phillipines be strengthened and that military assistance to the Phillippine Government be accelerated.

"*I have similarly directed acceleration in the furnishing of military assistance to the forces of France and the Associated States in Indochina* and the dispatch of a military mission to provide close working relations with those forces . . .".[9] (Emphasis supplied)

That same day, at the request again of the United States, the United Nations Security Council met and passed a resolution recommending that "Members of the United Nations furnish such assistance to the Republic of Korea as may be necessary to repel the armed attack and to restore international peace and security in the area."[10] This resolution was passed by a vote of 9 to 0 with one abstention (Yugoslavia) and one absence (the Soviet Union).

On July 7, 1950, the United Nations Security Council passed another Resolution recommending that all nations furnishing military assistance to the Republic of Korea make such assistance available to a unified command under a commander to be furnished by the United States.[11] This resolution was passed by a vote of 7 to 1, with two abstentions (India and Egypt) and one absence (the Soviet Union). Yugoslavia cast the negative vote. India later accepted the resolution, having indicated that it had abstained originally because of lack of instructions from its government.

In January 1950, the Soviet Union had walked out of the Security Council because of that body's refusal to deny Nationalist China its seat. Had the Soviet Union not taken that drastic step of boycotting the Security Council, it could have vetoed both resolutions.

The absence of the Soviet Union from the Security Council at that fateful time and the representation of the Communist countries on the Council by Yugoslavia, which was at that time feuding with the Soviet Union and was itself the object of Stalin's wrath, is highly significant not alone in terms of what subsequently happened in Korea but also in understanding what subsequently happened in Vietnam and what is happening in Vietnam today.

At the time, President Truman and his advisers viewed the Berlin blockade (which had been overcome), the invasion of South Korea by North Korea, Mao Tse-tung's threats against Formosa, the Communist supported Huk rebellion in the Philippines, and Ho Chi Minh's fight against the French recolonializers as all being part and parcel of the same monolithic threat by the imperialist, international Communist conspiracy.

President Truman's associating of these five events was entirely in keeping with the adoption of Ambassador Kennan's concept of containment and of the doctrine of the monolithic, international Communist conspiracy under which other nations acted and reacted as Moscow directed.

The Berlin blockade had indeed been Soviet probing of the Free World's defenses.

But on June 24, 1950, when the demarcation line at the 38th parallel in Korea was violated, did Moscow and/or Peking pull the strings which made the Communist trained leaders in North Korea jump?

That seems hardly likely.

It has been shown above that in its efforts to carry out the Moscow agreements for the unification of Korea, the United States had repeatedly turned to the United Nations and its organs to obtain whatever sanctions the organized international community could bring to bear upon those blocking unification. In Korea the United States had not been very successful, but still it tried.

Was there anything in the past which would have given the Soviet Union any expectation that if North Korea marched across the thirty-eighth parallel the United States would not immediately seek United Nations support?

If the invasion had been directed out of Moscow—or even Peking —by a monolithic, international, imperialist Communist conspiracy controlled by Stalin would the Soviet Union, in the light of past United States reliance upon the United Nations, have deliberately walked out of the United Nations in January 1950, and then five months later—while still boycotting the United Nations—have ordered North Korea to invade South Korea?

Two years before, on June 28, 1948, the Stalin-Tito break had shown the world that the concept of a Communist world dominated by Stalinist Russia was not correct and that control by the Soviet Union over *all* Communist nations was not as absolute as the dogma of "containment" had envisaged.

The earlier break away from Soviet domination by Mao Tse-tung, when he decided that Communist fomented revolution in China had to be Chinese—not Russian—oriented, should have shown the world the same thing. In developing the theory of "containment" the factor of nationalism had been given too little weight. Yet in the case of Mainland China, the 19th century theories of Marx had to contend with the centuries old economic and cultural heritage of China.

In the care of Vietnam the factor of "nationalism" has also been given too little weight in evaluating what has happened and what is happening in that country.

Could North Korea, in this episode, have been relying upon promises of support from Mao Tse-tung who, only seven months earlier, had succeeded in driving Chiang Kai-shek and his Nationalist Chinese forces from the Chinese mainland to Formosa? If that theory is tenable, then it is most curious that the Mainland Chinese did not enter the war in Korea until after the thirty-eighth parallel had been crossed by the United Nations forces and Mainland China proper was in danger.

On the other hand, the North Koreans might have been acting on "their own" and seized the opportunity to capture South Korea militarily. Such action would have been an attempt to unify what had been a unified country for centuries before the Moscow agreement to divide the country at the 38th parallel only for purposes of accepting the surrender of the Japanese forces. Even under the Japanese occupation of Korea, which took place in 1910, Korea had been ruled by the Japanese as a united country.

In its report to the United Nations Secretary General on June 25, 1950, the United Nations Commission on Korea stated:

"Pyongyang [North Korean] radio allegation at 13:35 hrs. of South Korean invasion across parallel during night declared entirely false by President and Foreign Minister [of South Korea] in course of conference with Commission members and secretary. Allegations also stated Peoples Army instructed repulse invading forces by decisive counterattack and placed responsibility for consequences on South Korea."[12]

The most illuminating aspect of the United States reaction to the invasion of South Korea by North Korea, however, is the linking of that invasion to the war in Vietnam.

Until the war broke out in Korea on June 24, 1950, President Truman and his Secretary of State, Dean Acheson, had been strongly resisting all pressures, especially by the so-called "China Lobby," for a United States commitment in the Pacific to equal the United States commitment to Europe under the NATO Treaty which had been signed a little over a year before on April 4, 1949.

At that moment in time Generalissimo Chiang Kai-shek of Nationalist China was in deep trouble. The State Department's White Paper, issued on August 6, 1949, had placed the blame for the loss of mainland China squarely on the Generalissimo. Simultaneously, the Department of State had announced that no further economic or military aid would be furnished to Chiang Kai-shek. On January 5, 1950, the United Kingdom had broken relations with Chiang Kai-shek's Government. The following day, the United Kingdom had recognized the Communist Government of Mao Tse-tung in Peking.

In an article in the *U. S. News & World Report* on May 5, 1950 entitled "Chiang Awaits End—Or World War III" the headings read:

"Chinese Communists can take what's left of Chiang Kai-shek's power almost at will. He's practically down to his last island.

"Chiang's Nationalists, crowded onto Formosa, are in hostile territory. They are exposed to air attack and invasion.

"Way out, as Chiang's friends see it, is a U. S.-Russian war. Only American arms, on a grand scale, could help him hold on." The article went on to say:

"His [Chiang Kai-shek's] remaining hope is that, in some way, war will break out soon between Russia and the United States, leading to full-scale American help to protect him in his present position and eventually to restore him to rule over China itself."

By coincidence, that same issue of the *U. S. News and World Report* contains the report of an interview with Senator Tom Connally (D., Texas), Chairman of the Senate Foreign Relations Committee, in which, among other things, he gave his opinion that neither Russia nor Red China wanted to or were prepared to wage war against the United States at that time. Yet, exactly fifty days after the interview the Soviet Union supposedly gave North Korea the "go ahead" to invade South Korea.

Considerable doubt has been cast as to which side moved first in Korea. Did South Korea goad the North Koreans into attacking, knowing that this would bring—as it did—massive aid to South Korea from the United States?[13]

It is clear that at the time of the attack, the President of South Korea, Syngman Rhee, had lost the popular elections which the United States had insisted on his having. North Korea had intensified its propaganda campaign for reunification. There was always a chance that the new government might make a "deal" for unification with North Korea, in which event, under the then existing provisions of the United States foreign aid law, aid to South Korea would terminate.

But Syngman Rhee was not the only person to benefit from the outbreak of hostilities between North and South Korea. His close friend, Generalissimo Chiang Kai-shek, also was in trouble and in imminent danger of having Red China invade the island of Formosa to which he had retreated. Chiang Kai-shek also benefited from the outbreak of hostilities in Korea. As has been seen, President Truman's immediate reaction was to send troops and aid to Korea and to send the 7th fleet to patrol off the coast of Formosa to prevent an invasion from mainland China.

The facts also fit a theory which has been advanced that the outbreak of hostilities in Korea was a result not of orders to invade, directed to North Korea, either from Moscow or Peking, but rather an attempt by two of the lesser powers—South Korea and Nationalist China—to enter upon a military adventure to bolster or even to save their own positions.

But for President Truman the hostilities in Korea meant that Moscow had given the signal to probe our defenses again. To him that meant that the probings in the Philippines and in Vietnam would also be intensified.

The United States had already been giving vast financial and limited military aid to France in trying to reconquer Indochina because of the assistance she had been giving us in carrying out the military containment concepts of NATO in Europe. In Truman's and Acheson's view of the world through 1950 glasses, it was relatively easy to equate the resistence put up by Ho Chi Minh to French recolonialization efforts with Communist probing of the Free World defenses. After all, Ho Chi Minh was admittedly a Moscow-trained Communist and Communists played a major role in the running of the Viet Minh. The French and the Bao Dai Vietnamese Government were anti-communist. Therefore the cause of the latter was just and deserving of United States support.

In this kind of viewing of the world in 1950, there were no greys—only blacks or whites. You were either anti-communist or you were against the Free World and in favor of imperialist, international Communism and its desire to take over the world. The French failed to realize that colonialism was dead and could not be resurrected. The fact that the Vietnamese people had fought against subjugation by the Chinese, the Japanese, and the French since long before Karl Marx and his concepts of the proleterian revolution was ignored.

But there was another factor influencing the reaction of President Truman in deciding to send troops to fight in Korea—the climate of the times.

A hunt for a scapegoat had been going on in the United States. The "China Lobby" insisted that a simple explanation be found as to why Chiang Kai-shek had been driven off mainland China and had permitted the island of Hainan, between Formosa and the mainland, to be taken by the Communists so easily.

There was also the need for a simple explanation as to how the Soviet Union had been able to explode an atomic bomb on September 23, 1949, thus putting itself in a position to gain equality with the United States in the field of nuclear power.

However, the explanation that it was Chiang Kai-shek's own ineptness and his failure to heed the advice of General George Marshall and others to institute needed reforms to give his people something to fight for—that was largely responsible for mainland China going behind the Bamboo Curtain would not satisfy the "China Lobby."

A Communist conspiracy in this country was conjured up to account for the loss of the Chinese Mainland.

Similarly, the fact that the Soviet Union might conceivably have had trained scientists capable, as the United States scientists were, of discovering the secrets of the atom eventually, even without espionage, was also discarded. To many people in the United States in those years the answer could only lie in betrayal at the highest levels in our own Government. The witch hunt grew in sound and fury.

On February 11, 1950, Senator Joseph McCarthy (R.-Wisc.) had stated in Wheeling, West Virginia:

"This . . . give you somewhat of the picture of the type of individuals who have been helping to shape our foreign policy. In my opinion the State Department, which is one of the most important government departments, is thoroughly infested with Communists.

"I have in my hand 57 cases of individuals who would appear to be either card carrying members or certainly loyal to the Communist Party, but who nevertheless are still helping to shape our foreign policy."[14]

Senator McCarthy was never able to produce the name of a single one of the 57 cases to which he referred.

In England, on March 1, 1950, Dr. Klaus Fuchs, a physicist who had had access to atomic secrets, was found guilty of espionage on behalf of the Russians.

Here in the United States, on March 7, 1950, Judith Coplon and Valentin Gubichev were found guilty of espionage. (The convictions were later reversed.)

These were added factors in determining President Truman's reactions to the outbreak of hostilities in Korea.

It is curious that at the time President Truman equated what was happening in Korea with what was happening in the Philippines and in Vietnam, the obvious dissimilarities of the situations were not more widely pointed out.

The government of Syngman Rhee in South Korea had come into being after popular elections on May 10, 1948, supervised by the United Nations. It was a legally constituted government under the Charter of the United Nations and a full-fledged member of that body. There could be no question as to the legality of United States military involvement in Korea along with other members of the United Nations acting in accordance with the Charter of the United Nations and pursuant to a resolution of the Security Council.[15]

The United States had sent military and economic aid to the Philippines to help that country put down a Communist trained and led, but indigenous, revolt against a duly constituted, legally recognized government which was a member of the United Nations. The United States sent no fighting men to the Philippines, although it did send military advisers to help train Philippine military personnel.

But what was the legal status of France in Vietnam when President Truman announced to the Congress on June 27, 1950, that he had directed the acceleration in the furnishing of military assistance "to the forces of France and the Associated States in Indochina"?

Up until the fall of France in 1940, France's sole claim to a legal status in Laos, Cambodia, and Vietnam was that of a military conquerer of those three countries. France's rule was based on might and not on the consent of those it governed in Indochina. Its government of that area through both French and indigenous civil servants could be considered legal only to the extent that "might made right" and that the international community of nations had not yet taken a firm stand against the widespread practice of colonialism by all the major powers.

The era of self-determination had not yet arrived.

During World War II, after the fall of France in 1940 and until 1945 when the Japanese landed in force, imprisoned the French and took over direct rule, France's role was that of agent or caretaker for the Japanese.

After VJ Day, in accordance with the Potsdam agreement, the British landed in the south to accept the surrender of the Japanese troops south of the 16th parallel. The British commander freed the French prisoners who promptly, with British blessing, executed a coup in Saigon.

It will be recalled that when the Chinese, also according to the Potsdam agreement, moved south in Vietnam to secure that area north of the 16th parallel against Japanese troops, they brought with them two non-communist parties — the Kuomintang sponsored Dong Minh Hoi and the VNQDD (the Vietnamese Nationalist Party).[16]

On March 6, 1945, the French Rrepresentative at Hanoi, Jean Sainteny, tried to reach an accomodation with Ho Chi Minh. They signed an agreement in which France recognized the Republic of Vietnam as a Free State having its own government, parliament, army, and treasury, and belonging to the Indochinese Federation and the French Union.

It should be noted that this agreement referred neither to North Vietnam nor South Vietnam but to all of Vietnam as a "Free State."

The agreement also provided:

"A total of 15,000 French troops were to be stationed north of the 16th parallel, to be relieved progressively by Vietnamese troops within five years, and France was to train and equip the Viet Minh forces."[17]

The agreement also provided for a French sponsored referendum to determine whether Tonkin, Annam, and Cochinchina — which had been separately ruled while Indochina had been a French colony should be united.

Ho Chi Minh left Vietnam for France on May 31, 1946, to try to work out the details of the agreement. The day before Ho Chi Minh left, the High Commissioner of Indochina, Admiral Thierry d'Argenlieu recognized Cochinchina as a "Free State" using the same words as were contained in the March 6, 1946, agreement between Ho Chi Minh and Jean Sainteny and the precise meaning of which Ho Chi Minh was then on his way to France to determine.[18]

Bernard Fall stated that this declaration by Admiral d'Argenlieu was "without authorization from Paris." In any event, to the Viet Minh it looked as though they had been duped into agreeing to permit French soldiers to be stationed in the north.

While Ho Chi Minh was negotiating at Fontainebleau with the French—the conference reached an impasse on "what constituted a 'free state' within the French Union and the status of Cochinchina"—Admiral d'Argenlieu took that moment to call a conference at Dalat to which he invited representatives from Laos, Cambodia, Cochinchina and Southern Annam. He did not invite the Viet Minh. Ho Chi Minh walked out of the conference in Fontainebleau.

When fighting broke out in Haiphong on November 22, 1946, France's legal status in Vietnam had not changed—it was still a colonial power trying to impose its rule upon a former colony. Its legal status did not and could not change by its almost simultaneous recognition of two separate states in Vietnam. Bao Dai had turned over his legal powers to Ho Chi Minh.

France continued in the position of dubious legality of a colonial power seeking to regain control of a colony for almost two years.

Then on June 5, 1948, the French entered into an accommodation with the ever-present Bao Dai under which the State of Vietnam, within the French Union, was recognized with Bao Dai as Chief of State. This agreement was put into effect on July 1, 1949. Both Great Britain and the United States extended *de jure* recognition to Vietnam six months later.

It should be noted that the agreement with Bao Dai recognized —as did the earlier agreement with Ho Chi Minh—the State of Vietnam, and not the State of South Vietnam or the State of North Vietnam.

These attempts by France both before and after the outbreak of the Indochina war—to set up puppet governments wholly amenable to its control—can only be considered attempts to hide behind a facade. France could not lift itself up by its bootstraps, so to speak, but by installing a puppet government tried to conceal the fact that it was attempting to recapture Vietnam.

This then was the situation vis-a-vis France and the Viet Minh on June 24, 1950, when hostilities broke out in Korea.

The Vietnamese war had not theretofore been brought before the United Nations, even though the fighting there increased in intensity.

Why had a complaint not been lodged before the United Nations?

The situation will permit only of surmises based on the state of world affairs during those years.

The United States was forging a ring of Free World countries around the Soviet Union in Western Europe and probably did not want to take action which would embarass its strong NATO ally, France. The Soviet Union was busy subverting its neighbors and creating satellites out of them. It probably did not want too much scrutiny of its own methods by an international body.

And so the world drifted along the road to the near involvement of the United States in a land war in Vietnam in aid of France in 1954, to the tragic battle of Dien Bien Phu and to the Geneva Conference in that year.

CHAPTER VII

THE FRENCH-INDOCHINA WAR

It is not the purpose of this volume to present an analysis of French or Viet Minh military tactics from November 22, 1946, to Dien Bien Phu in 1954, except as those tactics may have a bearing upon the situation in which the United States now finds itself involved in a land war in Vietnam with a 10,000 mile supply line.

Much has already been written on the fighting in Vietnam from 1946 to 1954. The war was fought with extreme violence and cruelty. It raged across the country for nearly eight years and caused great suffering among the people.[1]

When war broke out France was on the road to economic and physical recovery. The road would be long and hard, but with enormous amounts of United States economic aid it would eventually recover handsomely.

As we have seen, even before the outbreak of hostilities between the French and Viet Minh, Ho Chi Minh had begun to reorganize his party—and it definitely was *his* party.

At the beginning, the French tried to win on the basis of strictly military tactics—and classical military tactics at that. The Viet Minh would not stand and fight—as the Viet Cong refused to stand and fight when the Americans took over after the French had given up with the signing of the Geneva Accords.

While Ho Chi Minh had been in France in the summer of 1946—before war had broken out—there had been many long, parliamentary debates in the French Parliament as to what French policy should be toward Indochina. The members on the left proposed that the three States comprising Indochina-Vietnam, Laos and Cambodia—be "given equality of status and the right of secession." Prime Minister George Bidault was opposed, indicating that "recognition of dominion status after the model of the British Commonwealth would start a dangerous precedent for North Africa and Madagascar. The form of federation, therefore, that was finally accepted by the French Parliament, provided for federal bodies with purely advisory functions. The French Parliament was to retain legislative power over all important matters."[2]

This intransigence on the part of the French Parliament was one of the reasons for war breaking out between the French and the Viet Minh shortly thereafter. It is futile now to speculate on what the course of the world later might have been if the French leaders had, in 1946, been given the wisdom to realize that colonialism was dead and that it would have been wiser at that time for colonial powers such as France to recognize that fact and make the best adjustment possible.

But France at that time was rent with political problems. It has been said that one of the reasons why Ho Chi Minh was so adamant at the Fontainebleau Conference in the summer of 1946 was the belief of the French Communists that they would win the next elections in France and that they therefore would not back him so as not to "rock the boat."[3]

Be that as it may, on March 24, 1947:

"Ho Chi Minh made a firm statement of Vietnamese policy. If France would do to Vietnam, he said, what the United States had done to the Philippines and Britain to India, the Vietnamese people would bring to France friendly cooperation. If not, they would continue to resist. To this the reply of d'Argenlieu's successor, Emile Bollaert, was: 'We shall remain . . . The Constitution makes the French Union, of which Indo-China is an integral part, an institution of the Republic'."[4]

Before 1950, the Viet Minh—the Democratic Republic of Vietnam—worked energetically to build a popular base among all classes of people. The class struggle of the Communist doctrine was toned down.

"Ho Chi Minh stated: 'We do not advocate class struggle for an obvious reason. All the classes of Viet-Nam have been bled white beyond recovery by the French imperialists . . . The yellow five-cornered star (of Viet-Nam) . . . symbolized the solidarity of the five classes of people, namely the intellectuals, the farmers, the workers, the traders, and the soldiers . . . Nearly all the present members of the government are intellectuals.' "[5]

It was not until after the Communist victory on mainland China that Ho Chi Minh openly acknowledged the Communist character of his regime. At about the same time (January, 1950) Mainland China and Russia recognized the regime of Ho Chi Minh. Britain and the United States in February 1950, recognized the de facto existence of the regime of Bao Dai.

And the issue was joined.

After, coincident with, or before the cessation of hostilities in Korea on July 27, 1953, the Chinese Communists were able to ship to Ho Chi Minh increased supplies and weapons, some of Chinese manufacture, many of Russian manufacture, and very many American weapons captured in Korea by Chinese fighters.[6]

Earlier, in 1952, Ho Chi Minh had issued peace feelers to France, which had been rejected after pressure from Washington which feared that peace in Vietnam would enable Communist China to devote even more men and material to the struggle in Korea.

Bernard Fall claims that there was an agreement between the United States and France "guaranteeing that neither would conclude a peace without the other" and that the United States pressured France "not to pursue peace feelers extended by the Viet Minh in 1952" because of United States fears that any settlement would release men and supplies to fight in Korea. Negotiations going on then "could perhaps have brought about a cease fire on a far more acceptable basis than the one obtained two years later in the shadow of crushing military defeat."[7]

He charges that the armistice which President Eisenhower brought about in July, 1953, was, therefore, a breach of faith with France.

During the period from 1946 to 1953, Ho Chi Minh was able to capitalize, propaganda-wise, on the fact that France had paid only lip service to the principle of self-determination. The infusion into the struggle in Vietnam of large amounts of United States arms and material gave those Vietnamese, fighting against a reinstitution in their country of French colonial status, the idea that the United States was definitely on the side of France in its efforts.

Finally, on July 3, 1953, the French Government "announced its intention of completing the process of transferring to the Governments of the three Associated States (Laos, Cambodia, and Vietnam) all those remaining powers that are needed to perfect their independence to their own satisfaction."

Thus, after six years of fierce fighting, the promise could be wrung out of France that ultimately the three countries would be free—but still sometime vaguely in the future.

At about the same time—July 3, 1953—General Henri Navarre became the new French Commander-in-Chief in Indochina and the famous Navarre plan was approved by the United States. This was described by Secretary of State John Foster Dulles at his news conference on March 23, 1954—a month before the Geneva talks were to begin and while the Battle for Dien Bien Phu was raging—in these words:

"We have seen no reason to abandon the so-called Navarre plan, which was, broadly speaking, a two-year plan, which anticipated, if not complete victory, at least decisive military results during the fighting season which would follow the present fighting season, which is roughly a year from now.

"As you recall, that plan contemplated a very substantial buildup of the local forces and their training and equipment. It was believed that under that program, assuming there were no serious military reversals during the present fighting season, the upper hand could definitely be achieved in the area by the end of the next fighting season. There have been no such military reverses, and, as far as we can see, none are in prospect which would be of a character which would upset the broad timetable and strategy of the Navarre plan."[8]

A few days later Secretary of State Dulles was to fly to London and Paris in a vain attempt to secure the agreement of the former to join the United States in sending American and British troops to Indochina.

When Senator Mike Mansfield (D., Mont.), a shrewd student of the Far East, had returned to Washington from that area on an inspection trip for the Senate Committee on Foreign Relations, he reported to the Committee on October 27, 1953, saying in part:

"The basic problem which confronts the three governments and particularly that of Vietnam is to put down firm roots in their respective populations. They will be able to do so only if they evolve in accord with popular sentiment and they deal competently with such basic problems as illiteracy, public health, excessive populations in the deltas, inequities in labor, and land tenure, and village and agricultural improvements . . . essential that there be a constant rising of ethical standards of government and a determination to use the armies . . . strictly for national rather than private purposes."

On February 8, 1954—even before Secretary of State Dulles was to give the complacent news expressed at his news conference quoted above—Senator Mansfield elaborated on what he had seen in Vietnam and the worsening situation at that point:

"If not closely observed this crises might easily resolve itself into a Communist victory or the entanglement of the United States in another Korea. . . . Approximately 40 military posts in Cochin-China [the southern portion of Vietnam] have been seized by Communist-led rebels during the last two weeks. At least half fell through treason or desertion. Vietnamese troops have gone over to the Viet Minh, evidently without a struggle and of their own volition. . . ."[9]

Sharp debate began on the Senate floor the next day, February 9, 1954, with the announcement that the French had asked for and been promised 200 United States armed services' mechanics to service the planes the United States had given France.

Senator Stennis (D.-Miss.) led the debate saying:

" . . . it proves my contention that, step by step, we are moving into this war in Indochina, and I am afraid that we will move to a point from which there will be no return. . . . We are going to war inch by inch . . . ."[10]

Senator Mansfield joined the colloquy to add:

"I do not see what we could gain by sending troops to Indochina . . . The French and Associated States have approximately 400,000 men under arms. The Communists, the Viet Minh under Ho Chi Minh, have approximately 300,000 men . . . In a war in which there is no front, in a war which a great many people would like to forget, I will admit, I do not see that there is much that could be done by our country sending combat troops into that area."

Despite the worsening military situation in Vietnam, the siege of the French forces at Dien Bien Phu and the Viet Minh advances, the Eisenhower Administration sought to brush these facts aside. Speaking in Chicago before the Chicago World Trade Conference on February 23, 1954, Under Secretary of State Walter Bedell Smith said:

"The military situation in Indochina is favorable. Contrary to some reports, the recent advances by the Viet Minh are largely 'real estate' advances.

"Tactically," he said, "the French position is solid and the officers in the field are confident of their ability to deal with the situation."[11]

This was two and one half months before France lost the tragic battle of Dien Bien Phu.

Regardless of how much Administration officials could dissemble in public, privately they realized that morale in France was low and that the French people wanted to pull out entirely from Indochina. As Senator Mansfield had warned only two weeks before Under Secretary Smith spoke:

"Of great concern is the effect of these victories of Ho Chi Minh's forces on Paris. The French mood parallels that of some Americans in the grim winter of 1950 when our forces were withdrawing from North Korea. Many wish to abandon Indochina. And if the French quit the struggle the gateway of South Asia is open to the onward march of Communist imperialism."[12]

When, on February 8, 1954, Senator Mansfield had raised the fear that the sending of Air Force mechanics to Indochina seemed to be the first step in sending a fighting force there in real strength, he had been given assurances by the Majority Leader, Senator William Knowland (R.-Calif.) that that was not to be.

Senator Knowland stated:

"I think the action does not indicate, either directly or in-directly, any intention or desire on the part of the Government of the United States to send any ground forces to that area of the world."[13]

The discussions in the Senate, however, did operate to impose a damper on rushing efforts to send American troops to Indo-china. President Eisenhower agreed that their stay there would be limited to June, 1954.[14]

With the military battle going against the French, with constant desertions of the Vietnamese to Ho Chi Minh's banners, the Eisen-hower Administration believed that in the forthcoming Geneva meetings, in the latter part of April, the Administration's hand needed strengthening in dealing with the Russians and the Mainland Chinese at those meetings which would discuss both the Korean and the Indo-chinese situations.

Secretary of State John Foster Dulles, with President Eisenhower's blessing, set about trying to obtain a "united front" among the principal allies, well in advance of the Geneva Conference.

CHAPTER VIII

BRINKSMANSHIP—1954 STYLE

For Secretary of State John Foster Dulles in the Spring of 1954, the issues were simple and could be set forth in black and white.

Ho Chi Minh was a Moscow-trained Communist—that was admitted and known to all. He was leading the fight against the French in Indochina.

Therefore, as Dulles saw it, the Russian and Mainland Chinese Communists were "calling the shots." They were sending Ho supplies. Without them there would be no problem.

Therefore, eliminate them and their influence on Ho Chi Minh.

If this were done, Dulles felt, there would no longer be a Communist menace in Indochina—the French would rule there as they had in the past—the people of Indochina would docilely accept French rule—the old landowners would continue to receive their rents as they had in the past—the world could return to normalcy (i.e., the world before World War II).

President Eisenhower's Majority Leader in the Senate, Senator Knowland, spoke as though he realized that conditions had changed. In the Senate on February 8, 1954, he said:

" . . . the French have not been able to get the same wholehearted support for the war effort on the part of the Vietnamese that the Republic of Korea had on the part of the people of

Korea in resisting Communist aggression . . . . Ho Chi Minh has had some advantage, because he has posed as the leader in freeing that area from colonialism, whereas Korea . . . had been an independent country which was attacked from the outside . . . if the French were in a position to give assurances to the people of Vietnam, Laos, and Cambodia that, as of a certain day in the future, those people would have their independence we would see a remarkable change in that area of the world."[1]

Secretary of State Dulles *talked* as though he knew and appreciated the "facts of life" enunciated by Senator Knowland. Speaking before the General Assembly of the United Nations on September 17, 1953, he had said:

"Let me turn to Indochina. There the fighting continues. Communist forces are seeking to gain political power by military violence. Their military strength comes from a steady flow of military supplies from Communist China and Soviet Russia and from the Soviet-controlled Skoda munitions works. The pretext, until now, has been that the Associated States of Indochina were mere colonies and that the Communist war was designedd to promote 'independence' rather than to expand by violence the Soviet camp.

"It is no longer possible to support such a pretext. The French Government, by its declaration of July 3, 1953, has announced *its intention of completing the process of transferring* to the Government of the three Associated States all those remaining powers that are needed to perfect their independence to their own satisfaction."[2] (Emphasis supplied)

But the French declaration had been one of intent only. It had not been implemented. Since 1946 the French, with United States economic and military aid, had been seeking to reimpose colonial rule upon Laos, Cambodia, and Vietnam. Ho Chi Minh had taken advantage of these actions on the part of the French, with which the United States had aligned itself. It was not until seven years later, in 1953, that the French had issued a declaration saying that they intended to complete the process of granting independence to Laos, Cambodia, and Vietnam.

Apparently Secretary of State Dulles, the State Department, and the Eisenhower Administration wanted by their statements to wipe out the maimings and the deaths of the Vietnamese in their struggle against colonialism. They also wanted to give the impression and possibly believed that for all those long bitter years the French had stood for independence for three Associated States, even though their actions during those years had been to deny such independence.

In the Spring of 1954, Secretary of State Dulles, with Dien Bien Phu under severe attack from the Viet Minh, faced the possibility— the probability—of negotiating from weakness at Geneva in April, 1954.

He sought desperately to secure some strong cards at the negotiating table.

The pressures had begun late in January 1954, when Secretary of State Dulles met in Berlin with the Foreign Ministers from Britain, France, and the Soviet Union to arrange for a meeting to discuss a future meeting on Korea. French Foreign Minister Bidault, with public sentiment mounting in France for a settlement of the Indochinese war, was determined to include that area on the agenda for the April meeting at Geneva.

As President Eisenhower has related it:

"On February 9 (1954) Foster (Secretary of State John Foster Dulles) notified me from Berlin that French pressure for a conference on Indochina at Geneva was mounting. He held little hope of being able to withstand it, and said if the United States was held responsible for blocking such a conference, the moral obligation to carry on the war in Indochina might be shifted from French shoulders to ours. Finally, Foster himself found it necessary to propose a restricted four-power conference on the Far East."[3]

President Eisenhower cabled Dulles on February 10, 1954 concerning the Senate debates and the private conversations he had had with Senate leaders concerning the further involvement of the United States in Indochina.[4]

When the Viet Minh launched an all-out attack on Dien Bien Phu on March 30, 1954, the critical stage of United States relations with the French was reached. Of that period, President Eisenhower writes:

"Part of my fundamental concept of the Presidency is that *we have a constitutional government and only when there is a sudden, unforeseen emergency should the President put us into war without congressional action.*"[5] (Emphasis supplied)

The Eisenhower Administration, in the early days of 1954, did consider military intervention in Indochina on the side of the French, but, as a prerequisite, set three conditions:

(1) Intervention was to be in accordance with international law. If the French invited the United States to intervene, the United States could do so if the French request reflected "without question, the desire of the local government."[6]

(2) United States military intervention must meet with a favorable climate of world opinion. This was recognized as difficult to achieve without acting in concert with other nations which would "lend real moral standing to a venture that otherwise could be made to appear as a brutal example of imperialism. *This need was particularly acute because there was no incontrovertible evidence of overt Red Chinese participation in the Indochina conflict.*"[7] (Emphasis supplied).

(3) "Favorable action by the Congress."

On January 12, 1954, Secretary of State Dulles, laying the groundwork for strengthening the United States position at Geneva, had stated:

"The way to deter aggression is for the free community to be willing and able to respond vigorously at places and means of its own choosing."[8]

On March 29, 1954, Secretary of State Dulles, speaking before the Overseas Press Club at the Waldorf Astoria in New York, announced a new United States policy that shook the United States—and the world—saying in part:

"Under the conditions of today, the imposition on Southeast Asia of the political system of Communist Russia and its Chinese Communist ally, by whatever means, would be a grave threat to the whole free community. *The United States feels that that possibility should not be passively accepted, but should be met by united action.* This might involve serious risks. But these risks are far less than those that will face us a few years from now, if we dare not be resolute today."⁹ (Emphasis supplied)

The question was, what did the policy of "united action" entail? Did it mean that the United States was prepared to send ground troops into Indochina to aid the French?

As has subsequently been made public, such action was seriously considered but only in accordance with the three prerequisites laid down by President Eisenhower.

On the Sunday following Dulles "united action" speech, President Eisenhower sent Prime Minister Winston Churchill a message in which he said that the hands of the Free World must be strengthened before the Geneva Conference.

Without enthusiasm, Churchill replied that if Secretary of State Dulles came to London, the British Government would discuss the problem with him.

Following the announcement of the new policy of "united action" and in view of the worsening situation in Vietnam, high level talks were held in the Pentagon, in the State Department and at the White House.

The French Chief of Staff, General Paul Ely, came to Washington and secretly told U.S. leaders that American intervention was needed to save Indochina. When the Joint Chiefs of Staff met, Admiral Radford, Chairman of the Joint Chiefs of Staff, advocated air strikes from United States carriers against the Vietminh positions around Dien Bien Phu.

Admiral Robert B. Carney, chief of naval operations, and Gen. Nathan F. Twining, Air Force chief of staff, said that an airstrike would be effective in aiding the defenders of Dien Bien Phu, but doubted that this was enough to win the war for France.

Representing the Army at these discussions was General Matthew B. Ridgway, Army Chief of Staff, formerly commander of the U. N. troops in Korea. He opposed the air strike as leading inevitably to commitment of ground forces. He felt American ground forces were already overcommitted, and in no event should ground forces be committed to a land war in Vietnam.

Earlier, at the direction of President Eisenhower, General Ridgway had sent a team of experts to study the military possibilities in Vietnam. They reported:

"The area (Vietnam) . . . was practically devoid of those facilities which modern forces such as ours find essential to the waging of war. Its telecommunications, highways, railways —all the things that make possible the operation of a modern combat force on land—were almost nonexistent. Its port facilities and airfields were totally inadequate, and to provide the facilities we would need would require a tremendous engineering and logistical effort."[10]

On Saturday, April 3, 1954, Secretary of State Dulles and Admiral Radford met with eight Congressional leaders and revealed to them that the United States was seriously considering sending ground troops into action in Vietnam. However, it appeared to Secretary Dulles that Congressional approval would not be forthcoming unless:

" (1) United States intervention must be part of a coalition to include the other free nations of Southeast Asia, the Philippines, and the British Commonwealth;

"(2) The French must agree to accelerate their independence program for the Associated States so there could be no interpretation that United States assistance meant support of French colonialism;

"(3) The French must agree not to pull their forces out of the war if we put our forces in."[11]

The New York Times the next day reported the two hour and ten minute meeting at the State Department to discuss the "situation in Indochina and that Secretary of State Dulles spent 45 minutes with French Ambassador Henry Bonnet discussing strategy for the forthcoming Geneva Conference, scheduled to convene three weeks later.

That same Sunday edition of *The New York Times* reported reaction in certain parts of the world to the policy of "united action" enunciated by Secretary of State Dulles at the Overseas Press Club the preceding Monday night.

From Hong Kong the *Peiping Peoples Daily,* a Communist organ, was reported as saying that Dulles was "determined to maintain his attitude of hostility" and was "afraid of negotiation, afraid of peace and afraid of the Geneva Conference."

From New Delhi, India, it was reported that "New suspicion of U. S. motives in Asia has been aroused in some influential Indian quarters . . . Some Indians interpreted Dulles's speech of this week as an extension of the Monroe Doctrine to Asia."

The reaction in Saigon was mixed. *The New York Times* reported an increase in anti-American feeling among Communists and pro-Communists, by those who dislike Communism but "do not consider it a system so objectionable that it must be fought at the terrible cost in blood and treasure that seems to be necessary to defeat it, by those who believe Communism could be contained by compromise, by those who felt that nationalism was the 'predominant factor in the Communist movement in the Asian area' . . . and by those who resent the growing American influence in Vietnam."

The report from Saigon concluded with this significant observation: "The majority of Vietnamese people want peace at almost any price and a large proportion, now as in the past, seem to want the Viet Minh to win."

The Dulles policy, it was reported, greatly heartened the Nationalist Chinese on Formosa and those who favored them in Hong Kong.

On the same day, James Reston, writing in the *New York Times,* observed:

"M. Bidault [the French Foreign Minister] cannot return to Paris and announce that the truce talks failed and that the French must merely carry on the war as before . . . He will have to 'create a new situation' and the 'new situation' Washington expects is to be invited to carry out the logic of Mr. Dulles's speech of last Monday and enter the conflict . . . *For an Administration that has made so much of ending the fighting in Korea, this will be a tough decision. There is an election here in November and control of both the House and the Senate are at stake, but Mr. Dulles's judgement is that it will not profit the Republicans to win the House and lose a large part of Asia.*" (Emphasis supplied)

On the same day columnist William S. White wrote:
"The Democrats were not consulted before Mr. Dulles's speech in New York last Monday night warning the Communists that Southeast Asia would not be allowed to fall to them."
This reaffirmed the complaint made by Senator Mansfield the previous February when the sending of mechanics to Vietnam was under discussion.

He had said at that time:

"In other words, to use a phrase which was in high esteem during the period of the previous administration, when the Republicans were in the minority, we today, like them at that time, would like to be in on the takeoff as well as the crash landing, if there is to be a crash landing."[12]

These comings and goings about Washington that first weekend in April 1954, and these hints in the papers that the Eisenhower Administration was about to commit the United States to a vast new program abroad, as well as the reactions abroad, were noticed in the Congress.

In the Senate the explosion came on Tuesday, April 6, 1954. It was led by Senator John F. Kennedy (D.-Mass.) who first reviewed the confusion in the official releases on the actual situation in Indochina.

"Either we have not frankly and fully faced the seriousness of the military situation, or our intelligence estimates and those of the French have been woefully defective."[13]

In rapid succession, Senator Kennedy reviewed the series of optimistic statements and forecasts which had been made over the years:

(1) In February 1951, Brigadier General Francis G. Brink, head of the U. S. Military Advisory Group in Indochina, told of "the favorable turn of events" as a result of the adoption of new tactics;

(2) In the fall of 1951, French General de Lattre de Tassigny voiced optimism in a speech at the National Press Club in Washington, predicting victory, "under certain circumstances," in 18 months to 2 years;

(3) In June, 1952, an American and French joint communique stated:

"The military situation appears to be developing favorably . . . Aggression has been checked and recent indications warrant the view that the tide is now moving in our favor . . . We can look to continued favorable developments."

(4) In March 1953, French officials in Washington issued a communique predicting a new goal of "decisive military victory" in 2 years;

(5) In May 1953, President Eisenhower and Secretary of State Dulles told Congress, in support of the mutual security program for France and Indochina, that such a program would "reduce this Communist pressure to manageable proportions";

(6) In the fall of 1953, General "Iron Mike" O'Daniel, who had been sent to Indochina to discuss the situation, stated that he was "confident that the French-trained Vietnam Army when fully organized would prevail over the rebels";

(7) In September 1953 a French and American communique announced "an early and victorious conclusion";

(8) On December 2, 1953, Assistant Secretary of State for Far Eastern Affairs Walter S. Robertson announced that "In Indochina . . . we believe the tide is now turning";

(9) Later, that same month, Secretary of State Dulles stated that he did not believe that "anything that has happened upsets appreciably the timetable of General Navarre's plan (which called for a decisive military victory by about March 1955);"

(10) In February 1954, Defense Secretary Charles Wilson said a French victory was "both possible and probable" and that the war was going "fully as well as we expected it to at this stage. I see no reason to think Indochina would be another Korea";

(11) Two weeks before (the latter part of March 1954), Admiral Radford, Chairman of the Joint Chiefs of Staff, had stated "the French are going to win";

(12) At about the same time as Admiral Radford's statement, Secretary of State Dulles, at a press conference, was predicting that the French would gain the upper hand over the Viet Minh "by the end of this next fighting season."

Senator Kennedy reminded the Senate that contrary to this long series of optimistic statements, "every Member of the Senate knows that such victory today appears to be desperately remote, to say the least, despite tremendous amounts of economic and material aid from the United States, in view of a deplorable loss of French Union manpower. The call for negotiations or additional participation by other nations underscores the remoteness of such a final victory today, regardless of the outcome at Dien Bien Phu."[14]

Senator Kennedy then gave his frank assessment of the situation:

". . . no amount of American military assistance in Indochina can conquer an enemy which is everywhere and at the same time nowhere, 'an enemy of the people' which has the sympathy and covert support of the people."

Senator Kennedy referred to his own report on the situation in November 1951, after he had returned from an inspection trip to the Far East. He wrote at that time:

"In Indochina we have allied ourselves to the desperate effort of a French regime to hang on to the remnants of empire. There is no broad, general support of the native Vietnam Government among the people of that area. To check the southern drive of communism makes sense but not only through reliance on the force of arms. *The task is rather to build strong native non-Communist sentiment within these areas and rely on that as a spearhead of defense rather than upon the legions of General de Lattre. To do this apart from and in defiance of innately nationalistic aims spells foredoomed failure."* (Emphasis supplied)

Senator Kennedy also reminded the Senate of the report of the Judd (Dr. Walter H. Judd, Republican Congressman from Minnesota) Subcommittee of the House Committee on Foreign Affairs made on February 1, 1954,[15] which had stated:

"Until political independence has been achieved, an effective fighting force from the Associated States cannot be . . . expected * * *. The apathy of the local population to the menace of Viet Minh communism disguised as nationalism is the most discouraging aspect of the situation. That can only be overcome through the grant of complete independence to each of the Associated States. Only for such a cause as their own freedom will people make the heroic effort necessary to win this kind of struggle."

Senator Kennedy stated the dilemma confronting the United States in these terms:

". . . if the French persist in their refusal to grant the legitimate independence and freedom desired by the peoples of the Associated States; and if those peoples and the other peoples of Asia remain aloof from the conflict as they have in the past, then it is my hope that Secretary Dulles, before pledging our assistance at Geneva, will recognize the futility of channeling

American men and machines into that hopeless internecine struggle."

During the course of the ensuing debate, Senator Henry Jackson (D.-Wash.) expressed the belief that in the situation confronting the country the "President ought to come before the Congress and outline the policy and the program of the United States in relation to Indochina ... during the 80th Congress, a very serious situation arose in Greece, when Greece was about to fall. The President of the United States came before Congress and recommended a policy, which later became known as the Truman doctrine."

To this suggestion, Senator Everett Dirksen (R.-Ill.) took exception on grounds that the situations differed:

". . . in Greece, we were dealing with a sovereign power. In Indochina we are dealing with a colonial power which has exercised tutelage in Indochina ever since 1865."

Senator Kennedy pointed out that, while all those discussing the matter on the floor of the Senate were agreed that France must take some steps toward granting independence to Indochina, nevertheless, the French had granted concessions only after military victories on the part of the Viet Minh.

Senator Dirksen gave his opinion that there was no need to send United States troops to fight in Vietnam.

Senator Stennis (D., Miss.) joined in the discussion to assert his firm belief that the Congress would never vote to go into Indochina militarily on a unilateral basis.

Thus, two major themes were reiterated in the Senate debate on April 6, 1954. Senator after Senator—Senator Anderson (D., N. Mex.), Senator Dirksen (R., Ill.), Senator Kennedy (D., Mass.), Senator Jackson (D., Wash.), Senator Knowland (R., Calif.), Senator Magnuson (D., Wash.), and Senator Stennis (D., Miss.)—without dissent reiterated the same two themes:

(1) If the United States had to enter into the conflict in Indochina militarily, it should not do so "on its own" and (2) it should do so only if it were clearly understood that France would immediately agree to give the Associated States composing Indochina—Laos, Cambodia, and Vietnam—their independence.

Subsequent events would show that even until the end, France was not willing to do so—even to the point of rejecting the United

States offer to intervene militarily on condition that the fighting in Indochina be "internationalized."

What is amazing about this debate in the Senate on April 6, 1954, is that it came after the United States had been aiding France to re-establish its rule in Indochina for about 8 years. United States aid had been in the form of financial assistance—not in manpower. But the fact remains that financial aid to France had at that time amounted to over $2 billion and the United States did not become really insistent on the independence of Indochina until the question was raised about sending United States forces into Vietnam.

Theretofore, while paying lip service to the principle of independence, the United States had aided France in its recolonization efforts. One is forced to conclude that the official thinking of the late forties and the early fifties condoned aiding a great recolonialization power to recapture a colony so long as that aid were confined to economic and military material assistance—even though without such assistance that colonial power could not have sought to achieve its objectives.

The day after the Congressional debates, President Eisenhower held a press conference in which he enunciated his famous "domino theory." In response to a question on "the strategic importance of Indochina to the free world." Eisenhower stated:

"You had a row of dominos set up, and you knocked over the first one, and what would happen to the last one was the certainty that it would fall over very quickly . . . So you could have a beginning of a disintegration that would have the most profound influence . . . the possible sequence of events, the loss of Indo-China, of Burma, of Thailand, of the peninsula, and Indonesia following . . . the so-called island defensive chain of Japan, Formosa, of the Philippines and to the southward . . . to threaten Australia and New Zealand."

Almost within a month, Secretary of State Dulles was forced to bow to the unwillingness of Congress to act as he wished, for word went down from Congress on April 6, 1954, that it would not stand for the United States "going it alone" in Vietnam and imposing as an added condition that France must take meaningful action to accord independence to Vietnam.

This message was received in Foggy Bottom and Secretary of State Dulles prepared to leave for London and Paris to secure compliance with the Congressional requirements, well in advance of the convening of the Geneva meetings on April 26, 1954.

His departure date was set for the following Saturday, April 10, 1954.

But even before he could leave Washington, word was received from Paris that the French Cabinet had met and had refused to join the United States in warning Mainland China against intervention in the Indochinese War.

President Eisenhower states that Secretary of State Dulles had told him that "if the French wanted our open participation, this would call for a greater degree of philosophical and practical partnership than had prevailed to that time, notably in relation to proclaiming plainly their intentions regarding independence for the Associated States and in working cooperatively to expand training programs for indigenous forces."[16]

Thus, even in the face of a worsening military situation in Vietnam, France clung to the forlorn hope that somehow, in some miraculous way, France could preserve its Empire—and retain intact the ties that bound Vietnam, the richest of the three Indochinese States, to the French Union.

Hanson Baldwin military columnist of the *New York Times* on April 8, 1954, in an article entitled "Dulles' Views on Indochina Strategy Are Considered To Be Too Optimistic," pointed out that "the unpleasant truth is that the enemy still controls the major part of Vietnam; but the strategic position of the French and Vietnamese in Indochina has not changed appreciably since last year; but the few French military gains have been offset by the increasing war-weariness, political instability, and frustration in France, and that there is no quick military end in sight."

In the face of this gloomy assessment of the military situation in Vietnam by a noted military writer, Secretary of State Dulles took off for London and Paris for what would prove to be a series of bitter setbacks in terms of what he had sought.

At the Washington airport Dulles held a press conference at which he called his trip a "Mission for Peace Through Strength" and stated:

"I am going in order to consult with the British and French Governments about some of the very real problems that are involved in creating the obviously desirable united front to resist Communist aggression in Southeast Asia.

"There is danger to the entire area. It affects the vital interests of many nations in Southeast Asia and in the Western Pacific, including the Philippines and Australia and New Zealand, with whom we have mutual security treaties."

CHAPTER IX

FAILURE OF THE "MISSION OF PEACE THROUGH STRENGTH"

Secretary of State Dulles arrived in London on Sunday, April 11, 1954, and immediately plunged into a series of talks with Prime Minister Eden and other members of the British Government.

From the available information, there is a wide disparity of views as to what actually occurred.

An informal dinner meeting was held at the American Embassy in London on April 11. Eden states that he found that Dulles had modified his ideas and no longer wanted to issue a joint warning to China that further aggression would be met by armed force.

". . . (Dulles said) the United States Chiefs of Staff had suggested three weeks ago that American naval and air forces should intervene in the Indo-China war. He told us that some aircraft carriers had already moved from Manila towards the Indo-China coast. On reflection, Mr. Dulles had considered that the United States should not act alone in this matter and that before a decision to intervene were taken two conditions should be met. First there must be some assurance that the French Government were willing to grant the Associated States real independence within the French Union, so as to provide the necessary political basis for effective resistance. Second, the United States Government must ascertain whether their allies, especially the United Kingdom, Australia and New Zealand, took an equally grave view of the situation."[1]

Therefore Dulles put forward his newest proposal. He wanted to form at once an *ad hoc* Southeast Asia defense organization, thinking this would deter China from further interference in Indochina and show evidence of solidarity at Geneva.[2]

Dulles's proposal met with a cool reception. Eden took the opportunity to set Dulles straight with respect to the gloomy views held by the Americans as to the ability of the British to hold out in Malaya, especially if Indochina fell. He assured Dulles that the British were doing quite well there and that their security position had improved.

In his reply to Dulles, Eden discussed both the short range and the long range points of view.

With respect to the long range, Eden said he welcomed the concept of a Southeast Asia collective security organization "but that it would require the most careful thought and study, particularly on the question of membership. I emphasized that on no account should India and the other Asian Commonwealth countries be deliberately excluded."

Eden's problem was that in trying to hold the British Commonwealth together he was faced with a diversity of views among its members. India was militarily neutralist at that time; other members of the Commonwealth were strongly anti-Communist; others were wavering.

Eden told Dulles that the British were committed to a discussion of the Indochina question with the Soviet and Chinese Communist Governments at Geneva about two weeks from then and could not agree to military intervention before at least seeing what proposals those governments presented at Geneva. His view also was that it was doubtful "whether the situation in Indochina could be solved by purely military means."

The furthest he would go, therefore, Eden told Dulles, would be to issue a communique containing a warning that the United States and Great Britain would not permit the results of the Geneva Conference "to be prejudiced by Communist military action."

The informal talks begun on Sunday night were continued on Monday and Tuesday. They brought little change except that Eden, who had been pessimistic on Sunday night about the communiqué to be issued as a result of the talks containing any mention of collective security, was now persuaded to include the communiqué a promise to take part "with the other countries principally concerned" in examining the possibility of establishing a collective defense.

Eden was insistent, however, that the communiqué contain no specific naming of the "countries involved."[3]

During their conversations, Eden told Dulles that he could not approve the statement that the situation in Southeast Asia was analogous to the Japanese invasion of Manchuria or Hitler's invasion of the Rhineland. He flatly told Dulles that the British people would not stand for the threat of a land invasion of Indochina with promised peace talks less than two weeks away.

When Eden insisted that India should not be precluded in advance from joining any collective security arrangement, Dulles was equally insistent that no mention should be made of the possibility that India might be asked to join the group since, in that event, Dulles would have to insist that both Nationalist China and Japan also be invited.

The Dulles report to President Eisenhower on his meetings with Eden differs from that reported by Eden.

"Foster (Secretary of State John Foster Dulles) reported back with some optimism, expressing the belief he had accomplished much toward dispelling the British reluctance to say or do anything before Geneva. He noted that the communique issued that day indicated a large measure of acceptance of our view of the danger and necessity for united action. Differences remained, however. The British, fearful of becoming involved with ground forces in Indochina, took a more optimistic view of the results, in the event that the French lost northern Vietnam, than did the military in our country."[4]

From London, Dulles flew on to Paris to meet with French Foreign Minister Bidault. It will be recalled that even before Dulles left Washington for London and Paris, the French Cabinet had met and decided not to issue a warning to the Communist Chinese against further aggression.[5]

Thus Dulles' journey to Paris, after his rebuff by Eden, seemed futile.

The communiqué issued at Paris on April 14, 1954, after meetings between Dulles and Bidault and their advisors, stated:

"We deplore the fact that on the eve of the Geneva Conference, this aggression has reached a new climax in Vietnam, particularly at Dien Bien Phu, and has been renewed in Laos and extended to Cambodia.

"The independence of the three Associated States within the French Union, which new agreements are to complete, is at stake in these battles.

"We recognize that the prolongation of the war in Indo-China, which endangers the security of the countries immediately affected, also threatens the entire area of Southeast Asia and of the Western Pacific. In close association with other interested nations, we will examine the possibility of establishing, within the framework of the United Nations Charter, a collective defense to assure the peace, security and freedom of this area.

"We recognize that our basic objective at the Geneva Conference will be to seek the reestablishment of a peace in Indo-China which will safeguard the freedom of its people and the independence of the Associated States. We are convinced that the possibility of obtaining this objective depends on our solidarity."[6]

It is interesting to note that the communiqué talks of the "independence of the Associated States" as an accomplished fact although it had not been fully granted. President Eisenhower commented on this when he said:

"The French Government's statement, issued at this time, so long and tragically delayed, should have, by its wording, assured the world that the French were fighting for freedom and against Communist penetration. But the problem of achieving understanding and belief among the populations most affected was never completely solved."[7]

So Secretary of State John Foster Dulles returned to Washington to report to President Eisenhower on his "Mission of Peace through Strength."

As he had told Eden that first night in London, after his arrival, he wanted two things: a firm assurance from France for independence for the Associated States and an indication from the allies of the United States of their belief in the seriousness of the situation to be evidenced by the immediate establishment of an *ad hoc* common defense organization for the Southeast Asia area without defining the scope of the organization. He had, to some extent, secured a promise of independence for the Associated States. But on the second objective he had sought, he had received only an agreement to consider the proposition.

Secretary of State Dulles' "Mission for Peace through Strength," so openly conducted, did not escape comment in the American press.

On the first day of Dulles' meeting in London with Eden, Arthur Krock noted in the *New York Times*:

"The British Government opposition in Parliament attacked the proposal [for a statement on a united front before the Geneva Conference convened] and so did [French] Premier Laniel's variegated opposition. Therefore, Secretary Dulles's task was made much more difficult and the prospects for failure increased, with the added and basic disadvantage of a show of allied disunity on a brilliantly lighted world stage with Soviet Russia and Communist China among the spectators. In such condition, diplomacy requires a miracle to be effective."

James Reston, in an article entitled "Art of Sudden Diplomacy by John Foster Dulles," stated:

"It is hard to imagine . . . that he (Dulles) could have persuaded congressional leaders of the British or the French in advance to go along with a calculated policy of announcing that we might send troops to Indochina. Politicians don't like to do that, especially in election years.

"At the same time, neither governments nor Senators on Capitol Hill like to feel that decisions which might involve peace or war are being taken in haste or that they are being cornered into accepting United States policy with which they disagree."

Upon his return to the United States, Dulles flew to the "Little White House" at Augusta, Georgia, to report to President Eisenhower, and set in motion a course of events which infuriated Eden.

On April 16, 1954, Eden was informed by the British Ambassador to the United States, Sir Roger Makins, that Dulles had called a meeting in Washington of the Ambassadors to the United States from the United Kingdom, Australia, New Zealand, France, the Philippines, Thailand, and the three Associated States to establish an informal working party to consider the problems involved in the collective defense of Southeast Asia. This was Dulles's way, it appeared to Eden, to foreclose the composition of the membership of the Southeast Asia defense group. At the same time, Makins informed Eden that "the State Department has also repeated its warning that any attempt to include India would be countered by the inclusion of Formosa."

To Eden, this was an "extremely serious matter . . . To hold a mass meeting at this stage would be insulting to both (India and Burma) and consequently harmful in its effects on the Geneva Conference."

Dulles's action and Eden's reaction, should be considered in the light of a further difficulty to success at Geneva; namely that, two days after the Geneva meeting was to open, five Southeast Asian Prime Ministers were scheduled to assemble in Ceylon to consider common problems. The Prime Ministers would be from India, Ceylon, Burma, Indonesia and Pakistan.

"Ceylon is openly anti-communist and aware of the Communist threat. Pakistan is aligned with the Free World; the others, and notably India, are pursuing a policy of 'neutralism' and evaluating the present situation as a struggle between two equally culpable power blocks."[8]

So wrote Eden, making the strongest representations to Washington. His memorandum to the British ambassador in Washington was caustic:

"Americans may think the time past when they need consider the feeling or difficulties of their allies . . . We, at least, have constantly to bear in mind all our Commonwealth partners, even if the United States does not like some of them; and I must ask you to keep close watch on this aspect of our affairs, and not hesitate to press the United States."[9]

As a result of the representations made by Sir Roger Makins to the United States Department of State, it agreed to convert the meeting into a briefing session on the forthcoming Geneva Conference.

President Eisenhower recalls the incident thus:

". . . even before Foster (Secretary of State John Foster Dulles) left for Paris and Geneva, they had, possibly through misunderstanding, repudiated what he had thought was a firm agreement for the ambassadors of nine countries to meet in Washington to discuss unified action."

Meanwhile, another crisis had arisen.

The New York Times for Saturday, April 17, 1954, carried a story under a Washington dateline of April 14 that a "high administration source" said that, if France stopped fighting, the United States would have to send troops to fight the Communists in Indochina. The source was quoted as saying:

"In the event of a French withdrawal, Indochina probably would be Communist dominated within a month of that act. The situation in Southeast Asia relates to a war we might have to fight in the future and that we might lose."

In that unnamed official's opinion, the main target of the Communists in Korea and Indochina was Japan. Loss of Indochinese and Korean trade, if, as he anticipated they came under Communist domination and control, would make Japan an economic satelite of the Soviet Union, which was the Soviet aim. However, "he saw no reason why the French forces with the greater manpower and tremendous advantage in materials should not win."

The next day — Sunday, April 18 — the "high administration source" was identified as Vice President Richard M. Nixon, who had been addressing a meeting in Washington of the American Society of Newspaper Editors.

Public reaction to Nixon's remarks was quick.

Senator Majority Leader Knowland said that the troops should be sent to keep Southeast Asia from falling into the hands of Communists.

However, when questioned, Senators Saltonstall (R., Mass.), Hickenlooper (R-Iowa) and Kefauver (D-Tenn.) were opposed to sending troops to Southeast Asia.

Senators Lausche (D-Ohio), Flanders (R-Vt.), Kennedy (D-Mass.), Kefauver (D-Tenn.), and Humphrey (D-Minn.) expressed the need for assurances that the United States backed complete independence for the three Indochina States.

Mark Ethridge of the Louisville Courier-Journal said that the issue should be put to the people and that it was "very risky and dangerous for a man so high (as Vice President Nixon) by indirection to make such a proposition."

Colonel McCormick of the Chicago Tribune said that Nixon's remark was "the next thing to insanity. He talks like a jibbering idiot. We should stay out of Indochina no matter what happens."

Frank E. Gannett, publisher of the Gannett papers said:

"If troops are to be sent to Indochina that's a decision for Congress to make, not for any Administration officer. I have been in that part of the world and have flown over Indochina. It would be worse than Korea if we became involved there. I think it is the toughest part of the world to carry on a military operation."

The Vice President's remarks also touched off a debate in the Senate the next day, April 19, by Senator Hubert Humphrey (D-Minn.) who asked — rhetorically — how the Administration could reconcile its criticism of the Korea-type war for the year and a half past and its promises "not to have what we call struggles or wars on the periphery of the world" with the words emanating from the Administration "that it may be necessary for the United States to enter, full scale, into the Indochina conflict." He called upon the Administration to explain how its policy of "massive retaliation" fitted into what seemed to be its intentions of sending men to fight on the land in Indochina.

Senator Herbert H. Lehman (D-N.Y.) said that the speech by Vice President Nixon "has confused the people of the United States and frightened them . . . and made them very much concerned with regard to its meaning. Certainly it has confused and frightened our allies abroad, on whom we must rely to a very considerable extent and without whom we cannot possibly make an adequate defense of the freedoms of the world."

Other senators supported Senator Lehman's point of view.

For the American people who had come within a hair's breadth of becoming involved in a land war in Indochina, they could give thanks to the realism and stubbornness of the British, to the intransigence of the French, to blunt "stop, look, and listen" signals raised on the floor of the United States Senate, to the free American press which had not hesitated to cry out warnings, and for the down to earth practicality of a tough experienced soldier such as General Ridgway who later was to write:

". . . when the day comes for me to face my Maker and account for my actions, the thing I would be most humbly proud of was the fact that I fought against, and perhaps contributed to preventing, the carrying out of some hair-brained tactical schemes which would have cost the lives of thousands of men. To that list of tragic accidents that fortunately never happened I would add the Indo-China intervention."[10]

CHAPTER X

FOUR DAYS THAT ALMOST SHOOK THE WORLD

On April 20, 1954, with Secretary of State John Foster Dulles about to leave that evening for Paris and Geneva, Senator Lyndon B. Johnson (D.-Texas) attacked the so-called "Nixon War" saying:

"I am against sending American G.I.'s into the mud and muck of Indochina on a bloodletting spree to perpetuate colonialism and white man's exploitation in Asia. The Monroe Doctrine and Asia for Asians should be the foundation of our foreign policy."[1]

Senator Lyndon B. Johnson was reflecting the feelings of the people in the United States at that time.

Only a few days earlier, the 78,000 American Legionnaires in the First Division of the First Department of Illinois had resolved:

" . . . the United States should refrain from dispatching any of its Armed Forces to participate as combatants in the fighting in Indochina or in southeast Asia . . ."[2]

That same morning the *Washington Post and Times Herald* had, in its editorial pages, struck a blow against Dulles's concept that the monolithic, international Communist conspiracy was actively seeking to prevent peace in Indochina as it had done in Korea.

The editorial declared:

"No greater mistake can be made than to compare Indochina with Korea where there was a clear case of external aggression and the nation (Korea) rallied behind a strong leader. *There is neither the leader nor the popular support in Indochina; nor are there natural features for good defense . . . .*" (Emphasis supplied)

The mood of the country on April 20, 1954, was clearly against a military involvement in a land war in Southeast Asia.

Yet Dulles, as he flew to Paris, was in a most difficult position. The Presidential campaign waged less than two years before was on such issues as "the Democratic Party had been soft on Communism," "the Democratic Party lost China to Communism," and President Eisenhower's pledge to "go to Korea" to stop the killing of American boys there—which he did. Then there were the policies Dulles himself had publicly proclaimed of the United States not permitting itself to be nibbled to death in small wars around the globe while the Soviet Union and Communist China sat on the sidelines— their own men unscathed—watching the United States becoming mired in one quagmire after another. And finally, there was the McCarthy inspired anti-Communist hysteria sweeping the country, about to reach a climax of sorts in weeks of nationally televised hearings.

On the other hand, Secretary of State Dulles faced the prospect of being a participant at meetings in Geneva which could result in a large segment, if not all, of Vietnam—and possibly also Laos and Cambodia—being delivered into Communist hands. That prospect was difficult to face with mid-term elections six months away.

In the face of the crumbling defenses at Dien Bien Phu, the United States had agreed to air-lift French troops to that beleaguered area. Even that emergency operation was not having smooth sailing. India, observing a strict course of neutrality, forbade the American planes to over-fly its territory. This resulted in violent congressional reactions, with Senate Majority Leader Knowland and Senator Styles Bridges (R.-N. H.) both angrily demanding that the entire question of continued foreign economic assistance to India be "reexamined."

With all these factors shaping future events, Dulles went about attending the meetings of the NATO Council in Paris, but continuing his talks at every opportunity with French Foreign Minister Bidault and British Foreign Minister Eden.

On Friday evening, April 23, 1954, while at dinner at the Quai d'Orsay with Eden, Dulles was handed an urgent message. It was from the French Government passing on an urgent dispatch from General Navarre, commanding the French troops in Indochina, to the effect that, unless the United States could mount an immediate air strike against the Viet Minh at Dien Bien Phu, the situation there could not be saved.

Eden sent a personal message to Prime Minister Churchill giving Eden's opinion that it was too late for an air strike to do much good at Dien Bien Phu. However, Eden did tell Churchill that, if the United States wanted to discuss the possibility of putting troops into Indochina in the event that French resistance there totally collapsed as a result of the fall of Dien Bien Phu, Eden was prepared to recommend to Churchill that he agree to such discussions.

However, at Eden's request, Dulles assured him that the United States would take no action in the meantime without consulting the British.[3]

The next day Dulles told Eden the French could not be kept in the fight in Indochina unless they—the French—were convinced that the United States "would do what we can within the President's constitutional powers to join them in the fight." Dulles explained to Eden that there was no possibility of the United States giving France the air strike at Dien Bien Phu as General Navarre wanted because the President, under the Constitution, just could not act that fast.

However, according to Prime Minister Eden, both Dulles and Admiral Radford, Chairman of the Joint Chiefs of Staff, who had joined them, were quite vague as to just what action they did propose taking.

Eden and Dulles went to see Bidault.

Dulles told Bidault that if the French could assure them that the French would continue to fight, the United States, for its part, "would at once set about organizing the defense of the entire region."[4]

Eden immediately set Dulles straight. He reminded Dulles that the joint communiqué issued by Dulles and Eden in London earlier in the month did *not* commit the United Kingdom to armed intervention in Indochina.

At that point Dulles handed Bidault a letter, after first permitting Eden to glance at it. The letter was to the effect that the United States was willing to join the United Kingdom, France, and other allies to move troops into Indochina and "internationalize" the fighting there.

After the meeting broke up, the French first informed Eden that they would probably accept the United States offer. Later the French called back and told Eden that they would probably reject the offer if pressed by Dulles.

Alarmed at the United States proposal that there should be armed intervention by England and the United States before the Geneva Conference had an opportunity to negotiate a settlement, Eden flew to England and went immediately to Chequers to report to Prime Minister Churchill that he did not believe that the limited type of intervention contemplated by Dulles could achieve the results needed and that such military aid, without ground troops, would prove ineffective.

Churchill replied that he thought the British were being asked "to assist in misleading the [United States] Congress into approving a military operation, which would in itself be ineffective, and might well bring the world to the verge of a major war."[5]

Both Churchill and Eden agreed that the proper strategy before and during the Geneva Conference was to keep both the Soviet Union and Communist China guessing as to just what action England and the United States might take and that the nature of such action would depend on the results of the Conference. To them, Dulles's proposals, insofar as they could understand what they were, not only would "telegraph their punches" but would also give little room for maneuverability.

The next morning, at a special session, the British Cabinet approved a carefully worded directive containing eight points, the effect of which was to reserve Britain's position with respect to the negotiations at Geneva, making clear that Britain was committing itself to no course of action at all except to "give all possible diplomatic support to the French delegation at Geneva in efforts to reach an honorable settlement."[6]

Following that morning Cabinet meeting, however, the French informed Eden that Dulles had approached them with the proposal that the United States, the United Kingdom, France, the Philippines, and the Associated States (Laos, Cambodia, and Vietnam) should immediately issue a joint declaration to the effect that they were prepared to use "eventual military means" to stop the spread of communism. Dulles had told the French that if such a declaration were issued "President Eisenhower would be prepared to seek Congressional approval for intervention. United States naval aircraft would go into action at Dien Bien Phu on April 28."[7]

In the light of the previous Senate discussions on United States military intervention in Indochina, it is evident that Dulles, in order to save the French position in Indochina, was prepared to risk not only an acrimonious debate in the Congress but also a possible public repudiation of his position.

But the British would have none of it.

At a hastily called British Cabinet meeting that same afternoon, the United States proposal was turned down and Eden was instructed to notify both France and the United States of that decision.

The above is what transpired in France during those fateful four days, late in April 1954, as seen through Eden's eyes.

President Eisenhower gives a slightly different and less complete version of those events.

At 8 p.m. on April 23, Eisenhower received a message from Dulles in Paris passing on Navarre's message to Bidault in which Navarre wanted immediate United States B-29 air strikes from bases outside Indochina. The alternative, according to the message, was an immediate cease-fire—which Dulles interpreted to mean a cease-fire only at Dien Bien Phu. Eisenhower called Under Secretary of State Walter Bedell Smith and both agreed that "Foster's [John Foster Dulles] position should stand unchanged. There would be no intervention without allies."[8]

Eisenhower reports that Dulles had informed Eden that "major combat action by the United States forces in Indochina would need the consent of Congress."[9]

Commenting on the British Cabinet decision that there would be no unified action on Indochina prior to the Geneva Conference, Eisenhower says:

"This ended for the time being our efforts to find any satisfactory method of Allied intervention. I was disappointed but such was my confidence in Prime Minister Churchill and the British Government that I accepted their decision in the confidence that it was honestly made, and reflected their best judgment of what was best for Britain and, from their viewpoint, for the Free World."[10]

Those comings and goings by high officials of the United States, Britain, and France, those late evening flights from Paris to London and the emergency meetings of the British Cabinet could not escape public notice.

Drew Middleton, reporting in the *New York Times* from London on April 12, stated that partition of Indochina was already being discussed in British Government circles. The British believed that the best solution would be if Communist China would stop aiding the Viet Minh and "France and the Indochina States would be free to complete the pacification of the country." It was felt that the Soviet Union and Communist China would accept such a solution only at the price either of the admission of Mainland China to the United Nations or the recognition of Mainland China by the United States, or both.

The press was at that time reporting that many in the Administration were critical of Dulles for publicly overemphasizing the military situation in Indochina as being so vital to the interests of the United States without being in a position to do something about it, for urging United States military intervention, for building up the battle for Dien Bien Phu as the turning point of the Indochina war, and of jeopardizing negotiations for "united action" by antagonizing India through the conclusion of a military assistance pact with its enemy, Pakistan.[11]

Dulles left Paris for Geneva on April 24, 1954. His attempt at "united action" before the Geneva Conference had been rebuffed by both France and England. Worse than that, because the negotiations had been so openly conducted, all the world knew he had tried to strengthen the hand he was to play at Geneva—and failed.

Most importantly, the Soviet Union and Communist China knew it.

CHAPTER XI

THE 1954 GENEVA CONFERENCE

Even before the opening of the Geneva Conference on Korea and Indochina on April 26, 1954, there had been considerable speculation in some of the world's capitals about how the fighting in Indochina could be brought to an end.

One plan advanced was the partitioning of Vietnam. With two Berlins and two Koreas already in existence, why not two Vietnams?

Partition was bitterly opposed by the Vietnamese—Communist and non-Communist alike. They pointed out that even as part of the French colony of Indochina, Vietnam had been ruled as an entity.

The Vietnamese Governor of North Vietnam, echoed in Hanoi the outcry of his Emperor, Bao Dai, when he said bitterly that "the Vietnamese people would never accept partition." In his words, Vietnam was "Vietnam from Langon [north on the Chinese border] to Camau [south in the Mekong Delta]." It was reported that what the Vietnamese resented most about the proposal to partition their country was that it was "being treated like merchandise to be disposed of by the big powers at will."[1]

The Viet Minh, under Ho Chi Minh, also strongly opposed any partition of Vietnam because they saw no need for it. While it was true that the French Union forces held Hanoi, Haiphong, Hue and Saigon, most of the northern part of Vietnam was in Viet Minh hands or under Viet Minh control, as was a good portion of the south, including much of the valuable Mekong Delta. The battle for Dien Bien Phu was going very badly for the French Union forces and there was every indication—from the standpoint of the Viet Minh—that what they then did not control militarily they would control within a short time. It was also no secret that the attempts by the United States to secure allied military intervention in Indochina prior to the Geneva Conference had failed. Thus, although for different reasons, Ho Chi Minh and his followers were united with the remainder of the Vietnamese people in opposing partition.

The British were inclined to favor partition not as the best possible solution but as the only practical course of action in the light of the steadily deteriorating French situation—militarily in Indochina, politically in France.

Before and during the early stages of the Geneva Conference, the United States strongly opposed partition. That would mean that additional land and people would disappear behind the bamboo and iron curtains. After vigorously charging during the 1952 Presidential elections that the Democrats had been "soft on Communism" and had been responsible for the loss of China to the Communists, the Eisenhower Administration felt it could not be a party to any arrangement which conceded any part of Vietnam to the Communists.

On the other hand, the United States had been unsuccessful— publicly and privately—in persuading the British to join it in coming to the aid of France. Thus the United States was in the unenviable position, at the start of the Geneva Conference, of urging the French to fight on to avoid partition or worse, without being able to fight at their side.

Political columnist Marquis Childs pointed out at the time in a dispatch from Geneva that, in the view of the British, Australians, and Canadians, "the United States is proposing to use arms in Indochina to put down an internal revolution which is not in actual fact Communist imperialism."[2]

The first and foremost desire on the part of the French was to bring about an end to the fighting in all of Indochina. France desperately needed a cease fire there, especially after the fall of Dien Bien Phu on May 8, 1954, the day before the Geneva Conference turned to consider how to bring peace in Indochina, having reached an impasse on the Korean situation.[3]

To discuss the Indochina situation with them at Geneva, France, the United States, Great Britain and the Soviet Union had invited representatives from the Chinese Peoples' Republic, Laos, Cambodia, Vietnam and the Viet Minh.

The first proposal was advanced by the French on May 8, 1954. It provided for a cease fire for Laos, Cambodia, and Vietnam. In addition, for Vietnam, it proposed the regrouping of regular units of both sides in "zones of assembly," the exact areas to be determined on the basis of proposals received from the Commanders-in-Chief. All those not members of the army or the regular police forces were to be disarmed. The cease fire was to be effective upon the signing of the agreement. The disarmament and regrouping would take place a certain number (to be determined) days afterward. The agreement would be guaranteed by all the nations participating in the Geneva Conference. Violations of the agreement would call for "consultation with a view to taking appropriate measures individually or collectively."[4]

With respect to Laos and Cambodia, the French proposal called for the withdrawl of all foreign troops.

The French proposals made no provision for the political settlement of the dispute in Vietnam. The French wanted an end to the fighting in Indochina and that was all they proposed. So long as the fighting ceased, a political settlement could be argued out later. Even at that late date, France, facing a political crisis at home and with the military situation in Indochina deteriorating rapidly, was still unwilling to offer Vietnam its complete independence.

President Eisenhower, upon learning of the French proposition, summed it up as follows:

"Essentially these proposals treated the problem in two parts: (1) that of Laos and Cambodia, where the Viet Minh had created aggression from without, and (2) that of *Vietnam, where the situation was officially recognized as being primarily internal.*"[5] (Emphasis supplied)

Two points worried the President about the French proposal. In the first place, as he viewed it—although the actual text did not reveal any such intention—the regrouping of the armed forces would amount to a partition of Vietnam which "would probably lead to

Communist enslavement of millions in the northern, partitioned area."[6]

In addition, the French plan had the further defect that it provided no machinery for enforcement coming into *before* the cease fire became effective. For Eisenhower, no agreement with Communists was worth anything "unless it contains its own self-enforcing procedures."[7]

Two days after the French proposal was made public, the Viet Minh, on May 10, 1954, offered their solution to the Indochina crisis. The Viet Minh proposal dealt with both the military and political settlement of that crisis. For the first time at the Conference the proposal was advanced, in the Viet Minh plan, that general elections should be held with freedom of activity for "patriotic parties, groups, and social organizations in preparing for and holding the general elections." No provision was contained in the proposal for any outside supervision of the elections. It did contain a provision, however, for the recognition by France of the sovereignty of Vietnam throughout Vietnam, for a cease fire, for mutual exchange of prisoners, no prosecution of persons who had collaborated with the other side, no further importation of arms, for French troops to leave the country, and for a complete and simultaneous cease fire. The only supervision which would have been established, according to the Viet Minh offer, would be in the hands of mixed commissions composed of representatives from both sides.[8]

The lack, in the Viet Minh proposal, of any provision for neutral supervision of the elections cannot, in the light of the circumstances existing at the time, be interpreted as indicating an intention to "rig" the elections. Irrespective of neutral supervision of an election held in Vietnam at that time, Ho Chi Minh would have won overwhelmingly. As President Eisenhower put it:

"I have never talked or corresponded with any person knowledgeable in Indochinese affairs who did not agree that had elections been held as of the time of the fighting, possibly 80 percent of the population would have voted for the Communist Ho Chi Minh as their leader rather than Chief of State Bao Dai . . ."[9]

Bao Dai's proposal, put forward on May 12, 1954, asked a cease fire, without regroupment, and a United Nations' supervised election *after* Bao Dai's "authority over all Vietnam had been explicitly recognized and State of Vietnam control established throughout the country."[10]

With the Vietnamese and the Viet Minh both strongly opposing any partition, it looked, at that time, as if even part of Vietnam could not be saved from falling into Ho Chi Minh's hands. With that kind of a "settlement" the Eisenhower Administration could not be associated.

Secretary of State Dulles left the Geneva Conference and returned to Washington, where he still had quite a problem on his hands when he faced newsmen at his press conference on May 11, 1954.

Both he and President Eisenhower had publicly supported United States intervention in the Vietnam conflict on the basis of their so-called "domino theory." At that moment it seemed likely that all of Indochina would be swallowed up by the Communists. According to the "domino theory," if Indochina fell into Communist hands, the rest of Southeast Asia—and maybe more—would fall like a "row of dominos."

Of necessity, therefore, at his news conference, Dulles was forced to retreat from the inevitability of events under the "domino theory."

Dulles was reminded by a reporter that he had said that if one country fell the others would inevitably go Communist.

"We are trying," Dulles replied, "to change it so that would not be the case. That is the whole theory of collective security . . . As the nations come together, then the 'domino theory,' so called, ceases to apply."

The difficulty with Dulles' reply—which he quickly recognized—that the inevitability of the "domino theory" could somehow be changed by a collective security pact, was that there was no Southeast Asia collective security treaty. It was, of course, not non-existent by reason of any lack of effort on Dulles's part. But the fact remained that there was no such pact and Indochina was about to fall, it seemed. Therefore Dulles had to change the "domino theory" right then and there.

This retreat from the inevitability of the "domino theory" was properly headlined over an article by William H. Waggoner in next day's *Washington Post and Times Herald*:

"DULLES NOW CALLS DEFENSE FEASIBLE MINUS INDOCHINA—SAYS SOUTHEAST ASIA CAN BE HELD EVEN IF ASSOCIATED STATES ARE CONQUERED— 'DOMINO THEORY' OFFSET—SECRETARY CONTENDS IT DOES NOT APPLY."

Meanwhile, back at the Geneva Convention, the Soviet Union's Molotov, on May 14, proposed that the elections called for in the Viet Minh's proposal should be supervised by a commission of neutral states. This was an important modification of the Viet Minh proposal and indicated a desire for a settlement on the part of the Soviets. It was a concession which Russia would not agree to with respect to Korea. In view of Ho Chi Minh's great popularity throughout Vietnam, it was a concession which, under the then-existing conditions, would not alter the ultimate political outcome.

On June 8 Molotov backed the Viet Minh demand that the Conference settle both the military and political questions involved in the Vietnam situation, thus rejecting the French earlier proposals. In France it meant more than that. There had been hope up to that time that M. Bidault, the French Foreign Minister, might somehow obtain the consent of the Mainland Chinese and the Soviets to a cease fire while the more complicated political questions were debated. Now, with Molotov throwing Soviet support behind the Viet Minh proposals, the fighting, the killing, and the dying would continue in Vietnam while the talks at Geneva dragged on interminably.

Promptly, French Premier Laniel's government fell on the issue of Vietnam and, on June 18, Pierre Mendes-France became French Premier, pledging that unless the fighting in Vietnam were at an end by July 20, 1954, he would resign. He became his own Foreign Minister.

The next day, Under Secretary of State Walter Bedell Smith, who had taken Dulles's place at the Geneva Conference, met with Mendes-France in Paris. The French Premier said he hoped that the fighting in Vietnam could come to a speedy conclusion, but promised not to agree to any compromise "even a disguised one"—that would yield to the Viet Minh.

"Mendes-France had only one request: that we use our influence with the Vietnamese Premier, Ngo Dinh Diem—newly appointed by Bao Dai—to prevent him from needlessly obstructing any honorable truce which the French might reach with the Viet Minh."[11]

When Churchill and Eden met with Eisenhower and Dulles in Washington on June 25, 1954, they drafted a seven point program on which they agreed for the settlement of the Indochina dispute. Two of these points were that Laos and Cambodia must remain free and independent states and, if partition of Vietnam became necessary, everything south of the 18th parallel should remain non-Communist, but that any agreement reached could not preclude the later reunification of Vietnam by peaceful means.[12]

Premier Mendes-France met with Chou En Lai in Bern, Switzerland. According to Eisenhower, Chou En Lai agreed that the conflict in Vietnam should be settled in two phases, first a military ceasefire and then a political settlement. Chou En Lai agreed that the two states could be unified later on by "direct negotiations."[13]

At Mendes-France's urgent request, Dulles flew to Paris to meet with him and Eden on July 12. There Mendes-France reported that the Viet Minh had agreed to withdraw from Laos and Cambodia and recognize those two countries. Dulles still refused to return to Geneva, as France was requesting, but sent Under Secretary of State Walter Bedell Smith.

Even though the Chinese insisted up to the last minute that the United States should sign the agreements reached, the United States refused. Reasonable or not, that was Dulles's last word. The United States would not sign.

To get around the Mainland Chinese insistence on the United States signing the Geneva Agreement, Molotov and Eden agreed that no one except the French and Viet Minh military chiefs would sign and the heading of the declaration would list the governments participating.

The Accords were signed on July 21, 1954, slightly after the deadline that Mendes-France had given himself.

"The result," said Eden, "was not completely satisfactory, but we had stopped an eight-year war, and reduced international tension at a point of instant danger to world peace. This achievement was well worthwhile. All now depended on the spirit in which the agreements were carried out."[14]

CHAPTER XII

THE GENEVA ACCORDS

Many of those advancing peace proposals for Vietnam have often urged that the participants return to the Geneva Accords of 1954 as a basis for a settlement there.

In order to determine whether those Accords offer a valid starting point to work out a peace in Vietnam today, it is essential that their provisions be carefully examined and analyzed in the light of the circumstances surrounding their drafting.

When we talk about the Geneva Accords we are talking about four different documents:

(1) Agreement on the cessation of hostilities in Vietnam, July 20, 1954; (See Appendix)

(2) Agreement on the cessation of hostilities in Cambodia, July 20, 1954;

(3) Agreement on the cessation of hostilities in Laos, July 20, 1954;

(4) Final declaration of July 21, 1954, of the Geneva Conference. (See Appendix)

For purposes of this volume we are concerned with an analysis of the first and fourth documents.

The Agreement on the cessation of hostilities in Vietnam—and the similar agreements on Cambodia and Laos—deal with the cease-fire and regroupment of troops.

This agreement was signed for the Viet Minh by Ta-Quang Buu, Vice Minister of National Defense of the Democratic Republic of Vietnam, and for the French by Brigadier General Delteii. As will be seen later, much is made by the South Vietnamese that since South Vietnam did not sign this agreement it is not bound by its provisions. The fact is that the agreement was signed by the parties doing the fighting—the Viet Minh and the French. The Vietnamese had not yet been given their independence and their external affairs were still being conducted for them—as for the other French colonies— by France. When South Vietnam was finally given its independence it agreed to honor all foreign commitments made on its behalf by France.

The cessation of hostilities agreement established two Commissions for Vietnam.

The first was a joint commission composed of an equal number of representatives of the Commanders of the Viet Minh and the French. Its task was to ensure the execution of the following:

(a) A simultaneous cease-fire for Vietnam;

(b) Regroupment of the armed forces;

(c) Observance of demarcation lines between the regrouping zones and the demilitarized sections.

The second was an International Commission—which came to' be known as the International Control Commission (ICC). Its membership was to consist of Canada, Poland, and India, with India to act as Chairman. The decisions of the Commission had to be unanimous. The Commission was given the following four tasks:

(a) Controlling the movement of the armed forces of the two sides;

(b) Supervising the demarcation lines between the demilitarized areas and zones;

(c) Controlling the release of prisoners of war and civilian internees;

(d) Supervising those provisions of the agreement "regulating the introduction into the country of armed forces, military personnel and of all kinds of arms, munitions and material."

As will be seen, the enforcement of the ban on the introduction of new arms became an impossible task for the International Control

Commission. An analysis of how it went about its task and how its reports were flouted will be made later.

The agreement recognized that it would take time to evacuate French troops and therefore provided that the troops in Vietnam could be rotated, but set limits on the number so rotated in any quarter, required notification in advance to the International Control Commission, and set forth by specific name the points of entry for rotation of personnel and replacement of material in the zones north and south of the provisional demarcation line.

The agreement established three provisional assembly areas:

(1) The North around Hanoi and Haiphong was to be occupied by the French troops, who were given a maximum of 300 days to withdraw;

(2) Two areas in Central Vietnam for the Viet Minh, who were also given a maximum of 300 days to evacuate, although some sections of these areas were to be evacuated before that time;

(3) In South Vietnam for the Viet Minh, where a maximum of 200 days for evacuation was specified.

It should be noted that even this agreement for the cessation of hostilities, in dealing with political and administrative matters in the two regrouping zones on either side of the 17th parallel, specifically states that the provisions are established pending "the general elections which will bring about the unification of Vietnam."

One additional provision in the agreement on the cessation of hostilities in Vietnam—of great importance today—relates to military bases and military alliances.

With respect to military bases, Article 18 states:

". . . the establishment of new military bases is prohibited throughout Vietnam territory."

The agreement is equally adamant and absolute when it deals with foreign bases and alliances. Article 19 states:

". . . no military base under the control of a foreign State may be established in the regrouping zone of either party; the two parties shall ensure that the zones assigned to them do not adhere to any military alliance and are not used for the resumption of hostilities or to further an aggressive policy."

The Final Declaration of the Geneva Conference, announced the same day as the signing of the three agreements relating to the cessation of hostilities in Laos, Cambodia and Vietnam, attempted to deal with political and military matters in those three countries.

With respect to Vietnam, the Declaration contained four important provisions, the strict adherence to which would have had a profound effect upon the latter maintenance of peace in that area.

The first—Article 6—deals with the temporary character of the line of demarcation. It provides:

"The Conference recognizes that the essential purpose of the agreement relating to Vietnam is to settle military questions with a view of ending hostilities and that *the military demarcation line is provisional and should not in any way be interpreted as constituting a poliitcal or territorial boundary*. The Conference expresses its conviction that the execution of the provisions set out in the present declaration and in the agreement on the cessation of hostilities creates the necessary basis for the achievement in the near future of a political settlement in Vietnam." (Emphasis supplied)

It is difficult to conceive of language which more clearly spells out the temporary character of the demarcation line or negates any contention that those participating in the Geneva Conference intended by their actions in any way to attempt to bring about the establishment of two new, sovereign nations where there had been one before.

What the conferees in Geneva intended to do by regrouping the former combatants in zones in the north and the south, separated by a demilitarized zone—and they so state in section 6 quoted above —was to establish conditions under which political discussions and activities could take place.

How was the temporary demarcation line to be obliterated and the nation of Vietnam reunited? Through general elections to be held in all of Vietnam in July 1956. This is provided for by section 7 of the Geneva Declaration consisting of three concise and important sentences.

The first sentence reads:

"The Conference declares that, so far as Vietnam is concerned, the settlement of political problems, effected on the basis of respect for the principles of independence, unity and territorial integrity, shall permit the Vietnamese people to enjoy the fundamental freedoms, guaranteed by democratic institutions as a result of free elections by secret ballot."

Even for an international document, in which every word is generally scrutinized with special care, the first sentence was concisely and precisely drafted. Its meaning is entirely clear, despite later attempts to read into it other meanings.

In the first place, it reaffirms the ultimate uniting of Vietnam. Thus, the settlement of the political problems of Vietnam should be brought about based on "respect" for principles of:

Independence: At that time South Vietnam was not free from the control of France, despite the repeated urgings by the United States. North Vietnam had obtained its independence from France the "hard way";

Unity: The settlement of political problems should be based on the unification of all Vietnam;

Territorial integrity: This principle, for example, would not be satisfied if all of Vietnam were free and united except for territorial concessions given to the French, i.e., in Saigon.

Under this sentence, the settlement of the political problems should be such as to allow the Vietnamese people to enjoy fundamental freedoms. This sentence says those fundamental freedoms should be "guaranteed." How guaranteed? Guaranteed by "democratic institutions established as a result of free general elections by secret ballot."

In defending Diem's decision not to hold elections two years later, this sentence has been misinterpreted. It does not say that there must be democratic institutions in both north and south Vietnam *before* "free general elections by secret ballot" were to be held. The reverse is true. The framers of the Geneva Declaration were only reiterating the truism that the way to democratic institutions is through holding free general elections by secret ballot.

The second sentence reads:

"In order to ensure that sufficient progress in the restoration of peace has been made, and that all necessary conditions obtain for free expression of the national will, general elections shall be held in July 1956, under the supervision of an international commission composed of representatives of the Member States of the International Supervisory Commission (India, Poland, and Canada) . . ."

This sentence has also been misinterpreted, even more so than the first sentence of this section. Thus it has often been said that the reason the elections called for by this section in July, 1956, were never held was because, since North Vietnam was a Communist police state and there were not the necessary conditions there for "free expression of the national will."

Those who use this interpretation have *recast* the sentence to read: "General elections shall be held in July 1956 ONLY IF sufficient progress in the restoration of peace has been made and all the necessary conditions obtain for free expression of the national will."

But that was not intended and that is not what the sentence means or says.

Draftsmen of documents that are intended to have a legal effect must use words precisely. If the draftsmen of the Geneva Declaration had intended to attach conditions precedent to the holding of elections they would have clearly expressed themselves to that effect.

What the draftsmen were saying was:

We know that there have been considerable negotiations about when to hold general unifying elections. But, remember, before such elections can be held, there is much work to be done in bringing about conditions in which it is possible to hold such elections. At present, war-torn Vietnam is not in such a condition, even though Ho Chi Minh argues that it is.

In the first place, the evacuation of certain areas provided for in the Agreement on the Cessation of Hostilities in Vietnam could legally take up to as much as 300 days.

Then we have the problem of those from the north who want to go to the south and vice versa.

Let us compromise and *decide here and now* that in two years sufficient progress can be made in the restoration of peace and that the necessary conditions will prevail so that a free expression of national will can be obtained.

We here and now decide that such conditions will prevail at the end of two years. However, no matter how much, if any, progress has been made in the restoration of peace and whether or not the necessary conditions prevail for the free expression of the national will, we here declare and agree that general elections *shall* be held in July 1956.

It should be noted that the date set for the holding of the general elections in all Vietnam was not in any way qualified, as it would have been if the conferees had intended that a condition-precedent would have to be met before the elections could be held.

The exact date in July was to be determined on the basis of the consultants called for by the third and last sentence of section 7 which read:

"Consultations will be held on this subject between the competent representative authorities of the two zones from 20 July 1955 onwards."

Here too the conferees did not in any way modify or condition the holding of consultations. The fiat is laid down that the consultations were to be held from July 20, 1955, on. They were to be held regardless of conditions north or south of the demilitarized zone.

The third important provision of the Geneva Convention, as it related to Vietnam, dealt with refugees. Section 8 provides:

"The provisions of the agreements on the cessation of hostilities intended to secure the protection of individuals and property must be most strictly applied and must, in particular, allow everyone in Vietnam to decide freely in which zone he wishes to live."

This referred to that provision of the agreement on the cessation of hostilities in Vietnam which read:

". . . any civilians residing in a district controlled by one party who wish to go and live in the zone assigned to the other party shall be permitted and helped to do so by the authorities in that district."

The implementation of this provision was destined to give rise to violent charges and counter-charges on both sides.

From the standpoint of a discussion of what was supposed to happen in Vietnam according to the Geneva Accords and what did happen, these three provisions are the most important.

A fourth provision is related to the enforcement of the agreements on the cessation of hostilities. It is contained in Section 13 and reads as follows:

"The members of the Conference agree to consult one another on any question which may be referred to them by the International Supervisory Commission in order to study such measures as may prove necessary to ensure that the agreements on the cessation of hostilities in Cambodia, Laos, and Vietnam are respected."

Under Secretary Walter Bedell Smith, in Geneva, issued a unilateral statement saying that the United States "is not prepared to join in a declaration by the Conference such as is submitted."

Unilaterally, however, on behalf of the United States, Under Secretary of State Smith stated that the United States took note of the agreements on the cessation of hostilities and of articles 1-12, inclusive, of the Geneva Declaration and that the United States would "refrain from the threat or use of force to disturb them" and "would view any renewal of the aggression in violation of the aforesaid agreements with grave concern and as seriously threatening international peace and security."

He also called attention to the statement made in Washington on June 29, 1954, that:

"In the case of nations now divided against their will, we shall continue to seek to achieve unity through free elections supervised by the United Nations to insure that they are conducted fairly."

At the same time Under Secretary of State Smith was issuing that statement in Geneva, President Eisenhower issued a statement in Washington reading in part as follows:

". . . the United States has not itself been a party to or bound by the decisions taken by the Conference, but it is our hope that it will lead to the establishment of peace consistent with the rights and needs of the countries concerned. The agreement contains features which we do not like, but a great deal depends on how they work in practice."

President Eisenhower then went on with a reiteration of the pledge "not to use force to disturb the settlement" and that "any renewal of Communist aggression would be viewed by us as a matter of grave concern."

In the very same statement, President Eisenhower announced that the United States was pursuing discussions with other "free nations" to organize rapidly a collective defense in Southeast Asia "to prevent further direct or indirect Communist aggression in that general area."

In the light of subsequent events and the efforts of the United States to prevent the elections called for by the Geneva Declaration, United States' conduct during the Geneva Conference was most curious.

After the first few days in Geneva, Secretary of State Dulles left, never to return.

On June 15, with the Conference seemingly deadlocked, Under Secretary of State Walter Bedell Smith received a message in Geneva from President Eisenhower telling him to do everything in his power to bring the Conference to a speedy close, on the ground that the Communists seemed to be stalling.

British Foreign Minister Eden says:

"This implied that to keep hostilities going would be to help the French and their allies. I was sure that the reverse was the case."[1]

Three days later—after both Molotov and Chou En Lai had made concessions which would set in motion military talks leading to an armistice, without waiting for a political settlement—Assistant Secretary of State for Far Eastern Affairs, Walter S. Robertson, launched an attack on the Chinese Communists which Eden thought would surely wreck the Conference, but which did not do so.[2]

Secretary of State Dulles was persuaded at the last minute to send Under Secretary of State Smith back to the Conference "only after Mendes-France and Eden pointed out that the United States would not escape its obligations (or save the Vietnamese from 'slavery') by not participating at Geneva."[3]

The United States refused to endorse the Geneva Declaration, and, even when it unilaterally agreed not to use force or the threat of force to disturb the agreements on the cessation of hostilities, it refused to agree to join in consultations at some later time to decide what measures might be taken to ensure that those agreements were respected.

The United States did not sign the Geneva Declaration—but then *none* of the conferees did. *It is an unsigned document.*

The reason for this is that Communist China, up until the very end, refused to sign the Declaration unless the United States did. This Dulles refused to do. As a way of getting around this, all the participants in the Geneva Conference, including the United States and South Vietnam, were listed in the preamble as having taken part in the Conference.

All the participants except the United States and South Vietnam expressed themselves in one way or another as approving of the Geneva Declaration.

The United States issued the statements referred to above.

South Vietnam protested the fixing of the date for the elections and reserved its right of action.[4]

The cease-fire provided for by the Agreement for the Cessation of Hostilities in Vietnam came to North Vietnam on July 27, 1954, at 8:00 A.M. local time. On August 1, it was extended to Central Vietnam. By August 11 a cease-fire existed in all of Vietnam.

Now began the arduous task of rebuilding a divided country, devastated by years of a cruel war.

CHAPTER XIII

THE SEATO TREATY—AND WHAT IT REALLY MEANS

Within less than one month after a cease-fire became effective in southern Vietnam, the Southeast Asia Collective Defense Treaty —known as the SEATO treaty—was signed at Manila on September 8, 1954. (See Appendix)

Signatories of the treaty were the United States, Britain, France, Australia, New Zealand, the Philippines, Pakistan, and Thailand.

The groundwork had been laid for such a treaty by President Eisenhower and Secretary of State Dulles in the months before and during the Geneva Conference. For Britain, the Geneva Accords had, for the time being at least, staved off a World War. It was now ready to discuss a defense treaty for all of Southeast Asia which, because of the cessation of hostilities in Vietnam, would not result in an immediate British military involvement in Vietnam, as Dulles had proposed before the Geneva Conference.

The major issue at the Manila Conference was the type of commitment which would be made by the United States under the proposed treaty. Thailand, the Philippines, and Pakistan wanted a strong treaty—a solemn covenant where member nations are pledged to act immediately in case of aggression, "one for all and all for one." What they wanted was a North Atlantic Treaty Organization-type-of-treaty where the military response to aggression was automatic and where there was no need to come before the Congress for authority to commit United States military forces.

It was reported, from Manila, that the United States was holding out for an arrangement similiar to that which the United States had with Australia and New Zealand stopping "short of an automatic commitment to fight if an ally is attacked . . . The attitude is generally interpreted in the other delegations as arising from apprehension that any treaty resembling NATO in Asia would have had difficulty passing Congress."

The New York Times on September 5, 1954, editorialized: "Threatened States . . . would like to see a firm pledge of instant intervention by force in the case of aggression . . . the support of the United States, and probably Britain, will be given a more flexible type of commitment that provides for instant consultation and subsequent action 'within the limitations of constitutional processes' . . . This . . . is regarded in this country as an essential element in assuring the Senate's ratification of any accord that may be reached."

The Washington Post editorialized along the same line: "The Constitutional power of Congress to declare war is a proper safeguard against hasty military action in cases not involving immediate peril to our security. SEATO can be made meaningful and effective, as it should be, without abandoning this safeguard and without sacrificing the balance and flexibility that our defense policy ought to have."

Secretary of State Dulles himself had, just before leaving for the opening of the Geneva Conference in late April, 1954, told C. L. Sulzberger of *The New York Times* of his concept of how a Southeast Asia treaty would work:

"Were there an operational Southeast Asia alliance with France and the United States as members, Congress would have to approve American participation (in the Vietnam war). Then, perhaps, in a fashion similar to Korea, the United States might be able to intervene."[1]

Thus, Dulles did not entertain the idea that he could, at Manila, fashion a treaty acceptable to the Congress which would bypass that body. Therefore, the entreaties of the Philippines, Thailand, Pakistan and others for a NATO-type treaty were bound to fall on deaf ears.

As will be shown, the other two members of the United States Delegation at Manila were of like-mind with Dulles. Those members were Senator H. Alexander Smith (R.-N.J.) and Senator Mike Mansfield (D.-Mont.).

As will be shown by an analysis and comparison of the SEATO treaty with the NATO treaty, what was adopted at Manila in 1954 was a non-automatic treaty under which the consent of Congress to military action in Southeast Asia was a requirement. The other signatories to the SEATO treaty knew this and realized that those who had wanted a NATO type treaty had failed to persuade the United States Delegation to go along with them, despite Dulles' efforts to persuade them that what they finally got was just as good as a NATO-type treaty.

Dulles, who had set out to obtain a SEATO-non-automatic treaty rather than a NATO-automatic treaty, was successful. But Thailand, Pakistan, and the Philippines would not classify what they obtained as just as good as a NATO-type treaty.

The area defined in the treaty as covered by it is the general area of Southeast Asia., including "the entire territories of the Asian Parties" to the Treaty and the general area of the Southwest Pacific not including the Pacific area north of 21 degrees 30 minutes north latitude—thus excluding Formosa from coverage under the pact. By special protocol approved at the same time, the States of Laos and Cambodia and the free territory under the jurisdiction of the State of Vietnam were included in the territory covered by the SEATO Treaty.

The major military provisions of the Treaty are contained in Article IV.

Paragraph 1 of that Article states first that each party to the treaty "recognizes that aggression by means of armed attack in the "treaty area . . . would endanger its own peace and safety." It then provides that in that event each party agrees to take "action to meet the common danger *in accordance with its own constitutional processes.*" All "measures" taken under this paragraph must be reported "immediately" to the Security Council of the United Nations.

This paragraph relates to armed aggression. It was further restricted by a special provision inserted in the Treaty, relating only to the United States. That provision stated that, insofar as the United States was concerned, the only type of aggression and armed attack it would consider as coming within the provisions of paragraph 1 would be "Communist aggression and armed attack." The United States would consider any other type of aggression and armed attack as falling within the provisions of paragraph 2, which deals with subversion.

Earlier in the Manila Conference, Secretary of State Dulles had attempted to restrict paragraph 1 entirely to Communist aggression by means of armed attack. He sought to do so because he wanted to undertake no commitment on behalf of the United States if either Thailand or Pakistan were attacked by one of their non-Communist neighbors, a not too unlikely prospect in that part of the world. The other conferees, however, did want guarantees against just such attacks. Finally, as a compromise, Dulles was permitted to limit the United States commitment, and the United States commitment only, to Communist aggression and armed attacks, without in any way defining "Communist."

It should be especially noted that paragraph 1 contains a further limitation with respect to the action each nation obligated itself to take under its provisions. The action pledged to be taken under Article IV, paragraph 1, had to be in accordance with a nation's "own constitutional processes." For the United States, this meant that any action had to be specifically authorized by the Congress—this the nations signatory to the SEATO Treaty knew full well.

Paragraph 2 of Article IV relates to subversion and provides that if the "inviolability or the integrity" of any part of the area covered "is threatened by a fact or situation which might endanger the peace of the area, the Parties shall consult immediately" as to what to do about it.

The third and final paragraph of Article IV of the SEATO Treaty requires that any action taken under paragraph 1 could only be taken with the consent of, or at the invitation of, the government concerned.

Wherein does a SEATO-type treaty differ from a NATO-type treaty? A side-by-side comparison will readily indicate the important differences.

NATO	SEATO
"The Parties agree that an armed attack against one or more of them . . . shall be considered an attack against them all . . . each of them . . . will assist the Party . . . so attacked by taking . . . action . . . including the use of armed forces . . . ."	"Each Party . . . recognizes that aggression by means of armed attack . . . would endanger its own peace and safety . . . to take action . . . in accordance with its own constitutional processes...."

Thus, under a NATO-type treaty—ratified by the Senate—it is agreed in advance to the use of troops to repel attack. A SEATO-type treaty only promises action—without specifically mentioning the use of armed forces—but only after consultation between the signatories and then only in accordance with the signatory's own constitutional processes.

This was made abundantly clear in 1955 when the Treaty came before the Senate for its advice and consent on February 1, 1955.

Senate Floor Manager for the Treaty was Senator Walter George (D.-Georgia) who, in the aftermath of the 1954 elections in which the Democrats assumed control of the Senate, had succeeded to the position of Chairman of the Senate Committee on Foreign Relations.

Senator George immediately drew the distinction between the NATO Treaty under which "an attack made upon one of the parties is regarded as tantamount to an attack upon the United States" and the SEATO Treaty, saying:

"By contrast, the present (SEATO) treaty leaves no doubt that the constitutional powers of the Congress and the Presirent are exactly where they stood before . . . The treaty does not call for automatic action; it calls for consultation. If any course of action shall be agreed upon or decided upon, then that course of action must have the approval of Congress, because the constitutional process is provided for . . . ."

Senator H. Alexander Smith (R.,-N.J.), who had been a member of the United States Delegation to the SEATO Conference in Manila, indicated why the NATO device would not work in that part of the world:

"In southeast Asia a unique situation existed which did not lend itself to precisely the same measures of collective defense that have come into practice elsewhere in the world. It was necessary to develop a defense against aggression that would take into consideration the sensitivity of the Asian nations to any suggestion of western domination."

Senator Smith went on to point out that under the SEATO Treaty "we are not committed to the principle of NATO" and that if any emergency arose *"it will be brought before the Congress by the President* . . . under our constitutional process."

The other member of the United States Delegation to the SEATO Conference, Senator Mansfield (D., Mont.), pointed out that the new treaty did "not dedicate any major elements of the United States Military Establishment to form any army of defense in this area . . . . A NATO-type organization in the Far East would be an overextension of our military power as it stands today."

On the basis of these assurances the Senate, by the overwhelming vote of 82 to 1, gave its advice and consent to the ratification of the SEATO Treaty.

In the light of these facts, it is difficult to understand how President Johnson in his State of the Union Message to the Congress, delivered in person to a Joint Session, on the evening of January 10, 1967, could say:

"We are in South Vietnam because the United States of America and its allies are committed by the SEATO Treaty to act to meet the common danger of aggression in Southeast Asia."

It should be remembered that the SEATO Treaty had within it several built-in brakes against precipitous action.

First, there was the brake requiring specific Congressional action before troops could be committed. That had to be in accordance with United States constitutional processes.

Second, whatever action was taken had to be taken in accordance with the Charter of the United Nations.

Article I of the SEATO Treaty provides that the "Parties undertake, *as set forth in the Charter of the United Nations,* to settle any international disputes in which they may be involved by peaceful means in such manner that international peace and security are not endangered . . . ." (Emphasis supplied).

Article 2, of Chapter 1, Paragraph 4 of the Charter of the United Nations provides:

"All members shall refrain in their international relations from the threat or use of force against the territorial integrity or political independence of any state, or in any other manner inconsistent with the purpose of the United Nations."

Article 33 of Chapter 6 provides:

"The parties to any dispute, the continuance of which is likely to endanger the maintenance of international peace and security, shall first of all, seek a solution by negotiation, inquiry, mediation, conciliation, arbitration, judicial settlement, resort to regional agencies or arrangements, or other peaceful means of their own choice."

If the SEATO Treaty were to be applied, the preconditions required by the United Nations Charter—as well as the preconditions required by the Constitution of the United States—would have to be compiled with.

There are other restrictions in the SEATO Treaty which have not been adhered to.

The basic provision of the SEATO Treaty is Article IV.

Section 1 of that Article refers to aggression by means of armed attack. In that event the parties to the SEATO Treaty agree to do two things:

(1) To act in accordance with their constitutional processes— in the United States that would mean Congressional action. No such Congressional support was sought until after the Gulf of Tonkin incident—even though there had been a United States military build-up in South Vietnam before that time.

(2) To inform the Security Council of the United Nations immediately concerning measures taken against "armed attack." This was not done until after the Tonkin Gulf incident.

It is obvious, therefore, that until the Tonkin Gulf incident, the United States was operating under the second section of Article IV relating to threats "in any way other than by armed attack." This section relates to "any fact or situation which might endanger the peace of the area." In other words, this section relates to subversion, which is what the United States originally claimed was occurring in South Vietnam. But in that case the only obligation undertaken by the United States was to consult with the other signatories—which it did not do.

CHAPTER XIV

NGO DINH DIEM TAKES OVER IN SOUTH VIETNAM

Why did Ho Chi Minh accept the decision of the Geneva Conference to divide Vietnam into two parts, subject to unifying elections being held in July 1956?

After all, the government of Bao Dai—which was to become the Government of South Vietnam—denounced the declaration, reserving for itself the decision as to what future course of action it would take.

Why did not Ho Chi Minh do the same? It was obvious—especially after the loss of Dien Bien Phu—that the Viet Minh were winning on the military field of battle and would, within a short time, have under their political and military jurisdiction all of Vietnam, both north and south. Why then did Ho Chi Minh settle for "half a loaf"?

Dispatches from Geneva at that time indicated that Ho Chi Minh was very unhappy about the compromise. Many members of the Viet Minh delegation to the Geneva Conference made no secret of why they had acquiesced. They "declared openly that pressure from Chinese Communist Premier Chou En Lai and Soviet Foreign Minister Vyacheslav M. Molotov forced their regime to accept less than it rightfully should have obtained . . ."[1]

Many factors influenced Chou En Lai and Molotov to exert pressure upon Ho Chi Minh to accept the compromise.

135

The major factor motivating both Communist leaders was that neither of their countries was in any position to wage a major war at that particular time—and the United States had indicated (much to the dismay of both Churchill and Eden) that it was prepared to risk a third World War over Vietnam. While military intervention had originally been conditioned by President Eisenhower on having Great Britain as an ally, even he had gone so far on May 20, 1954, as to indicate that even that precondition was not necessarily absolute.

Asked whether he could build an effective Southeast Asia pact "without Great Britain's support," President Eisenhower had replied at his news conference:

". . . with the proper Asiatic nations, which, of course, he laid down as a *sine qua non,* and Australia and New Zealand, they might possibly work out something that would be maybe not as satisfactory or as broad as you would like it, but would be, could be workable."[2]

Unless something could be worked out at Geneva—especially something which would satisfy both Great Britain and France, both Chou En Lai and Molotov faced the distinct possibility that their countries would be drawn into a major war over Indochina.

Neither country was at that time prepared to run such a risk.

In the Soviet Union, Stalin had died only about a year before the Geneva Conference opened, giving rise to the usual political unrest attendant upon the death of any dictator. Within the Soviet Union, moreover, there were worries that the unrest could spread to its satellite Eastern European nations, spurred on by the example given by Yugoslavia's break with the Soviet Union. (Hungary and Poland revolted two years later.)

Mainland China too—in 1954—needed a time for consolidation and building. It was just completing a bloody purge of opponents and alleged opponents of the 5-year-old Mainland regime— a purge which resulted in the deaths of an estimated half a million Chinese. Moreover, Communist China had lost a considerable number of men and expended large amounts of materiel fighting in Korea. Its First Five-Year-Plan was barely a year old. To show the people of China tangible economic results, Communist China had to have peace.

Thus, Chou En Lai yielded on who would be charged with supervising the unifying elections in July 1956. In Korea, Chou En Lai and the Soviet Union had insisted that the unifying elections have no outside supervision—that they be supervised by the North and South Koreans themselves.

To obtain agreement, Chou En Lai, with respect to Vietnam, agreed to international supervision of the reunifying elections.

Both Molotov and Chou En Lai could point out to Ho Chi Minh, to overcome his objections when military victory seemed so close, that Ho's popularity in all of Vietnam was so great that he could easily win in an election even if it were not rigged. And they could point out to Ho that the Geneva Declaration was written in such a way that it was not a question of determining at some future date when the reunifying elections would be held—the Declaration was clear that the elections would be held, come what may, in July 1956.

And so, Ho Chi Minh accepted the compromise and both South and North Vietnam proceeded to live under, if not entirely up to, the Agreement on the Cessation of Hostilities and the Geneva Declaration.

In the face of the general acknowledgment that the Geneva settlements had been a serious blow to the prestige of the West and, that all things being equal, Ho Chi Minh was bound to win the election two years later, *The New York Times,* in an editorial pointed out on July 25, 1954, what had to be done to prevent Ho Chi Minh from winning that election:

"Manifestly, the Vietnamese and their French defenders must find and build up some real personality to offset the leadership quality in the adversary. It cannot be done from a chateau on the Riviera [where Bao Dai habitually took his pleasures]. It must be done in the most direct way, in hundreds of villages. There are undoubtedly free Vietnamese patriots of splendid ability. One must be chosen now to lead, and he must have strong support both within and without. The choice of such a leader must be made by the Vietnamese. But both the French and ourselves can do many things to add to his prestige. With solid political backing from France and economic backing from the United States, he should be able to go into the villages and offer a prospect of a better country and a free one under strong leadership."

This editorial prescription for what it would take to win the 1956 reunifying Vietnamese elections was eminently sound and fore-sighted. The odds were fantastic against winning those elections in the face of Ho Chi Minh's enormous popularity for having defeated the French colonialists.

Whether any South Vietnamese leader chosen to rebuild South Vietnam in so short a time could have overcome Ho Chi Minh's popularity lead by July 1956, must remain a matter of speculation. The difficulties encountered by Ho Chi Minh in North Vietnam dur-ing that period could lead to speculation today that had South Viet-nam been moving, noticeably, along the road to becoming a show-case of freedom, democracy, and economic progress, there might have been a chance for a South Vietnamese leader to win in free, internationally-supervised elections—but, at best, only a chance.

The South Vietnamese leader chosen was Ngo Dinh Diem, who took up his duties as Premier in Saigon toward the end of June 1954 when, as it turned out, the Geneva Conference was entering its last few weeks. It was obvious at that time that only through partition could any part of Vietnam be kept free of the rule of Ho Chi Minh.

Who was Ngo Dinh Diem?

How did he come to be selected Premier at that particularly crucial time?

Much has been written—some of it contradictory—about Diem, his background, his character, his abilities, and how he came to be selected.

All reports seem to agree that Diem was born on January 3, 1901. His birth is generally accepted as having taken place at Hue.[3] He was a mandarin, an ascetic, a devout Catholic, educated in the French schools in Hanoi, who entered the French-Vietnamese bu-reaucracy and rose to become Bao Dai's Minister of Interior at Hue, where he did a very respectable job. When the Japanese, in 1945, established a collaborationist regime in Vietnam, Diem refused to accept an offer of a post with that puppet government. He did the same with respect to the post-World War II government established by the Viet Minh under Ho Chi Minh.[4]

Diem came to the United States first, briefly, in 1950 and returned, after a trip to Europe, for a lengthier stay early in 1951. He lived mostly at the Maryknoll Seminary, a Catholic men's school located in New York state. During the course of his lectures in the United States on behalf of the cause of complete Vietnamese independence, Diem made powerful friends in Catholic circles. These friends included Francis Cardinal Spellman, Senator John F. Kennedy (D., Mass.), Senator Mike Mansfield (D., Mont.), Joseph P. Kennedy, the father of the Senator, and a powerful behind-the-scenes political figure in the United States, and a host of others. Earlier, he had greatly impressed Mr. Justice William O. Douglas of the Supreme Court who, after a trip to Vietnam, had written in praise of Diem's abilities.

Early in 1954 Diem was among the few nationalist leaders who could be considered "untainted." He had not, as many non-communists had, joined the Viet Minh, nor had he joined the post-war French-Bao Dai government, considered by many to be appeasers of colonialism. At that time, to find a ruler of the southern part of Vietnam who would have at least a chance of winning the loyalty of the people away from Ho Chi Minh, without bringing to his office a collaborationist record, was not easy. Professor Richard G. Scigliano of Michigan State University states: "Ngo Dinh Diem was the best known and most respected representative of the dwindling group which had committed itself neither to the Viet Minh nor to Bao Dai."[5]

There can be little doubt that United States pressure upon France was responsible for the selection of Diem by Bao Dai as Premier. The United States was in an excellent position to do so since it was, and had been, pouring vast sums of money into Vietnam in aid of the French. The French war in Vietnam was going badly. The French and the non-Communist Vietnamese already knew that they were through. If anything was to be saved in Vietnam it would have to be done with United States' aid. In addition, continuing United States' assistance would be needed in rebuilding and defending France. Reporter Sam Castain wrote:

"As a civil administrator under the French, he [Diem] had enjoyed a certain measure of popular support. Most important, he was an avowed anti-Communist. That was it. Secretary of

State John Foster Dulles picked him. Senator Mike Mansfield endorsed him. Francis Cardinal Spellman praised him. Vice President Richard M. Nixon liked him and President Dwight D. Eisenhower OK'd him."[6]

This statement neatly combines the two motives which have been advanced for the selection by the United States of Diem as Premier.

The first is that a group of powerful Catholic figures in and out of the Government in the United States combined to select Diem.[7]

The second is that the United States had decided to fight against South Vietnam coming under the eventual domination of Ho Chi Minh and it was using Diem as its instrument.

Under both theories, Diem was hand-picked by the United States and was its "man in Saigon."

In a special dispatch to *The New York Times* it was reported that when Diem arrived in Saigon on June 25, 1954, to assume the duties of his office he "received an enthusiastic welcome from his Roman Catholic supporters. However, the great mass of the Saigon population stayed home."

The French found Diem intractable and not at all agreeable to their objectives. Looking ahead, the French desired to build bridges to Hanoi so as to protect their interests both in the North and in the South. In September 1954, a French mission arrived in Washington to discuss aid not only to the French (betwen 1949 and 1957, France received $2.7 billion in U.S. aid) but also to the Associated States of Cambodia, Laos, and South Vietnam. It was at that time that the French proposed that Diem be replaced with someone more amenable to their objectives.

"This was contrary to the aims of the Americans, who . . . wanted to build up a single army that would be trained by American officers and could serve as the instrument for pacification in the countryside, where a land distribution program would be introduced."[8]

The communiqué issued in Washington on September 29, 1954, as a result of the French Mission's talks, promised that both France and the United States would continue to assist Laos, Cambodia, and Viet Nam "in their efforts to safeguard their freedom and independence and to advance the welfare of their people," promising continued assistance in the resettlement of the Vietnamese "who have of their own free will moved to free Vietnam and who already number some 300,000." The communiqué went on to state that France was prepared to retain its military forces in Vietnam. In its turn the United States expressed its willingness to consider financial assistance for those French military forces, as well as those of the three Associated States. Thereafter United States' aid to the three Associated States would go to them directly .

On October 23, 1954, President Eisenhower addressed his now famous letter to Diem proffering United States' aid. This has since been cited by United States officialdom as one justification for the present United States military involvement in Vietnam.

A careful analysis of President Eisenhower's letter to Diem— even without General Eisenhower's disavowal on August 17, 1965, of any such commitment—will indicate that no such commitment was intended or given.

The first paragraph of the Eisenhower letter, after noting that Eisenhower had been following with great interest the developments in Vietnam, goes on to say that the implications of the Geneva Agreement with respect to Vietnam "have caused grave concern regarding the future of a country *temporarily divided by an artificial grouping,* weakened by a long and exhausting war and faced with enemies without and by their subversive collaborators within." (Emphasis supplied.)

The second sentence of President Eisenhower's letter to Diem referred to the latter's request for aid to assist in the "formidable project" of moving several hundred thousand "loyal Vietnamese citizens" from the north to the south—from a "*de facto* rule and political ideology which they abhor." He told Diem that his request for that aid was being fulfilled.

In the third paragraph of President Eisenhower's letter to Diem he stated that the United States was exploring ways to make United States aid to Vietnam "more effective and to make a greater contribution to the welfare and stability" of Diem's government. He went on to tell Diem that he was asking the United States Ambassador to Vietnam to explore how that aid could assist Vietnam *"provided that your government is prepared to give assurances as to the standards of performance it would be able to maintain in the event such aid were supplied."* (Emphasis supplied)

Even this limited offer was conditioned on the Government of Vietnam giving the United States assurances as to the standards of performance it would maintain if the aid were given.

The fourth and last paragraph of President Eisenhower's letter to Diem stressed the purpose of the aid to be given. It was to help the Government of Vietnam develop and maintain "a strong, viable state, capable of resisting attempted subversion or aggression through military means."

However, President Eisenhower further conditioned the aid on "performance on the part of the Government of Vietnam in *undertaking needed reforms*." (Emphasis supplied)

As will be seen, even though the proffered aid was given, the reforms on which such aid was conditioned were never carried out.

President Eisenhower concluded his letter to Diem with the hope that the aid given by the United States "combined with your own continuing efforts" would contribute to an independent Vietnam "endowed with a strong government."

"Such a government," he wrote at the end, "would . . . be so responsive to the nationalist aspirations of its own people, so enlightened in purpose and effective in performance, that it will be respected both at home and abroad and discourage any who might wish to impose a foreign ideology on your free people." (See Appendix)

It is indeed difficult to see how on the basis of this limited, conditional offer of aid—conditions which were not fulfilled—the Johnson Administration could, eleven years later, repeatedly say that one of the reasons for the subsequent military involvement of the United States in vast military operations in Vietnam was the commitment made by President Eisenhower, especially in the face of the denial by President Eisenhower himself that he had made any such commitment.

At a news conference on August 17, 1965, in Washington, former President Eisenhower interpreted his letter of October 23, 1954, to Diem as follows:

"We said we would help that country. We were not talking about military programs, but foreign aid . . . there was no commitment given in a military context, except that as part of SEATO."

At the time of the cessation of hostilities in Vietnam, the United States had a military mission in Saigon consisting of 300 members. The functions of that Mission were only to report "to its Government the progress of the war and to supervise the American aid to the French Expeditionary Corps."[9]

The Mission had no other duties or responsibilities!

The Mission was accredited to the French Colonial Government in Vietnam and not to the Diem Government.

On November 3, 1954, the White House announced that the President had designated General J. Lawton Collins as Special United States Representative in Vietnam with the rank of Ambassador. The United States, the announcement stated, "has been particularly concerned over developments in Vietnam, a country . . . confronted by dangerous forces threatening its independence and security." General Collins was to explore with Prime Minister Ngo Dinh Diem "how a program of American aid given directly to Vietnam can best assist that country."[10]

What the statement meant by citing that Vietnam was "confronted by dangerous forces threatening its independence and security" became clear in a few days.

On November 8, 1954, Sir Anthony Eden announced in the House of Commons that, based on United States and French intelligence reports, the Viet Minh in the northern part of Vietnam had increased its armed forces by "twice as many field divisions as before the Geneva Agreement." Two days later the French charged that vast quantities of arms were flowing into North Vietnam from Mainland China.[11]

Both these reports were later found by the International Control Commission to be without foundation![11]

However, without waiting for confirmation of these reports, and without the International Control Commission having been asked to investigate the charges, the United States immediately changed the character of its Military Mission in Saigon. After Secretary of State Dulles had been restrained by the French Premier Mendes-France in Washington from taking more drastic action, General Collins announced in Saigon on November 17, 1954, that a special United States Military Mission "will soon take charge of instructing the Vietnamese Army in accordance with special American methods which have proven effective in Korea, Greece, and Turkey and other parts of the world."[12]

It is difficult to see how the changed functions of the United States military observer group in South Vietnam could be reconciled with the commitments of the French under the Geneva Accords and the unilateral pledge of the United States to respect those Accords.

Article 19 of the Geneva Agreement on the Cessation of Hostilities in Vietnam provided:

". . . the two parties (the French and Viet Minh) shall ensure that the zones assigned to them do not adhere to any military alliance and are not used for the resumption of hostilities or to further an aggressive policy."

Although at that time Diem spoke boldly about the reunification of all of Vietnam, Robert Shaplen states that "there is every reason to believe that Diem realized from the start that the division of Vietnam was likely to be permanent—short of another world war—and that he had to set his sights solely on South Vietnam."[13]

In this determination to rebuild his strength in and to hold the south, Diem had the wholehearted support of the United States.

"In effect the United States gave to the Diem government a 'blank cheque' and since then [after General Collins's all-out statements] Diem could find support in the American Embassy in Saigon and the State Department in Washington which he could not find among his own people. However, on the recommendation of General Collins the United States decided to continue and expand support for South Vietnam."[14]

The total commitment of the United States to support the regime of Ngo Dinh Diem in South Vietnam was underscored in a special report filed in the Senate on October 15, 1954, by Senator Mike Mansfield (D., Mont.).

Senator Mansfield was a delegate to the Manila Conference which worked out the SEATO Treaty. En route and returning from that Conference, Senator Mansfield spent some time in Vietnam, Laos, and Cambodia. In reporting on his trip, he said:

"In the event the Diem government fails . . . I believe that the United States should consider an immediate suspension of all aid to Vietnam and the French Union forces there . . . preliminary to a complete reappraisal of our present policies in

Free Vietnam. Unless there is reasonable expectation of fulfilling our objectives the continued expenditure of the resources of the citizens of the United States is unwarranted and inexcusable."[15]

CHAPTER XV

NGO DINH DIEM CONSOLIDATES HIS POSITION— AND HIS POWER

In his report to the Senate on October 15, 1954, Senator Mansfield pointed out that the Geneva Agreement provided for general elections in 1956 and that unless "the political difficulties of South Vietnam are overcome quickly the area now remaining outside Communist hands may pass to the Viet Minh at that time. Even before 1956, South Vietnam could give way to complete internal collapse."[1]

When Ngo Dinh Diem took his position as President of the Council of Ministers on July 7, 1954, he faced complete and utter chaos in South Vietnam—and the prospect that things would get worse before they could, if ever, get better.

Diem's power came from his appointment by Chief of State Bao Dai, who continued to reside in France. The French had not yet given South Vietnam complete independence so that Bao Dai's power derived both from French acceptance of his exercise of power and from his former position as Emperor. But, as Diem found out quickly, the powers granted to him as President of the Council of Ministers by Bao Dai were severely prescribed.

Diem did not control the South Vietnamese Army—that power still remained in the hands of General Nguyen Van Hinh, Chief of Staff of the Vietnamese Army, who not only was directly responsible to Bao Dai in France but who was also an officer in the French Army.

Diem did not control the civilian police force in the Saigon area. By special arrangements with Bao Dai the control of the police forces rested with the Binh Xuyen, a bandit-originated group operating "lucrative gambling and prostitution establishments in Saigon in addition to its control of the opium trade, a good segment of the fish and charcoal trade, and some hotels and rubber plantations."[2] A portion of the "take" by the Binh Xuyen from these "concessions" in the Saigon area was paid over to Bao Dai.

Northwest of Saigon, a large area was controlled by the Cao Dai, a religious sect claiming two million followers.

To the southwest of Saigon, another large area was controlled by another religious sect, the Hoa Hao, claiming a million and one-half followers.

In 1954, both these groups "constituted a considerable political threat, both as separatist groups and as quasi-nationalist elements that Saigon politicians sought to use to further their own ends. As such, they presented an obvious danger to the shaky Diem regime, and one that had to be dealt with cautiously."[3] These two groups had about 35,000 men under arms, collected taxes from the populations they ruled, and governed their own territories.[4]

All three groups had in the past resisted successfully any attempts by the central government in Saigon to impose any control over them. Corruption in and out of public office had been and continued to be a way of life in South Vietnam.

Diem found that the French had made no attempt to train the Vietnamese in administering a government. Those Frenchmen who had been in public office in South Vietnam were going home, leaving Diem with no trained Vietnamese government administrators.

Adding to all of Diem's troubles was the fact that refugees from the North were streaming South and some provision had to be made for their feeding, clothing, and housing. By the middle of September 1954, 300,000 of such refugees had come South; by the time the deadline established for relocation by the Geneva Accords was reached, some 800,000 refugees would have come South, the vast majority of them Catholics. While these refugees were to form a valuable political base of support for Diem, nevertheless, their care put a strain on his government in the early, unsure days.

"Saigon," Senator Mansfield reported, "has seethed with intrigue and counter-intrigue, with rumors and counter-rumors. The political plotting goes on in army circles, government circles, foreign circles, in party headquarters, in police headquarters, and even in the demi-monde of ill-disguised gangsters, pirates, and extortionists."

As he saw it, no independent non-Communist government could survive in South Vietnam—nor could it retake North Vietnam from the Communists-unless:

    (1) it represented genuine nationalism;

    (2) it were prepared to deal effectively with corruption; and

    (3) it demonstrated a concern in advancing the welfare of the people.

As President of the Council of Ministers, Diem could not even begin to move toward the attainment of any of these objectives until he could gain control of the government, since at that time he was "a virtual prisoner in his own residence."

In September 1954, Diem moved to consolidate his position—and his power. He ordered the Vietnamese Army Chief of Staff, General Hinh, back to France. Hinh refused to go. However, any move by the Army to oust Diem was quickly stopped by clear United States threats to withdraw all United States aid if such a move were made. General Collins made this unmistakably clear to the Vietnamese Army dissidents on November 17, 1954, the same day he made the strong statement in support of Diem and announced that the United States Military Aid mission would begin to train the Vietnamese Army.[5] Two days later Bao Dai was persuaded to re-call General Hinh, who was relieved of his command after he left Saigon.[6]

The strategy adopted by Diem to wrest power from the Bao Dai and the Hoa Hao sects and the Binh Xuyen was to divide and conquer. The three groups, theretofore, had had a loose sort of alliance to present a united front against any attempts by the central government to reduce their authority.

> "The general plan was to isolate the Binh Xuyen and eventually to destroy it, while bringing over most of the sect leaders through persuasion, through promises of political position, and the incorporation of sect troops into the national army, and through outright bribery."[7]

In September, 1954, Diem set his plan in motion by inviting each of the sects to appoint four leaders to become part of his cabinet. The invitation was accepted.

On December 31, 1954, the United States announced that henceforth economic and military aid would go directly to Vietnam rather than through the French. This gave Diem control of millions of American dollars to further his plan to get rid of the sects and the Binh Xuyen.

In January, 1955, Diem moved against the Binh Xuyen by closing the gambling casinos, a major source of their revenues, even though they paid the Diem Government 750,000 piastres a day in royalties.[8] With direct United States aid now flowing into the treasury, Diem was in a better position than the Binh Xuyen to absorb the loss caused by the closing of the casinos.

In February 1955, the French withdrew their subsidies to the sects, putting them in a position where they could no longer afford to pay for their private armies. This, too, the French were forced to do because of the loss of United States financial payments.

In February 1955, Diem tried to integrate the armies of the sects into the National Army, a move resisted by the sects because it would have left them defenseless and at Diem's mercy. It would have also meant the end of their rule in their own little fiefdoms.

The sects joined with the Binh Xuyen and met with them on March 10, 1955, to form an organization called the National United Front, seeking to replace Diem's government.

Two days earlier, reporting to the people of the United States on the first meeting of the Southeast Asia Treaty Organization and having stopped in Saigon on the way back, Secretary of State Dulles did a "laying on of hands" to show that Diem was still the United States' "man in Saigon."

But the new coalition did not seem to be impressed by Dulles's expression of continued support for Diem. Since his advent to power nine months before, Diem had sought in every way possible to consolidate his power and wipe out the opposition. For this reason, the United National Front had difficulty seeing that much progress was being made toward achieving an "efficient, loyal military force and sounder economic conditions." With the suppression of civil liberties continuing, it also had difficulty in seeing in Diem an individual dedicated to "the enjoyment by his people of political and religious freedoms."

The United National Front said as much when it issued an ultimatum on March 21, 1955 to the Diem government complaining "that in his nine months in office, the Prime Minister Diem had failed to put in motion any programme; the press was without any liberty; and the Prime Minister's family 'notably his several brothers' made life impossible for the army and the people."

Diem rejected the ultimatum saying that the real problem facing South Vietnam was the merging of the private armies controlled by the sects and the Binh Xuyen. In Diem's viewpoint, no political settlement of that problem was possible.

The Americans and the French, as well as many of Diem's followers, urged him to compromise. Diem refused; he wanted no coalition government, even a coalition government with non-Communists. Diem was determined to run the whole show, assisted only by his family.

On March 29, 1955, the eight ministers representing the sects resigned from the Diem cabinet and the United National Front announced that it had appealed to Bao Dai to intervene.

By that time Diem felt more militarily secure. He had been busily utilizing United States foreign aid money—at least $12 million of it —to bribe Bao Dai and Hoa Hao generals to come over to his side with their armed forces. Once integrated into the Vietnamese Armed Forces, Diem promised he would pay their wages with funds derived from the same source. The sects' generals had few alternatives. The cessation of French subsidies had deprived them of the wherewithal to pay their troops. And the personal bribes—running into the millions—looked very good.[9]

Diem could well afford these bribes. He was to receive $325.8 million in United States aid that year.

Thus, on the night of March 29, 1955, after learning of the withdrawal from his government of the eight sect ministers and of the appeal to Bao Dai, Diem's government "deliberately pushed the United Front into armed combat against government forces."[10]

French General Ely arranged a truce while United States General Collins hurried back to Washington, determined to get rid of Diem.

General Collins went directly to President Eisenhower who promised to support him in whatever he did. After long consultations with personnel in the State Department, it was agreed that Diem would be "kicked upstairs"—to become President of Vietnam—but the functioning 'general manager,' perhaps as Premier, would be Dr. Phan Huy Quat . . . whose own nationalist credentials were honorable."

On the afternoon of April 28, 1955, Secretary of State Dulles signed a cable to the United States Embassy in Saigon relaying to it Washington's decision. General Collins left to return to Saigon. That same evening, word was received in Washington that fighting had broken out in Saigon between the forces of the government and those of the Binh Xuyen. Dulles sent a cable to Saigon countermanding his afternoon telegram.

Diem was determined to present not only the French and United, States missions, but also his own followers who wanted to compromise, with a fait accompli. Diem had already taken advantage of the month-long truce to "win over"—with bribes—more of the sect Generals and their soldiers so that his main opposition was from the forces of the Binh Xuyen.

However, Diem was well aware of the purpose of General Collins's mission to Washington and knew full well that, if that were accomplished, he would be out.

On the other hand, the French were urging the Binh Xuyen forces to attack, hoping that Diem would capitulate.

At any rate, fighting broke out on April 28, 1955. ". . . [the Binh Xuyen troops] were quickly driven from the city and forced to retreat in disorder to the swamplands near the mouth of the Saigon river. There they were bottled up until September, when the national army moved in to crush the last remnant of Binh Xuyen power. Hoa Hao resistance quickly crumbled in the Mekong delta under the double assault of government troops and special emissaries from Saigon carrying bribes and other inducements to Hoa Hao leaders. The few Bao Dai forces which had not already deserted to the government were peacefully disarmed in October."[11]

The leader of the Binh Xuyen was finally captured in April, 1956, and executed.

Meanwhile, Diem moved against the last remaining obstacle to his absolute rule of South Vietnam—Bao Dai.

On the first anniversary of his assumption of power, Diem called for a referendum to be held on October 23, 1955. The questions on the referendum were so phrased as to give the electorate a choice only between Bao Dai and Diem.

Thus the electorate was asked only two questions:

"Each voter was to receive a ballot paper in two parts— one with the picture of Diem in red, bearing the inscription 'I depose Bao Dai and recognize Diem as Head of State charged with the commission of setting up a democratic regime,' and the other with a picture of Bao Dai in green, and the inscription 'I do not depose Bao Dai and do not regard Diem as the Head of State charged with setting up a Democratic regime.' The ballot paper was to be detached from the counter-foil to facilitate subsequent identification of the voter."[12]

Obviously, a vote for Bao Dai was a vote against a "Democratic" regime.

Bao Dai did not go to Saigon from his villa in Cannes to campaign. All he did was to issue a statement to the effect that he considered the referendum illegal. He did issue an order dismissing Diem but that was unpublished in the controlled press and disregarded.

The referendum was fraudulent "but was only a shade more fraudulent than most electoral tests under a dictatorship," according to Bernard Fall.[13]

Diem received 98.2 percent of the vote.

Professor Scigliano has noted that "even considering Bao Dai's lack of popular strength, his absence from the country, and the employment of the public bureaucracy on behalf of his successful opponent, [Diem's margin of victory] recalls elections in Communist states."[14]

The fact that this election was "rigged" is important because, as Bernard Fall stated, "in a propaganda war in which one side constantly brandishes the argument of legality, the fact that all its subsequent elections were just as fraudulent as that first one does constitute a psychological handicap."[15]

Disregarding the well-known fraudulence of the referendum, the United States Ambassador in Saigon, G. Frederick Reinhardt, on

October 26, 1955, acting on instructions from Washington, sent Diem an acknowledgment of the notification that there was a new government in Saigon.

Even while he was destroying with guns and dollars the power of the sects and of the Binh Xuyen, Diem moved ahead to set up a ruthless police state.

The Diem regime did not know how "to use its victory to 'return' its opponents to its fold, although it had won over the sects and the crown. Having won a battle, it preferred war to peace," according to the noted French correspondent and author Jean Lacouture.[16]

The choice was due to the concept of government held by Diem and the close members of his family on whom he relied heavily and sometimes exclusively in running the government of South Vietnam.

Diem's "own background of paternalistic but absolute leadership put him in a difficult position 'to compete with Ho Chi Minh on Ho's own terms, as a man of the people.' "[17]

With such a background, Diem could not put together a government which brought into it representatives of other groups so as to begin to build up a popular base of support from the people. He relied most heavily on his brother Ngo Dinh Nhu, who carried the title of Adviser to the President. His brother's wife, Madam Nhu gained considerable influence with Diem as well as considerable unfavorable publicity for his regime because of her many impolitic and anti-American remarks.

Another brother, Ngo Dinh Thuc, was the Archbishop of Hue and "Dean of the Catholic episcopacy . . . [who exerted] his influence with the Catholic clergy and population on behalf of the regime."[18]

Another brother, also highly influential in the Diem regime, was Ngo Dinh Can who "ruled central Vietnam with a police force of his own and an ideological strictness that made Saigon look like a haven of liberty and license; newspapers that passed government censors in Saigon were often unavailable in Hue."[19]

More and more, as Diem eliminated his enemies, his government became a personal one, with a tight, organizational set-up serving as a political intelligence agency for Diem and his family and was used to detect Communists or anyone suspected of Communist or other oppositionist tendencies.[20]

Using United States economic aid liberally, Diem greatly enlarged the police forces and established his own personal, secret police force, whose salaries were also paid for by United States assistance funds.

Breaking with tradition, Diem quickly reached into the countryside to deprive the villages of their autonomy. This he did in the middle of 1956 by abolishing the elective village councils. This, in colonial times, the French had not sought to do because the French did not want a strong, national Vietnamese government. But Diem, desirous of pulling all control into Saigon, did this.

"The councils of South Vietnam's 2500 villages come under the selection of the province chiefs [appointed by the central government], usually on the recommendation of the district chiefs [appointed by the central government], with the Department of the Interior apparently reviewing and approving the choices."[21]

Diem's earliest moves in South Vietnam were to suppress all opposition to his rule and to permit as few individual liberties as were permitted in Ho Chi Minh's Communist regime in the North.

Withal, there attached to the Ngo family a widely discussed "aura of corruption." The extent of the corruption exceeded normal bounds for a country that has always been tolerant of corruption. Rumors of corruption became so widespread that on August 24, 1957, "both Nhu and his wife took advertisements in several Saigon newspapers to deny these charges explicitly. Needless to say, this official denial fed rather than quenched rumors."[22]

All during this period of 1954 to 1956, Diem had the immense task of resettling refugees from the North. Approximately 800,000 refugees came south, about 80 percent of them Catholics which added immeasurably to Diem's political base. According to Bernard Fall:

"Although there is no doubt that hundreds of thousands of Vietnamese would have fled Communist domination . . . the mass flight was admittedly the result of an extremely intensive, well-conducted . . . very successful American psychological warfare operation. Propaganda slogans and leaflets appealed to the devout Catholics with such themes as 'Christ has gone to the South' and the 'Virgin Mary has departed from the North' and whole bishoprics . . . packed up lock, stock, and barrel, from the bishops to almost the last village priest and faithful."[23]

The arrival of the refugees in the South tripled the number of Catholics there. The remainder of the refugees from the North were Vietnamese soldiers (about 110,000) who had been fighting with the French and French administrators who had been running the colonial government in the North.

Many of the Catholics from the North were more highly skilled than the South Vietnamese Buddhists and there was great need for their skills in the government to replace the French who had returned to France. However, the great influx of Catholics into the Saigonese Government caused not only North versus South resentment but also Buddhist versus Catholic resentment—resentments which increased as the years went on.

Under his new administrative organization—taking over the administration of the provinces by personnel appointed by Saigon rather than by locally elected village councils—many of the Catholic refugees from the north were also employed by Diem's government as province administrators.

Estimates as to the number of refugees who went North during the resettlement period vary from 110,000 to 150,000 Viet Minh soldiers and their families.

The nature and circumstances of the refugee exodus from and to the north and the south is important in view of later events and later charges.

The paper entitled "Aggression from the North," issued by the State Department in February 1965 contains this charge:

"When Viet-Nam was partitioned, thousands of carefully selected party members were ordered to remain in place in the South and keep their secret apparatus intact to help promote Hanoi's cause. Arms and ammunition were stored away for future use. Guerilla fighters rejoined their families to await the party's call. Others withdrew to remote jungle and mountain hideouts. The majority—an estimated 90,000—were moved to North Vietnam."[24]

The difficulty with this statement—which seeks to prove that Hanoi, from the beginning, has been behind the civil war which broke out in South Vietnam in 1959—is that it is based upon an erroneous assumption.

The first sentence makes the flat statement that when Vietnam was partitioned "thousands of carefully selected party members" were "ordered" to remain in place in the South to keep their "secret apparatus intact to help promote Hanoi's cause." This assumes that the Geneva Accords provided that all "party members" were to go north of the 17th parallel.

The Geneva Accords contained no such provision.

The regroupment north of the 17th parallel was only for Viet Minh soldiers, not for all who believed in the Viet Minh cause. The Geneva Aggreement on the Cessation of Hostilities provided that the "military forces" of each side should regroup north and south of the 17th parallel—not that all Communists should do so.

In the second place, there were many southern sympathizers who were southerners, not of the regular military forces of Ho Chi Minh but fighting alongside them against the French. With reunification elections due to take place in less than two years, with Ho Chi Minh being expected to win, why should the Communist-sympathizer who lived south of the 17th parallel have to be "ordered" to remain at home?

Why should Ho Chi Minh, having every expectation of winning the reunification effort, "order" thousands of "carefully selected party members" to take cover in the south?

It would have been more logical for Diem to urge as many anti-Communists as possible to flee south to strengthen his own political base in anticipation that the reunifying elections would never take place and that Vietnam would remain divided—which is exactly what happened!

And finally, the International Control Commission did investigate the charge of the French High Command that "ammunition dumps and arms depots had been left behind by the People's Army intentionally for subversive use." It examined seven dumps found in one province. "Even though the dumps were actually discovered, the local authorities failed to provide evidence that they were left behind by the People's Army with specific subversive intentions."

But the crowning blow to disprove this charge was that the dumps "consisted of discarded and worn out materials which were not capable of any use." The Commission came to the conclusion that the charges had not been proven. Thereafter, further investigations were dropped "because the French High Command felt that further investigations would not serve any useful purpose."[25]

Like any unorganized guerilla force, when the cease fire came to Vietnam in 1954, the Viet Minh guerilla forces from the South, who were not part of Ho Chi Minh's regular forces, went to their homes in the South taking their weapons with them. That was the most natural thing for them to have done. It was only after Diem, with the blessing of the United States, had refused to hold the re-unifying elections in July, 1956, and Diem's oppression became so intolerable as to result in open revolt, that the fact that many of the Viet Minh from the south had taken their weapons home with them was turned into a sinister plot on the part of Ho Chi Minh to take over South Vietnam by force and that such a plot had existed since 1954.

If he expected to have to fight to conquer South Vietnam in 1956, and therefore ordered thousands of his followers to go underground in 1954, why did Ho Chi Minh agree to a cease fire in 1954 when he was winning?

CHAPTER XVI

WHY THE VIETNAM ELECTIONS WERE NOT HELD IN 1956

Right after the close of the Geneva Conference in 1954, those followers of Ho Chi Minh who were in the south began campaigning in anticipation of the 1956 elections that were required by the Geneva Accords to be held in July 1956.

It has been estimated that "the Viet Minh at the end of February 1955, prior to their withdrawal to the North, were masters of 60 to 90 percent of the villages in the South, except for those areas under the control of the sects."[1]

Ho Chi Minh and General No Nguyen Giap, the military leader who had successfully led the Viet Minh against the French, enjoyed in those villages "the status of national heroes." In preparation for the 1956 reunifying elections, Ho Chi Minh's followers went from village to village carrying pictures of Ho Chi Minh and Bao Dai, asking the villagers to choose between the two.

If Diem were to win in the 1956 elections he would have to win over these villagers with their fierce loyalty, their intense nationalism, and their burning anti-colonialism. Supplanting Ho Chi Minh in the affections of the inhabitants of these villages would be an extremely difficult task for Diem, who had not fought at their side against the French—who had not even been in the country during that struggle. In the eyes of the villagers, he was a "Johnny-come-lately."

But Diem, as events would show, had no intention of getting

into a popularity contest with Ho Chi Minh. Diem's opposition to an election was supported by the United States over the objections of the British, the French, the Soviet Union, and Mainland China.

Ho Chi Minh, with everything to gain, not only started his campaign in the south to win votes, but began an attempt to get international support for the beginning of the talks called for by the Geneva Declaration to work out the details of how the elections were to be held. According to that Declaration those consultations were to begin after July 20, 1955, and were to culminate in the reunification elections of July 1956.

North Vietnamese Foreign Minister Pham Van Dong, in April 1955, visited New Delhi where he, together with India's Prime Minister Jawaharial Nehru, issued a joint communiqué stating that both governments attached great importance to the holding of the reunification elections as called for by the Geneva Declaration.

On June 6, 1955, Foreign Minister Dong issued a statement to the effect that North Vietnam was ready to begin consultations the following month on the details of the reunification elections.

In July, Ho Chi Minh himself went to Peking and Moscow and in each place joint communiqués were issued stressing the importance of holding the reunification elections.

And finally, on July 19, 1955, Foreign Minister Dong, on behalf of Ho Chi Minh, sent Diem a formal note proposing that representatives of North and South Vietnam attend a "consultative conference" to discuss the holding of a conference on the reunification elections.[2]

Meanwhile, Washington began to sabotage not only the holding of the elections but also the preliminary consultations.

At his news conference on June 28, 1955, Secretary of State Dulles, when asked about the Vietnamese elections, reminded the newsmen that the United States had not signed the Geneva Agreements and that the Government of Vietnam had not signed them either. At the time, however, Under Secretary of State Walter Bedell Smith had agreed that the United States would "refrain from the threat or the use of force to disturb . . . [the Geneva Accords]." This was a legally binding obligation upon the United States.

"The United States," Secretary of State Dulles said at his news conference, "believes, broadly speaking, in the unification of countries which have a historic unity, where the people are akin. We also believe that, if there are *conditions of really free election,* there is no serious risk that the Communists would win." (Emphasis supplied)[3]

The words in the Geneva Declaration referring to free elections were:

" . . . the settlement of political problems, effected on the basis of respect for the principles of independence, unity and territorial integrity, shall permit the Vietnamese people to enjoy the fundamental freedoms, *guaranteed by democratic institutions established as a result of free general elections by secret ballot . . . ."* (Emphasis supplied)[4]

Secretary of State Dulles' statement above is thus strictly in accord with the provisions of the Geneva Declaration.

However, Dulles did not stop there. As he continued at his news conference, he twisted the meaning of the provisions of the Geneva Declaration in such a way as to give both South Vietnam and the United States an "out" for not holding the reunification elections called for by the Geneva Declaration. "We," he said, "are not afraid at all of elections, provided they are held *under conditions of genuine freedom* which the Geneva armistice agreement *calls for. If those conditions can be provided* we would be in favor of elections, because we believe that they would bring about the unification of the country under free government auspices." (Emphasis added)

Thus, from "conditions of really free elections"—which, provided there were sufficient international supervision before, during, and after the elections, could theoretically take place even in a nation otherwise a dictatorship—Secretary of State Dulles switched by the end of his statement to require "conditions of genuine freedom." These, of course, did not exist in Communist North Vietnam nor, for that matter, did they exist in Diem's South Vietnam.

At about the same time, Diem set in motion his own campaign to nullify any chances for holding the reunification elections.

Diem took little time in picking up the "Dulles line."

On July 16, 1955, Diem "stated that he favored free elections in principle but could not consider holding them until the DRV [Democratic Republic of Vietnam—North Vietnam] had given him proof of its readiness to place national interests before its Communist creed. It is 'out of the question . . . for us to consider any proposal from the Viet Minh, if proof is not given us that they put the superior interests of the national community above those of Communism; if they do not give up terrorism and totalitarian methods, if they do not cease violating their obligations . . . ." Diem also reasserted that the State of Vietnam did not consider itself bound by the Geneva Agreements."[5]

Meanwhile, Diem had turned the full force of his propaganda apparatus, in the establishment and perfection of which he had been and would continue to be assisted by United States economic aid and technical assistance, against not only the Geneva Accords but also the International Control Commission.

Inspired street demonstrations became the vogue in Saigon. On July 19, 1955, the South Vietnamese armed forces issued a statement expressing their determination "to fight the inhuman, despotic, ungrateful and wily Viet Communists and to fight the Pro-Communist, ineffective and incompetent International Commission."[6]

July 20, 1955—the first anniversary of the Geneva Accords—was declared to be "national humiliation day" and a demonstration was called for. As B. S. N. Murti, an employee of the International Control Commission, stated:

"The Saigon demonstration [on July 20, 1955] was most significant because it was organized by the authorities and the demonstration degenerated into a violent riot in which the two hotels, Majestic and Gallieni, where the International Commission personnel were staying, were looted and destroyed before the very eyes of the security police who were present and did nothing to prevent the disgraceful acts of the mob."

Both France and England during this period were urging Diem to agree to hold consultations looking toward the reunification elections.

Finally, on August 9, 1955, Diem replied to Dong's note of July 19, 1955, requesting consultations. He reiterated what he had previously said and continued that "nothing constructive [with respect to elections] will be done as long as the Communist regime of the North does not permit each Vietnamese citizen to enjoy democratic freedoms and the basic fundamental rights of man.'"[7] Diem also repeated his assertion that South Vietnam was not bound by the Geneva Accords.

At his press conference the next day, Secretary of State Dulles said that he agreed with Diem that South Vietnam was not bound by the Geneva Accords.

On August 30, 1955, Secretary of State Dulles added the final blow to hopes of reunification elections. He said: "We certainly agree that conditions are not ripe for free elections." Thus Dulles was reverting to his previous stand taken at his press conference on June 28, 1955, when he changed the meaning of the Geneva Declaration.

"In view of the U.S.'s heavy economic aid to the State of Vietnam and its fervent backing of Diem in the face of British and French urgings that he be replaced, the importance to Diem of U.S. backing for his election stand must have been considerable. Apparently encouraged by Dulles's strong support, Diem declared bluntly on 21 September that there could be 'no question of a conference, even less of negotiations' with the DRV."[8]

This forthright statement by Diem should have been sufficient to shatter Ho Chi Minh's hopes that there would ever be reunification elections. But it did not. Diem's statement was made before the October rigged-referendum and Ho Chi Minh could still hope that Diem might fall and be replaced by someone who would be more amenable to participating in such elections.

Ho Chi Minh moved in two directions.

In South Vietnam, through his loyal followers there, he stepped up demands for elections. Diem's reply was to intensify repressive measures, using police forces now much better trained and equipped through United States aid. "South Vietnamese police arrested more than 100 men and women in Saigon for having demonstrated in favor of consultations between the South and North." Elsewhere in South Vietnam "people were arrested and kept in prison for the fault of explaining the provisions of the Geneva Agreement to their friends."[9]

On the international scene, Ho Chi Minh, through Foreign Minister Dong, appealed to Britain and the Soviet Union as the co-chairmen of the Geneva Conference demanding that France and the State of Vietnam guarantee the implementation of the agreements. India and Communist China added their support to Ho Chi Minh's appeal. Neither co-chairman acted vigorously.

"On 20 December [1955], the co-chairmen reported the delivery of the various messages they had received to the members of the Geneva Conference and said they would be 'grateful' to receive comments and suggestions. By the end of 1955, it is likely that the DRV's hopes of obtaining action by appealing to the co-chairmen had been greatly diminished."[10]

At the end of January 1956, Chou En Lai suggested—since in their letter of December 20, 1955, the co-chairmen had asked for suggestions—that the Geneva Conference be reconvened. On February 14, 1956, the North Vietnamese made the same suggestion. On February 18, 1956, the Soviet Union sent a note to the British joining in Mainland China's request. The British replied on March 9, 1956, that there should be a meeting of the co-chairmen to discuss the matter.

As a result, meetings between the British and the Soviet Union were held in London during April and May, 1956. For Ho Chi Minh the results of these meetings were disappointing. For Diem they were considered a victory. The notes sent by Great Britain and the Soviet Union to both the North Vietnamese and South Vietnamese Governments merely "expressed their concern about the present situation in relation to the fulfillment of the Geneva Agreements . . . . In particular, consultations have not taken place about the preparation and holding of free, nation-wide elections in Vietnam . . . ."

The real concern of both co-chairmen seemed to be about the keeping of the peace in Vietnam, since the International Control Commission was encountering a growing lack of cooperation on the part of both North and South Vietnam in fulfilling its duties, concerning which the co-chairmen stated that they were "confident that the authorities in both parts of Vietnam will show effective cooperation and that these difficulties [lack of cooperation with the Commission] will in practice be removed."

However, pending "the holding of free general elections for the reunification of Vietnam, the two co-chairmen attach great importance to the maintenance of the cease fire . . . ."

Each government was invited to transmit to the co-chairmen "their views about the time required for the opening of consultations on the organization of nation-wide elections in Vietnam and the time required for the holding of elections as a means of achieving the unification of Vietnam."[11]

On this appeal to the international community for support in his efforts to secure the holding of reunification elections, Ho Chi Minh had lost ground—badly. The messages from the co-chairmen were dated May 8, 1956, and had made no mention of the fact that the Geneva Declaration had flatly stated that the reunification elections had to take place in July, 1956. On the contrary, the request contained in the message concerning suggestions as to when the elections might take place by implication inferred that there was no hope that the elections would take place in July 1956. Without the military pressures that existed at the time of the Geneva Conference, the hope of selecting a new date—with both co-chairmen seeming to shy away from a reconvening of that Conference—seemed as slight as it turned out in fact to be.

On May 11, 1956, North Vietnam sent Diem a letter, referring to the co-chairmen's message and "requesting the start of the consultation, but also pledging to maintain peace."[12]

Diem, of course, felt he was in a stronger position since he had "won" the referendum in October and had declared the independent Republic of Vietnam.

In a rush to have another election to enhance his strength, Diem had already called for the election of a National Assembly. The election took place on March 4, 1956. The South Vietnamese Government "clearly reserved the right to veto candidates not to its liking." Those elected to the Assembly would be immune from arrest only if they did not support "the policies of Communists or rebels." All those who entered as contestants "had to depend on the administration for their campaigning, finances, transport and propaganda."

The elections for the National Assembly were marked by arrests of suspected candidates, by the boycotting of the elections by all opposition parties, and by the establishment of concentration camps where "all the families of former Viet Minh supporters and opponents of Government had been detained."[13]

So on March 4, 1956, in a "free" election more repressive than the 1955 referendum which had renounced Bao Dai, a National

Assembly was "elected." It is therefore not surprising that one of its first measures was a denunciation of the Geneva Agreements.

Commenting on these elections on June 1, 1956, before the American Friends of Vietnam, Assistant Secretary of State for Far Eastern Affairs, Walter S. Robertson, said:

"Perhaps no more eloquent testimony to the new state of affairs in Vietnam could be cited than the voice of the people themselves as expressed in their free election of last March. At that time the last possible question as to the feeling of the people was erased by the overwhelming majority for President Diem's leadership. The fact that the Viet Minh was unable to carry out its open threats to sabotage these elections is impressive evidence of the stability and prestige of the Government."[14]

When Diem, on May 29, 1956, answered the co-chairmen's letter he could afford to feel more secure. He repeated what he had said before, stating that the "absence of all liberty in North Vietnam makes the question of electoral and pre-election campaigns practically unattainable for the moment."[15]

So July 1956 came and went and the reunifying elections required to be held during that month under the terms of the Geneva Declaration were not held.

The record is clear that they were not held because Secretary of State John Foster Dulles did not want them held and backed Diem in refusing to hold them.

It is indeed unfortunate that the United States, which throughout its history has stood for the principle of free elections, should today stand before the world with the sorry record of having prevented free elections in Vietnam because it was afraid it would lose the elections.

In an effort to change the clearly documented record of United States involvement in the prevention of free elections in Vietnam, attempts are being made to change recorded history.

Thus Deputy Under Secretary of State for Political Affairs, U. Alexis Johnson, speaking in Montreal on March 14, 1966—almost ten years after the reunifying elections were supposed to be held in Vietnam—affirmed that in "1955 and 1956 the South Vietnamese Government maintained that it would agree to such elections if they were genuinely free and internationally supervised throughout Vietnam and not just in South Vietnam."[16]

This Diem did not maintain. As the record shows, it was Diem who held elections only in South Vietnam elections which were not only not internationally supervised but were obviously controlled by the South Vietnamese Government.

The Deputy Under Secretary of State also affirmed at that meeting that the United States "although not a party to the Geneva Accords, consistently favored genuinely free elections under UN supervision . . . ." This is what Under Secretary of State Walter Bedell Smith said at Geneva in 1954. But the subsequent actions of the United States were at variance with this interpretation of the United States' position.

Continuing, Deputy Under Secretary of State Johnson stated that "in 1956 no more than any other Communist government was the Hanoi government prepared to hold such elections and accordingly the elections were not held . . . . In fact, it was the North that was not willing to submit itself to the test of free elections under international control."

Was Ho Chi Minh bluffing when he went through all those motions seeking international intervention to obtain reunifying elections and exhorting his Viet Minh followers in the south to agitate for them?

No one will really ever know for certain!

It has, of course, been true that no dictatorship—whether it be a dictatorship of the right or the left—can permit free elections, let alone elections supervised by some impartial body. Those who argue that Ho was bluffing in 1956 support their argument on this broad generalization. They argue that Ho was an absolute Communist dictator and therefore he would not have permitted free, internationally supervised elections in all of Vietnam.

In Vietnam in 1956, all qualified observers were agreed that in a popularity contest with Diem, Ho Chi Minh would win overwhelmingly. The worst that might have happened in a free, internationally supervised election was that it would have revealed that in the North there were a few dissidents who were not entirely committed to the rule of Ho Chi Minh.

It is also agreed that Ho Chi Minh had considerable following in the south, not only among the southern Viet Minh who had remained in the south, but among many of the non-Communists groups, whom Diem was already alienating.

It should also be remembered that there were many non-Communists in the south who bitterly resented the decision to partition their country and hence were resentful about Diem's decision not to meet with the North Vietnamese to try to unite the country.

If Ho Chi Minh in 1956 was not bluffing about wanting free, internationally supervised reunification elections, why did he let the deadline of July, 1956, go by without taking some action?

What could he have done about it?

Ho Chi Minh had appealed to Communist China, India, Britain, and the Soviet Union. The net result was the letter from the co-chairman on May 8, 1956, which indicated that they were more interested in the maintenance of peace than in reunification elections in Vietnam.

On the other hand, there was no doubt that the United States was backing Diem in an all-out manner. It had shown its determination to keep Diem in Saigon even in the face of opposition from the French and the British. Whether Ho Chi Minh would have used force at that point even with the backing of Mainland China and the Soviet Union is doubtful. But, without such aid, he was not about to take on the United States and its vast power.

In addition, the United States, by forging the Southeast Asia Treaty Organization shortly after the Geneva Conference, had erected some sort of an umbrella over South Vietnam. Ho Chi Minh, in 1956, had no way of knowing how leaky that umbrella was to prove in 1965 when the United States received only token support from its SEATO allies when it escalated its military involvement in Vietnam to an all-out land, sea and air war.

Ho Chi Minh in the summer of 1956 was having troubles at home. His agrarian reform measures had failed miserably and, as a result, rioting which had to be severely repressed occurred in several places in North Vietnam. Word of the rioting and the harsh measures taken to repress it had reached the south. That was definitely not the time to take to the stump to extol the virtues of the Communist system to the people of the south who at least had enough to eat.

One added factor in Ho Chi Minh's lack of direct action in 1956, when the time for the July elections came and went, was the war weariness of his followers.

"The conclusion seems inescapable that the 1956 elections were not held because the Diem government, with important United States backing, was more interested in maintaining itself as a separate, anti-Communist government than in risking its survival to achieve the national unity to which all Vietnamese ostensibly were committed."[17]

CHAPTER XVII

CEASE-FIRE, REGROUPMENT, EXODUS AND REPRESSION

Under the Geneva Agreement for the Cessation of Hostilities in Vietnam, the enforcement machinery established to supervise the carrying out of the Agreement's provisions was the International Control Commission, consisting of representatives of India, Canada, and Poland. The Commission had been envisaged by the conferees at the Geneva Conference as only a temporary device established on the assumption that the parties to the Geneva Accords intended to carry out their provisions in good faith.

The Commission was intended to have only a very short life. After the reunification elections of July 1956, there would be established the reunited, independent nation of Vietnam, which would govern itself and decide its own internal affairs without international supervision. Since the reunification elections would be internationally supervised to make certain they were free, the government that the Vietnamese people would then have, after the elections, would thus be a government freely chosen by them.

The International Control Commission was not designed or intended to control Vietnamese affairs forever.

In view of the circumstances—and despite them—some of the supervisory tasks assigned to the Commission were carried out surprisingly well.

One of these was the arrangement for a cease-fire in all of Vietnam and the establishment and maintenance of the demilitarized zone, which was to consist of a strip five kilometers on either side of the 17th parallel.

The actual cease-fire was arranged and actually took place with a minimum of difficulty. In the light of the situation which existed at the time, the success of the Commission in this area of responsibility is not too surprising. All three sides—the French, the Viet Minh, and the other Vietnamese—after eight years of fierce and bloody fighting wanted an end to the killing. Diem had still to consolidate his position and at that time was a virtual prisoner in his own house. Ho Chi Minh had every reason to believe that he had won at Geneva and had only to bide his time before he would control all of Vietnam.

As for the demilitarized zone, complaints were continually made by both sides alleging violations of the rules governing the demilitarized zone. The artificial division of Vietnam at the 17th parallel could be accomplished more easily by drawing a line on a map than in reality. It is all very well to provide in an agreement that the area for a distance of five kilometers on either side of the 17th parallel should be demilitarized. However, it was dealing with a formerly unified country. People had been living and continued to live in that ten kilometer area. Frictions, misunderstandings, and violations of the rules were bound to occur.

Another responsibility assigned to the International Control Commission in which it was successful was the regroupment of the armed forces north and south of the demilitarized zone at the 17th parallel. This was a more difficult task than it might appear to be since it involved more than merely moving troops from one area to another. It also meant that arrangements had to be carefully worked out in advance for the take-over of essential civilian functions in the areas of regroupment. Included in those areas were Hanoi and Haiphong, both of which were held and administered by the French with their own and Vietnamese troops and administrators.

Well before each takeover, the people living in these regroupment areas had to be prepared for the assumption of civilian rule by the new authority.

The International Control Commission had high praise for both sides with respect to the orderly and peaceful manner in which the regroupment took place.[1]

A third area of responsibility in which the Commission did well was with respect to the refugees, both from the north and from the south.

The movement of 800,000 refugees from the north to the south with as few incidents as did occur was a truly remarkable performance. Incidents did occur where some who wanted to go south were prevented from doing so by Ho Chi Minh. There were also complaints that some persons in the south who wanted to go north were denied permits to do so.

While relatively successful in carrying out its responsibilities under the Geneva Agreement in the areas of the cease fire, regroupment and the exodus, the Commission failed completely in carrying out its responsibilities in three other areas: elections, prevention of retaliation against former resistance workers, and the prohibition against the importation of arms into Vietnam.

Since reunification elections were never held when Diem, with United States approval, refused to abide by that requirement of the Geneva Accords, the Commission cannot be faulted for not having supervised well the elections which were not held.

In the matter of Diem's retaliation against the former resistance workers and the families of the soldiers who went north with Ho Chi Minh, the Commission failed because it was up against the deliberate decision of the Diem government to refuse to cooperate with the Commission. The lack of cooperation stemmed from the fact that repression—cruel repression—of anyone who disagreed with Diem's government was a deliberate policy of the Diem Government. And all during the time Diem was engaged in the execution of such a policy he owed his continuance in office to United States military and economic aid.

In July 1956, although he had bribed, imprisoned or liquidated the sects and had killed or driven the Binh Xuyen into the hills, Diem still faced considerable opposition from the resistance workers loyal to Ho Chi Minh who had remained in the south and from the families of the soldiers who had gone north with Ho Chi Minh.

As has been pointed out, the Geneva Accords did not require all those who favored Ho Chi Minh to go north—only members of Ho Chi Minh's regular army were required to do so. Many of the soldiers in Ho Chi Minh's army were from the south and had left their families behind on the land they had tilled because the reunification elections were supposedly only 14 months away, after which they expected to return.

By July 1956, many persons had been jailed by Diem's army and police forces because they were agitating and demonstrating in favor of holding the reunification elections prescribed by the Geneva Accords. Many more were in jail merely because they had attempted to explain the provisions of the Geneva Accords. In addition, many families of Viet Minh soldiers had been put in concentration camps prior to the March 4, 1956 election of the National Assembly.

After July 1956, Diem felt himself more secure.

He had successfully resisted all moves to force him to hold the reunification elections—or even to sit down with Ho Chi Minh to discuss them. He had strong United States backing for this stand and also had United States money, materiel, and technical assistance. Especially did he have help in building up his army, police force, and his own special secret police force, whose members were paid with funds supplied by the United States.

Except for the Catholic minority and the doubtful personal loyalty of the military and police forces, Diem had little popular following. Had he been so inclined in 1956, he could have set about building a broad basis of popular support. Diem could have established democratic institutions, permitting freedom of speech and press; giving the villages a say in their own government, instituted, with the help of the vast amount of United States economic aid he was receiving, the economic reforms so badly needed in his war-torn land; ending the graft and corruption which openly pervaded his entire administration, from top to bottom; and utilizing every other possible means available to build a viable democratic society.

In short, Diem could have and should have done what the United States was telling the American people he was in fact doing.

On June 1, 1956, the day after Diem announced that he would not consent to the holding of reunification elections, the Assistant

Secretary of State for Far Eastern Affairs. Walter S. Robertson, praised Diem's actions and went on to report to the American Friends of Vietnam, meeting in Washington, D.C., that Vietnam was "progressing rapidly to the establishment of democratic institutions by elective processes, its people resuming peaceful pursuits, its army growing in effectiveness, sense of mission, and morale . . ."

The facts, however, were not in accord with this glowing description.

The building of democratic institutions was alien to Diem's nature. Far removed from the people, lacking the common touch, with a mandarin background and viewpoint, surrounded by and relying almost solely on the advice of his family, Diem took the opposite course of action, ruling with an iron hand and ruthlessly attempting to crush any opposition to his rule.

Diem instituted a reign of terror against the resistance workers, against the families of Ho Chi Minh's soldiers who had gone north with him, and against non-Communists who opposed his policies.

The eight year attempt by France to reconquer Vietnam had the characteristics of both a civil and an international war. For many reasons, there were a considerable number of Vietnamese fighting alongside the French troops against the Vietnamese. The French, during the Geneva Conference, were quite concerned about possible reprisals after the cease-fire against those who had taken the French side. Ho Chi Minh also feared that the South Vietnamese guerilla workers and the families of the soldiers who would go north with him would be retaliated against in the south by the French and their Vietnamese allies.

Accordingly, both the Agreement on the Cessation of Hostilities in Vietnam and the Geneva Declaration contained express prohibitions against any form of retaliation.[2]

An increasing number of complaints against the Diem government were made to the International Control Commission alleging the establishment of concentration camps, tortures, murders, secret arrests and other terroristic tactics. Complaints alleging reprisal measures were also filed against Ho Chi Minh's government, but he was not faced with the same problems as Diem. Ho Chi Minh had "pacified" most of the area in the north, outside of the areas held by the French, before the Geneva Conference. Any dissidents who remained fled to the French areas and were evacuated to the south, after the Geneva Accords, together with those who had collaborated with the French and the Vietnamese soldiers who had fought with the French armies. There thus remained in the north few against whom Ho Chi Minh had reason to take reprisal measures.

In the early years after the Geneva Accords, Diem cooperated with the International Control Commission—but slowly. Ho Chi Minh's cooperation with the Commission was at the same pace.[3] The Commission's own bureaucratic procedures militated against speed.

At that time—1955 to 1958—Diem was acting under a law promulgated on January 11, 1956, which permitted the arrest, imprisonment, and assignment of residence (confinement in a place other than a prison) "of any person considered to be a danger to the defense of the State."

In 1958, the rumor spread that a thousand persons had been poisoned at the concentration camp at Phu Loi, 30 miles outside Saigon. This was grist for the propaganda mills of Ho Chi Minh and he made the most of it. He complained to the International Control Commission, but Diem would not agree to any investigation. Finally, in the face of international pressures from non-Communist countries, Diem did permit an investigation by P. J. Honey, a Western specialist in Vietnamese affairs. He could verify only twenty deaths, ". . . but the attitude of the Southern regime indicated that it definitely had things to hide."[4]

To cloak with the air of legality the even harsher measures he intended to use, Diem had adopted, in 1959, Law No. 10, which permitted special "drumhead" military tribunals to pronounce the death penalty or to impose a sentence of life imprisonment for a variety of acts considered contrary to Diem's ideas about the welfare of the State.[5]

While Law 10/59 did not specifically name the former resistance workers, it was aimed at and used against them—although it was all-embracing and caught many others in its net.

Ho Chi Minh complained to the International Control Commission that the law was a thinly disguised weapon used harshly against the resistence workers. The Commission found that the Diem government was engaged in "a systematic plan to violate the provisions of Article 14 [prohibiting reprisals] of the Geneva Agreement."

Diem launched a major campaign against so called "Communists" and throughout the country—at least that part of it controlled by Diem—"catch a Communist" campaigns were put on with the citizenry encouraged to denounce persons suspected of being Communist —or, at least, opposed to the Diem Government.[6]

By 1960 the situation in South Vietnam was so bad that, despite the repression of all complaint against the government, on April 26, 1960, "eighteen highly respected [South Vietnamese] citizens, including several former Cabinet ministers, submitted" a list of complaints to Diem.[7]

The indictment of the Diem regime made, among others, the following charges:

"The people do not know a better life or more freedom under the republican regime which you have created . . . A constitution had been established in form only; . . . deliberations [of the National Assembly] always fall in line with the government; . . . antidemocratic elections . . . Continuous arrests fill the jails and prisons to the rafters; . . . public opinion and the press are reduced to silence; . . . discouragement and resentment of the people . . . Political parties and religious sects have been eliminated . . . elimination [of the religious sects] has opened the way to the Viet Cong; . . . number of civil servants has increased . . . The administrative machinery of government, already slowed down, is about to become completely paralyzed . . . graft impossible to hide . . . Favoritism based on family or party connections should be banished; the selling of influence, corruption, and abuse of power must be punished . . . Distrust, jealousy, rancor among colleagues [in the Army] should be eliminated . . . many people are out of work . . . Sources of revenue are in the hands of speculators who use the [government] party and group to mask monopolies operating for certain private interests . . ."

Despite the evident respectibility of those signing this letter, making these complaints and issuing these warnings, Diem took no action to institute reforms.

This was not the only warning sign of deteriorating conditions which Diem failed to heed.

A month earlier—in March, 1960— a document appeared in the country-side in South Vietnam and in Paris entitled "Declaration of Former Resistence Fighters on the Present Situation in South Vietnam." (See Appendix)

This Declaration made many of the same points as would be contained in the open letter to Diem a month later by the eighteen citizens of Vietnam, except that the Declaration was much more vivid in its description of the enumerated abuses.

There is, however, one important difference between the Open Letter to Diem and the Declaration of Former Resistence Fighters.

The Open Letter did not talk about the reunification elections which were never held or the eventual reunification of the two parts of Vietnam. Instead, the Open Letter pointed out that with its "geographic conditions of a fertile and rich soil yielding agricultural, forestry, and fishing surpluses, South Vietnam should have been able to begin a definitive victory in the historical competition with the North, so as to carry out the will of the people and to lead the country on the way to hope, liberty, and happiness."

Thus, in 1960, these South Vietnamese political figures had accepted the idea that there would be two Vietnams for the foreseeable future and they were only trying to make South Vietnam a better country by ridding it of graft, corruption and gross economic and political mismanagement.

Surprisingly, the Declaration of Former Resistence Fighters, while it did bitterly mention the refusal of Diem to hold the reunification elections, was more concerned with the failure of Diem to work out with Hanoi agreements for normalizing relations between the two parts of Vietnam, even though separated, and was especially concerned about Diem's repressive tactics.

The Declaration made no demand for the immediate holding of reunification elections. But it wanted the Diem Government to undertake "realistic measures to consult with the Democratic Republic of Vietnam for holding general elections for unification, and, *first of all, to establish normal relations between the people of the two zones in postal, economic, cultural and travel matters, etc.*" (Emphasis supplied)

The major portion of the Declaration—like the Open Letter to Diem—contains a vivid description of the repressive measures taken against the people by the Diem regime. Some of the incidents cited, such as the reference to the poisonings at the Camp Phu Loi, were exaggerations, but many of them, on the basis of reports by other observers, accurately reflect what was going on in South Vietnam at that time under Diem. The Declaration is violently anti-American, calling Diem an American puppet and deploring the American intervention in South Vietnam with its attendant disruption of the economy and its emphasis upon increasing the army and police forces. It mentions the terrorist tactics employed against Communists and non-Communists alike.

Some of the complaints were:

" . . . the invasion of American goods, which stifle local manufacturers . . . [ruining] the South Vietnamese economy which is . . . daily more dependent on the United States . . . thousands and thousands of prisons and concentration camps burden the country and presently contain more than 200,000 people . . . the sadism of physical torture is only equalled by the methods of moral torture . . . this policy of terror and repression has been transformed into a veritable war . . . since the enactment of the fascist law 10/59, directed against the unarmed masses of South Vietnam . . . Diemist troops . . . armed, equipped, maintained and commanded by the Americans, have set loose against the people vast 'sweeps,' 'punitive expeditions,' killing, plundering and burning everything in their path . . . the 10/59 law not only threatens the lives of the people, but is the sword of Damocles hanging over the head of the collaborators of the present regime . . . the main thrust of the attacks of the American-Diemists was against the former Resistance Fighters and the most stubborn guerrilla bases . . . these 'gangsters' have been given *carte blanche* for assassinating former Resistance Fighters . . . summary executions number in the thousands . . . [the Diem Government] dispossess the peasants by direct action or help reactionary landlords who want to evict peasants from land distributed by the Resistance . . . by means of American equipment, they have annihilated whole villages, razed cemetaries, destroyed pagodas, Caodist temples, homes, gardens and rice fields . . . horrible atrocities have been commited . . . the South Vietnamese regime, in feudal submission to the Americans, and sole property of the Ngo-dinh-Diem family, does not tolerate any opposition, opinions or activity; it even goes so far as to persecute those who only demand reforms and disapprove of certain government measures . . ."

In the light of these conditions, is it any wonder that it was estimated at that time that more and more of the countryside came under the control of the guerrillas?[8]

CHAPTER XVIII

THE ORIGINS AND CHARACTER OF THE CIVIL WAR IN VIETNAM

Both the Open Letter to Diem and the Declaration of Former Resistance Fighters had clearly warned that time was running out and that, unless the necessary reforms were instituted, more direct action would be taken.

In the countryside, the people started fighting back against Diem's repressive measures. It was during the period from 1956 to 1961 that the National Liberation Front for South Vietnam was born.

According to the official United States version of that birth, the National Liberation Front for South Vietnam is "Hanoi's creation; it is neither independent nor southern, and what it seeks is not liberation but subjugation of the South."[1]

Under the United States official version, the North Vietnamese Communist Party, meeting in Hanoi in September, 1960, called for the liberation of South Vietnam and for the formation of the "Front for the Liberation of the South," describing the task that lay ahead as "a protracted, hard, and complex struggle, combining many forms of struggle of great activity and flexibility, ranging from lower to higher, and taking as its basis the building, consolidation, and development of the revolutionary power of the masses."

The U. S. official version continues:

". . . three months later Hanoi announced creation of the 'Front for Liberation of the South.' This is the organization that Communist propaganda now credits with guiding the forces of subversion in the South; it is pictured as an organization established and run by the people in the South themselves."

This official United States version of the beginnings of the National Liberation Front for South Vietnam and of its creation as a creature of North Vietnam just does not fit the facts, however much it bolsters the case that the United States did not interfere in a civil war in South Vietnam but instead went to the aid of a friendly country which had requested help to meet aggression from the North.

And, as will be seen, the adoption by the United States of this version of the birth of the National Liberation Front for South Vietnam amounted to the United States being taken in by North Vietnam propaganda seeking to claim credit for the inconvenient birth of a movement which Hanoi, because of the circumstances, would have preferred never to have been conceived or had been stillborn.

The official United States version of how the National Liberation Front for South Vietnam came into being must be carefully read.

The statement that "three months later Hanoi announced creation of the 'Front for Liberation of the South' " is misleading, although accurate as far as it goes. The statement seeks to give the impression that, because Hanoi announced the creation of the National Liberation Front for South Vietnam, it followed that Hanoi had in fact *created* the Front. The announcement could have been made by any radio in any country which picked up the announcement of the formation of the Front as broadcast over a clandestine radio located in South Vietnam.

Many serious students of the Vietnamese scene have raised grave doubts as to the United States version of the formation of the National Liberation Front for South Vietnam.

A realistic appraisal of the who, where, when, what and how of the origin of the Front can be had only in the context of what was happening in South Vietnam at that time.

Gerald Hickey, in his excellent analysis of a village in South Vietnam in the late 1950's entitled "Village in Vietnam" says:

"By 1958, Khanh Hau [the village in the MeKong Delta in South Vietnam which Hickey studied intensively and in depth at that time] also for the first time experienced the activities of a relatively new political movement—the Mat Tran Dan Toc Giai Phong Mien Nam Viet Nam (*National Front for the Liberation of South Vietnam*), referred to by the South Vietnamese government as the Viet Cong or Vietnamese Communists . . . and invariably called the Viet Minh by the villagers."[2]

Gerald Hickey was in the Mekong Delta at that time making an in-depth study of life in one South Vietnamese village (Khanh Hau) in a research capacity for Michigan State University. He, therefore, had an excellent opportunity to study the rise of what the Diem Government called the Viet Cong—Vietnamese Communists—but which the villagers continued to refer to by the name used to designate the Vietnamese fighters against the French colonial regime, the Viet Minh.

The rise of the National Liberation Front for South Vietnam— the circumstances and character of its birth and its subsequent development—can be properly assessed only when viewed in the context of conditions existing in Vietnam—both North and South— during the period from the signing of the Geneva Accords to the end of 1960.

We have already noted the repressive measures taken by Diem to stifle ruthlessly all opposition to his rule, to consolidate his grip on the country, to permit graft and corruption to run riot, and, with his law 10/59, to weed out through killings, tortures, and imprisonments the former resistance fighters, their families, and the families of Ho Chi Minh's South Vietnamese soldiers who had gone north in compliance with the Geneva Agreement. It has also been pointed out that Diem, with the encouragement of the United States, had refused to hold the reunification elections in 1956 as called for by the Geneva Accords.

Commenting on the situation existing in South Vietnam in the early part of 1956, *The Times* (London) stated:

"The liberal intellectuals have been silenced in one way or another; the gangster organization of the Binh Xuyen has disintegrated; the Cao Dai General Nguyen Than Phuong has brought his forces over to the Government and deposed his 'pope.' By no means all of the countryside is firmly administered by the Government in Saigon. But at any rate organized armed resistance has been ended . . . A year ago [1955] Mr. Diem refused national elections on the grounds that there was no guarantee of democratic freedom in the north. If he has asserted his own power by equally undemocratic methods, it has nevertheless been asserted."[3]

Bernard Fall, in his excellent studies on the organizational techniques and abilities of the Viet Minh which had controlled much of the countryside of South Vietnam during the war with the French, shows clearly that after Ho Chi Minh's forces moved north, in accordance with the precepts of the Geneva Accords, he left behind in the countryside a vast governmental organization, well disciplined, not organized on a national or South Vietnamese unified scale but, as was customary, village oriented. This was confirmed by the excellent account by noted columnist Joseph Alsop who traveled in the Mekong Delta during that period.[4]

Ho Chi Minh was also having his difficulties in the North. His economic problems were great not only because of his own economic policies in attempting to "communize" North Vietnam but also because he was trying to rule one half of a divided country, both halves of which had economically complemented the other before the temporary division agreed to at Geneva. Thus, because of the artificial partition of Vietnam, Ho Chi Minh was ruling the portion which was not economically self-sufficient. He had to seek outside help and when his attempts to secure such help from the French failed, he turned to Communist China and to the Soviet Union and its East European satellites.[5]

Foreign aid received by North Vietnam, expressed in the equivalent of millions of United States dollars, was:

	Grants	Credit	Total
1955-1957	$300.0	$ 50.0	$350.0
1958-1960	25.0	188.5	213.5
1961-1965	5.0	327.5	332.5
Total	$330.0	$566.0	$896.0

The major portion of this economic assistance came from the Soviet Union and Communist China.[6]

In contrast, foreign economic assistance received by South Vietnam from the United States, expressed in millions of United States dollars, was:[7]

1953-1957	$ 733.9	$ 50.0	$ 783.9
1958-1960	519.5	29.2	548.7
1961-1966	1,327.5	8.8	1,336.3
Total	$2,580.9	$ 88.0	$2,668.9

These figures do not include military assistance received by either North or South Vietnam.

Ho Chi Minh was also having trouble on the agricultural front. His efforts to communize the farms resulted in riots and an uprising which were put down with military force in November 1956.

"Hastily trained political cadres were put in charge of this
(agrarian) 'reform' and were overzealous in their interpretation
of the agrarian laws. In the resultant confusion, 'middle' and
'rich' peasants frequently were classified erroneously as landlords and indiscriminately brought to trial and condemned.
Many of them were killed."[8]

At about the same time, Ho Chi Minh tried to liberalize freedom of expression and suddenly found his government faced with more criticism from all segments of the populace than he had bargained for. He beat a hasty retreat.

When, in June 1956, Ho Chi Minh realized that the reunification elections were not going to take place and that he was receiving only tepid support from Communist China and the Soviet Union, he issued a statement that reunification would have to wait and that the North "is the foundation, the root of the struggle for complete national liberation and the reunification of the country. That is why everything we are doing in the North is aimed at strengthening both the North and the South. Therefore, to work here is the same as struggling in the South, to struggle for the South and the whole of Vietnam."[9]

In other words, he was bluntly telling the Vietnamese in the South to bide their time and that they could expect no help from him.

But as repression under Diem intensified, it became more and more difficult for those in the South to avoid striking back. In February 1955 Diem had turned down Ho Chi Minh's proposal "to grant all facilities to persons on both sides of the border in sending mail, carrying out business enterprises, and facilitating exchanges of a cultural, scientific, sporting and social nature."[10]

This refusal on the part of Diem meant that persons in the South having relatives in the north could not openly visit or correspond with them, and vice versa, and that all business ties—north and south—had to be severed. But, more importantly, those southern members of Ho Chi Minh's armed forces who had been regrouped in the North in accordance with the Geneva Agreement and had left their families behind for the few months until the country was reunified could not be reunited with their families for a longer period than they had anticipated.

Disillusioned on the chances for the early reunification of their country, facing increased terroristic tactics by Diem's police, with every criticism of the government labeled as "communistic," and cut off from their relatives in the north, the South Vietnamese began to fight terror with terror and resistance.

Hickey, from his vantage point in the village of Khanh Hau in the Mekong Delta, was able to record the growth of that resistance.

"Early in 1958, . . . the director of the UNESCO School . . . awoke one morning to find a Viet Cong flag stuck in the ground before the entrance to his house. Several months later, banners bearing antigovernment slogans were strung across the spur road . . . but after dark the area of security dwindled as it did during the Indochina War to the barbed wire enclosure around the Council House . . . By the end of 1958 the ever-increasing number of assassinations throughout South Vietnam, of which most victims were public servants [appointed by Diem], was attributed by the government to the Viet Cong . . . Viet Cong activities increased in Khanh Hau through 1959 . . . according to some villagers young men responded favorably to Viet Cong recruitment efforts . . . the situation worsened steadily in 1960 . . . ."[11]

The time was ripe for the formalization of the organization of the resistance fighters of the South—to disregard the words of caution from the North to go it alone, letting Hanoi come along or not, as it pleased. After all, they had the organizational know-how drilled into them by Ho Chi Minh during the long years of their struggle against the French. They also had the fighting know-how learned during the same period and by having been given a refresher course by resisting Diem's police forces and army.

According to the French author, Jean Lacouture:

"Probably the actual birth of the National Liberation Front must be traced back to March 1960. At that time a group of the old resistance fighters, assembled in Zone D (eastern Cochinchina) [in South Vietnam], issued a proclamation calling the prevailing situation 'intolerable' for the people as a result of Diem's actions, and called upon patriots to regroup with a view toward ultimate collective action . . . No actual signal was given; the principal decisions were made only six months later. *But the little Congress of March 1960 was in some ways the 'general call' for the creation of the Front,* the signal, coming from the South, was to force the government of the North to assume its responsibility."[12]

In March of 1960 the former resistance fighters in South Vietnam had much for which to reproach their former brothers-in-arms who had gone to or remained in the north in 1954-55.

The time for the 1956 reunification elections had come and gone without their being held—and Ho Chi Minh had done nothing about it except to protest to the International Control Commission.

The United States Miliary Assistance Advisory Group in South Vietnam was increasing rapidly—and Ho Chi Minh had done nothing about it except to protest to the International Control Commission.

The United States was supplying more and more arms to South Vietnam in contravention of the express terms of the Geneva Accords—and Ho Chi Minh had done nothing about it except to protest to the International Control Commission.

Diem was using the hated law 10/59 to mop up former resistance fighters—and Ho Chi Minh had again done nothing about it except to protest to the International Control Commission.

Another French writer, Philippe Devillers, has pointed out that the resistance fighters in South Vietnam actually forced Hanoi to support them.

"The members of the Viet Minh cadre in the south . . . had to listen to bitter remarks that were made to them about the inability of the North to do anything about the Diem dictatorship. The overriding strategy of the Socialist camp meant little or nothing to guerrilla fighters being hunted down in Nam-Bo [South Vietnam]. It was in such a climate of feeling, in 1959, that responsible elements of the Communist Resistance in Indochina came to the conclusion that they had to act, whether Hanoi wanted them to or not. They could no longer stand by while their supporters were arrested, thrown into prison, and tortured, without attempting to do anything about it as an organization, without giving some lead to the people in the struggle in which it was to be involved. Hanoi preferred diplomatic notes, but it was to find that its hand had been forced."[13]

Thus, when the third Communist Party Congress was held in Hanoi in September 1960 and announced that what was needed was a National Front for the Liberation of the South, North Vietnam was only getting on a bandwagon that had already begun to roll in South Vietnam. It was an obvious attempt to take over the leadership of the movement in the south that it had, until then, not led.

Philippe Devillers, in conversations with the authors, related that when, in March of 1960, the Proclamation of the Former Resistance Fighters was broadcast over the clandestine South Vietnamese radio, the Hanoi radio attacked the movement as a trick by Diem and the United States to lure former resistance fighters into revealing themselves so they could be hunted down. It is, of course, difficult to determine whether Hanoi actually believed this interpretation of what was happening in the south or was trying to hold back the resistance workers in the south because the "call to arms" was coming at a time inconvenient for Hanoi.

It took the North Vietnamese Government a while to realize that a resistance movement had in fact begun in the south and that that movement was no longer going to wait on Hanoi's pleasure before standing up to Diem's excesses.

The resistance workers in the South became strengthened by the attempted coup by the military against Diem on November 11, 1960 in their will to fight Diem and his police. The coup failed but it indicated that Diem was vulnerable and that his apparent support from the military forces he had been building up might be more apparent than real—as it turned out to be three years later.

"Five weeks after the coup, on December 20, 1960, about a hundred persons who had gone underground announced from 'somewhere in Nam Bo [South Vietnam] the creation of the 'National Liberation Front of South Vietnam.' If that organization could hardly be identified by the personalities of its leaders, which were kept secret, one could obtain an idea of its orientation from the ten point program that was soon broadcast over Radio Hanoi."[14]

This is the broadcast by the Hanoi Radio of the ten point program adopted by the National Liberation Front for South Vietnam that is referred to in the official United States version of the formation of the Front as: "Hanoi announced the creation of the 'Front for Liberation of the South.' "

The so-called ten-point program of the National Liberation Front of South Vietnam refers to the headings under which many proposals are made. The ten major headings are:

"I. Overthrow the camouflaged colonial regime of the American imperialists and the dictatorial power of Ngo Dinh Diem, servant of the Americans . . .

"II. Institute a largely liberal and democratic regime.

"III. Establish an independent and sovereign economy, and improve the living conditions of the people.

"IV. Reduce land rent; implement agrarian reform . . .

"V. Develop a national and democratic culture and education.

"VI. Create a national army . . .

"VII. Guarantee equality between the various minorities and between the two sexes . . .

"VIII. Promote a foreign policy of peace and neutrality.

"IX. Re-establish normal relations between the two zones . . .

"X. Struggle against all aggressive war . . ."[15]

The document itself contains many curious items.

While there can be no doubt of the ten point document being "marxist" oriented, it contains several points which mitigate against its being a northern document and strongly indicate it's origin as being southern.

The program called for neutrality, which was a point also made in the Declaration of the Former Resistance Fighters issued in South Vietnam nine months earlier. Since the document also called for the reunification of Vietnam, it would be difficult to imagine Hanoi—even for propaganda purposes—announcing that upon reunification it would stop its alignment with Mainland China and the Soviet Union.

The reunification provision is also a curious one. Instead of calling for immediate reunification, it calls for *ultimate* reunification and in the meantime for the regularization of trade and travel between the two zones. The Declaration of the Former Resistance Fighters had also called for this.

Lacouture states that the "text was patently the result of a hasty compromise between Southern democrats desirous of gaining the sympathy of the masses and Communist cadres anxious to maintain their contact with the North."[16]

Thus began the civil war in South Vietnam into which the United States barged with ever increasing military involvement.

In the face of that uprising, Hanoi—whether it wanted to or not—HAD to come out in support of the insurgents to the south. The former resistance fighters who were being hunted down in the south by Diem's forces had, after all, fought or aided Ho Chi Minh to fight against the French.

Other than moral support, how much support by way of men and materiel did Ho Chi Minh give his compatriots fighting against Diem and his United States' equipped and trained armed forces?

How did the amount of that aid given by Ho Chi Minh compare with the amount of military aid given by the United States to Diem?

CHAPTER XIX

BEGINNING OF UNITED STATES MILITARY ESCALATION

Under the Agreement of 1954 for the Cessation of Hostilities in Vietnam—which the United States agreed not to disturb—North Vietnam and France, on behalf of itself and of the remaining southern portion of its colony of Vietnam, and North Vietnam agreed:

(1) " . . . the introduction into Vietnam of any troop reinforcements and additional military personnel is prohibited . . ." (Article 16);

(2) " . . . the introduction into Viet-Nam of any reinforcements in the form of all types of arms, munitions and other war material, such as combat aircraft, naval craft, pieces of ordnance, jet engines and jet weapons and armoured vehicles, is prohibited." (Article 17)

(3) " . . . the establishment of new military bases is prohibited throughout Vietnam territory . . ." (Article 18);

(4) " . . . no military base under the control of a foreign State may be established in the regrouping zone of either party . . ." (Article 19)

(5) " . . . the two parties [France and North Vietnam] shall ensure that the zones assigned to them do not adhere to any military alliance and are not used for the resumption of hostilities or to further an aggressive policy . . ." (Article 19)

The prohibition contained in Article 19 against adherence to "any military alliance" posed a considerable problem for Secretary of State Dulles right after the Geneva Conference. He was determined to carry out his original purpose in uniting the allies of the United States in a treaty designed to defend Southeast Asia against aggression. A treaty to which South Vietnam would be a signatory would focus the attention of the world on an obvious breach of the Geneva Accords after only a few short weeks. And yet, if Dulles were to complete his objective of insuring "united action," he had to find some way out of his dilemma.

The way out was found in not permitting Laos, Cambodia, and South Vietnam to sign the SEATO Treaty but covering their territories in a separate protocol. It was a veneer spread over the first crack in the Geneva Accords. The device covered the crack only thinly and, for former colonies in that area, it constituted a dangerous precedent. It was highly reminiscent of the days when the great colonial powers declared—unilaterally or in concert with each other—that certain areas constituted "spheres of influence" for one or more of the colonial powers.

Prime Minister Nehru of India considered this approach "dangerous . . . from the point of view of any Asian country" since such spheres of interest could be established with or without the consent of the country "protected."[1]

Immediately after the signing of the SEATO Treaty, it became obvious that South Vietnam was one of the places where the United States had determined to build up barriers against further growth of Communism in Southeast Asia and that at least a portion of those barriers would be military in nature.

At the time of the Geneva Accords, the United States already had a Military Assistance Advisory Group (MAAG) in Vietnam. Since the United States had been supplying the French with a considerable amount of military material to enable it to carry on its fight against the Viet Minh, the MAAG had been stationed there as observers to make certain that the weaponry got into the right hands, to observe and report on how well it performed in combat or in supply, and what defects needed correcting.

The agreement for the maintenance of the MAAG in Vietnam had originally been concluded with France, Laos, Cambodia, and

Vietnam on December 23, 1950, when, following the outbreak of hostilities in Korea, President Truman had requested of the Congress and had received increased aid for the French to resist "Communist aggression" in Vietnam. The United States maintained that it had a right to continue its Military Mission in South Vietnam despite the prohibition in the Geneva Accords, and even after the French high command left South Vietnam on April 28, 1956. The United States based this claim on its interpretation of the Agreement as prohibiting additional foreign military personnel from coming to South Vietnam *after* the Geneva Agreement was signed.

The United States maintained this claim even after the roles of the MAAG changed from observation to training the South Vietnamese Army, following the special mission of General Lawton Collins to Saigon in November 1954.[2]

Having by means of the protocol to the SEATO Treaty "disturbed" the Geneva Accords with respect to the prohibition against South Vietnam's entering into "any military alliance," the United States proceeded to "disturb" the Geneva Accords with respect to the prohibition against "the introduction into Vietnam of any troop reinforcements and additional military personnel."

In its Fifth Interim Report, dated January 8, 1956, covering the period from August 11, 1955 to December 10, 1955, the International Control Commission reported receiving from North Vietnam complaints that "foreign military missions" were making trips to South Vietnam without reporting in advance to the Commission, which was a clear violation of the provisions of the Geneva Agreement.

"As a result of the first complaint, the Commission has stated that notifications should be given by both parties regarding visits of Foreign military missions."

However, from an examination of subsequent reports by the Commission, it is evident that this injunction was honored in the breach. United States military aircraft continued to arrive and depart from South Vietnam without complying with the Commission's rules and with the provisions of the Geneva Agreement for advance notification to the Commission and giving the Commission's inspecting teams an opportunity to inspect the aircraft. (See Appendix)

In that same report the Commission complained about the restrictions imposed by South Vietnam on the Commission's investigating personnel. These restrictions, an examination of later Commission reports reveals, continued unabated despite repeated protests by the Commission. Complaints were also made about similar restrictions imposed by North Vietnam.

The Fifth Report of the Commission stated:

"Difficulties were also encountered about the control of the Saigon airport, as in August [1955] the [Commission's investigating] team's movements came to be restricted to the V.I.P. stand and the parking area [at the Saigon airport]."

The pattern of harrassment of the Commission's investigating teams at the Saigon airport was quite simple.

The Commission's investigating teams were not permitted in the V.I.P. enclosure or in the customs building. Thus they could not inspect the material loaded on or off arriving planes. A United States military aircraft would land and taxi directly to the customs building. The V.I.P.s aboard would go directly to the V.I.P. enclosure and then be driven directly to downtown Saigon. The plane would be unloaded and then taxi to the parking area. It was only then that the Commission's teams would be given the opportunity to inspect the empty plane.

Later reports show that when, in an attempt to circumvent the restrictions under which they operated, the Commission's teams requested the planes' manifests, in very many instances they could not be found or were otherwise unavailable.

During the years from 1954 through 1960, therefore, the Commission was unable to determine just how much and what kind of United States military materiel was flowing into South Vietnam in violation of the Geneva Agreement. Here, in the United States, the exact amount of military assistance to South Vietnam was given a "security" classification and hence was not known outside of official circles.

As later revealed, however, during the fiscal years 1958 through 1960, United States military assistance, including training assistance for South Vietnamese soldiers brought out of South Vietnam for training, amounted to $166 million.

During this period, charges were filed with the International Control Commission by South Vietnam against North Vietnam, and vice versa, alleging violations of those sections of the Geneva Agreements of Article 16 (troop reinforcements) and Article 17 (increased armaments) relating to preparations for the resumption of hostilities. Some were admitted and excused—some were denied. But a reading of the Commission's Reports shows that the largest number of allegations of violations was filed against South Vietnam.

From the Commission's reports it is obvious that lack of cooperation on both sides was a constant problem for the Commission. As it stated in its Sixth Report:

"Neither party has fulfilled in their entirety these obligations [of cooperating with the Commission]. As has been revealed in the preceding paragraphs, the degree of cooperation given to the Commission by the two parties has not been the same. While the Commission has experienced difficulties in North Vietnam, the major part of its difficulties has arisen in South Vietnam."

The greatest difficulty encountered by the Commission, in addition to its inability to ascertain what military material was being introduced into South Vietnam by sea and air, was in keeping track of United States military personnel stationed on South Vietnamese soil.

On April 25, 1956, the Commission received a request from the French and the South Vietnamese for permission for the entry of 350 military personnel of the United States Army into South Vietnam. This group was called TERM—Temporary Equipment Recovery Mission—and was being sent to South Vietnam to select excess United States' military equipment for shipment back to the United States.

The Commission informed the French and the South Vietnamese that it wanted further information—such as numbers and names of personnel and length of stay—and that, pending a decision of the Commission, "no entry should be effected. In spite of this, 290 United States military personnel belonging to the 'TERM' had been introduced into South Vietnam, thus facing the Commission with a *fait accompli*."

The Commission then asked for information as to the length of stay of this group. The South Vietnamese Government replied that it was impossible to determine when the mission would be completed. The Commission informed the Government of South Vietnam that, in its opinion, the work of TERM should be completed by the end of June 1959, and that "TERM should cease to exist thereafter and its personnel should leave the Republic of Vietnam."

In reply, the Government of South Vietnam informed the Commission that TERM could complete its work by the end of December 1960, and all its personnel would leave South Vietnam by December 31, 1960.

During December 1960, January and February of 1961, North Vietnam complained that the members of the TERM mission had not left South Vietnam but had been absorbed into MAAG "under the assumed name of the Logistics Section."

South Vietnam replied that of the 350 members of the TERM mission, 261 had left South Vietnam while the remaining 89 had been absorbed into MAAG, but that MAAG was not over its authorized strength.

The Polish member reiterated North Vietnam's contention that the entire TERM mission had been absorbed into the MAAG.

Early in 1960, South Vietnam informed the Commission that it had approached the United States with a request that it increase MAAG from "the figure as it then stood, 342, to 685." The contention of the South Vietnamese Government was that even with this increase the strength of the MAAG "would still be well below the combined strength of 888 MAAG and French instructors present in Vietnam at the time of the Armistice."

The Commission agreed, with the Polish delegate dissenting. North Vietnam protested, alleging that South Vietnam had "requested the Commission to let the United States armaments and military personnel into South Vietnam to replace the French Expeditionary Corps which had invaded Vietnam."

Previously, the Commission in its Tenth Report, for the period of February 1, 1959 to January 31, 1960, over the objection of the Polish Delegation, had entertained a complaint from South Vietnam expressing "concern over the problem of subversion in

South Vietnam and urged the Commission to look into the complaints submitted by it concerning alleged acts of sabotage, subversion and espionage committed on the territory of South Vietnam." The Polish Delegation argued that such complaints had not theretofore been accepted by the Commission and that they were not covered by the Genva Agreement.

In this same report, North Vietnam again complained about the former resistance fighters being detained and tortured at the Phu Loi concentration camp.

In its Eleventh Report for the period February 1, 1960 to February 28, 1961, the Commission asked the South Vietnamese Government to clarify the legality of the introduction into South Vietnam from the United States, during the period beween June 1956 and April 1960, of "war materials . . . such as heavy artillery equipment, modern radar equipment, aircraft and other kinds of armaments." Ostensibly these were brought in for the use of the MAAG. The Commission reported that in answer to a similar inquiry, the South Vietnamese Government had replied that "all war materials though imported in the name of MAAG . . . were actually destined for the Army of the Republic of Vietnam."

These are typical of the incidents related in the reports of the International Control Commission through its Eleventh Report.

Thus, the military situation in South Vietnam when John F. Kennedy was sworn in as President on January 20, 1961, was as follows:

The United States was in South Vietnam with a relatively small MAAG training mission of about 600 men. At the time of the cessation of hostilities in Vietnam in 1954 the MAAG Mission had numbered about 300. Since the Geneva Accords, the number had gradually increased.

In addition, huge quantities of war material had been introduced by the United States into South Vietnam.

It has been estimated that 78 per cent of all American aid given to Vietnam between 1956 to 1960 went into supporting the Army and related military groups. "In short, from 1956 to 1960 the South Vietnamese government spent two-fifths of its total revenues, including over three-quarters of the money it obtained from the United States, in order to maintain its military establishment."[3]

Within a short space of time after President Kennedy took office, the military assistance program to South Vietnam was increased greatly. Military assistance, which was $65 million in fiscal year 1961 increased to $144 million in fiscal year 1962 (the period between July 1, 1961 and July 1, 1962).

This caused the International Control Commission, in its Special Report of June 2, 1962, to the co-chairmen (Great Britain and the Soviet Union) of the Geneva Conference on Indo-China to find, *without dissent*, that "from 3rd December, 1961, up to 5th May, 1962, the Commission's Teams have controlled the entry of 72 military personnel, and observed but not controlled 173 military personnel, 62 helicopters, 6 reconnaissance aircraft, 5 jet aircraft, 57 fighters/fighter bombers, 25 transport aircraft, 26 unspecified types of aircraft, 102 jeeps, 8 tractors, 8 105-mm howitzers, 3 armoured carriers (tracked), 29 armoured fighting vehicle trailers, 404 other trailers, and radar equipment and crates, 5 warships, 9 LSTs (including 4 visiting LSTs), 3 LCTs, 5 visiting aircraft carriers and spares of various kinds."

It is interesting to note that, except for the vast increase in quantity, the types of material of a military nature observed being unloaded in South Vietnam between December 3, 1961, and May 5, 1962, in many respects paralleled that mentioned in the Eleventh Report of the Commission for the period February 1, 1960 to February 28, 1961.

The Special Report of the Commission also found that there had been incitement to revolution in the South from North Vietnam. As will also be noted, that incitement came after years of military buildup in the South by the United States which continued in an ever-increasing scale both before and after South Vietnam refused to hold the reunifying elections called for by the Geneva Accords.

The Special Report of the Commission found, the Polish Delegation dissenting:

" . . . in specific instances there is evidence to show that armed and unarmed personnel, arms, munitions and other supplies have been sent from the Zone in the North to the Zone in the South with the object of supporting, organizing and carrying out hostile activities including armed attacks directed against the Armed Forces and Administration of the Zone in the South . . .

". . . there is evidence to show that the PAVN [North Vietnam] has allowed the Zone in the North to be used for inciting, encouraging and supporting hostile activities in the Zone in the South, aimed at the overthrow of the Administration in the South . . ."

Speaking of this period, Murti, an Indian with the International Control Commission, stated:

"But when the MAAG completely took over the military operations in South Vietnam the International Commission could no longer shut its eyes to the realities. The Commission requested the South Vietnam Government to let them know whether the increased strength of MAAG personnel and the war materials imported by them, such as heavy artillery equipment, modern radar equipment, aircraft and other kinds of armaments were brought in legally or otherwise. There was no secret about the arrival of the aircraft carrier U.S.S. "CORE" in December 1961 in Saigon with a large number of airplanes, pilots and maintenance men of the U.S. Air Force. "CORE" made repeated visits to Saigon with arms, ammunition, aircraft and U.S. military personnel."[4]

Pulitzer Prize Winner Malcolm Browne, who was on the scene in Saigon when the "CORE" arrived there "with the first load of American helicopters and helicopter crewmen." It docked in front of the Majestic Hotel "in full view of one of the city's busiest streets. Thousands were looking on." When a group of reporters asked the United States Information Office about it, the reply was: "Carrier in front of the Majestic Hotel? What carrier? We don't see any carrier. We're not authorized to see any carrier."[5]

Why did President Kennedy, less than twelve months after his inauguration, increase so greatly the United States military commitment in South Vietnam?

What were President Kennedy's objectives?

How far was President Kennedy prepared to go in involving United States military personnel in a ground war in Southeast Asia?

CHAPTER XX

KENNEDY AND VIETNAM—YEAR OF DECISION—1961

In the course of the 1960 Presidential campaign, between the Democratic ticket of Kennedy and Johnson and the Republican ticket of Nixon and Lodge, the issue of United States foreign policy was prominent.

During the third, nation-wide television debate between Kennedy and Nixon, on October 13 ,1960, Nixon stated:

"As far as Indochina was concerned, I stated over and over again that it was essential during that period that the United States make it clear that we would not tolerate Indochina falling under Communist domination.

"Now as a result of our taking the strong stand that we did, the civil war there was ended, and today at least in the south of Indochina *the Communists have moved out and we do have a strong free bastion there.*"[1] (Emphasis supplied)

In reply, Kennedy said:

". . . on Indochina, Mr. Nixon talked before the newspaper editors in the spring of 1954 about putting . . . American boys into Indochina. The reason Indochina was preserved was the result of the Geneva Conference which partitioned Indochina."[2]

In like vein, Kennedy had said the day before, in speaking before the Democratic National and State Committees in New York, that

Nixon was a "risk taker" abroad and a "conservative" at home. He reminded his listeners that, in 1954, Nixon had said: "We must take the risk of putting our boys·in Indochina" if needed to "avoid further Communist expansion." "If ever there was a war," Kennedy continued, "where we would have been engaged in a hopeless struggle without allies, for an unpopular colonialist cause, it was the 1954 war in Indochina . . . a peace-loving people do not want a trigger-happy President in the White House."[3]

Kennedy had expressed the same sentiments upon his return from an inspection trip to Indochina in 1951.[4]

Kennedy had expressed the same sentiments on the floor of the United States Senate during the course of the debates, in 1954, about sending troops to Indochina.[5]

When Kennedy took office on January 20, 1961, he faced two formidable tasks. First, he had to get his ambitious domestic program—including far-reaching civil rights legislation—through the Congress. Second, he had to meet the foreign crises that faced the United States in many quarters of the globe.

On the international scene, the four immediate trouble spots were Cuba, the Congo, Laos, and Vietnam. These crises were caused, said Walt W. Rostow, Deputy Special Assistant to the President for National Security Affairs, by "a successful Communist breaching . . . of the cold-war truce lines which had emerged from the Second World War and its aftermath. In different ways each had arisen from the efforts of the International Communist movement to exploit inherent instabilities of the underdeveloped areas of the non-Communist world, and each had a guerrilla-warfare component."[6]

Cuba, Rostow admitted, was a "broad-based national insurrection" against Batista, the former ruthless dictator of that island, whose regime had been bolstered by United States financial aid. Less than three months after Kennedy's inauguration, the United States, on April 15, 1961, was to suffer a tragic loss of prestige when the attempted invasion of Cuba, at the Bay of Pigs by United States trained and partially supported Cuban guerrillas failed.

To what extent Kennedy's later views on United States' involvement in international affairs, and especially in Vietnam, were to be colored by the disaster at the Bay of Pigs will probably never be known. Theodore C. Sorenson, one of Kennedy's biographers and Special Counsel to Kennedy throughout his term of office, states that Kennedy's scepticism was greatly increased by that experience. Because the United States had suffered a serious setback at the Bay of Pigs which enhanced the prestige of the Communist bloc countries and deepened the suspicions of the non-aligned countries, it may well be that Kennedy was resolved, at all costs, not to suffer another reverse on the international scene.

In the Congo, when Kennedy took office, the United Nations was having, and would continue to have, grave difficulites in maintaining some semblance of peace and order among the various warring factions.

In Laos, fighting among the various groups—the Communist Pathet Lao, the neutralists led by Souvanna Phouma, and the conservatives led by General Phoumi Nosavan, reputedly backed by the United States Central Intelligence Agency—had already intensified by the time Kennedy was sworn in as President.

The Department of State had, on January 7, 1961, issued a statement proposing as the solution for the Laotian problem the recognition of the role of the Communists in Laos, a clear showing that the United States did not want a military position there, and joining "with other free nations to support and maintain the independence of Laos through whatever measures seem most promising."

A Geneva Conference of 14 nations was convened on May 16, 1961, to consider the situation in Laos. In attendance were Burma, Cambodia, Canada, People's Republic of China, Democratic Republice of Vietnam [North Vietnam], France, India, Poland, Republic of Vietnam [South Vietnam], Thailand, the United Soviet Socialist Republic, the United Kingdom and the United States. Agreement on the neutrality of Laos was reached on July 23, 1962, and a coalition government began to administer an uneasy and fragile truce.

In Vietnam Kennedy felt he faced a different problem. In this area Kennedy was no novice. He had made a report on its situation to the Senate in 1951 after a visit there. As already noted, he had spoken out on Vietnam and against the sending of troops there in the Senate in 1954.

By the time Kennedy took office in January 1961, the situation in South Vietnam had seriously deteriorated. The unsuccessful military coup of November 11, 1960 had been followed by an increase in repressive measures by Diem. The killings and sabotage by the South Vietnamese, many of whom were old Viet Minh fighters combatting Diem's oppression, were increasing.

One of the chief architects of Kennedy's policies in South Vietnam was his Secretary of State, Dean Rusk. By a curious coincidence, Dean Rusk had also been one of the architects of President Truman's policy on Vietnam. Secretary of State Rusk had been Assistant Secretary of State for Far Eastern Affairs during 1950-52 when Truman had decided, after fighting broke out in Korea, to step up United States' aid to France in its efforts to recolonialize Vietnam, since he viewed the Viet Minh resistance to France's efforts as part of the international, aggressive Communist movement of conquest.

The Kennedy Administration's view of the situation in Vietnam apparently was that nothing had changed there since 1950. It was as though nothing had happened in the intervening years except the banishment of the communist Ho Chi Minh, north of the 17th parallel. The broken pledge of holding reunification elections in all of Vietnam in 1956 was forgotten. The repressive measures of Diem against his own people were overlooked. Just as the strong nationalist motivation of the Vietnamese people was discounted when the United States went to the aid of France in 1950 so, in 1961, the resistance of the South Vietnamese to the oppressions of Diem was laid at the doorstep of Ho Chi Minh, who was being told what to do by Peking and Moscow.

The facts were made to fit the theory. Those that did not fit were not mentioned. Thus the declaration of the former resistance workers in South Vietnam, issued in March 1960, was ignored. The announcement in 1960 from South Vietnam of the formation of the National Liberation Front for South Vietnam was brushed aside. The request for the redress of grievances by the 18 prominent South Vietnamese leaders was given no heed. What was played up was the announcement from Hanoi of the creation of the National Liberation Front for South Vietnam to give the impression that it was a creature of Hanoi. The killings and murders in South Vietnam were interpreted as being directed from Hanoi to overthrow Diem's government rather than as reactions to Diem's tortures and imprisonments and his refusal to hold the promised elections. Those members of Ho Chi Minh's armies who were originally from the South but who had gone north of the 17th parallel with Ho Chi Minh after the Geneva Accords—as they were required to do by the Geneva Agreement—were portrayed as "infiltrators" when in 1958-1961 they returned to the South, either to rejoin their families and/or to fight against Diem. Prominence was given to the encouragement by the Lao Dong (Communist) Party in North Vietnam of the efforts of the National Liberation Front for South Vietnam "to overthrow the U.S.—Diem clique" and to "liberate the south."

Apparently little attention was paid, during the Kennedy appraisal of the situation in South Vietnam in 1961, to comparing it with the situation that existed there in 1950 or 1954. The acceptance of the theory that the international, aggressive, monolithic communist conspiracy, directed either from Peking, Moscow, or Hanoi, was behind the shootings, the beheadings, and the disembowelings in South Vietnam seemed to brook no deep analysis in 1961 in relation to the facts as they really were.

The fact that many of Ho Chi Minh's regular troops were from the south has been repeatedly swept aside. Under the Geneva Agreement, they were required to regroup north of the 17th parallel. They did so in the expectation that by the end of July 1956—about a year later—after the reunification elections, all Vietnam would be one and that they could then go South to rejoin their families.

In 1961—almost five years after they had gone north—the question of reunification elections was heard no more both in the north and the south.

In the period from 1958, the southerners in the north were receiving word that Diem had systematically begun to ferret out, torture, and imprison their former comrades in arms against the French who had remained in the South.. Not having been part of Ho Chi Minh's regular troops, they were not required to go north.

As noted student of the scene, Robert Shaplen, has put it: "In their campaign to isolate villages, particularly in the [Mekong] delta, the Communists had begun to smuggle in armed guerrillas from the north. These were southerners who had gone north in 1954 and been retrained as the vanguard of the new revolutionary army to 'liberate' South Vietnam; they now joined the stay-behinds who for four years had been organizing militant cells and were engaging in widespread terrorism, including assassination of hamlet and village chiefs, teachers, local security heads, and other government officials."[6]

In the classic sense, therefore, there was a civil war going on in South Vietnam when Kennedy took office. At that time, the fighting was between southerners fighting the southerners (and the northerners) composing Diem's regime. That had been going on at an increasing tempo since 1958. They were joined in ever greater numbers during 1960 by other southerners, who had been living north of the 17th parallel and who had come south—as southerners —to fight the southern regime of Diem. That there may have been some northerners among them did not change the southerners versus southerners character of the conflict. The fact that there were many norhterners in Diem's regime did not make his regime a northern one.

A civil war is defined as "a war between different sections or parties of the same country or nation." The fact that some of the southerners fighting the Diem government in South Vietnam were Ho Chi Minh trained Communists did not change the character of the fighting in South Vietnam. It was a civil war regardless of the political persuasions of the combatants.

This is not to say that Ho Chi Minh did not at all times want or would have spurned an opportunity to rule a united Vietnam or was not giving aid and comfort to the South Vietnamese fighting to overthrow the Diem government. After all, the objective of a united Ho Chi Minh-ruled Vietnam had been snatched from his grasp at Geneva by the failure of Mainland China and the Soviet Union to back a more adamant stand in his favor.

But that is a far cry from saying that if, in the period from 1954 to 1961, all of North Vietnam had been obliterated from the map, peace and tranquility would have reigned in South Vietnam. Diem's refusal to compromise with his opposition, his autocratic rule, and his ruthless repression of all dissent led to unrest in South Vietnam and to open resistance to his actions.

It should also be remembered that the southerners who came South to fight had been fighters in the Viet Minh. They had been trained and had fought against the French—and fought well. The

White Paper issued by the Kennedy Administration late in 1961 admitted that the weapons they used were captured from Diem's own forces.

"By hitting such targets [police stations, army outposts, etc.] suddenly and in superior force, the VC [Viet Cong] are able to assure themselves a supply of arms and ammunition. This reduces their dependence on the long supply line from the North. The weapons of the VC are largely French-or U.S.-made or handmade on primitive forges in the jungles."[7]

It is curious to note the great pains to which the U.S. Government has gone to deride the notion that the fighting in South Vietnam started as a civil war. Thus the 1961 State Department's "White Paper" is entitled: "A Threat to Peace: North Vietnam's Effort to Conquer South Vietnam." The 1965 "White Paper," issued at the time of the 1965 United States military escalation is entitled "Aggression From the North: The Record of North Viet-Nam's Campaign to Conquer South Viet-Nam."

Why this intense effort to rewrite history and to give a different connotation to the known facts?

One answer, of course, might be the blind belief in 1961, as in 1950, in the theory of monolithic, international, aggressive Communist conspiracy. Under this theory, many of the southerners fighting Diem were Communists. Ho Chi Minh was a Communist. Therefore, the southern Communists are not really fighting to overthrow Diem because they were reacting to being tortured and put in concentration camps but because, as Communists, they were forced to obey the orders of Ho Chi Minh. Hence, this became "Aggression from the North."

There may, however, be another or additional reason for the insistence that the fighting in South Vietnam did not start as a civil war but was "Aggression from the North."

It will be recalled that when the SEATO Treaty was agreed to at Manila on September 5, 1954, Secretary of State Dulles had insisted that the Treaty be circumscribed so as to preclude the United States involvement in petty wars that, fueled by old enmities, might erupt in the Pacific. A special provision, applicable only to the United States, was, therefore, written into the Treaty, stating clearly that the aggression and armed attack referred to in Paragraph I, Article IV of the Treaty would "apply only to Communist aggression." Obviously, therefore, if the fighting in South Vietnam were declared to be a civil war, the United States could not use this provision to justify armed intervention in such a civil war. The United States had to contend and maintain that what was taking place in South Vietnam in 1961 was "Aggression from the North"— a Communist aggression within the meaning of the SEATO Treaty.

This then was the factual situation in Vietnam that confronted Kennedy upon his inauguration. The trouble in South Vietnam was presented to him as stemming from, directed by, and supplied by Ho Chi Minh from Hanoi as part of the overall international Communist conspiracy to rule the world.

Arthur M. Schlesinger, Jr., in his biography of Kennedy, wrote that Vietnam was to occupy more of Kennedy's attention than "anything else in Asia" during his brief years in office.

"The civil war had begun the year after the cancellation of the elections. Diem's authoritarianism . . . produced a spreading resistance . . . . Nearly all those who came from North Vietnam in the Kennedy years . . . were South Vietnamese who had gone north in 1954; most of the Viet Cong in any case continued to be recruited in South Vietnam; and most Viet Cong arms and equipment were captured from Diem's army."[8]

Immediately after taking office in January 1961, Kennedy created a special Task Force on Vietnam consisting of representatives from the Department of State, the Department of Defense, the Central Intelligence Agency and the White House staff. The Task Force reported to Kennedy in late April of 1961. At the same time, a report on the situation in Vietnam was submitted by the Joint Chiefs of Staff. Both reports recommended sending combat troops to Vietnam.[9]

Theodore C. Sorensen, in his biography of Kennedy, states that Kennedy did not approve either the Task Force report or the report of the Joint Chiefs of Staff that combat troops be sent to Vietnam.

Instead, according to Sorenson, Kennedy approved a "more limited program." He tripled the number of advisers to be sent to Vietnam "with officers assigned at the batallion level as well as to regiments, to advise in combat as well as training, and to aid in unconventional as well as conventional warfare." United States logistical support was increased (helicopters to fly South Vietnamese soldiers from place to place and, ultimately, as it turned out, into battle.) In addition, more money and more instructors were made available to the South Vietnamese Civil Guard and Self-Defense Forces.

Thus did the United States "back into" an undeclared ground war in Vietnam—quietly, without fanfare, and without Congressional approval.

It should have seemed inevitable to those making this decision in 1961 that:

(1) when "advisers" are sent in to advise under actual combat circumstances, they would inevitably have to fire back when fired upon;

(2) when a United States' helicopter ferrying trops into combat is fired upon it will fire back; and,

(3) inevitably some of the United States planes would be flown into combat without South Vietnamese soldiers aboard.

In the light of Kennedy's previously expressed opinions on United States' military involvement in a land war in Southeast Asia without allies, why did Kennedy make the decision to embroil the United States in such a land war?

In Schlesinger's opinion, Kennedy had no choice but to escalate. He claims the commitment was made in 1954 by Eisenhower, saying:

"Whether we were right in 1954 to undertake this commitment will long be a matter of interest to historians, but it had ceased by 1961 to be of interest to policy-makers. Whether we had vital interests in South Vietnam before 1954, the Eisenhower letter created those interests. Whether we should have drawn the line where we did, once it was drawn we became every succeeding year more imprisoned by it. Whether the domino theory was valid in 1954, it had acquired validity seven years later, after neighboring governments had staked their own security on the ability of the United States to live up to its pledges in Saigon."[10]

This statement is curious in the light of the situation in which Kennedy found himself in 1961 when called upon to decide what to do about South Vietnam.

In the face of increasing insurgency in the South Vietnamese countryside, the Eisenhower Administration did not view its commitment as greater than that of doubling the MAAG mission from around 300 to around 600 men in 1960, BUT not in changing its mission from that of training the South Vietnamese Army to fighting the Vietcong.

Kennedy would, the following year, agree to a neutralist government in Laos under a "troika" arrangement which recognized that the Communists should play a part in the Government of Laos. But such an arrangement was not put forward for South Vietnam. Why? Schlesinger says:

" . . . but the survival of that policy [a coalition government which would include Communist representation] in South Vietnam, where the government was stronger and the army more willing to fight, left us in 1961 no alternative but to continue the effort of 1954."[11]

But the Kennedy Administration in 1961 did not merely "continue the effort of 1954." While there is some basis for questioning the legality, under the Geneva Accords, of the Eisenhower Administration's changing the nature of the United States MAAG mission to Vietnam from that of merely observing to actually training the South Vietnamese army, from 1954 to 1960 the Eisenhower Administration went no further than that. It was in 1961, under the Kennedy Administration, that the MAAG was greatly increased in size and given quasi-combat assignments.

Comparing the relative strengths of the Diem Government in South Vietnam with the Government in Laos is to compare two weak governments to determine not which is stronger but which is weaker. The strength of the Diem Government in 1961 and the willingness of its army to fight could have been ascertained easily from any knowledgeable—and there were some—newspapermen in Saigon at the time. Even as Schlesinger, writing in 1967, states:

"In our whole time in Vietnam, there has never been a government in Saigon which had the active loyalty of the peasants; indeed, in the past, when the Saigon government has recovered control of territory from the Viet Cong, its first camp-followers have often been stooges of the oligarchy collecting back rents and taxes."[12]

Sorensen gives another view of how Kennedy escalated the war in Vietnam to the extent he did. Sorenson also was of the opinion that—rightly or wrongly—a commitment had been made by his predecessor which was not one "that President Kennedy felt he could abandon without undesirable consequences throughout Asia and the world."[13]

"Unfortunately," writes Sorenson, "he [Kennedy] inherited in Vietnam more than a commitment and a growing conflict. He also inherited a foreign policy which had identified America in the eyes of Asia with dictators, CIA intrigue and a largely military response to revolution. He inherited a military policy which had left us wholly unprepared to fight—or even to train others to fight—a war against local guerrillas."

In May of 1961 Kennedy sent Vice President Johnson to South Vietnam to assure Diem of his continuing support, to assess the situation, and to report back to Kennedy. Earlier, on May 5, 1961, at a press conference Kennedy announced that "consideration" was being given to the use of United States troops to fight the Communists in Vietnam.

The day before, Secretary of State Dean Rusk had held a news conference at which he told reporters that the President had authorized an "increase in the amount of military assistance, and a number of other measures have been determined upon. Furthermore the United States has undertaken training and advisory measures which are designed to strengthen both materially and militarily the ability of the Vietnam armed forces to overcome this increased Communist threat."[14]

Asked whether corruption in South Vietnam was the "cause of the situation" there, Secretary Rusk said that "corruption is [not] the root cause of the situation there, in the face of amounts of determined activity by those coming in from the outside . . ."

At that time, graft in South Vietnam was open and notorious—and was to continue that way all during the Kennedy and Johnson years.

The Manifesto of the Eighteen Notables of Saigon had made a point of this, as had the Declaration of the Former Resistance Fighters—both issued in South Vietnam in 1960.

And yet, in May of 1961 Secretary of State Rusk saw the issue in South Vietnam as only "Agression from the North" rather than repression by and corruption in the Diem government in the South.

Vice President Johnson, from Saigon on May 13, 1961, issued a rosy joint communique which mentioned "the determination, energy and sacrifices of the Vietnamese people, under the dedicated leadership of President Ngo Dinh Diem . . . a brave country in defense of its liberties . . . Diem . . . is in the vanguard of those leaders who stand for freedom . . . high priority to restoration of a sense of security . . . to pursue vigorously appropriate measures in other fields to achieve a prosperous and happy society . . . an increase and acceleration of United States assistance to the Republic of Vietnam . . . ."[15] During this trip, Vice President Johnson had called Diem the Winston Churchill of Asia.

Upon his return to Washington, Vice President Johnson, reporting to Kennedy, recommended "a major effort to help."

"The Vice-President did not envisage the commitment of American troops beyond training missions. American combat involvement at this time, he said, was not only unnecessary but undesirable because it would revive anti-colonial emotions throughout Asia. Instead, Johnson favored the reorientation of the military effort along with programs of political and economic reform."[16]

In the months in 1961 following the return of the Vice President, the situation in South Vietnam steadily deteriorated. United States advisers were being shot at—and killed. The casualties were not large but they were growing.

Late in October, a new mission was sent to Vietnam headed by General Maxwell Taylor and Walt Rostow. Upon their return with recommendations, Kennedy, says Sorenson, once again faced the decision of whether to send combat troops to fight in Vietnam. "American troops were needed less for their numerical strength than for the morale and will they could provide to Diem's forces . . ."

All Kennedy's principal advisers were pressuring him to send combat troops to fight in Vietnam. "But," says Sorensen, "the President *in effect* voted 'no'—and only his vote counted." (Emphasis supplied)

According to Schlesinger, Kennedy's "in effect" voting "no" was based on the statement made by him on the floor of the Senate in 1954, previously quoted, when the question was whether the United States would send ground troops to help France in her re-colonializing efforts. He had said at the time that "unilateral action by our own country . . . would be virtually impossible . . . an enemy which is everywhere and at the same time nowhere . . . ."

The facts are, however, that, when in May 1961 Kennedy had changed the role of the "American advisers" in South Vietnam to permit them "to advise in battle mission," Kennedy had "in effect" voted "yes" to send combat troops to fight in Vietnam. The casualty lists attested to that. If Kennedy's voting "no" meant that he was opposed to sending large numbers of troops to fight in South Vietnam but would send a few, then in 1961 that "no" vote held true since by the end of that year only about 1500 additional advisers were sent to fight in Vietnam. However, by the end of 1963, there were to be over 15,000 advisers there.

To make it more difficult for those who wanted him to inter-vene "to charge him privately with weakness," Kennedy according to Sorensen, never formally made a "final negative decision on troops." Instead, he escalated the troops and types of missions sent to South Vietnam.

"He [Kennedy] steadily expanded . . . by sending in combat support units, air combat and helicopter teams, still more military advisers and instructors and 600 of the green-hatted Special Forces to train and lead the South Vietnamese in antiguerrilla tactics."

By pre-arrangement between the Government of the United States and the Government of South Vietnam, Diem, on December 7, 1961, sent Kennedy a letter in which he complained about the long history of Communist aggression against his government, of the announced plan of the Communists to take over in South Vietnam, and of a growing number of incidents (1800 in October with more than 2000 casualties).

"If we lose this war," Diem told Kennedy, "our people will be swallowed by the Communist Bloc . . . the forces of International Communism now arrayed against us are more than we can meet with the resources at hand. We must have further assistance from the United States . . . ."

Diem's letter made no mention of carrying out needed social and economic reforms—reforms which President Eisenhower had made conditional to granting aid seven years earlier—reforms which Diem had promised Vice President Johnson he would carry out seven months earlier. (See Appendix)

Kennedy's reply to Diem, dated December 15, 1961, also made no mention of Diem's carrying out the promised social and economic reforms.

Kennedy's answer mentioned the "dangerous condition" in South Vietnam caused by "North Vietnam's efforts to take over your country." It noted what "our own information has convincingly shown— that the campaign of force and terror now being waged against your people and your Government is supported and directed from the outside by the authorities at Hanoi." The letter also contained the promise to "help the Republic of Vietnam to protect its people and to preserve its independence. We shall promptly increase our assistance to your defense effort . . ." (See Appendix)

The latter sentence was actually superfluous, except for the record. Increased aid had already openly been dispatched to South Vietnam. It openly arrived in Saigon on December 11, 1961 and caused the International Control Commission to sit up and take notice.

There was no need for Kennedy to mention in his letter to Diem that combat troops were being sent to South Vietnam. They were already there. Some had already been killed. More had been wounded.

In December 1961, the State Department released a "White Paper" entitled "A Threat to Peace; North Vietnam's Effort to Conquer South Vietnam." It is in many respects similar to a "White Paper" released by the State Department in February 1965, after the massive escalation of the United States military effort in Vietnam and the institution of United States' bombings against North Vietnam. (See Appendix)

The 1961 "White Paper" sought at every turn to give the impression that but for Ho Chi Minh and his cohorts in the North there would be nothing but peace and prosperity in South Vietnam. No mention is made in the 1961 "White Paper" of Diem's repressive rule, of the large numbers of South Vietnamese, many of them non-Communists, even then languishing in Diem's concentration camps; of the graft and corruption running rampant throughout Diem's Government; of the Manifesto of the Eighteen respected South Vietnamese citizens issued the year before; of the Declaration of the South Vietnamese former resistance fighters; of the announcement in South Vietnam of the formation of the National Liberation Front; of the growing unrest in Diem's armed forces which had culminated in an unsuccessful coup in November 1960, which Diem had overcome by promising reforms (which he never carried out); and of the increasing personalism and favoritism of Diem's Government.

The 1961 "White Paper" was but one of the long series of official United States Government's incorrect presentations designed to gloss over the increasing involvement of the United States in military action in South Vietnam. It was but one episode in the large number of deceptions of the American people which were to follow and to create the widening "credibility gap" between the American people and their Government.

But withal, the question remains why President Kennedy, in the light of his often expressed views against getting the United States embroiled in a land war in Southeast Asia without allies, should have committed United States troops to such an adventure in May 1961.

CHAPTER XXI

KENNEDY AND VIETNAM — THE LATER YEARS

The twenty-three months that elapsed between President Kennedy's assurances to President Diem that increased United States aid for South Vietnam would be forthcoming and the assassinations of both Presidents were increasingly turbulent years for South Vietnam.

That period witnessed:

(1) A widening role for United States military involvement in South Vietnam not only in terms of numbers of men sent to Vietnam (more than a seven-fold increase to over 15,000 men at the end of 1963) but also in actual participation in the fighting, with an increasing number of United States casualties;

(2) Failure to win "the hearts and minds" of the South Vietnamese people to the support of the Diem Government;

(3) A growing estrangement of many of the working press in South Vietnam (and in the United States) from both Vietnamese and United States' news sources in the face of ever-increasing attempts to "manage the news" and to paint a false picture of what was actually going on in South Vietnam and of the United States combat involvement there; and,

(4) Increased opposition to Diem and his government, culminating, on November 1, 1963, in the assassination of Diem and the

overthrow of the government, to be followed by a series of military coups.

Both Schlesinger and Sorensen are in agreement that during this period the United States paid more attention to the military side of the problem in South Vietnam than to the social and economic reforms that Diem had promised but never effected.

The sending of General Maxwell Taylor and Walt Rostow to report on conditions in South Vietnam in October 1961 is interpreted by Schlesinger as a yielding by Secretary of State Rusk of the problem to the military. Sorensen, on the other hand, was of the opinion that the military side of the struggle in South Vietnam took precedence because of the inability of the State Department "to compete with the Pentagon."[1]

In any event, the Taylor-Rostow report recommended increased United States military intervention. General Taylor recommended "that American troops perform certain tasks, like airlift and air reconnaisance . . . he even envisaged sending an American military task force - perhaps 10,000 men - capable of conducting combat operations for self-defense and perimeter security and, if the Vietnamese Army were hard pressed, of providing an emergency reserve."[2]

Schlesinger states that Kennedy was "impressed by its [the Taylor-Restow report] description of the situation as serious but not hopeless and attracted by the idea of stiffening the Diem regime through an infusion of American advisers." This is exactly what Kennedy did, even though Schlesinger states that Kennedy did not like the proposal that United States troops be sent into combat. Kennedy pointed out that sending some troops would lead to a request for more and more and more troops and that the war in Vietnam "could be won only so long as it was their war. If it were ever converted into a white man's war, we would lose as the French had lost a decade earlier."

Inevitably, the Americans sent into South Vietnam as "advisers" took an increasingly active role in actual combat. Reporter Malcolm Browne has recounted how he was in Danang as early as April 1962, when two American fighter bombers - two-seaters - landed with their "bomb racks empty, and fresh smoke stains trailed back over the wings from their guns." American "advisers"

were in the front seats - the "seats from which strafing and bombing missions are flown." To keep up the pretence that the Americans were only "advising," each of the back seats was occupied
by a South Vietnamese soldier.[3]

There can be no doubt but that the infusion into South Vietnam in 1962 of $287.3 million in United States economic and mili-
tary aid helped stem the tide that was running against Diem in late
1961. The use of new weapons in the war, especially helicopters,
brought a new mobility to the guerrilla war. Pulitzer Prize-winning
reporter David Halberstam wrote that the helicopters, "fighter
bombers and armored personnel carriers had given a shot in the
arm to the Vietnamese regulars."[4]

But the military aid, in the opinion of the American advisers
on the scene in South Vietnam, also had its disadvantages. Against
the lightly armed Vietcong, these modern weapons were giving the
Vietnamese soldiers a "false sense of security." They noted that the
South Vietnamese soldiers did not like to fight at night, were not
using the Vietcong tactics of ambushes, and were not using "psychological warfare against the enemy. All that the Government
troops had done so far was to seize a momentary advantage because of the new weaponry—and they had even failed to exploit
this fully."[5] That was in September, 1962.

Social and Economic Reforms—Promises Without Fulfillment

In his letter to Diem on October 23, 1954, President Eisenhower
conditioned United States' aid "on performance on the part of the
Government of Vietnam in undertaking needed reforms."

The needed reforms were never made by Diem.

In President Kennedy's notification to Diem on December 14,
1961, that United States' aid would be increased, no mention was
made of the need for Diem's undertaking to make the requested, but
never carried out, reforms.

However, on January 4, 1962, after the amount of military aid
to South Vietnam had been more than doubled, while economic aid
stayed at the same level, a joint communiqué was issued by the
United States and South Vietnam dealing with the expansion of the
latter's economic development program. Included in that program
were training facilities for village officials, rural health programs,

expanded education programs, additional agricultural credit, and resettlement villages.

The communiqué made no mention of carrying out needed reforms, especially land reform.

Over the years land reform has been one of the basic needs—a hitherto unfulfilled need—to begin to reach the minds and hearts of the people. According to Bernard Fall, in South Vietnam "2 percent of the landowners hold 45 percent of the [rice] land, and 72 percent hold 15 percent [of the rice land]." Most of the 2 percent are absentee land owners.[6]

Fall relates that during the French-Indochina War "the former owners arrived literally in the baggage train with the advancing French and Vietnamese soldiers and very often used the troops to force the peasants not only to surrender part of the current crops but to make payments on past crops as well . . . such practices—which still have not entirely ceased today—play into Communist hands."

Bernard Fall wrote that description in 1964.

On March 31, 1967, columnist Clayton Fritchey, wrote in the Washington *Evening Star*:

" 'Absentee landlords are still riding in with pacifying troops,' reports the *London Times,* 'not merely to grab back their lands but to extort back rents for the time they fled the Viet Cong,' Although an old law limits rents to 25 percent of the crop, the *Times* reports that 'landlords still extort rents as high as 60 percent.' "

The difficulty with land reform in South Vietnam is that the very government that would have to institute such reforms is in the hands of the absentee landlords. Everyone is for land reform, Fritchey wrote, "except the only three groups that matter—namely, the Ky military junta, the landowning class that supports him, and the U.S. Government, which supports both."

One innovation given top billing by both Washington and Saigon in 1962 as their newest weapon in the arsenal to be used in the "other war"—the war for "the hearts and minds" of the people—was the "strategic hamlet." This was widely hailed as copying a successful experiment used by the British in the pacification of Malaya. It was to be the United States' answer to the

Communists' "wars of national liberation." Brigadier R.G.K. Thompson, who had been connected with the Malaysian experiment, was brought from Britain to Saigon, together with a team of experts, to advise.

According to Roger Hilsman, then Director of Intelligence and Research for the Department of State, speaking in 1962, the concept was to "cut the major routes of supply and deny the Communists access to thousands of unprotected villages." The program called for putting "barbed wire, watchtowers, and ditches filled with bamboo spikes and booby traps" around the villages. Each fortified village would be given a radio to call for help, which could be flown in quickly by helicopter. In this way, the village could be tied into the central government which would provide each village with "health, education, agricultural services, police protection, and good village administration." The South Vietnamese Government would establish "civic-action teams," each of which would include "a medical technician, a school teacher, an agricultural credit representative, a public information representative, two or three public administration advisers, and a youth activities representative, as well as a police adviser, a civil guard liaison officer . . . and a squad of soldiers to issue weapons to the villagers and provide training in their use."[7]

To many this may sound surprisingly similar to the program so loudly hailed at Honolulu in February 1966.

Why did the strategic hamlet program of 1962 fail?

For that matter, why did Diem's fortified hamlet program—agroville program begun in 1959—fail?

Why did the scheme work in Malaya and not in South Vietnam?

In an excellent study by Milton E. Osborne, published in 1965 by the Department of Asian Studies of Cornell University, the comparison is made between the strategic hamlet program and the agroville program and both are compared with the Malayan pacification program.

We can here only summarize the highlights of the Osborne report. It is, however, important to understand the differences between the Malayan pacification efforts and those undertaken in South Vietnam in order to differentiate between the substance of what went on in Malaya and the shadow of what has gone on and is going on in South Vietnam under whatever title is given to the program of rural pacification.

Before World War II, Malaya had been a British colony. It was occupied by Japan during the war. Afterwards, Britain recolonialized it and, as it did with its other colonies, promised and began working toward independence for Malaysia.

In that country there were two groups of people: the Malays and the Chinese. The Malays "were not actively involved as opponents of the existing [British] regime. The Chinese were divided between support for the Malaya [non-Communist] Chinese Association and support for the Malaya Communist Party. During the war, there had sprung up a group of about 500,000 Chinese squatters living in settlements. Some settlements had sprung up around cities and towns, with the squatters obtaining urban employment. Some settlements had developed, during the Japanese occupation, on forest lands which the Chinese squatters cleared and cultivated. And finally there were squatter settlements on the edge of estates working on plantations and mines.

The important factor, however, is that these squatter settlements were impermanent and had no deep roots or long history.

The Chinese Communists, right after the war, tried to exploit whatever good-will they had gained by their resistance to the Japanese "into political action in the form of strikes and demonstrations against the returning British administration."[8] Through threats and terror the Chinese Communists received support—"food, information and recruits"—from the Chinese squatters.

The squatter settlements therefore became the main threat to the British and Malays. It was therefore decided to resettle them in new areas, preferably close to where they were then living.

The British recognized that when they resettled the squatters in new villages, security had to be guaranteed since most of the squatters, although not Communists or even Communist sympathizers, would yield to Communist threats and pressures and supply them with food and information. Security was maintained and food and information denied the Communists. This is in contrast to what happened in some of the fortified villages in Vietnam where often arms were not supplied by the Vietnamese Government to the resettled villagers.

One important difference to bear in mind in comparing Malasian insurgency with that encountered in South Vietnam is the different type of problem encountered. In Malaya the challenge came from an ethnically separate group, the Chinese, who in most cases had had no long association with the country in which they mounted their insurgency.

In South Vietnam, on the other hand, "it was not a case of transferring an alien population with little social cohesiveness . . . but an effort to resettle established communities with very strong ritual ties to the soil which they had occupied over periods at times exceeding one, and sometimes even two, hundred years."[9]

Another basic difference between what was attempted under the "strategic hamlet" program in South Vietnam and the resettlement program in Malaysia was that in the former too much was undertaken too fast.

On April 20, 1962, the National Assembly of South Vietnam gave enthusiastic endorsement to Diem's "strategic hamlet" program. On December 29, 1962—8 months later—Diem announced that 4,077 strategic hamlets had been completed, out of a total of 11,182 to be built, and that 39 percent of the South Vietnamese population—over 5 million people—were living in those hamlets.

By contrast, it took over two years to resettle 66,000 people in the State of Johore in Malaysia. Johore was thought to present the most acute problem and resettlement was started there.

Even given the wide discrepancies pointed out by Osborne in the official figures for completed strategic hamlets, the pace of resettlement was obviously too fast and contrasted with the care and meticulousness with which the British and the Malays proceeded.

In Malaya, the insurgents could not, as the Vietcong can in South Vietnam, live off the jungle.

Osborne also points out that, unlike Malaya, in South Vietnam "the challenge came from people who were indistinguishable, in ethnic terms, from the supporters of the established government, or those peasants who did not have loyalties either way . . . . It is probably impossible to stress too strongly that the insurgency in Vietnam is a civil war and this fact permeates the entire struggle."

Because the military and the police had been trained to expect an invasion from the north they were not prepared for an insurrection and the security accorded to the strategic hamlets left much to be desired.

Another factor in the failure of the strategic hamlet program was the fact that the villagers who were forcibly resettled had to leave the graves of their ancestors whom they venerated.[10]

Two other factors are cited by Osborne for the failure of the strategic hamlet concept. One was that the people were aware that the South Vietnamese governmental authorities "were supported by a foreign power." Also, it was the Government which, "in the peasants' minds, represented the absentee landlords who sought rent on lands which the peasants had farmed without charge over many years."

One major difficulty with the strategic hamlet concept was that the fence around the village faced both ways. It had been erected to keep the Vietcong out—it also kept the Vietnamese peasant inside.

The Vietnamese farmer detests controls and being forced to live in a fortified strategic hamlet was like living on a fortified "collective farm." This the farmers resented and that resentment was one of the strongest aids for the Vietcong.[11]

Osborne is highly critical of those who made the decision to start the strategic hamlet program and claims that there was sufficient information available at the time to show that there was a vast difference between Malaya and South Vietnam. There was, he states, "insufficient analysis" of these differences leaving him with the "uncomfortable feeling that too many important decisions were made on the basis of hope and supposition rather than on the basis of careful analysis."

Managed News from Saigon, The Pentagon and Foggy Bottom

During 1962 and 1963, three wars were going on in South Vietnam simultaneously.

First, there was the military war against the Vietcong, to the winning of which the United States was dedicating more and more money, material and so-called "advisers."

Second, there was the war for the "hearts and minds of the people," without whose support Diem's days were numbered. As we have seen, he was losing that war because he did not institute the needed social and economic reforms.

The third war was being waged against the truth—against the correspondents in South Vietnam who wanted to get the facts to the American people and were having every conceivable roadblock put in their way to prevent their doing so.

One of the problems was that the United States Ambassador to South Vietnam, Frederick Nolting, and the Chief of the Military Mission to South Vietnam, General Paul Harkins, were convinced that the United States just had to "sink or swim" with Diem and therefore fed back to President Kennedy rosy reports all during this period as to how well Diem was doing.

However, some of the reporters in South Vietnam—such as Malcolm Browne and David Halberstam, to mention only two—were not "sold" on Diem.

They saw all too well the dangers to the United States in tying its entire program to Diem's star.

They were all too well aware of the graft and corruption that pervaded the Diem regime. As one reporter, Sam Castain wrote in LOOK: "To his [Diem's] personal credit, he allegedly managed, again with American aid, to amass a personal fortune of some $50 million. . . ."[12]

These reporters could see the strategic hamlet concept being perverted in many instances into concentration camps, playing right into the hands of the Vietcong and making enemies for Diem's government. Castain describes the resettlement of the villagers of one hamlet thus:

" 'The soldiers forced us out of our huts,' said the village chief . . . 'and told us that a fortified village was ready for us in the valley. 'Can we take our land'? we asked. Two men refused to leave our ancestral home and were shot. It took us 60 days to march here. We have no land to farm, and if the Government does not give us food soon, we'll have to sell the pigs and buffalo we brought with us. The Vietcong come at night for our weapons. We give them the weapons. Why should we die for weapons?' "

These reporters realized that Diem's much-touted land reform program was a farce and that the land-hungry people of South

Vietnam were still land-hungry and even more embittered against the absentee landowners and their governmental supporters. Writing in the *Reporter,* Bernard Fall related how, when Diem came in, he disarmed the plantations. Now the plantation managers "keep in business by closing their eyes" when the Vietcong come to levy tribute on their men. "They silently pay millions of piasters of ransom to the Vietcong—and as much again to bribe the South Vietnamese authorities to allow them to operate."[13]

These same reporters could see the American "advisers" being used more and more in combat, without the American people permitted to get the true facts. Thus Browne, in connection with the incident of the two fighters which had been flown in combat by American "advisers," relates that United States security guards confiscated the pictures he had taken of the two American "advisers." His pictures "would have shown blond, blue-eyed 'Vietnamese,' which would have given the lie to the official line."

Speaking of the courageous reporters who managed to get the story through—or at least as much of it as they were permitted to learn—Schlesinger stated:

"They did not believe Diem's communiqués; and, when Harkins and Nolting insisted they were true, they stopped believing Harkins and Nolting."[14]

Secretary of Defense Robert S. McNamara made his first inspection trip to South Vietnam in May 1962. Homer Bigart cabled from Saigon to *The New York Times* on May 11, 1962, that McNamara "after 48 hours in South Vietnam" said he was "tremendously impressed." According to Bigart, McNamara gave this impression to the Vietnamese and the Americans in Saigon:

"First, the Kennedy Administration still is rigidly following its 'sink or swim with Diem line';

"Second, the administration regards President Diem as a remarkable national leader whose loss would be a great setback to the anti-Communist cause in Southeast Asia;

"Third, the administration believes the American correspondents here are giving a distorted picture to Congress of American involvement in the shooting war."[15]

This "distorted picture" of American involvement in a shooting war, which McNamara complained about, it should be remembered, was one month after reporter Malcolm Browne had seen two American "advisers" land at Danang returning from a combat mission.

A year later—and less than four weeks before the assassination of Diem—after his second trip to South Vietnam, the White House reported:

"Secretary McNamara and General Taylor reported that in their judgment the major part of the U.S. military task can be completed by the end of 1965, although there may be a continuing requirement for a limited number of U.S. training personnel."

In that same White House release McNamara and Taylor were said to believe that by the end of that year—1963—"1000 U.S. military personnel assigned to South Vietnam can be withdrawn."

During all this time considerable pressure was being put on the reporters who did not stop at reporting the official Diem or United States Embassy communiques but insisted on reporting the truth.

Thus, Browne was called in by Admiral Harry D. Felt, Commander in Chief of United States forces in the Pacific and asked "Why don't you get on the team."

Halberstam relates how when Arthur Ochs Sulzberger, the publisher of *The New York Times*—his employer—went to see President Kennedy, he asked: "What do you think of your young man in Saigon?" Sulzberger replied that he thought Halberstam was "doing fine." Kennedy said that he thought that Halberstam was "too close to the story, and too involved." Sulzberger disagreed. Then Kennedy asked whether the publisher was thinking of transferring Halberstam to another area. Again the President received a negative answer. Halberstam was supposed to go on vacation at that time but *The New York Times* immediately canceled it "lest it appear to have acquiesced in this pressure."[16]

Browne also related how, in South Vietnam, all accredited reporters are given an Identification Card entitling them to be "admitted to briefings . . . fly on any military transport plane and many helicopters . . . talk to top American officials . . . accompany American units in the field." It also entitled the reporter to Post Exchange privileges and hospitalization at reduced rates.

"If a reporter is discredited for some reason, he is deprived of this card, and in effect excommunicated from the American community. This is a powerful weapon to aim at a man who depends on the American community for news."[17]

Schlesinger reports that in 1962 and 1963, there was a group of dissenters in the White House, led by Averell Harriman, Assistant Secretary of State for Far Eastern Affairs, who believed the United States was on the wrong course in South Vietnam. The Secretary of State, Dean Rusk, was content to go along "with military predominance in the formation of United States policy toward Vietnam."[18]

But the question remains: In the face of highly respectable opposition within the White House to continuing to seek a military solution to a political problem, in the face of what should have been disturbing reports by many capable reporters—Browne and Halberstam were given Pulitzer prizes for their reporting from South Vietnam—in the face of ever increasing losses of Americans killed or wounded in South Vietnam, in the face of the recommendation of the military for more and more escalation, why did not Kennedy at least order a major review of the United States commitment— why did he not at least propose a neutralization of Vietnam along the lines of the Laos solution—rather than continuing the policy of "sink or swim with Ngo Dinh Diem"?

Schlesinger states that Kennedy's "confidence in McNamara, so wholly justified in so many areas, led the President to go along with the optimists on Vietnam."

As a matter of fact, Sorensen paints a picture of an even more divided staff of advisers in the White House as to what policy the United States should follow in Vietnam.

Sorensen's assessment of Kennedy's actions was that "Kennedy was increasingly doubtful that the war could be won by Diem, for whom he retained great personal admiration," but felt that the United States could not move to oust him and his only hope was "to change Diem's policies and personnel, not remove him."

But events moved too swiftly in 1963 for "Diem's policies and personnel" to be changed by persuasion.

For the civil war in South Vietnam, 1963 started just about normally with the usual spate of optimistic statements.

Admiral Felt and General Harkins conferred in Saigon and Admiral Felt issued a statement, on January 11, 1963, predicting the inevitable defeat of the Vietcong saying: "I am confident the Vietnamese are going to win the war."

In Los Angeles, in a major address on February 13, 1963, Secretary of State Rusk said flatly that the "momentum of the Communist drive has been stopped . . ."

Less than three months later, on May 8, 1963, there were riots in the South Vietnamese city of Hue, 400 miles north of Saigon. The riots had serious political overtones. The Buddhists wanted to fly their flag in celebration of Buddha's birthday. Permission was refused and rioting broke out. The Buddhists claimed that government soldiers fired into the mob, killing 12 people including some children. The government denied that its troops had fired into the crowd, claiming the Communists did it. In the face of continued Buddhist demonstrations in Hue, martial law was imposed.

The quarrel in Hue had begun because of an overlapping of religious celebrations. The 2,507th anniversary of Buddha's birth overlapped the period set aside for the celebration of the 25th anniversary of Catholic Archbishop Thuc's consecration as a bishop. The Buddhists wanted to fly their flag because the Archbishop had flown the Vatican flag and, even after the refusal to fly the Buddhist flag was withdrawn, the Buddhists decided to hold a mass meeting to protest against religious persecution.[19]

Diem managed to quiet the Buddhists in Hue but on June 11, 1963, the demonstrations in Saigon reached a climax when a Buddhist monk burned himself to death before the Cambodian Embassy. Acting on a tip, Malcolm Browne was there and took picture of the actual immolation of the monk—pictures which appeared throughout the United States and shocked the American people.

Even after the government reached an agreement with the Buddhists on June 15, 1963, to end religious persecution, rioting continued and government troops were called out in Saigon. Clubs were used against the Buddhists by the police on July 17 when 1000 Buddhists assembled in front of a pagoda in Saigon to protest religious persecution.

President Kennedy, on the same day at his news conference, stated that the crisis over religious persecution in South Vietnam was hurting the war effort and that he hoped both sides would "reach an agreement on the civil disturbances and also respect for the rights of others." Schlesinger points out that the last phrase was censored out of the statement by Saigon.

From June 15 to November 1, 1963, the events that were to result in the overthrow of Diem and the assassination of Diem and his brother moved at an increasing pace. Reporters on the scene wrote excellent, detailed accounts of those fatal four and one-half months.

On August 21, 1963—six days after Ambassador Nolting had left Saigon and before his successor arrived—Diem attacked the Buddhist pagodas.

"It was a carefully coordinated military operation. In Hue and Saigon heavily armed Special Forces troops and police assaulted the barricaded Buddhists. Midst screams, gunfire, grenade explosions, and the eerie banging on gongs, they rounded up hundreds of bonzes [Buddhist priests] and haulded them away in trucks."[20]

When Senator Gruening commented on this episode on the floor of the Senate later, he said; "The United States won no friends and influenced no Vietnamese people when Buddhist priests were driven off to concentration camps in AID vehicles by Diem's secret police, who were paid by U.S. funds."

On September 2, 1963, in a televised interview over the Columbia Broadcasting System between President Kennedy and newscaster Walter Cronkite, Kennedy said:

"I don't think that unless a greater effort is made by the Government to win popular support that the war can be won there. In the final analysis, it is their war. They are the ones who have to win it or lose it. We can help them, we can give them equipment, we can send our men out there as advisers, but they have to win it—the people of Vietnam— against the Communists . . . . In the last two months the Government has gotten out of touch with the people."

On the repression of the Buddhists, Kennedy said: "The repressions against the Buddhists . . . were very unwise . . .

all we could do is make it very clear that we don't think this is the way to win."

But time had run out. Despite the United States' efforts to cut back on aid to Diem as a means of bringing pressure to bear on him to make his peace with the Buddhists and get on with fighting the war, that pressure—which might have been effective much, much earlier—came too late.

On November 1, 1963, a military junta deposed Ngo Dinh Diem and killed him and his brother.

Three weeks later to the day President Kennedy lay dead of an assassin's bullet in Parkland Hospital in Dallas, Texas and Vice President Lyndon Baines Johnson was sworn in as President of the United States.

CHAPTER XXII

GROWING DISENCHANTMENT AND
INCREASING INVOLVEMENT

The period between the assassination of President Kennedy on November 22, 1963, and the Gulf of Tonkin incident in the early days of August 1964 was marked by a growing uneasiness on the part of an ever-widening circle of people in the United States as to the exact nature and extent of the United States' commitment in Vietnam and the directions in which United States' policies there were tending.

That period also witnessed a serious decline in the credence which the people of the United States gave to the utterances of their Government, caused in no small measure by the wide variance between the contents of the official news handouts and the on-the-scene reports sent back to their newspapers by the many courageous reporters in South Vietnam. The war against the American newspapermen in South Vietnam continued.

The fears of the people of the United States that this country was getting deeper and deeper into what might well prove to be an inextricable morass were not lessened by the continued instability of the South Vietnamese Government, with its frequent coups and threatened coups.

It was during this period also that Secretary of State McNamara continued to shuttle back and forth between Saigon and Washington, each time issuing, upon his return, contradictory statements which confused the American public more and more.

It will be recalled that on his first trip to South Vietnam in May 1962, while John F. Kennedy was still President, Secretary McNamara had issued a statement—after a full 48 hours in South Vietnam—that he was "tremendously encouraged," giving newsmen the clear impression that the Kennedy Administration would "sink or swim with Diem."

After Secretary McNamara's second visit to South Vietnam, the White House issued a statement, on October 3, 1963, that both McNamara and General Taylor reported that "the major part of the U.S. military task can be completed by the end of 1965" and that "by the end of this year [1963] . . . 1,000 U.S. military personnel assigned to South Vietnam can be withdrawn."

Three months later—and after President Kennedy's death—following McNamara's third visit to South Vietnam, the signals were changed and it was announced that all plans for the 1965 recall of U.S. troops had been dropped. As Hedrick Smith wrote in *The New York Times* on December 21, 1963:

"Some diplomatic observers maintained that the goal . . . was never meant as an inflexible commitment. They suggested that it was intended primarily for domestic political purposes."

In May of 1964 Secretary McNamara made his fourth trip to South Vietnam. This time *The New York Times* story by Jack Raymond on May 15, 1964, was headed:

"McNAMARA URGES FURTHER U.S. AID FOR VIETNAM WAR; BACK FROM SAIGON, HE GIVES PRESIDENT A PLAN TO SEND MORE MONEY AND MEN."

Curiously enough, on May 4, 1964, writing from Saigon, Jack Raymond had reported that the then Premier Khanh of South Vietnam had stated that "American aid—which involves 16,000 men and money at the rate of $500 million a year—was adequate . . . and he had no plans to ask McNamara for more when he visits Saigon again next week."

This caused Senator Gruening to raise the question on the Floor of the Senate on May 22, 1964, as to "who wants this aid: Secretary McNamara or Premier Khanh?"

The early months of 1964 also witnessed more and more voices being raised in the Congress and the press concerning the increasing United States involvement in Southeast Asia and where it was all leading.

In one of the earliest major speeches on the subject in the Senate on March 10, 1964, entitled "The United States Should Get Out of Vietnam," Senator Gruening reviewed the entire history of United States involvement in Vietnam, first on the side of the French in their attempts to make Indochina once again a French colony, and then on its own to preserve the "freedom" of South Vietnam.

In his speech Senator Gruening supported Senator Mike Mansfield's statement three weeks earlier for a reassessment of United States foreign .policy, in which Mansfield had asked the United States "to face up to the realities of today, and not depend so much on the wishes of yesterday." Gruening pointed out that President Johnson had inherited the United States involvement in South Vietnam, was not wedded to Dulles' "domino theory," and was in the best possible position to avoid any further or increased military involvement in South Vietnam. At that time Laos had been neutralized by the Geneva Agreement of 1962 and one of the other "dominoes" would in May 1964 complain to the United Nations against United States violation of its borders in hot pursuit of the Vietcong — a violation which the United States would publicly admit and for which it would publicly apologize.

On March 10, 1964, Gruening advocated: "All our military should immediately be relieved of combat assignments. All military dependents should be returned home at once. A return of the troops to our own shores should begin . . . . I consider the life of one American worth more than this putrid mess . . . Let us get out of Vietnam on as good terms as possible—but let us get out."

He was joined by Senator Morse, who also said there was no justification for killing a single American boy in Vietnam and that it was "about time the American people awakened to what is going on in South Vietnam and recognized that South Vietnam is beyond the perimeter of American defense."

Two years later their assessment of the strategic value of South East Asia to the United States was to be echoed in May, 1966 by

General David M. Shoup, retired Commandant of the United States Marine Corps and Congressional Medal of Honor winner, who said in Los Angeles, at the Junior College World Affairs Day:

"I want to tell you, I don't think the whole of Southeast Asia, as related to the present and future safety and freedom of the people of this country, is worth the life or limb of a single American."

All during the early months of 1964—and thereafter as well—both Morse and Gruening stood up on the Floor of the Senate to urge United States military withdrawal from South Vietnam, and repeatedly they warned of the dangers that lay ahead for the United States if there were further escalation of the United States commitment there. They spoke daily sometimes and sometimes two or three times a week.

Other questioning voices began to be heard in and out of Congress. These voices intensified as more and more United States' troops were killed or wounded in South Vietnam either by Vietcong fire or by plane crashes.

On March 7, 1964, John S. Knight—a past president of the American Society of Newspaper Editors with an outstanding military record—wrote a widely published newspaper column entitled "Vietnam: It Isn't Worth the Cost" in which he stated that "the white man is through in Asia and there is nothing we can do to turn the rising tide of nationalism . . . there is also . . . the risk of escalating the war and finding ourselves in mortal combat with millions of Red Chinese. In such a struggle, the United States would have no allies at our side."[1]

Mr. Knight went on to advise that the United States should recognize "the impossibility of a military victory and negotiate for whatever political advantages can be found in a stalemate."

This suggestion was applauded in the leading editorial in *The New Republic* for March 28, 1964, which pointed out that "U.S. commitment deepens month by month with no end in sight."

Columnist Chalmers M. Roberts, writing in *The Washington Post* on May 3, 1964, put the question squarely:

"Is it in the vital interest of the United States that, even at a cost of further American lives, this country continue to bolster the regime in Saigon against its Communist led and oriented foes?

"And on that point, in this election year neither party is fully agreed either among its leaders or with the opposition. That is the agony of uncertainty which troubles so many in the United States today."

On May 21, 1964 *The New York Times* editorialized: "We must confront the Communists with options short of unacceptable defeat, options to which they can turn, once some of their leaders begin to conclude that victory may be unattainable or too expensive. In brief, we must define our peace aims . . . . But an increased military effort alone, without an offer to negotiate, would simply compound the errors of the past."

In May of 1964 voices were heard on both sides of the question on what should be the best course for the United States to follow in South Vietnam.

Senator Barry Goldwater discussed the possibility of using nuclear weapons to defoliate the trees along the jungle trails used as supply routes. *The Washington Post,* on May 27, 1964, came out four-square against defoliation saying:

"This sort of unselective and nondiscriminating warfare (defoliation), like the use of napalm and similar weaponry, simply is not suited to the pursuit of guerrilla infiltrators. We are burning the barn to get at the rats . . . open to all sorts of ethical doubts. . . ."

Walter Lippmann stated in his column in the *Washington Post* on May 28, 1964, that the United States should frankly admit it had made a mistake in becoming militarily involved in South Vietnam and take the matter to the conference table.

"It is not easy for any country to repair its mistakes, especially those in which it has invested lives, money, and moral judgments. But the original mistake in Southeast Asia has to be repaired. The way to do this is to go to a conference. The chances of its being successful are not brilliant. . . . But the military outlook in South Vietnam is dismal beyond words."

The St. Louis (Mo.) Post Dispatch on June 1, 1964, also proposed that the United States admit to the error of its ways.

Meanwhile, on May 21, 1964, Ambassador Adlai Stevenson presented the United States' answer, in the U.N., to the charges by Cambodia that both the United States and South Vietnamese forces had violated its borders—which Stevenson admitted, pleading extenuating circumstances. In the course of this talk, Stevenson stated that the United States had consistently sought to adhere to the provisions of the 1954 Geneva Accords. In an editorial on Stevenson's speech, *The St. Louis (Mo.) Post-Dispatch* termed the statement "cynical because as Ambassador Stevenson well knows the United States participated in negotiation of the Geneva agreement of 1954 . . . and has violated it repeatedly. The agreement has also been violated by China, North Vietnam, and the Vietcong. And it has been violated by South Vietnam, acting on American advice."

But the mere fact that the Security Council was debating Vietnam gave people the idea that somehow the Vietnam conflict should be turned over to the United Nations, as had been done with the Korean conflict.

Early in June, Senators Morse and Gruening, on the Senate Floor, called for an immediate United Nations sponsored and enforced cease fire in South Vietnam.

Events were moving fast in the early months of 1964 and the movement was growing both for escalation of the United States military effort in South Vietnam and for negotiations that would lead to a neutral South Vietnam.

In Paris, on June 12, President de Gaulle called for ending all foreign intervention in South Vietnam.

In Saigon, Premier Khanh on July 19 called for pushing the war into North Vietnam to liberate it.

Complaints continued to pour into Washington in the daily press reports out of South Vietnam that both the wars in South Vietnam—the military war and the war for the hearts and minds of the people of South Vietnam—were going badly.

The May 18 issue of *U. S. News and World Report* carried a story entitled "True Story of War in Vietnam" that set out in detail the whole sorry story of what was and what was not happening in South Vietnam. "U.S. involvement in Vietnam," the report stated, "reveals a series of classic military and political errors from which it may be hoped that the Government will eventually profit . . . . American servicemen and reporters have long been saying we are losing the war."

Under a series of very revealing headlines, the report, written by Robert L. Moore, Jr., set forth, among others, the following observations:

"Lacking a Will to Win": The South Vietnamese officers and officials never had it so good. The vast majority of them lack the "will to fight, endure privations and win." Those who are benefitting from the infusions of American military and economic aid realize that if the war is ended, so will the "dole";

"Advisers in Combat": Half of the U.S. casualties have been suffered by the so-called advisers "although they make up only about 6 percent of the total U.S. force in Vietnam."

"Officers Picked by Politics": The officers of the so-called special forces were picked not on the basis of merit but on the basis of "political favors to the sons of friends and supporters of President Diem and his family."

"Luxury in Midst of War: "Most of the officers have a batman to serve them tea in bed." The officers often refuse to see their American advisers if they think they will try to get them to undertake combat operations;

"Cowardice and Laziness": The Vietnamese officers were most reluctant to engage the Vietcong. When they realized that a Vietnamese patrol was about to find a Vietcong patrol, the Vietnamese became noisy in the hopes the Vietcong would go away;

"Graft and Corruption": Graft and corruption were widespread even in combat areas. Deserters were not reported until after payday so the officers could pocket the extra pay. "There is little confidence among Americans working at the combat level that corruption will be significantly reduced" by Premier Khanh;

"Redtape and Delay"; The Vietnamese military system cannot react quickly. The example is cited of how two Americans were downed in the jungle on March 26 and that it took eight days to get permission from the Vietnamese authorities for Vietnamese rangers to join the search for the Americans;

"How to Handle Snipers: 'Withdraw' ": "Vietcong snipers pick-ing off a few men were routing whole companies and batallions":

"U.S. Equipment wasted": " . . . by and large, the Vietnamese have no concept of maintenance, much less preventive maintenance";

"Rescue—or Flight?": Vietnamese-flown helicopters, going to the rescue of wounded, were repeatedly driven off by the slightest groundfire;

"Why Villagers Desert": "Until the Vietnamese muster the courage to go out at night and patrol the areas they are supposed to be securing, the entire 'clear and hold' concept is a joke."

The solution given in the report was "for the United States to take operation control of the war away from the . . . Vietnamese officer corps. . . ."

This was the solution proposed on June 29, 1964, by a G.O.P. House group led by Congressman Gerald R. Ford (R., Mich.) when it advocated that "American forces must take command of the forces in Vietnam and not simply remain as advisers" and that U.S. strategy "ought to be aimed at sealing off South Vietnam, preventing the infiltration from North Vietnam."

Thus, at the end of July, 1964, President Johnson's handling of the conflict in South Vietnam was coming under attack from all sides. The "hawks" and the "doves" were assailing him in Congress, in the press, and in periodicals. France was calling for the neutrality of Indochina. Cambodia had begun to accept Russian military aid. Civil strife had broken out in Laos over which the United States had begun reconnaissance flights and had lost two planes early in June, 1964. Editorials had begun to appear in influential papers across the country questioning United States' actions in South Viet-nam. United States' casualties were mounting. A Presidential election would take place in November and, in all likelihood—in one form or another—Vietnam would be an issue.

Then came the incidents in the Gulf of Tonkin on the 2d and 4th of August, 1964, and the opportunity for President Johnson to secure overwhelming Congressional approval for his actions and an unlimited commitment of power for the future. In addition it served to provide an opportunity to rouse the people of the United States to support the Nation's war effort—behind the Commander-in-Chief—without going to war.

CHAPTER XXIII

THE GULF OF TONKIN INCIDENT AND RESOLUTION

On the evening of August 4, 1964, President Johnson preempted prime radio and television time for a nationwide broadcast to the American people.

He announced that, for the second time within as many days, there had taken place "hostile actions against United States ships on the high seas in the Gulf of Tonkin."

"The initial attack on the destroyer *Maddox* on August 2," he said, "was repeated today by a number of hostile vessels attacking two U.S. destroyers with torpedoes. The destroyers and supporting aircraft acted at once on the orders I gave after the initial act of aggression. We believe at least two of the attacking boats were sunk. There were no U.S. losses."

He announced that he believed that "such acts of violence against the Armed Forces of the United States" should be met not only defensively but with "positive reply." Even as he spoke to the people, he said air action was going on against "gunboats and certain supporting facilities in North Vietnam which have been used in these hostile operations."

President Johnson then told the American people that aggression "by terror against the peaceful villagers of South Vietnam has now been joined by open aggression on the high seas against the United States of America."

The United States' response to this "outrage," however, would be "limited and fitting. We still seek no wider war."

He continued to outline the four actions, in addition to the retaliatory air strikes, which he had taken or was about to take:

(1) He had instructed the Secretary of State to make the position of the United States perfectly clear to all foreign nations;

(2) He had requested Ambassador Stevenson "to raise this matter immediately and urgently before the Security Council of the United Nations";

(3) He had consulted with Congressional leaders of both parties; and,

(4) He would ask the Congress to pass a resolution "making it clear that our Government is united in its determination to take all necessary measures in support of freedom and in defense of peace in Southeast Asia."

To heighten both the drama and the urgency of the situation, Secretary of Defense McNamara held a press conference at midnight that very same night, even while United States aircraft from the carriers *Ticonderoga* and *Constellation* were flying 64 attack sorties over North Vietnam, bombing four patrol boat bases and a petroleum dump.

The next day—August 5, 1964—the President sent a Special Message to the Congress. In it he asked the Congress" on its part, to join in affirming the national determination that all such attacks will be met, and that the United States will continue in its basic policy of assisting the free nations of the area to defend their freedom."

The President asked Congress to enact the resolution he proposed "promptly." He gave two reasons for requesting prompt action.

First, "the events of this week would in any event have made the passage of a congressional resolution essential."

Second, the United States was entering on "3 months of political campaigning." It was therefore essential for hostile nations during that time to understand that "the United States will continue to protect its national interests, and that in these matters there is no division among us."

On the same day—August 5, 1964—Ambassador Stevenson appeared before the Security Council of the United Nations not for the purpose of asking the Council to take action either with respect to the entire conflict in Vietnam or the Gulf of Tonkin incident but merely to inform the Council that the incident had taken place. At no time did Ambassador Stevenson ask the Council to assume jurisdiction of the Vietnam conflict.

At the Security Council Ambassador Stevenson repeated the official United States version of the Tonkin Gulf incident—the version given to the press that day by Secretary of Defense McNamara at a press conference and repeated by him at a closed-door joint meeting of the Senate Armed Services and Foreign Relations Committees.

In Secretary McNamara's words, what had happened in the Gulf of Tonkin on August 2 and 4, 1964, was as follows:

"At about noon [on August 2] when the USS Madddox [a U.S. destroyer "engaged in a routine patrol in International waters of the Gulf of Tonkin off the North Vietnam coast"] was about 30 miles from the coast, she reported that three torpedo boats were on a southerly course heading toward the ship at a range of over 10 miles.

". . . at approximately 2:40 P.M., the Maddox was approached by a high speed . . . craft . . . [with] . . . the apparent intention . . . to conduct a torpedo attack. . . . She was attacked by the three PT craft at 3:08 P.M. She opened fire . . . after three warning shots failed to slow down the attackers . . . two of the PTs closed to 5,000 yards, each firing one torpedo. . . . The two torpedoes passed on the starboard side at a distance of 100 to 200 yards. . . . The USS Ticonderoga . . . operating in waters to the southeast . . . advised she was sending four . . . fighters. . . . At about 3:21 P.M., the third hostile PT moved up to the beam of the Maddox and received a direct hit . . . machine gun fire from the PTs was directed at the Maddox . . . no injury to personnel and no damage . . . Ticonderoga aircraft commenced attacking the PTs . . . strafing attacks were directed against two of the PTs and they were damaged. The third PT remained dead in the water. . . . At 3:29 P.M. the engagement terminated. . . ."

That is the official McNamara account of the engagement in the Gulf of Tonkin on August 2, 1964.

The second incident occurred two days later—on August 4, 1964 —but this time at night.

Again, in Secretary McNamara's own words, the official version of what occurred:

"In the early evening of [Tuesday] August 4 . . . the *Maddox* reported radar contact with unidentified surface vessels who were paralleling its track and the track of the *Turnerjoy* [its sister destroyer] . . . the *Maddox* reported [at 7:40 P.M.] that . . . an attack . . . appeared imminent . . .the *Maddox* was heading southeast near the center of the Gulf of Tonkin in International waters approximately 65 miles from the nearest land. . . . The *Maddox* at 8:36 P.M. established new radar contact with two unidentified surface vessels and three unidentified aircraft. . . . U.S. fighter aircraft were launched from the *Ticonderoga*. . . . Shortly thereafter, the *Maddox* reported that the unidentified aircraft had disappeared from its radar screen. . . . At 9:30, additional unidentified vessels were observed on the *Maddox* radar, and . . . began to close rapidly . . . from the west and south . . . destroyers reported at 9:52 P.M. that they were under continuous torpedo attack and were engaged in defensive counterfire. Within the next hour, the destroyers relayed messages stating that they had avoided a number of torpedoes, that they had been under repeated attack, and that they had sunk two of the attacking craft. . . By Midnight . . . the destroyers reported that . . . they had suffered no hits nor casualties . . . at least two enemy aircraft had been sunk . . . At 1:30 A.M. . . . the attacking craft had . . . broken off the engagement."

Secretary of Defense McNamara's elucidation of what had happened at the Gulf of Tonkin on August 2 and 4 left more questions unanswered than answered.

First, what had motivated three lone North Vietnamese PT boats to take on a United States destroyer, 30 miles off-shore, protected by air-cover from two United States aircraft carriers nearby? If the North Vietnamese intelligence was that poor that it did not realize that the aircraft carriers were that close to the destroyer's position, why did they attempt the same maneuver two days later—at night?

Second, why was there such a massive response on the part of the Johnson Administration to such relatively minor incidents?

The United States naval units involved had acquitted themselves bravely and well. In the first incident, one PT boat had been destroyed—two others had been damaged. In the second incident two PT boats had been sunk.

Why then the need for the adoption—on an emergency basis—of a Congressional resolution giving approval to the action taken?

Slowly—very slowly—over the years the true facts have come to light.

Meanwhile, Secretary of Defence McNamara had revealed at his press conference—and later to the Senate and to the House, what further steps had been taken as a result of the Tonkin Gulf incidents to increase the United States military involvement in Vietnam.

In his testimony before the joint Senate Armed Services and Foreign Relations Committees' hearings, McNamara stated that "in view of the unprovoked and deliberate attacks in International waters on our naval vessels" the President and his principal advisers concluded that "additional precautionary measures were required in Southeast Asia." These measures were taken, the Committees were told by Secretary of Defense McNamara, because one must bear in mind that the "best way to deter escalation is to be prepared for it."

This is tantamount to saying that the best way to deter escalation is to escalate!

In retrospect—and as additional facts have come to light—it is now evident that the Johnson Administration had, prior to the Gulf of Tonkin incident, decided to escalate the war in Vietnam at least to the extent of preparing for aerial bombardments of selected targets in North Vietnam.

However, the policy was also adopted to play down the decision to escalate. This was done with consummate public relations skill, even as an experienced magician diverts the attention of the audience away from where the action is taking place.

The spotlight was kept focused on the allegedly unprovoked attack by North Vietnamese PT boats on two United States destroyers allegedly in International waters on a routine patrol. Highlighted also were the United States retaliatory raids on the North Vietnamese PT bases and petroleum dump. The United States response, in the words of the President in his dramatic nationwide broadcast, would be "limited and fitting." These were terms which the United States people were to hear often after the open escalation of United

States military might in Vietnam in February 1965.

But in August 1964, there was no similar focusing of public attention on the beginnings of the United States buildup in Vietnam. Instead, at his news conference at 9:00 o'clock on the morning following his dramatic press conference at midnight the night before, Secretary of Defense McNamara slipped in a paragraph setting forth the steps taken to escalate United States' military involvement in Vietnam. At his news conference—and later in the day before the joint meeting of the Senate Armed Services and Foreign Relations Committees—McNamara stated that the following steps had been taken:

"a. Transfers of an attack carrier group from the Pacific Coast to the Western Pacific.

"b. Movement of intercepter and fighter bomber aircraft into South Vietnam [A prelude to more direct and intense United States military involvement in the shooting war in Vietnam—both North and South—which was to begin six months later, almost to the day];

"c. Movement of fighter bomber aircraft into Thailand [Also a prelude to the beginning of the large-scale military build-up in that country];

"d. Transfer of interceptor and fighter bomber aircraft from the United States to advance bases in the Pacific [Part of the preparations for building up the troops in South Vietnam six months later];

"e. Movement of an antisubmarine force into the South China Sea;

"f. The alerting and readying for movement of selected Army and Marine forces."

All these military reinforcements were avowedly instituted because two United States destroyers were attacked by a few North Vietnamese PT boats—the former came through unscathed, two of the latter were sunk and others damaged!

A proposed resolution, drafted in the White House, was sent to the Congress at the same time as the Presidential Message requesting it on August 5, 1964. Public testimony before the Senate Foreign Relations Committee—almost two years later during May 1966, brought out that the draft of the proposed resolution had been prepared well before the Tonkin Gulf incident, so that the White House would be prepared just in case![1]

At 9:05 A.M. on August 6, a joint, closed-door hearing was held by the Senate Armed Services and Foreign Relations Committees. The witnesses heard were Secretary of Defense McNamara, Secretary of State Rusk, and General Earle G. Wheeler, Chairman, Joint Chiefs of Staff. The hearing lasted one hour and forty minutes, including the time necessary to poll the Committees on the vote on approving the resolution. All members present voted in favor of the resolution except Senator Morse—a member of the Foreign Relations Commitee. The hearings were not printed until November 1966, more than two years later. They were thus not available to individual Senators, not members of these Committees, when consideration of the resolution was begun in the Senate later that day.

The House Foreign Affairs Committee also held closed-door hearings on the Resolution that same day—August 6. A transcript of those hearings had not been printed even late in 1967.

Both the Senate Committees and the House Committee reported the resolution favorably without change. Identical resolutions were under consideration by the respective Committees of both Houses so that upon passage by both Houses, a conference—which would have caused delay—could be avoided and upon passage by both Houses the resolution could be rushed to the President for his signature, as was in fact done.

The Resolution has three "whereas" clauses and three "operative" [power giving] clauses. (For text, see Appendix)

The first "whereas" clause recites that "naval units of the Communist regime in Vietnam . . . have deliberately and repeatedly attacked United States naval vessels lawfully present in International waters." The clause goes on to assert that these actions were in violation not only of the Charter of the United Nations but also in violation of principles of International law. The clause charges that these actions "created a serious threat to International peace."

The second "whereas" clause alleged that these attacks were part of "a deliberate and systematic campaign of aggression" being waged by the Communist regime in North Vietnam not only against its neighbors but also against "the nations joined with them in the collective defense of their freedom."

The third "whereas" clause recites the motives of the United States in being in Southeast Asia. Three motives are set forth. The United States:

(1) "is assisting the peoples of Southeast Asia to protect their freedom;

(2) "has no territorial, military, or political ambitions in that area; and,

(3) "desires only that these people should be left in peace to work out their own destinies in their own way."

"Whereas" clauses as a part of legislation do not have the force and effect of law. They can be used, however, as Congressional findings of fact setting forth the reasons for the enactment of legislation or to clarify the objectives of such legislation. In the case of the Southeast Asia Resolution, the "whereas" clauses were useful because their adoption by the Congress put that body squarely behind the Administration's versions of what happened in the Gulf of Tonkin on August 2 and 4, as well as behind the Administration's interpretation of what it had been and was trying to do in Vietnam, i.e., fighting aggression from the North and not interfering in a civil war in South Vietnam.

The first "operative" clause of the Southeast Asia Resolution is both retroactive and prospective. In it Congress states that it both "approves and supports the determination of the President, as Commander in Chief, to take all necessary measures to repel any armed attack against the forces of the United States and to prevent further aggression. . . ." It is clear that this clause puts the Congressional stamp of approval on whatever action President Johnson ordered to be taken to repel the attack against the destroyers on August 2 and 4, 1964. That would cover the actions taken by the destroyers and their fighter cover against the attacking PT boats. During the course of the debate on this provision in the Senate and the House, it was conceded by all that this power was already vested in the President in his capacity as Commander in Chief.

But what about the retaliatory raids against the PT bases and the petroleum dump? That could not be called repelling an "armed attack against the forces of the United States." To cover that action the words "to prevent further aggression" were used. But it should be noted that the words "to prevent further aggression" are not modified by the words "against the forces of the United States." The clause just speaks about "aggression." For its interpretation, we must refer back to the second "whereas" clause which linked the attacks against United States naval vessels to a "deliberate and systematic campaign of aggression" by North Vietnam not only against its neighbors but also against all nations aiding those neighbors "in the collective defense of their freedom."

Thus the first operative clause of the Southeast Asia Resolution gives the President advance approval to "take all necessary measures" without in any way limiting those measures so long as their purpose was to "prevent further aggression" by North Vietnam.

The second "operative" clause makes the additional finding that the United States "regards as vital to its national interest and to world peace the maintenance of International peace and security in Southeast Asia."

Then this clause goes on to say that the United States is prepared *"as the President determines,* to take all necessary steps, *including the use of armed forces,* to assist" members of SEATO or Laos, Cambodia, or South Vietnam if any of them should request "assistance in defense of their freedom." [Emphasis supplied] All this is modified by the recitation that the United States is thus prepared to act "consonant with the United States Constitution and the Charter of the United Nations and in accordance with its obligations under the Southeast Asia Defense Treaty."

The third operative clause sets time limits on the Resolution. It is to expire when the President determines that "the peace and security of the area is reasonably assured by International conditions created by action of the United Nations or otherwise." The Resolution could also be made to expire by a concurrent resolution passed by the Congress, which does not need the approval of the President.

The Southeast Asia Resolution came before the Senate on August 6 and 7, 1964, and before the House on August 7, for consideration and passage.

In the House, the Resolution (H.J.Res. 1145) received scant debate. Most of those who spoke echoed the words of the Chairman of the House Committee on Foreign Affairs, Dr. Thomas E. Morgan (D.-Penna.) when he said:

"The resolution provides us the opportunity to demonstrate to the Communist aggressors that the people of the United States are united in their firm resolve to protect ourselves, to resist attack, and to take prompt and appropriate means to prevent aggression."[2]

Congressman Morgan did state that the Resolution "is definitely not an advance declaration of war. The Committee has been assured by the Secretary of State that the constitutional prerogative of the Congress in this respect will continue to be scrupulously observed."

No one questioned the scope of the powers granted to the President by the proposed Resolution.

The Resolution was adopted by the House by a vote of 416 to 0.

In the Senate, the debate on the Southeast Asia Resolution (S.J. Res. 189) was somewhat different, but not so different as to change the result appreciably.

Floor Manager for the Resolution in the Senate was Senator Fulbright, Chairman of the Senate Committee of Foreign Relations. His presentation of the necessity for the resolution followed the Administration's presentation to the American people and to the Congress as to what had happened in the Gulf of Tonkin. Speaking of the attacks on the destroyers, Senator Fulbright said:

"The action taken by the United States was appropriate as policy as well as justified in law. An act of unambiguous aggression cannot be tolerated or ignored without inviting further provocations, especially when the act is committed by a regime which has been engaged in consistent and repeated aggression against its neighbor states."[3]

But already doubts and questions were beginning to be heard in the Senate Cloakrooms and in other quarters as well—doubts that not all the facts had been given to the American people about the Gulf of Tonkin incidents—questioning as to whether the incidents were in fact unprovoked—doubts whether the destroyers were actually in International waters—questions as to whether the incidents were not being used to stampede the Congress into voting unlimited military powers to the President to be used at some future time to escalate the war in Vietnam—questions as to whether the incidents were "too convenient" in serving to offset the urgings of a few weeks earlier by U Thant, Secretary General of the United Nations, for peace in Southeast Asia.

And the doubts and questions revolved around the simple question: Why should a few North Vietnamese PT boats "take on" two United States destroyers protected by two United States airplane carriers? Why the attempt at suicide?

This quesion had been raised two days before by Adlai Stevenson in the Security Council when he said:

"The Acts of aggression by the North Vietnamese in the Gulf of Tonkin make no sense whatsoever standing alone."

He, however, answered:

". . . the kidnapping of village officials in the Republic of South Vietnam makes no sense either. . . ."

For many that explanation was too simple. The question was raised on the Floor of the Senate early in the debate on the Southeast Asia Resolution.

Following the opening presentation by Senator Fulbright, Senator George McGovern (D.,-S.D.) addressed a question to the former:

"All of us have been puzzled, if not baffled, as to why a little state such as North Vietnam should seek a deliberate naval conflict with the United States—with the overwhelming naval and air power that we have in that area."

Senator McGovern then referred to a column that appeared in *The Washington Post* the day before (August 5, 1964) which quoted Hanoi on Sunday as charging "the United States and South Vietnam had sent warships 'to shell the Hon Me and Hon Ngu Islands in the territorial waters of North Vietnam. Those islands are near the area where the *Maddox* was attacked Sunday. Hon Me is used as a naval base . . . and Communist PT boats have been seen in the area." The column pointed out that the United States State Department had denied that United States warships shelled the islands but did not "exculpate South Vietnam. It only denied American participation."

"There are some indicaions," the column continued, "that the South Vietnamese may in fact have attacked the two islands. . . . U.S. warships on occasion reportedly have escorted South Vietnam vessels part way to their targets."

To this, Senator Fulbright replied: "The best information that I have from high officials in our Government in this field is to the effect that our boats did not convoy or support or backup any South Vietnamse naval vessels that were engaged in such attacks."[4]

Senator Allen Ellender (D.-La.) then asked Senator Fulbright categorically "whether or not the evidence showed any act on our part which might have provoked this attack."

Senator Fulbright replied:

"I would say categorically that that was not shown. Whatever provocation there may have been, arose, if it did arise, from the activity of the North Vietnamese ships."

Later questioning by Senator Gaylord Nelson (D.,-Wis.) of Senator Fulbright brought out the further fact that the MADDOX was as close as 11 miles to the shore of North Vietnam "to show that we do not recognize a 12 mile limit, which . . . North Vietnam had asserted."

To that Senator Nelson replied that "if patrolling that close does not have a direct, necessary bearing upon the accomplishment of our mission, I am wondering whether we should be taking the risk of the sinking of our ships. . . . Assume a situation in which Cuba was firing on the coast of Florida with PT boats. It would be a risky thing for Russia to be out there testing our viewpoint about their patrols within 11 miles of our coast."

Senator Fulbright agreed to the interpretation put forth by Senator John Sherman Cooper (R.,-Ky.) that "we . . (are) . . . now giving the President advance authority to take whatever action he may deem necessary respecting South Vietnam and its defense, or with respect to the defense of any other country included in the [SEATO] treaty."

Toward the close of the first day of debate, Senator Morse gave a version of what had happened in the Gulf of Tonkin that came much closer to explaining why the North Vietnamese PT boats had taken on the United States Navy.

"On July 31, the war was escalated . . . This was a well-thought out military operation. These islands were bombed.

"When these islands were bombed, American destroyers were in Tonkin Bay, and they were not 60 or 65 miles away. . . .

It is undeniable that in the patrolling operations of our destroyers in Tonkin Bay the destroyers have patrolled within 11 miles and more than 3 miles off the coast of North Vietnam. . . . The presence of those ships in that proximity to the North Vietnamese coast [the islands bombed were 3 to 5 miles off the coast] while an act of war was being committed against the North Vietnamese coast by the bombings of those islands, was bound to implicate us . . . it is bound to be looked upon by our enemies as an act of provocation; and it makes us a provocateur under the circumstances."

The fact that Senator Morse was correct in bringing out these facts was—almost two years later—confirmed by Senator Fulbright when he said:

". . . since that time [the hearings on the Southeast Asia resolution] there has come to my attention suggestions that the whole affair was very questionable as to the character of the attack upon our ships on the high seas. . . . Any suggestion at the time that this might have been a deliberate provocation on our part to invite the incident or that we had been inside the territorial waters of North Vietnam in connection with some boats of South Vietnam . . . was brushed aside in the emotions that naturally arose from an allegation by the Administration that this was a deliberate and unprovoked attack upon our ships upon the high seas. . . ."

Senator Gruening, during the course of the debate, declared that the Tonkin Gulf incident was "'an inevitable development of the U.S. steady escalation of our own military activities in Southeast Asia in recent weeks. I do not justify or condone that attack on our ships. I do not at all disagree with the Administration's policy of countering this attack and of not merely repelling the attackers but destroying them and giving them the same medicine which they seek to inflict on our vessels. But that does not mean that I can approve the whole U.S. policy of active, unilateral military intervention in Southeast Asia. . . .'"

In agreeing with Senator Gruening in his support of the Administration's repelling of aggression, Senator Morse pointed out that there had been two actions taken in response to the armed attack against the destroyers. The first had been to repel the attack and destroy or attempt to destroy the attackers. In this the United States was clearly justified. However, in the retaliatory raids the United States was on much more doubtful legal grounds. The United States in that instance was acting as judge, jury, and executioner. The United States—unilaterally—decided that the raid on its destroyers—in which no damage was inflicted—should result in North Vietnam's losing, by bomb destruction, certain of its bases and petroleum dump. Under such circumstances, who could gainsay the United States placing a higher price on the attack than the destruction of the bases and the petroleum dump?

This is a forerunner of the thinking which underlay the decisions after the Plieku raid when the "eye for an eye" concept was announced, which was later elevated into more widespread bombings of North Vietnam facilities and installations, including civilian buildings.

Finally, as the debate on the Southeast Asia Resolution was drawing to a close, Senator Nelson sought further clarification. He was, he said, "most disturbed to see that there is no agreement on what the joint resolution means. I would like to see it clarified."

He proposed to offer an amendment which would approve and support the President's efforts to bring the problem of peace in Southeast Asia to the Security Council, and the President in "seeking no extension of the present military conflict, will respond to provocation in a manner that is 'limited and fitting.' " He proposed adding to his amendment the limition:

"Our continuing policy is to limit our role to the provision of aid, training assistance, and military advice, and it is the sense of the Congress that, except when provoked to a greater response, we should continue to attempt to avoid a direct military involvement in the Southeast Asian conflict."

Senator Fulbright replied that he could see nothing objectionable in Senator Nelson's amendent but he could not accept it. The House at that moment was voting on the resolution. To accept the amendment would cause delays, confusion, and would mean a conference with the House.

The Nelson amendment was never brought to a vote.

A vote was then taken on the Southeast Asia Resolution—in the form in which it had been reported by the Senate Committees and in the form in which it was being adopted by the House. The resolution was adopted by a vote of 88 to 2, with only Senators Morse and Gruening voting against it.

Senator Fulbright has since that time on many occasions publicly apologized for rushing through the resolution.

He has said: "My role in the adoption of the resolution of August 7, 1964, is a source of neither pleasure nor pride to me today . . . it was adopted during an election campaign in which the President was telling the American people that it would be a mistake for the United States to become involved in a major war in Asia while criticizing his opponent for proposing just that. This may explain the perfunctory debate of August 1964 but hardly excuses the Congress for granting such sweeping authority with so little deliberation. It was a mistake which I trust will not soon be repeated."[5]

In his press conference on November 1, 1967, President Johnson admitted that the Administration "began discussing at this table (in the White House) in May of that year (1964—more than two months before the Gulf of Tonkin incident) the desirability of asking Congress to join with us in deterring aggression."

Can we, therefore, conclude that the "unprovoked" attack against United States naval vessels in the Gulf of Tonkin was anticipated more than two months before it took place?

CHAPTER XXIV

BUILDING THE IMAGE, "A MAN OF PEACE"

President Johnson signed the Southeast Asia Resolution into law on August 10, 1964.

With a copy of the resolution safely in his pocket, Lyndon Baines Johnson was off to the hustings to campaign vigorously for election to his first full term as President of the United States.

He also faced the task of repairing his image.

Senator Barry Goldwater (R.-Ariz.), his Republican opponent, was already being pictured by the Democrats as a trigger-happy Westerner who had discussed—months before—the possibility of using atomic weapons to defoliate the supply lines into South Vietnam. The Democrats were seeking to give the voters the impression that Goldwater, if elected President, would involve the United States in a land war in Southeast Asia that might lead to a nuclear World War III.

The Gulf of Tonkin incident had alarmed the country and had tarnished, somewhat, the Johnson image as a man of peace who would keep the United States out of a massive land war in Southeast Asia. Johnson's sudden nation-wide broadcast on the Gulf of Tonkin incident, his ordering instant retaliatory air strikes against North Vietnamese bases, his Secretary of Defense's midnight press conference, his stern message to the Congress, and the passage of the Southeast Asia Resolution had all contributed in some quarters of the country to arousing a sense of unease—vague feelings that perhaps the war was, in fact, being escalated.

In his campaigning, therefore, Johnson sought to lay to rest these fears and to dispel decisively the notion that the only choice the voters had was between a trigger-happy Arizonan and a trigger-happy Texan.

On August 12, 1964—two days after he signed the Southeast Asia Resolution—President Johnson appeared before the members of the American Bar Association assembled at the Waldorf Astoria Hotel in New York City.

He took this occasion to attack Senator Goldwater—but not by name—for his alleged advocacy of the use of nuclear weapons in Vietnam, saying:

"It has never been the policy of any American President to sympathetically or systematically place in hazard the life of this Nation by threatening nuclear war. No American President has ever pursued so irresponsible a course. Our firmness at moments of crisis has always been matched by restraint—our determination by care."[1]

For those who argued "that we have lost almost 200 lives there [in Vietnam] in the last four years, and should come home," Johnson replied that "The United States cannot and must not and will not turn aside and allow the freedom of a brave people to be handed-over to Communist tyrrany."

Such an alternative, he said, was "morally unthinkable."

"Some others," he continued, "are eager to enlarge the conflict. They call upon us to supply American boys to do the job that Asian boys should do. They ask us to take reckless action which might risk the lives of millions and engulf much of Asia and certainly threaten the peace of the entire world. Moreover, such action would offer no solution at all to the real problem of Vietnam. America can and America will meet any wider challenge from others, but our aim in Vietnam, as in the rest of the world, is to help restore peace and to re-establish a decent order."

Seventeen days later—on August 29, 1964—speaking at a barbecue in the local rodeo arena in Stonewall, Texas, given in honor of his 56th birthday anniversary, President Johnson again sought to contrast himself with a trigger-happy would-be President.

Telling of giving the order "the other day to send the boys off that carrier with the bombs to destroy the nests of those PT boats that had fired on our destroyer, that was an order I didn't want to give."

"I have had advice," he continued, "to load our planes with bombs and drop them on certain areas that I think would enlarge the war and escalate the war, and result in our committing a good many American boys to fighting a war that I think ought to be fought by the boys of Asia to help protect their own land. And for that reason, I haven't chosen to enlarge the war. Nor have I chosen to retreat and turn it over to the Communists."[2]

He sought to give the same image of great restraint almost a month later—September 25, 1964—when he dedicated the Eufaula Dam in Oklahoma.

"There are those who say," he told the audience, "you ought to go north and drop bombs, to try to wipe out the supply lines, and they think that would escalate the war. We don't want our American boys to do the fighting for Asian boys. We don't want to get involved in a nation with 700 million people and get tied down in a land war in Asia."[3]

He had similarly resisted the advice "to go south and get out and come home."

Instead, he promised, "we are not about to start another war and we're not about to run away from where we are." His words varied only slightly when he spoke three days later at the Carpenter Motor Inn in Manchester, New Hampshire, before the New Hampshire Weekly Newspaper Editors Association on September 28, 1964.

He reminded his audience that some of "our people—Mr. Nixon, Mr. Rockefeller, Mr. Scranton, and Mr. Goldwater—have all . . . suggested the possible wisdom of going north in Vietnam." He pointed out that he had rejected these suggestions and that, on his part, he wanted to be "very cautious and careful."

"So just for the moment," President Johnson informed the assembled editors, "I have not thought that we were ready for American boys to do the fighting for Asian boys. What I have been trying to do, with the situation that I found, was to get the boys in Vietnam to do their own fighting with our advice and with our equipment. That is the course we are following. So we are not going north and drop bombs at this stage of the game, and we are not going south and run out and leave it for the Communists to take over."[4]

Thus went the image-painting during the 1964 Presidential campaign.

As Theodore H. White pointed out in his book on that campaign, the Democrats did not try to make the issue between Johnson and Goldwater one of a choice between peace and war "but a choice, nevertheless—between peace and the risk of war." It was at that time that the Democrats twisted the Goldwater slogan from "In your heart you know he's right" to read: "IN YOUR HEART, YOU KNOW HE *MIGHT*."[5]

For the Johnson campaign, therefore, it was vital that he give the impression that he was a man of moderation.

Thus he continued in that vein when he addressed Democratic party workers of Indiana and Kentucky on October 9, 1964, at the Sheraton Seelbach Hotel in Louisville, Kentucky:

"We are trying as best we can not to enlarge that war, not to get the United States tied down in a land war in Asia, and not for American boys starting to do the fighting that Asian boys ought to be doing to protect themselves. We don't want to pull out and come home and say, 'We will turn it all over to you.'

"So if you don't want to enlarge it and you seek no larger war, and you don't want to pull out and run home, the only thing you can do is what we are doing. We let them know that when they shoot at us in the Tonkin Gulf, we will make prompt, adequate, and sufficient reply."[6]

Speaking at Akron University 12 days later on October 21, 1964, President Johnson repeated the pledge not to enlarge the war and not to send American boys to fight in a land war in Asia and defined the foreign policy issue of the campaign as follows:

"The issue is whether we will use our great power with judgment and restraint.

"The issue is whether we will continue the long, the hard, the patient search for a lasting peace."

"But," he continued, "we are not about to send American boys 9 or 10,000 miles away from home to do what Asian boys ought to be doing for themselves."

In the remaining days of the 1964 Presidential campaign he became more blunt.

In Columbia, South Carolina, on October 26, 1964, President Johnson told the people assembled on the steps of the State Capitol: "You know the policies of one man who seeks your trust. That man offers a policy of brinkmanship with nuclear power. He urges that we consider using nuclear weapons in Vietnam, even in Eastern Europe, if there should be an uprising."

Johnson continued:

"And I say here tonight to you that the next man that sits there as the President may be called upon to move his thumb up toward that nuclear button that could wipe out 300 million people in a short time; that that next President may hear that phone ring that is there by his bed and by his desk, that 'hot line' from Moscow, and you have to select the man that you want to answer it."[7]

In giving the electorate the impression that he was speaking with the voice of moderation during the 1964 Presidential campaign, President Johnson was contrasting his proposed policies in Vietnam not only with the early statements of Candidate Goldwater concerning the interdiction of the supply lines into South Vietnam by the use of nuclear weapons, but also with the proposals by some Republican leaders for a complete take-over by United States military forces of the war in South Vietnam.

In the latter part of June, a Republican task force in the House of Representatives, headed by Congressman Gerald R. Ford (R.-Mich.), had proposed that: "American forces must take command of the forces in Vietnam and not simply remain advisers. He called the present policy one reason why we haven't done as well as we should have done. U.S. strategy ought to be aimed at sealing off South Vietnam, preventing the infiltration from North Vietnam."[8] Mr. Ford said this could be done by sending more U.S. special forces to Vietnam.

Even while President Johnson and Senator Goldwater were criss-crossing the country, the economic and political situation in South Vietnam was steadily worsening and appeals for peace from President de Gaulle, United Nations Secretary General U Thant and even Ho Chi Minh were bruskly rejected or quietly ignored.

At his news conference on July 23, 1964, de Gaulle stated: ". . . locally, a military solution cannot be expected. Some people imagine . . . that the Americans could achieve a military victory by carrying the war to the North as far as it would be necessary. But, although they certainly have at their disposal all the desired means, it is difficult to believe that they wish to take the tremendous risk of a generalized conflict . . . peace must be made . . . this implies returning to what was agreed upon ten years ago, and, this time, complying with it; in other words, this implies that in North and South Vietnam, in Cambodia, and in Laos, no foreign power may any longer intervene in any way in the affairs of these unfortunate countries. . . ."[9]

DeGaulle then went on to propose a meeting "of the same order" as the Geneva meeting of 1954 "to which each participant must come without conditions or recriminations."

Both the de Gaulle suggestion and a similar suggestion by U Thant in July 1964, for a reconvening of the Geneva Conference were rejected by the United States.[10]

It was not until more than a year later—after the death of United States Ambassador to the United Nations, Adlai Stevenson, in July 1965—that the people of the United States and of the world were to learn that in September 1964, during the presidential campaign, a peace feeler was transmitted from Ho Chi Minh to the United States. A reply to this peace feeler by the United States was first postponed by the United States until after the election and was then rejected.

As commentator Eric Sevareid told the story in *Look* magazine on November 30, 1965:

"In the early autumn of 1964 . . . U Thant . . . had privately obtained agreement from authorities in North Vietnam that they would send an emissary to talk with an American emissary, in Rangoon, Burma. Someone in Washington insisted that this attempt be postponed until after the Presidential election. When the election was over, U Thant again pursued the matter. Hanoi was still willing to send its man. But Defense Secretary Robert McNamara . . . opposed the attempt. He said the South Vietnamese Government would have to be informed and that would have a demoralizing effect on them; that government was shaky enough, as it was. . . . U Thant was furious over this failure of his patient efforts. . . ."

Not only was the South Vietnamese Government shaky after the Presidential elections of 1964 in the United States, it was shaky both before and during the election campaign. The military coup that overthrew and killed Diem on November 1, 1963, was followed by a succession of coups.

As John Mecklin, at the time Public Affairs Officer for the United States Information Agency in Saigon, stated it:

"A parade of meaningless names marched across the headlines, mixed with reports of new Viet Cong gains."

The military leaders chose former Vice President Nguyen Ngoc Tho to succeed Diem. He was succeeded by a military triumvirate headed by Major General Duong (Big Minh) Van Minh on January 6, 1964. Twenty-four days later, on January 30, 1964, another military coup installed Major General Nguyen Khanh in power. On February 8, 1964, Major General Khanh announced the formation of a new government with himself as Premier and Major General Duong Van Minh as nominal Chief of State. The latter was thrown out of the government on August 16 and General Khanh was installed as Chief of State. And so on and on with a long succession of heads of state, provisional leaders, each being installed and ousted by the military leaders.

The musical chair government in Saigon inspired humorist, Art Buchwald, to write "Lodge in Orbit" in which he imagined a conversation wherein United States Ambassador to South Vietnam, Henry Cabot Lodge, is trying to explain the shifts in government in Saigon:

"'. . . the United States has the situation in Vietnam well in hand. Under the firm leadership of Gen. Nguyen Khanh many new reforms have been instituted . . . [courier hands him a telegram] . . . General Khanh has been dividing the country, and

"OUR MEN IN SAIGON"

UPI Photo

Washington, D. C.   May 9, 1957.
Secretary of State John Foster Dulles
and President Ngo Dinh Diem of
South Vietnam.

UPI Photo

"NO JETS IN WAR"

Saigon, South Vietnam.   May 13, 1964.
"U. S. Secretary of Defense Robert
McNamara (2nd from left) chats with Viet-
namese Premier, Maj. Gen. Nguyen Khanh,
in Saigon, May 13. Flanking them are U. S.
Ambassador Henry Cabot Lodge (left) and
Chairman of the Joint Chiefs of Staff, Gen.
Maxwell D. Taylor (right).   McNamara left
here, May 13, saying U. S. has decided not
to inject jet planes into guerrilla war."

UPI Photo

Agana, Guam.   March 19, 1967.   "Standing at attention during
playing of the national anthems are (left to right) Rear Admiral
Horace Bird, commander of U. S. naval forces in the Marianas;
Secretary of State Dean Rusk; Secretary of Defense Robert
McNamara; South Vietnamese Chief of State Nguyen Van Thieu;
President Lyndon B Johnson and Premier Nguyen Cao Ky of
South Vietnam."

the United States feels he can no longer control the various factions . . . [courier hands him a telegram] . . . the best solution to the problem would be a three-man military junta . . . Gen. Khanh has been a handicap and we intend to support Gen. Minh whom Gen. Khanh disposed of several months ago with our help . . . [courier hands him a telegram] . . . Dr. Nuyen Xuan Oanh is now in charge of the Saigon government . . . [courier hands him a telegram] . . . we have not ruled out Gen. Khanh's contribution to our effort in Vietnam . . . he still holds the title of Premier . . . Our main objective is to win the war, but we realize that this cannot be done until there is a stable government in Vietnam. We feel we have such a government with Dr. Oanh. . . . The phone rings . . . and Ambassador Lodge answers it wearily. 'Yes sir. Whom did you say? Madame Nhu? Thank you.' "[11]

All during the Presidential campaign, and after it as well, there was more wrong in Saigon than the inability of a single government to remain in power for any appreciable length of time.

When Lodge left Saigon to return to the United States, he was replaced on June 23, 1964, by General Maxwell Taylor who had been Chairman of the Joint Chiefs of Staff.

As Mecklin commented on this appointment: "Taylor was one of the Nation's most respected soldiers, though some critics noted that he also shared with McNamara responsibility for the shortsighted American military policy in Vietnam during the previous two and one-half years."[12]

The instability of the South Vietnamese Government could not help being reflected in the war being fought against the Vietcong.

The retaliatory air strikes after the Gulf of Tonkin incident "momentarily heartened" the Khanh regime.

"In the months that followed, the news from Vietnam became increasingly incomprehensible and ugly. Repeated outbreaks of bloody, senseless rioting in the streets of Saigon among students, Catholics, and Buddhists. Mounting indications of Viet Cong influence in the mobs, especially Buddhist mobs."[13]

After the Gulf of Tonkin incident, Premier Khanh, with the encouragement of the United States, "moved to establish total power with a very strong central government. Riots started again in the streets; the result was not that Khanh became stronger, but that his government fell."[14]

Peter Grose wrote in *The New York Times* from Saigon on August 7:

... insofar as United States policy makers encouraged General Khanh in his bold moves to centralize power, they bear a major responsibility for the present situation. The risk they encouraged was not ... well calculated ... the Americans made the basic error of assuming that the primary interest of the Vietnamese people is the same as the primary interest of the American mission in Vietnam: defeat of the Vietcong insurgency."

Five weeks later, Grose wrote from Saigon to *The New York Times* on September 12 that there were rumors in Saigon that "Buddhist leaders ... have called on both the Government army commanders and Vietcong leadership to 'slow down' the war, if not actually cease fighting ... independent military observers detect signs ... of increasing numbers of de facto cease-fire understandings growing up in recent weeks among individual units in widespread parts of the country."[15]

Six days later, the Defense Department reported that United States destroyers again in the Gulf of Tonkin had fired on and "presumably hit four or five hostile targets." Commenting on this incident, editor I.F. Stone stated:

"Neither Washington nor Moscow nor Peking nor Hanoi can calculate clearly because none of them seems to be sure of what happened. We say we shot at some blips on a radar screen; Peking and Hanoi say, in substance, that nothing at all happened; and Moscow says we sank three ships. Now Washington says it thinks maybe we did. This is beginning to resemble a bar-room brawl with the lights out."[16]

The incident—whatever it was—must have given added encouragement to those in Saigon determined to fight on against the Vietcong and resist the voices raised on behalf of an early end to the fighting.

The Presidential elections in the United States were held amidst reports from Saigon of a rapidly deteriorating political and military situation there.

President Johnson won his first full term handsomely. There is little room for doubt but that the overriding motive of the voters casting their ballots in favor of Lyndon Baines Johnson did so, as far as foreign issues were concerned, because of the fear that Goldwater would surely lead us into a nuclear, world-wide conflagration.

CHAPTER XXV

OPEN ENDED ESCALATION

By the end of 1965, in a masterful, unanimous report to the Senate by a study team composed of Senator Mike Mansfield (D., Mont.), Senate Majority Leader, Senator Edmund S. Muskie (D., Maine), Senator Daniel K. Inouye (D., Hawaii), Senator George D. Aiken (R., Vt.) and Senator J. Caleb Boggs (R., Del), it was said of the United States military involvement in Vietnam:

"Despite the great increase in American military commitment, it is doubtful in view of the acceleration of Vietcong efforts that the constricted position now held in Vietnam by the Saigon government can continue to be held for the indefinite future, let alone extended, without a further augmentation of American forces on the ground . . . the question is not one of applying increased U. S. pressure to a defined military situation but rather of pressing against a military situation which is . . . open ended. How open is dependent on the extent to which North Vietnam and its supporters are willing and able to meet increased force by increased force."[1]

What events had transpired in 1965 that caused President Johnson to disregard his promise to the American electorate that "We don't want our American boys to do the fighting for Asian boys"? Why had United States troop commitments to Vietnam been raised from 23,000 at the end of 1964 to over 165,000 by the end of

1965, with more on the way, incurring United States casualties in 1965 of 1,365, killed and 6,110 wounded?

From the time of the Presidential election on November 4, 1964 —even as before the election—economic and political conditions in South Vietnam continued to deteriorate, while the Vietcong terrorist and military activities increased in quantity and ferocity. Military coup followed military coup—needed reforms were not made, even though repeatedly promised.

From November 4, 1964, to the end of January 1965, events moved swiftly both in South Vietnam and in the United States.

More and more voices were being raised in the United States stressing the need for a negotiated settlement of the United States military involvement in Vietnam. It was during this period, it will be recalled, that U.N. Secretary General U Thant was pressing the Administration for an answer [which ultimately turned out to be a refusal] to Ho Chi Minh's willingness to send an emissary to Rangoon to discuss the Vietnamese situation. President de Gaulle's suggestion for a neutral Indochina was being more and more discussed.

Others espoused the Goldwater approach of interdicting the supply lines from North Vietnam, but using only conventional weapons.

"Barry Goldwater was censured during the election campaign for wanting to extend the Vietnam war." *The New Republic* wrote in its December 5, 1964 leading editorial. "Now General Maxwell Taylor, the U. S. Ambassador to Saigon, will try to sell the same plan to President Johnson in Washington this week . . . Those who recommend extending the war have not satisfactorily explained how bombing Laotian jungle trails or North Vietnamese ports or training centers would stop the rot in Saigon, undermine the will of the Viet Cong or transform the soldiers of the South into an effective, winning force."

Speaking of the possibility of the war in Vietnam being enlarged, William P. Bundy, Assistant Secretary of State for Far Eastern Affairs, stated on January 23, 1965:

"As for enlarging our own actions, we cannot speak surely about the future, for the aggressors themselves share the responsibility for such eventualities. We have shown in the Gulf of Tonkin that we can act, and North Vietnam knows it and knows its own weaknesses. But we seek no wider war, and we must not suppose that there are quick or easy answers in this direction."[2]

In that same address, speaking of the then Prime Minister of South Vietnam, Tran Van Huong, the Assistant Secretary described him as "a man of determination and character, dedicated to fairness to all groups," who was trying to solve the problems of his country—"the same kind of problems Diem faced and overcame in 1954, but in the far more difficult internal security crises brought on by the Viet Cong aggression, which has been slowly extending the areas of Communist control in the countryside and the pace of guerrilla and terrorist activity, even to Saigon itself." Four days later— on January 27, 1965—Prime Minister Huong was ousted by General Khanh.

Some looked upon this latest coup as possibly auguring a negotiated settlement of the conflict in South Vietnam. Joseph Kraft, writing in *The Washington Star* that same day, stated that it now might be possible for a settlement to come about—a settlement "negotiated between the Saigon Government and the Vietnamese Communists, with the U. S. edged obscurely into the background, and the Chinese Communists excluded altogether."

On January 31, 1965, writing from Saigon to *The New York Times,* Seymour Topping noted that plans were already drafted "to deal with a situation in which Americans might have to leave South Vietnam hastily."

In the Gallup poll of January 31, 1965, the people were asked:

"Do you favor efforts by President Johnson to arrange a conference with leaders of Southeast Asia, including China, to see if a peace agreement can be worked out?"

81 percent of the American people said that that was what they favored. Eleven percent dissented. Eight percent had no opinion.

At the end of January, 1965, it looked as though popular sentiment in the United States was for a negotiated settlement in Vietnam and that there might well be coming upon the scene in Saigon a government which might be inclined to negotiate. But that was by no means certain.

On February 6, 1965, Russian Premier Kosygin arrived in Hanoi for what some believed would be an attempt to persuade Ho Chi Minh to negotiate a settlement of the Vietnamese conflict.

On February 7, 1965, in what the United States stated was retaliation for an attack on the United States' outpost at Pleiku, United States' planes struck targets in North Vietnam, even while Kosygin was still in Hanoi and coincidental with a proposal by President Shastri of India that there should be a meeting between Russian and United States' leaders to solve the problems of Southeast Asia.

From that first "retaliatory" strike against North Vietnam, bombing raids on North Vietnam would increase in number and intensity so that by November, 1967, the number of missions flown over North Vietnam to bomb targets there would amount to more than 31,000 and the number of ground troops at that time would be more than 500,000.

What happened at Pleiku on February 7, 1965, that justified such a massive escalation of United States military involvement in Vietnam?

The "retaliatory" air strikes against North Vietnam were announced in a statement issued by the White House on February 7, 1965.

The statement read in part as follows:

" . . . yesterday . . . two South Vietnamese airfields, two U. S. barracks areas, several villages, and one town in South Vietnam were subjected to deliberate surprise attacks. Substantial casualties resulted.

"Our intelligence has indicated, and this action confirms, that Hanoi has ordered a more aggressive course of action against both South Vietnamese and American installations.

"Moreover, these attacks were made possible by the continuing infiltration of personnel from North Vietnam . . . .

"Today's joint response was carefully limited to military areas which are supplying men and arms for attacks in South Vietnam. As in the case of the North Vietnamese attacks in the Gulf of Tonkin last August, the response is appropriate and fitting.

" . . . we seek no wider war . . ."

Curiously enough, while the statement gives the impression that the retaliatory action was taken as an instant response to "deliberate surprise attacks" after a discussion with the National Security Council "last night," the action seemed to have been anticipated almost a week before in a February 1, 1965, statement by the President announcing the "orderly withdrawl of American dependents from South Vietnam" and stating:

"It has become clear that Hanoi has undertaken a more aggressive course of action against both South Vietnamese and American installations, and against Americans who are in South Vietnam assisting the people of that country to defend their freedom. We have no choice now but to clear the decks and make absolutely clear our continued determination to back South Vietnam in its fight to maintain its independence."

The same announcement stated that the deployment to South Vietnam of a Hawk air defense battalion had been ordered and that "other reinforcements, in units and individuals, may follow."

In his statement issued on February 7, 1965, describing the incident at Pleiku, Secretary of Defense McNamara stated:

"The first attack in the Pleiku area was carried out by a company of Viet Cong using 81-mm. mortars, the mortar fire was directed against the United States military compound at the Second Corps Headquarters of the South Vietnamese military forces, and simultaneously elements of the same company attacked the airstrip at Camp Holloway, at which were located United States helicopter forces on the outskirts of Pleiku.

"This latter attack on the airstrip was accompanied by a ground probe during which smallarms fire was used, rifle grenades, demolition charges, and recoilless rifles. Following competition of the attacks a Viet Cong four-tube, 81-mm. mortar position was located outside the perimeter defense of the airstrip. Nearby were containers for 61 mortar rounds. The United States cascualties in the Pleiku area were 7 killed, 109 wounded, and, of the 109, 76 of the wounded required evacuation.

"In addition 5 United States helicopters were destroyed, 9 to 11 damaged, and 6 United States fixed wing aircraft were damaged."

Secretary McNamara's statement gave the impression that the attacks on Pleiku were launched by North Vietnamese infiltrators who had come down the trail to attack the United States base. Thus he said:

"As I say, elements of the U. S. and South Vietnamese Air Forces were directed to launch joint retaliatory attacks against . . . the areas which Hanoi has used as bases for the infiltration of men and equipment out of the southern portion of North Vietnam across the border into Laos, down the corridor through Laos, and into South Vietnam. The infiltration routes are pictured on the map. One comes into the Pleiku area . . . . "

In reporting the incident and the retaliatory raids to the Security Council of the United Nations, the United States Ambassador to the United Nations, Adlai E. Stevenson, made this contention clear.

He said:

"These attacks by the Viet Cong, which operates under the military orders of North Vietnamese authorities in Hanoi, were a concerted and politically timed effort to sharpen and intensify the aggression at a moment designed for broader effect in the field of International politics, and to test the will of the Republic of Vietnam and the United States to resist aggression . . . there is a pattern of military operations directed, staffed and supplied in crucial respects from outside the country. Up to 34,000 armed and trained soldiers have infiltrated into South Vietnam from the north since 1959. In addition, key items of equipment, such as mortars of the type employed in the attacks of February 7th, have come from North Vietnam. During 1964, the infiltration of men and equipment has increased sharply, and virtually all of those now coming in are natives of North Vietnam."[3]

The factual basis for the account of what happened at Pleiku was immediately challenged in many quarters.

Writing in *The New York Times* the very next day—February 8, 1965—Charles Mohr raised a number of questions.

He first pointed out that the attackers used, as their heaviest weapon, 81-mm. American-made mortars.

"The question is," he asked, "that if the Vietcong unit at Pleiku was—as is so often the case—using captured weapons, would this sustain the argument that North Vietnam made possible this particular attack?"

Mohr also pointed out that the attacks were made by only a company or less of Vietcong. "This was not a large Vietcong assault. Many are much larger. . . ."

Commenting on the fact that the Administration had pointed to the three attacks in one night as indicating "a pattern of overall direction, probably from Hanoi," Mohr asked:

"Since larger numbers of Vietcong attacks have taken place throughout South Vietnam on other nights . . . why should this be?"

Malcolm Browne arrived there shortly after the attack. He was of the opinion that the attackers numbered no more than 50 men and that their weapons were "wire cutters to get through the perimeter fence, American hand grenades, and a large number of TNT blocks wrapped into pole bombs . . . the explosives [in the mortars fired from a nearby village] appeared to have been extracted from captured American shells."

Reporter Drew Pearson, in an article in *The Washington Post* on February 28, 1965, entitled "Pleiku Attack Not a Hanoi Plot," stated that the attackers at Pleiku were able to achieve success only "because of the sheer stupidity and lack of alertness by the Americans and the South Vietnamese . . . Hanoi could not have planned to have all South Vietnamese personnel and all Americans asleep."

"What happened," Pearson stated, "was that Ambassador Taylor . . . seized this opportunity to recommend retaliatory raids. He sincerely believed this was a Hanoi plot. Ordinarily his recommendation might have been discounted in Washington, but it happened that McGeorge Bundy, White House adviser on security matters, was in Saigon at precisely that time.

"Bundy's brother, William, is Assistant Secretary of State for the Far East and has long advocated a stronger hand in Vietnam, including bombing the North. When McGeorge Bundy . . . joined Taylor in rushing back a premature, exaggerated account of the Pleiku raid, the White House finally yielded to advice which the Bundy brothers had been giving for some time. . . ."

In its issue of February 20, 1965, *The New Republic* had its own explanation for the retaliatory air strikes against North Vietnam:

"On the face of it, last week's air raids on North Vietnam were made to divert public attention from the bungled defenses of the military installations in South Vietnam which the guerrillas pounded and penetrated, and to appease public wrath over American soldiers killed and wounded in their beds. But the Administration naturally preferred to offer loftier motivations for retaliatory bombing of another country."

However plausible these official explanations of the reasons back of the retaliatory air raids against North Vietnam may have seemed at the time, the subsequent steady escalation of United States military involvement on the sea and in the air over North Vietnam do raise the question as to whether all the decisions made in February 1965 have yet come to light. Recent writings shed new light on the incident.

According to reporters Rowland Evans and Robert Novak, writing of the Pleiku incident, President Johnson had made no decision to "go North" at that time.

"The President's caution," they wrote, "brought a cold chill to advisers in the Pentagon and State Department who foresaw a dreary chain of events: the crumbling of the Saigon government, South Vietnam eventually being sucked into the Communist orbit, and Communist subversion or influence spreading into all of Southeast Asia and from there to the Philippines. They were not at all certain that Johnson would send bombers north of the 17th parallel to abort this chilling scenario. But all speculation became academic on February 7 when the United States Air Force barracks at Pleiku . . . were attacked by mortar fire and hand grenades from a Vietcong raiding party . . . Johnson showed the same toughness and swift reaction to the Pleiku raid that he had displayed six months earlier in the Bay of Tonkin."

According to these observers, the "purposes of the bombing were . . . to bolster confidence and morale in Saigon and, secondarily, to make it more costly for Ho Chi Minh to send his legions South to help the Vietcong."

" 'If he had not retaliated to the attack on Pleiku in early February, he said one afternoon a week before going to Baltimore [to make his famous Johns Hopkins speech], he would have been impeached. How could the United States sit back quietly and accept the atrocities that were being staged by the Vietcong?' "[4]

However other writers give a different version of the Pleiku incident and the events which followed.

Writing in the *Saturday Evening Post* for March 27, 1965, in an article entitled "Vietnam: Where Do We Go From Here," author Stanley Karnow reported that the decision to bomb North Vietnam had been made well before February 7, 1965.

In this article, Stanley Karnow relates that on a visit to Washington in late November 1964, General Maxwell Taylor suggested "two operations to President Johnson: (1) retaliatory forays into North Vietnam for Vietcong terrorism against Americans or attacks against U. S. installations; (2) air strikes against supply lines and staging areas in Laos, possibly phasing such hits on such North Vietnamese targets as bridges and powerplants. The President was cautious. He consented in principle to limited escalation—on condition that the Vietnamese generals and politicians stop wrangling . . . Returning to Saigon, Taylor conveyed that message to the Vietnamese."

However, the wrangling did not stop but "the United States had no intention of being forced out of Saigon. And out of that determination evolved the feeling that whether or not the South Vietnamese Government was stable, some kind of action would have to be taken against the north . . . President Johnson gradually came around and told Taylor the United States would attack north 'on the next appropriate occasion'."

In the words of General Taylor, as quoted by Karnow:

"Once that decision was reached, all that was required was a circumstance that justified reprisal. The Vietcong handed us the chance at Pleiku and Quinhon . . . ."

Mr. Roger Hilsman, then Assistant Secretary of State for the Far East states that the decision to bomb the North Vietnamese was made in February 1965 and that after the decision was made, a plausible excuse was sought.

Says Hilsman:

"The public position . . . tended to justify the bombing of North Vietnam as a retaliation for attacks on American installations in South Vietnam, such as the attack on the American barracks at

Pleiku, or as retaliation for increased use of the infiltration routes. Many outside observers felt that all this was merely a rationalization and excuse—that the decision had been made on the grounds described above [to punish Hanoi—to cut off flow of supplies—it would make the whole North Vietnamese effort more costly and painful] and then delayed until a suitable incident provided the justification. In any event the public case was weak."

Buttressing his assertion that the public case was weak, Roger Hilsman cites the small number of previous attacks on United States officials and installations, the insignificant amount of infiltration, and the lack of "evidence that there had been such a significant introduction of North Vietnamese in 1964 as to justify retaliation."

Commenting on the white paper issued by the Department of State at the time, Roger Hilsman is highly critical of it as a supporting document and notes that it did not present any evidence "of the presence of regular North Vietnamese units except the allegations of two [of the four ethnic North Vietnamese captured] and two other captured Viet Cong of southern origin."[5]

"Although it was not offered at the time," Hilsman continues, "another reason for the decision to bomb North Vietnam was probably the conviction that the struggle in the south was at a crisis point and the whole of South Vietnam would be lost unless desperate measures were taken promptly."

In view of the fact that, as both Roger Hilsman and General Taylor have said, the decision to bomb North Vietnam was made before the Pleiku incident and the Johnson Administration was only waiting for "a circumstance that justified reprisal," the question remains why the Pleiku incident—which occurred while Premier Kosygin of the Soviet Union was in Hanoi—was chosen?

The Pleiku incident was followed by a similar incident three days later at Quinhon where a U. S. billet was blown up, killing 23 soldiers.

Thus in these two incidents alone—occurring in the space of four days—the number of servicemen killed almost totalled the United States losses for the whole year 1962 and almost half the number killed in 1963.

An uneasiness spread throughout the country as more and more people became uncertain as to the exact aims of the Johnson Administration.

On February 10, 1965, Mr. James Reston in an article entitled "A Time for Reflection on Vietnam" in *The New York Times* commented on the President's statement with respect to the retaliatory raids that: "We seek no wider war. Whether or not this course can be maintained lies with the North Vietnamese aggressors."

"Nobody," Mr. Reston stated, "should underestimate the seriousness of this remark. It is a clear threat that the war will be extended unless Hanoi withdraws, and there is absolutely no indication by Hanoi or its Communist backers that withdrawal is intended . . . The President . . . has compromised between those here who want him to go on about as before and those who want him to use his airpower on the Communist industry in the north."

Reston's conclusion was that a Korean type solution on either side of the 17th parallel "is probably the best anybody can get out of it, and the first step in this is clearly a self-imposed cease fire on both sides of the line."

On February 11, 1965, Secretary General U Thant called for international negotiations on Vietnam inside or outside the United Nations. Secretary of State Rusk answered U Thant at his news conference on February 25, 1965, saying:

" . . . the proposals I know about thus far have been procedural in nature. The missing piece continues to be the absence of any indication that Hanoi is prepared to stop doing what it is doing against its neighbors.

" . . . This question of calling a conference, under what circumstances—these are procedural matters. What we are interested in, what is needed to restore peace to Southeast Asia, is substance, content, an indication that peace is possible in terms of the appetites and the attitudes of the other side."

That same day, in an article entitled: "United States Should Not Shun a Parley," Walter Lipmann observed in *The Washington Post*:

"The military policy of holding on in South Vietnam, supplemented with retaliatory strikes, needs to be accompanied by a full-scale peace offensive. The United States ought not to be afraid to say and should not hesitate to say that it is seeking a negotiated settlement in southeast Asia . . . . The administration has always shrunk from talking about a negotiated peace."

On February 12, Joseph Kraft, in his column in *The Washington (D.C.) Evening Star* entitled: Political Track Needed in Vietnam," observed:

" . . . there is more than an innocent connection between the Hanoi government and the Vietcong guerillas. But the two are not one and the same thing. To act as though they are is to U. S. power in the hands of the least responsible party to the the whole Vietnamese affair . . . it is possible for a handful of Vietcong troublemakers, with a couple of well placed grenades or plastic bombs, to unleash the might of U. S. sea and air power against North Vietnam . . . Washington has every right to refer the matter either to the United Nations or to the Geneva powers. Either of these bodies could generate enough diplomatic movement to justify an easing off of the military action."

These reiterated calls for a negotiated settlement in Vietnam, coming as they did from so many divergent sources, coupled as they were by persistent rumors in Washington that the war in Vietnam was again about to be escalated, resulted in a debate in the Senate on February 17, 1965.

In a major speech in the Senate that day, Senator Frank Church (D., Idaho) stated:

"The weakness in Saigon emanates from Saigon itself, where we, as foreigners, are powerless to unite the spoiling factions. A family feud is never settled by outsiders. Only the Vietnamese themselves can furnish the solution . . . . Peiping is now able to pose as the champion of Asia for the Asians . . . . It would be to our national advantage . . . to seek an international agreement for the neutralization of the whole great region that used to be French Indochina . . . ."[6]

Senator Church cited with approval, and inserted in the Congressional record, editorials and columns from newspapers and periodicals calling for negotiations, including the columns by Reston, Lippmann, and Kraft.

Earlier Senator Stephen Young (D.-Ohio) had said:

" . . . we must not and we shall not be bogged down in a land war on the Asiatic mainland . . . The Communist dictators are now fully aware of our determination to fulfill our commitments to South Vietnam. It would be no sign of weakness to negotiate toward a peaceful solution of that conflict."[7]

Senator Gaylord Nelson (D.-Wisc.) stated that it was "in our national interest to seek ways and means of negotiating a constructive settlement" and cited with approval an editorial from the *Milwaukee Journal* which recommended:

"Where do we go from here? Logically to a negotiated settlement . . . . Nothing could be lost by recalling the Geneva pact powers for negotiation. President de Gaulle is right when he says that Southeast Asia should be a neutral zone and that steps should be taken now to that end."[8]

Senator George McGovern (D.-S.D.) observed that "the time for the United States to explore the possibility of a negotiated settlement is now, before the forces are out of control and before a trend is started that might lead to World War III."[9]

The Progressive for February 20, 1965, pointed out that:

"It is a very sanguine State Department or Pentagon official who imagines that the North Vietnamese under threat of still further American air blows will advise the guerrillas in the South to cease and desist their increasingly successful forays, and that the guerrillas will obey."

On February 24, 1965, on the Senate Floor, Senator Gruening, pleading that the President not follow the advice of the so-called "hawks" for escalating the war in Vietnam and noting that an "honorable way out of the mess in Vietnam has been afforded the United States by the pleas for negotiation made by the Pope, by the Secretary General of the United Nations, by India, and by France, and by numerous private citizens, including some of our colleagues," inserted in the Congressional Record an article which proved to be, by later events, a remarkably accurate forecast of the course of action which the United States would take in escalating its military involvement in Vietnam.

The article was by the military writer, Hanson W. Baldwin, and appeared in *The New York Times* Magazine for Sunday, February 21, 1965, under the title:

"We Must Choose—(1) 'Bug Out', (2) Negotiate, (3) Fight—A Military Commentator Argues for a Greater Use of Our Power in Vietnam: 'We Must Fight A War to Prevent an Irreparable Defeat' ".

In his article, Mr. Baldwin advocated these steps:

"First: . . . we must recognize . . . that we are fighting a war in Vietnam not merely advising how to fight one."

Second: ". . . the United States itself must provide maximum possible security in Vietnam to major U. S. installations . . . ."

Third: ". . . simplification and streamlining of both the high military command and the 'country team' units . . . ." He pointed out that combined United States and South Vietnamese military units have been successful in clearing an area of Vietcong, but that the Agency for International Development was responsible for supervising the South Vietnamese internal security forces in holding the area thereafter and that they "rarely have been able to hold an area once it has been cleared of the Vietcong."

"Perhaps," Mr. Baldwin suggested, "military troops should be charged with the 'hold' as well as the 'clear' part of the operations."

Fourth: "Continuous and heavy air and sea attacks" would be necessary, "targets in North Vietnam probably would have to be broadened," a "naval blockade and naval gunfire may well supplement the air bombardment . . . ."

Fifth: Much larger and better led South Vietnamese forces would be necessary. They would have to be supplemented by U. S. ground troops . . . ."

How many U. S. soldiers would be needed? "Perhaps 200,000 to 1 million Americans would be fighting in Vietnam."

"Vietnam," Mr. Baldwin concluded, "is a nasty place to fight. But there is no neat and tidy battlefield in the struggle for freedom; there is no 'good' place to die. And it is far better to fight in Vietnam—on China's doorstep—than fight some years hence in Hawaii, on our own doorsteps."

Earlier in his article, in discussing the possibility of China's retaliation against United States escalation by entry into the war, Mr. Baldwin had stated:

" . . . China itself, with an obsolete air force and minimal naval power, could not defend itself effectively against a determined air and sea attack."

In his article, Mr. Baldwin did not explain how with such an "obsolete air force and minimal naval power" China could wage war against the United States on the shores of Hawaii.

Four days later—on February 28, 1965—in a low key announcement from Saigon—not Washington—United States and South Vietnamese officials signalled the next stage of United States escalation of its military involvement in Vietnam by announcing that President Johnson had decided to open continuous, limited air strikes against North Vietnam "in order to bring about a negotiated settlement." The retaliatory air strike stage of escalation was past. The announcement came out of Saigon on a Sunday.

The day before, at a hastily called Saturday morning press briefing, the State Department had handed the assembled reporters a white paper entitled "Aggression From the North: The Record of North Viet-Nam's Campaign to Conquer South Viet-Nam."

A copy of that white paper is set forth in the Appendix together with an excellent analysis by I. F. Stone, of its misleading statements and lack of candor.

In analyzing the white paper *The New Republic* for March 8, 1965, stated that;

> "The best that can be said about the State Department's white paper on Vietnam is that it is entirely unconvincing. The worst is that it is contradictory, illogical and misleading."

For example, the white paper cited the findings of the International Control Commission in 1962 "that there was 'sufficient evidence to show beyond reasonable doubt' that North Vietnam had sent arms and men into South Vietnam to carry out subversion with the aim of overthrowing the legal Government there." Not one single word appears in the white paper referring to the findings by the International Control Commission, in the same report in 1962, that the United States had also violated the Geneva Accord by the introduction into South Vietnam of arms and armed services personnel. (See Appendix)

The white paper states that the majority of the infiltrators are from the North and cites 19 examples. Of these 19, "16 are South Vietnamese natives who were returning to their homeland, 1 is unidentified by place of birth, and only 2 are North Vietnamese."

"The second conclusion . . . is that war material from North Vietnam and its Communist bloc allies is pouring into the south . . . the long inventory of all Communist made weapons captured from Vietcong in an 18 month period . . . showed only 22 crew served weapons . . . and 155 small arms, hardly enough to equip one of the Vietcong companies . . . Before it became necessary to deny the existence of a civil war in South Vietnam, American military men admitted that about 80 percent of the Vietcong weapons were unwittingly supplied by the United States by loss, theft, or sale by enterprising South Vietnamese."[10]

But if the purpose in issuing the white paper was to still the steadily mounting voices of the critics of the United States policy of escalating its military involvement in Vietnam that purpose was not achieved.

Senator George McGovern, writing in *The Progressive* for March 1965 stated:

"I . . . am very much opposed to the policy . . . of extending the war to the North . .. Attacks on North Vietnam will not seriously weaken guerrilla fighters a thousand miles away, fighters who depend for 80 percent of their weapons on captured United States equipment and for food on a sympathetic local peasantry . . . Bombing North Vietnam is not calculated to reduce their [the guerrillas'] determination, but . . . would antagonize many other Asians . . . The only viable policy for the United States in Vietnam is negotiation and a political settlement."

On the very day—February 28, 1965—that the announcement was made in Saigon that the President of the United States had approved open, continuous, limited air strikes against North Vietnam, Drew Pearson, in his column in *The Washington Post* noted three fallacies in the United States position with respect to Vietnam:

First: "We contend that we are in South Vietnam at the request of the popular government to protect freedom. This is pure bunk. The government has changed so often that no one can keep track of whether Big Minh, Little Minh, or Minnie Mouse is in power."

Second: "We believe that the best way to stop Vietnamese

fighting is by retaliatory raids against the North. There are many indications that this also is pure bunk."

Third: "The United States has told our allies privately that we are ready to negotiate a settlement in Indochina but that we want to negotiate from strength. Unfortunately, the longer we remain in South Vietnam the more our strength deteriorates."

February 28, 1965, also saw the publication in *The New York Times* of an open letter to the President, signed by hundreds of academicians from many universities and colleges in New York, urging that he "seek a negotiated settlement by every possible means in order to create an independent neutralized government and to bring about the withdrawal of U.S. troops." The following day, March 1, 1965, another open letter to President Johnson appeared in *The New York Times* signed by hundreds of academicians from many leading East coast colleges and universities stating that "if we are not to widen the war beyond all conscience, as reasonable men we must initiate negotiations while there is still time." The years that followed were to witness many similar open letters to the President signed by persons in all walks of life. These will be commented on in detail at a later point.

Adding to the growing clamor for a beginning to negotiations for the settlement of the war in Vietnam, was a column in the *Long Island Press* for February 28, 1965, by Bob Considine, entitled "Why Not Negotiate in Vietnam?" in which he stated:

" . . . if we continue to support the insupportable chaos of Vietnam, we will lower the high regard our allies hold for us as sensible, hard-nosed realists . . . The peoples of Southeast Asia have been fighting Chinese of all ideological hues for several thousand years. They are not going to stop resisting them the day the ink dries on a negotiated peace . . . It's time to fish or cut bait, a time to halt not doing either, and to hell with face."

On March 8, 1965, Secretary General U Thant proposed a six nation preliminary conference on Vietnam. The nations to attend would be the U.S.S.R., Great Britain, France, Communist China, and North and South Vietnam. The next day, Secretary of State Rusk rejected the proposal until North Vietnam stopped its aggression against South Vietnam.

Commenting on this abrupt rejection of U Thant's proposal, *The New York Times,* in its leading editorial on March 10, 1965, stated.

"The words were hardly out of Secretary General Thant's mouth when the United States rejected his proposal . . . The State Department gave the same old reply. 'We still await some indication that the aggressors are prepared to talk about stopping the aggression,' it said, adding that 'Washington would require advance evidence that negotiations would produce an agreement acceptable to the United States in Vietnam.' In other words, the United States will negotiate if our terms are accepted before negotiations begin. So why negotiate?"

On March 15, 1965, seventeen so-called non-aligned nations, meeting in Belgrade, issued a statement expressing concern about the "aggravation of the situation in Vietnam and are convinced that it is the consequence of foreign intervention in various forms, including military intervention, which impedes the implementation of the Geneva Agreement in Vietnam." It should be noted that these nations spoke only of Vietnam—not South Vietnam or North Vietnam.

"We are firmly convinced," the statement continued, "the only way leading to the termination of the conflict consists in seeking a peaceful solution through negotiations. We therefore make an urgent appeal to the parties concerned to start such negotiations, as soon as possible, without posing any preconditions, so that a political solution to the problem of Vietnam may be found in accordance with the legitimate aspirations of the Vietnamese people."

The so-called non-aligned countries signing the declaration were Afghanistan, Algeria, Cyprus, Ceylon, Ethiopia, Ghana, Guinea, India, Iraq, Kenya, Nepal, Syria, Tunisia, United Arab Republic, Yugoslavia, Zambia, and Uganda.

The declaration was handed to Secretary of State Rusk for delivery to President Johnson on April 1, 1965. On the same day it was handed to the Secretary General of the United Nations, and to the Governments of Canada, Mainland China, France, Poland, the U.S.S.R., the United Kingdom, the Republic of Vietnam, North Vietnam, and the National Front for the Liberation of South Vietnam.

Earlier—on March 24, 1965—the first "teach-in" protesting the United States involvement in the war in Vietnam had been held on the campus of the University of Michigan—setting a pattern for similar teach-ins in colleges and universities from coast to coast. The rise and development of this unique form of public protest will be discussed at greater length later. It did add to the growing sentiment that the United States agree to unconditional negotiations to end its involvement in the Vietnam conflict.

On April 2, 1965—the day after the receipt of the declaration by the 17 non-aligned nations—the Administration announced that it intended to send several thousand additional troops to Vietnam.

However all during this period efforts were made by the Administration to win over to its side the ever-growing voices of dissent. Senators and Congressmen, and their principal assistants, were invited in groups to the White House for so-called briefings. These were not, as one might suppose, free flowing "give and take" discussions between the Members of Congress and their advisers, and the President and his advisers. Instead, those assembled were "talked at" by the President, Secretary of State Rusk, Secretary of Defense McNamara and any other advisers of the President who happened to be there.

Many in the President's audience were irked by his habit of taking a copy of the Southeast Asia Resolution from his pocket, waving it in the air and telling the assemblage that he had been given authority to do what he was doing in Vietnam by the Congress by an overwhelming vote.

Many recalled that in the closing moments of debate on the Southeast Asia Resolution, Senator Gaylord Nelson of Wisconsin had indicated that he was inclined to offer an amendment which would have limited the effect of the Resolution. His amendment would have read in part:

"Our continuing policy is to limit our role to the provision of aid, training assistance, and military advice, and it is the sense of Congress that, except when provoked to a greater response, we should continue to attempt to avoid a direct military involvement in the Southeast Asia conflict."

Senator Nelson's amendment was not accepted because it would mean that the Senate-passed version of the Resolution would differ from that passed by the House, thus necessitating a conference. Senator Fulbright, Chairman of the Foreign Relations Committee and Floor Manager of the Resolution in the Senate, informed Senator Nelson at the time that: "I do not at all disagree with the amendment as a general statement of policy."

And yet, in these briefings given members of Congress some six months after the passage of the Resolution, they were told that the Resolution gave the President boundless power (which in fact it did!).

In a further effort to win over his critics, President Johnson delivered a major policy address at Johns Hopkins University on the evening of April 7, 1965. The speech was in great measure a repetition of the White Paper issued on February 27, 1965. (See Appendix).

President Johnson did admit that "some of the people of South Vietnam are participating in an attack on their own government. But trained men and supplies, orders and arms, flow in a constant stream from North to South. This support is the heartbeat of the war."

"Our objective," President Johnson said at Johns Hopkins, "is the independence of South Vietnam and its freedom from attack . . . attacks on South Vietnam were stepped up . . . it became necessary for us to increase our response and to make attacks by air. This is not a change of purpose. It is a change in what we believe that purpose requires."

He stated that the escalation had been undertaken to slow down aggression, to increase the confidence of the "brave people of South Vietnam . . . and to convince the leaders of North Vietnam . . . we will not be defeated . . . we will not grow tired. We will not withdraw."

" . . . peace demands an independent South Vietnam," he continued, "securely guaranteed and able to shape its own relationship to all others—free from outside interference—tied to no alliance—a military base for no other country."

How to attain this peace?

"There may be many ways to this kind of peace: in discussion or negotiation with the governments concerned; in large groups or in small ones; in the reaffirmation of old agreements or their strengthening with new ones . . . . And we remain ready with this purpose for unconditional discussions."

Then President Johnson went on to propose a huge, $1 billion economic development program for the countries of Southeast Asia. He called upon the Secretary General of the United Nations to "use the prestige of his great office and his deep knowledge of Asia to initiate, as soon as possible, with the countries of that area, a plan for cooperation in increased development."

He announced that he was naming a team of outstanding experts to inaugurate United States participation in the program, naming Eugene Black, former president of the World Bank, to head that team. The use of the words "unconditional discussions" in the Johns Hopkins speech seemed, without further analysis, to be a major concession to those of President Johnson's critics who had, in increasing numbers, urged him to undertake negotiations to end the war in Vietnam. But the speech contained two sleepers.

In the first place, he stated that one of the ways to peace could be in "discussion or negotiation with the *governments* concerned." (Emphasis supplied) Since, under the United States' version of "aggression from the north" the fighting in the south was all directed from the north, the National Liberation Front would not be considered a government and the United States, therefore, was not prepared to enter into discussions or negotiations with it.

In the second place, the only thing that President Johnson promised was that the "discussions" would be unconditional, not the negotiations. And it should be noted that in the language President Johnson used in his speech a careful distinction was made between "discussion" and "negotiation."

Commenting on the President's speech on the Floor of the Senate the next day, Senator Morse stated:

" . . .nothing in the President's speech . . . suggests to me he has any negotiations in mind at all. There was a lot of lip service paid to the theory of peace, grandiose utopian verbiage was plentiful, and the dollar sign was liberally displayed . . . the enemy the United States must deal with if there are to be any real peace negotiations for South Vietnam are the rebels within South Vietnam. They control much of the territory and much of the population of the south . . . We will not have any real negotiations until we talk to the people we are fighting . . . ."

Senator Gruening similarly pointed out, in commenting on the President's speech:

"The refusal to concede that the fighting in South Vietnam is essentially a civil war and that to bring that fighting to a halt it is necessary to discuss the issues with the principles—the Vietcong—is tantamount to retaining a pre-condition to our willingness to negotiate. In addition, our continued bombing of North Vietnam is not conducive to bringing about peace in Vietnam— it is asking North Vietnam to parley with a gun at its head."

Curiously, when President Johnson replied to the declaration by the 17 non-aligned nations on April 8, 1965, a subtle condition was inserted on how peace could be attained.

" . . . peace can be achieved in Southeast Asia," the reply stated, "the moment that aggression from North Vietnam is eliminated." What is that aggression? "It has meant the training and infiltration of agents and armed forces—the procurement and supply of munitions . . . When these things stop and the obstacles to security and stability are removed, the need for American supporting action will also come to an end. And when conditions have been created in which the people of South Vietnam can determine their own future free from external interference, the United States will be ready and eager to withdraw its forces from South Vietnam."

An analysis of this statement will show that in effect the United States was asking for the unconditional surrender not only of the North Vietnamese but of the Vietcong as well. This statement should be read in the light of the United States' reiterated contention that the support of Hanoi for the fighting in the South "is the heartbeat of the war." Under this concept, to ask Hanoi to discontinue to supply not only the Vietcong but its own troops in the South was thus asking for Hanoi to abandon both its troops and the Vietcong or to withdraw its troops and to abandon the Vietcong as a pre-condition for peace.

Apparently in May of 1965, contemplating a further increase in ground troops in South Vietnam—which he was to order on July 28, 1965—the President, on May 4, 1965, sent a message to the Congress requesting an authorization of $700 million solely to prosecute the war in Vietnam for the remaining month and one-half of the fiscal year 1965, which would end on June 30, 1965. On an annual basis, that would be tantamount to an increase of $5.6 billion to prosecute the Vietnam war.

But in requesting the authorization, which the Administration admitted was not really needed at the time, the President stated he really wanted an additional approval, by the Congress, of his war efforts.

His message stated:

"This is not a routine appropriation. For each Member of Congress who supports this request is also voting to persist in our effort to halt Communist aggression in South Vietnam. Each is saying that the Congress and the President stand united before the world in joint determination that the independence of South Vietnam shall be preserved and Communist attack will not succeed."

CHAPTER XXVI

CONGRESS ABDICATES

"I am a Congressional man," said Senator Richard Russell (D., Ga.) on the Senate Floor on March 1, 1966, during the consideration of a supplemental authorization of funds for escalating the war in Vietnam. "I have stood here for more than 30 years," he continued, "and deplored—almost wept over—the slow erosion of Congressional power that has placed this body in a position inferior to the other branches of the Government. The whole genius of our Government was to provide three coequal branches—legislative, executive, and judicial."[1]

Congressional action—and inaction—with respect to the escalated involvement of the United States in Vietnam amply illustrates the truth of the words uttered by Senator Russell who, as Chairman of the Senate Armed Services Committee strongly warned, originally, against the United States becoming involved in a land war in Southeast Asia. However, disregarding his own personal feelings with respect to the policies being pursued, he has done an exceedingly able job of securing the passage in the Senate of the legislation needed to support those policies.

As we have seen, the abdication of the Congress with respect to exercising an effective role in determining how deep United States involvement in South Vietnam would become was manifested first in its hasty passage of the Gulf of Tonkin resolution.

The second manifestation of abdication of its responsibilities by Congress was with respect to the request by the President for an added appropriation of $700 million to prosecute the war in Vietnam. That request was made on May 4, 1965.

Just a few days before—on April 26, 1965—Secretary of Defense McNamara had told his press conference:

" . . . the current . . . strikes against North Vietnam have been designed to impede this infiltration of men and materiel, an infiltration which makes the difference between a situation which is manageable and one which is not manageable internally by the Government of South Vietnam."

In answer to reporters' questions, Secretary McNamara stated:

"We don't have plans to increase procurement above the previously established levels . . . the cost of the U. S. forces operating in the waters of South Vietnam and in the air and the cost of our advisory and logistical support, is running on the order of $800 million a year."

That McNamara was correct and that he did not intend to step up procurement was concurred in by the House Appropriations Committee in its report on the resolution appropriating the $700 million requested by the President. The Committee stated:

"Sections 512 and 536 of the Defense Appropriation Act, 1965, contain language which has been carried in the bill for several years making certain additional funding immediately available without further action by the Congress.

"The authorities in existing law could have been utilized in lieu of the proposed appropriation."

Thus, as the President had told Congressional leaders in the East Room of the White House before making the request to the Congress, it was not money the President wanted, it was, rather, Congressional approval for what he had done, and for what he might decide to do.

The day after the request was made to the Congress, and after a short, hasty meeting of the House Appropriations Committee, the House of Representatives debated the resolution making the $700 million appropriation, under a restriction limiting all debate on the measure to one hour. The resolution passed by a vote of 408-7.[2]

Voting against the resolution in the House of Representatives were: Representatives George E. Brown, Jr. (D.-Calif.); Philip Burton (D.-Calif.); John J. Conyers (D.-Mich.); John G. Dow (D.-N.Y.); Don Edwards (D.-Calif.); Edith Green (D.-Ore.); and, William Fitts Ryan (D.-N.Y.).

Presenting the Administration's case for the resolution in the House was Representative George H. Mahon (D.-Texas), Chairman of the House Appropriations Committee. He told how the members of the House Committees on Foreign Affairs, on Armed Services and Appropriations had been called to the White House on Sunday evening, May 2, 1965, "for the purpose of discussing the situation with them."

"I must point out," he continued, "that, by the transfer of funds and within the framework of existing law, the President could have met this emergency without the action we will take today . . . I do not believe this action to be necessary to show that Congress is behind the President in his determination to follow a firm policy in dealing with Communist aggression. The President and the country already know it. This will simply reaffirm our position established on August 10, 1964, when the last Congress passed a resolution [Tonkin Gulf Resolution] placing itself squarely on record in favor of a firm policy in Southeast Asia."

As he concluded his remarks, Representative Mahon said that "by providing these funds and participating in this action we shall set a good example of democracy at work."!

Many Representatives who voted against the resolution also spoke against it.

However, there were also some who voted for the resolution, while expressing openly their doubts about the course being pursued in Vietnam.

Thus, Representative John V. Lindsay (R.-N.Y.)—later Mayor of the City of New York—voted in favor of the resolution but explained that he did so only because "the President has requested us to present a united front to the world on our involvement in Vietnam."

However, he warned that his vote "was not to be construed as an approval of the administration's whole policy in Vietnam; nor does it imply the endorsement of a blank check for the unexamined spending of more and more millions, the unilateral commitment of more and more of our Armed Forces and the expansion of the ground and air conflict into a major war, without allies and without the exercise of great diplomacy."

How many other Representatives voted in favor of the resolution appropriating $700 million to escalate the war in Vietnam with similar doubts and misgivings cannot, of course, be ascertained.

When the same resolution was debated in the Senate on the 5th and 6th of March, 1965, many of the same doubts and criticisms were heard—but the vote in approving the resolution was still lopsided—88 to 3 in favor of the resolution.

It is important to recall that the debates in both the House and the Senate took place in the shadows of events taking place much closer to the shores of the United States—in the Dominican Republic —to which, on the night of Wednesday, April 28, 1965, President Johnson had sent 20,000 United States marines on the ground that they were necessary to prevent a Communist take-over of the coup which had begun there the previous Saturday.

The marines were sent into the Dominican Republic on Wednesday night, April 28, 1965. On the following Sunday evening, May 2, 1965, President Johnson summoned Congressional leaders to the White House and informed them he wanted the $700 million Vietnam supplemental appropriation passed as a matter of great urgency to show the world that at least on Vietnam—however much grumbling there might be about his Dominican Republic intervention—the Congress was behind the President. By Thursday afternoon, May 6, 1965, the appropriation resolution had passed both houses of Congress.

It is of course difficult to tell the extent to which the Johnson Administration at that time felt it needed the expression of Congressional approval it would obtain by the passage of the Vietnam $700 million supplemental appropriation as an offset to its Dominican Republic intervention or needed it to lay a basis for its ground troop escalation of the war in Vietnam two and one-half months later.

In any event, on the morning of May 6, 1965—the day on which the appropriation resolution was to be voted on in the Senate—in its leading editorial entitled: "The Illusion of Omnipotence," *The New York Times* stated:

"... the Johnson doctrine means that the emphasis is now going to be on resisting the advance of Communism anywhere in the world with military force rather than on differentiating between various kinds of Communism or trying to coexist with any of them. The United States gives the appearance of heading toward the unenviable, self-righteous and self-defeating position of world policeman."

During the debates in the Senate on May 5 and 6, 1965, the admitted lack of need for the funds requested was pointed out repeatedly, as was the fact that the appropriation resolution was being used by the Johnson Administration to secure Congressional approval for its past and future policies in Vietnam.

Senator Nelson noted that "a very substantial number of this body is gravely troubled by the unseemly haste of our action here today . . . My dissent is based upon the conviction that when a matter of this import is before us we owe it to ourselves and the Nation to discuss it deliberately and fully. There is a continuing public confusion about where we are going and why."

"What is at issue right now," Senator Nelson continued, "is the wisdom of acting within hours upon this requested appropriation— acting without printed hearings and with precious little discussion— acting posthaste, not because this money is required immediately, but rather this precipitous action is supposed to demonstrate our support for the President's conduct of foreign affairs as well as our unity of purpose in opposing Communist aggression . . . at a time in history when the Senate should be vindicating its historic reputation as the greatest deliberative body in the world we are stumbling over each other to see who can say 'yea' the quickest and the loudest. I regret it, and I think some day we shall all regret it."

Announcing that he would vote against the appropriation resolution, Senator Nelson concluded by noting that "obviously you need my vote less than I need my conscience."[3]

"The speed with which this request was . . . brought to the floor," said Senator Joseph Clark (D.-Penna.), "under a time limitation which limits debate to 5 hours, makes the determination of this serious judgment question much more difficult." Senator Clark reviewed at length how the United States had become involved militarily in Vietnam. He pointed to three myths and three realities with respect to the conflict there.

"Myth No. 1 is that we have a mission to conduct a holy war against godless Communism . . .

"Reality No 1 is that holy wars . . . have never succeeded in the past, are not likely to succeed in the present, and will not succeed in the future . . .

"The second myth is that to have a pro-Western South Vietnam is essential to our national security . . .

"The second reality is that the United States has no business getting sucked into a ground war on the land mass of Asia . . .

"The third myth is that military solutions to political problems are likely to succeed in the world of today . . .

"The third reality is that the best hope for achieving a just and lasting peace lies in an earnest effort, painstakingly pursued by the diplomats of all countries, to settle the differences between the nation-states they represent without recourse to war."

Senator Clark's conclusion was that "the passage of this appropriation for use of our military forces in Vietnam will do nothing to upgrade, streamline, and modernize our foreign policy. It is all too likely to do just the opposite."

However, Senator Clark announced that "with great reluctance and a heavy heart I have concluded to vote for the pending appropriation."[4]

Senator Robert Kennedy (D.-N.Y.) announced that he would vote in favor of the appropriation resolution. "I do so," he said, "in the understanding that, as Senator Stennis (D.-Miss.) said yesterday: 'It is not a blank check . . . We are backing up our men and also backing up the present policy of the President. If he substantially enlarges or changes it, I would assume he would come back to us in one way or another."

Both Senators Morse and Gruening spoke at length against the appropriation resolution, both pointing out that it was not the money that President Johnson wanted but an endorsement of his past policies in Vietnam and authority to escalate further.

"This requested appropriation," Senator Gruening said, "coupled with the President's message, is in fact tantamount to giving the President a blank check . . . We should resent being dragged around like a dog on a leash and given 48 hours to pass bills with which the administration seeks to gird up its shaky policies and which admittedly are not needed at this time . . . By this message the President has

sought to give the clear impression that a vote against this appropriation is a vote in aid of Communism. This implication is totally unwarranted. It should be resented by every Member of Congress . . .
I yield to no one in the intensity of my opposition to the International
Communist conspiracy and in my determination to do what I can to
defeat that conspiracy . . ."[5]

"Last August," Senator Morse reminded the Senate, "many
Senators . . . [explained] . . . that their votes for the [Tonkin
Gulf] resolution should not be construed to support an expansion
of the war, or of bombing North Vietnam, or of U.S. troops fighting in Asia. Within 8 months, all those things had come to pass, and
the administration needed only to cite the Vietnam resolution as
the source of its authority to expand the war in any way it saw
fit."

"It is only votes that are binding upon the Pentagon or the White
House, not the opinions of Senators," Senator Morse pointed out.
"Let me say to the Senators who claim that they intend to be consulted again before there is another escalation of the war: 'You are
being consulted right now.' This is the President's consultation. When
the President has this consultation under his belt, he is going to
announce the landings of thousands more of American troops in
Vietnam. When he starts sending those hundreds of thousands of
troops into Asia, the moment that the Chinese start moving on the
ground—that is exactly a part of the war plans—he will cite the
pending joint resolution and the resolution of last August which
give him that authority."[6]

Nevertheless, the joint resolution appropriating an additional
$700 million for prosecuting the war in Vietnam was passed on May
6, 1965, by a vote of 88 to 3, with only Senators Morse, Nelson,
and Gruening voting against it.

On July 28, 1965, in a nationally televised press conference,
President Johnson announced:

"I have today ordered to Vietnam the Air Mobile Division
and certain other forces which will raise our fighting strength
from 75,000 to 125,000 almost immediately. Additional forces
will be needed later, and they will be sent as requested. This
will make it necessary to increase our active fighting forces by
raising the monthly draft call from 17,000 over a period of

time to 35,000 monthly, and for us to step up our campaign for voluntary enlistments."

At that same press conference, President Johnson annouced that he had "directed Ambassador [to the United Nations] Goldberg to go to New York today and to present immediately to Secretary General U Thant a letter from me requesting that all of the resources, energy, and immense prestige of the United Nations be employed to find ways to halt aggression and to bring peace to Vietnam." Ironically, Ambassador Goldberg had been sworn in as Ambassador only two days before.

Reporters Rowland Evans and Robert Novak report that the night before he was to make the announcement to the American people of the escalation, President Johnson summoned Congressional leaders to the White House for a briefing. According to them, Senate Majority Leader Mike Mansfield took out "a three page typed statement and read it in full . . . While promising Johnson to stand behind him *publicly* on the large reinforcements to be sent to Vietnam, Mansfield made it clear he was privately opposed to it and just about everything else the United States had done in Vietnam since Diem's murder, particularly the bombing in the North."[7]

Thus President Johnson, with the Congressional appropriation resolution, approving his policies, safely in his pocket, to buttress the power previously given him by the Tonkin Bay resolution, went ahead to escalate the United States involvement in a massive land war in Southeast Asia. The reservations expressed in the House and in the Senate were but words—the President had his resolutions and felt free to act. As Senator Morse had said, the Pentagon and the White House recognized votes—not words.

Thus the Congress had abdicated its power to deescalate the war in Vietnam for the second time.

CHAPTER XXVII

U. S. "PEACE OFFENSIVES"

In the months following the Pleiku incident in the early days of February, 1965, the intensity and type of bombing raids against North Vietnam had undergone a significant change.

At first these raids were supposed to be in retaliation for specific incidents; then to interdict vital communication links to South Vietnam; and then to destroy the military potential of North Vietnam and drive it to the negotiating table.

The mass protests, the teach-ins and the open letters to the President printed in newspapers around the country used the bombings against North Vietnam as the focal point of the vocal and written protests. Many could not accept the Administration's simple explanation of what was happening in South Vietnam as "Aggression from the North." Given the more factual explanation that an indigenous civil war was taking place in South Vietnam with the Vietcong being aided by North Vietnam, they reasoned that bombing North Vietnam would not affect the will of the Vietcong to fight on.

It was also obvious that, even assuming the Administration's thesis that the heart, the mind, and the will of the Vietcong resided in Hanoi, bombing North Vietnam was bound to stiffen the determination of the North Vietnamese to resist, for to agree to negotiate while being bombed would be an admission to the world that North Vietnam was negotiating out of fear and weakness.

A widely publicized national teach-in was scheduled for May 15, 1965, in Washington, D.C. One of the central themes of the teach-in would be that the bombings of North Vietnam should be stopped.

On May 13, 1965 the bombings of North Vietnam were stopped. This was announced in Washington on May 15, 1965—the very day of the teach-in. The reason for stopping the bombing was given as "operational."

It was announced that the bombing pause would be continued "into next week." The bombings were resumed on May 19, 1965.

Not until December 10, 1965—seven months later—was it revealed that Secretary of State Rusk had sent a secret note to the Government of North Vietnam announcing the bombing pause. The world learned of the text of the note from the Hanoi radio which broadcast its full text. In printing the text of the note as an "Exclusive" in I. F. Stone's Weekly for December 20, 1965 enterprising editor I. F. Stone headed the column: "How to Make a Peace Note Sound as Offensive and Unacceptable as Possible."

The letter to Hanoi from Secretary of State Rusk announced there would be "no air attacks on North Vietnam for a period beginning . . . 12 May [13 May Saigon time] and running into next week . . . the U. S. Government has taken account of repeated suggestions . . . that there can be no progress toward peace while there are air attacks on North Vietnam. The U. S. Government remains convinced that the underlying cause of trouble in Southeast Asia is armed action against the people and Government of South Vietnam by forces whose actions can be decisively affected from North Vietnam. The United States will be very watchful to see whether in such period there are significant reductions in such armed actions by such forces . . . the end of armed attacks against the people and Government of Vietnam is the only road . . . to bring a permanent end to . . . air attacks on North Vietnam . . . if this pause should be misunderstood . . . [as an indication of weakness] . . . by any party, it would be necessary to demonstrate more clearly than ever . . . that the United States is determind not to accept aggression without reply in Vietnam . . . But my Government is very hopeful that there will be no such misunderstanding and that this first pause in air attacks will meet with a response . . ."

In commenting, Hanoi radio called the letter "an ultimatum to the Vietnamese people, urging the South Vietnamese to abandon their patriotic struggle as a condition for a halt in the bombing of [North Vietnam] . . . Who gives the U. S. the right to bomb, stop bombing, then resume bombing . . . Who gives them the right to invade South Vietnam, massacre the South Vietnam people, then to urge them to lay down their arms . . . otherwise they should bomb the north more intensively . . . Who gives the U.S. the right to urge the North Vietnamese people [to] . . . let the aggressors freely massacre their kith and kin in the South?"

After the July 28, 1965, escalation announcement, United States forces in Vietnam increased rapidly. At the end of 1964, United States forces in Vietnam totalled 23,000 men. When President Johnson announced the increase in fighting men being sent to Vietnam on July 28, 1965, there were 75,000 men in Vietnam. By the end of 1965, that total had increased to over 165,000.

In 1964 the United States' losses in Vietnam were 146 killed and 1,038 wounded.

In 1965 the United States' losses in Vietnam were 1,365 killed and 6,110 wounded.

Many Free World leaders, noting the huge outpourings of United States fighting men and war materials into South Vietnam, were fearful that the course of action on which the United States had embarked would lead—unless the United States could somehow be deterred from following it to its logical conclusion—to a nuclear world war. In viewing the situation, these leaders were not bound by previous decisions or misconceptions—they had no face to save, no error to confess, no "Aggression from the North" to rewrite.

From July 28, 1965, even as the escalation of United States' bombing of North Vietnam intensfied and the buildup of United States' troops in South Vietnam increased, without any discernable limit on either, many more voices in the United States and abroad were raised in an insistent clamor that the United States should negotiate an end to its military involvement in Vietnam. There were teach-ins, marches, and open letters to the President to halt the bombings.

Adding his voice to those of U Thant, Secretary General of the United Nations, and of Charles de Gaulle, President of France, on October 4, 1965, in a dramatic, unprecedented and moving scene, Pope Paul VI flew to New York to appear before the General Assembly of the United Nations to make an eloquent plea for peace in Vietnam.

Also during the fall of 1965, a "series of forced disclosures of rejected opportunities for peace talks added emphasis to increasing domestic pressures for negotiations."[1]

An excellent account of the peace efforts by all parties to the Vietnam war is set forth in "The Politics of Escalation" by Franz Schurman, Peter Dale Scott, and Reginald Zelnick.

It will be recalled that the November 30, 1965, issue of *Look* magazine carried the report by Eric Sevareid concerning the peace feeler from Hanoi that lay dormant during the Presidential elections of 1964 and was then rejected.[2]

A similar incident took place during November and December, 1965. On November 20, 1965, a letter was sent to President Johnson by Amintore Fanfani, Foreign Minister of Italy, that on Thursday, November 11, 1965, in Hanoi "Ho Chi Minh and the President of the Council, Van Dong, expressed to two persons (known to me) the strong desire to find a peaceful solution to the conflict in Vietnam."

The letter continued that in order for peace negotiations to come about there would have to be a cease fire in all of Vietnam, meaning the cessation of all belligerent operations including the cessation of debarkation of further American troops; "a declaration according to which the Geneva Agreements of 1954 will be taken as the basis for the negotiations"—a declaration made up of the four points formulated by Hanoi, "points that are in reality the explanaion of the Geneva text and which, therefore, can be reduced to a single point: application . . . of the Geneva Accords."

The Foreign Minister then went on to say that according to the report he had received "the government in Hanoi is prepared to initiate negotiations without first requiring actual withdrawal of the American troops."

Secretary of State Rusk did not reply to the letter from the Italian Foreign Minister until December 4, 1965. The reply was received by Mr. Fanfani in New York on December 6, 1965, although its contents had been communicated to him on November 29, 1965.

Ho Chi Minh's four points may be summarized as follows:

"(1) Recognition of the basic national rights of the Vietnamese people . . . U. S. Government must withdraw from South Vietnam all U. S. troops . . . dismantle all U. S. military bases there, cancel its 'military alliance' with South Vietnam. It must end its policy of intervention and aggression in South Vietnam. . . . the U. S. Government must stop its acts of war against North Vietnam . . . .

"(2) Pending the peaceful reunification of Vietnam, while Vietnam is still temporarily divided into two zones . . . the two zones must refrain from joining any military alliance . . . no foreign military bases, troops and military personnel in their respective territories.

"(3) The internal affairs of South Vietnam must be settled by the South Vietnamese people themselves, in accordance with the program of the South Vietnam National Front for Liberation, without any foreign interference.

"(4) The peaceful reunification of Vietnam is to be settled by the Vietnamese people in both zones themselves, without any foreign interference."

In his reply, Secretary of State Rusk noted that the four points were not exactly in accord with the Geneva Accords, since the reunification elections according to those Accords were to be supervised by the International Control Commission. "Nevertheless," Secretary of State Rusk repled to Fanfani, "we are prepared to include these four points for consideration in any peace talks along with any proposals which the United States, South Vietnam, and other governments may wish to advance." He did also point out that if "there were a cessation of certain military activities on the one side, there would have to be an equivalent cessation of military activities on the other."

A New York lawyer, Peter Weiss, who interviewed the Italian go-between, Professor La Pira, had forwarded a long memorandum to Ambassador Arthur Goldberg that "Ho would not enter peace negotiations with the U. S. if the Hanoi-Haiphong area were bombed."

On December 15, 1965—two days after Foreign Minister Fanfani informed Secretary of State Rusk that he was of the opinion that the Rusk reply had been delivered in Hanoi that day (December 13, 1965)—United States "planes bombed the Haiphong area for the first time, destroying a power station at Uong Bi, fourteen miles outside of Haiphong."

On December 18, 1965, reports out of Hanoi called stories of Hanoi's peace feelers "sheer groundless fabrications."[3]

The negotiations which President Johnson conducted from December 24, 1965, to January 31, 1966, in "search of peace" were negotiations conducted under the searchlight of publicity. No doubt was left in anyone's mind that President Johnson had sent his emissaries to the far corners of the world seeking peace. The comings and goings of the Johnson Peace Ambassadors were trumpeted throughout the world.

However, what was not trumpeted were the terms on which President Johnson would agree to a cessation of hostilities in Vietnam.

As Evans and Novak described this era:

" . . . on December 29, [1965], on notice of only a few hours, he [President Johnson] dispatched his emissaries around the world to talk peace, stage managing the leading actors and their itineraries himself with just enough secrecy to give the whole enterprise the aura of international intrigue. This was the kind of theatre that Johnson gloried in. With foreign heads of government part of his cast and the whole world watching the drama unfold, the great peace offensive of 1965 was a thrilling challenge, activated by the full power of the presidency.

"One by one, his special ambassadors were propelled to the four corners of the globe."[4]

Even while President Johnson's emmisaries were "country hopping" in what turned out to be a fruitless quest for "peace," the Department of State, on January 7, 1966, issued a list of fourteen elements which, it said, could go into peace making in Southeast Asia:

"1. The Geneva Agreements of 1954 and 1962 are an adequate basis for peace in Southeast Asia;

"2. We would welcome a conference on Southeast Asia or on any part thereof;

"3. We would welcome 'negotiations without preconditions' as the 17 nations put it;

"4. We would welcome unconditional discussions as President Johnson put it;

"5. A cessation of hostilities could be the first order of business at a conference or could be the subject of preliminary discussions;

"6. Hanoi's four points could be discussed along with other points which others might wish to propose;

"7. We want no U. S. bases in Southeast Asia;

"8. We do not desire to retain U. S. troops in Southeast Asia;

"9. We support free elections in South Vietnam to give the South Vietnamese a government of their own choice;

"10. The question of reunification of Vietnam should be determined by the Vietnamese through their own free decision;

"11. The countries of Southeast Asia can be non-aligned or neutral if that be their option;

"12. We would much prefer to use our resources for the economic reconstruction of Southeast Asia than in war. If there is peace, North Vietnam could participate in a regional effort to which we would be prepared to contribute at least $1 billion;

"13. The President has said: 'The Vietcong would not have difficulty being represented and having their views represented if for a moment Hanoi decided she wanted to cease aggression. I don't think that would be an insurmountable problem.'

"14. We have said publicly and privately that we could stop the bombing of North Vietnam as a step toward peace although there has not been the slightest hint or suggestion from the other side as to what they would do if the bombing stopped."

Point No. 13 is the stock answer given by any Administration spokesman who is asked whether the Vietcong or the National Liberation Front would have a place at the conference table, on an equal footing with the other participants in the fighting in Vietnam, at any "unconditional discussions" or "negotiations without preconditions." A straight "yes" or "no" answer is not given. Instead the questioner is referred to the President's previous statement as though that statemen did in fact provide such a straightforward answer.

In reality, this circumlocution is meant to answer "no" while giving the impression that the answer is "yes". This is in accord with the Johnson Administration's theory of how the war in Vietnam began and how it has been carried on. It assumes that the National

Liberation Front is the creation of Hanoi and that it, as well as the Vietcong, are absolutely controlled by Hanoi. On that assumption if Hanoi is admitted to the conference, since Hanoi, according to the United States theories, is in fact the Vietcong and the National Liberation Front, then those two would, of course, be represented there.

This overlooks the large amount of South Vietnam territory and the large number of South Vietnamese people controlled by the Vietcong and the National Liberation Front.

Meanwhile the flurry of peace overtures by President Johnson throughout the world had caused uneasiness in Premier Ky's government in Saigon. On January 15, 1966, Secretary of State Rusk and United States Ambassador at large Averell Harriman met with Premier Ky in Saigon allegedly to allay South Vietnamese fears that U. S. peace efforts would be detrimental to the Saigon regime.

In the communique issued on January 16, 1966, by Prime Minister Nguyen Cao Ky and Secretary of State Dean Rusk, it was stated that South Vietnam reaffirmed "that peace in Vietnam must (A) accord with the pledges and desires of the Vietnamese people: an end to aggression; independence and liberty; in order to permit eventually unification of Vietnam; (B) be accompanied by guarantees in the absence of which there could be resumption of aggression which would endanger both Southeast Asia and the peace of the world."

Both parties agred that they "must continue to take all necessary military measures, while remaining alert to all proposals and initiatives that might lead to peace."

CHAPTER XXVIII

THE CONGRESS DISSENTS

The second session of the 89th Congress began in Washington on January 10, 1966, in the midst of a lull in the bombing of North Vietnam which had been going on since December 24, 1965, and in the midst of the most widely publicized "peace offensive" of the war.

The Congressmen and Senators had been "home" for about two and one-half months since the adjournment of the first session of the 89th Congress. They had met their constituents face to face—had heard their queries—had listened to their doubts about where the United States was heading in Southeast Asia. Members of Congress returned to Washington in a much more questioning mood than when they had left it in October after adjournment.

Also while in their home States they had read the news of Secretary of Defense McNamara's meeting with military leaders in Saigon on the 28th and 29th of November, 1965—that he thought "it would be a long war" and read from other sources that the military leaders were asking for an increase in United States forces to bring the total up to 350,000 or 400,000 men.

For the entire House of Representatives and for one-third of the Senate, this was an election year and the mood of the electorate was troubled.

On January 8, 1966, Senator Mike Mansfield (D.-Mont.) had filed with the Senate Foreign Relations Committee his report (See Appendix) entitled: "The Vietnam Conflict: The Substance and the Shadow."

The report's conclusions were that the introduction of large numbers of United States troops and huge quantities of military weapons and supplies, have "blunted but not turned back the drive of the Vietcong . . . [who] . . . have responded to the increased American role with a further strengthening of their forces by local recruitment in the south and reinforcements from the north."

Predicting that more United States' forces would be needed, the report stated that "if present trends continue, there is no assurance as to what ultimate increase in American military commitment will be required before the conflict is terminated." Because of the nature of the conflict, United States' commitment was "open ended," i.e., there was no stable number of Vietcong; as the United States increased its forces, the Vietcong force would be increased and it was as though caught on a rising escalator.

One point made by the report—especially in view of the urgings by many to escalate the bombings of North Vietnam—was that the Vietcong had the power to commit terrorist attacks in Saigon at will. "Indeed . . . Saigon with its many vulnerabilities to sabotage and terrorism and Hanoi with its exposure to air attack are mutual hostages, one for the other."

The truth and significance of this statement becomes abundantly evident as one walks through the streets of Saigon—as one of the authors of this volume did in May 1967—and realizes that the front in this guerrilla war is all around one and that the Vietnamese peasant, clad in black pajamas, approaching you rapidly along the sidewalk may just as easily as not be a Vietcong and that the package he carries may contain a plastic bomb. While one quickly adjusts and gives the idea no further thought, the potential is there. There can be no adequate protection against sabotage and acts of terrorism and Saigon is in fact hostage for Hanoi.

As much bemedaled Army Green Berets Sergeant, Donald Duncan described the war in Vietnam:

"This isn't like Korea . . . This is the first war I know of where a ground soldier can be in the middle of the blood,

stink, and death one minute and be in a cool bar drinking a
gin and tonic twenty minutes later."[1]

President Johnson, in his State of the Union message to the
Congress on January 12, 1966, broadcast to a nationwide audience, in
discussing the situation, echoed the grimness of the Mansfield report that "the days may become months, and the months may become years, but we will stay as long as aggression commands us to
battle . . . we just cannot know what the future may require. We
may have to face long, hard combat or a long, hard conference, or
even both at once."

On January 14, 1966, on the floor of the Senate, Senator Stephen
Young (D.-Ohio) reported to the Senate on his study trip to Saigon
where he had stayed from September 28, 1965 to October 20, 1965,
and concluded that "the conflict raging in Vietnam is a civil war."
He related that General Westmoreland had told him that the "bulk
of the Vietcong fighting in South Vietnam were born and reared in
South Vietnam." He said he knew that the President was being given
advice to bomb North Vietnam "back into the stone age" and urged
the President to resist such advice.[2]

More and more voices were being heard in the Congress and
in the press to continue the halt in the bombings of North Vietnam.

On January 19, 1966, President Johnson sent a message to the
Congress requesting $12.76 billion in supplemental funds primarily
for the war in Vietnam stating:

"In the last 2 years, in repeated acts of authorization and
appropriation, the Congress has provided continuing support for
our national decision 'to prevent further aggression' in Southeast Asia. The quoted words come from the joint resolution of
the Congress that was approved on August 10, 1964 [Tonkin
Gulf Resolution]. It is in the letter and the spirit of the resolution that I request this supplementary appropriation. While that
resolution remains in force, and until its obligations are discharged, we must persevere."[3]

This was the device President Johnson had used in the past,
obtaining approval from the Congress of his past and future actions
through a request for the approval of additional funds for the war
in Vietnam. Again, as will be shown, the hearings brought out that

the funds were not needed at that time but, as a prelude to the resumption of bombing of North Vietnam less than two weeks later, the Johnson Administration evidently felt that Congressional approval was needed.

But this time there was not to be "instant" Congressional approval as of the Tonkin Gulf Resolution in 1964 and of the $700 million appropriation resolution in 1965. Now President Johnson's request triggered a debate in the Senate from February 16, 1966, to March 1, 1966.

That debate—which was little reported in the press—was itself preceded by certain Congressional happenings on the basis of which the debate could have been predicted.

On January 21, 1966, 77 Democratic Members of Congress sent a carefully worded letter to the President expressing their support for President Johnson's efforts "to bring the war in Vietnam to the conference table. Specifically we applaud you for the moratorium on bombing North Vietnam." They suggested one further step: "that we formally request the United Nations to seek an effective cease fire and that we pledge our support and resources to such an effort." They expressed concern that "unless we can halt or reverse the escalation of the last months it will become increasingly difficult to achieve a further pause, a ceasefire and meaningful negotiations."

---

*Representatives Brock Adams (D.-Wash.), Joseph Addabbo (D.-N.Y.), Thomas Ashley (D.-Ohio), Jonathan Bingham (D.-N.Y.), John Blatnik (D.-Minn.), John Brademas (D.-Ind.), George E. Brown, Jr. (D.-Calif.), James Byrne (D.-Pa.), Ronald B. Cameron (D.-Calif.), Jeffery Cohelan (D.-Calif.), James Corman (D.-Calif.), Winfield Denton (D.-Ind.), John Dow (D.-N.Y.), Ken Dyal (D.-Calif.), Don Edwards (D.-Calif.), Leonard Farbstein (D.-N.Y.), Donald Fraser (D.-Minn.), Samuel Friedel (D.-Md.), Richard Fulton (D.-Tenn.), Robert Giaimo (D.-Conn.), Jacob Gilbert (D.-N.Y.), John Gilligan (D.-Ohio), Henry Gonzales (D.-Tex.), Bernard Grabowski (D.-Conn.), George W. Grider (D.-Tenn.), Martha Griffiths (D.-Mich.), Harlan Hagan (D.-Calif.), William Hathaway (D.-Maine), Augustus Hawkins (D.-Calif.), Ken Hechler (D.-W. Va.), Floyd Hicks (D.-Wash.), Chet Holifield (D.-Calif.), Elmer Holland (D.-Pa.), Harold Johnson (D.-Calif.), James Kee (D.-W. Va.), Paul Krebs (D.-N.J.), Robert Leggett (D.-Calif.), Clarence Long (D.-Md.), Rodney Love (D.-Ohio), Richard McCarthy (D.-N.Y.), Harris McDowell, Jr. (D.-Del.), James Mackay

The 77 legislators did not come out four-square for a continuation of the bombing pause. They hinted at it with the statement that they realized that "there were those who urge a resumption of bombing of North Vietnam and a premature abandonment of our peace efforts."

A communication from so large a segment of the members of his own party in the House of Representatives could not be ignored by President Johnson. He replied the very next day.

Referring to the suggestion by the 77 Congressmen for the utilization of the United Nations, President Johnson replied that he had reviewed the matter often with Ambassador Goldberg and that "he and I are firmly determined to make every possible use of the United Nations in moving toward peace, and toward an effective ceasefire as part of that purpose."[4]

As for the continuation of the pause in the bombing of North Vietnam, President Johnson reported that, all during the pause, the infiltration of the "aggressor's forces has continued and so have his attacks on our allies and on our own men . . . we have a heavy obligation not to add lightly to the dangers our troops must face."

President Johnson's reply of January 22, 1966, to the Congressmen's letter of the preceding day was lengthy and extremely cordial.

When he heard from fifteen members of the Senate five days later, on January 26, 1966, President Johnson's response was quite different.

Leadership in sending the Senatorial letter was taken by Senator Vance Hartke (D.-Ind.). On that day, January 26, 1966—in a mat-

---

*Continued from preceding page.
(D.-Ga.), John Mackie (D.-Mich.), Ray Madden (D.-Ind.), Lloyd Meeds (D.-Wash.), George P. Miller (D.-Calif.), William Moorhead (D.-Pa.), John Moss (D.-Calif.), Lucien Nedzi (D.-Mich.), Barratt O'Hara (D.-Ill.), James O'Hara (D.-Mich.), Alec Olson (D.-Minn.), John Race (D.-Wis.), Rolland Redlin (D.-N. Dak.), Thomas Rees (D.-Calif.), Henry Reuss (D.-Wis.), George Rhodes (D.-Pa.), Edward Roybal (D.-Calif.), William St. Onge (D.-Conn.), James Scheuer (D.-N.Y.), B. F. Sisk (D.-Calif.), Herbert Tenzer (D.-N.Y.), Paul Todd (D.-Mich.), John Tunney (D.-Calif.), Morris Udall (D.-Ariz.), Weston Vivian (D.-Mich.), Charles Weltner (D.-Ga.), Lester Wolff (D.-N.Y.), Frank Thompson, Jr. (D.-N.J.), Andrew Jacobs, Jr. (D.-Ind.), Benjamin S. Rosenthal (D.-N.Y.), Edward P. Boland (D.-Mass.), Joseph E. Karth (D.-Minn.).

ter of a few hours and without fanfare—Senator Hartke showed the draft letter to a number of his colleagues who agreed with its contents. By afternoon the letter to President Johnson had been signed by fourteen other Senators, in addition to Senator Hartke, and was on its way by messenger to the President.

The letter stated that the signers agreed with the recent statements of the Majority Leader, Senator Mike Mansfield; of the senior member of the Republican Party, Senator George Aiken (R.-Vt.), and of the Chairman of the Senate Committee on Foreign Relations, Senator Fulbright.

> "Senator Fulbright said . . . that he was opposed to the resumption of the bombing of North Vietnam by United States forces 'for the foreseeable future'; Senator Mansfield said that there should be an 'indefinite' suspension of these bombings; and Senator Aiken endorsed the foregoing views by stating, 'bombing should be suspended until it becomes perfectly clear that the Communist nations intend to fight the war to the finish.'
> " . . . *We believe you should have our collective judgment before you, when you make your decision.*"

In addition to Senator Hartke, the letter was signed by Senators E. L. (Bob) Bartlett (D., Alaska), Quentin Burdick (D., N. Dak.), Frank Church (D., Idaho), Joseph S. Clark (D., Pa.), Ernest Gruening (D., Alaska), Eugene McCarthy (D., Minn.), George McGovern (D., S. Dak.), Lee Metcalf (D., Mont.), Wayne Morse (D., Oreg.), Gaylord Nelson (D., Wis.), Maurine Neuberger (D., Oreg.), William Proxmire (D., Wis.), Harrison A. Williams, Jr. (D., N.J.), and Stephen Young (D., Ohio).

President Johnson's reply, sent to Senator Hartke on January 28, 1966, was curt.

After acknowledging receipt of the letter and expressing his thanks for "this expression of opinion," the President's letter stated:

> "I continue to be guided in these matters by the resolution of the Congress approved on August 10, 1964 . . . by a vote of 504 to 2. My views of the present situation remain as stated in my recent reply to a group of members of the House, of which I enclose a copy."

For many Senators who had signed the letter to the President, the curt reply was particularly galling because of the authority cited by President Johnson in justifying his actions.

Except for Senators Morse and Gruening, all the signatories of the letter had voted in favor of the Tonkin Gulf resolution.

At the time of its passage, Senator Nelson had sought in vain to amend it so as to restrict the powers seemingly granted to the President and to prevent him from doing exactly what he was doing—enlarging the war in Vietnam. Senator Nelson had been persuaded by Senator Fulbright, Chairman of the Foreign Relations Committee, not to press his amendment.

On the very day that the President replied to the Senatorial letter the Senate Foreign Relations Committee had begun a series of hearings on the Vietnam war—hearings which had nationwide press, radio and television coverage. This was an attempt by Senator Fulbright to go directly to the people and to apprize them of dissenting views on the Vietnam war.

Evans and Novak stated that in those days "the cloakrooms hummed with complaints and criticisms over the President's Vietnam policy. What had started in 1964 with the two-man opposition of Wayne Morse and Ernest Gruening and then grew to half a dozen or more in 1965, now had mushroomed to perhaps half the sixty-six Democratic Senators in 1966."

According to these reporters, the "outright opposition of the Hartkes and the McCarthys dramatized the harsh political fact that Johnson's problems had assumed a new and far more ominous dimension."[5]

President Johnson's second reply to this appeal by so many members of his own party in the Senate was to order the resumption of the bombing of North Vietnam on January 31, 1966.

At the same time he instructed the United States Ambassador to the United Nations, Arthur Goldberg, to write the Secretary General of that organization asking for an urgent meeting of the United Nations Security Council to consider the Vietnam situation.

The Security Council met the next day—February 1, 1966—and on February 2, 1966, voted to consider the Vietnam war. The vote was 9 in favor, two opposed (the Soviet Union and Bulgaria), with four abstentions (France, Mali, Nigeria, and Uganda). The United States has not taken the next step needed to have the matter acted upon by the Security Council. That next step would be to put the topic on the agenda of the next monthly meeting of the Security Council. Placing an item on the agenda of the Security Council requires only nine votes and, since it is a procedural action, is not subject to veto.

Thus, if a full scale debate on Vietnam in the Security Council of the United Nations is desired, the way lies open.

According to columnist Drew Pearson, writing in *The Washington Post* February 25, 1966, there were two reasons why the United States marched up the hill to the Security Council and marched right down again.

"Reason No. 1 was because Prime Minister Harold Wilson of England asked us to.

"Reason No. 2 was because the Russians, while not asking a postponement, made it diplomatically clear that it would put them in a better position with the Chinese."

According to Pearson, Wilson was going to Russia and thought he "could do some good with the Russians prior to any forensic slugging match in the Security Council." Having refused to accede to Wilson's request to hold up on the resumption of the bombings of North Vietnam, Pearson said, "it was decided that the United States could at least honor the [Wilson] request for debate postponement in the U. N."

Commenting on this United States move in the United Nations, Senator Morse on February 28, 1966, on the Floor of the Senate, pointed out that the United States "went to the United Nations with an olive branch in one hand and bombs in the other. Members of the United Nations are still talking about the bombs." Calling for an open debate of the matter by the Security Council, Senator Morse asked: "Could it be that we are not too enthusiastic about getting it out in the open?"[6]

The widely publicized hearings of the Senate Foreign Relations Committee which began a month earlier had been preceded on January 24, 1966, by a three hour, closed door session of the Committee with Secretary of State Rusk at which, it was reported, the Secretary opposed Chairman Fulbright's suggestion that the Vietcong be invited to peace talks before the resumption of the bombings of North Vietnam. With the approval of President Johnson, Secretary of Defense McNamara refused to appear publicly before the Committee on the grounds of security.

The Committee hearings did much to focus public attention on the underlying factors of United States involvement in the war in Vietnam and especially upon the proposal of Lieutenant General James M. Gavin for a method of United States de-escalation of its involvement. However, in terms of effectiveness in stopping the determination of the Johnson Administration to escalate the war in Vietnam the Committee hearings were no more productive than the letters of the 77 Members of Congress or the 15 Senators were in preventing the resumption of the bombing of North Vietnam. The debate in the Senate in the latter part of February on the authorization of supplemental funds to prosecute the war in Vietnam would prove to be just as ineffectual.

General James M. Gavin was due to testify before the Senate Foreign Relations Committee on Tuesday, February 8, 1966. On Friday afternoon, February 4, 1966, the White House announced that President Johnson was flying the next day to Honolulu for discussions with Premier Ky of South Vietnam and other South Vietnamese officials. At Honolulu on February 8, 1966, a Declaration of high-sounding purpose was issued jointly in the name of the Governments of South Vietnam and the United States. The Declaration made no mention of the eventual reunification of North and South Vietnam. In the Declaration, the Government of South Vietnam promised:

"(1) We must defeat the Viet Cong and those illegally fighting with them on our soil;

"(2) We are dedicated to the eradication of social injustice among our people;

"(3) We must establish and maintain a stable, viable economy and build a better material life for our people;

"(4) We must build true democracy for our land and for our people."

Ignoring the resumption of the bombing of North Vietnam the week before, General Ky pleaded with the Vietcong:

"Come safely to join us through the open arms program; Stop killing your brothers, sisters, their elders and their children; Come and work through constitutional democracy to build together that life of dignity, freedom, and peace those in the north would deny the people of Vietnam."

The United States pledged to help the people of Vietnam "to build while they fight . . . stabilize the economy—to increase the production of food—to spread the light of education—to stamp out diseases."

"Honolulu," Evans and Novak state, did not "achieve Johnson's purpose of drawing attention away from the Peace Block. The transparent effort to steal the headlines from the Fulbright hearings received almost as much attention, all of it adverse, as did the substance of the conference itself."

The Honolulu Conference did succeed in proclaiming Premier Ky as the "United States man in Saigon" just as much as Diem was given that stamp of approval throughout his reign. It would make Ky less cooperative in supporting United States demands for economic and social reforms.

In the welter of publicity flowing out of Honolulu, General Gavin's suggestions for the United States conduct of the war in Vietnam took second place and consequently did not have as much impact on the American people as it deserved.

General Gavin stated in part to the Senate Committee on Foreign Relations:

" . . . today we have sufficient forces in South Vietnam to hold areas along the coast, where sea and air power can be made fully effective, and then we can use this power as we see fit to do so . . . We must do the best we can with the forces we have deployed in Vietnam now . . . keeping in mind the true meaning of global strategy in world affairs today . . . tactical mistakes that are allowed to escalate at the initiative of an enemy could be disastrously costly . . . . We should maintain enclaves on the coast, desist in our bombing attacks on North Vietnam and seek to find a solution through the United Nations . . . . In the budget request figures for . . . fiscal year '67, we are going into $10.5 billion into Vietnam . . . . Is Vietnam at this point worth this investment of our national resources, with all the other commitments we have world wide?"

When former Ambassador to South Vietnam, General Maxwell D. Taylor appeared before the Senate Committee on Foreign Relations on February 17, 1966, he disagreed with General Gavin, saying such a course of action would sacrifice our troops' "unique attributes of mobility and fire power . . . would assign a most inglorious mission to our troops . . . effect of such behavior on our Vietnamese allies could be disastrous . . . destroy all confidence in Vietnam in ultimate success."

In a letter later released, General Mathew B. Ridgway told Chairman Fulbright he agreed with General Gavin.

When former Ambassador to the Soviet Union, George F. Kennan —the author of President Truman's containment doctrine in 1950— appeared before the Senate Committee on February 10, 1966, he was asked by Senator Lausche (D.-Ohio) what he proposed "that we do now to bring this to a settlement without damage to our prestige and without danger to our security."

Mr. Kennan proposed that the United States limit its aims and military commitment in that area, "that we decide what we can safely hold in that region with due regard to the security of our forces, that we dig in and wait and see whether possibiliites for a solution do not open up."

CHAPTER XXIX

THE CONGRESS DISSENTS—BUT CONSENTS

On February 16, 1966, a new front opened for the Congressional debates on United States Vietnam policies. On that day the Supplemental Appropriations authorization bill was made the Senate's pending business and, off and on until March 1, 1966, the subject would be discussed in the Senate away from the television cameras and with very little publicity.

The debate began on February 16 amid increased grumbling in both Republican and Democratic Senate cloakrooms as to where the Johnson Administration's policies were leading. In the ensuing debate these rumblings would spill onto the Senate floor.

To understate the situation, the televised hearings by the Senate Foreign Relations Committee had been extremely displeasing to the Johnson Administration which suddenly found new and powerful voices being given national forums to reach millions of people throughout the country and to question not only the Administration's policies but also the Administration's facts. Heretofore such nationwide coverage had been reserved for Presidential addresses and press conferences by the President, the Secretary of State, and the Secretary of Defense. No nationwide opportunity had been given to question the policies or the facts enunciated in those addresses and press conferences.

Only two more days of hearings—February 17 and 18—were scheduled, when, on February 16, 1966, even before the Vietnam authorization bill had been made the pending business before the Senate, an attempt was made to stifle debate on the bill.

Senator Russell Long (D.-La.), a constant defender of the Administration's policies in Vietnam, took the Floor to denounce those who would voice dissent with the Administratioin's actions: "Those advocates of retreat, defeat, surrender and national dishonor," he said, "have not been doing the country any good when they went before a television network suggesting that this Nation was not committed to fighting aggression in this area. The Senate voted for the resolution last year . . . He [the President] was authorized to send troops wherever necessary to resist aggression . . . It is not helping our country when Senators go before the Nation and express their fears that the Red Chinese might come in and that we are losing American boys."[1]

Defending the televised hearings, Senator Gruening pointed out that "if the hearings continue to be televised, the American people may learn of the mistaken concept stated by our distinguished majority whip [Senator Long] that we have a solemn commitment. They will learn there was no such commitment . . ."

"I do not believe it is helpful," Senator Long then continued, "to go on national television and suggest that we are the international criminal when we are, in fact, the international good guys . . . Our children will call us blessed and courageous if we stand fast and defeat Communist aggression."

"It is easy for gentlemen," said Senator McGovern (D., S.D.), "to talk about our children calling us blessed if we get involved in war with China. But if that happens, there may not be any children left to call us blessed."

Senator Gruening pointed out to Senator Long that "Abraham Lincoln . . . opposed the entry of the United States in the Mexican War, spoke out against it in the Congress and elsewhere and today no one vilifies the memory of Abraham Lincoln or castigates him for that courageous and proper attitude."

Senator McGovern took exception to the suggestion that those Senators who were concerned about "a major war in Asia are somehow lacking in patriotism and willingness to defend our country's interest." Senator McGovern reminded his colleagues that General MacArthur had said that anyone who committed the United States to a major war on the Asian mainland "ought to have his head examined" and that in 1954, "during discussion of whether we should send forces into Southeast Asia . . . General Ridgway . . . vigorously opposed it and said that he regarded it as a harebrained idea."

"No one," Senator McGovern continued, "would be foolish enough to suggest that General MacArthur or General Gavin are lacking in patriotism or in knowledge of the problems we are up against if we get into a major war in Asia."

"The issue," said Senator Gore, (D., Tenn.), "is not 'defeat, retreat, surrender', as Senator Long had stated, but rather whether this war is to be held within bounds which we can reasonably anticipate to be manageable, whether the goal be limited and the commitments limited, or whether this be an open end commitment for total victory militarily against whatever forces may appear in opposition in Southeast Asia. The issue is rather whether this war is a global war."

"Statements have been made," Senator Gore stated, "that this debate would be an aid to the enemy . . . Debate is necessary for our democratic processes. A government conducted under such a system must be conducted in the main in public . . . I am pleased for those behind the Iron Curtain who may not be pleased with their lot to know that there is one place in the world where the most critical issues can be the subject of free debate."

Later in the day, in calling up the bill, Senator Richard Russell (D.-Ga.), Chairmen of the Senate Armed Services Committee and Floor Manager for the bill, sought to allay fears and head off what those in the cloakroms were predicting would be a debate in depth.

He had two objectives.

The first was speed. Neither he nor the Administration wanted protracted debate. Earlier in the day, Senator Vance Hartke had served notice that he would object to any request for unanimous consent to limit debate on the bill.

The second was to head off amendments seeking to dictate the policy on carrying on the war in Vietnam or to repeal the Tonkin Gulf Resolution.

"It is important" Senator Russell stated, "that the Senate and the Nation clearly recognize this bill for what it is: an authorization of defense appropriations. It could not properly be considered as determining foreign policy, as ratifying decisions made in the past, or as endorsing new commitments."

Then Senator Russell stated that "an unreasonable delay in approving this bill or a close vote on it is hardly the way to demonstrate appreciation for their [the Armed Forces in Vietnam] sacrifices in our behalf."

If an impasse arose between the Congress and the Executive Branch about providing for United States troops in Vietnam, they would have "no medical facilities, no food, no ammuniiton, no shells, and no fuel for the airplanes and helicopters now in that area."

Of course, even though the bill before the Senate made no provision for any of these items, since they needed no authorization but are merely appropriated for, the idea was projected that speed was of the essence.

The Senate Committee on the Armed Services in its report did not point out—as the House Committee would point out the following week—that "many of the items involved . . . may simply have been moved from the regular 1967 authorization to the supplemental without any real program for acceleraiton. Obviously no military advantage would be gained by such a bookkeeping situation." But this was also ascertainable from a close examination of the hearings released by the Senate Committee on the Armed Services, despite the many security deletions from the text.

This lack of a real need for authorization at that time, coupled with the statement in the President's message of January 19, 1966, transmitting the request, that it was being made "in the letter and the spirit of the [Tonkin Gulf] resolution," was a clear indication that this authorization would again be used in the future to point to as an endorsement of a policy of escalation.

Shortly after Senator Richard Russell (D.-Ga.) had made the opening statement on the bill, Senator George Aiken (R.-Vt.), Senior Republican in the Senate, raised the question:

"Does the Senator from Mississippi," (Senator John Stennis, Chairman of the Senate Armed Services Preparedness Subcommittee, who was aiding Senator Russell's Floor management of the bill) "interpret the approval of this request for supplemental appropriations as either approving or disapproving our policy in South Vietnam?"

Senator Stennis replied that it would constitute neither approval nor disapproval.

Senator Aiken expressed the thought that it was important to have this interpretation "so that the action of Congress on this proposal may not be so badly misinterpreted or misconstrued as was the resolution of August 1964" [Tonkin Gulf resolution].

Senator Gore, stating that he would support the bill but that such support should not be interpreted as "approval on my part of the policies and decisions that have led to our involvement in Vietnam in its current proportions . . . commitment of U. S. combat forces to Vietnam was a serious mistake, and will prove to be . . . an historic mistake, that has increased rather than diminished the danger of a major war . . . I voice my deep concern . . . in the hope that a review of the past and a searching public analysis and debate of the present may possibly be of some help in shaping the momentous decisions in the days and months ahead. The responsibility of a U. S. Senator and the dictates of conscience impel me to participate in this discussion and to express these views."

Senator Gore recalled that when "President Eisenhower undertook our initial commitment I counseled against it." He had also advised President Kennedy and President Johnson against widening that commitment. He had not publicly dissented before "in deference to the constitutional responsibility and to a feeling that strident public opposition and dissent" to publicly declared policies might lessen any chance of their being effective.

"Upon reflection," he admitted, "this was a mistake and I am sorry I did not speak out publicly more often and sooner than I did."

During the course of his presentation of a thorough analysis of how the United States had become involved in Vietnam "step by step." Senator Gore reminded his colleagues that "we have inched into this Asian morass through three Administrations. Three Presidents have assured the American people that combat forces would not be sent to Vietnam. Upon many occasions it was said that the steps being taken were not to be followed by subsequent events which some of us foresaw."

Senator Fulbright, Chairman of the Senate Foreign Relations Committee, said that he agreed with Senator Gore that "Vietnam, per se—and leaving for later discussions the influence of China— is not vital to the security of the United States"; and that Vietnam "does not constitute the balance of power between the major powers of the world."

Speaking about the Senate Foreign Relations Committee's televised hearings on Vietnam, Senator Fulbright apologized to the Senate and stated "I regret that I did not initiate them, and that the committee did not initiate them long ago. I can only say that I did not realize earlier how serious is this commitment in Southeast Asia. At the time of the 1964 resolution I really had no realization of what we were about to get into, or how it was about to escalate, or certainly I would have held hearings then. I regret that we did not do this earlier. However, it is better to have the hearings now than not at all."

On Friday, February 18, 1966—the third day after the debate had started in the Senate on the appropriation authorization and after there had been in all not more than twelve hours of debate on the bill itself—Senator Russell, Chairman of the Armed Services Committe, stated that in his opinion there was a filibuster going on. "If Senators continue this delay interminably, we risk losing the war in Vietnam by a process of attrition and a lack of ammunition which our forces must have to defend themselves."[2]

Senator McGovern stated that he thought that "a few days discussion of an authorization of nearly $5 billion should not quite so quickly be labeled a 'filibuster'."

He went on to say that he was one of a group of Senators who had considered offering an amendment to the bill to limit its impact to "sustaining the forces already in being in Vietnam, but also in some fashion to reflect the opposition or at least the concern of a number of Members of the Senate about the dangers of any larger war in Vietnam."

Senator McGovern stated that in the light of Senator Russell's assurance that "nothing in this legislation can properly be considered as determining foreign policy, as ratifying decisions made in the past or as endorsing new commitments," he—Senator McGovern—would not propose such an amendment.

There were reasons for the Senate Leadership's raising the cry of "filibuster" in the Senate that Friday afternoon, February 18, 1966. There had just been, in its opinion, too much attention and publicity given to the critics of the Administration's Vietnam policies.

The Senate Foreign Relations Committee's nationally televised hearings on Vietnam had just concluded that morning. There had been six days of those hearings and the Senate Leadership was faced with the prospect, unless debate were closed and a vote taken that afternoon, of two more weeks of debate on the Senate Floor.

Another reason for wanting to foreclose debate was given by Senator McGovern. In the cloakrooms and in Senatorial offices much attention was being paid to drafting amendments which would do exactly as Senator McGovern had stated: Prohibit the further escalation of the United States military commitment in South Vietnam.

Senator Gruening, in addition, had given notice that he would propose an amendment prohibiting draftees from being sent to Southeast Asia involuntarily unless Congress thereafter passed a law to the contrary.

Senator Morse had already announced that he would propose an amendment repealing the Tonkin Gulf Resolution.

In the Senate, amendments beget amendments since there is no rule that an amendment offered has to have any relevance to the subject matter of the bill itself. Once amendments began to be offered there was no telling what type of amendment would be offered or what amendments might be adopted. The House still had to act on the bill and if the House Members saw the Senate tacking on amendments there was also the prospect that amendments would be offered and accepted there.

And finally, the Senate Leadership faced a bleak prospect of obtaining a speedy vote during the following week. Lincoln's birthday fell in the middle of that week—a time for Republican Senators traditionally to be absent—to fulfill speaking engagements all around the country. Similarly, Democratic Senators would be away from Washington at Jefferson-Jackson Day speaking engagements.

However, the only practical way to end debate on the bill that afternoon in the Senate was by unanimous consent. The Senate Leadership knew that there were sufficient Senators in the Chamber who wanted the issues involved to be fully debated so that at least one Senator would object if it attempted to obtain unanimous consent to limit debate on the bill—especially since there had been actually only twelve hours of debate on the bill itself.

When the debate finally reached its climax and votes were taken on March 1, 1966, two amendments were presented—Senator Gruening's amendment on draftees and Senator Morse's amendment to repeal the Gulf of Tonkin resolution.

Senator Gruening had long advocated the draft amendment he was to propose.

The sharp escalation of the United States involvement in fighting a land war in Southeast Asia had raised questions throughout the country as to whether draftees should be sent to fight in Southeast Asia if they did not want to go. United States involvement there came into being after the draft law had been extended at a time when the United States was at peace. In the summer and fall of 1965 the question was being actively raised by many youths facing the draft—those who did not object to war as such—and hence under legal precedents in effect at that time would not be classified as conscientious objectors. Their objections were to fighting in Vietnam and not to service elsewhere, for although the Vietnam war was the only war in which the United States was engaged at that time, U. S. troops were stationed in many other parts of the world.

Whether draftees should be sent to Vietnam against their will deserved, Senator Gruening stated, the "fullest possible debate in Congress" and was a question which "Congress itself should decide."

Accordingly, on August 19, 1965, Senator Gruening had prepared an amendment to the then pending Defense Department Appropriation Bill which would prohibit draftees from being sent to Southeast Asia without their consent unless Congress, by law, thereafter permitted them to be sent involuntarily. That amendment had been drafted and was lying on Senator Gruening's desk when, as he recounted the story on the floor of the Senate on February 24, 1966:

"The President asked to see me at the White House. The

purpose of our meeting was to enable me to explain to the President in detail my opposition to our military involvement in Vietnam, which I had been voicing on the floor of the Senate for a year and a half. I told the President that I disagreed completely with his administration's position: namely, that three Presidents had pledged support to this policy—that there was in fact no national pledge or an unavoidable commitment—that we had in fact asked ourselves in into Vietnam. I also elaborated on my other reasons for believing that our involvement was folly—that it was a war we could not win—that continuation there would lead to greater and greater disaster.

"While there, after I expressed my views, I told him I intended to introduce an amendment that very afternoon forbidding draftees to be sent to Southeast Asia involuntarily without the consent of the Congress. The President earnestly urged me not to introduce the amendment. He said that in any event no draftees would be sent to Vietnam before January. After repeating his request that I take no such action, he said that if we were not out of Vietnam by January, I would be free to do anything I pleased . . . In accordance with the President's urgent request that I not offer the amendment at the time and his hopeful expectation that our troops would be out of Vietnam by January, I naturally refrained from submitting the amendment."[3]

Senator Gruening called up his draftee amendment on March 1, 1966. After the briefest of debates, the amendment was met by a "sudden death" motion—a motion to table it, which is not debatable —and the amendment was defeated by a vote of 93 to 2 (Senators Morse and Gruening).

Senator Morse's amendment to rescind the Gulf of Tonkin resolution was met similarly with a tabling motion and was tabled by a vote of 92 to 5 (Senators Fulbright, Gruening, McCarthy (D.-Minn.), Morse, and Young, (D.-Ohio).)

The vote was not as overhelming a reaffirmation of the Gulf of Tonkin resolution as appears on the surface.

Reference has previously been made in this chapter to reservations openly proclaimed by some Senators that their vote was not to be construed as a confirmation of past or future actions of the Administration. Many also gave that as their view in the privacy of the cloakroom.

Thus Senator Fulbright pointed to Senator Russell's statement in presenting the bill that "nothing in this legislaion can properly be construed as determining foreign policy, as ratifying decisions made in the past, or as endorsing new commitments. I think we are entitled to rely upon that statement by the Senator."

Senator Morse replied that there was "no question as to the policy of the Administration in the bill. There is nothing that the Senator from Georgia can say to change that policy. The policy is set out with complete clarity in the bill itself and in the statements of the witnesses of the Administration."

Senator Fulbright replied that Senator Morse had put into words the difficulty confronting him. "I am very reluctant to vote for this measure," he said, "for the reasons the Senator has stated. The alternative . . . proposed by the Senator from Oregon [Senator Morse] would result in a situation which would force a decision on the floor as to whether the Senate should reaffirm policies [Tonkin Gulf Resolution] which I do not wish to reaffirm . . ."

Senator Clark (D.-Pa.) stated:

"I shall vote against the Morse amendment and shall vote in favor of the bill. I do both with a heavy heart, most reluctantly, as the least acceptable of all available choices. But I wish to make it very clear indeed that my votes . . . do not indicate an endorsement of the policy which I fear the Administration is following."

Senator Clark was referring to his remarks the day before in which he called the attention of the Senate to a report out of Saigon by Seymour Topping, in *The New York Times,* predicting that the military effort in South Vietnam would be stepped up.

Topping reported senior United States and South Vietnamese officials in Saigon as saying that "in their planning . . . the war will last 3 to 7 years . . . additional troops are to be brought in . . . Air strikes at communication lines in North Vietnam and infiltration routes in Laos are to be continued . . . it is expected that American casualties each month will average about 400 to 500 dead and about 15,000 wounded . . . Official planning in Saigon no longer

takes account of any possibility of peace negotiations with the Vietcong."

That report out of Saigon was dated February 25, 1966.

On the vote on March 1, 1966 for final passage of the Supplemental Appropriations Authorization for the Department of Defense
for Vietnam, only Senators Morse and Gruening voted against the
bill.

By coincidence, the House version of the Senate Supplemental
Vietnam Appropriation Authorization bill was considered on the
same day that the Senate voted on it—March 1 ,1966.

Debate in the House was limited to three hours.

Early in the debate, Representative Jeffery Cohelan (D.-Calif.)
filed a statement on behalf of 78 Representatives* stating that "we

---

*William Anderson (D.-Tenn.), Thomas Ashley (D.-Ohio), Jonathan Bingham,
(D.-N.Y.), John Blatnik (D.-Minn.), John Brademas (D.-Ind.), James Byrne
(D.-Pa.), Ronald Cameron (D.-Calif.), Emanuel Celler (D.-N.Y.), Jeffery
Cohelan (D.-Calif.), James Corman (D.-Calif.), Dominick Daniels (D.-N.J.),
William Dawson (D.-Ill.), Charles Diggs (D.-Mich.), John Dow (D.-N.Y.),
Ken Dyal (D.-Calif.), Don Edwards (D.-Calif.), George Fellon (D.-Md.),
Leonard Farbstein (D.-N.Y.), Donald Fraser (D.-Minn.), Samuel Friedel
(D.-Md.), Richard Fulton (D.-Tenn.), Edward Garmatz (D.-Md.), Robert
Giaimo (D.-Conn.), Jacob Gilbert (D.-N.Y.), John Gilligan (D.-Ohio), Martha
Griffiths (D.-Mich.), Richard Hanna (D.-Calif.), Julia Butler Hansen (D.-
Wash.), William Hathaway (D.-Maine), Augustus Hawkins (D.-Calif.), Ken
Hechler (D.-W.Va.), Henry Helstoskei (D.N.J.), Floyd Hicks (D.-Wash.),
Chet Holifield (D.-Calif.), James Howard (D.-N.J.), J. Oliva Huot (D.-N.H.),
Charles Joelson (D.-N.J.), Harold Johnson (D.-Calif.), James Kee (D.-
W. Va.), Cecil King (D.-Calif.), Paul Krebs (D.-N.J.), Robert Leggett (D.-
Calif.), Clarence Long D.-Md.), Torbert Macdonald (D.-Mass.), Harris Mc-
Dowell, Jr. (D.-Del.), Roy McVicker (D.-Colo.), James Mackay (D.-Ga.),
John Mackie (D.-Mich.), Spark Matsunaga (D.-Hawaii), Walter Moeller (D.-
Ohio), Lloyd Meeds (D.-Wash.), Patsy Mink (D.-Hawaii), William Moor-
head (D.-Pa.), John Moss (D.-Calif.), Lucien Nedzi (D.-Mich.), Robert Nix
(D.-Pa.), James O'Hara (D.-Mich.), Arnold Olsen (D.-Mont.), Edward Pat-
ten (D.-N.J.), Melvin Price (D.-Ill.), Rolland Redlin (D.-N.Dak.), Thomas
Rees (D.-Calif.), Joseph Resnick (D.-N.Y.), Henry S. Reuss (D.-Wis.),
George Rhodes (D.-Pa.), Benjamin Rosenthal (D.-N.Y.), Edward Roybal (D.-
Calif.), Fernand St. Germain (D.-R.I.), James Scheuer (D.-N.Y.), Carlton
Sickles (D.-Md.), Robert Sweeney (D.-Ohio), Herbert Tenzer (D.-N.Y.),
Frank Thompson, Jr. (D.-N.J.), Paul Todd, Jr. (D.-Mich.), Morris Udall
(D.-Ariz.), Lionel Van Deerlin (D.-Calif.), Weston Vivian (D.-Mich.), Lester
Wolff (D.-N.Y.)

. . . reject any contention that approval of this legislation will constitute a mandate for unrestrained or indiscriminate enlargement of the military effort, and we strongly support continued efforts to initiate negotations for a settlement of the conflict."[4]

Curiously of the 78 Representatives signing this statement, only 45 had signed the letter of January 21, 1966, to the President with respect to the continuation of his efforts to find peace in Vietnam and implying that he should continue the pause in the bombing of North Vietnam. But again, all 78 signers of the statement were Democrats. It would be logical to assume the sentiments of most of the signers of the letter to the President were the same as those signing the statement introduced by Represenative Cohelan against escalation of United States military activities in Vietnam. It could thus be said that over one third of the members of President Johnson's own party in the House of Representatives were against further escalation of the war in Vietnam.

With total debate in the House limited to three hours, there was only time for brief statements.

Representatives William F. Ryan (D., N.Y.) pointed out that it was "not a matter of support for men in combat, but whether they should be in combat at all, or if they are, what their missions should be in the context of what strategy and what policy. This is a bill to finance escalation, not to finance an existing policy. It is now before us, and our responsibility is a heavy one."

Representative Ryan voted against the bill.

Representative Paul A. Fino (R., N.Y.) voted in favor of the passage of the bill but said that his "vote is for our soldiers, and for their splendid endurance in the face of this nerve-shattering war. I do not support the way in which the Administration is conducting our overall cold war policy."

However, his objection to the Administration's policies were not the same as Rrepresentative Ryan's. In Ryan's view there should be a "switch to military and diplomatic tactics aimed at putting us in a position to negotiate a successful conclusion to this war before we have spent tens of thousands of lives and tens of thousands of dollars."

Representative Don Edwards (D., Calif.), who was paired on the final vote, announced himself as "for this measure because

I don't want to see our boys die in the wrong war, at the wrong time, in the wrong place for lack of domestic support. But I would hope that our efforts for peace in Southeast Asia would be intensified to end not only that war but also the threat of World War III." Representative Edwards advocated that the United States be "ready to sit with the Vietcong at the conference table and to allow them participation in the future political life of South Vietnam." He also came out strongly for a cessation of the bombing of North Vietnam.

Representative Benjamin S. Rosenthal (D., N.Y.) announced that he was voting in favor of the bill "with reluctance and apprehension."

"If we continue along this course and wander ever more deeply into the jungle mists of Asia," Representative Phillip Burton (D., Calif.) warned, "I fear that many more innocent Vietnamese will die, many more brave American soldiers will perish, many mothers and fathers will weep, and the honor of this great Nation will be cast over with a shadow that only time will dispel." He voted against the bill.

Representative Jonathan Bingham (D., N.Y.) stated that he was voting for the bill but that his "vote does not mean that I am wholly satisfied with the Administration's policies with respect to Vietnam."

"In voting for this supplemntal defense authorization," said Representative Edward A. Roybal (D., Calif.), "I wish to make it clear that my vote should not be construed as an unqualified endorsement of all aspects of our policy in Vietnam . . . does not constitute a mandate for unrestrained or indiscriminate enlargement of the military effort, and most certainly, not a blanket approval of present or future action in that part of the world . . . vital . . . that this country exercise the most careful prudence . . . so as to limit the conflict as much as possible."

The bill was passed by a vote of 392 to 4, Representatives Brown (D., Calif.), Burton (D., Calif.), Conyers (D., Mich.), and Ryan (D., N.Y.) voting against it.

To the man in the street, it looked like an overwhelming vote of confidence in the policies being carried on by the Johnson Administration in Vietnam. The 392-4 vote in the House and the 94-2 vote in the Senate on the same day made headlines — the reservations expressd by so many members of both Houses did not.

Thus ended the great debate on Vietnam in the Congress on March 1, 1966.

Neither House of Congress had come close to applying the brakes to the Johnson Administration's determination to escalate the United States military involvement in Vietnam.

Why?

Why, at a time when so many voices were raised on the Floor of the Senate, in the House Chamber, in the cloakrooms of both Houses, at the sit-ins, the teach-ins and in the open letters in the newspapers to the President by tens of thousands of respected individuals, was the Congress so ineffectual in changing the Johnson's Administration's escalation policies or, at least, in slowing them down?

Was it, as Senator Richard Russell had said, that it was due to the slow erosion "of Congressional power that has placed this body (the Senate) in a position inferior to the other branches of the Government?"

The lack of action by the Congress to restrain the Johnson Administration from ever greater escalation of the United States military involvement in Vietnam was due not, as Senator Russell put it, to the erosion of Congressional power over the years — and there has been that — but rather to the refusal or reluctance to utilize the power which, under the constitution, is vested in the Congress.

The Federal Government can expend only such monies as are appropriated by the Congress. With respect to the escalation of the war in Vietnam, the Congress, through the purse strings, could have said: "Thus far and no further." It did not do so — although it was given the opportunity to call a halt.

The reason for not stopping the passage of the Tonkin Gulf resolution can be ascribed to two weaknesses in the system of checks and balances. Hasty legislation will often as not turn out to be bad legislation. Some may think of the Congress as slow, ponderous and as moving with the speed of cold molassas. It is all of these but therein lies its ability to "check" the Executive

Branch. Caught up as it was in the patriotic hysteria of the Tonkin Gulf incident and requested to act immediately, the Congress did not bring into play the system — full Committee hearings, printed and available for study by the members before they are called upon to debate and vote, full and open debate — at least in the Senate — for whatever time was needed to debate all sides of the grave issue.

Another difficulty lies with the misuse that was made by the Administration of the Congressional Committee system. Committee Chairmen and Subcommittee Chairmen are specialists in their subjects — they have to be because of the vast number of subjects handled by Congress. All other Members must place reliance on the Chairmen and members of the Subcommittees for their information as to the effects of the legislation presented.

Senator Morse was the only member of the Foreign Relations Committee to vote against the Tonkin Gulf Resolution both in the Committee and on the Floor. Given the opportunity to vote to rescind that resolution in 1966, the only two members of that Committee to join Senator Morse were Senators Fulbright and McCarthy.

The major reason why the Congress was so ineffectual in applying the brakes to the Vietnam escalation has been attributed to the refusal of so many members of the Congress "to put their votes where their mouths were."

As Senator Morse said:

"It is only votes that are binding upon the Pentagon or the White House, not the opinions of Senators."

The Senator from Pennsylvania, Joseph Clark, has written a book on the shortcomings of the Congress entitled: "Congress, The Sapless Branch."

If one were to write a book on the shortcomings of the Congress with respect to United States military involvement in Vietnam, one could, perhaps, entitle it: "Congress, The Spineless Branch."

CHAPTER XXX

VIETNAM FOLLY—ITS EFFECTS AT HOME

At home to date, the major effects of the massive United States military involvement in Vietnam can be grouped under three headings:

First, a growing credibility gap between the Government of the United States and the people;

Second, the steady erosion of the Great Society programs; and,

Third, the mounting uneasiness of the ever larger number of people in the United States as manifested in teach-ins, public protests, and shrill cries of "why don't we win in Vietnam."

The Credibility Gap

The credibility gap with respect to the United States' military involvement in Vietnam is not a creation of the Johnson Administration — it has only widened under that Administration.

It will be recalled that[1] in 1954 the late President John F. Kennedy, then a United States Senator from Massachusetts, in discussing on the floor of the Senate the possibility of sending United States troops to fight a land war in Vietnam cited many examples of misstatements issued by leading officials of the Eisenhower Administration about Vietnam.

Unfortunately, those misstatements continued when John F. Kennedy became President. They are most clearly illustrated by the many conflicting statements made by Secretary of State Rusk, Secretary of Defense McNamara, and Lyndon Johnson — then Vice President — as each reported from the scene in Saigon. These misstatements are also illustrated by the attempt to gloss over the semi-military status given to United States' so-called advisers in South Vietnam in the face of reports sent back by on-the-scenes reporters that the advisers were in fact going out on combat missions.

But the credibility gap under the Eisenhower and Kennedy Administration was as nothing compared to its width under the Johnson Administration.

Numerous examples have been given throughout this volume of "stage managed" news emanating from official administration sources.

The Pleiku incident serves as an illustration of how the credibility gap widened under the Johnson Administration.

After the Pleiku incident, the White House announced on February 7, 1965:

". . . Hanoi has ordered a more aggressive course of action against both South Vietnam and American installations. Moreover, these attacks were only made possible by the continuing infiltration of personnel and equipment from North Vietnam. This infiltration markedly increased during 1964 and continues to increase."

Yet Roger Hilsman, former Assistant Secretary of State for the Far East, shows "Viet Cong Infiltrated from North Vietnam" as follows:

Year	Number
1961	5,400
1962	12,400
1963	7,400
1964	7,400
1965	19,000

We have already cited responsible writers to the effect that the decision to bomb the North was made before the Pleiku incident and that once the decision was reached, all that was required was a circumstance that justified reprisal.[2]

Veteran *Newsweek* White House correspondent, Charles Roberts, places the decision to bomb North Vietnam as having been made as early as October 1964. President Johnson's "decision that night," (February 7, 1965) he wrote, "the order that sent U.S. bombers roaring over a remote North Vietnamese village named Dong Hoi, was far from impulsive. As a matter of fact, he had made that momentous **decision** to bomb North Vietnam four months earlier. That decision was made . . . in October 1964, at the height of the Presidential election campaign."[3]

Correspondent Roberts's statement raises this interesting question: If, as he says, the decision to bomb North Vietnam was made in October 1964 could it not, more logically, have been made months earlier — say in June 1964, at the time (June 23, 1964) of the appointment of General Maxwell Taylor as Ambassador to South Vietnam — thereby explaining the seeming over-reaction of the Johnson Administration to the Gulf of Tonkin incident?

With its decision made in June or July 1964 to escalate the war in Vietnam, could not the Johnson Administration, in rushing the Gulf of Tonkin resolution through the Congress, have been arming itself in advance with sufficient Congressional approval of what it had already decided to do?

Senator George McGovern (D., S.D.) bluntly questioned the validity of the Tonkin Gulf incident when he said, in an article in *The Atlantic Monthly* for January 1967:

"Looking back on the Bay of Tonkin incidents of August 1964, one wonders if a crisis were manufactured by the Administration to justify a politically popular aerial reprisal against Hanoi backed by a strongly worded congressional resolution—all of this at the beginning of a national election when Administration firmness was being questioned by the political challenger."

But whether the decision to bomb North Vietnam was made in June or July or October of 1964, there is raised the corollary question: Did that decision include the decision to increase radically the United States ground forces in South Vietnam? If the answer is in the affirmative, then the credibility gap becomes wide indeed in the light of candidate Johnson's repeated pledges in the Presidential campaign in the Fall of 1964 against "committing a good many American boys to fighting a war that I think ought to be fought by the boys of Asia to help protect their own land."[4]

"As the founding fathers well knew," the lead editorial in *The Nation* stated on July 25, 1966, "undistorted information about public affairs is as vital to democracy as universal suffrage. As we are now being taught modern techniques of management of the news are destructive of the democratic process . . . These millions of self-satisfied Americans had better learn to read the news, to be sophisticated about news management, and to be utterly skeptical about anything this Administration tells them. Otherwise they will find themselves with the forms of democracy but none of the substance."

Richard Goodwin, former special assistant to President Kennedy and Johnson, stated that with full ". . . allowance for necessary uncertainties I believe there has never been such intense and widespread deception and confusion as that which surrounds this war. The continual downpour of contradiction, misstatements and kaleidoscopically shifting attitudes has been so torrential that it almost numbed the capacity to separate truth from conjecture and falsehood."[5]

Or, as Secretary General of the United Nations U Thant had stated on February 24, 1965:

"I am sure the great American people, if only they know the true facts and the background to the developments in South Vietnam, will agree with me that further bloodshed is unnecessary . . . in times of war and of hostilities the first casualty is truth."[6]

The Erosion of the Great Society

President Johnson came before a joint session of the Congress on the night of January 12, 1966 — while the bombing pause was still on — to tell the assembled legislators and a nationwide television and radio audience in what state the Union found itself. In his address, President Johnson, while not in the least minimizing the war in Vietnam, sought to give the impression that the United States could have both guns AND butter.

"This nation is mighty enough," he said, "its society is healthy enough, its people are strong enough to pursue our goals in the

"There's Money Enough To Support Both Of You—
Now, Doesn't That Make You Feel Better?"

rest of the world while still building a great society at home."

He then talked of the many areas of the Great Society programs, which he had so skillfully gotten through the Congress, that would require strengthening and extension.

"I recommend," he told the Congress, "that you provide the resources to carry forward with full vigor the great health and education programs . . . prosecute with vigor and determination our war on poverty . . . rebuild completely on a scale never before attempted entire central and slum areas . . . attack the wasteful and degrading poisoning of our rivers . . . clean completely entire large river basins . . . meet the growing menace of crime in the streets by building up law enforcement . . . equal justice to all our citizens . . . we will continue to meet the needs of our people by continuing to develop the Great Society."

In the face of such military escalation in Vietnam, the President's "guns and butter" speech, "came as a shock," columnists Evans and Novak report, "to those who had expected partial suspension of the Great Society to finance the war in Vietnam. The former Senator from Texas, who in 1950 had rapped Harry Truman for seeking both guns and butter, was now doing precisely the same thing."[7]

Concerning the war in Vietnam, President Johnson did not sugarcoat the pill for the assembled Members of Congress.

He reviewed his most recent peace efforts and reported that able "and experienced spokesmen have visited, in behalf of America, more than 40 countries. We have talked to more than a hundred governments — all 113 that we have relations with, and some that we don't. We talked to the United Nations and we have called upon all of its members to make any contribution that they can toward helping obtain peace."

As for the course of the United States in the time ahead the President said: "We will strive to limit the conflict, for we wish neither increased destruction nor do we want to invite increased danger . . . the days may become months, and the months may become years, but we will stay as long as aggression commands us to do battle."

Many in his audience that night—people both in the Congress and throughout the country—who had been aware of the steady and projected buildup of United States armed forces in Vietnam were sceptical of President Johnson's ability to have "business as usual" in the United States while waging what looked like a major war in Southeast Asia.

The anwer was not long in coming.

On January 24, 1966, President Johnson sent to the Congress his budget message for the fiscal year July 1, 1966 to June 30, 1967. His message stated that the budget provided a "program for action." It was founded on two premises:

"In international affairs, we are determined to seek peace with every means at our command—but we are fully prepared to meet the costs of opposing aggression.

"In domestic affairs, we are determined to press confidently forward toward the Great Society—but we shall do so in an orderly and responsible way, and at a pace which reflects the claims of our commitments in Southeast Asia upon the Nation's resources."

Actually the Great Society programs had been cut for fiscal year 1967, and fiscal year 1966 programs would be cut back by impounding funds already appropriated by the Congress.

Commenting on the budget in an editorial entitled: "Half a War," the *Washington Post* on January 26, 1966, pointed out that "President Johnson's budget for the war on poverty is a disappointment to hopes that the President himself has raised. It represents a sharp cut in the plans that the Johnson administration itself had held before cities throughout the country and a drastic reduction in the goals that the President in his own speeches has enunciated to the Nation."

The editorial noted that the President had stated in his original message on the poverty program: "We are citizens of the richest and most fortunate nation in the history of the world . . . . That is still true. 'The new program I propose is within our means . . . .' And that also still is true. But the program that is projected in the new budget does not reflect either of these truths."

Even as the President was delivering his State of the Union message to the Congress, his Bureau of the Budget began impounding funds from various agencies.

One of the first programs cut back was the school milk program. Mrs. Barbara D. McGarry, Executive Director of the American Parents Committee, protested the cut in a letter dated January 18, 1966, addressed to President Johnson. "Surely," Mrs. McGarry wrote the President, "in humanitarian as well as economic terms, our Nation's children represent our greatest national investment." She reminded him of his State of the Union "pledges that our children shall not be the victims of a false economy."

The school milk program was only one of the many Federal programs curtailed to make way for the guns for Vietnam.

On September 8, 1966, the President sent the Congress his economic message announcing which programs had been either deferred or reduced. It was announced at that time that Federal program levels would be reduced by from one and one-half billion dollars to two billion dollars. Later that figure was revised, sharply upward, to $5.2 billion.

Senator Morse, Chairman of the Senate Subcommitte on Education, has estimated that between $2.5 and $2.7 billion would be needed for the poverty program for fiscal year 1968. The budget request for that fiscal year called for only $1.86 billion.

The Library and Services Construction Act which authorized for fiscal year 1968 the sum of $50 million was to be funded instead at $27 million.

Under Title I of the Elementary and Secondary Education Act $2.4 billion was authorized for fiscal year 1968 for educationally deprived children. Only $1.2 billion was included in President Johnson's 1968 budget for this purpose.

And so on and on, program after program of the Great Society is cut back or inadequately funded. The effects of the erosion of the Great Society cannot be measured alone by the number of billions of dollars not appropriated. The effects of these cutbacks will manifest themselves upon the future social and economic strength of the United States:

(1)—in the thousands upon thousands of children throughout the nation whose educations will be inadequate because of the schools that were not built and the teachers who were not trained during the "war years." These deficiencies will not have their maximum effects this year or next. They will make themselves felt when the children whose educations are sacrificed now—in the cause of the United States' Vietnam Folly—become adults. Even if they escape becoming tax consumers rather than taxpayers, their lack of an adequate education will prevent their making the maximum contribution to the economy of the United States or to their leading the most productive and fruitful lives of which they are capable;

(2)—in the lack of the maximum economic growth of the United States because of the needed hydroelectric projects that were not constructed, the markets that were not opened because the roads were not built, the housing that will not be there to meet the growing population of the United States, and the resulting lessened employment in construction, lessened profits and lessened revenue to the U. S. treasury.

Already—to a greater or a lesser extent—the effects of the United States' Vietnam Folly are felt by every citizen in every walk of life in every part of the United States. As the Vietnam war continues to escalate, its effects will probe ever deeper into the economic and social fiber of the United States.

The Public Protests

On February 19, 1965—just 12 days after the Plieku incident and the United States bombing of targets in North Vietnam in "retaliation," a large advertisement appeared in the *New York Times* under the heading:

"VIETNAM: AMERICA MUST DECIDE BETWEEN A FULL-SCALE WAR AND A NEGOTIATED TRUCE."

The advertisement noted that the escalation of the war "can lead to a major war involving the United States and China—a war nobody wants and no one can win." Those signing the advertisement then pleaded:

"Stop the widening of the war—Bombing North Vietnam will not stop the conflict in South Vietnam. Widening the war only serves to invite the intervention of the North Vietnamese regular army, the U.S.S.R., and China.

"Seek a cease fire—No issues will be decided by prolonging the bloody and fratricidal conflict in South Vietnam . . . .

"Negotiate an international settlement . . . means must be

found and found urgently to take the issue from the field of battle to the conference table."

The advertisement was signed by over a hundred persons from all walks of life and from all parts of the United States. The co-chairmen of the group signing the open letter were Dr. Benjamin Spock, noted pediatrician, and Professor H. Stuart Hughes of Harvard.

Among those signing the open letter were religious leaders, authors, union leaders, doctors, professors, bankers, scientists, a former counseler of the United States Department of State (Benjamin V. Cohen), a cartoonist (Jules Feiffer), actors, and the national chairman, at that time, of the Americans for Democratic Action, (Professor John P. Roche) who later became a staunch supporter of the Johnson Administration's policies in Vietnam and the "Intellectual in Residence at the White House."

The following week, on February 28, 1965, another advertisement appeared in the *New York Times* and was headed: "An Open Letter to President Johnson on Vietnam." It was signed by over four hundred men and women of the academic community who were teaching at colleges and universities in the New York area.

This advertisement also urged the President ". . . to seek a negotiated settlement by every possible means in order to create an independent, neutralized government and to bring about the withdrawal of U.S. troops. We ask you to lay the problem immediately before an international body and to put an end to our unilateral and illegal actions . . . *The longer we persist in our present policy, the fewer will be the alternatives open to us."* [Emphasis Supplied]

Signing the statement were members of the faculties of Adelphi University, Albert Einstein College of Medicine, Brooklyn College, City College of New York, Columbia University, Cornell University, Hofstra College, Long Island University, New York University, Polytechnic Institute of Brooklyn, Pratt Institute, Queens College, Rutgers University, Rockefeller Institute, Sarah Lawrence College, Sloan-Kettering Institute for Cancer Research, State University of New York, Stevens Institute of Technology, Yeshiva University, and others.

The very next day *The New York Times* carried another "Open Letter" to President Johnson dealing with the war in Vietnam. This letter was signed by almost two hundred members of the academic

community on the East Coast, adding their voices to the 400 who
had signed a similar advertisement on February 16, 1965, from colleges and universities in the Boston, Massachusetts, area.

This advertisement, at a time when United States troops in Vietnam numbered about 23,000 "advisers," asked the questions: "We
have widened the war—how wide will it become? . . . Would it not
be both prudent and just to take the initiative toward peace in Vietnam?" It concluded with the plea:

"If we are not to widen the war beyond all conscience, as
reasonable men we must initiate negotiations while there is
still time."

This letter was sponsored by the "Ad Hoc Committee for an
Open Letter on Vietnam," chaired by Professor Arno J. Mayer of
the Princeton history department.

About one month later, on April 4, 1965, a telling advertisement signed by 2,700 ministers, priests, and rabbis appeared in *The
New York Times*.

The full page advertisement, bordered by some of the names of
those signing it, was headed:

"MR. PRESIDENT: *IN THE NAME OF GOD, STOP IT!*"

Part of this advertisement read:

"It is not a light thing for an American to say that he is
dismayed by his country's actions. We do not say it lightly,
but soberly and in deep distress. Our Government's actions in
Vietnam have been and continue to be unworthy either of the
high standards of our common religious faith, or of the lofty
aspirations on which this country was founded . . . in Vietnam
this Nation, so proudly self-described as 'under God' is not content even with an 'eye for an eye' retaliation, but returns evil
for evil on a multiplying scale."

Heading the list of signers of this advertisement were Bishop
John Wesley Lord, Washington, D.C. area, Methodist Church; Dr.
Dana McLean Greeley, president, Unitarian Universalist Association;
Dr. Edwin T. Dahlberg, former president, National Council of Church-
es; Father Peter Riga, moderator, Catholic Council on Civil Liberties;
Dr. Isidor B. Hoffman, chaplain to Jewish students, Columbia Uni-
versity; and Dr. Henry J. Cadbury, biblical scholar, former chairman
of the American Friends Service Committee.

An equally telling advertisement appeared in *The New York Times* on January 23, 1966 under the caption:

"THEY ARE OUR BROTHERS WHOM WE KILL!"

containing an eloquent plea for peace in Vietnam by the International Committee of Conscience on Vietnam, a group affiliated with the Clergymen's Emergency Commitee for Vietnam of the Fellowship of Reconciliation. This moving "call to conscience" was signed by, among others, Alfred Hassler, Executive Secretary of the Fellowship of Reconciliation, Rabbi Abraham J. Heschel of the Jewish Theological Seminary, Dr. Martin Luther King of the Southern Christian Leadership Conference, Monsignor Paul Hanly Furfey of the Catholic University in Washington, D. C., Dr. Howard Schomer of the Chicago Theological Seminary, and Dr. Howard B. Radest, Executive Director of the American Ethical Union.

In the years that followed, other groups, in papers all over the country, inserted advertisements and open letters to President Johnson protesting the escalating United States' military involvement in Vietnam.

A sampling of these—as examples of a widely used form of protest and to indicate the broad spectrum of the people involved—: is contained in the Appendix.

Even the lawyers took to the public press to present the arguments supporting the contention that the "military involvement of the United States in Vietnam is illegal under international law." Taking a full page advertisement in the *New York Times* on January 15, 1967, a group calling itself "Lawyers Committee on American Policy Towards Vietnam" summarized the salient points it had made in a Brief it had previously issued.

The legal conclusions reached in the advertisement appeared under the following captions:

"I. The unilateral military intervention of the United States in Vietnam violates the Charter of the United Nations. The Charter's exceptional authorization of individual and collective self-defense [Article 51] 'if an armed attack occurs against a member of the United Nations' does not apply in the case of Vietnam;

"(1) There has been no 'armed attack' upon South Vietnam within the meaning of Article 51 of the Charter;

"(2) The United States failed to fulfill its Charter obligation to seek a peaceful solution in Vietnam;

"(3) The doctrine of 'collective self defense' cannot justify the United States military intervention in the civil war in South Vietnam;

"(4) The 'request' of the 'Government' of South Vietnam does not provide a legal basis for 'collective self defense';

(5) The Korean precedent does not justify the unilateral intervention of the United States in Vietnam;

"II. The military presence of the United States in Vietnam violates the Geneva Accords of 1954;

"III. The United States is not committed by the SEATO Treaty or otherwise to intervene in Vietnam;

"IV. The intensity and destructiveness of United States warfare in Vietnam is contrary to international law;

"V. United States actions in Vietnam violate treaties which are part of the Supreme Law of the land, and hence violate the United States Constitution."

The legal analysis of the United States' position was prepared in consultation with an advisory group of eminent lawyers. Their names follow:

Richard A. Falk, chairman, Milbank professor of international law, Princeton University;

John H. E. Fried, rapporteur, professor of political science, City University of New York;

Richard J. Barnet, codirector, Institute for Policy Studies, Washington, D. C.;

John H. Herz, professor of international relations, City University of New York;

Stanley Hoffman, professor of international law, Harvard University;

Sol H. Mendlovitz, professor of international law, Rutgers University School of Law;

Wallace McClure, professor of international law, World Rule of Law Center, Duke University;

Richard S. Miller, professor of international law, Ohio State University, College of Law;

Hans J. Morgenthau, Michelson distinguished service professor of political science and modern history, University of Chicago;

William G. Rice, professor of international law, University of Wisconsin Law School; and,

Quincy Wright, professor of international law, University of Chicago, Rice University.

The Lawyers Committee Brief of Sepember 1965 was answered by a State Department Brief on March 4, 1966.

The New York Times advertisement of the Lawyers Committee as well as pertinent extracts from the State Department Brief are set out in the Appendix.

In the meantime, another form of public protest began to evolve.

On March 16, 1965, the Senate of the State of Michigan adopted Senate Resolution No. 71 "condemning the currently threatened classes cancellation at the University of Michigan." The resolution stated that:

"The action of the twenty instructors at the University of Michigan who have threatened cessation of classes on March 24, 1965, is not only totally ill-advised but represents a clear violation of their duties as instructors at a State University to their students and to the people of the State of Michigan, and hereby is condemned."

Despite this condemnation, a unique phenomenon of the Vietnam war was launched—the campus teach-in—and it spread like wildfire from coast to coast.

In an article in the July 1, 1965, issue of the *Manchester Guardian Weekly,* Anatol Rapoport, Professor of Mathematical Biology at the University of Michigan, described the origins of the teach-in concept.

Early in March 1965, ". . . a dozen of our [University of Michigan] faculty members had spent an evening arguing about what to do about the escalated Vietnam war . . . . At one point some people went into another room and came out with the idea of calling a 'work moratorium.' Classes were to be cancelled for a day, and students were to be invited to participate in a day-long analysis of historical, political, military, and moral aspects of the Vietnam war. The call for a 'work moratorium' . . . issued on March 12, 1965, was signed by 49 faculty members. Reactions ranged from enthusiasm among the students to 'concern' among our colleagues . . . . After eight hours of nerve-frazzling debate between the 'militants' and the rest, the teach-in movement was born . . . At 8 P.M. on March 24, 3,000 students showed up. About 70-80 of these constituted a counter-demonstration . . . . The next night Columbia had their teach-in. The chain reaction was on: Michigan State, Western Reserve, Buffalo, Chicago, Pennsylvania . . ."

The teach-ins, as they spread from one end of the United States to the other, took many forms. Many, especially at the beginning, were devoted to serious discussions of the issues involved in the United States' escalation of its military involvement in Vietnam; others turned into denunciations of United States policies.

According to former Ambassador John Kenneth Galbraith, the "Teach-in movement might never have occurred had not many in our Government tried to manipulate the American people into consensus about the war in Vietnam."

It was but natural that the teach-ins should have as their offshoots the off-campus mass demonstrations by interested and concerned citizens. The majority of these mass demonstrations were held to voice opposition to the United States policies in Vietnam. Some were held in support of those policies.

It was also natural that the mass demonstrations should attract not only the immature who so often seek to call attention to themselves by draft card burnings and desecration of the United States' flag but also Communists and their sympathizers who rush to join mass movements—especially those of protest in the hopes of taking over the movement or just to cause trouble.

It should be noted that even before the signed advertisements, the teach-ins, and the mass demonstrations, all of which began early in 1965, national peace organizations such as the American Friends Commitee, The Fellowship of Reconciliation and The National Committee for a SANE Nuclear Policy had begun to hoist warning signals early in 1964 that United States involvement in Vietnam could grow greater.

To the voices of these peace organizations were added, in 1965, the voices of those who were not necessarily opposed to all war—those who had supported the United States military efforts in Korea as well as those who had supported United States military involvement in World War II—but who objected to the particular military involvement of the United States in Vietnam.

One reason for the vehemence of the public protests after the bombings of North Vietnam began in February 1965, and after the Pleiku incident, could be ascribed to the reaction of the public to the breach of the promises made during the Presidential campaign of 1964. The American people had been deeply involved in that campaign—they had been opposing what they believed was an imminent danger that the United States, if Senator Goldwater were elected, would immediately be plunged not only into a land war in Asia but, ultimately, into a nuclear world war.

After the 1964 election, with Johnson's victory, many believed that the danger had been averted and breathed sighs of relief.

Then came the bombings of North Vietnam. The sighs of relief seemed premature.

Exercising the right of freedom of speech—for which professedly the United States was fighting in Vietnam—some Americans, feeling that President Johnson was openly betraying his campaign promises, voiced their protests by the tens of thousands through teach-ins, through demonstrations, through petitions in the press, and by writing to their Senators and Congressmen.

The extent and intensity of the public protests against the Johnson Administration's escalation of the United States military involvement in Vietnam is all the more surprising in view of President Johnson's consistent efforts to "play down" the escalation of the war in Vietnam.

Thus Evans and Novak are critical of President Johnson's method of announcing his decision on July 28, 1965, to send a land army into Southeast Asia:

"The President's nationally televised message to the country the next day, July 28, was low-keyed and undramatic—purposely scheduled in midday, not in the evening when, as Johnson knew better than anyone, the audience would have been much greater. The timing of the speech, the decision not to call up the reserves, and the subdued tone all added up to the loss of another opportunity to galvanize the American people and arouse their support for the war."[8]

The decision to continue to defer college students coupled with the decision not to call up the reserves played a great part in minimizing resistance to the escalation of the United States military commitment in Vietnam among what could otherwise have been a very articulate, vociferous, and politically powerful segment of the populace.

That policy was continued by President Johnson in the extension of the draft law he signed on June 30, 1967.

What of the reactions of the Johnson Administration and its supporters to these protests?

There can be no doubt but that many of the signers of the advertisements and the participants in the teach-ins against further United States military involvement in Vietnam faced subtle, future penalties by way of teaching contracts not renewed, research grants not given, or governmental appointments not made.

The American Civil Liberties Union cites the following as "symptoms of a gathering storm":

"—General Westmoreland's warning that dissent threatens military morale and encourages North Vietnam;

"—The White House statement that the FBI is making reports on 'Communist influence' in the Spring Mobilization for Peace March 9, conveniently disclosed for the press on the day of the April 15 march;

"—Demands by Congressmen for the jailing of those who, by speech, urge resistance to the draft, despite Assistant Attorney General Vinson's calm comment that the Constitution forbids it;

"—The cry of 'conspiracy' hurled by Representative Mendel Rivers, Chairman of the House Armed Services Committee, against the Justice Department and certain Federal judges whom he feels are preventing prosecution of those who advocate defiance of the draft;

"—The wide-spread practice of city police of photographing and checking the license plates of those participating in anti-Vietnam War meetings (and who reserve this technique for use against those with whom they disagree);

"—The penalization of professors who publicly advocate an end to the war."

The more recent form of criticism of those who voice dissent with the Administration's Vietnam policies takes the form of saying that Hanoi is listening to the dissenters and misreads the extent of the dissent, believing that it represents a wide segment of the population and if Hanoi would only hold on, the spirit of the American people will weaken and America will withdraw. The critics of the dissenters then attempt to say that dissent is thus responsible for a prolongation of the fighting in Vietnam.

"The best one can say for this argument," says former Ambassador Galbraith, "is that it is subversive of meaningful commitment to democracy. Those concerned about the expansion of the war in Vietnam are concerned for the fate of many hundreds of thousands of more lives—American lives as well as the lives of others, than are presently committed to battle . . . . Does an American have the right to remain silent if his reasoned judgment is that lives are presently being pointlessly jeopardized by our Government? This question need only be asked, and the answer becomes obvious."

Retaliation against dissenters from the United States' involvement may become even more subtle in the future than it has been in the past.

The *Washington Post* on July 20, 1967, carried the story of a University of Wisconsin professor of history—a Vietnam dissenter—who was asked to join the President's Panel on Educational Research and Development and then was not appointed because "it was very essential that everybody on the panel be above suspicion. There wasn't any question about my loyalty, he [Dr. Donald R. Hornig, President Johnson's science adviser and the appointing officer] didn't put it that way. But he felt that I would be a liability to the Panel." The professor had served on the panel for many years while it was in its formative stage.

As the American Civil Liberties Union stated on June 4, 1967:

"Such instances show that dissent is now the object of official and private intimidation and harassment. Unless these, and others, are vigorously and courageously opposed, unless the right and importance of dissent are reaffirmed and defended, the nation could slip back into a new era of McCarthyism with its dangers to a free society—fear, conformity and sterility."

CHAPTER XXXI

VIETNAM FOLLY—ITS EFFECTS ON
SOUTH VIETNAM

On January 17, 1966—at the height of the nationally televised Senate Foreign Relations Committee's hearings—General Wallace M. Greene, Jr., Commandant of the United States Marine Corps, returning from a 13-day tour of Southeast Asia, stated:

"You can kill every Vietcong and North Vietnamese in Vietnam and still lose the war unless you make a success of the pacification program."[1]

All observers of the Vietnamese scene are convinced that the "other war"—the war for the "hearts and minds" of the people—is as important as the military war.

How goes the "other war"?

According to *U. S. News and World Report* for May 22, 1967:

"Half the country's area—or more—still is outside the control of the South Vietnamese Government. Nor is all of the 'secure' portion firmly under Saigon's influence. Some of it is regarded as safe only by day—and virtually all of it is prey to Communist hit-and-run attacks at almost any time . . . between 40 and 50 percent of South Vietnam's 11,700 villages and hamlets are participating in the local elections."

According to that report, at the beginning of 1966, the South Vietnamese Government claimed control of over 57 percent of the population. In May 1967;

"Under Government control: 8.54 million, or 56.8 percent;

"Under Communist control: 2.74 million, or 18.2 percent;

"In contested areas: 3.77 million, or 25.0 percent."

It cannot be too strongly or too often emphasized that the term "under Government control" is entirely a relative concept. The front is all around in Saigon.

"There is considerable evidence," columnist Ray Cromley wrote in the *Saigon Post* on February 23, 1967, "that the Viet Cong have penetrated the Vietnamese staffs of a good many—perhaps most—of the American offices in South Vietnam and most offices of the Vietnamese Government, including the police, army and air force."

Security for United States armed forces and civilian forces stationed in Vietnam is, because of the nature of the conflict, a major problem.

When one of the authors of this volume was in South Vietnam in May 1967, he was driven to a building occupied by the United States Agency for International Development (AID). The entrances were barricaded by squat, cement posts providing a sort of obstacle course preventing anyone from driving up to the entrance without first being stopped in a small courtyard where, under the watchful eyes of armed United States and Vietnamese guards, a local Vietnamese employee walked slowly around his automobile with a geiger-like instrument testing for concealed bombs. Such precautions are well taken—if only the individual holding the instrument had kept his eyes on the gauge instead of on the sky!

The AID building itself was located only a short distance back from a heavily traveled major public highway in downtown Saigon. Any of the thousands of automobiles or cycles speeding by could have carried a Vietcong with a concealed bomb suitable for hurling over the barricade.

The outside barricades are no protection against infiltration and sabotage from within.

One of the AID officials there did not seem embarassed to relate that a short time before when he hired a Vietnamese secretary, she had requested an advance on her wages so that she would have sufficient money to bribe the Vietnamese security officers to sign her security clearance papers!

The problem is just as acute outside of Saigon. Stewart Alsop relates the question posed to him by an Air Cavalry commander:

"One of my best sergeants was leading the patrol, and he saw two peasants squatting by a house, and he went over and tapped one of them on the shoulder, and the other one shot him dead, through the head. So what should he have done—shot those guys first without asking questions?"

"An old woman," Alsop continued, "or a squatting peasant can turn out to be the enemy in this war. So can a child. A 10-year-old boy volunteered to lead a platoon of Marines through a minefield. Nine of the Marines died—the boy had laid the minefield himself."[2]

Because the Vietcong and the North Vietnamese are indigenous to Vietnam and because a civil war is going on in South Vietnam with Vietnamese fighting Vietnamese, the result has been that noncombatant civilians—caught in the middle—have been killed or wounded in large numbers.

On December 22, 1966, the Associated Press reported that the 1966 civilian death toll averaged about 1,000 per month and that the injured civilians ran three times as many.

Yet the civilians killed and wounded are the very persons whose hearts and minds the entire pacification program was intended to reach.

Desmond Smith in *The Nation,* June 12, 1967, cites the following:

"From a briefing on how the First Cav 'softened up' the Bong-Son plain preparatory to moving in: 'Three hundred and sixty-five air strikes . . . more than thirty B-52 strikes . . . . Then we lobbed in better than a million shells . . . We dumped more than a million psywar [psychological warfare] leaflets on the plain . . . . Well, do you correspondents have any questions'? "According to your handout, all you have captured so far in OPERATION PERSHING is thirty hand grenades, four rounds of large ammunition, 3 tons of rice and 3 tons of salt!

" 'Sir'?

" 'It appears that you've leveled virtually every village and hamlet, killed or driven more than 50,000 peasants off the land with your firepower. My question is, how do you intend to go about winning the hearts and minds of these people'? " 'I'm afraid you'll have to take that up with S.5 sir, but jeeze, it's a real good question.' "

Basically the military effort has been of two varieties: search and destroy or secure and hold operations.

The New Republic commented on a search and destroy operation in January 1967 "in what is called the 'Iron Triangle,' a 60-square-mile area about 30 miles north of Saigon. All Vietnamese in this area are being moved out, whether they like it or not. The region is to be made uninhabitable. Ward Just of the *Washington Post* describes the operation in these words: "The most powerful military juggernaut yet assembled by the Americans in the Vietnam war is now roaring through the hardcore Communist areas in three provinces to the north and west of Saigon, literally laying waste the countryside."

The New Republic editorial pointed out that over 6,000 Vietnamese had been removed by the time it was written on January 28, 1967, "along with their cattle, pigs and oxcarts, and were living in some sort of temporary camps. The homes of the refugees have been or will be destroyed by fire, explosives and bulldozers."

Vietnamese men, women and children moved by white alien Americans out of villages that they have occupied all their lives and then seeing those same Americans putting their homes to the torch are not likely prospects to have their hearts and minds easily won either by them or by the South Vietnamese, who stood watching or were there actively helping the Americans.

The refugee camps to which such forcibly displaced persons are sent are also not especially conducive to winning their hearts and minds. These camps are used for refugees who have been forcibly removed from their villages as well as for refugees who come to get away from the bombings of the villages that are known or suspected of being Communist strongholds.

"The Vietcong," wrote correspondent Neil Sheehan of *The New York Times,* "and the North Vietnamese regulars habitually fortify hamlets with elaborate trenchwork and bunker systems. Infantry attacking in classic style across open paddy fields would suffer prohibitive casualties. Under these circumstances, military commanders can only be expected to use whatever force is at their disposal."

However, Sheehan cites an additional reason for sometimes bombing South Vietnamese hamlets.

"Hamlets are also habitually bombed and shelled at the request of a South Vietnamese province or district chief who has been told by some paid informer that Communist troops are present there . . . since the peasants are often not responsible for the presence of the Communists and, since ground units do not exploit the bombings and shellings, these attacks seem to have a negligible military value."[3]

Sheehan states that the American officials give as their excuse for such practices the legal argument that the Vietnamese "as the legal authorities have the right to destroy their own villages, even if Americans perform the destructive acts."

The refugee camps to which the people from these bombed villages flee or to which the refugees from the razed villages are taken are depressing sights.

General Moishe Dayan, Israeli war hero, visited Vietnam in the summer of 1966 and described such a refugee camp that he visited which held 200 families.

The refugees lived in long, narrow tin huts, with each family occupying space approximately 12 by 15 feet long, with no partitions between each family space. In the center of each space was a wide wooden bed on which the entire family ate and slept. In the corner of the space used as a kitchen was a coal stove with a cluster of blackened crockery. In and around the huts, women were bent over cooking pots and washtubs. Innumerable bare-bottomed and dirty children milled around the huts, begging with outstretched hands. The refugees were sullen and refused to be interviewed.[4]

Sheehan, writing in October 1966, placed the number of refugees at over a million—out of a population of slightly over 15 million. "It takes a good deal," Sheehan observed, "to make a Vietnamese peasant forsake his land and the graves of his ancestors."

General Dayan concluded that the resettlement of the refugees "on the land" was not really the building of farm villages but the creation of slums around United States' military establishments.

The efforts of the Saigon Government to resettle refugees has been entirely inept.

"If resettled properly," Sheehan reports, "the refugees could conceivably develop into an asset for the Saigon Government. Yet true to its usual behavior, the regime neglects them and the majority are left to shift for themselves. Refugee slums have risen in the cities almost as fast as G.I. bars."

Since the Vietnamese National Assembly approved, on April 20, 1962, the establishment by Diem of thousands of "strategic hamlets" the concept has continued from one failure to another under various high-sounding names such as "rural reconstruction," "rural pacification," and the current program, formulated at the Honolulu Conference in February 1966, under the term "revolutionary development."

The workings of the strategic hamlet program under Diem and the reasons given by observers as to why it failed have already been described.[5]

Many of the activities under the current revolutionary development program are repeating some of the mistakes made under Diem's "strategic hamlet program."

Ward Just, veteran *Washington Post* reporter, described what is happening in the revolutionary development program as an inability on the part of the South Vietnamese "to absorb Lyndon Johnson's Great Society, a concept not especially rooted in Asian tradition or especially congenial to it."

While in South Vietnam, one of the authors of this volume found considerable dismay at the so-called Washington "numbers game" under which AID is under great pressure to report to Washington on progress in the revolutionary development—how many schools, how many clinics.

"In Washington," Ward Just stated, "the President can ask why there aren't more schools. In the provinces, the problem is more complex. Are there books? Teachers? Who will build the school? Does the village need one? Want one? How much squeeze (local jargon for graft) must be taken off the top?" Ward Just continued:

"The bewildering variety of American programs, from advisers on tax collection to experts in animal husbandry to projects involving health, auto repair and journalism, is beyond the capacity of the Vietnamese to absorb. The Americans are trying to stuff ten pounds of sugar into a five pound bag. And the bag more often than not is labeled 'Made in America.' "

In an article appearing in the *Washington Post* on July 1, 1967, staff writer Richard Harwood, writing from South Vietnam, gave an illuminating report on how the revolutionary development program was going. He compared two villages.

The first was Tuylon Village, 150 miles south of the Demilitarized Zone. Tuylon is occupied by a Marine Combined Action Committee (CAC) consisting of 15 United States Marines and 60 local Vietnamese recruited as soldiers. Their mission "is to protect Tuylon and to raise the standard of living." Night after night, Tuylon is attacked by the Vietcong, and each time the Vietcong are driven off with great losses. The Marines arranged for a loan so that the village could purchase much needed irrigation pumps and "then organized the farmers into a cooperative to buy the dam, to buy seed, and to market their crops. The village is now pacified. The Vietcong have not been around since last November."

The leader of the CAC groups stated:

"This village knows two things, that we will die for them and that we will not be driven out."

He contrasted Tuylon village with Anphu village just beyond the suburbs of Saigon, where no such security for the resettled villagers exists. This village is being "pacified" by a Revolutionary Development 59-man cadre. That is, it was being pacified until the Vietcong came in April 1967, and badly mauled the officials from the Saigon Government. "The situation . . . is so bad that the province chief has been asked to set up roadblocks at night to prevent the Revolutionary Development cadres from deserting their villages on motor scooters at sundown."

"The cadres," Harwood wrote, "are an invention of the U. S. Central Intelligence Agency and are patterned after the cadres of the Vietcong, have adopted in many cases the bureaucratic habits of the Government of South Vietnam. They are not disposed to social action."

Lt. Colonel William Corson commands the Marine CAC units. He frankly does not think the Revolutionary Development program will work. In his view, the "other war" is doomed to failure. According to him:

"The Revolutionary Development teams and the Government of South Vietnam must inevitably be in conflict whenever they operate together. The Government of Vietnam wants obedience and the status quo; obedience to its edicts, not to laws. But the Revolutionary Development teams, in theory, are designed to disturb the status quo. So conflict is inevitable."

One aspect of the status quo which must be disturbed if the Revolutionary Development program is to work is the much needed land reform.. No progress has been made.

We have already set forth how the lack of such land reform leads to instability and a lack of will to fight on the part of the South Vietnamese.[6]

Neil Sheehan wondered why the American press repeated reports of promises of land reform by officials in Saigon and are taken seriously in Washington "since the promises are never carried out and the speeches made today are practically identical in content and phraseology to those made four years ago by some other Government leaders."

Pulitzer prize-winning Harvard historian, Arthur M. Schlesinger, Jr., former Special Assistant to both President Kennedy and President Johnson, suggests that only a "government which enlists enthusiastic support by the countryside, i.e. a government not dominated by the landlords—would stand a chance of dealing with guerrilla resurgence, even should the North Vietnam forces be withdrawn."[7]

Since 1965, the United States has introduced into South Vietnam and on the high seas around all of Vietnam an enormous amount of fire-power that has been used by both United States and South Vietnamese troops to destroy targets in both North and South Vietnam, and, in South Vietnam, to raze whole civilian villages, to defoliate forests, and to destroy rice paddies.

But long before 1965 the United States had been importing into South Vietnam a commodity equally destructive of the social and economic life of the South Vietnamese—money.

That money, and the goods and services it bought, kept in power in Saigon corrupt officials—generals, mandarins, mandarin types, and lesser bureaucrats—intent only on their own enrichment and the preservation of the status quo at all costs, with a total disregard for bettering the social and economic conditions of the masses of people in the country.

The corrosive effect of the vast sums of money poured into South Vietnam has, in some ways, been as devastating as the shells, bombs and bullets poured out over that land.

In the years since Diem, United States economic assistance to South Vietnam has amounted to approximately $2.6 billion—from fiscal year 1953 through fiscal year 1966. Military assistance has amounted to at least $1.5 billion.[8]

These figures are only those sums given to the South Vietnamese Government. They do not include sums spent directly by the Department of Defense for equipping and maintaining its troops in the field in Vietnam.

Described in non-technical terms, the United States economic assistance program for the private sector of the South Vietnamese economy, called the commercial import program, works as follows: Suppose a Saigon importer wants to import an item costing $1000 in the United States. He goes to the proper South Vietnamese Government bureau and obtains an import license for that item, paying to the government 73,500 piasters at the official rate of 73.5 piasters to the dollar. The Government of South Vietnam is supposed to use those 73,500 piasters for the economic development of the country.

The seller of the item in the United States is paid in dollars out of AID funds allocated for economic assistance to South Vietnam.

However, the importer in Saigon, with a black market exchange rate of about 140 piasters to the dollar, can immediately sell his import license for 140,000 piasters and make an immediate profit of 66,500 piasters. Or, if he decides to sell the item, he will sell it at a price of 140,000 piasters plus costs and profit.

The effect is, of course, inflationary. The 73,500 piasters deposited with the South Vietnamese Government for the economic development of the country buys less and less, requiring the United States Government to pump more and more dollars into the economic aid program for South Vietnam. For the fiscal year 1966, the commercial import program was expected to "deliver approximately 35 major types of commodities to Vietnam for an estimated total cost of $370 million." The largest categories are: rice ($35.3 million); iron and steel mill products ($72 million); medicine and pharmaceuticals ($21 million); fertilizers ($17 million); petroleum fuels and products ($27.1 million); industrial machinery and parts ($70.9 million); and motor vehicles and parts ($17.8 million).

"U. S. officials," said Kenneth L. Whiting in an *Associated Press* dispatch from Saigon on January 13, 1967, "say continued inflation is the worst threat to Vietnam's fragile economy in 1967. No knowledgeable Vietnamese or American pretends the economic crisis is past. Tax collection is inadequate, heavy rice imports are necessary, labor unrest continues and corruption is widespread."[9]

Economic assistance to South Vietnam is also used to purchase materials in the United States for use in programs such as education, agriculture and fisheries, health, public safety, refugee relief, transportation and communication of the Government of South Vietnam.

And finally, the United States' economic aid is used to make up budgetary deficits incurred by the Government of South Vietnam.

Goods imported under any of these three programs are subjected to a high degree of theft. Much of this pilfered material also finds its way into the hands of the Vietcong.

According to the findings of a two-month study on the scene in Vietnam by the Associated Press:

". . . close observers of the Vietnam scene have made estimates ranging up to 40 percent of United States' assistance funds and goods . . . [is lost through] . . . theft, bribery, blackmarketing, currency manipulation, and waste."[10]

AID officials contend that the figure is not that high, but when their rebuttal is analyzed, it is found that the AID officials are referring only to the portion of the economic assistance program designed for use by the South Vietnamese Government and that in addition the lower figure they cite refers only to pilferage from the docks where the goods are unloaded and not to the losses between the docks and the ultimate destination of the goods.

That same *Associated Press* report found:

"Inevitably, some goods, particularly the drugs and rice . . . wind up in the hands of the Vietcong . . . [who] . . . control most of the roads and waterways in Vietnam, which enables them to exact money and a part of cargoes—including supplies from America—as tribute . . . bribery and payoffs appear to be part of everyday life. Low paid public officials expect payoffs as part of the fruits of holding office."

The *Associated Press* report also concentrated on the rampant black market in Saigon which flourished on one of that city's streets around the corner from the United States Embassy and was nicknamed PX Alley because in the stalls lining the streets could be found "Post Exchange luxury items: champagne, Scotch and bonded Bourbon, transistor radios and tape recorders, expensive cameras . . . army shirts, socks . . ."

Saigon authorities gave the sidewalk stalls until November 18, 1966, to close up shop but the *Associated Press* report predicted that they would soon be back in business at a different location.

When one of the authors of this volume was in Saigon in May 1967, he found the prediction had come true.

The black market stalls had moved to the back streets and were being openly operated. Many of the goods in the stalls still bore the PX marked prices and some of the shirts were in wrappers bearing what purported to be contract numbers. According to those who had been there before the move, the only changes were that the stalls seemed to be of a more permanent construction and bore Government license numbers. [The pictures in this volume of the new stalls in which the black market is still being carried on were taken with the coopertion of the Saigon Police Department!]

The extent of the black marketing, profiteering and graft in Vietnam is aptly illustrated by a special dispatch to the *New York Times* dated July 1, 1967, describing the scene at Maxim's restaurant on Tu Do Street in Saigon, labeled as "one of the most expensive night clubs" where any drink—including Coca Cola—was $3.50 rising to $6.00 on holidays." An evening for two can cost "$50 without dinner."

" . . . on one recent night," the dispatch continued, "as always, at least three-quarters of the club's patrons were . . . Vietnamese. A number . . . were junior officers in the South Vietnamese Army. None of them are paid as much as $50 a week."

One Vietnamese businessman told the reporter he went to Maxim's with his wife one night to celebrate their 15th wedding anniversary.

BLACK MARKET—SAIGON STYLE

Before "Clean-up"

During "Clean-up"

UPI Photo

UPI Photo

SAIGON BLACK MARKET

Saigon, South Vietnam. Oct. 6, 1966. "A woman (left) counts her receipts as she sits beside sidewalk counter laden with such black market staples as whiskey, cigarettes and canned goods. The sidewalk stalls are a prime repository of black market merchandise."

"AXE FALLS ON SAIGON BLACK MARKET"

Saigon, South Vietnam. Nov. 17, 1966. "A Saigon policeman leans over a counter laden with canned goods in Saigon's black market recently as he orders its owners to 'move along.' The day of reckoning arrived Nov. 17 for the black marketplace, long a repository for contraband goods including merchandise stolen from U.S. military post exchanges. Vietnamese combat police swooped down on the market, tore the place apart and burned it."

THE "CLEANED-UP" SAIGON BLACK MARKET
JUNE 1967

Photo by Saigon Police Department

Photo by Saigon Police Department

" 'It was horrible', he said, 'I ordered some champagne. They charged me $30, and then I saw—still on the bottle—the price tag from the American PX. It said $3 or $3.50.' "

The Americanization of the war in South Vietnam is nowhere more evident than in Saigon where the "Americans," according to Ward Just in the *Washington Post* on January 1, 1967, "have taken the best villas and apartments . . . drive up in taxis, fill the best restaurants, and often squire the prettiest girls."

"Tensions," he reported, "between the Vietnamese and Americans have been tightened by growing inflation, the deterioration of the cities, and the increasing habit of the Vietnamese to regard the war principally an American effort."

Putting half a million American GI's into a country as small as South Vietnam is bound to cause resentment. A walk or a drive down Tu Do Street in Saigon shows the American presence almost everywhere—the big-boned (by contrast to the South Vietnamese men) GI's walking everywhere—outbidding the Vietnamese for pedi-cabs and girls—the crowded bars obviously catering to the American GI—the garish neon signs over the bars—and the Army and Air Force scurrying through the crowded Saigon streets.

"The moral degeneration," wrote Neil Sheehan in the *New York Times,* "caused by the GI culture that has mushroomed in the cities and towns is another malady. Bars and bordellos, thousands of young Vietnamese women degrading themselves as bar girls and prostitutes, gangs of hoodlums and beggers and children selling their older sisters and picking pockets have become ubiquitous features of urban life."[11]

Thus goes the "other war" in South Vietnam.

It is a struggle between the advocates of "search and destroy" and those who would "secure and hold."

It is also a struggle between the Northerners and the Southerners in South Vietnam for the control of all of South Vietnam.

Tran Van Dinh, former Chargé d'Affaires and Acting Ambassador of Vietnam to the United States, in January 1967 predicted the June 1967 showdown between General Nguyen Van Thieu (who comes from central Vietnam) and General Nguyen Cao Ky (who comes from North Vietnam). He told of the "increasing resentment of the Southerners . . . [that] all the key posts in the Government of South Vietnam are now held by men from North Vietnam. General Nguyen Cao Ky, the prime minister, is a Northerner; so are the secretary general of the National Leadership Committee which advises Ky; the minister for National Reconstruction (in charge of pacification); the director general of police and military security; the chief of staff; and the commander of the troops that surround Saigon and protect Ky against a coup d'état. Northerners control the army, the police, the pacification, the propaganda, have all the money, all the power, and thus control 14 million South Vietnamese."

In contrast, Tran Van Dinh pointed out that "63 of the 64 members of the Central Committee of the National Liberation Front, the political arm of the Viet Cong that both the State Department and Ky say is a puppet of Hanoi and Peking, are Southerners." The one exception, though born in Hanoi, spent all his adult life in the South and taught school in Saigon.

Since 1954, the Government in Saigon, which was established at the behest of the United States and supported by it, has been a carpetbag government of Northerners. Diem, from the central part of Vietnam, remained in power only so long as he continued to receive the support of the United States and the Northern-born Generals commanding the armed forces in the South. When he lost support from both quarters he was removed.

Since Diem's day Northerners have been set up to govern Southerners even down to the district, province, and village levels. When these bureaucrats diverted aid funds into their own pockets or taxed the people so that they could pass part of it back to heir superiors as kick-backs for obtaining their positions, their actions were doubly resented because they were Northerners.

In the February 8, 1966 Declaration of Honolulu the Government of South Vietnam pledged that it would "create on the basis of elections . . . an elected government."

In September, 1966 the Government of South Vietnam proceeded to hold an election of a Constituent Assembly under conditions which guaranteed the election of an Assembly bound to do the bidding of the Military Junta. Those who advocated or were thought to be sympathetic to peace or neutrality were barred from being candidates or from voting.

Before, during and after the elections a strict press, radio and television censorship was maintained by the Saigon government.

It was this hand-picked Constituent Assembly which adopted not only a new Constitution for South Vietnam but also the rules for the general elections.

The election rules were obviously slanted to insure the election of General Thieu or General Ky in the September 3, 1967 elections for President.

Thus, on May 16, 1967 the Constituent Assembly voted that the winning Presidential candidate need only secure a plurality, not a majority, of the votes cast. With the deputies in the Constituent Assembly representing the Military Junta firmly united, a proposal for a run-off election between the two leading candidates was handily defeated.

Another election rule limited electioneering to one month. General Thieu and General Ky were well known through their official trips, which they continued to make right up to the time the other candidates were even permitted to begin their campaigns.

To avoid the possibility that the pro-military vote in South Vietnam would be split, in a Military Junta power play it was announced that Thieu and Ky would run on the same ticket, with General Thieu winning out for first place.

For the September 3 elections to select a President, Vice-President and members of the Senate the same ground rules were laid down for both candidates and voters as had prevailed during the elections for the Constituent Assembly. No one advocating peace or neutrality was permitted to be a candidate or to vote.

In a stormy session held on July 19, 1967, the Constituent Assembly met to pass on the qualifications of those who wanted to run in the general elections.

The session was especially stormy because the Assembly's elections committee had recommended that the military ticket of Thieu and Ky not be permitted to run. The Committee's reason was that, under the constitution, all military and civil service candidates were required to take leave without pay from their posts while campaigning. Thieu and Ky had taken leave without pay from the armed services but continued to hold their civilian jobs as Chief of State and Premier.

According to R. W. Apple, Jr., in *The New York Times,* even though the Military Junta seemed confident of winning "they called an emergency meeting, put the national police and some military units on alert and began a daylong effort to line up votes. Ky's Chief of the security police went into the gallery during the debate accompanied by two bodyguards with pistols jammed into their hip pockets."

The military show of force won out. The Thieu-Ky slate was approved by a show of hands in which 56 of the 75 deputies supported the slate.

Not so fortunate were two popular would-be candidates: economist Au Truong Thanh and General Duong Van (Big) Minh.

Thanh was ruled out on charges, supported by the Ky Government, that he was "pro-Communist and neutralist even though he served until last fall as Economics Minister in the Ky Cabinet." He had resigned at that time in the revolt of a number of Ministers in the Cabinet protesting the large number of Northerners running the South Vietnamese Government. In the Constituent Assembly, he was accused of having said that there was "only one way to end the war, neutralization . . . South Vietnam will have to take a really neutral position . . . our generation can never accept it (Communism) for ourselves."

General "Big" Minh, in exile for two years in Thailand, had led the 1963 putsch against Diem and was too popular in South Vietnam among both civilians and military men to be permitted to run for President.

Two days later on the Constituent Assembly cut the slates of Senatorial candidates from 640 to 480, eliminating two slates allied with militant Buddhist leader Thich Tri Quang. Also eliminated were slates having peace candidates and one ticket of the trade unions which was expected to run very strongly.

Throwing a sop to American public opinion and the Constituent Assembly which had previously called for such action, the Military Junta in Saigon on July 19 announced that "newspaper censorship will be relaxed." A close reading of the "fine print" showed that the penalties for newspapers printing articles objectionable to the Ky government had actually been increased. Instead of deleting the offending article and permitting the remainder of the paper to be printed and distributed, the rules were changed to provide that if there were an offending article in an edition of a newspaper, the entire edition could be seized.

A few days before the September 3 elections, one newspapr was completely shut down for printing something offensive to the government.

Not content with these steps to insure that the military ticket of Thieu-Ky would win the election, General Ky went further. Word came back from Saigon on August 1, 1967 that a new military committee was being formed to keep on running things regardless of who won the election. R. W. Apple, Jr. reported in *The New York Times* that such a move was practically confirmed by General Ky when he told correspondents that it was still being discussed secretly and that "if you write about it in any paper, you will be brought to court."

This brazen revelation that the elections were to be a mere sham and that the Military Junta was already preparing to continue its rule was too much for many in the United States.

The New York Times, in its August 3, 1967 editorial, noted that the Military Junta seemed "determined to convert the . . . election . . . into a farcical matter of 'heads we win, tails you lose' " and warned that if the junta were permitted to continue in this manner nothing would change "in Saigon, in the somber conduct of the war or in the world's estimate of legitimacy of American war aims."

Heated debate erupted in the Senate on August 11, 1967. Participants were: Senators Jacob Javits (R.-N.Y.), Robert Kennedy (D.-N.Y.), Senate Majority Leader Mike Mansfield (D.-Mont.), Chairman of the Senate Foreign Relations Committee J. William Fulbright (D.-Ark.), John O. Pastore (D.-R.I.), George McGovern (D.-S. Dak.), Stuart Symington (D.-Mo.), Joseph Clark (D.-Pa.) John Sherman Cooper (R.-Ky.), Frank Church (D.-Idaho), Stephen Young (D.-Ohio), and Senator Gruening (D.-Alaska).

Senator Robert Kennedy said, "There is mounting and distressing evidence of efforts to interfere with the free choice of the people. Candidates have been barred, some because their views were 'unacceptable,' though they were loyal citizens . . . If such acts continue, if candidates are stifled, or silenced in advance, then no matter how free the balloting, there will have been no election. And

"I'm Looking After The Little Tyke All The Time"

the Vietnamese people will be denied the chance to chart their own future."

Senator Gruening applauded the statements by Senator Kennedy and the others "as evidence that resistance to this war is growing, that they are seeing a new light, that they are groping for a way to get out of this mess, and I devoutly hope we may succeed."

Senator Pastore, until then an unswerving supporter of the Administration, began to reflect the "discouragement and disappointment" he found among his constituents. "If this ballot box is going to become shackled, if we are going to tell a society who can run for office and who cannot run, then I think that the people of this country have a reason to doubt the moral justification we claim— indeed, a reason and right to question our involvement at all."

Senator McGovern joined in the chorus, "We cannot export freedom or stability to Vietnam. We can only bring more death and destruction of our own men and of the people we are supposedly trying to assist . . . The best way to back our men in Vietnam is to change the policy that sent them there."

This furor did not pass unnoticed in the Administration.

Ambassador Ellsworth Bunker, in Saigon, stated it was grossly unfair to judge the campaign against a standard "of perfection which does not prevail even in the United States." Columnist Roscoe Drummond echoed Ambassador Bunker and stated that all we should hope for was that the election should be fairer than elections "we sometimes hold in the United States—whether in Chicago or Texas, Mississippi or Alabama." Columnist William S. White accused those who had spoken out in the Senate as "demanding of South Vietnam a perfectionism in 'clean' elections that has never been found in the United States itself." Both these columns appeared on the same page in the *Washington Post* on August 16, 1967.

In another effort to shore up the election slated to be held on September 3, 1967, President Johnson appointed a group of prominent Americans to go to South Vietnam to observe the election. The group was headed by former Ambassador to South Vietnam, Henry Cabot Lodge.

As expected, the Thieu-Ky ticket won in the September 3, 1967 election.

The percentage of votes received by the tickets coming in in the first four were:

Thieu-Ky	35%
Dzu-Chieu	17%
Suu-Dan	11%
Huong-Truyen	10%

It should be noticed that the tickets coming in second, third and fourth advocated peace and, together, received 38% of the votes cast—more than the winning ticket.

The election observers were on hand in South Vietnam and, on their return, "reported virtually unanimously," Max Frankel reported in *The New York Times* on September 7, 1967, "that the vote was fair and even admirable. Some White House officials felt the exercise had exceeded all their expectations."

Columnists Drummond and White, in the *Washington Post* for September 6, 1967, also hailed the Vietnamese elections.

"The integrity of South Vietnamese's elections," wrote White, had been "established overwhelmingly and beyond all question by independent observers."

According to Drummond, "the elections brought into being a government that can legitimately speak for the people of South Vietnam."

However, assessing the election on October 11, 1967 at the time the Thieu-Ky was sworn in, reporter R. W. Apple, Jr., in *The New York Times,* observed that the "army delivered the votes that enabled the general (Thieu) to defeat his civilian rivals . . . Whether the generals will apply pressure on the new regime informally or through a council has not been decided."

Many in South Vietnam did not agree with the assessment of President Johnson's election committee.

Under the election rules, the Constituent Assembly was required to certify the validity of the elections.

October 2, 1967 marked another tense day at the Constituent Assembly. It had before it a report from its committee which had looked into the election and had recommended by a vote of 16 to 2 that the election be voided because of irregularities.

Four days before, militant Buddhist Monk, Thich Tri Quang had started a "sit in" in a park near the Assembly's meeting place. According to *The New York Times* his press representatives had issued a news release "accusing the Government of giving 50 million piasters, or $424,000 to four (pro Government) deputies . . . to be distributed to deputies who would agree to vote in favor of validation."

Outside also students were demonstrating in the streets, the police charged in, 30 persons were beaten, some severely. Among the injured were Columbia Broadcasting System employees Keith Kay, Jack Laurence, and Bert Quint.

When the vote was taken on sustaining the September 3, 1967 election, it was found valid—but by a narrow margin—58 to 43.

In the aftermath of the September 3, 1967 election, it was difficult to see evidences that democracy had come to Saigon. On September 15, 1967 Dzu, the peace candidate who ran second in the election, was convicted in absentia in a Saigon court of passing a bad check and of illegally transferring money to the United States. A Saigon newspaper was banned the day before the vote in the Constituent Assembly on validating the elections because it had printed a story, which was true, that a committee had recommended against validating the election. On September 21, 1967, Au Truong Thanh, former Cabinet Minister who had been ruled off the ballot because he wanted to run as a peace candidate, was arrested, with no charge being placed against him, and hustled off to jail. After strong United States protests he was released. On October 9, 1967, *Newsweek* was banned in South Vietnam because it had published a story criticizing the South Vietnam Army and had correctly stated that it was turning more and more of the fighting over to the United States and "opting out" of the shooting war.

From the standpoint of the attainment of the objectives sought by the United States in pressing for elections, the banning of *Newsweek* was highly significant. One of the basic objectives of the elections was the attainment of a government which would have the support of the people in the prosecution of the war. And yet—after the elections which were to be a step toward the attainment of that

Freedom From The Press

objective—the article which caused the banning of *Newsweek* was one which showed even less support on the part of the Vietnamese armed forces for the war effort and the turning of that task over to the United States forces.

The military struggle in South Vietnam also presents the picture of the United States intervening militarily in a civil war on a "go it alone" basis—without any except token allies.

On March 12, 1967, the New York Times carried the story that "State Department officials said today that 37 nations had joined the United States in helping South Vietnam. Most are providing nonmilitary assistance."

The following were listed as the contributions (other than those of the United States) of the signatories of the SEATO Treaty;

"Australia: 4,500 combat troops with more on the way; economic aid ranging from medical teams to school books . . . .

"France: Professional and training personnel; low-interest credits for economic development . . . .

"New Zealand: Combat forces being increased to about 300 men; economic assistance in medicine and education . . . .

"Pakistan: Flood relief . . . .

"Philippines: a 2000-man military engineering unit; civil action personnel including military and civilian medical teams . . . .

"Thailand: Armed forces totalling about 12,000 men and economic aid ranging from rice to roofing materials and medical supplies . . . .

"United Kingdom: Economic aid ranging from road building equipment to education and medical help . . . ."

South Korea was listed as sending 45,000 combat troops and medical supplies.

It should be noted that the Philippines, South Korea, and Thailand receive economic and military assistance from the United States and that in both South Korea and Thailand the United States had many more troops stationed than either country sent to South Vietnam. Troops from these three countries sent to South Vietnam are fed, clothed, and paid by the United States.

These three countries, and Australia, were the only ones included in the list of the "37 nations [that] had joined the United States in helping South Vietnam" which sent troops. The aid sent by the other countries was minimal.

Part of the lack of success in winning the hearts and minds of the people of South Vietnam to the support of the government in Saigon is attributable to the repressions against the people exercised by that government.

Exactly one week after President Johnson appeared on May 13, 1965, before the Association of American Editorial Cartoonists and said: "I am continuing and I am increasing the search for every possible path to peace," an emergency decree was published in the Saigon Daily News on May 20, 1965.

That decree made it a crime, punishable by imprisonment for from one to five years, for advocating in any way "peace and neutrality."

The sincerity of statements made by the United States is obviously brought into question around the world when it sees the United States "client Government" in Saigon punishing individuals by imprisonment for advocating the very peace which the President of the United States publicly proclaims he seeks so constantly and earnestly.

There obviously is no hope for the selection of a genuinely representative Government in South Vietnam—even in the part under the control of Saigon—if freedom of speech and press are repressed, or if individuals are not permitted to be candidates for public office or even to vote if they express the hope for peace or neutrality.

"We know," said Desmond Smith in *The Nation* for December 5, 1966, upon his return from South Vietnam, "that the Americans and the Cao Ky government are not ready (and have never been ready) to give a voice [in the political reconstruction process following a cease fire] to anyone who is not anti-Communist. The American political conditions, put forward on November 17, 1965, and confirmed to me by William Bundy [Assistant Secretary of State for the Far East] on December 14, have not been softened. As long as Washington, at the request of South Vietnamese cliques, closes the door in this manner to movements struggling for social justice, democratic government, and genuine national independence, there will be no end to the fighting."

One wonders at the reactions of South Vietnamese as they learn about the deaths of near relatives in bombing raids in South or North Vietnam. Are their hearts and minds won over solidly to the "democratic" Government in Saigon?

One wonders at the reactions of the South Vietnamese in the countryside as South Vietnamese, with United States weapons, assist the agents of absentee landlords as they collect back rent at exorbitant rentals. Are their hearts and minds won over solidly to the "democratic" Government in Saigon?

One wonders at the reactions of the men in Saigon or Danang or Hue as they see their wives, daughters or sisters sell themselves into prostitution to an American GI because a bar girl can earn more than a cabinet minister. Are their hearts and minds won over solidly to the "democratic" Government in Saigon?

One wonders at the reactions of the people of South Vietnam as they see high and low bureaucrats living in luxury because the wheels of the South Vietnam Government will not move without bribes. Are their hearts and minds won over solidly to the "democratic" Government in Saigon?

The hearts and minds of people so long denied fundamental economic, social, and political freedoms are not being won by bombs, grenades and napalm.

CHAPTER XXXII

TOWARD PEACE IN VIETNAM

We have shown that:

Vietnam is an ancient nation with its own history, culture, customs and traditions as a unified country dating back as far as 500 B. C. (Chapter II).

China conquered Vietnam and held it captive for 1000 years but failed in its attempts to make Vietnam a part of Chinese civilization—it drove out the Chinese in the 10th Century and remained Vietnamese (Chapter II);

By 1893 France had, by force of arms, made all of what it called Indochina—Laos, Cambodia and Vietnam—a French colony (Chapter III);

During World War II, Vietnam was conquered and ruled by the Japanese through the French (Chapter IV);

After World War II, the United States aided Ho Chi Minh, Communist-trained, Vietnamese nationalist leader, in his attempts to drive out the Japanese and to gain control of his country (Chapter V);

Later, the United States came to the aid of France with $2 billion worth of financial aid and military supplies—but no troops—in France's attempts to recolonialize Vietnam, thus identifying the United States, in the eyes of both the Communist and the non-Communist Vietnamese people, as standing on the side of French colonialism and opposing their peoples' desires for independence (Chapter VII);

In 1954 President Eisenhower considered and then declined to commit United States troops to fight a land war in Vietnam alongside French forces unless Congress approved and Great Britain joined—both refused (Chapters VII-X, incl.);

In 1954, the United States publicly agreed that it would not "disturb" the Geneva Accords under which there was to be a cease fire in all of Vietnam. That country was to be *temporarily* but only temporarily divided at the 17th parallel only until internationally supervised reunifying elections could be held in July, 1956 (Chapter XII);

Under the 1954 Geneva Accords, Ho Chi Minh's *regular* troops were to regroup north of the 17th parallel but did not require Ho Chi Minh's southern sympathizers, who, as guerrillas, had aided him in his war against the French, to go north or to give up their arms (Chapter XVII);

Even before the Geneva Accords were agreed to, the United States installed a puppet government in Saigon under a ruler brought from monastic retirement in the United States—Ngo Dinh Diem—who had, "sat out" the French-Indochinese war. (Chapter XIV);

In 1954, in violation of the Geneva Accords, which the United States had agreed to support and which prohibited either North or South Vietnam to enter into military alliances, the United States formed the Southeast Asia Treaty Organization that, unilateraly, extended military protection to South Vietnam (Chapter XII);

In 1954, President Eisenhower offered to send economic aid to Diem provided Diem would undertake "needed reforms" which Diem never did—no military aid was offered or promised to South Vietnam (Chapter XIV);

Almost immediately after the Geneva Accords were agreed to, the United States began to violate the provisions of the Accords prohibiting the introduction of new arms or troops into North or South Vietnam by sending in ever-increasing amounts of weapons and members of its armed forces (Chapter XIX);

In 1956, Diem—with United States approval—refused to hold the promised reunifying elections despite Ho Chi Minh's repeated requests that such elections be held and his appeals to the Soviet Union and Great Britain for the enforcement of the provisions of the Geneva Accords requiring such elections (Chapter XVI);

Diem became increasingly repressive of all who disagreed with his policies. The officials of his government and those who had an "in" with that government became increasingly corrupt. Thousands of South Vietnamese were imprisoned for opposing Diem's policies and finally in 1958-59 the people of South Vietnam began to revolt (Chapter XVIII);

The National Liberation Front was formed in South Vietnam by those who had formerly fought against the French and now issued a call for help from North Vietnam. Those who responded from North Vietnam were mostly southerners from Ho Chi Minh's regular army who had gone north in accordance with the provisions of the Geneva Accords to await the reunifying elections. It was those whom the United States labelled "infiltrators from the North" (Chapter XVIII);

Into this civil war in South Vietnam, which, by its installation of Diem and their joint reneging on the promise to hold elections, the United States had played a large part in precipitating, the United States now injected huge quantities of arms, large sums of money and increased its military forces there to 16,500 by the end of 1963 and 23,000 by the end of 1964 (Chapters XX and XXI);

President Kennedy did not make any commitment to Diem that he would send United States troops to fight in South Vietnam. Even though President Kennedy did build up the number of United States "advisers" there to 16,500, he maintained up to his death that "they have to win it—the people of Vietnam." It was *their* war. (Chapter XXIV:

The minor Tonkin Gulf incident in August 1964 was used to rush through the Congress a broadly phrased resolution drafted in the White House giving the President wide powers to take action in Southeast Asia including the use of U. S. armed forces (Chapters XXIII, XXVIII and XXIX);

During the 1964 Presidential elections, President Johnson repeatedly promised the American people that United States boys would not be sent to fight a land war in South Vietnam (Chapter XXIV);

At the time of the Pleiku incident on February 7, 1965—after which the United States began to bomb North Vietnam on an ever-widening basis—there were fewer than 400 North Vietnamese regular troops in all of South Vietnam (Chapter I);

In ordering the bombing of North Vietnam after the Pleiku incident President Johnson stated the attacks were only against "military facilities in North Vietnam used by Hanoi for the training and infiltration of Vietcong personnel into South Vietnam." (Chapter XXV)

The cost of the Vietnam war to the United States is (November 1967) about $3 billion a month and has resulted in drastic cuts in much needed domestic programs (Chapter XXX);

The opposition to United States military involvement in a land war in Southeast Asia has been greater than to any previous military involvement of the United States (Chapter XXX);

United States military involvement in Vietnam violates:

- the Constitution of the United States which authorizes only the Congress to declare war (Chapters I and XXX);
- the Geneva Accords which the United States agreed it would not disturb (Chapters I, XII, XIV, and XIX);
- the SEATO Treaty under which the United States agreed to consult with its allies and to act in accordance with its constitutional processes (Chapters I, XIII, and XXX);
- the Charter of the United Nations which calls upon all members to refrain from use of force and to seek a variety of peaceful means to settle disputes, none of which the United States has used (Chapters I and XXX);

The "other war"—the war to win the hearts and minds of the South Vietnamese people talked about for the last eight years—is being lost because of the failure to carry out long promised and much needed social and economic reforms so that today:

- in the countryside, the peasant farmers are being ruthlessly exploited by absentee landlords and by corrupt officials sent from Saigon to govern them;
- in the cities, venal, grafting government officials, military officers, and profiteering businessmen are more interested in lining their own pockets than in the welfare of the people who are left to eke a bare living in the midst of rampant inflation:

- freedom of speech and press are suppressed so that hundreds have been sent to prison by drum-head military courts merely for advocating peace or neutrality;
- the meaning of the word "election" has been perverted not only by the suppression of freedom of speech and press but by permitting only those who pass government inspection to run for election or to vote;
- because of the harsh, repressive measures of the government in Saigon, those who oppose the graft, corruption, and inefficiency and who earnestly seek social, economic and political reforms are left with no place to go except to join National Liberation forces known as the Vietcong;
- the practice of napalm burning or bombing of South Vietnamese villages out of existence on suspicion that they harbor some Vietcong, the search and destroy military operations, and the practice of moving villagers and destroying their homes are making converts not for the Government in Saigon but for the National Liberation Front (Chapters I and XXXI);

The only foreign troops fighting in South Vietnam are those of the United States and a few of its allies; otherwise, the North and South Vietnamese are fighting the North and South Vietnamese—the dictionary definition of a civil war in which foreign powers have intervened (Chapters I, XVIII, and XXX);

All key posts except one in the South Vietnamese Government, are held by people from North Vietnam; but 63 of the 64 members of the Central Committee of the National Liberation Front are from South Vietnam (Chapter XXX);

While United States troop strength in South Vietnam rose by 142,000 men in 1965, by 150,000 more men in 1966, and 350,000 more men to September, 1967, desertions from the South Vietnam armed forces rose from 96,000 men in 1965 to 110,000 men in 1966, (Chapter I);

The United States was not attacked (as at Pearl Harbor in World War II);

Vietnam—and all of Southeast Asia—is not essential to the security of the United States. More than that, as former Marine Corps Commandant General Shoup has asserted, all Southeast Asia is not worth the life or limb of a single American (Chapters I, VIII, IX, XI, and XII).

United States military involvement in Vietnam is open-ended and, unless there is de-escalation on the part of the United States, the extent of future United States military involvement will be determined by North Vietnam and not by the United States (Chapter XXV).

U. S. military escalation in Vietnam instead of stopping Communism, as contended by its advocates, actually benefits the Soviet Union and Communist China which, without committing a single man to combat there, see more and more U. S. armed forces engaged in combat with a primitive peasant people and more and more U. S. resources diverted to meet military needs. (Chapters I and XXXI);

The so-called "domino theory"—that if South Vietnam fell under Communist domination the surrounding countries would also fall—has been disproved by subsequent events in Cambodia, Laos and Indonesia. (Chapters I and X);

The fragmentation of the International Communist Party in Eastern Europe, and the schism between the Soviet Union and Mainland China, as well as the Johnson Administration's attempts to "build bridges to the East" make outmoded the concept of an aggressive, monolithic, international Communist Conspiracy upon which United States' involvement in South Vietnam has been from time to time allegedly based.

While professing to seek "negotiations without preconditions," the Johnson Administration has in fact insisted upon terms which are the equivalent of an unconditional surrender by Hanoi and the National Liberation Front and attached one important precondition to negotiations, i.e. it refuses to recognize the National Liberation Front—which is the adversary—and is entitled to participate in negotiations in its own right, since it is not only playing the major role in the fighting in South Vietnam but controls large areas and considerable numbers of people in South Vietnam. (Chapters I and XXVII);

How to Bring Peace to Vietnam?

Between a policy of "cut and run" and a policy of unlimited military escalation, what is the "third alternative" which the United States could adopt to extricate itself from the Vietnam morass?

As General James M. Gavin stated in an interview published in *Newsweek* on October 16, 1967: ". . . our policy today in Southeast Asia is serving Communist interest perfectly. It does so in two ways. In the *nation,* it drains our resources—not merely economic, but intellectual and emotional—so that we are neglecting the fierce needs of our own society. In the *world,* it fastens our attention on Asia so intensely that all other areas—like the Middle East—become more open than ever to successful Soviet penetration."

To achieve peace in Vietnam it is essential that the *United States* which has on its own "taken over" there, first establish a climate for peace in that war-torn country.

Such a climate can be established only if the United States, as the major economic, military, and political power in that area, takes certain fundamental actions, announcing in advance that it is taking these actions **simultaneously.**

• *ACTION: Establish in Saigon a "Government for all South Vietnamese-held territory and its controlled people that is truly representative of all elements—other than the Vietcong.*

The time has long since run out when the United States can continue to delude itself—or attempt to delude the world—that the military juntas ruling in Saigon are representative of any but the military class and those war profiteers and black marketeers who have a vested interest in continuing the struggle in South Vietnam and in promoting their own interests.

It will be said that the United States cannot impose upon the South Vietnamese people a representative government—that they must do that by themselves through democratic processes. This is probably true in the long run. No foreign power can impose a government satisfactory to the people that will last after the imposing force is withdrawn.

Since 1954 the United States, through its economic and military might, has kept in power as the so-called legitimate Government of South Vietnam one repressive, corrupt, undemocratic, military government after another.

In the light of this history, the United States is in no position to argue that it cannot use its economic and military might in South Vietnam—now augmented by over 500,000 men of its armed forces —to establish in Saigon a government which is truly representative of all elements of South Vietnam's economic, religious and military life—for the time being other than the Vietcong, and having done so leave its future to the Vietnamese people.

In South Vietnam, the bullets for the rifles, the shells for the mortars, the gasoline for the jeeps, the tanks and the airplanes, and the food for the people—these are all available through and *as* the United States armed forces decide.

The vast economic and military power which the United States now possesses in South Vietnam should be used to bring about a government in South Vietnam which is dedicated to stopping, rather than in prolonging, the war. So long as the military junta in Saigon severely punishes all public discussions for peace, how can the conditions for peace exist?

• *ACTION: The United States should announce that all bombing of North Vietnam by both United States and South Vietnamese forces has been stopped permanently and unconditionally.*

The bombings of North Vietnam have achieved none of the various objectives claimed for them. They have proven a complete failure—have killed many non-combatants and caused the physical destruction of non-military targets that remain to be rebuilt.

The bombings of North Vietnam have not made for a more stable government in Saigon.

The bombings of North Vietnam have not forced Hanoi to come to the conference table.

• *ACTION: The United States should announce that all bombing in South Vietnam by both United States and South Vietnamese forces has been stopped.*

As Vietnamese Buddhist monk Thich Nhat Hanh reports:

"Between 1961 and 1964, even modest estimates of the casualties indicated that more than half a million such (South Vietnamese) civilians had been killed . . . is it a matter for surprise that more and more Vietnamese are drawn to the ranks of the National Liberation Front? It needs only the sight of a red Viet Cong flag in a village or some, often unconfirmed, report that Viet Cong are in the village to draw down American firepower."[1]

• *ACTION: The United States should announce that search and destroy operations by United States and South Vietnamese forces would no longer be made.*

Sweeping down and surrounding a South Vietnamese village suspected of aiding, harboring, or sympathizing with the Vietcong, rounding up the inhabitants, forcing them to gather up their life-long possessions, herding them into refugee camps that are no more or better than concentration camps, and then putting the homes in the village to the torch are not operations calculated to "win the hearts and minds of the people."

These operations are along the lines of the "strategic hamlet" program under Diem. It, too, failed. It, too, strengthened the Vietcong.

• *ACTION: The new civilian government in Saigon should call upon all belligerents in South Vietnam—the North Vietnamese, the Viet Cong and the United States— to agree to an immediate, in-place cease fire.*

A Columbia Broadcasting System public opinion poll of the secure areas of South Vietnam (those not controlled by the Vietcong) in March 1967 reported that "more than four out of five respondents express a wish for an end to the war. Sample comments:

"No more of this fratricidal war.

"As long as there is war everyone has to suffer.

"We could live again in peace and hear no more gunfire."[2]

If such a call for an immediate, in place cease fire were made and well publicized, and if it were adhered to by the South Vietnamese and United States forces, the Vietcong and the North Vietnamese would be in an untenable position if they continued hostilities. A war-weary population in South Vietnam would turn against them, and both—especially the Vietcong—depend for continued resistance upon the support they receive from the surrounding population.

As Buddhist monk Thich Nhat Hanh has put it:

" . . . the Vietnamese people with twenty years of war behind them, will turn with trust and longing to a government that combines the concerns of peace and independence . . . A refusal to participate in an effort that is clearly in the direction of peace combined with independence would brand the Front as the enemy of the people rather than their friends, and its own image would be tarnished and degraded hopelessly."[3]

• *ACTION: The United States should announce that it is turning over to the newly constituted South Vietnamese Government all peace-keeping functions in the areas it controls* in South Vietnam.

Under the circumstances outlined, it would be normal to return police functions to the South Vietnamese Government rather than to have them performed by United States forces.

• *ACTION: The United States should announce that it will immediately discontinue all aid of all kinds—including the payment of salaries directly or indirectly—to any units of the South Vietnamese armed services which attempt to interfere by force with the carrying out by the South Vietnamese Government of its police functions.* . .

Without United States aid a successful military coup against the new Saigon Government would be impossible.

• *ACTION: The newly constituted South Vietnamese Government should announce that thereafter freedom of speech, press, and religion would be guaranteed in all areas under its control; that all repressive measures that theretofore had been used against the exercise of such freedoms were repealed; and all persons imprisoned under such laws would be freed and pardoned.*

A government which professes to seek peace cannot condone the punishment of those who seek the same goals.

A government which seeks to be broadly representative of all elements of the population cannot condone religious persecution.

A government which seeks to be representative of the people cannot hope to do so if it represses freedom of speech and press.

• *ACTION: The United States should announce that as the South Vietnamese forces take over the policing of the areas under South Vietnam government control, United States forces will be withdrawn to certain large city areas preparatory to their return to the United States; that no further troops will be brought to South Vietnam; and that construction of all military bases and facilities will be stopped immediately.*

If the Vietnamese are ever to control their own destinies, they must first be permitted to do so. In 1954 they were prevented from doing so—long before there were any North Vietnamese regular troops in South Vietnam—by a United States puppet government in Saigon, supported by United States arms and money, and showing no desire to be truly representative of the will of the people.

The United States today has an opportunity to undo what it did in 1954—again using United States arms and money—but this time by installing in Saigon a truly representative government and getting out of South Vietnam.

The way to withdraw, as the United States professes it wants to do, is to withdraw.

As Professor Howard Zinn of Boston University has described the process:

"The United States controls the air, the ports, the sea; it can make the most graceful, the most majestic withdrawal in history. Of course it could not do this in a day or a week; it would need to pull its troops from the interior to the coast (so that temporarily there would be something like 'enclaves'), and then transport them away from Vietnam as quickly as ships and planes can carry them."[4]

Those who have advocated a planned withdrawal, as has been here described, have been accused of advocating that the United States "turn tail and run" from Vietnam.

It could be argued that unilateral withdrawal, however unlikely under present policies would be preferable to continuing the fruitless disastrous course—unendingly costly in lives and treasure—that the United States is pursuing.

What is advocated is a realistic appraisal of the situation in which the United States has trapped itself, and a realization that Vietnam belongs to the Vietnamese and, as President Johnson said on one occasion:

"We are not going north and we are not going south; we are going to continue to try to get them to save their own freedom with their own men, with our leadership and our officer direction, and such equipment as we can furnish them."[5]

Turning South Vietnam back to the South Vietnamese and obligating them to assume their responsibilities is-short of pulling out completely—the only way to reverse the dangerous trend to Americanize the war in Vietnam to a much greater extent than it is Americanized today.

• *ACTION: The newly constituted Government of South Vietnam should invite the National Liberation Front to meet with it to plan free, internationally-supervised elections for the formation of a truly representative government for South Vietnam, with freedom of speech and press guaranteed in all of South Vietnam, including the portions held by the Vietcong.*

On July 15, 1965, a group of Catholic intellectuals in South Vietnam stated publicly:

"The key to peace in Vietnam is the establishment of a non-Communist movement that can enter into dialogue with the National Liberation Front and be strong enough to compel the Front to abide by the decisions made in those negotiations."[6]

A non-Communist government broadly representative of all factions in non-Communist South Vietnam, as has been outlined, should be strong enough to deal with the National Liberation Front. This can be achieved if the military junta is curbed and basic freedoms are protected.

The Catholic intellectuals continued.

"The basic condition of peace cannot be other than to establish a democratic force, not aligned with any power bloc, in which all basic liberties and freedoms are respected, in which Communists and non-Communists can co-operate to build a progressive society, according to the ideals of justice and freedom."

Even free, internationally-supervised elections in South Vietnam would probably mean a coalition government. Would that necessarily lead to the ultimate taking over of the Government of South Vietnam by the Communists?

This would not necessarily follow.

The Buddhist monk Thich Nhat Hanh does not believe that this take-over would follow in the wake of a coalition government.

"If the National Liberation Front were 100 percent Communist, then the fear would be justified, but it is not. Only a very small proportion of its membership, though admittedly including much of its top leadership, is Communist. The rest . . . . are in the Front because it is the only possibility they have for expressing their patriotic and nationalist resentment of the presence of foreign troops. Given a different choice, there would be strong pressures within the Front to cooperate genuinely with a representative non-Communist force."[7]

• *ACTION: The newly constituted Government of South Vietnam should call for the immediate withdrawal of all North Vietnamese troops from South Vietnam, coinciding with similar action by the United States, and should also announce its willingness to discuss with North Vietnam the resumption of trade and intercourse between North and South Vietnam, and it should discuss what steps must be taken ultimately to hold free, internationally supervised elections to determine whether Vietnam should, once more, be united.*

As has been shown, Vietnam as a unified country was economically interdependent. Its division at the 17th parallel worked economic hardship on both parts.

Even if Vietnam should remain divided for some time to come, there is no reason to continue the artifical barriers between the North and the South.

Whether ultimately in free, internationally supervised elections Vietnam votes for or against unification depends to a great extent on the leadership which grows up in the South and the efforts it makes to satisfy the needs of the people.

* * * * * * * *

The actions suggested above which the United States could take along the road to peace in Vietnam are not intended as a detailed list of guideposts needed on that road.

Will the United States follow that road to peace—or will it continue along the road to more and more military escalation in Vietnam?

It should be clear that all the United States so-called peace offenses, staged with much fanfare, have failed and were bound to fail because:

First, they were based on a refusal to concede that the United States was not fighting aggression, but was itself the aggressor;

Second, the proposal tentatively advanced as United States' objectives for the return to the Geneva Accords—which were predicated on a united Vietnam—while the United States insisting on an independent South Vietnam were incompatible and hence just double talk;

Third, the real adversaries were the Viet Cong or National Liberation Front with whom the United States has persistently refused to deal.

Until the present approach is changed to conform with reality there is little prospect of bringing the adversaries to the conference table.

The United States today is the richest and most powerful nation in the world. No one, anywhere, could doubt but that the United States —if it desires to do so—could raze all of South Vietnam as it is now doing to considerable parts of it. The withdrawal of the United States from its military involvement in South Vietnam would not be interpreted as an act of weakness but rather as an act of great moral strength.

When Great Britain made the decision that it could not crush, at the point of a Hessian bayonet, the great yearning for freedom of the American colonists, and decided not to continue further its military efforts to put down the rebellion, it became the greater for it.

When France decided that the spirit of freedom of the Algerian people could not be crushed by bullet and bomb, and gave them their freedom, France, too, became the greater for it.

Neither country "lost face."

So, too, with the United States' involvement in South Vietnam.

In a nation—as in an individual—it takes great moral fortitude to confess error. Has the United States the moral fortitude—on a scale with its great strength and wealth—to confess that it has acted in error in Vietnam?

The United States stands today at the crossroads of a great moral decision and must ask itself: "What shall it profit" a nation if it "gain the whole world but loses" its own soul?

The time has come for the United States to institute in South Vietnam its own style of War of National Liberation. Let the United States show the world that its strength lies not in its wealth and military might but rather in the ideals for which it stands.

Let the United States stop raining death and destruction over the people in the countryside of North and South Vietnam.

Let the United States turn aside from its support of cruel, corrupt military dictatorship in South Vietnam and embrace there instead a government that will recognize, support, and defend the worth, the dignity, and the fundamental freedom of each individual in South Vietnam.

The course the United States now pursues in Vietnam is fraught with the gravest dangers for all mankind. It is a collision course destined—unless changed-to bring about a world holocaust.

Under dictatorships, the people have no opportunity to affect the decisions of their dictators.

In a democracy, such as the United States, the people, by making their voices heard and by expressing themselves through the ballot, can change national decisions.

On the issue of Vietnam, will those voices be raised too late—will those ballots be cast too late?

> "No doubt but ye are the people—
> absolute, strong and wise . . . .
> "On your own heads, in your own hands,
> the sin and the saving lives!"*

It may be doubted from the record whether such South Vietnamese as the United States has supported are "strong and wise" when *as a whole* the Vietnamese have shown their determination for independence and freedom from foreign domination.

The United States, as the intruder, which has sought, unsuccessfully, to impose its purposes and policies on the Vietnamese should harken to the words of a real American Statesman, Thomas Brackett Reed.

Reed, Maine Congressman, was the great Speaker of the House of Representatives in the 1890's. In protest against what he deemed the imperialist policies of his Party under President William McKinley, who seemed headed for annexation of the Philippines and possibly Cuba and Puerto Rico without their peoples' consent, he retired from public life stating:

> "The best government of which any people is capable is a government they establish for themselves. With all its faults, with all its imperfections, it is much better than the best government established for them even by wiser men."

---

*From "The Islanders", by Rudyard Kipling

There has been no evidence in Southeast Asia that the United States has demonstrated that its policies have been those of "wiser men."

Thomas Brackett Reed's advice offers a hopeful alternative to United States folly in Vietnam—if the United States will permit the people of Vietnam to follow it.

Unfortunately, the Vietnamese have not, due to circumstances detailed in this volume, been permitted to devise their own government for themselves.

The governments which the French, the Japanese, and, in the last decade, the United States, have sought to devise for them were bound to fail and have failed. They brought about rebellion which has lasted a quarter of a century. What the Vietnamese people have sought and continue to aspire to, is a government which they devise themselves, free from the imposition of alien control, whether it be of the Chinese, the French, the Japanese, or the Americans.

That they want independence for which they have fought with such tenacity and courage against overwhelming odds—should really command the world's admiration and sympathy—especially the respect of Americans, since the United States was born of a similar struggle, even though different in some respect, but primarily inspired by the same objectives and hope.

There should be an early end of the folly of America's intervention and the return by the United States to principles which it has long cherished, and by and large exemplified. This should lead to the independence of the Vietnamese in their own way and, hopefully, would enable them to obtain their age old quest for freedom.

But the primary pre-occupation of the United States should be for Americans. Attemping to inculcate democracy in Vietnam—which should be none of our business—is part of our delusion and one of the paths to our folly. What should be our concern, almost our whole, if not our sole, concern, should be for what our involvement has done, does, and will do to America. By November 1967 it has meant the needless sacrifice of over 14,000 fine American lives, with 90,000 wounded, some horribly crippled for life, the erosion of our overdue pressing domstic needs, the loss of our image in the world, and departure from past performance, as a peace loving, treaty abiding nation.

Another crucial delusion is the assumption that opponents of our Vietnam folly should refrain from criticism unless they can propose a solution. While recommendations for extrication—"honorable" is the adjective usually attached—have been variously advanced, that is *not* their responsibility (although the authors have proposed one). It *is* the responsibility of those who got us into the Southeast Asia mess.

There is still another fundamental approach which, as a final note, should be re-emphasized. It is based on the little appreciated fact, consistently concealed by the official pronouncements, that it is the United States—barging into Vietnam unilaterally and unasked, in violation of all treaties, engaging in combat and bombing North and South—which is the aggressor. This unpalatable truth would, in seeking a solution, require a confession of error and unilateral withdrawal, an alternative at present unlikely of realization but preferable to a continuation of the blind, unproductive, unending and utterly destructive current policy. An analysis of the United States' Southeast Asian involvement cannot omit this concluding somber judgment.

NOTES ON CHAPTER I*

1. Under President Truman, financial aid was given to France in this attempt. Many of our problems today in South Vietnam stem from the identification of the United States with the United States backing of France's attempt to reimpose upon Vietnam its previous status of a non-self governing colony of France, preserving thereby French financial investments in Vietnam. See Chapters I and VI.
2. Washington Star, Dec. 16, 1966
3. *Hearings on Supplemental Foreign Assistance, Fiscal Year 1966—Vietnam, Before the Senate Committee on Foreign Relations, 89th Cong., 2d Sess. 567 (1966)*
4. 112 CONG. REC. 3975 et seq. (daily ed. Feb. 25, 1966).
5. The Washington Post, June 18, 1967.
6. Senator Mike Mansfield, Senate Majority Leader, in a speech at Yashiva University in New York on June 16, 1966.

NOTES ON CHAPTER II

1. "By Southeast Asia we mean the peninsula jutting out from the Asian mainland between India and China, the vast archipelago south and east of it which includes Indonesia and the Philippines." J. BUTTINGER, THE SMALLER DRAGON 17 (1958).
2. G. KAHIN, GOVERNMENTS AND POLITICS OF SOUTHEAST ASIA at 379 (2d Ed. 1964). See also: B. FALL, THE TWO VIETNAMS 12-13 (Rev. Ed. 1964).
3. BUTTINGER, supra Note 1 at 72.
4. FALL, *supra* Note 2 at 9.
5. "The word 'Viet' has always designated the people of Vietnam, with additional word 'Nam' (south) indicating that they were located to the south of their Chinese-dominated kinsmen." *Id.*
6. KAHIN, GOVERNMENT AND POLITICS OF SOUTHEAST ASIA Note 2 at 377 (1964)

*For fuller descriptions of works cited see "Selected Bibliography."

7. BUTTINGER, *supra* Note 1 at 26 and 61, note 38.
8. D. HALL, A HISTORY OF SOUTHEAST ASIA 4 (1955).
9. BUTTINGER, *supra* Note 1 at 95.

It should be noted that anti-Chinese feelings were intensified on the part of the Vietnamese when especially harsh measures of repression were adopted by the Chinese when they reconquered Vietnam in 1406 for a brief span of 25 years.

10. *Id*. Ch. II; FALL, *supra* Note 5 Ch. 2.
11. BUTTINGER, *supra* Note 1 at 173.
12. *Id* at 131.
13. *Id*. at 132. See also: HALL, *supra* Note 8 at Ch. 22.
13. HALL, *supra* Note 8 at 359-60.
15. BUTTINGER, *supra* Note 1 at 132.

NOTES ON CHAPTER III

1. "One last Vietnamese leader, De Tham, held out in the Yen-The area north of the Red River Delta until he was betrayed in 1913." B. FALL, THE TWO VIETNAMS 25 (Rev. Ed. 1964).
2. J. CADY, THE ROOTS OF FRENCH IMPERIALISM IN EASTERN ASIA 1, 12-13 (1954).
3. *Id,* at 79
4. *Id*. at 87
5. *Id*. at 213
6. *Id*. at 272-273.
7. *Id*. at 384-385.
8. *Id* at 385-386.
9. FALL, *supra* Note 1 at 35.
10. KAHIN,´ GOVERNMENT AND POLITICS OF SOUTH-EAST ASIA 386-389 (1964).
11. *Id*. at 389
12.

"Nguyen Ai Quoc (Nguyen the Patriot) was the pseudonym used by Nguyen Tat Thanh, better known to the world today as Ho Chi Minh. Born in 1890, he left Vietnam in 1911 as a cabin boy on a merchant vessel and was known to be in Paris at the time of the Versailles conference. He became active in the French Socialist Party and attended its congress in 1920, voting with the majority which split off and formed the French Communist Party. In 1923 he was sent to Moscow as the French Communist Party delegate to the Peasant International . . . He remained there for more than a year to study communism and attended the Fifth Congress of the Communist International (Comintern) in 1924. He then accompanied Mikhail Borodin, the senior Soviet adviser to the Kuomintang, to Canton, where he ostensibly worked as a translator, a cover for his task of organizing an Indochinese Communist movement. In 1925 he created the Association of Revolutionary Youth, a precursor of the ICP." KAHIN, *supra* Note 10 at 389 n 33.

13. *Id.* at 390.

NOTES ON CHAPTER IV

1. B. FALL, THE TWO VIETNAMS 49 (Rev. Ed. 1964).
2. *Id.* at 58
3. E. ROOSEVELT, AS HE SAW IT 115-116 (1946).
4. H. R. DOC. NO. 144, 87th Cong., 1st Sess. 325 (1961).
5. H.R. DOC. NO. 161, Vol. I, 86th Cong., 1st Sess. 918 (1960).
6. *Id.* at 915 et seq.
7. FALL,*supra* Note 1 at 68-70.
8. G. KAHIN, GOVERNMENTS AND POLITICS OF SOUTHEAST ASIA 390 (2d Ed. 1964).
9. FALL, *supra* Note 1 at 69.
10. G. TANHAM, COMMUNIST REVOLUTIONARY WARFARE 67 (1961).
11. FALL, *supra* Note 1 at 70.
12. B. FALL, THE VIET MINH REGIME 3 (Rev. Ed. 1956)
13. M. GETTLEMAN, VIET NAM 57 (1965).
14. FALL, *supra* Note 12 at 6.
15. FALL, supra Note 1 at 74.

NOTES ON CHAPTER V

1. J. BYRNES, ALL IN ONE LIFETIME 317 (1958).
2. 45 FOREIGN AFFAIRS 575-576 (1947).
3. H. R. DOC. NO. 171, 89th Cong., 1st Sess. 4 (1947).
4. SENATE COMMITTEE ON FOREIGN RELATIONS, A DECADE OF AMERICAN FOREIGN POLICY, S.DOC.-NO. 123, 81st Cong., 1st Sess. 1268-9 (1950).
5. *Id*. at 678.

NOTES ON CHAPTER VI

1. THE RECORD OF KOREAN UNIFICATION, 1943-1960, DEPARTMENT OF STATE PUBLICATION 7084 at 69 (1960).
2. *Id*. at 73.
3. *Id*.
4. *Id*. at 75.
5. DEPARTMENT OF STATE BULLETIN, January 9, 1949, 59-60.
6. DEPARTMENT OF STATE BULLETIN, June 9, 1949, 781-783.
7. DEPARTMENT OF STATE BULLETIN, June 19, 1949, 781.
8. U. N. Doc. S/1501 (1950).
9. DEPARTMENT OF STATE BULLETIN, July 3, 1950, 5.
10. U. N. DOC. S/INF/4 (1951) 6.
11. *Id*. at 6-7.
12. U. N. Doc. S/1496.
13. I. STONE, THE HIDDEN HISTORY OF THE KOREAN WAR (1952).
14. 96 CONG. REC. 1956 (1950)
15. Chapter VII, United Nations Charter
16. G. KAHIN, GOVERNMENTS AND POLITICS OF SOUTHEAST ASIA 393 (1964).
17. B. FALL, THE TWO VIETNAMS 73 (Rev. Ed. 1964). See also: KAHIN, *supra* Note 16 at 393.
18. FALL, *supra* Note 17 at 73-74.
19. KAHIN, *supra* Note 16 at 394.

NOTES ON CHAPTER VII

1. See "Selected Bibliography," especially B. FALL, THE TWO VIETNAMS (Rev. Ed. 1964); B. FALL, STREET WITHOUT JOY (3d Rev. Ed. 1963); J. ROY, THE BATTLE OF DIENBIENPHU (1965). G. KAHIN, GOVERNMENTS AND POLITICS OF SOUTHEAST ASIA (1964).

2. D. HALL, A HISTORY OF SOUTHEAST ASIA 716 (1955).

3. KAHIN, *supra* Note 1 at 394 n. 46.

4. HALL, *supra* Note 2 at 717.

5. KAHIN, *supra* Note 1 at 397 n. 54.

6. D. EISENHOWER, MANDATE FOR CHANGE 338 (1963).

7. B. FALL, THE TWO VIETNAMS 122-124 (Rev. Ed. 1964).

8. DEPARTMENT OF STATE BULLETIN, September 28, 1953, 405

9. 100 CONG. REC. 1503 (1954).

10. *Id.* at 1550-1552.

11. DEPARTMENT OF STATE BULLETIN, March 8, 1954, 359.

12. 100 CONG. REC. 1503 (1954).

13. *Id.* at 1505

14. EISENHOWER, *supra* Note 6 at 341.

NOTES ON CHAPTER VIII

1. 100 CONG. REC. 1505 (1954).

2. DEPARTMENT OF STATE BULLETIN, September 28, 1953, 405.

3. D. EISENHOWER, MANDATE FOR CHANGE 343 (1963).

4. *Id.* Part of the cable read: ". . . It is true that certain legislators have expressed uneasiness concerning any use of American maintenance personnel in Indochina. They fear that this may be opening the door to increased and unwise introduction of American troops into that area. Administration has given

assurances to guard against such developments . . ."
See also Chapter VII, *supra*.

5. *Id*. at 345.
6. *Id*. at 340.
7. *Id*.
8. DEPARTMENT OF STATE PUBLICATION 6446 at 2376 (1957).
9. 100 CONG. REC. 4046 (1954).
10. M. RIDGWAY, SOLDIER 276-277:

"The land was a land of rice paddy and jungle—particularly adapted to the guerrilla-type warfare at which the Chinese soldier is a master. This meant that every little detachment, every individual, that tried to move about that country, would have to be protected by riflemen. Every telephone lineman, road repair party, every ambulance and every rear-area aid station would have to be under armed guard or they would be shot at round the clock.

"If we did go into Indo-China, we would have to win. We would have to go in with a military force adequate in all its branches, and that meant a very strong ground force—an Army that could not only stand the normal attrition of battle, but could absorb heavy casualties from the jungle heat, and the rots and fevers which afflict the white man in the tropics. We could not again afford to accept anything short of decisive military victory.

"We could have fought in Indo-China. We could have won, if we had been willing to pay the tremendous cost in men and money that such intervention would have required—a cost that in my opinion would have eventually been as great as, or greater than, that we paid in Korea. In Korea, we had learned that air and naval power alone cannot win a war and that inadequate ground forces cannot win one either. It was incredible to me that we had forgotten that bitter lesson so soon—that we were on the verge of making that same tragic error."

11. EISENHOWER, *supra* Note 3 at 347.
12. 100 CONG. REC. 1552 (1954).
13. *Id*. at 4672.

14. *Id.*
15. H. R. REPORT NO. 2025, 82nd Cong., 1st Sess. (1951).
16. EISENHOWER, *supra* Note 3 at 345.

NOTES ON CHAPTER IX

1. A. EDEN, FULL CIRCLE 106-7 (1960).
2. *Id.* at 107.
3. *Id.*
4. D. EISENHOWER, MANDATE FOR CHANGE 348 (1963).
5. *Supra,* Chapter VIII.
6. NEW YORK TIMES, April 15, 1954.
7. EISENHOWER, *supra* Note 4 at 348.
8. NEW YORK TIMES, April 26, 1954.
9. EDEN, *supra* Note 1 at 110.
10. M. RIDGWAY, SOLDIER 278.

NOTES ON CHAPTER X

1. WASHINGTON POST AND TIMES HERALD, April 21, 1954.
2. 100 CONG. REC. A-3449-3450 (1954).
3. A. EDEN, FULL CIRCLE 113-114 (1960).
4. *Id.* at 115.
5. *Id.* at 117.
6. *Id.* at 118. As set forth by Eden, the following is the full text of the directive:

"1. We do not regard the London communique as committing us to join in immediate discussions on the possibility of Allied intervention in the Indo-China War.

"2. We are not prepared to give any undertaking now, in advance of the Geneva Conference, concerning United Kingdom military action in Indo-China.

"3. But we shall give all possible diplomatic support to the French delegation at Geneva in efforts to reach an honourable settlement.

"4. We can give an assurance now that if a settlement is reached at Geneva, we shall join in guaranteeing that settlement and in setting up a collective defense in South-East Asia, as foreshadowed in the London communiqué, to make that joint guarantee effective.

"5. We hope that any Geneva settlement will make it possible for the joint guarantee to apply to a least the greater part of Indo-China.

"6. If no such settlement is reached, we shall be prepared at that time to consider with our allies the action to be taken jointly in the situation then existing.

"7. But we cannot give any assurance now about possible action on the part of the United Kingdom in the event of failure to reach agreement at Geneva for the cessation of hostilities in Indo-China.

"8. We shall be ready to join with the United States Government now in studying measures to ensure the defense of Thailand and the rest of South-East Asia, including Malaya, in the event of all or part of Indo-China being lost."

7. *Id*. at 119.
8. D. EISENHOWER, MANDATE FOR CHANGE 351 (1963).
9. *Id*.
10. *Id*.
11. NEW YORK TIMES, April 24, 1954.

NOTES ON CHAPTER XI

1. NEW YORK TIMES, April 29, 1954.
2. WASHINGTON POST AND TIMES HERALD, April 28, 1954.
3. The deadlock on the Korean question hinged on whether the elections to be held would be under the supervision of the United Nations.
4. For full text of French proposal see Appendix p.———.
5. D. EISENHOWER, MANDATE FOR CHANGE 357 (1963).
6. *Id*.
7. *Id*.
8. For full text of Vietminh proposal see Appendix p.———.
9. EISENHOWER, *supra* Note 5 at 372.

10. F. WEINSTEIN, VIETNAM'S UNHELD ELECTIONS 5 (1966).
11. EISENHOWER, *supra* note 5 at 366.
12. *Id.* at 368. See also A. EDEN, FULL CIRCLE 149 (1960) According to Eden, Eisenhower and Churchill agreed on "an armistice agreement on Indochina which:

"1. Preserves the integrity and independence of Laos and Cambodia and assures the withdrawal of Vietminh forces therefrom.

"2. Preserves at least the southern half of Vietnam, and if possible an enclave in the delta; in this connection we would be unwilling to see the line of division of responsibility drawn further south than a line running generally west from Dong Hoi.

"3. Does not impose on Laos, Cambodia, or retained Vietnam any restrictions materially impairing their capacity to maintain stable non-Communist regimes; and especially restrictions impairing their right to maintain adequate forces for internal security, to import arms and to employ foreign advisers.

"4. Does not contain political provisions which would risk loss of the retained area to Communist control.

"5. Does not exclude the possibility of the ultimate reunification of Vietnam by peaceful means.

"6. Provides for the peaceful and humane transfer, under international supervision, of those people desiring to be moved from one zone to another of Vietnam, and

"7. Provides effective machinery for international supervision of the agreement."

13. EISENHOWER, *supra* note 5 at 369.
14. EDEN, *supra* note 12 at 160.

NOTES ON CHAPTER XII

1. A. EDEN, FULL CIRCLE 144 (1960).
2. *Id.* at 145.
3. B. FALL, THE TWO VIETNAMS 231 (Rev. Ed. 1964).

4. F. WEINSTEIN, VIETNAM'S UNHELD ELECTIONS 12 (1966).

NOTES ON CHAPTER XIII

1. C. SULZBERGER, THE DAY IT ALL BEGAN, NEW YORK TIMES, January 11, 1967.

NOTES ON CHAPTER XIV

1. NEW YORK TIMES, July 25, 1954.
2. NEW YORK TIMES, May 19, 1954.
3. B. FALL, THE TWO VIETNAMS 235 (Rev. Ed. 1964). Fall states that there is some question as to whether Diem was born in Hue or north of the 17th parallel in Dai Phuong.
4. More detailed accounts of Diem's earlier years can be found in: B. FALL, THE TWO VIETNAMS (Rev. Ed. 1964); R. SCIGLIANO, SOUTH VIETNAM: NATION UNDER STRESS (1963); D. WARNER, THE LAST CONFUCIAN (1963).
5. SCIGLIANO, *supra*, Note 4 at 16-17.
6. S. CASTAIN, VIETNAM'S TWO WARS, LOOK, January 28, 1964.
7. Syndicated columnist Drew Pearson in his column in the WASHINGTON POST AND TIMES HERALD on January 5, 1967 entitled "Hierarchy, Spellman Differ on Vietnam" stated that "it was Cardinal Spellman who arranged for a public relations firm to build up President Diem as the Catholic puppet of South Vietnam, and that Diem's brother, the Catholic bishop of Saigon (sic), beat a well-worn path to Spellman's door to 'promote the war' . . . Cardinal Spellman enlisted the support of Joseph P. Kennedy, wealthy father of the late President . . . the two . . . arranged for the Harold Oram public relations firm, at a fee of $3000 a month to build up Diem as the man who could save Vietnam." See also R. SHEER and W. HINCKLE, THE VIETNAM LOBBY, RAMPARTS, July, 1965.
8. R. SHAPLEN, THE LOST REVOLUTION 118 (1966).
9. R.MURTI, VIETNAM DIVIDED 56 (1964).

10. DEPARTMENT OF STATE BULLETIN, November 22, 1954, 777-778.
11. MURTI, *supra* note 9 at 54-55.
12. *Id.* at 51.
13. SHAPLEN, *supra* at 120.
14. MURTI, *supra* Note 9 at 146.
15. 100 CONG. REC. 16253 (1954).

NOTES ON CHAPTER XV

1. 100 CONG. REC. 16252 (1954).
2. R. SCIGLIANO, SOUTH VIETNAM: NATION UNDER STRESS 20 (1963).
3. R. SHAPLEN, THE LOST REVOLUTION 117 (1966).
4. SCIGLIANO, *supra* Note 2 at 20.
5. *Supra,* Chapter XIV.
6. SCIGLIANO, *supra* Note 2 at 18.
7. *Id.* at 21.
8. B. MURTI, VIETNAM DIVIDED 138 (1964).
9. B. FALL, THE TWO VIETNAMS 243-244 (Rev. Ed. 1964).
10. SCIGLIANO, *supra* Note 2 at 21 n. 32.
11. *Id.* at 21-22.
12. MURTI, *supra* Note 8 at 142.
13. FALL, *supra* Note 9 at 257.
14. SCIGLIANO, *supra* Note 2 at 23.
15. FALL, *supra* Note 9 at 258.
16. J. LACOUTURE, VIETNAM: BETWEEN TWO TRUCES 28 (1966).
17. FALL, *supra* Note 9 at 253.
18. SCIGLIANO, *supra* Note 2 at 57-58.
19. FALL, *supra* Note 9 at 252-253.
20. SCIGLIANO, *supra* Note 2 at 76.
21. *Id.* at 32
22. FALL, *supra* note 9 at 252.
23. *Id.* at 153-154.
24. DEPARTMENT OF STATE PUBLICATION 7839 at 26 (February 1965).
25. MURTI, *supra* Note 8 at 67.

NOTES ON CHAPTER XVI

1. R. SCIGLIANO, SOUTH VIETNAM: NATION UNDER STRESS 134 (1963).
2. F. WEINSTEIN, VIETNAM'S UNHELD ELECTIONS (1966). This is one of the most penetrating analyses of why the reunification elections were not held.
3. DEPARTMENT OF STATE BULLETIN, July 11, 1955, 50.
4. Geneva Declaration, Art. 7. See Appendix p.———.
5. WEINSTEIN, *supra* Note 2 at 31. See also B. MURTI, VIETNAM DIVIDED 183 (1964).
6. MURTI, *supra* Note 5 at 158.
7. WEINSTEIN, *supra* Note 2 at 32.
8. *Id.* at 33.
9. MURTI, *supra* Note 5 at 157.
10. WEINSTEIN, *supra* Note 2 at 37.
11. Cmmd. 9763 at 10 (1956).
12. WEINSTEIN, *supra* Note 2 at 38.
13. MURTI, *supra* Note 5 at 192-193.
14. DEPARTMENT OF STATE BULLETIN, June 11, 1956, 973.
15. WEINSTEIN, *supra* Note 2 at 39.
16. DEPARTMENT OF STATE BULLETIN, April 4, 1966, 530.
17. WEINSTEIN, *supra* Note 2 at 52.

NOTES ON CHAPTER XVII

1. B. MURTI, VIETNAM DIVIDED 32, 35 (1964).
2. See Article 9 of the Geneva Declaration and Article 14(6) of the Agreement on the Cessation of Hostilities in Vietnam, Appendix.
3. See Reports of the International Commission for Vietnam, Appendix.
4. J. LACOUTURE, VIETNAM: BETWEEN TWO TRUCES 29 (1966)

5. FALL, THE TWO VIETNAMS 272 (1964); LACOUTURE *supra* Note 4 at 30; M. GETTLEMAN, VIETNAM 256 et seq. (1965).
6. MURTI, *suupra* Note 1 at 68.
7. FALL, *supra* Note 5 at 271 and Appendix III therein.
8. MURTI, *supra* Note 1 at 197.

NOTES ON CHAPTER XVIII

1. AGGRESSION FROM THE NORTH, DEPARTMENT OF STATE PUBLICATION 7839, February 1965, at 20.
2. G. HICKEY, VILLAGE IN VIETNAM 10 (1964)
3. Quoted in F. WEINSTEIN, VIETNAM'S UNHELD ELECTIONS 43 n. 177 (1966).
4. B. FALL, THE VIETMINH REGIME (Rev. Ed. 1956); B. FALL, STREET WITHOUT JOY (4th Ed. 1964); J. ALSOP, THE NEW YORKER, June 25, 1955.
5. B. FALL, THE TWO VIETNAMS 191-3 (Rev. Ed. 1964).
6. G. KAHIN, GOVERNMENTS AND POLITICS OF SOUTHEAST ASIA 507 (1955).
7. U. S. OVERSEAS LOANS AND GRANTS, July 1, 1954—June 30, 1966, HOUSE FOREIGN AFFAIRS COMMITTEE.
8. G. KAHIN AND J. LEWIS, THE UNITED STATES IN VIETNAM 89 (1967).
9. *Id*. at 89.
10. WEINSTEIN, *supra* Note 3 at 27.
11. HICKEY, *supra,* Note 2 at 10-11
12. J. LACOUTURE, VIETNAM: BETWEN TWO TRUCES 53-54 (1966).
13. P. DEVILLERS, DGO DINH DIEM AND THE STRUGGLE FOR REUNIFICATION IN VIETNAM, IN M. GETTLEMAN, VIETNAM 225-226 (1965).
14. LACOUTURE, *supra* Note 12 at 55.
15. FALL, *supra* Note 5 at 449-453.
16. LACOUTURE, *supra* Note 12 at 55.

NOTES ON CHAPTER XIX

1. B. MURTI, VIETNAM DIVIDED 50 (1964).
2. See Chapter XIV, *supra.*
3. R. SCIGLIANO, SOUTH VIETNAM: NATION UNDER STRESS 113 (1963).
4. MURTI, supra Note 1 at 56-57.
5. M. BROWNE, THE NEW FACE OF CENSORSHIP, TRUE, April 1967 at 38.

NOTES ON CHAPTER XX

1. S. REP. 994, Part 3, 87th Cong., 1st Session 211 (1961).
2. *Id.* at 212.
3. SENATE REP. 994, Part 1, 87th Cong., 1st Sess. at 573 (1961).
4. See Chapter IX, *supra.*
5. Id.
6. R. SHAPLEN, THE LOST REVOLUTION 140 (1966).
7. DEPARTMENT OF STATE PUBLICATION 7308 (December 1961).
8. A. SCHLESINGER, JR., A THOUSAND DAYS (538-539 (1965).
9. T. SORENSEN, KENNEDY 736 (1965).
10. SCHLESINGER, *supra* Note 8 at 537-538.
11. *Id.* at 538.
12. A. SCHLESINGER, JR., THE BITTER HERITAGE 114 (1967).
13. SORENSEN, *supra* Note 9 at 734.
14. DEPARTMENT OF STATE BULLETIN, May 22, 1961, 758.
15. DEPARTMENT OF STATE BULLETIN, June 19, 1961, 956-957.
16. SCHLESINGER, *supra* Note 8 at 542-543.

NOTES ON CHAPTER XXI

1. T. SORENSEN, KENNEDY 739 (1965).
2. A. SCHLESINGER, JR., A THOUSAND DAYS 546 (1965).
3. M. BROWNE, THE NEW FACE OF CENSORSHIP, TRUE, April, 1967 at 31.
4. D. HALBERSTAM, THE MAKING OF A QUAGMIRE 81 (1964, 1965).
5. *Id.*
6. B. FALL, THE TWO VIETNAMS 308-9 (Rev. Ed. 1964).
7. DEPARTMENT OF STATE BULLETIN, October 8, 1962 at 532.
8. M. OSBORNE, STRATEGIC HAMLETS IN SOUTH VIETNAM (1965).
9. *Id.* at 11.
10. *Id.* at 23. See also: G. HICKEY, VILLAGE IN VIETNAM, Ch. I (1964).
11. M. BROWNE, THE NEW FACE OF WAR 197 (1965).
12. S. CASTAIN, VIETNAM'S TWO WARS, LOOK, January 28, 1964.
13. B. FALL, WHAT DE GAULLE ACTUALLY SAID ABOUT VIETNAM, THE REPORTER, October 24, 1963.
14. SCHLESINGER, *supra* Note 2 at 983.
15. NEW YORK TIMES, May 12, 1962.
16. HALBERSTAM, *supra* Note 4 at 268.
17. BROWNE, *supra* Note 11 at 94.
18. SCHLESINGER, *supra* Note 2 at 984-986.
19. R. SHAPLEN, THE LOST REVOLUTION 192 (1966).
20. J. MECHLIN, MISSION IN TORMENT 180 (1965)

NOTES ON CHAPTER XXII

1. CHICAGO DAILY NEWS, March 7, 1964.

NOTES ON CHAPTER XXIII

1. Hearings on S. 2793 before the Senate Committee on Foreign Relations, 89th Cong., 2d Sess. 618-620 (1966).
2. 110 CONG. REC. 18539 (1964).
3. *Id.*
4. 110 CONG. REC. 18402 (1964).
5. J. FULBRIGHT, THE ARROGANCE OF POWER 52 (1966).

NOTES ON CHAPTER XXIV

1. PUBLIC PAPERS OF THE PRESIDENTS, 1963-64, Book II, at 953-954 (1965).
2. *Id.* at 1022.
3. *Id.* at 1126.
4. *Id.* at 1164.
5. T. WHITE, THE MAKING OF THE PRESIDENT 1964 at 358 (1966).
6. PUBLIC PAPERS, *supra* Note 1 at 1267.
7. *Id.* at 1456.
8. NEW YORK TIMES, June 30, 1964.
9. M. RASKIN and B. FALL, VIETNAM READER 270 (1965).
10. F. SCHURMANN, P. SCOTT, R. ZELNIK, THE POLITICS OF ESCALATION IN VIETNAM, Ch. III (1966).
11. THE WASHINGTON POST, September 3, 1964.
12. J. MECKLIN, MISSION IN TORMENT 288-289 (1965).
13. *Id.* at 290.
14. D. HALBERSTAM. THE MAKING OF A QUAGMIRE 312, (1964, 1965).
15. I. F. STONE WEEKLY, September 21, 1964.
16. I. F. STONE WEEKLY, September 28, 1964.

NOTES ON CHAPTER XXV

1. THE VIETNAM CONFLICT: THE SUBSTANCE AND THE SHADOW, REPORT OF SENATOR MIKE MANSFIELD (D., Mont.), SENATOR EDMUND S. MUSKIE, (D.,

Maine), SENATOR DANIEL K. INOUYE (D., Hawaii), SENATOR GEORGE D. AIKEN (R., Vermont) and SENATOR J. CALEB BOGGS (R., Del.) TO THE SENATE COMMITTEE ON FOREIGN RELATIONS, January 3, 1966.

2. DEPARTMENT OF STATE BULLETIN, February 8, 1965, at 175.

3. DEPARTMENT OF STATE BULLETIN, March 15, 1965, at 362-371.

4. R. EVANS and R. NOVAK, LYNDON B. JOHNSON: THE EXERCISE OF POWER 535 (1966).

5. R. HILSMAN, TO MOVE A NATION 531n (1967).

6. 111 CONG. REC. 2871 (1965).

7. *Id.* at 2823.

8. *Id.* at 2878.

9. *Id.* at 2880.

10. THE NEW REPUBLIC, March 8, 1965.

NOTES ON CHAPTER XXVI

1. 112 CONG. REC. (daily ed. March 1, 1966) 4192.

2. 111 CONG. REC. 9518-9541, incl. (1965).

3. *Id.* at 9759.

4. *Id.* at 9752-9754.

5. *Id.* at 9729.

6. *Id.* at 9763.

7. R. EVANS and R. NOVAK, LYNDON B. JOHNSON: THE EXERCISE OF POWER 551 (1966).

NOTES ON CHAPTER XXVII

1. F. SCHURMANN, P. SCOTT, and R. ZELNIK, THE POLITICS OF ESCALATION IN VIETNAM 101 (1966).

2. *Supra*

3. SCHURMANN, *supra* Note 1 at 103-107.

4. R. EVANS and R. NOVAK, LYNDON B. JOHNSON: THE EXERCISE OF POWER 555 (1966).

NOTES ON CHAPTER XXVIII

1. D. DUNCAN, THE NEW LEGIONS 67 (1967).
2. 111 CONG. REC. 2823 (1965).
3. 112 CONG. REC. (daily ed. January 12 ,1966) 129.
4. 112 CONG. REC. (dailey ed. January 24, 1966) 844-845.
5. R. EVANS and R. NOVAK, LYNDON B. JOHNSON: THE EXERCISE OF POWER 563 (1966).
6. 112 CONG. REC. (daily ed. February 28, 1966) 4129.

NOTES ON CHAPTER XXIX

1. 112 CONG. REC. (daily ed. February 16, 1966) 2911 *PASSIM.*
2. 112 CONG. REC. (daily ed. February 18, 1966) 3302.
3. 112 CONG. REC. (daily ed. February 24, 1966) 3813.
4. 112 CONG. REC. (daily ed. March 1, 1966) 4254.

NOTES ON CHAPTER XXX

1. *Supra.*
2. *Supra.* R. HILSMAN, TO MOVE A NATION 529 (1967).
3. C. ROBERTS, L.B.J.'S INNER CIRCLE 20 (1965).
4. *Supra.*
5. R. GOODWIN, REFLECTIONS ON VIETNAM, NEW YORKER, April 16, 1966.
6. THE NEW LEADER, November 7, 1966 at 10.
7. R. EVANS and R. NOVAK, LYNDON B. JOHNSON: THE EXERCISE OF POWER 559 (1966).
8. *Id.* at 551.

NOTES ON CHAPTER XXXI

1. NEW YORK TIMES, January 18, 1966.
2. SATURDAY EVENING POST, January 14, 1967 at 12.
3. NEW YORK TIMES MAGAZINE, October 9, 1966.
4. WASHINGTON POST AND TIMES HERALD, October 16, 23, and 30, 1966.

5. *Supra.*
6. *Supra.*
7. A. SCHLESINGER, JR., A THOUSAND DAYS 114 (1965)
8. U .S. OVERSEAS LOANS AND GRANTS, July 1, 1945-June 30, 1966, HOUSE FOREIGN AFFAIRS COMMITTEE.
9. WASHINGTON POST AND TIMES HERALD, January 14, 1967.
10. NEW YORK TIMES, November 13, 1966.
11. NEW YORK TIMES MAGAZINE, October 19, 1966.
12. THE NEW REPUBLIC, January 21, 1967 at 21.

NOTES ON CHAPTER XXXII

1. T. HANH, VIETNAM: LOTUS IN A SEA OF FIRE 66-67 (1967).
2. COLUMBIA BROADCASTING SYSTEM, THE PEOPLE OF SOUTH VIETNAM: HOW THEY FEEL ABOUT THE WAR, March 13, 1967.
3. HANH, *supra* Note 1 at 85.
4. H. ZINN, VIETNAM: THE LOGIC OF WITHDRAWAL 110 (1967).
5. *Supra.*
6. HANH, *supra* Note 1 at 87.
7. *Id.* at 84-85.

APPENDIX TO VIETNAM FOLLY

(1) Proposed Vietminh Peace Plan, May 11, 1954 408

(2) Vietnam Peace Terms, May 13, 1954 410

(3) Agreement on the cessation of hostilities in Vietnam, July 20, 1954 412

(4) Final declaration of July 21, 1954, of the Geneva Conference— 429

(5) The cease-fire agreements in Indochina: Statement by the President, July 21, 1954 432

(6) Statement by the Under Secretary of State at the concluding plenary session of the Geneva Conference, July 21, 1954 433

(7) Southeast Asia Collective Defense Treaty and protocol thereto, September 8, 1954 434

(8) Aid to the State of Vietnam: Message from President Eisenhower of the United States to the President of the Council of Ministers (Diem) of Vietnam, October 23, 1954 439

(9) Excerpts from the declaration of former resistance fighters on the present situation in South Vietnam, March, 1960 441

(10) Exchanges of messages between President Kennedy and President Ngo Dinh Diem of the Republic of Vietnam, December 14 and December 7, 1961 450

(11) Department of State statement commenting on the report of the Control Commission for Vietnam, June 25, 1962 454

(12) President Kennedy's TV interviews, September 2 and 9, 1963 (excerpts) 456

(13) Message from President Johnson to Gen. Duong Van Minh, Chairman of the Military Revolutionary Council of the Republic of Vietnam, December 31, 1963 459

(14) United States to increase economic and military aid to Vietnam: Statement by the White House, March 17, 1964 461

(15) President's Message to Congress, August 5, 1964 462

(16) Security Council hears U. S. charge of North Vietnamese attacks: Statement by Adlai E. Stevenson, U. S. representative in the Security Council, August 5, 1964......465

(17) Southeast Asia resolution......470

(18) Serious Vietcong attacks: Statement by Secretary of Defense Robert S. McNamara, February 7, 1965......471

(19) Harvard East Asia Specialists Speak Out on Vietnam...... 473

(20) Examples of Vietnam newspaper protests......475

(21) Joint United States-South Vietnam statement on attacks on North Vietnam, Saigon, February 11, 1965......536

(22) Aggression from the North: State Department report, February 27, 1965......537

(23) A reply to the White Paper, by I. F. Stone, March 8, 1965......562

(24) Legal basis for U. S. actions against North Vietnam: Department of State memorandum, March 8, 1965......569

(25) Leading American Authorities on International Law Reply 574

(26) Pattern for peace in Souheast Asia: Address by President Johnson, Johns Hopkins University, April 17, 1965......587

(27) Additional appropriation to meet mounting military requirements in Vietnam: Message from the President of the United States, May 4, 1965......593

(28) Excerpt from letter from Assistant Secretary of State MacArthur to Senator Fulbright, August 2, 1965, transmitting a paper entitled: "The U. S. Commitment to Assist South Vietnam"......597

(29) Excerpt from "The Vietnam Conflict: The Substance and The Shadow"—Report to Senate Committee on Foreign Relations, January 6, 1966......601

(30) Remarks of the President on the submittal to Congress of the supplemental appropriation for 1966, January 19, 1966......603

(31) Declaration of Honolulu, February 8, 1966......604

(32) Excerpts from the Reports of the International Commission for Supervision and Control in Vietnam relating to Articles 16-20 banning the introduction of fresh troops, military personnel, arms and munitions 608

NEW YORK TIMES, May 11, 1954
PROPOSED VIETMINH PEACE PLAN

In order to achieve the re-establishment of peace in Indo-China the following shall be deemed necessary:

[1]

Recognition by France of the sovereignty and independence of Vietnam throughout the territory of Vietnam and also of the sovereignty and independence of Khmer [Cambodia] and Pathet Lao [Laos].

[2]

Conclusion of an agreement on the withdrawal of all foreign troops from the territory of Vietnam, Khmer and Pathet Lao within time limits to be agreed upon between the belligerents. Pending the withdrawal of troops, the dislocation of French troops in Vietnam shall be agreed upon, particular attention being paid to limit to the minimum the number of their dislocation points. Provision shall be made that the French troops should not interfere in the affairs of local administration in the areas of their dislocation.

[3]

Holding of free general elections in Vietnam, Khmer and Pathet Lao. Convening of advisory conferences of the representatives of the Governments of both sides in Vietnam, Khmer, and Pathet Lao, in each of the states separately, and under conditions securing freedom of activity for patriotic parties, groups and social organizations in the preparation and the holding of free general elections to establish a unified government in each country: while interference from outside should not be permitted. Local commissions will be set up to supervise the preparation for and the carrying out of the elections.

Prior to the establishment of unified governments in each of the above-mentioned states, the Governments of both sides will respectively carry out their administration after the settlement has been carried out in accordance with the agreement on the termination of hostilities .

[4]

A statement by the delegation of the Democratic Republic of Vietnam on the readiness of the Government of the Democratic

Republic of Vietnam to examine the question of the entry of the Democratic Republic of Vietnam into the French Union in conformity with the principle of free will and on the conditions of this entry. Corresponding statements should be made by the Governments of Khmer and Pathet Lao.

[5]

The recognition by the Democratic Republic of Vietnam as well as by Khmer and Pathet Lao of the economic and cultural interests of France existing in these countries.

After the establishment of unified governments in Vietnam, Khmer and Pathet Lao, the economic and cultural relations of these states with France should be subject to settlement in conformity with the principles of equality and mutual interest. Pending the establishment of the unified governments in the three states, the economic and cultural relations of Indo-China with France will temporarily remain without a change as they exist now. However, in the areas where communications and trade ties have been broken off, they can be re-established on the basis of understandings between both sides.

The citizens of both sides will enjoy the privileged status to be determined later in matters pertaining to domicile, movement and business activities on the territory of the other side.

[6]

The belligerent sides undertake not to prosecute persons who collaborated with the other side during the war.

[7]

Carrying out mutual exchange of prisoners of war.

[8]

Implementation of measures referred to in Paragraphs 1 to 7 should be preceded by the cessation of hostilities in Indo-China and by the conclusion to this end of appropriate agreements between France and each of the three states which should provide for:

A. Complete and simultaneous cease-fire throughout the whole of the Indo-China territory by all armed forces of the belligerent sides, ground, naval and air. Both sides in each of the three states of Indo-China, for the purpose of strengthening the armistice, will carry out a necessary settlement of territories and of the areas occupied by them, and it should also be provided that both sides should not hinder each other during the passage, for the purpose of the above-mentioned settlement, by the troops of the other side over the territory occupied by the other side.

B. Complete termination of transportation into Indo-China from abroad of new ground, naval and air units or personnel, or any kind of arms and ammunition.

C. To set up control over the implementation of the terms of agreement on the cessation of hostilities and to establish for this purpose in each of the three states mixed commissions composed of the representatives of the belligerent sides.

NEW YORK TIMES, May 13, 1954
VIETNAM PEACE TERMS

The Berlin conference, recommended the re-establishment of peace in Indo-China. This re-establishment implies a military settlement to establish peace on a real and durable basis.

Military Settlement

[1]

The delegation of the State of Vietnam declares itself ready to examine any working document submitted to the conference. Such documents must present a serious, positive effort, likely to lead in good faith to a satisfactory military settlement.

[2]

They must include sufficient guarantees to assure a real and durable peace and prevent any possibility of new aggression.

[3]

They must not lead to a direct or indirect, definitive, or provisional partition of the national [Vietnamese] territory, de facto or de jure.

[4]

They must foresee an international control of the execution of the cease-fire conditions.

As regards the relations between the State of Vietnam and France:

These relations will be based on the joint French-Vietnam declaration of April 28, 1954, which foresees the signature of two fundamental treaties. The first of these treaties recognizes the total independence of the State of Vietnam and its full and complete sovereignty. The second establishes a French-Vietnam association in the French Union on a basis of equality.

AS REGARDS THE INTERNAL POLITICAL SETTLEMENT IN VIETNAM:

[1]

In view of the territorial and political unity of Vietnam, recognition of the principle that the only state qualified to represent Vietnam legally is the state incarnated by His Majesty Bao Dai, Chief of State. This state is the only one to be invested with the powers deriving from the internal and external sovereignty of Vietnam.

[2]

Recognition of the principle of a single army on the entire territory. This army is the National Army placed under the direction and responsibility of the State of Vietnam.

Settlement of the status of the soldiers of the Vietminh [rebels] within the framework of the legal army of Vietnam in conformity with the above-mentioned principle and according to a procedure to be determined. International control of the application of the said settlement.

[3]

Within the framework and competence of the State of Vietnam, free elections on the entire territory, after the establishment of the fact by the [United Nations] Security Council that the authority of the state has been established on the entire territory and that the conditions of freedom are present. To insure the freedom and honesty of these elections, international control operating under the auspices of the United Nations.

[4]

Representative government formed under the aegis of His Majesty Bao Dai, Chief of State of Vietnam, following, and according to the results of, the elections.

[5]

Undertaking on the part of the State of Vietnam to prohibit any persecution of persons having collaborated during the hostilities with the Vietminh.

[6]

International guarantee of the political and territorial integrity of the State of Vietnam.

[7]

Assistance by friendly nations to develop the national resources and raise the standard of living.

AGREEMENT ON THE CESSATION OF HOSTILITIES IN VIETNAM, July 20, 1954[1]

Chapter I—Provisional Military Demarcation Line and Demilitarized Zone

Article 1

A provisional military demarcation line shall be fixed, on either side of which the forces of the two parties shall be regrouped after their withdrawal, the forces of the People's Army of Vietnam to the north of the line and the forces of the French Union to the south.

The provisional military demarcation line is fixed as shown on the map attached (omitted).

It is also agreed that a demilitarized zone shall be established on either side of the demarcation line, to a width of not more than 5 kms. from it, to act as a buffer zone and avoid any incidents which might result in the resumption of hostilities.

Article 2

The period within which the movement of all the forces of either party into its regrouping zone on either side of the provisional military demarcation line shall be completed shall not exceed three hundred (300) days from the date of the present Agreement's entry into force.

Article 3

When the provisional military demarcation line coincides with a waterway, the waters of such waterway shall be open to civil navigation by both parties wherever one bank is controlled by one party and the other bank by the other party. The Joint Com-

---

[1]IC/42/Rev. 2, 20 July 1954.

mission shall establish rules of navigation for the stretch of waterway in question. The merchant shipping and other civilian craft of each party shall have unrestricted access to the land under its military control.

Article 4

The provisional military demarcation line between the two final regrouping zones is extended into the territorial waters by a line perpendicular to the general line of the coast.

All coastal islands north of this boundary shall be evacuated by the armed forces of the French Union, and all islands south of it shall be evacuated by the forces of the People's Army of Vietnam.

Article 5

To avoid any incidents which might result in the resumption of hostilities, all military forces, supplies and equipment shall be withdrawn from the demilitarized zone within twenty-five (25) days of the present Agreement's entry into force.

Article 6

No person, military or civilian, shall be permitted to cross the provisional military demarcation line unless specifically authorized to do so by the Joint Commission.

Article 7

No person, military or civilian, shall be permitted to enter the demilitarized zone except persons concerned with the conduct of civil administration and relief and persons specifically authorized to enter by the Joint Commission.

Article 8

Civil administration and relief in the demilitarized zone on either side of the provisional military demarcation line shall be the responsibility of the Commanders-in-Chief of the two parties in their respective zones. The number of persons, military or civilian, from each side who are permitted to enter the demilitarized zone for the conduct of civil administration and relief shall be determined by the respective Commanders, but in no case shall the total number authorized by either side exceed at any one time a figure to be determined by the Trung Gia Military Commission or by the Joint Commission. The number of civil police and the arms to be carried by them shall be determined by the Joint Commission. No one else shall carry arms unless specifically authorized to do so by the Joint Commission.

Article 9

Nothing contained in this chapter shall be construed as limiting the complete freedom of movement, into, out of or within the demilitarized zone, of the Joint Commission, its joint groups, the International Commission to be set up as indicated below, its inspection teams and any other persons, supplies or equipment specifically authorized to enter the demilitarized zone by the Joint Commission. Freedom of movement shall be permitted across the territory under the military control of either side over any road or waterway which has to be taken between points within the demilitarized zone when such points are not connected by roads or waterways lying completely within the demilitarized zone.

CHAPTER II—PRINCIPLES AND PROCEDURE GOVERNING
IMPLEMENTATION OF THE PRESENT AGREEMENT

Article 10

The Commanders of the Forces on each side, on the one side the Commander-in-Chief of the French Union forces in Indo-China and on the other side the Commander-in-Chief of the People's Army of Vietnam, shall order and enforce the complete cessation of all hostilities in Vietnam by all armed forces under their control, including all units and personnel of the ground, naval and air forces.

Article 11

In accordance with the principle of a simultaneous cease-fire throughout Indo-China, the cessation of hostilities shall be simultaneous throughout all parts of Vietnam, in all areas of hostilities and for all the forces of the two parties.

Taking into account the time effectively required to transmit the cease-fire order down to the lowest echelons of the combatant forces on both sides, the two parties are agreed that the cease-fire shall take effect completely and simultaneously for the different sectors of the country as follows:

Northern Vietnam at 8:00 a.m. (local time) on 27 July 1954
Central Vietnam at 8:00 a.m. (local time) on 1 August 1954

Southern Vietnam at 8:00 a.m. (local time) on 11 August 1954

It is agreed that Peking mean time shall be taken as local time.

From such time as the cease-fire becomes effective in Northern Vietnam, both parties undertake not to engage in any large-scale offensive action in any part of the Indo-Chinese theatre of operations and not to commit the air forces based on Northern Vietnam outside that sector. The two parties also undertake to inform each other of their plans for movement from one regrouping zone to another within twenty-five (25) days of the present Agreement's entry into force.

Article 12

All the operations and movements entailed in the cessation of hostilities and regrouping must proceed in a safe and orderly fashion:

(a) Within a certain number of days after the cease-fire Agreement shall have become effective, the number to be determined on the spot by the Trung Gia Military Commission, each party shall be responsible for removing and neutralizing mines (including river- and sea-mines), booby traps, explosives and any other dangerous substances placed by it. In the event of its being impossible to complete the work of removal and neutralization in time, the party concerned shall mark the spot by placing visible signs there. All demolitions, mine fields, wire entanglements and other hazards to the free movement of the personnel of the Joint Commission and its joint groups, known to be present after the withdrawal of the military forces, shall be reported to the Joint Commission by the Commanders of the opposing forces;

(b) From the time of the cease-fire until regrouping is completed on either side of the demarcation line:

(1) The forces of either party shall be provisionally withdrawn from the provisional assembly areas assigned to the other party.

(2) When one party's forces withdraw by a route (road, rail, waterway, sea route) which passes through the territory of the other party (see Article 24), the latter party's forces must provisionally withdraw three kilo-

metres on each side of such route, but in such a manner as to avoid interfering with the movements of the civil population.

Article 13

From the time of the cease-fire until the completion of the movements from one regrouping zone into the other, civil and military transport aircraft shall follow air-corridors between the provisional assembly areas assigned to the French Union forces north of the demarcation line on the one hand and the Laotian frontier and the regrouping zone assigned to the French Union forces on the other hand.

The position of the air-corridors, their width, the safety route for single-engined military aircraft transferred to the south and the search and rescue procedure for aircraft in distress shall be determined on the spot by the Trung Gia Military Commission.

Article 14

Political and administrative measures in the two regrouping zones, on either side of the provisional military demarcation line:

(a) Pending the general elections which will bring about the unification of Vietnam, the conduct of civil administration in each regrouping zone shall be in the hands of the party whose forces are to be regrouped there in virtue of the present Agreement;

(b) Any territory controlled by one party which is transferred to the other party by the regrouping plan shall continue to be administered by the former party until such date as all the troops who are to be transferred have completely left that territory so as to free the zone assigned to the party in question. From then on such territory shall be regarded as transferred to the other party, who shall assume responsibility for it.

Steps shall be taken to ensure that there is no break in the transfer of responsibilities. For this purpose, adequate notices shall be given by the withdrawing party to the other party, which shall make the necessary arrangements, in particular by sending administrative and police detachments to prepare for the assumption of administrative responsibility. The length of such notice shall be determined by the Trung Gia Military Commission. The transfer shall be effected in successive stages for the various territorial sectors.

The transfer of the civil administration of Hanoi and Haiphong to the authorities of the Democratic Republic of Vietnam shall be completed within the respective time-limits laid down in Article 15 for military movements.

(c) Each party undertakes to refrain from any reprisals or discrimination against persons or organizations on account of their activities during the hostilities and to guarantee their democratic liberties.

(d) From the date of entry into force of the present agreement until the movement of troops is completed, any civilians residing in a district controlled by one party who wish to go and live in the zone assigned to the other party shall be permitted and helped to do so by the authorities in that district.

Article 15

The disengagement of the combatants, and the withdrawals and transfers of military forces, equipment and supplies shall take place in accordance with the following principles:

(a) The withdrawals and transfers of the military forces, equipment and supplies of the two parties shall be completed within three hundred (300) days, as laid down in Article 2 of the present Agreement;

(b) Within either territory successive withdrawals shall be made by sectors, portions of sectors or provinces. Transfers from one regrouping zone to another shall be made in successive monthly installments proportionate to the number of troops to be transferred;

(c) The two parties shall undertake to carry out all troop withdrawals and transfers in accordance with the aims of the present Agreement, shall permit no hostile act and shall take no step whatsoever which might hamper such withdrawals and transfers. They shall assist one another as far as this is possible;

(d) The two parties shall permit no destruction or sabotage of any public property and no injury to the life and property of the civil population. They shall permit no interference in local civil administration;

(e) The Joint Commission and the International Commission shall ensure that steps are taken to safeguard the forces in the course of withdrawal and transfer:

(f) The Trung Gia Military Commission, and later the Joint Commission, shall determine by common agreement the exact procedure for the disengagement of the combatants and for troop withdrawals and transfers, on the basis of the principles mentioned above and within the framework laid down below:

1. The disengagement of the combatants, including the concentration of the armed forces of all kinds and also each party's movements into the provisional assembly areas assigned to it and the other party's provisional withdrawal from it, shall be completed within a period not exceeding fifteen (15) days after the date when the cease-fire becomes effective.

The general delineation of the provisional assembly areas is set out in the maps[1] annexed to the present Agreement.

In order to avoid any incidents, no troops shall be stationed less than 1,500 metres from the lines delimiting the provisional assembly areas.

During the period until the transfers are concluded, all the coastal islands west of the following lines shall be included in the Haiphong perimeter:

    —meridian of the southern point of Kebao Island
    —northern coast of the Ile Rousse (excluding the island), extended as far as the meridian of Campha-Mines
    —meridian of Campha-Mines.

2. The withdrawals and transfers shall be effected in the following order and within the following periods (from the date of the entry into force of the present Agreement):

Forces of the French Union	Days
Hanoi perimeter	80
Haiduong perimeter	100
Haiphong perimeter	300

Forces of the People's Army of Vietnam

Ham Tan and Xuyenmec provisional assembly area	80
Central Vietnam provisional area— first installment	80
Plaine des Joncs provisional assembly area	100
Point Camau provisional assembly area	200
Central Vietnam provisional assembly area— last installment	300

CHAPTER III — BAN ON INTRODUCTION OF FRESH TROOPS, MILITARY PERSONNEL, ARMS AND MUNITIONS, MILITARY BASES

Article 16

With effect from the date of entry into force of the present Agreement, the introduction into Vietnam of any troop reinforcements and additional military personnel is prohibited.

It is understood, however, that the rotation of units and groups of personnel, the arrival in Vietnam of individual personnel on a temporary duty basis and the return to Vietnam of individual personnal after short periods of leave or temporary duty outside Vietnam shall be permitted under the conditions laid down below:

(a) Rotation of units (defined in paragraph (c) of this Article) and groups of personnel shall not be permitted for French Union troops stationed north of the provisional military demarcation line laid down in Article 1 of the present Agreement, during the withdrawal period provided for in Article 2.

However, under the heading of individual personnel not more than fifty (50) men, including officers, shall during any one month be permitted to enter that part of the country north of the provisional military demarcation line on a temporary duty basis or to return there after short periods of leave or temporary duty outside Vietnam.

(b) "Rotation" is defined as the replacement of units or groups of personnel by other units of the same echelon or by personnel who are arriving in Vietnam territory to do their overseas service there;

(c) The units rotated shall never be larger than a battalion— or the corresponding echelon for air and naval forces;

(d) Rotation shall be conducted on a man-for-man basis, provided, however, that in any one quarter neither party shall introduce more than fifteen thousand five hundred (15,500) members of its armed forces into Vietnam under the rotation policy.

(e) Rotation units (defined in paragraph (c) of this Article) and groups of personnel, and the individual personnel mentioned in this Article, shall enter and leave Vietnam only through the entry points enumerated in Article 20 below:

(f) Each party shall notify the Joint Commission and the International Commission at least two days in advance of any arrivals or departures of units, groups of personnel and individual personnel in or from Vietnam. Reports on the arrivals or departures of units, groups of personnel and individual personnel in or from Vietnam shall be submitted daily to the Joint Commission and the International Commission.

All the above-mentioned notifications and reports shall indicate the places and dates of arrival or departure and the number of persons arriving or departing.

(g) The International Commission, through its Inspection Teams, shall supervise and inspect the rotation of units and groups of personnel and the arrival and departure of individual personnel as authorized above, at the points of entry enumerated in Article 20 below.

Article 17

(a) With effect from the date of entry into force of the present Agreement, the introduction into Vietnam of any reinforcements in the form of all types of arms, munitions and other war material, such as combat aircraft, naval craft, pieces of ordnance, jet engines and jet weapons and armoured vehicles, is prohibited.

(b) It is understood, however, that war material, arms and munitions which have been destroyed, damaged, worn out or used up after the cessation of hostilities may be replaced on the basis of piece-for-piece of the same type and with similar characteristics. Such replacements of war material, arms and munitions shall not be permitted for French Union troops stationed north of the provisional military demarcation line laid down in Article 1 of the present Agreement, during the withdrawal period provided for in Article 2.

Naval craft may perform transport operations between the regrouping zones.

(c) The war material, arms and munitions for replacement purposes provided for in paragraph (b) of this Article, shall be introduced into Vietnam only through the points of entry enumerated in Article 20 below. War material, arms and munitions to be replaced shall be shipped from Vietnam only through the points of entry enumerated in Article 20 below;

(d) Apart from the replacements permitted within the limits laid down in paragraph (b) of this Article, the introduction of war material, arms and munitions of all types in the form of unassembled parts for subsequent assembly is prohibited;

(e) Each party shall notify the Joint Commission and the International Commission at least two days in advance of any arrivals or departures which may take place of war material, arms and munitions of all types.

In order to justify the requests for the introduction into Vietnam of arms, munitions and other war material (as defined in paragraph (a) of this Article) for replacement purposes, a report concerning each incoming shipment shall be submitted to the Joint Commission and the International Commission. Such reports shall indicate the use made of the items so replaced.

(f) The International Commission, through its Inspection Teams, shall supervise and inspect the replacements permitted in the circumstances laid down in this Article, at the points of entry enumerated in Article 20 below.

Article 18

With the effect from the date of entry into force of the present

Agreement, the establishment of new military bases is prohibited throughout Vietnam territory.

Article 19

With effect from the date of entry into force of the present Agreement, no military base under the control of a foreign State may be established in the regrouping zone of either party; the two parties shall ensure that the zones assigned to them do not adhere to any military alliance and are not used for the resumption of hostilities or to further an aggressive policy.

Article 20

The points of entry into Vietnam for rotation personnel and replacements of material are fixed as follows:

—Zones to the north of the provisional military demarcation line: Laokay, Langson, Tien-Yen, Haiphong, Vinh, Dong-Hoi, Muong-Sen;

—Zone to the south of the provisional military demarcation line: Tourane, Quinhon, Nhatrang, Bangoi, Saigon, Cap St. Jacques, Tanchau.

CHAPTER IV—PRISONERS OF WAR AND CIVILIAN INTERNEES

Article 21

The liberation and repatriation of all prisoners of war and civilian internees detained by each of the two parties at the coming into force of the present Agreement shall be carried out under the following conditions:

(a) All prisoners of war and civilian internees of Vietnam, French and other nationalities captured since the beginning of hostilities in Vietnam during military operatons or in any other circumstances of war and in any part of the territory of Vietnam shall be liberated within a period of thirty (30) days after the date when the cease-fire becomes effective in each theatre.

(b) The term "civilian internees" is understood to mean all persons who, having in any way contributed to the political and armed struggle between the two parties, have been arrested for that reason and have been kept in detention by either party during the period of hostilities.

(c) All prisoners of war and civilian internees held by either party shall be surrendered to the appropriate authorities of the other party, who shall give them all possible assistance in proceeding to their country of origin, place of habitual residence or the zone of their choice.

CHAPTER V—MISCELLANEOUS

Article 22

The Commanders of the Forces of the two parties shall ensure that persons under their respective commands who violate any of the provisions of the present Agreement are suitably punished.

Article 23

In cases in which the place of burial is known and the existence of graves has been established, the Commander of the Forces of either party shall, within a specific period after the entry into force of the Armistice Agreement, permit the graves service personnel of the other party to enter the part of Vietnam territory under their military control for the purpose of finding and removing the bodies of deceased military personnel of that party, including the bodies of deceased prisoners of war. The Joint Commission shall determine the procedures and the time limit for the performance of this task. The Commanders of the Forces of the two parties shall communicate to each other all information in their possession as to the place of burial of military personnel of the other party.

Article 24

The present Agreement shall apply to all the armed forces of either party. The armed forces of each party shall respect the demilitarized zone and the territory under the military control of the other party, and shall commit no act and undertake no operation against the other party and shall not engage in blockade of any kind in Vietnam.

For the purposes of the present Article, the word "territory" includes territorial waters and air space.

Article 25

The Commanders of the Forces of the two parties shall afford full protection and all possible assistance and co-operation to the Joint Commission and its joint groups and to the International

Commission and its inspection teams in the performance of the functions and tasks assigned to them by the present Agreement.

Article 26

The costs involved in the operations of the Joint Commission and joint groups and of the International Commission and its Inspection Teams shall be shared equally between the two parties.

Article 27

The signatories of the present Agreement and their successors in their functions shall be responsible for ensuring and observance and enforcement of the terms and provisions thereof. The Commanders of the Forces of the two parties shall, within their respective commands, take all steps and make all arrangements necessary to ensure full compliance with all the provisions of the present Agreement by all elements and military personnel under their command.

The procedures laid down in the present Agreement shall, whenever necessary, be studied by the Commanders of the two parties. and, if necessary, defined more specifically by the Joint Commission.

CHAPTER VI—JOINT COMMISSION AND INTERNATIONAL COMMISSION FOR SUPERVISION AND CONTROL IN VIETNAM

28. Responsibility for the execution of the agreement on the cessation of hostilities shall rest with the parties.

29. An International Commission shall ensure the control and supervision of this execution.

30. In order to facilitate, under the conditions shown below, the execution of provisions concerning joint actions by the two parties, a Joint Commission shall be set up in Vietnam.

31. The Joint Commission shall be composed of an equal number of representatives of the Commanders of the two parties.

32. The Presidents of the delegations to the Joint Commission shall hold the rank of General.

The Joint Commission shall set up joint groups the number of which shall be determined by mutual agreement between the parties. The joint groups shall be composed of an equal number of officers from both parties. Their location on the demarcation line between the regrouping zones shall be determined by the parties whilst taking into account the powers of the Joint Commission.

33. The Joint Commission shall ensure the execution of the following provisions of the Agreement on the cessation of hostilities:

(a) A simultaneous and general cease-fire in Vietnam for all regular and irregular armed forces of the two parties.

(b) A re-groupment of the armed forces of the two parties.

(c) Observance of the demarcation lines between the re-grouping zones and of the demilitarized sectors.

Within the limits of its competence it shall help the parties to execute the said provisions, shall ensure liaison between them for the purpose of preparing and carrying out plans for the application of these provisions, and shall endeavor to solve such disputed questions as may arise between the parties in the course of executing these provisions.

34. An International Commission shall be set up for the control and supervision over the application of the provisions of the agreement on the cessation of hostilities in Vietnam. It shall be composed of representatives of the following States: Canada, India and Poland.

It shall be presided over by the Representative of India.

35. The International Commission shall set up fixed and mobile inspection teams, composed of an equal number of officers appointed by each of the above-mentioned States. The fixed teams shall be located at the following points: Laokay, Langson, Tien-Yen, Haiphong, Vinh, Dong-Hoi, Muong-Sen, Tourane, Quinhon, Nhatrang, Bangoi, Saigon, Cap St. Jacques, Tranchau. These points of location may, at a later date, be altered at the request of the Joint Commission, or of one of the parties, or of the International Commission itself, by agreement between the International Commission and the command of the party concerned. The zones of action of the mobile teams shall be the regions bordering the land and sea frontiers of Vietnam, the demarcation lines between the re-grouping zones and the demilitarized zones. Within the limits of these zones they shall have the right to move freely and shall receive from the local civil and military authorities all facilities

they may require for the fulfillment of their tasks (provision of personnel, placing at their disposal documents needed for supervision, summoning witnesses necessary for holding enquiries, ensuring the security and freedom of movement of the inspection teams etc. . .). They shall have at their disposal such modern means of transport, observation and communication as they may require. Beyond the zones of action as defined above, the mobile teams may, by agreement with the command of the party concerned, carry out other movements within the limits of the tasks given them by the present agreement.

36. The International Commission shall be responsible for supervising the proper execution by the parties of the provisions of the agreement. For this purpose it shall fulfill the tasks of control, observation, inspection and investigation connected with the application of the provisions of the agreement on the cessation of hostilities, and it shall in particular:

(a) Control the movement of the armed forces of the two parties, effected within the framework of the regroupment plan.

(b) Supervise the demarcation lines between the re-grouping areas, and also the demilitarized zones.

(c) Control the operations of releasing prisoners of war and civilian internees.

(d) Supervise at ports and airfields as well as along all frontiers of Vietnam the execution of the provisions of the agreement on the cessation of hostilities, regulating the introduction into the country of armed forces, military personnel and of all kinds of arms, munitions and war material.

37. The International Commission shall, through the medium of the inspection teams mentioned above, and as soon as possible either on its own initiative, or at the request of the Joint Commission, or of one the parties, undertake the necessary investigations both documentary and on the ground.

38. The inspection teams shall submit to the International Commission the results of their supervision, their inevstigation and their observations, furthermore they shall draw up such special reports as they may consider necessary or as may be requested from them by the Commission. In the case of a disagreement within

the teams, the conclusions of each member shall be submitted to the Commission.

39. If any one inspection team is unable to settle an incident or considers that there is a violation or a threat of a serious violation the International Commission shall be informed; the latter shall study the reports and the conclusions of the inspection teams and shall inform the parties of the measures which should be taken for the settlement of the incident, ending of the violation or removal of the threat of violation.

40. When the Joint Commission is unable to reach an agreement on the interpretation to be given to some provision or on the appraisal of a fact, the International Commission shall be informed of the disputed question. Its recommendations shall be sent directly to the parties and shall be notified to the Joint Commission.

41. The recommendations of the International Commission shall be adopted by majority vote, subject to the provisions contained in article 42. If the votes are divided the chairman's vote shall be decisive.

The International Commission may formulate recommendations concerning amendments and additions which should be made to the provisions of the agreement on the cessation of hostilities in Vietnam, in order to ensure a more effective execution of that agreement. These recommrndations shall be adopted unanimously.

42. When dealing with questions concerning violations, or threats of violations, which might lead to a resumption of hostilities, namely:

(a) Refusal by the armed forces of one party to effect the movements provided for in the regroupment plan;

(b) Violation by the armed forces of one of the parties of the regrouping zones, territorial waters, or air space of the other party;

the decisions of the International Commission must be unanimous.

43. If one of the parties refuses to put into effect a recommendation of the International Commission, the parties concerned or the Commission itself shall inform the members of the Geneva Conference.

If the International Commission does not reach unanimity in the cases provided for in article 42, it shall submit a majority report and one or more minority reports to the members of the Conference.

The International Commission shall inform the members of the Conference in all cases where its activity is being hindered.

44. The International Commission shall be set up at the time of the cessation of hostilities in Indo-China in order that it should be able to fulfill the tasks provided for in article 36.

45. The International Commission for Supervision and Control in Vietnam shall act in close co-operation with the International Commissions for Supervision and Control in Cambodia and Laos.

The Secretaries-General of these three Commissions shall be responsible for co-ordinating their work and for relations between them.

46. The International Commission for Supervision and Control in Vietnam may, after consultation with the International Commissions for Supervision and Control in Cambodia and Laos, and having regard to the development of the situation in Cambodia and Laos, progressively reduce its activities. Such a decision must be adopted unanimously.

47. All the provisions of the present Agreement, save the second sub-paragraph of Article 11, shall enter into force at 2400 hours (Geneva time) on 22 July 1954.

Done in Geneva at 2400 hours on the 20th of July 1954 in French and in Vietnamese, both texts being equally authentic.

For the Commander-in-Chief of
the People's Army of Vietnam
TA-QUANG BUU,
*Vice-Minister of National
Defence of the Democratic
Republic of Vietnam*

For the Commander-in-Chief of
the French Union Forces in
Indo-China
Brigadier-General DELTEII

FINAL DECLARATION OF GENEVA CONFERENCE, JULY 21, 1954[1]

Final declaration, dated July 21, 1954, of the Geneva Conference on the problem of restoring peace in Indo-China, in which the representatives of Cambodia, the Democratic Republic of Vietnam, France, Laos, the People's Republic of China, the State of Vietnam, the Union of Soviet Socialist Republics, the United Kingdom, and the United States of America took part.

1. The Conference takes note of the agreements ending hostilities in Cambodia, Laos and Vietnam and organizing international control and the supervision of the execution of the provisions of these agreements.

2. The Conference expresses satisfaction at the ending of hostilities in Cambodia, Laos and Vietnam; the Conference expresses its conviction that the execution of the provisions set out in the present declaration and in the agreements on the cessation of hostilities will permit Cambodia, Loas and Vietnam henceforth to play their part, in full independence and sovereignty, in the peaceful community of nations.

3. The Conference takes note of the declarations made by the Governments of Cambodia and of Laos of their intention to adopt measures permitting all citizens to take their place in the national community, in particular by participating in the next general elections, which, in conformity with the constitution of each of these countries, shall take place in the course of the year 1955, by secret ballot and in conditions of respect for fundamental freedoms.

4. The Conference takes note of the clauses in the agreement on the cessation of hostilities in Vietnam prohibiting the introduction into Vienam of foreign troops and military personnel as well as of all kinds of arms and munitions. The Conference also takes note of the declarations made by the Governments of Cambodia and Laos of their resolution not to request foreign aid, whether in war material, in personnel or in instructors except for the purpose of the effective defense of their territory and, in the case of Laos, to the extent defined by the agreements on the cessation of hostilities in Laos.

---

[1] IC/43/Rev. 2, 21 July 1954, Original: French

5. The Conference takes note of the clauses in the agreement on the cessation of hostilities in Vietnam to the effect that no military base under the control of a foreign State may be established in the regrouping zones of the two parties, the latter having the obligation to see that the zones allotted to them shall not constitute part of any military alliance and shall not be utilized for the resumption of hostilities or in the service of an aggressive policy. The Conference also takes note of the declarations of the Governments of Cambodia and Laos to the effect that they will not join in any agreement with other States if this agreement includes the obligation to participate in a military alliance not in conformity with the principles of the Charter of the United Nations or, in the case of Laos, with the principles of the agreement on the cessation of hostilities in Laos or, so long as their security is not threatened, the obligation to establish bases on Cambodian or Laotian territory for the military forces of foreign Powers.

6. The Conference recognizes that the essential purpose of the agreement relating to Vietnam is to settle military questions with a view to ending hostilities and that the military demarcation line is provisional and should not in any way be interpreted as constituting a political or territorial boundary. The Conference expresses its conviction that the execuion of the provisions set out in the present declaration and in the agreement on the cessation of hostilities creates the necessary basis for the achievement in the near future of a political settlement in Vietnam.

7. The Conference declares that, so far as Vietnam is concerned, the settlement of political problems, effected on the basis of respect for the principles of independence, unity and territorial integrity, shall permit the Vietnamese people to enjoy the fundamental freedoms, guaranteed by democratic institutions established as a result of free general elections by secret ballot. In order to ensure that sufficient progress in the restoration of peace has been made, and that all the necessary conditions obtain for free expression of the national will, general elections shall be held in July 1956, under the supervision of an international commission composed of representatives of the Member States of the International Supervisory Commission, referred to in the agreement on the cessation of hostilities. Consultations will be held on this subject between

the competent representative authorities of the two zones from 20 July 1955 onwards.

8. The provisions of the agreements on the cessation of hostilities intended to ensure the protection of individuals and of property must be most strictly applied and must, in particular, allow everyone in Vietnam to decide freely in which zone he wishes to live.

9. The competent representative authorities of the Northern and Southern zones of Vietnam, as well as the authorities of Laos and Cambodia, must not permit any individual or collective reprisals against persons who have collaborated in any way with one of the parties during the war, or against members of such persons' families.

10. The Conference takes note of the declaration of the Government of the French Republic to the effect that it is ready to withdraw its troops from the territory of Cambodia, Laos and Vietnam, at the request of the governments concerned and within periods which shall be fixed by agreement between the parties except in the cases where, by agreement between the two parties, a certain number of French troops shall remain at specified points and for a specified time.

11. The Conference takes note of the declaration of the French Government to the effect that for the settlement of all the problems connected with the re-establishment and consolidation of peace in Cambodia, Laos, and Vietnam, the French Government will proceed from the principle of respect for the independence and sovereignty, unity and territorial integrity of Cambodia, Laos and Vietnam.

12. In their relations with Cambodia, Laos and Vietnam, each member of the Geneva Conference undertakes to respect the sovereignty, the independence, the unity and the territorial integrity of the above-mentioned states, and to refrain from any interference in their internal affairs.

13. The members of the Conference agree to consult one another on any question which may be referred to them by the International Supervisory Commission in order to study such measures as may prove necessary to ensure that the agreements on the cessation of hostilities in Cambodia, Laos and Vietnam are respected.

THE CEASE-FIRE AGREEMENTS IN INDOCHINA:
Statement by the President, July 21, 1954[1]

I am glad, of course, that agreement has been reached at Geneva to stop the bloodshed in Indochina.

The United States has not been a belligerent in the war. The primary responsibility for the settlement in Indochina rested with those nations which participated in the fighting. Our role at Geneva has been at all times to try to be helpful where desired and to aid France and Cambodia, Laos, and Vietnam to obtain a just and honorable settlement which will take into account the needs of the interested people. Accordingly, the United States has not itself been party to or bound by the decisions taken by the Conference, but it is our hope that it will lead to the establishment of peace consistent with the rights and the needs of the countries concerned. The agreement contains features which we do not like, but a great deal depends on how they work in practice.

The United States is issuing at Geneva a statement to the effect that it is not prepared to join in the Conference declaration, but, as loyal members of the United Nations, we also say that, in compliance with the obligations and principles contained in article 2 of the United Nations Charter, the United States will not use force to disturb the settlement. We also say that any renewal of Communist aggression would be viewed by us as a matter of grave concern.

As evidence of our resolve to assist Cambodia and Laos to play their part, in full independence and sovereignty, in the peaceful community of free nations, we are requesting the agreement of the Governments of Cambodia and Laos to our appointment of an Ambassador or Minister to be resident at their respective capitals (Phnom Penh and Vientiane). We already have a Chief of Mission at Saigon, the capital of Vietnam, and this Embassy will, of course, be maintained.

The United States is actively pursuing discussions with other free nations with a view to the rapid organization of a collective defense in Southeast Asia in order to prevent further direct or indirect Communist aggression in that general area.

---

[1] Department of State Bulletin, Aug. 2, 1954, p. 163.

STATEMENT BY THE UNDER SECRETARY OF STATE[1] AT THE CONCLUDING PLENARY SESSION OF THE GENEVA CONFERENCE, JULY 21, 1954[2]

As I stated on July 18, my Government is not prepared to join in a declaration by the Conference such as is submitted. However, the United States makes this unilateral declaration of its position in these matters:

Declaration

The Government of the United States being resolved to devote its efforts to the strengthening of peace in accordance with the principles and purposes of the United Nations takes note of the agreements concluded at Geneva on July 20 and 21, 1954 between (a) the Franco-Laotian Command and the Command of the Peoples Army of Vietnam; (b) the Royal Khmer Army Command and the Command of the Peoples Army of Vietnam; (c) Franco-Vietnamese Command and the Command of the Peoples Army of Vietnam and of paragraphs 1 to 12 inclusive of the declaration presented to the Geneva Conference on July 21, 1954 declares with regard to the aforesaid agreements and paragraphs that (i) it will refrain from the threat or the use of force to disturb them, in accordance with Article 2(4) of the Charter of the United Nations dealing with the obligation of members to refrain in their international relations from the threat or use of force; and (ii) it would view any renewal of the aggression in violation of the aforesaid agreements with grave concern and as seriously threatening international peace and security.

In connection with the statement in the declaration concerning free elections in Vietnam my Government wishes to make clear its position which it has expressed in a declaration made in Washington on June 29, 1954, as follows:

In the case of nations now divided against their will, we shall continue to seek to achieve unity through free elections supervised by the United Nations to insure that they are conducted fairly.

With respect to the statement made by the representative of the State of Vietnam, the United States reiterates its traditional position

---

[1]Walter Bedell Smith.
[2]Department of State Bulletin, Aug. 2, 1954, pp. 162-163.

that peoples are entitled to determine their own future, and that it will not join in an arrangement which would hinder this. Nothing in its declaration just made is intended to or does indicate any departure from this traditional position.

We share the hope that the agreements will permit Cambodia, Laos and Vietnam to play their part, in full independence and sovereignty, in the peaceful community of nations, and will enable the peoples of that area to determine their own future.

SOUTHEAST ASIA COLLECTIVE DEFENSE TREATY AND PROTOCOL THERETO, SEPTEMBER 8, 1954[1]

Text of Treaty

The Parties to this Treaty,

Recognizing the sovereign equality of all the Parties,

Reiterating their faith in the purposes and principles set forth in the Charter of the United Nations and their desire to live in peace with all peoples and all governments,

Reaffirming that, in accordance with the Charter of the United Nations, they uphold the principle of equal rights and self-determination of peoples, and declaring that they will earnestly strive by every peaceful means to promote self-government and to secure the independence of all countries whose peoples desire it and are able to undertake its responsibilities,

Desiring to strengthen the fabric of peace and freedom and to uphold the principles of democracy, individual liberty and the rule of law, and to promote the economic well-being and development of all peoples in the treaty area,

Intending to declare publicly and formally their sense of unity, so that any potential aggressor will appreciate that the Parties stand together in the area, and

Desiring further to coordinate their efforts for collective defense for the preservation of peace and security,

Therefore agree as follows:

---

[1] 6UST 81; Treaties and Other International Acts Series 3170.

Article I

The Parties undertake, as set forth in the Charter of the United Nations, to settle any international disputes in which they may be involved by peaceful means in such a manner that international peace and security and justice are not endangered, and to refrain in their international relations from the threat or use of force in any manner inconsistent with the purposes of the United Nations.

Article II

In order more effectively to achieve the objectives of this Treaty the Parties, separately and jointly, by means of continuous and effective self-help and mutual aid will maintain and develop their individual and collective capacity to resist armed attack and to prevent and counter subversive activities directed from without against their territorial integrity and political stability.

Article III

The Parties undertake to strengthen their free institutions and to cooperae with one another in the further development of economic measures, including technical assistance, designed both to promote economic progress and social well-being and to further the individual and collective efforts of governments toward these ends.

Article IV

1. Each Party recognizes that aggression by means of armed attack in the treaty area against any of the Parties or against any State or territory which the Parties by unanimous agreement may hereafter designate, would endanger its own peace and safety, and agrees that it will in that event act to meet the common danger in accordance with its constitutional processes. Measures taken under this paragraph shall be immediately reported to the Security Council of the United Nations.

2. If, in the opinion of any of the Parties, the inviolability or the integrity of the territory or the sovereignty or political independence of any Party in the treaty area or of any other State or territory to which the provisions of paragraph 1 of this Article from time to time apply is threatened in any way other than by armed attack or is affected or threatened by any fact or situation which might endanger the peace of the area, the Parties shall consult immediately in order to agree on the measures which should be taken for the common defense.

3. It is understood that no action on the territory of any State designated by unanimous agreement under paragraph 1 of this Article or on any territory so designated shall be taken except at the invitation or with the consent of the government concerned.

Article V

The Parties hereby establish a Council, on which each of them shall be represented, to consider matters concerning the implementation of this Treaty. The Council shall provide for consultation with regard to military and any other planning as the situation obtaining in the treaty area may from time to time require. The Council shall be so organized as to be able to meet at any time.

Article VI

This Treaty does not affect and shall not be interpreted as affecting in any way the rights and obligations of any of the Parties under the Charter of the United Nations or the responsibility of the United Nations for the maintenance of international peace and security. Each Party declares that none of the international engagements now in force between it and any other of the Parties or any third party is in conflict with the provisions of this Treaty, and undertakes not to enter into any international engagements in conflict with this Treaty.

Article VII

Any other State in a position to further the objectives of this Treaty and to contribute to the security of the area may, by unanimous agreement of the Parties, be invited to accede to this Treaty. Any State so invited may become a Party to the Treaty by depositing its instrument of accession with the Government of the Republic of the Philippines. The Government of the Republic of the Philippines shall inform each of the Parties of the deposit of each such instrument of accession.

Article VIII

As used in this Treaty, the "treaty area" is the general area of Southeast Asia, including also the entire territories of the Asian Parties, and the general area of the Southwest Pacific not including the Pacific area north of 21 degrees 30 minutes north latitude. The Parties may, by unanimous agreement, amend this Article to include within the treaty area the territory of any State acceding to this Treaty in accordance with Article VII or otherwise to change the treaty area.

Article IX

1. This Treaty shall be deposited in the archives of the Government of the Republic of the Philippines. Duly certified copies thereof shall be transmitted by that government to the other signatories.

2. The Treaty shall be ratified and its provisions carried out by the Parties in accordance with their respective constitutional processes. The instruments of ratification shall be deposited as soon as possible with the Government of the Republic of the Philippines, which shall notify all of the other signatories of such deposit.

3. The Treaty shall enter into force between the States which have ratified it as soon as the instruments of ratification of a majority of the signatories shall have been deposited, and shall come into effect with respect to each other State on the date of the deposit of its instrument of ratification.

Article X

This Treaty shall remain in force indefinitely, but any Party may cease to be a Party one year after its notice of denunciation has been given to the Government of the Republic of the Philippines, which shall inform the Governments of the other Parties of the deposit of each notice of denunciation.

Article XI

The English text of this Treaty is binding on the Parties, but when the Parties have agreed to the French text thereof and have so notified the Government of the Republic of the Philippines, the French text shall be equally authentic and binding on the Parties.

Understanding of the United States of America

The United States of America is executing the present Treaty does so with the understanding that its recognition of the effect of aggression and armed attack and its agreement with reference thereto in Article IV, paragraph 1, apply only to communist aggression but affirms that in the event of other aggression or armed attack it will consult under the provisions of Article IV, paragraph 2.

In witness whereof, the undersigned Plenipotentiaries have signed this Treaty.

Done at Manila, this eighth day of September, 1954.

For Australia:
R. G. Casey

For France:
G. La Chambre

For New Zealand:
Clifton Webb

For Pakistan:
Signed for transmission to my Government for its considera-
tion and action in accordance with the Constitution of Pakistan.
Zafrulla Khan

For the Republic of the Philippines:
Carlos P. Garcia
Francisco A. Delgado
Tomas L. Cabili
Lorenzo M. Tañada
Cornelio T. Villareal

For the Kingdom of Thailand:
Wan Waithayakon Krommun Naradhip Bongsprabandh

For the United Kingdom of Great Britain and Northern Island:
Reading

For the United States of America:
John Foster Dulles
H. Alexander Smith
Michael J. Mansfield

I CERTIFY THAT the foregoing is a true copy of the Southeast
Asia Collective Defense Treaty concluded and signed in the English
language at Manila, on September 8, 1954, the signed original of
which is deposited in the archives of the Government of the Republic
of the Philippines.

IN TESTIMONY WHEREOF, I, RAUL S. MANGLAPUS,
Undersecretary of Foreign Affairs of the Republic of the Philippines,
have hereunto set my hand and caused the seal of the Department of

Foreign Affairs to be affixed at the City of Manila, this 14th day of October, 1954.

[Seal]

Undersecretary of Foreign Affairs
RAUL S. MANGLAPUS
RAUL S. MANGLAPUS

Entered into force: February 19, 1955.

Protocol to the Southeast Asia Collective Defense Treaty

Designation of States and Territory as to Which Provisions of Article IV and Article III Are To Be Applicable

The Parties to the Southeast Asia Collective Defense Treaty unanimously designate for the purposes of Article IV of the Treaty the States of Cambodia and Laos and the free territory under the jurisdiction of the State of Vietnam.

The Parties further agree that the above mentioned states and territory shall be eligible in respect of the economic measures contemplated by Article III.

This Protocol shall enter into force simultaneously with the coming into force of the Treaty.

IN WITNESS WHEREOF, the undersigned Plenipotentiaries have signed this Protocol to the Southeast Asia Collective Defense Treaty.

Done at Manila, this eighth day of September, 1954.

AID TO THE STATE OF VIETNAM: Message From the President of the United States to the President of the Council of Ministers of Vietnam, October 23, 1954[1]

Dear Mr. President: I have been following with great interest the course of developments in Vietnam, particularly since the conclusion of the conference at Geneva. The implications of the agree-

---

[1]Department of State *Bulletin,* Nov. 5, 1954, pp. 735-736.

ment concerning Vietnam have caused grave concern regarding the future of a country temporarily divided by an artificial military grouping. weakened by a long and exhausting war and faced with enemies without and by their subversive collaborators within.

Your recent requests for aid to assist in the formidable project of the movement of several hundred thousand loyal Vietnamese citizens away from areas which are passing under a *de facto* rule and political ideology which they abhor, are being fulfilled. I am glad that the United States is able to assist in this humanitarian effort.

We have been exploring ways and means to permit our aid to Vietnam to be more effective and to make a greater contribution to the welfare and stability of the Government of Vietnam. I am, accordingly, instructing the American Ambassador to Vietnam to examine with you in your capacity as Chief of Government, how an intelligent program of American aid given directly to your Government can serve to assist Vietnam in its present hour of trial, provided that your Government is prepared to give assurances as to the standards of performance it would be able to maintain in the event such aid were supplied.

The purpose of this offer is to assist the Government of Vietnam in developing and maintaining a strong, viable state, capable of resisting attempted subversion or aggression through military means. The Government of the United States expects that this aid will be met by performance on the part of the Government of Vietnam in undertaking needed reforms. It hopes that such aid, combined with your own continuing efforts, will contribute effectively toward an independent Vietnam endowed with a strong government. Such a government would, I hope, be so responsive to the nationalist aspirations of its people, so enlightened in purpose and effective in performance, that it will be respected both at home and abroad and discourage any who might wish to impose a foreign ideology on your free people.

Excerpts from the March, 1960
DECLARATION OF FORMER RESISTANCE FIGHTERS ON THE PRESENT SITUATION IN SOUTH VIETNAM
(translation)

— I —

At the present time, South Vietnam has become a veritable colony of the American imperialists. State power in South Vietnam, monopolized by the reactionary clique of feudalists and capitalist compradores, led by Ngo-dinh-Diem, is only a puppet power, a lackey of the American imperialists who pull the strings. The American-Diemists have made great efforts in the construction of barracks, bases and military airports in the whole of South Vietnam. They have continuously raised troops and have pursued intensive military training. They have adhered, *de facto,* to the Manila Pact and are noisily vaunting a new military organization of aggression under cover of a "friendly economic alliance" obedient to America. All these military activities have no other end than to repress the South Vietnamese people and to prepare intensively for war in order to invade North Vietnam, to maintain constant pressure on neutral Cambodia and to threaten the security of Asia.

As regards the reunification of the country, the South Vietnamese authorities have systematically rejected all the reasonable proposals made by the government of the Democratic Republic of Vietnam, not only refusing conferences with the North and shamelessly rejecting the holding of general elections which should have taken place in July 1956, but also opposing any normal relations between the two zones.

South Vietnam having been seriously devastated by the war, the Diemist authorities should have taken concrete measures to review the economy and to raise the standard of living of all strata of society. However, since 1954, the economic policies of the South Vietnamese authorities have completely disdained the interests of the people and the nation. In South Vietnam, bent under the weight of taxes and fines, the people are mercilessly exploited. Moreover, the South Vietnamese authorities have instituted forced labor, robbed the people of property, land and ricefields . . . They have left the door open to the invasion of American goods, which stifle local manufacturers and merchants with their competition, ruin the South Vietnamese economy, which is consequently daily more dependent on the United States.

. . . The Amercian-Diemists have established a reign of terror and barbarous repression, elevating violence to a government principle. All democratic liberties, even the most elementary, have been abolished. It is a capital crime in the eyes of the American-Diemists to protest against American intervention, to speak of patriotism, peace and national unity or even humanity and justice! The people have no liberty of expression and organization, not even the right to form unions and fraternal organizations. Gatherings, even of 3 or 4 people, which have no political end, for example marriages and celebrations of the anniversary of the death of ancestors, are either forbidden or strictly controlled.

There is a complete lack of personal security. Legislation and practice in South Vietnam give the administrative organs discretionary power to arrest, imprison, torture and even kill citizens. Thousands and thousands of prisons and concentration camps burden the country and presently contain more than 200,000 people! Horrible atrocities have been committed there: they have broken the limbs of prisoners, mutilated women's breasts, inserted billy-clubs in genital organs, had prisoners eaten alive by specially trained dogs . . . in short, the sadism of physical tortures is only equalled by the methods of moral tortures. Finally, the Diemist authorities do not refrain from pure and simple elimination of prisoners, such as the notorious case of the poisoning of several thousand prisoners—resulting in more than 1,000 deaths—at the camp PHU-LOI, a mass assassination as yet unparalleled in the prison annals of the peace-time world.

This policy of terror and repression has been transformed into a veritable war, especially since the enactment of the fascist law 10/59, directed against the unarmed masses of South Vietnam. This persecution is expanding with measures which the worst of Hitler's supporters would have approved: rape, disembowelment with mutilation of the intestines, cannibalism . . . point blank machinegunning of crowds made up of women, old men and children . . . The bloody massacres at BING-THANH, MO-CAY, CHO-DUOC, DUY-XUYEN, HUONG-DIEN and recently at

LONG-MY, VI-THANH, HOA-LUU, THO-SON, LONG-PHU, CA-MAU, THANH-PHU and a great number of other places— massacres causing hundreds of deaths among innocent people— have thrown light on the extreme cruelty of the American-Diemists. Carrying the guillotine to all corners of the land, the American-Diemist summarily execute patriots. By means of American equipment, they have annihilated whole villages, razed cemeteries, destroyed pagodas, Caodaist temples, homes, gardens and ricefields; They have concentrated hundreds of thousands of inhabitants in huge camps cynically labelled "agricultural centers" or "prosperity zones." In a time of peace, Diemist troops composed of infantry and air-borne units, police, militia, supported by artillery, air cover and armored vehicles—troops armed, equipped, maintained and commanded by the Americans—have set loose against the people vast "sweeps," "punitive expeditions," killing, plundering and burning everything in their path.

This policy of fascist dictatorship is directed at all strata of society. Workers, peasants and working masses live in constant terror. Intellectuals and students are not exempt from arbitrary arrest. Caodaists, Hoa-hao, brutally repressed in 1955, are still the victims of coercion. A sizeable number of priests, bonzes and other religious men have been thrown in prison or murdered in a cowardly manner.

This unspeakable policy does not spare the refugees, forced or deceived by the American-Diemists in 1954-55, nor even the soldiers and civil servants of the Diemist political machinery. The 10/59 law does not only threaten the lives of the people, but is a sword of Damocles hanging over the head of the collaborators of the present regime.

The South Vietnamese regime, in feudal submission to the Americans, and sole property of the Ngo-dinh-Diem family, does not tolerate any opposition, opinions or activity; it even goes so far as to persecute those who only demand reforms and disapprove of certain government measures. It answers its critics with exile in remote posts, imprisonment or assassination. To be convinced of this, one has only to cite the cases of NGUYEN-HUU-CHAU and of General DUONG-VAN-DUC . . .

. . . Every social stratum has its share of suffering.

In the working world: unemployment, dismissal, starvation wages, an uncertain future.

For the peasants: lack of security which prevents all normal work, expropriation of land and ricefields, arbitrary legislation of the price of rice, monopoly of the so-called "cooperatives," sale at a loss of agricultural products, extremely unsettled daily life, famine.

For the working masses of the cities: lack of work, taxes, fines, extreme poverty.

Artisans are dying out, crushed under the weight of taxes and the competition of imported merchandise.

As for the national bourgeois, from bankruptcy to bankruptcy, it is lamentably impoverished.

Even the small landholders are prostrated by the policies of rice prices and other measures for exacting money.

The professional class has not escaped oppression. With the steep rise of prices they have ever increasing difficulties.

School children and university students suffer from a dramatic lack of educational institutions and money to pursue their studies. The curriculum is backward and reactionary and the mother tongue has been discarded! Once they have their degrees, most students cannot find work.

Our refugee compatriots, victims of American-Diemist lies, lead a sad and hopeless life. Not satisfied with reducing them to poverty, the clique in power has chased them from one camp to another with malicious fires, to finally put them off in "agricultural exploitation" camps and "prosperity zones" such as exist at CAI-SAN, BAN-ME-THUOT etc. . . . where they are pitilessly exploited.

— II —

While putting into effect this inhuman policy oppressing all the people of South Vietnam, the main thrust of the attacks of the American-Diemists was against the former Resistance fighters and the most stubborn former guerrilla bases. For the past 6 years they have undertaken a series of measures of horrible reprisal against the former Resistants, first of all measures of discrimination. South Vietnamese prisons contain hundreds of thousands of our number.

A tight network of security agents and informants spy on every one of our actions and words. These "gangsters" have been given *carte blanche* for assassinating Former Resistance Fighters. There have been atrocities worthy of medieval times: we cite, among others, the crime perpetrated against Mr. UT-LEP, Former Resistance Fighter at Tay-ninh, whose intestines were taken from his body and exhibited on the public square! Summary executions number by the thousands. Wives of Former Resistants or women who took part in the national struggle have been the victims of rape and serious coercion: They are forced, for example, to leave their husbands or fiances.

Furthermore, the American-Diemists pursue against us their oft-admitted policy of "total uprooting". How many of our children, newborn babies still unweaned, have been torn from their mothers to be abandoned on the road or placed in squalid orphanages, in order to deprive us of descendants!

Recently, the American-Diemists announced what they call their "policy as regards Former Resistance Fighters" which practically outlaws ordinary people as well as Former Resistance Fighters and throws them into the machine of repression.

As has been said, they have abolished all the attainments of the Resistance, the economic and democratic rights acquired by the peasants, including the property rights of the lands of colonialists and traitors. They dispossess the peasants by direct action or help reactionary landowners who want to evict peasants from land distributed by the Resistance.

They even go so far as to exhume and desecrate the graves of national heros who fell during the war of liberation.

The regions where formerly the people took active part in the Resistance have been placed under a special form of administration which can be reduced to the simple formula: kill, burn, sack.

The South Vietnamese authorities forced the Former Resistance Fighters and the people to take courses of "denunciation of Communism", in fact they forced us to abandon the patriotic ideal, repudiate the accomplishments and deeds of the Resistance, to insult the country, slander the struggle for liberation and enter the road of treason, their own road.

Their favorite slogan, "anti-communism" or "denunciation of Communism" is only a pretext for generalized repression of all patriots, the people as a whole, including soldiers and civil servants.

— III —

After the victorious Resistance, the popular army of South Vietnam was regrouped in the North. The people then re-converted the village-fortresses, filled in the traps, demolished the obstacles, built schools on the bomb craters, enthusiastically rebuilt the villages destroyed by the colonialists, in short we fervently undertook peaceful work, stimulated by the hope of seeing a lasting peace, our country united on the basis of independence and democracy, the life of slavery abolished forever, and parents and friends soon reunited. All the South Vietnamese desired the rigorous and integral application of the Geneva accords, the fruit of immense sacrifice in human lives of all our people.

Thus the people of South Vietnam had returned to normal life, having no more weapons in their possession.

However, for the past 6 years, the policies and the acts of the South Vietnamese authorities have not taken into account these aspirations and this desire. At the present time there is no indication of any desire on the part of South Vietnamese authorities to change to a policy based on respecting national interests. On the contrary, these same authorities have proven to be more decided than ever in carrying out their criminal designs.

Under these conditions:

WE

FORMER RESISTANCE FIGHTERS, leaders and members of the Vietminh-Lien Front, of organizations of the Resistance: Workers, peasants, youth, women, old people, high school and university students, Mother of Resistance Fighters, Pioneers;

Members of RELIGIOUS ORGANIZATIONS: Cao-dai, Hoahao, Buddhists, Catholics;

ASSOCIATIONS OF JOURNALIST RESISTANCE FIGHTERS, ARTIST RESISTANCE FIGHTERS, CHINESE NATIONALS FOR LIBERATION;

PARTIES: Communist or Workers Party, Vietnamese Democrat or Vietnamese Socialist;

CADRES and MEMBERS OF STATE ORGANISMS during the Resistance; INDIVIDUALS NOT ADHERING TO ANY PARTY;

comprising, therefore, the vast majority of the Vietnamese people,

CONSIDER that it is time once again to solemnly proclaim our position to internal and international opinion on the present situation in South Vietnam;

1— . . . Since peace has been reestablished the people, having laid down their arms, have not discarded peaceful means of struggle, even though the American-Diemists declared open war on them at a very early date. But since the South Vietnamese authorities savagely repress the most harmless forms of demands—thus, they greeted with shots a group of people who, struck by famine, came to ask help from an administrative body—they have by their own acts forced the people into legitimate self-defense.

Thus, recently, when the American-Diemists have undertaken savage attacks on the people, they have met armed resistance, approved by the patriotic soldiers in the ranks of the South Vietnamese army.

Although forced into legitimate self-defense, the people still hope that this situation will not degenerate into civil war. All they demand of the South Vietnamese authorities is the application of a domestic policy of peace and democracy, based on respecting national interests and the interests of the entire population.

The Resistance fighters, as well as the people as a whole, consider that the great majority of the soldiers, and civil servants of the South Vietamese regime, including top officials, are a part of the Diemist government machine only by necessity or force. These fellow citizens neither hate the Former Resistance Fighters nor desire to act as enemies of the people. They can be assured that we trust in their patriotism and will help them find the right path and choose the path suitable for the national, as well as their personal interests. They understand perfectly, we are convinced, that if the people take up arms to fight terror or punish bloodthirsty traitors, notorious criminals, and faithful lackeys of the American-Diemists, it is only to defend themselves.

2—The Former Resistance Fighters and all the people of South Vietnam consider that the American-Diemists are solely responsible for the present situation in South Vietnam. If, despite this widespread opposition, the American-Diemists stubbornly persist in pursuing their fascist, militarist policies, disdaining the people, peace, unity, independence, democracy and the improvement of living conditions, they should assume all responsibility for the serious developments in the situation in South Vietnam and its consequences.

3—For 6 years now the people of South Vietnam have valiantly struggled for the national welfare.

In the present circumstances,

WE LAUNCH AN URGENT APPEAL to all classes, all social strata, all milieu to struggle even more courageously, even more resolutely, to oblige the South Vietnamese authorities to:

—Change their policies, to put an end to bloody "sweeping" operations, abolish the fascist 10/59 law, annul the death sentences pronounced for patriots, liberate those in prison without valid cause, dissolve the concentration camps, the "agricultural development centers", the "prosperity zones", end the coercive policies directed at the populations of cities and the country;

Stop the repression of labor unions;

Eliminate all coercive measures against intellectuals, journalists, writers and members of liberal professions;

End the policy of repression of religious sects, ethnic minorities and progressive foreign nationals.

End the discriminatory rule of former zones of resistance, and the so-called "policy toward Former Resistance Fighters";

Respect and apply democratic liberties;

Re-establish security in the countryside;

Promote an independant, democratic economic policy, not subject to the Americans, eliminate the monopolies, protect national industry and commerce, reduce the import of American-made products, and eliminate the legislation of rice prices;

Reduce taxes, abolish unjustified taxes, eliminate the fines and other mthods designed to exact money from the people, forced labor; find solutions to unemployment, stop dismissals, introduce social security, be concerned with labor conditions and female civil servants, improve the situation of artists;

End the despoiling of land and rice fields and end the inflationary cost of farming;

Respect the desires of civil servants, soldiers, city officials and refugees;

Liberate themselves from submission to America, eliminate all U.S. bases in South Vietnam, expel the American military advisors and not accept any form of American interference in South Vietnam;

End the man-hunt to swell military ranks, and the enlisting of the "dan-ve" (self defense units) in the "bao-an" (militia), end the construction of military bases; reduce military expenditures and put into effect a budget for improving the material and cultural life of the people;

Reject the aggressive Manila Pact (SEATO) and the new "friendly economic alliance", another camouflaged aggressive pact;

Undertake realistic measures to consult with the government of the Democratic Republic; establish normal relations between the people of the two zones in postal, economic, cultural and travel matters, etc.;

Outlaw all depraved "culture" of American origin, revitalize and develop national culture, allow liberty of artistic expression and representation;

Build new schools, institute new scholarships, reform the teaching curriculum, respecting national feelings and democratic spirit, use the mother tongue in all classes,

4—The Former Resistance Fighters and all the people of South Vietnam struggle to end the colonial regime and the fascist dictatorship of the Ngo family, in order to form a National Democratic Union government in South Vietnam, composed of representatives of diverse political opinions and all social classes, accomplishing national independence and the democratic liberties guaranteeing a decent life for the people, respecting and integrally and rigorously applying the Geneva Accords, entering into conferences with North Vietnam for the peaceful reunification of the country. This government would pursue a foreign policy of peace and friendship based on the principles of the Bandung Conference.

The present struggle in South Vietnam is that of all the people and includes all political opinions, from the communists to individuals who merely desire reform, in other words the great majority of patriots. The force of our union, with the active support of our northern compatriots and the progressive peoples of the world, will prevail.

As in the past, during nine years of Resistance, faithful to our anti-imperialist traditions,

WE,

FORMER RESISTANCE FIGHTERS

UNITED WITH ALL COMPATRIOTS of South Vietnam,

WILL NOT SPARE OUR FORCES in the struggle for national independence, peace, democracy and a free Vietnam, united and prosperous . . .

NAM-BO, [South Vietnam] MARCH 1960
The Former Resistance Fighters of
South Vietnam

EXCHANGES OF MESSAGES BETWEEN PRESIDENT KENNEDY AND PRESIDENT NGO DINH DIEM OF THE REPUBLIC OF VIETNAM, DECEMBER 14 AND DECEMBER 7, 1961[1]

President Kennedy to President Diem

December 14, 1961.

Dear Mr. President: I have received your recent letter in which you described so cogently the dangerous condition caused by North Vietnam's efforts to take over your country. The situation in your embattled country is well known to me and to the American people. We have been deeply disturbed by the assault on your country. Our indignation has mounted as the deliberate savagery of the Communist program of assassination, kidnapping and wanton violence became clear.

---

[1]Department of State Bulletin, Jan. 1, 1962, pp. 13-14.

Your letter underlines what our own information has convincingly shown—that the campaign of force and terror now being waged against your people and your Government is supported and directed from the outside by the authorities at Hanoi. They have thus violated the provisions of the Geneva Accords designed to ensure peace in Vietnam and to which they bound themselves in 1954.

At that time, the United States, although not a party to the Accords, declared that it "would view any renewal of the aggression in violation of the agreements with grave concern and as seriously threatening international peace and security." We continue to maintain that view.

In accordance with that declaration, and in response to your request, we are prepared to help the Republic of Vietnam to protect its people and to preserve its independence. We shall promptly increase our assistance to your defense effort as well as help relieve the destruction of the floods which you describe. I have already given the orders to get these programs underway.

The United States, like the Republic of Vietnam, remains devoted to the cause of peace and our primary purpose is to help your people maintain their independence. If the Communist authorities in North Vietnam will stop their campaign to destroy the Republic of Vietnam, the measures we are taking to assist your defense efforts will no longer be necessary. We shall seek to persuade the Communists to give up their attempts of force and subversion. In any case, we are confident that the Vietnamese people will preserve their independence and gain the peace and prosperity for which they have sought so hard and so long.

John F. Kennedy.

President Diem to President Kennedy

December 7, 1961.

Dear Mr. President: Since its birth, more than six years ago, the Republic of Vietnam has enjoyed the close friendship and co-operation of the United States of America.

Like the United States, the Republic of Vietnam has always been devoted to the preservation of peace. My people know only too well the sorrows of war. We have honored the 1954 Geneva Agreements even though they resulted in the partition of our country and the enslavement of more than half of our people by Communist tyranny. We have never considered the reunification of our nation by force. On the contrary, we have publicly pledged that we will not violate the demarcation line and the demilitarized zone set up by the agreements. We have always been prepared and have on many occasions stated our willingness to reunify Vietnam on the basis of democratic and truly free elections.

The record of the Communist authorities in the northern part of our country is quite otherwise. They not only consented to the division of Vietnam, but were eager for it. They pledged themselves to observe the Geneva Agreements and during the seven years since have never ceased to violate them. They call for free elections but are ignorant of the very meaning of the words. They talk of "peaceful reunification" and wage war against us.

From the beginning, the Communists resorted to terror in their efforts to subvert our people, destroy our government, and impose a Communist regime upon us. They have attacked defenseless teachers, closed schools, killed members of our anti-malarial program and looted hospitals. This is coldly calculated to destroy our government's humanitarian efforts to serve our people.

We have long sought to check the Communist attack from the North on our people by appeals to the International Control Commission. Over the years, we have repeatedly published to the world the evidence of the Communist plot to overthrow our government and seize control of all of Vietnam by illegal intrusions from outside our country. The evidence has mounted until now it is hardly necessary to rehearse it. Most recently, the kidnapping and brutal murder of our Chief Liaison Officer to the International Control Commission, Colonel Noang Thuy Nam, compelled us to speak out once more. In our October 24, 1961, letter to the ICC, we called attention again to the publicly stated determination of the Communist authorities in Hanoi to "liberate the South" by the overthrow of my government and the imposition of a Communist regime on our people. We cited the proof of massive infiltration of Communist agents and military elements into our country. We outlined the Communist strategy, which is simply the ruthless use of terror against the whole population, women and children included.

In the course of the last few months, the Communist assault on my people has achieved high ferocity. In October they caused more than 1,800 incidents of violence and more than 2,000 casualties. They have struck occasionally in battalion strength, and they are continually augmenting their forces by infiltration from the North. The level of their attacks is already such that our forces are stretched to the utmost. We are forced to defend every village, every hamlet, indeed every home against a foe whose tactic is always to strike at the defenseless.

A disastrous flood was recently added to the misfortunes of the Vietnamese people. The greater part of three provinces was inundated, with a great loss of property. We are now engaged in a nationwide effort to reconstruct and rehabilitate this area. The Communists are, of course, making this task doubly difficult, for they have seized upon the disruption of normal administration and communications as an opportunity to sow more destruction in the stricken area.

In short, the Vietnamese nation now faces what is perhaps the gravest crisis in its long history. For more than 2,000 years my people have lived and built, fought and died in this land. We have not always been free. Indeed, much of our history and many of its proudest moments have arisen from conquest by foreign powers and our struggle against great odds to regain or defend our precious independence. But it is not only our freedom which is at stake today, it is our national identity. For, if we lose this war, our people will be swallowed by the Communist Bloc, all our proud heritage will be blotted out by the "Socialist society" and Vietnam will leave the pages of history. We will lose our national soul.

Mr. President, my people and I are mindful of the great assistance which the United States has given us. Your help has not been lightly received, for the Vietnamese are proud people, and we are determined to do our part in the defense of the free world. It is clear to all of us that the defeat of the Viet Cong demands the total mobilization of our government and our people, and you may be sure that we will devote all of our resources of money, minds, and men to this great task.

But Vietnam is not a great power and the forces of International Communism now arrayed against us are more than we can meet with the resources at hand. We must have further assistance from the United States if we are to win the war now being waged against us.

We can certainly assure mankind that our action is purely defensive. Much as we regret the subjugation of more than half of our people in North Vietnam, we have no intention, and indeed no means, to free them by use of force.

I have said that Vietnam is at war. War means many things, but most of all it means the death of brave people for a cause they believe in. Vietnam has suffered many wars, and through the centuries we have always had patriots and heroes who were willing to shed their blood for Vietnam. We will keep faith with them.

When Communism has long ebbed away into the past, my people will still be here, a free united nation growing from the deep roots of our Vietnamese heritage. They will remember your help in our time of need. This struggle will then be a part of our common history. And your help, your friendship, and the strong bonds between our two peoples will be a part of Vietnam, then as now.

Ngo Dinh Diem

The President
The White House
Washington, D.C.

DEPARTMENT OF STATE: STATEMENT COMMENTING ON THE REPORT OF THE CONTROL COMMISSION FOR VIETNAM, JUNE 25, 1962[1]

The report just issued by the International Control Commission for Vietnam demonstrates that the Communist North Vietnamese are engaged in a campaign of aggression and subversion aimed at the violent overthrow of the Government of South Vietnam. It

---

[1]Department of State Bulletin, July 16, 1962, pp. 109-110.

indicates clearly that the hostilities in Vietnam, which in the first 5 months of this year alone resulted in the death of more than 9,000 people, are planned, caused, and led by the Communist authorities in North Vietnam. These are the conclusions of the Commission's Legal Committee:

* * * there is evidence to show that armed and unarmed personnel, arms, munitions and other supplies have been sent from the Zone in the North to the Zone in the South with the object of supporting, organizing and carrying out hostile activities, including armed attacks, directed against the Armed Forces and Administration of the Zone in the South * * * there is evidence to show that the PAVN [People's Army of Vietnam] has allowed the Zone in the North to be used for inciting, encouraging and supporting hostile activities in the Zone in the South, aimed at the overthrow of the Administration in the South.

The Commission accepted these conclusions of the Legal Committee that there was sufficient evidence to show "beyond reasonable doubt" that the authorities in Communist North Vietnam committed these violations. The Commission also cited the Republic of Vietnam for its activities in importing military equipment and personnel above the limits imposed by the 1954 Geneva Accords. The report clearly demonstrates, however, that these actions were taken by South Vietnam as part of its effort to defend itself against aggression and subversion from the North. In December of last year President Diem requested increased military assistance from the United States. We have responded to this request.

President Diem and President Kennedy have both stated that they look forward to the discontinuance of the present level of military assistance when the Communist North Vietnamese halt their campaign to destroy the Republic of Vietnam. The report of the International Control Commission takes note of this position. The United States welcomes the Commission's report and recommends it for world attention. We hope that the Commission will continue its efforts to restore peace in Vietnam.

N.B. This statement does not indicate fully the findings of the International Control Commission with respect to United States arms build-up in South Vietnam. See Appendix for pertinent excerpts from the reports of the International Control Commission.

PRESIDENT KENNEDY'S TV INTERVIEWS, SEPTEMBER 2, AND 9, 1963 (Excerpts)[1]

(a) CBS Interview, September 2

*   *   *   *   *

MR. CRONKITE. Mr. President, the only hot war we've got running at the moment is of course the one in Vietnam, and we have our difficulties here, quite obviously.

PRESIDENT KENNEDY. I don't think that unless a greater effort is made by the Government to win popular support that the war can be won out there. In the final analysis, it is their war. They are the ones who have to win it or lose it. We can help them, we can give them equipment, we can send our men out there as advisers, but they have to win it—the people of Vietnam—against the Communists. We are prepared to continue to assist them, but I don't think that the war can be won unless the people support the effort, and, in my opinion, in the last 2 months the Government has gotten out of touch with the people.

The repressions against the Buddhists, we felt, were very unwise. Now all we can do is to make it very clear that we don't think this is the way to win. It is my hope that this will become increasingly obvious to the Government, that they will take steps to try to bring back popular support for this very essential struggle.

MR. CRONKITE. Do you think this Government has time to regain the support of the people?

PRESIDENT KENNEDY. I do. With changes in policy and perhaps with personnel, I think it can. If it doesn't make those changes, I would think that the chances of winning it would not be very good.

MR. CRONKITE. Hasn't every indication from Saigon been that President Diem has no intention of changing his pattern?

PRESIDENT KENNEDY. If he does not change it, of course, that is his decision. He has been there 10 years, and, as I say, he has carried this burden when he has been counted out on a number of occasions.

Our best judgment is that he can't be successful on this basis. We hope that he comes to see that; but in the final analysis it is

---

[1] Department of State Bulletin, Sept. 30, 1963, pp. 498-500

the people and the Government itself who have to win or lose this struggle. All we can do is help, and we are making it very clear. But I don't agree with those who say we should withdraw. That would be a great mistake. I know people don't like Americans to be engaged in this kind of an effort. Forty-seven Americans have been killed in combat with the enemy, but this is a very important struggle even though it is far away.

We took all this—made this effort to defend Europe. Now Europe is quite secure. We also have to participate—we may not like it—in the defense of Asia.

*   *   *   *   *

(b) NBC Interview, September 9

*   *   *   *   *

MR. HUNTLEY. Mr. President, in respect to our difficulties in South Vietnam, could it be that our Government tends occasionally to get locked into a policy or an attitude and then finds it difficul to alter or shift that policy?

THE PRESIDENT. Yes, that is true. I think in the case of South Vietnam we have been dealing with a Government which is in control, has been in control for 10 years. In addition, we have felt for the last 2 years that the struggle against the Communists was going better. Since June, however—the difficulties with the Buddhists—we have been concerned about a deterioration, particularly in the Saigon area, which hasn't been felt greatly in the outlying areas but may spread. So we are faced with the problem of wanting to protect the area against the Communists. On the other hand, we have to deal with the Government there. That produces a kind of ambivalence in our efforts which exposes us to some criticism. We are using our influence to persuade the Government there to take those steps which will win back support. That takes some time, and we must be patient, we must persist.

MR. HUNTLEY. Are we likely to reduce our aid to South Vietnam now?

The PRESIDENT. I don't think we think that would be helpful at this time. If you reduce your aid, it is possible you could have some effect upon the government structure there. On the other hand, you might have a situation which could bring about a collapse. Strongly in our mind is what happened in the case of China at the end of World War II, where China was lost—a weak government became increasingly unable to control events. We don't want that.

MR. BRINKLEY. Mr. President, have you had any reason to doubt this so-called "domino theory," that if South Vietnam falls, the rest of Southeast Asia will go behind it?

The PRESIDENT. No, I believe it. I believe it. I think that the struggle is close enough. China is so large, looms so high just beyond the frontiers, that if South Vietnam went, it would not only give them an improved geographic position for a guerrilla assault on Malaya but would also give the impression that the wave of the future in Southeast Asia was China and the Communists. So I believe it.

Mr. BRINKLEY. In the last 48 hours there have been a great many conflicting reports from there about what the CIA [Central Intelligence Agency] was up to. Can you give us any enlightenment on it?

The PRESIDENT. No.

Mr. HUNTLEY. Does the CIA tend to make its own policy? That seems to be the debate here.

The PRESIDENT. No, that is the frequent charge, but that isn't so. Mr. [John A.] McCone, head of the CIA, sits in the National Security Council. We have had a number of meetings in the past few days about events in South Vietnam. Mr. McCone participated in every one, and the CIA coordinates its efforts with the State Department and the Defense Department.

Mr. BRINKLEY. With so much of our prestige, money, so on, committed in South Vietnam, why can't we exercise a little more influence there, Mr. President?

The PRESIDENT. We have some influence. We have some influence and we are attempting to carry it out. I think we don't—we can't expect these countries to do everything the way we want to do them. They have their own interest, their own personalities, their own tradition. We can't make everyone in our image, and there are a good many people who don't want to go in our image. In addition, we have ancient struggles between countries. In the case of India and Pakistan, we would like to have them settle Kashmir.

That is our view of the best way to defend the subcontinent against communism. But that struggle between India and Pakistan is more important to a good many people in that area than the struggle against the Communists. We would like to have Cambodia, Thailand, and South Vietnam all in harmony, but there are ancient differences there. We can't make the world over, but we can influence the world. The fact of the matter is that with the assistance of the United States and SEATO [Southeast Asia Treaty Organization], Southeast Asia and indeed all of Asia has been maintained independent against a powerful force, the Chinese Communists. What I am concerned about is that Americans will get impatient and say, because they don't like events in Southeast Asia or they don't like the Government in Saigon, that we should withdraw. That only makes it easy for the Communists. I think we should stay. We should use our influence in as effective a way as we can, but we should not withdraw.

*   *   *   *   *

MESSAGE FROM PRESIDENT JOHNSON TO GEN. DUONG VAN MINH, CHAIRMAN OF THE MILITARY REVOLUTIONARY COUNCIL OF THE REPUBLIC OF VIETNAM, December 31, 1963[1]

Dear General Minh. As we enter the New Year of 1964, I want to wish you, your Revolutionary Government, and your people full success in the long and arduous war which you are waging so tenaciously and bravely against the Viet Cong forces directed and supported by the Communist regime in Hanoi. Ambassador [Henry Cabot] Lodge and Secretary of Defense Robert S. McNamara have told me about the serious situation which confronts you and of the plans which you are developing to enable your armed forces and your people to redress this situation.

This new year provides a fitting opportunity for me to pledge on behalf of the American Government and people a renewed partnership with your government and people in your brave strug-

---

[1]Department of State Bulletin, Jan. 27, 1964, pp. 121-122.

gle for freedom. The United States will continue to furnish you and your people with the fullest measure of support in this bitter fight. We shall maintain in Vietnam American personnel and material as needed to assist you in achieving victory.

Our aims are, I know, identical with yours: to enable your government to protect its people from the acts of terror perpetrated by Communist insurgents from the north. As the forces of your government become increasingly capable of dealing with this aggression, American military personnel in South Vietnam can be progressively withdrawn.

The United States Government shares the view of your government that "neutralization" of South Vietnam is unacceptable. As long as the Communist regime in North Vietnam persists in its aggressive policy, neutralization of South Vietnam would only be another name for a Communist takeover. Peace will return to your country just as soon as the authorities in Hanoi cease and desist from their terrorist aggression.

Thus, your government and mine are in complete agreement on the political aspects of your war against the forces of enslavement, brutality, and material misery. Within this framework of political agreement we can confidently continue and improve our cooperation.

I am pleased to learn from Secretary McNamara about the vigorous operations which you are planning to bring security and an improved standard of living to your people.

I wish to congratulate you particularly on your work for the unity of all your people, including the Hoa Hao and Cao Dai, against the Viet Cong. I know from my own experience in Vietnam how warmly the Vietnamese people respond to a direct human approach and how they have hungered for this in their leaders. So again I pledge the energetic support of my country to your government and your people.

We will do our full part to ensure that under your leadership your people may win a victory—a victory for freedom and justice and human welfare in Vietnam.

Sincerely,

Lyndon B. Johnson

UNITED STATES TO INCREASE ECONOMIC AND MILITARY AID TO VIETNAM: Statement by the White House, March 17, 1964[1]

Secretary McNamara and General Taylor, following their initial oral report of Friday, today reported fully to President Johnson and the members of the National Security Council. The report covered the situation in South Vietnam, the measures being taken by General Khanh and his government, and the need for United States assistance to supplement and support these measures. There was also discussion of the continuing support and direction of the Viet Cong insurgency from North Vietnam.

At the close of the meeting the President accepted the report and its principal recommendations, which had the support of the National Security Council and Ambassador Lodge.

Comparing the situation to last October, when Secretary McNamara and General Taylor last reported fully on it, there have unquestionably been setbacks. The Viet Cong have taken maximum advantage of two changes of government, and of more long-standing difficulties, including a serious weakness and overextension which had developed in the basically sound hamlet program. The supply of arms and cadres from the north has continued; careful and sophisticated control of Viet Cong operations has been apparent; and evidence that such control is centered in Hanoi is clear and unmistakable.

To meet the situation, General Khanh and his government are acting vigorously and effectively. They have produced a sound central plan for the prosecution of the war, recognizing to a far greater degree than before the crucial role of economic and social, as well as military, action to insure that areas cleared of the Viet Cong survive and prosper in freedom.

To carry out this plan, General Khanh requires the full enlistment of the people of South Vietnam, partly to augment the strength of his anti-guerrilla forces, but particularly to provide the administrators, health workers, teachers, and others who must follow up in cleared areas. To meet this need, and to provide a more

---

[1]Department of State Bulletin, Apr. 6, 1964, pp. 522-523.

equitable and common basis of service, General Khanh has informed us that he proposes in the near future to put into effect a National Mobilization Plan that will provide conditions and terms of service in appropriate jobs for all able bodied South Vietnamese between certain ages.

In addition, steps are required to bring up to required levels the pay and status of the paramilitary forces and to create a highly trained guerrilla force that can beat the Viet Cong on its own ground.

Finally, limited but significant additional equipment is proposed for the air forces, the river navy, and the mobile forces.

In short, where the South Vietnamese Government now has the power to clear any part of its territory, General Khanh's new program is designed to clear and to hold, step by step and province by province.

This program will involve substantial increases in cost to the South Vietnamese economy, which in turn depends heavily on United States economic aid. Additional, though less substantial, military assistance funds are also needed, and increased United States training activity both on the civil and military side. The policy should continue of withdrawing United States personnel where their roles can be assumed by South Vietnamese and of sending additional men if they are needed. It will remain the policy of the United States to furnish assistance and support to South Vietnam for as long as it is required to bring Communist aggression and terrorism under control.

Secretary McNamara and General Taylor reported their overall conclusion that with continued vigorous leadership from General Khanh and his government, and the carrying out of these steps, the situation can be significantly improved in the coming months.

PRESIDENT'S MESSAGE TO CONGRESS, AUGUST 5, 1964[1]

To the Congress of the United States:

Last night I announced to the American people that the North Vietnamese regime had conducted further deliberate attacks against

---

[1] Department of State Bulletin, Aug. 24, 1964, pp. 261-263.

U.S. naval vessels operating in international waters, and that I had therefore directed air action against gunboats and supporting facilities used in these hostile operations. This air action has now been carried out with substantial damage to the boats and facilities. Two U.S. aircraft were lost in the action.

After consultation with the leaders of both parties in the Congress, I further announced a decision to ask the Congress for a resolution expressing the unity and determination of the United States in supporting freedom and in protecting peace in southeast Asia.

These latest actions of the North Vietnamese regime have given a new and grave turn to the already serious situation in southeast Asia. Our commitments in that area are well known to the Congress. They were first made in 1954 by President Eisenhower. They were further defined in the Southeast Asia Collective Defense Treaty approved by the Senate in February 1955.

This treaty with its accompanying protocol obligates the United States and other members to act in accordance with their constitutional processes to meet Communist aggression against any of the parties or protocol states.

Our policy in southeast Asia has been consistent and unchanged since 1954. I summarized it on June 2 in four simple propositions:

1. *America keeps her word.* Here as elsewhere, we must and shall honor our commitments.

2. *The issue is the future of southeast Asia as a whole.* A threat to any nation in that region is a threat to all, and a threat to us.

3. *Our purpose is peace.* We have no military, political, or territorial ambitions in the area.

4. *This is not just a jungle war, but a struggle for freedom on every front of human activity.* Our military and economic assistance to South Vietnam and Laos in particular has the purpose of helping these countries to repel aggression and strengthen their independence.

The threat to the free nations of southeast Asia has long been clear. The North Vietnamese regime has constantly sought to take over South Vietnam and Laos. This Communist regime has violated the Geneva accords for Vietnam. It has systematically conducted a campaign of subversion, which includes the direction, training, and supply of personnel and arms for the conduct of guerrilla warfare in South Vietnamese territory. In Laos, the North Vietnamese regime has maintained military forces, used Laotian territory for infiltration into South Vietnam, and most recently carried out combat operations—all in direct violation of the Geneva agreements of 1962. In recent months, the actions of the North Vietnamese regime have become steadily more theatening. In May, following new acts of Communist aggression in Laos, the United States undertook reconnaissance flights over Laotian territory, at the request of the Government of Laos. These flights had the essential mission of determining the situation in territory where Communist forces were preventing inspection by the International Control Commission. When the Communists attacked these aircraft, I responded by furnishing escort fighters with instructions to fire when fired upon. Thus, these latest North Vietnamese attacks on our naval vessels are not the first direct attack on armed forces of the United States.

As President of the United States I have concluded that I should now ask the Congress on its part, to join in affirming the national determination that all such attacks will be met, and that the United States will continue in its basic policy of assisting the free nations of the area to defend their freedom.

As I have repeatedly made clear, the United States intends no rashness, and seeks no wider war. We must make it clear to all that the United States is united in its determination to bring about the end of Communist subversion and aggression in the area. We seek the full and effective restoration of the international agreements signed in Geneva in 1954, with respect to South Vietnam, and again in Geneva in 1962, with respect to Laos.

I recommend a resolution expressing the support of the Congress for all necessary action to protect our Armed Forces and to assist nations covered by the SEATO Treaty. At the same time, I assure the Congress that we shall continue readily to explore any avenues of political solution that will effectively guarantee the removal of Communist subversion and the preservation of the independence of the nations of the area.

The resolution could well be based upon similar resolutions enacted by the Congress in the past—to meet the threat to Formosa in 1955, to meet the threat to the Middle East in 1957, and to meet the threat in Cuba in 1962. It could state in the simplest terms the resolve and support of the Congress for action to deal appropriately with attacks against our Armed Forces and to defend freedom and preserve peace in southeast Asia in accordance with the obligations of the United States under the Southeast Asia Treaty. I urge the Congress to enact such a resolution promptly and thus to give convincing evidence to the aggressive Communist nations, and to the world as a whole, that our policy in southeast Asia will be carried forward—and that the peace and security of the area will be preserved.

The events of this week would in any event have made the passage of a congressional resolution essential. But there is an additional reason for doing so at a time when we are entering on 3 months of political campaigning. Hostile nations must understand that in such a period the United States will continue to protect its national interests, and that in these matters there is no division among us.

SECURITY COUNCIL HEARS U.S. CHARGE OF NORTH VIETNAMESE ATTACKS: Statement by Adlai E. Stevenson, U.S. Representative in the Security Council, August 5, 1964[1]

I have asked for this urgent meeting to bring to the attention of the Security Council acts of deliberate aggression by the Hanoi regime against naval units of the United States.

Naval vessels of my Government, on routine operations in international waters in the Gulf of Tonkin, have been subjected to deliberate and repeated armed attacks. We therefore have found it necessary to take defensive measures.

The major facts about these incidents were announced last night by the President of the United States and communicated to other governments at the same time I was instructed to request this meeting. I shall recount these facts for you, Mr. President, in chronological order so that all the members may have all the information available to my Government.

---

[1]Department of State Bulletin, Aug. 24, 1964, pp. 272-274.

At 8:08 a.m. Greenwich meridian time, August 2, 1964, the United States destroyer *Maddox* was on routine patrol in international waters in the Gulf of Tonkin, proceeding in a southeasterly direction away from the coast about 30 miles at sea from the mainland of North Vietnam. The *Maddox* was approached by three high-speed North Vietnamese torpedo boats in attack formation. When it was evident that these torpedo boats intended to take offensive action, the *Maddox,* in accordance with naval practice, fired three warning shots across the bows of the approaching vessels. At approximately the same time, the aircraft carrier *Ticonderoga,* which was also in international waters and had been alerted to the impending attack, sent out four aircraft to provide cover for the *Maddox,* the pilots being under orders not to fire unless they or the *Maddox* were fired upon first.

Two of the attacking craft fired torpedoes, which the *Maddox* evaded by changing course, All three attacking vessels directed machinegun fire at the *Maddox.* One of the attacking vessels approached for close attack and was struck by fire from the *Maddox.* After the attack was broken off, the *Maddox* continued on a southerly course in international waters.

Now, Mr. President, clearly this was a deliberate armed attack against a naval unit of the United States Government on patrol in the high seas—almost 30 miles off the mainland. Nevertheless, my Government did its utmost to minimize the explosive potential of this flagrant attack in the hopes that this might be an isolated or uncalculated action. There was local defensive fire. The United States was not drawn into hasty response.

On August 3 the United States took steps to convey to the Hanoi regime a note calling attention to this aggression, stating that United States ships would continue to operate freely on the high seas in accordance with the rights guaranteed by international law, and warning the authorities in Hanoi of the "grave consequences which would inevitably result from any further unprovoked offensive military action against United States forces." This notification was in accordance with the provisions of the Geneva accords.

Our hopes that this was an isolated incident did not last long. At 2:35 p.m. Greenwich meridian time, August 4, when it was nighttime in the Gulf of Tonkin, the destroyers *Maddox* and *C.*

Turner Joy were again subjected to an armed attack by an undetermined number of motor torpedo boats of the North Vietnamese navy. This time the American vessels were 65 miles from shore, twice as far out on the high seas as on the occasion of the previous attack. This time numerous torpedoes were fired. That attack lasted for over 2 hours.

There no longer could be any shadow of doubt that this was a planned, deliberate military aggression against vessels lawfully present in international waters. One could only conclude that this was the work of authorities dedicated to the use of force to achieve their objectives, regardless of the consequences.

My Government therefore determined to take positive but limited and relevant measures to secure its naval units against further aggression. Last night aerial strikes were thus carried out against North Vietnamese torpedo boats and their support facilities. This action was limited in scale, its only targets being the weapons and facilities against which we had been forced to defend ourselves. Our fervent hope is that the point has now been made that acts of armed aggression are not to be tolerated in the Gulf of Tonkin any more than they are to be tolerated anywhere else.

I want to emphasize that the action we have taken is a limited and measured response, fitted precisely to the attack that produced it, and that the deployments of additional U.S. forces to Southeast Asia are designed solely to deter further aggression. This is a single action designed to make unmistakably clear that the United States cannot be diverted by military attack from its obligations to help its friends establish and protect their independence. Our naval units are continuing their routine patrolling on the high seas with orders to protect themselves with all appropriate means against any further aggression. As President Johnson said last night, "We still seek no wider war."

Mr. President, let me repeat that the United States vessels were in international waters when they were attacked.

Let me repeat that freedom of the seas is guaranteed under long-accepted international law applying to all nations alike.

Let me repeat that these vessels took no belligerent actions of any kind until they were subject to armed attack.

And let me say once more that the action they took in self-defense is the right of all nations and is fully within the provisions of the Charter of the United Nations.

The acts of aggression by the North Vietnamese in the Gulf of Tonkin make no sense whatsoever standing alone. They defy rational explanation except as part of a larger pattern with a larger purpose. As isolated events, the kidnapping of village officials in the Republic of South Vietnam makes no sense either. Neither does the burning of a schoolhouse—or the sabotage of an irrigation project—or the murder of a medical worker—or the random bomb thrown into a crowd of innocent people sitting in a cafe.

All these wanton acts of violence and destruction fit into the larger pattern of what has been going on in Southeast Asia for the past decade and a half. So does the arming of terrorist gangs in South Vietnam by the regimes in Hanoi and Peiping. So does the infiltration of armed personnel to make war against the legitimate government of that nation. So does the fighting in Laos—and all the acts of subversion—and all the propaganda—and the sabotage of the international machinery established to keep the peace by the Geneva agreements—and the deliberate, systematic, and flagrant violations of those agreements by two regimes which signed them and which by all tenets of decency, law, and civilized practice are bound by their provisions.

The attempt to sink United States destroyers in international waters is much more spectacular than the attempt to murder the mayor of a village in his bed at night. But they are both part of the pattern, and the pattern is designed to subjugate the people of Southeast Asia, to an empire ruled by means of force of arms, of rule by terror, of expansion by violence.

Mr. President, it is only in this larger view that we can discuss intelligently the matter that we have brought to this Council.

In his statement last night, President Johnson concluded by emphasizing that the mission of the United States is peace. Under the explicit instructions of President Johnson, I want to repeat that assurance in the Security Council this afternoon: Our mission is peace.

We hoped that the peace settlement in 1954 would lead to peace in Vietnam. We hoped that that settlement, and the supplementary

Geneva accords of 1962, would lead to peace in Laos. Communist governments have tried aggression before—and have failed. Each time the lesson has had to be learned anew.

We are dealing here with a regime that has not yet learned the lesson that aggression does not pay, cannot be sustained, and will always be thrown back by people who believe, as we do, that people want freedom and independence, not subjection and the role of satellite in a modern empire.

In Southeast Asia we want nothing more, and nothing less, than the assured and guaranteed independence of the peoples of the area. We are in Southeast Asia to help our friends preserve their own opportunity to be free of imported terror, alien assassination, managed by the North Vietnam Communists based in Hanoi and backed by the Chinese Communists from Peiping.

Two months ago, when we were discussing in this Council the problems created on the Cambodia-South Vietnam frontier by the Communist Viet Cong, I defined our peace aims in Southeast Asia. I repeat them today:

There is a very easy way to restore order in Southeast Asia. There is a very simple, safe way to bring about the end of United States military aid to the Republic of Vietnam.

Let all foreign troops withdraw from Laos. Let all states in that area make and abide by the simple decision to leave their neighbors alone. Stop the secret subversion of other people's independence. Stop the clandestine and illegal transit of national frontiers. Stop the export of revolution and the doctrine of violence. Stop the violations of the political agreements reached at Geneva for the future of Southeast Asia.

The people of Laos want to be left alone.

The people of Vietnam want to be left alone.

The people of Cambodia want to be left alone.

When their neighbors decide to leave them alone—as they must —there will be no fighting in Southeast Asia and no need for American advisers to leave their homes to help these people resist aggression. Any time that decision can be put in enforcible terms, my Government will be only too happy to put down the burden that we have been sharing with those determined to preserve their independence. Until such assurances are forthcoming, we shall stand for the independence of free peoples in Southeast Asia as we have elsewhere.

That is what I said to this Council in May. That is what I repeat to this Council in August.

When the political settlements freely negotiated at the conference tables in Geneva are enforced, the independence of Southeast Asia will be guaranteed. When the peace agreements reached long ago are made effective, peace will return to Southeast Asia and military power can be withdrawn.

SOUTHEAST ASIA RESOLUTION[1]

Whereas naval units of the Communist regime in Vietnam, in violation of the principles of the Charter of the United Nations and of international law, have deliberately and repeatedly attacked United States naval vessels lawfully present in international waters, and have thereby created a serious threat to international peace; and

Whereas these attacks are part of a deliberate and systematic campaign of aggression that the Communist regime in North Vietnam has been waging against its neighbors and the nations joined with them in the collective defense of their freedom; and

Whereas the United States is assisting the peoples of southeast Asia to protect their freedom and has no territorial, military or political ambitions in that area, but desires only that these peoples should be left in peace to work out their own destinies in heir own way: Now,therefore, be it

Resolved by the Senate and House of Representatives of the United of America in Congress assembled, That the Congress approves and supports the determination of the President, as Commander in Chief, to take all necessary measures to repel any armed attack against the forces of the United States and to prevent further aggression.

Sec. 2. The United States regards as vital to its national interest and to world peace the maintenance of international peace and security in southeast Asia. Consonant with the Constitution of the United States and the Charter of the United Nations and in ac-

---

[1]Text of Public Law 88-408 [H.J. Res. 1145], 78 Stat. 384, approved Aug. 10, 1964.

cordance with its obligations under the Southeast Asia Collective Defense Treaty, the United States is, therefore, prepared, as the President determines, to take all necessary steps, including the use of armed force, to assist any member or protocol state of the Southeast Asia Collective Defense Treaty requesting assistance in defense of its freedom.

Sec. 3. This resolution shall expire when the President shall determine that the peace and security of the area is reasonably assured by international conditions created by action of the United Nations or otherwise, except that it may be terminated earlier by concurrent resolution of the Congress.

SERIOUS VIETCONG ATTACKS: Statement by Secretary of Defense Robert S. McNamara, February 7, 1965[1]

Good afternoon, ladies and gentlemen. In describing certain of the events which have taken place in South Vietnam and North Vietnam during the past 24 hours, I'll refer to this map which stands in front of us. On it we have shown the relative positions of China, Laos, North Vietnam, South Vietnam, Cambodia, Thailand, and the South China Sea.

Approximately 24 hours ago, at 2 a.m. Sunday morning, February 7, Saigon time, the Vietnam Communist guerrillas carried out three attacks, one against installations in the Pleiku area, which is in the central part of South Vietnam, a second at Tuy Hoa, with an airstrip adjacent to it, an area near the coast, and a third against Vietnam villages near Nha Trang.

The first attack in the Pleiku area was carried out by a company of Viet Cong using 81-mm. mortars, the mortar fire was directed against the United States military compound at the Second Corps Headquarters of the South Vietnamese military forces, and simultaneously elements of the same company attacked the airstrip at Camp Holloway, at which were located United States helicopter forces on the outskirts of Pleiku.

---

[1]Department of State Bulletin, Feb. 22, 1965, p. 239.

This latter attack on the airstrip was accompanied by a ground probe during which small-arms fire was used, rifle grenades, demolition charges, and recoilless rifles. Following completion of the attacks a Viet Cong four-tube, 81-mm. mortar position was located outside the perimeter defense of the airstrip. Nearby were containers for 61 mortar rounds. The United States casualties in the Pleiku area were 7 killed, 109 wounded, and, of the 109, 76 of the wounded required evacuation.

In addition 5 United States helicopters were destroyed, 9 to 11 damaged, and 6 United States fixed-wing aircraft were damaged.

The second attack at Tuy Hoa was directed against Vietnamese villages in the area and against the storage tanks for aviation gas for the Vietnamese Air Force stationed at the Chop Chi Airfield. Again, 81-mm. fire was used, the storage tanks of aviation gas were set on fire. There were no United States casualties in that area.

The third attack, as I mentioned earlier, was against a village or series of villages about 15 miles northeast of Nha Trang. The reports of operations in this area are fragmentary, and I can't give you the results other than to say that we believe that there were no United States casualties there. Immediately following, the United States representatives in Saigon met with representatives of the South Vietnamese Government. They jointly agreed that joint retaliatory action were required. The President's approval of this action was given after the action was discussed with and recommended by the National Security Council at a meeting held between 7:45 p.m. and 9 p.m. last night.

As a result of this action, elements of the U. S. and South Vietnamese Air Forces were directed to launch joint retaliatory attacks against barracks and staging areas in the southern portion of North Vietnam.

On this map you see Hanoi, the capital of North Vietnam, Saigon, the capital of South Vietnam, the line of demarcation between the two countries at the 17th parallel. The targets agreed upon for the joint retaliatory attacks were barracks areas and staging areas in the southern portion of North Vietnam. As I say, elements of the U. S. and South Vietnamese Air Forces were directed to launch joint retaliatory attacks against those targets. These are the areas which Hanoi has used as bases for the infiltration of men and equipment out of the southern portion of North Vietnam across the border into Laos, down the corridor through Laos, and into South Vietnam. The infiltration routes are picturized on the map. One comes into the Pleiku area in the central part of Vietnam, and others come further south.

U. S. aircraft took off from three U. S. carriers that were steaming in the South China Sea. These carriers were steaming south of the 17th parallel, which is the line of demarcation between North and South Vietnam, about 100 miles off the coast of South Vietnam. The three carriers were the U.S.S. *Ranger,* U.S.S. *Hancock,* and U.S.S. *Coral Sea.*

Of the aircraft which took off from the carriers, 49 struck the Dong Hoi barracks and staging area in the southern part of North Vietnam. Certain other U. S. aircraft and certain South Vietnamese aircraft aborted because of adverse weather conditions and did not proceed to their target areas. Photo reconnaissance of the results of the strike is not yet available, but the combat crews upon their return to the carriers reported seeing heavy fires, heavy smoke, and substantial damage to military targets in the target area. One U.S. aircraft, an A—4 from the carrier *Coral Sea,* was lost. The pilot was seen to eject into the sea. Air-sea rescue operations are underway. All other aircraft returned safely to their bases.

HARVARD EAST ASIA SPECIALISTS SPEAK OUT ON VIETNAM

We, the undersigned faculty, researchers, and graduate students in East Asian studies at Harvard, declare our opposition to present American policy in Vietnam. Not only is the United States destroying a society it professes to defend, but its actions are also increasing the danger of war with China. We urge the immediate cessation of bombing in North Vietnam. We further urge that the goal of a total military victory in the South be abandoned in favor of negotiations for a compromise settlement and the withdrawal of American troops. [May 29, 1967]

Faculty
Glen W. Baxter
Robert N. Bellah
John L. Bishop
Jerome A. Cohen
Albert Craig
Edwin A. Cranston
Peter Duus
Joseph F. Fletcher, Jr.
Howard S. Hibbett
J. R. Hightower
Max Loehr
Masatoshi Nagatomi
John M. Rosenfield
Henry Rosovsky
Benjamin Rowland, Jr.
Donald H. Shively
James C. Thomson, Jr.
Ezra F. Vogel
Edward W. Wagner
Researchers
Anne B. Clark
Paul A. Cohen
David Finkelstein
Merle Goldman
John Israel
Graduate Students
Elizabeth Akiya
Guy Alitto
Janet L. Anderson
R. David Arkush
Susan N. Arkush
Gail Bernstein
Richard P. Bernstein
Alexander Berzin
Jonathan W. Best
Herbert P. Bix
Julie Blattner
Vincent S. Brandt
John Brode
Michael Warren
  Brown-Beasley
Susan Bush
Fox Butterfield
Julia Chang

Sue Fawn Chung
Keith W. Clemens
Timothy Connor
Sharlie J. Conroy
Lloyd R. Craighill
Lewis S. W. Crampton
Michael T. Dalby
Deborah Davis
Owen de Long
Doris Dohrenwend
John W. Dower
Fred W. Drake
Alison Dray
Edward L. Dreyer
June T. Dreyer
Randle Edwards
Thomas M.
  Engelhardt
Loren W. Fessler
Peter Figdor
Louisa G. Fitzgerald
James J. Freeman
Edward Friedman
Frank L. Gniffke
Ralph F. Glenn
Peter J. Golas
Louis A. Goodman
Julian Gresser
Peter Grilli
Ben Haraguchi
Joseph S. Hayes, Jr.
David Hewson
Money L. Hickman
Daniel N. Hoffman
Mel Horwitch
Martha H. Howard
Ralph W. Huenemann
Martha Jenkins
Patricia M. Jones
Linda Klepinger
Richard A. Kraus
Edgar F. Lambert III
Robert Lee
Miriam L. Levering

Steven I. Levine
Lillian M. Li
John S. Major
Julie C. Martin
Julia B. Meech
Vreni Merriam
Harold Metzgar
Kenneth H. Miller
Richard H. Minear
Mark Mohr
James R. Morrell
Alden Myers
Kate Nakai
Andrew J. Nathan
Daniel I. Okimoto
Henry Alan Pattiz
Jim Peck
Willard J. Peterson
R. M. Pfeffer
Marshall Pihl
Don Price
Robert Quint
Thomas G. Rawski
Edward J. M. Rhoads
Jon L. Saari
Evelyn T. Sakakida
Jeremy S. Scanlon
Jonathan Schell
Susan S. Shin
Zenryu Shirtkawa
Bradford L. Simcock
Nancy F. Sizer
John N. Somerville
Douglas G. Spelman
Tina Han Su
Fumie Tateoka
Philip West
John K. Wheeler
Deborah White
Eric Widmer
Thomas B. Wiens
Suzanne Wilson
Ed Winckler
Christopher Winters
Anthony Zaloom

The above 129 signatures represent 78 per cent of all American faculty, researchers, and graduate students currently engaged at Harvard in the formal study of East Asian history, government, law, economics, and culture. All are United States citizens.

NEW YORK TIMES, April 4, 1965

2700 Ministers, Priests and Rabbis say;

MR. PRESIDENT:

IN THE NAME OF GOD STOP IT!

We are aware of the awesome responsibilities you carry; we can imagine the difficulties of making important decisions in the face of conflicting advice from many sources; nor do we doubt your devotion to this Nation or to the great goal of peace among all nations. Yet in offering our concerns over American involvement in Vietnam we must be as blunt as honesty requires us to be.

Mr. President, every one of us is deeply, personally dismayed by the role the United States is playing in Vietnam.

It is not a light thing for an American to say that he is dismayed by his country's actions. We do not say it lightly, but soberly and in deep distress. Our Government's actions in Vietnam have been and continue to be unworthy either of the high standards of our common religious faith, or of the lofty aspirations on which this country was founded.

Now the United States has begun the process of extending the war beyond the borders of South Vietnam, with all the attendant dangers of precipitating a far greater conflict perhaps even on a global and nuclear scale.

Mr. President, we plead with you to reverse this course. Let us admit our mistakes and work for an immediate cease-fire. Let us call a conference of all the nations involved, including China, not alone to conclude peace but to launch at once a major and cooperative effort to heal and rebuild that wounded land.

Let us declare our intention to withdraw our troops, calling on other states to do the same, thereby allowing the Vietnamese the right of self-determination. We cannot dictate their course, and we may well regret it, but the risk is to be preferred over the certainty that the moral bankruptcy of our present policy is setting the stage for the ultimate victory of totalitarian forces, and even of thermonuclear war.

The prophets and teachers of our Judeo-Christian faith admonished the people of their day, and of all times, to go beyond the old restraints by which injuries might be exactly recompensed, and instead to deal with their enemies with love and good deeds. Yet in Vietnam this Nation, so proudly self-described as "under God" is not content even with "eye for an eye" retaliation, but returns evil for evil on a multiplying scale.

No nation has ever saved either its life or its soul by such methods, and ours will not be an exception. As men and women who have committed their lives to the attempt to explain and interpret the will of God, we have no alternative but to assert on every occasion and in every way open to us our conviction that these methods are not God's methods, but will bring the judgment of God upon our Nation.

Mr. President, we plead with you with the utmost urgency to turn our Nation's course, before it is too late, from cruelty to compassion, from destruction to healing, from retaliation to reconciliation, from war to peace. (Clergyman's Emergency Committee for Vietnam.)

William B. Abbot,
  Anaheim, Calif.
Ralph C. Abele,
  St. Louis, Mo.
W. N. Abeloe,
  Oakland, Calif.
Melvin Abson,
  Geneva, New York
Eric O. S. B. Abts,
  Elkhorn, Nebr.
Lyman Achenbach,
  Columbus, Ohio
George A. Ackerly,
  Bronx, New York
Thomas B. Adams,
  Birdsboro, Pa.
Frank Adamson,
  El Cerrito, Calif.

Leon M. Adkins,
  Nashville, Tenn.
Roy Charles Agte,
  Brockport, N. Y.
Owen W. Akers,
  Kalamazoo, Mich.
James Albrecht,
  Oak Lawn, Ill.
Alton P. Albright,
  Leesport, Pa.
Ralph E. Albright,
  Amherst, Ohio
Comci M. Alden,
  Tucson, Ariz.
Robert D. Aldrich,
  Fargo, N. D.
Gross W. Alexander,
  La Quinta, Calif.

L. L. Alger,
  Modesto, Calif.
Jonathan P. Allbright,
  Sunbury, Pa.
Charles M. Allen, Jr.,
  Beresford, S. D.
Charles T. Allen,
  Chelsea, Mass.
Michael Allen,
  New York, N. Y.
Robert J. Allen,
  Portland, Oregon
William Wayne Allen,
  Portland, Oregon
Gerald T. Alles,
  Youngstown, Ohio
Fitz H. Alleyne,
  Brooklyn, N. Y.

John M. Allison,
Albany, N. Y.

Ralph D. Althouse,
Northampton, Pa.

Bruce F. Anderson,
Collinsville, Conn.

Charles E. Anderson,
Fort Wayne, Indiana

Donald W. Anderson,
Gardner, Mass.

Edward S. Andersen,
San Mateo, Calif.

Dwight H. Anderson,
Ann Arbor, Michigan

Emory C. Anderson,
Wessington Springs, S.D.

J. W. Anderson,
Wichita, Kansas

John C. Anderson,
Warwick, N. Y.

K. A. Anderson,
Everest, Kansas

Karl S. Andersen,
Amherst, Mass.

L. Vann Anderson,
Worcester, Mass.

Nina E. Anderson,
Delphos, Kansas

Olof Anderson, Jr.,
Louisville, Kentucky

Stuart LeRoy Andersen,
Berkeley, Calif.

William C. Anderson,
Austin, Texas

Leslie E. Andrews,
Wakeeney, Kansas

John W. Annas,
Skaneateles, N.Y.

H. W. Apel,
Topeka, Kansas

Helen A. Archibald,
Chicago, Ill.

W. D. Archibald,
Lebanon, Ind.

A. H. Armistead,
Brooklyn, N.Y.

Moss W. Armistead,
Floristant, Mo.

Ancel H. Arnold,
Buckeye, Arizona

Keith F. Arnold,
New Haven, Mich.

O. Arnold,
Burlington, Ohio

John K. Arnot,
La Grange Park, Ill.

Owen W. Arrington,
Bozeman, Montana

J. E. Arthur,
Saginaw, Mich.

Raymond Paavo Arvio,
Pomono, N.Y.

Richard Aselford,
Milford, Pa.

Charles H. Asplin,
Edmonds, Wash.

C. J. Atkinson,
Havertown, Pa.

Samuel H. Audelman,
Newton Center, Mass.

B. F. Auld,
Baltimore, Md.

F. Aussler,
Park Ridge, N.J.

James L. Austin,
Rockville, Conn.

Wayne G. Austin,
Plainville, Mass.

Charles E. Autenrieth,
Prairie Village, Kansas

Gilbert S. Avery,
Roxbury, Mass.

Clarence F. Avey,
Westfield, Mass.

Carlos A. Avila,
Ashland, Mass.

Joseph B. Axenroth,
Furham, N.H.

Jacob B. Ayers,
Baltimore, Maryland

Paul D. Babbitt,
Hartford, Conn.

Kenneth D. Babcock,
Toledo, Ohio

Joseph Baccus,
Rialto, Calif.

Ivan A. Backer,
E. Rutherford, N.J.

Walter W. Baese, Jr.,
Fort Worth, Texas

K. R. Bailey,
Omaha, Nebraska

Robert B. Bailey,
Minneapolis, Minn.

Stanley A. Bailey,
Madison Heights, Mich.

Glen M. Baird,
Union Bridge, Maryland

William T. Baird,
Chicago, Ill.

John D. Baker,
Washington, Kansas

Mervin F. Baker,
Grass Valley, Calif.

Richard H. Baker,
Westfield, N.Y.

Samuel A. Baker,
Rochester, N.Y.

George H. Baldridge,
Atwood, Ill.

Raymond E. Balcomb,
Portland, Oregon

A. Graham Baldwin,
Andover, Mass.

H. Burnell Baldwin,
New London, Minn.

L. E. Baldwin,
Fort Shaw, Montana

Russell E. Baldwin,
Madison, Wisconsin

Frederic E. Ball,
Chicago, Ill.

Lee H. Ball,
Ardsley, N.Y.

Warren Baltzer,
St. Louis, Mo.

Andrew Banning,
Bangor, Maine

Dan H. Barfield,
Fort Worth, Texas

C. Eugene Barnard,
Roseville, Calif.

Harold H. Barnard,
Barneveld, N. Y.

Joseph R. Barndt,
Berkeley, Calif.

Frederic H. Barnes,
East Berlin, Conn.

Roger Angus Barnett,
Lynn, Mass.

Glenn H. Barney,
Center, Colorado

R. W. Barney,
Brighton, Michigan

Floyd G. Bartel,
Topeka, Kansas

Gilbert Bartholmew,
Westminster, Ind.

M. E. Bartholmew,
Geneva, N.Y.

C. S. Bartolett,
Parkesburg, Pa.

Donald B. Barton,
Inwood, L.I., N.Y.

William E. Bartz,
Unadilla, N.Y.

V. Bass,
Mason, Mich.

Ruth S. Bast,
Claremont, Calif.

Lloyd A. Bates,
Shepherdstown, W.Va.

Richard L. Batzler,
Baltimore, Maryland

William H. Baudendistel,
Port Wash., N.Y.

Richard Bauer,
Staten Island, N.Y.

Vernon H. Baum,
York, Pa.

Jack H. Baumgart,
Reed City, Mich.

Karl F. Baur,
Springfield, Missouri

William F. Baur,
Stony Point, N.Y.

W. L. Baxter,
Stamford, Conn.

Jane Beach,
Tarrytown, N.Y.

Paul R. Beach,
Normal, Ill.

Alvin J. Beachy,
Sauderton, Pa.

T. F. R. Beale,
Sun City, Calif.

Samuel M. Beaty,
Columbus, Ohio

E. K. Beckett,
San Pedro, Calif.

Camille Bedord,
Mount Vernon, N.Y.

A. A. Bedikina,
Leonia, N.J.

George J. Beebe,
Hays, Kansas

Maynard Beemer,
Eudora, Kansas

John T. Beers,
Wellsburg, N.Y.

Robert W. Beggs,
Ithaca, N.Y.

Timothy H. Behrendt,
Castine, Maine

Alfred E. Behrer,
Taylor Ridge, Ill.

Edwin C. Beier,
Marissa, Ill.

Howard E. Beil,
Belleville, Wisc.

David W. Bell,
Brewer, Maine

J. S. Bellinger,
Corcoran, Calif.

La Mar Bender,
Richfield, Pa.

Victor C. Bendsen,
Boise, Idaho

David W. Bennett,
Cornwall, N.Y.

J. C. Bennett,
Scotia, Nebraska

O. E. Bennett,
Burlington, W. Va.

Roy L. Bennett,
San Francisco, Calif.

W. Roy Bennett,
Napa, Calif.

William T. Bennett,
West Southport, Maine

Oscar A. Benson,
Chicago, Ill.

Bruce Berg,
Wolworth, Wisconsin

Lloyd A. Berg,
Bronx, N.Y.

C. L. Bergenoff,
Bay Shore, L.I., N.Y.

William R. Berger,
Healy, Kansas

Robert E. Bergmack,
Jackson, Miss.

Ernest T. Berkely, Jr.,
Chatsworth, Calif.

Daniel Berrigan,
New York, N.Y.

Phillip Berrigan,
Newburgh, N.Y.

Raphael Berringer,
Saint Nazianz, Wisc.

S. Berven,
Austin, Minn.

Samuel L. Besecker,
Wilmington, Delaware

Richard K. Best,
Revere, Mass.

Karel F. Betermans,
San Anselmo, Calif.

R. J. Beuthin, Jr.,
Bridgeport, Mich.

R. D. Beving,
San Fernando, Calif.

Robert W. Blaney,
Los Angeles, Calif.

Carl F. Beyer,
Jackson, Michigan

Douglas Beyer,
  Ness City, Kansas
Daniel Biebighause,
  Brownton, Minn.
Kenneth Biel,
  Glendive, Montana
Vernon Bigler,
  Syracuse, N.Y.
James E. Bill,
  South Bend, Indiana
A. M. Billman,
  Harriship, Pa.
Francis M. Bishop,
  Hill City, Kansas
Clifford W. Bjorkund,
  Chicago, Ill.
Benjamin J. Black,
  Cleveland, Ohio
Ira D. Black,
  Montclair, N.J.
Donald K. Blackie,
  Grand Rapids, Michigan
Thomas J. Blakely,
  Cherry Valley, N.Y.
David A. Blaken, Sr.,
  Springfield, Ill.
Robert L. Blakesley,
  Cleveland, Ohio
Miles D. Blanchard,
  Monson, Mass.
H. Blanke,
  Chicago, Ill.
E. B. Blankenship,
  Shelleyville, Ill.
Ervin F. Block,
  Cleveland, Ohio
Gust F. Block,
  Stockton, Calif.
H. P. Bloesch,
  Chicago, Ill.
Gordon Blunt,
  Littleton, Colorado
Thomas T. Boates, Jr.,
  Beverly, Mass.
Robert W. Bockstruck,
  Erie, Pa.

Erwin R. Bode,
  Dittmer, Missouri
L. C. Boeker,
  Blue Springs, Mo.
George H. Boer,
  Florence State Coll., Ala.
Theodore W. Boetz,
  West Hartford, Conn.
Helen E. Boher,
  Baltimore, Maryland
Stanley Bohn,
  Kansas City, Kansas
Anton Boisen,
  Elgin, Ill.
Ralph C. Bolin,
  Napa, Calif.
John Hall Boller,
  Long Beach, Calif.
Paul F. Boler,
  Malverne, L.I., N.Y.
H. D. Bollinger,
  Nashville, Tennessee
Charles M. Bond,
  Lewisburg, Pa.
Lester L. Boobar,
  Portland, Maine
Ann D. Bostrom,
  Phoenix, Arizona
O. E. Bormy,
  Topeka, Kansas
David J. Bort,
  Orange, N.J.
Elizabeth Borteline,
  New York, N.Y.
Emory Lee Bothast,
  Keene, N.H.
George Borthwick,
  Troy, N.Y.
Robert D. Botley,
  San Mateo, Calif.
Augustus Botten,
  Athens, Pa.
Keith A. Bovee,
  Lowell, Michigan
Eugene L. Boutilier,
  Fresno, Calif.

Bruce H. Bowen,
  Rochester, N.Y.
Calvin H. Bowers,
  Los Angeles, Calif.
Arthur W. Bowler,
  Randolph, Mass.
Walter D. Bowman,
  Wichita, Kansas
Howard Box,
  Brooklyn, N.Y.
Cleo V. Boyd,
  Ypsilanti, Mich.
James O. Bradford, Jr.,
  Napa, Calif.
Frederic M. Bradley,
  Boulder, Colorado
J. W. Bradley,
  Machias, Maine
DeWitt J. Brady,
  Covina, Calif.
Donald D. Brady,
  Honor, Michigan
James A. Braker,
  Kingston, N.Y.
Alfred T. Bramsey,
  Detroit, Michigan
Harry A. Brandt,
  Laverne, Calif.
E. E. Brannon,
  Kansas City, Kansas
Frank M. Brannon,
  Madison, N.J.
Floyd Braun,
  Auburn, Mich.
William G. Braude,
  Providence, R.I.
Theodore A. Braun,
  Glen Ridge, N.J.
Howard N. Bream,
  Gettysburg, Pa.
James P. Breeden,
  Roxbury, Mass.
Donald L. Brenneman,
  Chicago, Ill.
Abraham Brenning,
  Lincoln, Nebraska

Charles T. Brewster,
Honolulu, Hawaii

Edward Eldridge Brewster,
Joliet, Ill.

James W. Bristah,
Detroit, Mich.

James E. Bristo,
Philadelphia, Pa.

Carl C. Brizer,
Chicago, Ill.

Margueritte H. Bro,
Park Forest, Ill.

Charles D. Broadbent,
Concord, N.H.

Herbert C. Brockman,
Kansas City, Kansas

Walter P. Brockway,
Exeter, N.H.

Herbert Bronstein,
Rochester, N.Y.

Hadfield Brook,
Saint James, L.I., N.Y.

Kenneth Brookes,
Augusta, Maine

Rachel G. Brooks
Elmira, N.Y.

John R. Bross,
Billings, Montana

Whitcomb J. Brougher,
Portland, Oregon

Arnold Brown,
Roxbury, Mass.

Arnold A. Brown,
Hood River, Oregon

Arthur M. Brown,
Lewiston, Maine

David Clifford Brown,
Niagara Falls, N.Y.

Derek Brown,
So. Walpole, Mass.

Donald S. Brown,
Gloversville, N.Y.

Edwin A. Brown,
Berea, Ohio

Frederick Crawford Brown
Cambridge, Mass.

M. Joe Brownrigg,
Boston, Mass.

Robert Brubaker,
Brighton, Mich.

A. L. Brueggemann,
Warrenton, Missouri

T. T. Brumbaugh,
New Rochelle, N.Y.

John Brunn,
Wakefield, Nebr.

John W. Brush,
Nashville, Tenn.

Donald Brushelt,
Latham, N.Y.

Bradford H. Bryant,
Oakland, Calif.

Walter E. Bucher,
Canton, Ill.

Albert W. Buck,
Chicago, Ill.

Earl G. Buck,
Milwaukee, Wis.

Joseph A. Buckles,
Chicago, Ill.

Donald A. Buckley,
Utica, N.Y.

Hartzell Buckner,
Auburn, Calif.

Robert C. Buckley,
Hempstead, L.I., N.Y.

Marshall H. Budd,
Marlborough, N.H.

Ruth W. Budd,
Marlborough, N.H.

Bernie A. Buehler,
Powhatan Point, Ohio

Daniel Buendorf,
Harris, Minn.

Howard F. Buies,
Syracuse, N.Y.

George Bulin,
Bellmore, N.Y.

Harold W. Buller,
Beatrice, Nebr.

R. N. Burda,
San Francisco, Calif.

Howard W. Burden,
Flint, Mich.

Earl R. Burdick,
Canisteo, N.Y.

Lloyd A. Burkhalter,
Seekonk, Mass.

Neilson C. Burn,
Orange, Conn.

Alfred W. Burns,
East Greenwich, R.I.

Robert G. Buttrick,
Monmouth, Ill.

Carol Buzzi,
Teaneck, N.J.

Sydney S. Byrne,
River Rouge, Mich.

Sidney D. Cahoon,
So. Dennis, Mass.

Terry Cain,
Greenwood, Neb.

Robert A. Caine,
Minneapolis, Minn.

Bruce Calkins,
Bronx, N.Y.

William S. Calkins,
Cortland, N.Y.

Melvin M. Cammack,
O'Neill, Neb.

A. N. Campbell,
Mahtomedi, Minn.

Arthur D. Campbell,
Tacoma, Wash.

Colin Campbell, Jr.,
Ann Arbor, Mich.

Fay Campbell,
Maryville, Tenn.

Irving C. Campbell,
Browntown, Miss.

Robert L. Campbell,
E. Weymouth, Mass.

Julius Cancel,
Ozone Park, N.Y.

James W. Canny,
Auburn, Ill.

Fred Cappuccino,
Takoma Park, Md.

Howard R. Carey,
Inglewood, Cal.
Albert Carlyle,
Fremont, Neb.
Donald D. Carpenter,
Montmorenci, Ind.
David C. Cargill,
Syracuse, N.Y.
Paul M. Cargo,
Caro, Mich.
Erland E. Carlson,
Escanaba, Mich.
John D. Carman,
New York, N.Y.
Russell J. Carpenter,
Pine City, N.Y.
Harold Carrell,
Morrill, Kan.
John W. Carrier,
Hutchinson, Kan.
Frank Cary,
Plainfield, Mass.
G. Arthur Casaday,
Palo Alto, Cal.
J. R. Case,
Vergennes, Vt.
Harold N. Caton,
San Jose, Cal.
P. W. Caton,
Dickinson, N.D.
Mario Cestaro,
Jeffrey, N.H.
Burns A. Chalmers,
Washington, D.C.
Bruce S. Chamberlain,
Rockdale, Mass.
William A. Chamberlain,
Winthrop, Me.
Eben T. Chapman,
Woodbury, Conn.
Don M. Chase,
Jackson, Cal.
Lewis A. Chase,
Scarborough, Me.
Keith W. Chidester,
Stamford, Conn.

Harry Childress,
Redding, Cal.
Lloyd E. Chorpenning,
Hamilton, Mass.
Jack K. Christian,
Broadlands, Ill.
Joseph H. Christian,
Dearborn Heights,
Ernest W. Churchill,
Pearl River, N.Y.
Gorie Ciaravine,
Detroit, Mich.
Edward T. Clapp,
Portland, Conn.
Thaddeus Clapp,
Worcester, Mass.
Allan W. Clark,
Sanbornville, N.H.
David W. Clark,
Santa Fe, N.M.
David L. Clark,
Holland, Mich.
Donald Clark,
Toledo, Ohio
Fred C. Clark,
Bloomfield, Conn.
Gordon M. Clark,
Johnsonville, N.Y.
George D. Clark,
Banning, Cal.
Arden Clute,
Mountain View, Cal.
Daw S. Clute,
Schenectady, N.Y.
Paul J. Cotton,
Geneva, Ohio
Clyde E. Coatney,
Wichita, Kan.
Orville A. Coates,
Boise, Idaho
Clarke M. Cockrane,
Almont, Mich.
John I. Coffman,
Pomona, Cal.
Jehuda M. Cohen,
Los Angeles, Cal.

Franklin Cohn,
Los Angeles, Cal.
Jordan D. Cole,
North Chatham, N.Y.
Maurice W. Coleb,
Brunswick, Me.
Harold C. Coleman,
Vallaje, Cal.
Percy E. Colton,
Houlton, Me.
K. Collier,
Sun Valley, Cal.
George L. Collins,
San Jose, Cal.
Alfred P. Coman,
Nashville, Ind.
Dale K. Compton,
Marysville, Kan.
Paul Conlay,
Baltimore, Md.
Rolfe J. Conrad,
Pacific Grove, Cal.
Albert L. Coomb,
Laconia, N.H.
James R. Cooper,
Bloomingdale, N.J.
Robert O. Cooper,
Kingville, Tex.
T. R. Cooper,
Averill Park, N.Y.
Raymond J. Cope,
Berkeley, Cal.
Glenn A. Copeland,
Champaign, Ill.
Martin J. Corbin,
Tivoli, N.Y.
Richard C. Cox,
New York, N.Y.
Robert M. Cox,
Rye, N.Y.
Edgar H. Coxeter,
Briarcliff Manor, N.Y.
Glenn A. Crafts,
Synder, N.Y.
Kenneth E. Crouch,
Rensselaer, N.Y.

Russell Craig,
Chelsea, Mich.

Warren H. Crain,
Anadarko, Okla.

Frederick M. Crane,
Pomona, Cal.

Henry Hitt Crane,
Detroit, Mich.

Harold E. Craw,
Meridan, Conn.

David L. Crawford,
Cadillac, Mich.

Edna L. Crede,
Peoria, Ill.

Harry L. Crede,
Peoria, Ill.

Howard Crenshaw,
Turon, Kan.

Haywood Crewe,
Norwich, Vt.

Don R. Crocker,
Mount Vernon, Ill.

Charles W. Crooker,
Rutland, Mass.

Winston C. Crosse,
Lourell, Del.

Norman Crotser,
St. Johns, Mich.

Forrest Crouch,
Mt. Eris, Ill.

Robert R. Croyle,
Bloomsburg, Pa.

Maurice E. Culver,
Kansas City, Kan.

Earnest Cummings,
Kalamazoo, Mich.

Ralph Cummins,
East Peoria, Ill.

J. C. Curry,
Flint, Mich.

Paul J. Custer,
Hartford, S.D.

Wolcott Cutler,
Cambridge, Mass.

Russell M. Dackson,
Winona, Minn.

Elmer L. Dadisman,
Astoria, Ill.

Harold A. Dagley,
Peoria, Ill.

Enise, Daher,
Paterson, N.J.

J. E. Dalke,
Hillsboro, Kansas

Gene D. Damewood,
Kansas

Alex Danaer,
Elyria, Ohio

John I. Daniel,
Franklin, Mass.

Raymond S. Daniel,
Columbus, Ohio

Willbar O. Daniel,
Pearl River, N.Y.

Kenneth L. Danskin,
Altadena, Calif.

Steven L. Darling,
Quincy, Ill.

John W. Darr,
Seattle, Washington

Richard D. Davey,
Rochester, N.Y.

Julius E. Davis,
Parlier, Calif.

Lewis H. Davis,
Dobbs Ferry, N.Y.

Newell E. Davis,
Winnetka, Ill.

Floyd Davidson,
Topeka, Kansas

John F. Davidson,
Lenox, Mass.

Ralph J. Davie,
Mechanicville, N.Y.

Charles D. Davis,
Newark, Del.

Jerome Davis,
West Haven, Conn.

John Rogers Davis,
Tucson, Arizona

Burton Davison,
Elmhurst, N.Y.

Richard A. Dawson,
Bakersfield, Calif.

Albert E. Day,
Falls Church, Va.

Ben F. Day,
Rockford, Ill.

John Warren Day,
Asheville, N.C.

Vergie Deal,
Derry, N.H.

Frank De Chambeau,
Jackson Heights, N.Y.

Allen C. Deeter,
North Manchester, Ind.

Edward L. Deighton,
Depew, N.Y.

Robert H. DeLancey,
Ogden, Utah

Charles A. Delay,
Gilman, Ill.

Alvin L. Dennan,
Boston, Mass.

Ray W. Denning,
Williamsport, Pa.

F. E. Densmore,
Hillsdale, Mich.

Robert C. Dentan,
New York, N.Y.

Wilford L. Denton,
Long Beach, Calif.

Richard C. Devor,
Meadville, Pa.

Charles De Vries,
Harwich, Mass.

Norman E. Dewire,
Detroit, Mich.

Jesse R. De Witt,
Royal Oak, Mich.

Selden C. Dickinson,
Oak Park, Ill.

Robert L. Dickson,
Wayne, Mich.

Elmer M. Ditch,
Oakland, Ill.

Theodore Dixon,
Simsbury, Conn.

Clyde Dodder,
San Bruno, Calif.

Allan T. Dodge,
Watertown, N.Y.

Samuel H. Dodge,
Paterson, N.J.

Carroll A. Doggett,
Baltimore, Md.

Herbert L. D. Doggett,
Silver Spring, Md.

George W. Dolch,
Camden, N.Y.

Frederic Dolfin,
Grand Rapids, Mich.

Howard P. Donahue,
Decatur, Ill.

Henry F. Donelson,
Louisburg, Kansas

Arthur G. Donnelly,
Cordova, Ill.

Paul Donovan,
St. Louis, Mo.

William V. Dorn,
Mazon, Ill.

Everett M. Dorr,
Fairfax, Va.

James B. Doughten,
Lincoln, Del.

Philip Douglas,
New Bedford, Mass.

Hugh A. Doughlin,
Norristown, Penna.

Everett J. Downes,
Douglastown, N.Y.

Francis A. Drake,
Schroon Lake, N.Y.

J. A. Drake,
Topeka, Kansas

Lowell Drake,
Eagle, Nebraska

Richard M. Drake,
Cleveland, Ohio

William F. Drake,
Flint, Mich.

Dan E. Driesen,
Reedly, Calif.

Allen E. Dripps,
Rochester, Minn.

William H. Dubay,
Santa Monica, Calif.

John S. Du Bois,
Auburn, Mass.

Wilton J. Dubrick,
Binghamton, N.Y.

Ralph H. Dude,
Galesburg, Ill.

Herbert H. Duenow,
Prairie View, Ill.

Joseph Duffy,
Hartford, Conn.

Hubert N. Dukes,
Berkeley, Calif.

Dale Dunbar,
Tucson, Arizona

Donald B. Duncan,
Wildwood, N.J.

Russell Dunlap,
Sodus, N.Y.

Lloyd A. Duren,
Huntington, L.I., N.Y.

Ralph A. Durham,
Montrose, Colo.

Dwight E. Dussair,
Olathe, Kansas

Harry J. Dutt,
Fairmount, N.D.

William H. Duvall,
Concord, Mass.

F. A. Dyckman,
Glens Falls, N.Y.

Linton J. Dwyer,
Taunton, Mass.

Ralph Dyer,
Nebraska City, Nebr.

Robert H. Eads,
Rochester, N.Y.

Edward L. Eastman,
Watertown, Conn.

Robert A. Edgar,
New York, N.Y.

Herbert Edmondson,
Pleasantville, N.J.

Hal Edward,
Santa Ana, Calif.

D. W. Edwards,
Mountain View, Calif.

Kenneth A. Edwards,
Santa Rosa, Calif.

R. H. Edwards,
Ossining, N.Y.

William H. Edwards,
Wappingers Falls, N.Y.

Benjamin Eitelgeorge,
Hygiene, Colo.

Emmet E. Eklund,
Tacoma, Wash.

Charles D. Ellewood,
West Liberty, W. Va.

Charles E. Elliott,
Juba City, Calif.

Murray A. Elliott,
West Newbury, Mass.

Ralph H. Elliott,
Albany, N.Y.

Willis E. Elliott,
New York, N.Y.

A. L. Ellis,
North Branford, Conn.

Blake S. Ellis,
So. Portland, Maine

Edwin L. Ellis,
Jamaica, N.Y.

M. W. Ellis,
St. Clair, Mo.

Robert C. Ely,
Attica, Kansas

John H. Emerson,
Santa Clara, Calif.

Laurence W. C. Emig,
Melrose, Mass.

George E. Emmons,
Danville, Ill.

Mark Emswiler,
Friend, Kansas

Frank W. Engstrom,
Natoma, Kansas

Charles O. Erickson,
Haslett, Mich.

Leif Edward Erickson,
Clayton, Indiana
Robert L. Erickson,
Chicago, Ill.
Edward L. Ericson,
Arlington, Va.
Fred Erion,
Audobon, Pa.
A. R. Eschliman,
W. Liberty, Ohio
Loy S. Estes,
Polson, Montana
Barry H. Evans,
Washington, D.C.
John L. Everett, Jr.,
Cortes, Colorado
Donald C. Everhart,
Indianapolis, Indiana
Norman J. Faramelli,
Phila., Pa.
Thomas K. Farley,
Riverside, Calif.
Harley W. Farnham,
Denver, Col.
Norman R. Farnum, Jr.,
Holyoke, Mass.
John Wesley Farr,
Bakersfield, Calif.
A. E. Farstrup,
Orinda, Calif.
C. A. Farthing,
Columbus, Ohio
Ronald M. Fassett,
Grand Rapids, Mich.
William J. Faulkner,
Wildwood, N.J.
R. E. Featherstone,
Watertown, N.Y.
Rudolph R. Featherstone,
Jamaica, N.Y.
Raymond Norman Fedje,
Needham Heights, Mass
R. A. Feenstra,
Falls City, Oregon
Joseph J. Feller,
Bridgeport, N.Y.

Shelby C. Felts,
Centralia, Ill.
Joe M. Fernandez,
Pico Rivera, Calif.
Folke Ferre,
Rochester, N.Y.
E. S. Ferris,
Great Neck, N.Y.
Theodore P. Ferris,
Boston, Mass.
John D. W. Fetter,
Ithaca, N.Y.
Richard M. Fewkes,
Middleboro, Mass.
Howard R. Feye,
Saratoga Springs, N.Y.
R. M. Field,
Watervliet, N.Y.
Murry A. Figg,
Akron, Ohio
Lester E. Fike,
Askley, Indiana
Oscan R. Fike,
Bellwood, Pa.
Hugh W. Findley,
Dorchester, Mass.
Elliott J. Finlay,
Bridgewater, Mass.
Nels Firre,
Newton Centre, Mass.
Julius Fischbach,
Minneapolis, Minn.
David R. Fisher,
Lansing, Mich.
Howard W. Fisher,
Kirkwood, Ill.
F. J. Fitch,
Muskegon, Mich.
Roger W. Fitzgerald,
Au Sable Forks, N.Y.
James A. Flad,
Norwich, Kansas
Sylvus D. Flora,
Carleton, Nebraska
Daniel C. Flory,
Paris, Indiana

Edgar Flory,
New Preston, Conn.
Robert Folkert,
Richmond, Mich.
Arthur Foote,
St. Paul, Minn.
Kenneth Ripley Forbes,
Phila., Pa.
Charles R. Ford,
Denver, Col.
Williston M. Ford,
San Diego, Calif.
G. Foster,
Neponset, Ill.
William L. Foster,
Canaan, Conn.
Ralph Fothergill,
Jerome, Idaho
John Fragale, Jr.,
Warwick, N.Y.
William J. Frain,
Jamaica, N.Y.
Greta Frankley,
New York, N.Y.
C. W. Franklin,
Springfield, Mass.
Alfred C. Fray,
Beach Haven, Pa.
Eugene N. Frazier,
Hutchinson, Kan.
Martin Freedman,
Paterson, N.J.
Forster W. Freeman,
DeWitt, N.Y.
William Freeman,
Omaha, Neb.
Porter French,
Chester, Ill.
Richard E. French,
Auburndale, Mass.
Edward S. Frey,
New York, N.Y.
Eric Friedland,
Chicago, Ill.
Albert H. Friedlander,
New York, N.Y.

Philip R. Friedeman,
Andover, Ohio
Elmer R. Friesen,
Newton, Kansas
John W. Frint,
Belleville, Kansas
Stephen H. Fritchman,
Glendale, Calif.
Don W. Frogge,
New Haven, Conn.

Victor M. Frohne,
Mt. Vernon, Indiana
Clifford E. Frost,
Marilla, N.Y.
Harold I. Frost,
Auburn, Maine
Henry D. Frost,
So. Bound Brook, N.J.
Harry T. Frownfelter,
Wellsboro, Pa.

Gerhard Fressen,
Newton, Kansas
L. Fruechte,
Lyons, Ill.
C. H. Frye,
New York, N.Y.
Franklin P. Frye,
Worcester, Mass.
Glenn M. Frye,
E. Lansing, Mich.

[NEW YORK TIMES, June 5, 1966]

ON VIETNAM:

Events of the past few months have further undermined the administration's stated rationale for involvement in Vietnam—that American armed force is there to defend the Vietnamese. The continuing demonstrations in Hue, Danang and Saigon, with their anti-Ky and anti-American slogans, have made it clearer than ever that the Saigon regime has virtually no popular support. Military activities have been steadily escalated, and American military power has been forced to assume the brunt of the fighting from the South Vietnamese army. An estimated 100,000 soldiers deserted this army in 1965 alone . . .

WE CALL UPON OUR GOVERNMENT

To cease all bombing, North and South, and all other offensive operations immediately;

To indicate that it will negotiate with the National Liberation Front and all other interested parties for a peaceful settlement;

To encourage in every way, and in no way to interfere with, the free exercise of popular sovereignty in Vietnam;

To evaluate seriously whether self-determination for the Vietnamese as well as our own national interests would not be best served by termination of our military presence in Vietnam.

MEMBERS OF THE ACADEMIC COMMUNITY

ALABAMA
  STILLMAN
  COLLEGE
Thorpe Butler
Donald R. Fletcher
Jonathan S. Golan
Richard King
Frederick L. Kuretski
Lawrence Rubin
Barbara P. Tinker
Robert F. Tinker
David M. Wax
Robert Weinberg
Joshua Williams
OTHER
  INSTITUTIONS
Theodore Klitzke
Harold A. Nelson
Melville Price
ARIZONA
  ARIZONA STATE
  UNIVERSITY
Marvin M. Fisher
Donald W. Geisen
Robert A. Heimann
Thomas Ford Hoult
Edmund G. Howells
Leo B. Levy
Audrey MacDonald
Robert Rein'l
Morris J. Starsky
T. Alexander Votichenko
UNIVERSITY OF
  ARIZONA
James R. Anthony
D. F. Fleming
Donald M. Freeman
Harold C. Fritts
Clifford M. Lytle
Hormoz Mahmoud
Paul S. Martin
Russell Sherman
Cornelius Steelink
C. E. Wilson

CALIFORNIA
  CALIFORNIA
  STATE COLLEGE,
  LONG BEACH
Harold Aspiz
Roscoe L. Buckland
Earl R. Carlson
Gene Dinielli
Leonard Fels
Alan Glasser
Raphael Hanson
Roy K. Heintz
Richard Lyon
Frank G. Nelson
Samuel Pollach
William M. Resch
Alfred Sheets
Robert Thayer
J. J. Thompson
David A. Williams
Alva Yano
CALIFORNIA STATE
  COLLEGES,
  OTHER BRANCHES
Huguette Bach
C. Wesley Bird
Marguerite Dunton
Leonard Feldman
Amnon Goldworth
Peter A. Griffin
Paul Hayner
Stanley P. Hughart
Elizabeth Huttman
Edward J. Jay
Bonnie B. Keller
Marvin E. Lee
Anthony R. Lovaglia
Bernard Marcus
Arnold Mechanic
Walter-Nelson
E. Nomikos
Peter R. Ori
Thomas H. Pagenhart
Gerald C. Preston

William Sawrey
Andrew Scott
Gerald S. Silberman
John Sperling
Hobart F. Thomas
Sylvia Vatuk
Robert L. Zeppa
William Otto Zoller
UNIVERSITY OF
  CALIFORNIA,
  BERKELEY
Max Alfert
Paul J. Alpers
Cyril P. Atkinson
Michael W. Baker
Jonas A. Barish
Edward N. Barnhart
Diana Baumrind
Ernest Becket
Albert M. Bendich
W. E. Berg
Gerald D. Berreman
Frederick A. F. Berry
Stephen Booth
Thomas C. Breitner
Lawrence D. Brown
Wallace L. Chafe
Seymour Chatman
Mark N. Christensen
Aaron V. Cicourel
John A. Clausen
Robert A. Cockrell
Philip A. Cowan
Hans G. Daellenbach
Joanne D'Andrea
William R. Dennes
Stephen P. Diliberto
Isadora Ding
Vincent Duckles
Richard M. Dudley
Joseph J. Duggan
J. W. Dyckman
Garrett Eckbo
John Edmunds

John Ernest
Paul Forman
Dorothy E. Gibson
Christian Gram
Robert Greene
Douglas E. Greiner
John J. Gumperz
Michael J. Harner
Robert A. Harris
John E. Hearst
Max Heirich
Robert F. Heizer
Morris W. Hirsch
Elina Holst
Karl Kasten
Jack F. Kirsch
David Kretch
Joseph R. Levenson
J. A. Levine
William Z. Lidicker
Leon F. Litwack
Norman Livson
M. Loeve
Sheldon Margen
Jonathan Middlebrook
Jacob Milgrom
Henry Miller
C. R. Mocine
Ralph L. Moellering
C. Bradley Moore
Forrest Mozer
Charles Muscatine
Paul Mussen
S. M. Newberger
John B. Nielands
Simon Nicholson
Raymond D. Oliver
Paul Omelich
Edward M. Opton, Jr.
A. Pabst
Oscar H. Paris
Sherwood Parker
Melvin L. Periman
Peter L. Petrakis
Rudolph L. Pipa
George O. Poinar, Jr.

Ralph W. Powell
Norman Rabkin
Lydia Rapoport
D. P. Reay
Jesse Reichek
Karen S. Renne
Gordon G. Roadarmel
Russell Hope Robbins
Walden K. Roberts
Raphael M. Robinson
William S. Robinson
Harry Rubin
Donald Sarason
Meyer J. Scharlack
Henry Scheffe
Irwin Scheiner
Mark Schorer
Peter H. Selz
William F. Shipley
Joseph H. Silverman
Dan I. Slobin
M. Brewster Smith
Ralph I. Smith
R. H. Somers
Kenneth M. Stampp
Pete Steffens
Gunther S. Stent
George W. Stocking, Jr.
Herbert L. Strauss
Fred Stripp
R. C. Strohman
Herbert Sussman
Edward S. Sylvester
Steve Talbot
P. Emery Thomas
Tony Tripodi
Donald Ultan
James Vlamis
Clyde Wahrhattig
Frederic Wakeman, Jr.
Lawrence Waldron
Richard P. Wiebe
Steven Weinberg
David W. Weiss
L. E. Weiss
Harold Widom

Clyde D. Wilson
Donald M. Wilson
Reginald E. Zelnick
Robert B. Zevin
Karl E. Zimmer
Michael Zimmerman
UNIVERSITY OF
 CALIFORNIA,
 DAVIS
Max Bach
William Biglow
Gulbank Chakerian
Edmond Costantini
Richard D. Cramer
S. Fishman
Gerald Friedberg
Charles R. Grau
Richard E. Grimm
Jay L. Halio
Charles A. Hayes, Jr.
Roland Hoermann
Clyde E. Jacobs
Kurt Kreith
Marshall Lindsay
John H. Madison
Allen G. Marr
Douglas L. Minnis
Lawrence Rappaport
Donald M. Reynolds
Alvin D. Sokolow
G. Ledyard Stebbins
Sherman Stein
Matthew Stolz
Edward Theil
Louis F. Weschler
UNIVERSITY OF
 CALIFORNIA,
 OTHER BRANCHES
Inge Bell
Frederick A. Eiserling
Carolyn Fisher
Bill Garoutte
Alan W. C. Green
Don L. Jewett
David R. Krieg
George G. Laties

Alexander Miller
Norman Miller
Ernest Newbrun
Stewart E. Perry
John Pickett
Eugene Rosenberg
Eli Sercarz
John P. Seward
Stephen A. Shapiro
Alfred Strickholm
Irving Zabin

MERRITT COLLEGE

Suzanne Adams
Douglas Baugh
Lloyd Baysdorfer
Helen Bersie
Kenneth Castellino
Harry Caughren
Deborah Dizard
Charles Duffy
Ronald Eberhart
Roland Gangloff
Beverly Gilbert
Mary Greer
James Harris
Edith A. Jenkins
Douglas E. Kyle
J. Elaine Lockley
James B. Lyons
Marian Malloy
Yale Maxon
Irwin Mayers
Doris A. Meek
Lois Michel
Alex Pappas
Jack Paul
Harriet Polt
Frank A. Poulos
Merle Quait
Robert Seward
Patricia Smeltzer
Glenand Spencer
Frank W. Storti
Thomas R. Trent
Helen Sande Truber
Eve St. Martin

Wallenstein
Wayne Welch
Maurice Wolfe

STANFORD
UNIVERSITY

Kenneth J. Arrow
Paul Berg
Barton J. Berstein
Marc Bertrand
William A. Bonner
Robert McAfee Brown
William Calin
W. B. Carnochan
Raymond B. Clayton
William A. Clebsch
Charles Drekmeier
Melvin Edelstein
Solomon Feferman
Naomi C. Franklin
H. Bruce Franklin
John G. Gurley
William Helpern
John C. Hotchkiss
Karel de Leeuw
John C. Lapp
Mark Mancall
Hubert Marshall
Thomas C. Moser
Ingram Olkin
Thomas F. A. Plaut
Yosal Rogat
Arnold A. Rogow
Irene Rosenthal-Hill
Nevitt Sanford
Leonard I. Schiff
Paul S. Seaver
Rudolph Sher
Albert E. Shirk, Jr.
George Stark
Charles M. Stein
Wilfred Stone
Paul Wallin
Charles Yanofsky

CONNECTICUT

UNIVERSITY OF
CONNECTICUT

Max M. Allen
Shirley Ariker
James H. Barnett
Rufus A. Blanshard
Edward G. Boettiger
Gary M. Brodsky
Joyce Brodsky
Eric W. Carlson
Joseph B. Cary
Thomas P. Churchill
Arthur Chovnick
William R. Clark
Albert K. Cohen
David J. Colfax
Irving P. Cummings
Douglas P. Crowne
Jack M. Davis
Norman T. Davis
Hollis F. Fait
Charles A. Fritz
Anita D. Fritz
Kenneth Forman
Amerigo Farina
Herbert I. Goldstone
Michael T. Gregoric
John Gregoropoulos
Mortimer Guiney
Joan J. Hall
Hugh M. Hamil
George Hemphill
David A. Ivry
Eleanore B. Luckey
Charles A. McLaughlin
Harry J. Marks
Robert G. Mead
Alexander G. Medicott
William T. Moynihan
Kent R. Newmyer
J. D. O'Hara
William C. Orr
Lawrence L. Parrish
Robert A. Peters
Matthew N. Proser

Max Putzel
Kenneth Ring
Compton Rees
Robert A. Rollin
William Rosen
Melvyn Rosenthal
Jay S. Roth
Lorraine A. Roth
Julian B. Rotter
James Scully
David A. Sonstroem
William C. Spengemann
Thomas K. Standish
Milton R. Stern
William G. Walker
Ellen L. Walker
Herbert Weil
Thomas Wilcox
William A. Wilson, Jr.
Roger Wilkenfeld
Sam Witryol
George E. Wolf
Nancy C. Wolf
David Zeaman
WESLEYAN
  UNIVERSITY
Edgar F. Beckham
Richard V. Buel, Jr.
Nathanael Green
Peter Kilby
James R. Lusardi
Basil J. Moore
Richard M. Ohmann
Philip Pomper
David E. Swift
John E. Theismeyer
David A. Titus
YALE UNIVERSITY
Albert Berry
E. J. Boell
Arthur Brandenburg
Robert A. Dahl
David Danelski
Edward S. Deevey, Jr.
David Egger
Thomas I. Emerson

Edmund Fantino
Charles W. Forman
Joseph Gall
Arthur W. Galston
Alan Garen
Joseph Goldstein
Dorothy M. Horstmann
Shane Hunt
Franklin Hutchinson
G. E. Hutchinson
Robert L. Jackson
Michael Kahn
David Kelsey
Friedrich Kessler
T. C. Koopmans
Christopher A. Larkin
David Little
Staughton Lynd
James A. Mau
David G. Miller
Paul S. Minear
Harold Morowitz
G. D. Nostow
Howard Pack
Janet Pack
Louis H. Pollak
D. F. Poulson
Charles A. Reich
Clark Reynolds
Harry Rudin
Alan E. Samuel
Herbert Scarr
Hames P. Sewell
Gaddis Smith
Albert J. Solnit
Julian Sturtevant
Clyde W. Summers
Sidney Tarrow
W. Silbey Towner
Robert Triffen
J. P. Trinkhaus
G. R. Wyatt
UNIVERSITY OF
  DELAWARE
R. J. Bresler
C. A. Carpenter, Jr.

D. E. Ingersoll
S. E. Koss
S. Lukachevich
G. Malz
F. Roberts
E. Seymour
B. Skyrms
R. Wolters
DISTRICT OF
  COLUMBIA
CATHOLIC
  UNIVERSITY
H. B. Atabek
Rev. Charles E. Curran
Richard des Jardins
A. J. Durelli
Mary E. Fitzpatrick
Rt. Rev. Msgr. Paul
  Hanly Furfey
Hans G. Furth
Gerald J. Goodwin
Rev. T. J. Harte
Gustav B. Hensel
John J. Hocker
Jasper Ingersoll
Gottfried O. Lang
Cecil P. Nelson
Rev. Carl J. Peter
John Renaldo
Rev. Walter J. Smith
Jerome Steffens
Mary Elizabeth Walsh
Y. C. Whang
James Youniss
Shuh-Jing Ying
IDAHO STATE
  UNIVERSITY
Sylvia Cline
Arthur B. Hillabold
Jane Hillabold
Wilbur Huck
F. G. Jarvis
Arthur Kincaid
Mary Kitaj
Ann Leger
R. A. Lyman

Nicole O'Connor
Gerald Priori
Mireille Solignac
John F. Walker
UNIVERSITY OF
  CHICAGO
Robert M. Adams
Hannah Arendt
Paul H. Strohm, Jr.
Phillip Thompson
Charles R. Tittle
Stephen H. Wedgewood
Eleanor Weinblatt
Robert Werman
Robert H. Whitman
Philip R. Wikelund
John R. Wilson
James G. Witte, Jr.
Irving M. Zeitlin
Paul N. Zietlow
MANCHESTER
  COLLEGE
Richard Bittinger
Kenneth Brown
Donald Colburn
Dean Frantz
Paul Keller
Roger Carasso
Merton Dillon
Raymond Ditrichs
Melvin Dubofsky
Emory Evans
Salvador J. Fajardo
Arnold B. Fox
Charles Freedeman
Charles H. George
Lynn B. Graves
Jack C. Gray
Michael Hays
Earl Hayter
Mazhar Hazan
Martin Kullich
Benjamin Keen
Samuel Kinser
Tilden J. Le Melle
John Lloyd

Andrew Mac Leish
R. L. Morgenthau
Frank Morrow Jr.
Donald Murray
C. Mason Myers
Kenneth Owens
J. Norman Parmer
Carl Parrini
Robert H. Renshaw
Albert Resis
Jesse P. Ritter, Jr.
Rosendo Rivera
Marvin S. Rosen
Saul Rosenthal
Hans-Jochen Schild
Robert Schneider
Martha E. Schrein
Jordan Schwarz
James Shirley
Lucien Stryk
D. Raymond Tourville
Charles Tucker
Bruce Von Zellen
David Wagner
Allen Weaver
Dale Weeks
David Welborn
Patrick White
James C. Wilcox
Alfred Young
INDIANA
  UNIVERSITY
James Allison
Howard Anderson
Philip Appleman
Frank G. Banta
Willis Barnstone
Ernest Berhardt-Kabisch
Mary Alice Burgan
William M. Burgan
N. John Castellan, Jr.
Norman S. Cohen
Dorrit Claire Cohn
Aubrey Diller
James A. Dinsmoor
Albert Eisen

Sheldon Gellar
Charlotte F. Gerrard
Rudolf B. Gottfried
Quentin M. Hope
Hans Jaeger
Peter K. Jansen
W. Nicholas Knight
Roger Lass
D. B. Lichtenberg
Charles Leonard Lundin
Karl Magnuson
Lewis H. Miller, Jr.
Bernard S. Morris
Herbert J. Muller
Raymond G. Murray
Roger G. Newton
Bernard B. Perry
Howard V. Rickenberg
Judy Rilling
Mark Rilling
Stefan H. Robock
Samuel N. Rosenberg
Norbert Samuelson
John H. Scandrett
Frederic C. Schmidt
UNIVERSITY OF
  ILLINOIS
Alexander Abashian
Norman Blackburn
M. K. Brussel
Letterio Calapal
Robert Carroll
Michael Glaubman
Joseph Landin
Michael Lewis
Oscar Lewis
E. F. Masur
Alan McConnell
John Pappademos
H. Y. Tienen
NORTHERN ILLINOIS
  UNIVERSITY
Harold Aikins
John Antes
R. M. Archer
Thomas Blomquist

Ralph Bowen
Donald M. Brayton
Waldo W. Burchard
William Bussen
Rufus King
Wilson Lutz
Robert Mock
Leon Neher
Philip Orpurt
T. Wayne Rieman
William Schuhle
Ernest Shull
David Waas
PURDUE
  UNIVERSITY
Kathryn Black
William C. Black
Ray B. Browne
Roland Duerksen
Jack W. Fleming
Michael Golomb
Anne M. Herouard
Albert Kahn
William E. Martin
Robert A. Miller
Neil Myers
J. Bennet Olson
Marc Pilisuk
J. J. Price
Eleanor L. Robinson
Nathan Rosenberg
Henry Salerno
Eugene Schenkman
Ramey Stanford
Robert R. Tompkins
Edwin Umbargar
G. N. Wollan
UNIVERSITY OF
  MAINE
George Almond
J. A. Antonitis
Robert Apostal
Ronald Banks
David Clark
George Davis
Stuart Doty

Frank A. Durbin, Jr.
Steve Finner
Rod Forsgren
Stanley Freeman
George Friend
E. Vaughn Gulo
James Henderson
Carol Holden
Edward Holmes
Arthur Johnson
Karl Kopp
John Lindlof
Douglas Miller
Ralph Minger
Edward Nadel
Fred Ohnmacht
Arnie Raphaelson
Walter Schoenberger
George Semsel
Dave Smith
Herman Trubov
Theodore Vrooman
Edward Wade
MARYLAND
  GOUCHER
    COLLEGE
Barbara Bradshaw
Allan Brick
John V. Chamberlain
Sara deFord
Sibylle Ehrlich
Marianne Githens
William L. Hedges
Florence Howe
Joseph Morton
Dee Ann Pappas
Frederic C. Wood, Jr.
MASSACHUSETTS
  AMHERST
    COLLEGE
Howell D. Chickering, Jr.
Joel E. Gordon
Harold Fruchtbaum
Richard Girsch
Allen Guttmann
Hugh D. Hawkins

Gilbert Lawall
N. Gordon Levin, Jr.
Ray A. Moore
Lewis S. Mudge
Donald S. Pitkin
John William Ward
Ralston E. Warner
Henry T. Yost
BOSTON UNIVERSITY
Joseph Ablow
Paul K. Ackerman
Jean Baierlein
Chester C. Bennett
Ludwig Bergmann
Morton Berman
Abraham Blum
Edgar M. Bottome
Jonathan B. Chase
John Clayton
Murray L. Cohen
Robert Cohen
Patricia A. Cole
Andrew S. Dibner
Samuel Y. Edgerton, Jr.
Richard Estes
Karl Fortress
Frank Garfunkel
Philip E. Kubzansky
Charles N. Leef
Herbert Lipton
Louis Lowy
Daniel G. MacLeod
Theodor R. Marcus
Daniel G. Partan
Murray Reich
S. Paul Schilling
Peter E. Siegle
Nancy R. Smith
Wilma Thompson
John Wilson
John S. Zawacki
BRANDEIS
  UNIVERSITY
Robert W. Berger
Leo Bronstein
Maurice E. Bush

Lewis Coser
George Cowgill
L. J. Cuprak
S. James Davidson
Gordon Fellman
Richard Fox
Lawrence Grossman
Jon E. Haebig
Louis B. Hersh
Sheridan Jones
David Kaplan
N. O. Kaplan
Earl Lazerson
Harold Levine
L. Levine
S. Lehrer
Henry Linschitz
Heinz Lubasz
Robert A. Manners
Michael Mazur
Behzad Mohit
Paul Monsky
David Prill
Michael Phillips
Barbara Riddle
Michael Rosen
Benson Saler
Morris S. Schwartz
S. S. Schweber
Edna Seaman
John R. Seeley
Robert T. Seely
William C. Seitz
Mitchell Siporin
Richard L. Sklar
Philip Slater
B. Z. Sobel
Maurice R. Stein
Jerome Targovnik
Tyson Tildon
Samuel E. Wallace
Alex Weingrad
Robert S. Weiss
Kurt G. Wolff
Sylvia D. Zalinger
Irving Zola

HARVARD
UNIVERSITY
Andrew S. Abraham
Lenore Abraham
Joseph B. Alpers
William B. Arveson
R. Baierlein
A. Clifford Barger
Gerald Barnes
Rhoda W. Baruch
Jonathan Beckwith
Robert Belenky
Allan Berlind
Marshall H. Berman
Arthur Bienenstock
Carl A. L. Binger
Elkan R. Blout
Dwight Bolinger
Lee Breckenridge
S. Bromberger
Elmer Brown
Nancy Bucher
Douglas L. Carmichael
George F. Carrier
Frank Casa
Courtney Cazden
Anne M. Cohlen
Bertran Cohler
Donald G. Comb
Ian Cooke
Albert H. Coons
Barry S. Cooperman
Marlene S. Cooperman
Vern Countryman
Harvey Cox
Robert Darrow
Bernard Davis
David Denhardt
Daniel Deykin
A. Richard Diebold
David H. Dressler
Gerald Dworkin
John Edsall
Monroe Engel
Edna Epstein
Wolfgang Epstein

Friedericka Erienmeyer
Leonard Faltz
Ned Feder
Michael M. Field
Wilma K. Fife
Jacob Fine
Roderick Firth
Fred Fox
Dan Fraenkel
George M. Frederickson
W. M. Frohock
Albert Gelpi
Naomi L. Gerber
Stephen Gewirtz
Stephen Gilman
Owen Gingerich
Warren Gold
Howard Goldfine
Alan Goodridge
Annamaria Gorini
Luigi Gorini
Lester Grinspoon
Charles G. Gross
Jerome Gross
John A. Haines
F. Harder
Peter Hartline
Stephen Heinemann
John Hershey
Kenneth J. Hertz
Howard H. Hiatt
Helene Z. Hill
Daniel Horowitz
Helen Horowitz
Mahlon B. Hoagland
H. Stuart Hughes
Judith M. Hughes
John W. Hutchison
William Irvine
Frederio R. Jameson
Robert L. Jungas
Herman Kaickar
Linda Kalver
Manfred L. Karnovsky
Eva Kataja
Jerry Kazdan

Martin Kilson
Jerome King
James P. Koch
Robert Kohler
Edward A. Kravitz
Max Krook
David Layzer
Cavin P. Leeman
Eric Lenneberg
Harry Levin
Edmund C. Lin
Theodore A. Litman
Arthur MacEwan
Edward Mark
Joanne D. Medalie
Arnold Meisler
Murray Melbin
Everett I. Mendelsohn
Matthew Meselson
Stanley Milgrim
Edwin E. Moise
Frederick L. Moolten
Barrington Moore, Jr.
David Morrison
Richard E. Mumma
Franz G. Nauen
Peter Neumeyer
Donald A. Norman
Robert Nozick
Richard F. Olive
Joseph R. Parrish
Edward Pattullo
Henry Paulus
Joseph R. Parrish
Martin Peretz
Elmer Pfefferkorn
Ed Pincus
Mordeca Jane Pollock
Charles P. Price
Mark S. Ptashne
Hilary Putnam
David L. Ragozin
Michael K. Rees
Peter Reich
David Riesman
Anne Roe

Lesley J. Rogers
Rose Sabaroff
Carl Sagan
J. Lyell Sanders, Jr.
Nilima Sarkar
Peter Schofield
Stanley G. Schultz
Stanley J. Segal
Richard Sennett
Bert Shapiro
George Shapiro
Linda N. Shapiro
Victor Sidel
Raymond Siever
Burrhus F. Skinner
Arlene Skolnick
Jerome H. Skolnick
David H. Smith
Joseph L. Snider
Mary Jane Spiro
Robert G. Spiro
Ervin Staub
Phil Stone
Bradford Sturtevant
Karl V. Teeter
Betty M. Twarog
George Wald
Donald Wallach
Paul L. Watson
Norman F. Watt
Earl M. Wedrow
James C. White
Mrs. J. C. White
Samuel H. Wilson
David E. Wolfe
John Womock, Jr.
Barbara E. Wright
Michael Young
Marvin Zatzman
Norman Zinberg
MASSACHUSETTS
    INSTITUTE OF
    TECHNOLOGY
Robert Adolph
Michael Artin
Maria L. Bade

Eugene Bell
Aron Bernstein
Carl John Black, Jr.
Michael J. Brower
Elinor Charney
Jule Charney
Ronald Chase
Lawrence Chasin
Noam Chomsky
Stephen L. Chorover
Samuel Clark
Charles D. Coryell
Martin Diskin
Murray Eden
Harold W. Fairbairn
Herman Feshbach
K. L. Fields
Jerry Fodor
Maurice S. Fox
Kenneth Frankel
Robert G. Gallager
Stephen Gilborn
Glen Gordon
Richard Greene
William C. Greene
Paul R. Gross
Albert R. Gurney, Jr.
Theodore Gurney, Jr.
Alan Heim
Richard Held
Norman N. Holland
Charles E. Holt
Thomas Jackson
Irwin M. Jacobs
Elizabeth W. Jones
Jonathan P. Kabat
Merton Kahne
Lewis Kampf
Jerrold J. Katz
Angus Kerr-Lawson
Michael Klagsbrun
Karl Kornacker
Edwin Kuh
R. L. Kyhl
Emmet Larkin
Mark Levensky

Cyrus Levinthal
Donald B. Lombardi
S. E. Luria
Kenneth F. Manly
Travis R. Merritt
Erik Mollo-Christensen
Philip Morrison
Duncan M. Nelson
Reginald E. Newell
Robert Pendleton
Norman Pettit
William H. Pinson, Jr.
Stephen Parrott
Frank J. Popper
Peter Ralph
Ronald H. Reeder
Phillips W. Robins
Peter N. Rosenthal
Herbert Saltzstein
C. P. Sargent
David Schachter
David L. Schalk
Carl Shakin
Ascher Shapiro
Moshe Siev
Allen Silverstone
Larry R. Squire
Victor P. Starr
Donald Stein
Martin T. Steinbach
Arthur Steinberg
Kenneth Stevens
Marvin Stodolsky
Henry Stommel
Dirk J. Struik
Vigdor Teplitz
William J. Thompson
W. Turchinetz
John Viertel
William B. Watson
Hurd C. Willett
John W. Winchester
Rodney Wishnow
George Wolf
S. A. Yankofsky
William M. Youngren

Paul L. Zubkoff
**UNIVERSITY OF
MASSACHUSETTS**
Dean A. Allen
Dorothy Sharp Carter
Thomas J. Crowe
John H. Foster
Robert W. Gage
John W. George
Rodney E. Harris
Joseph Havens
Julian F. Janowitz
Harold Jarmon
George Levinger
Elain Marks
John Piehle
John Ragle
Trevor Robinson
Evelyn H. Russell
Sargent Russell
Freda Salzman
George Salzman
A. J. W. Scheffay
Rachel Smith
Richard S. Stein
Everett E. Turner
**NORTHEASTERN
UNIVERSITY**
Philip N. Backstrom
Jacob Barshay
Robert F. Brightbill
Alan Cromer
Robert G. Feer
Mitzi Filson
Walter L. Fogg
Marvin H. Friedman
Norbert L. Fullington
Roberta Gordon
Joseph D. Gresser
W. F. Luder
Robert MacDonald
Bertram J. Malenka
Harold Naidus
Irene A. Nichols
J. David Oberholtzer
Norman Rosenblatt

Eugene Saletan
Gilbert A. Schloss
Donald Shelby
Stanley R. Stembridge
R. L. Stern
Harold Stubbs
H. T. Tien
David S. Wyman
SIMMONS COLLEGE
Frederick M. Anderson
Fredda R. Bloom
Laura C. Colvin
Jean Cotton
Dorothea P. Dutra
Tilden G. Edelstein
David Emerson
Richard Freedman
Frances H. Jacobs
Diane C. Hawthorne
Joseph L. Hozid
Leonard J. Kirsch
Kenneth F. Kister
Lawrence L. Langer
Ruth S. Leonard
William Manley
George W. Nitchie
Georgia T. Noble
C. Richard Rohrberg
Richard C. Sterne
Robert C. Vernon
SMITH COLLEGE
Leonard Baskin
David Cavirch
Ely Chinay
Louis Cohn-Haft
Robert Fabian
Myron Glazer
Philip Green
S. Ralph Harlow
Bruce Hawkins
Seymour W. Itzkoff
Mervin Jules
Morris Lazorowitz
Bert Mendelson
Jim Morrissey
Elliott Ottner

Harold Poor
Matile Poor
Dorothy M. Randall
Michael Rice
Peter I. Rose
Louis Ruchames
J. Diedrick Snoek
Melvin Steinberg
Kenneth Stern
Francis Stienon
Donald Trumpler
Renee Wasserman
Renee Watkins
Janice Wilson
Anthony N. Zahareas
TUFTS UNIVERSITY
Gerald Adler
Vasken Aposhian
Robert M. Asch
Reilly Atkinson
Sylvan Barner
Benjamin K. Bennett
Richard W. Black
Michael D. Bliss
Ashley S. Campbell
Ernest Cassara
Judith Chernaik
John Cornwall
Dorothea J. Crook
Morris A. Cynkin
Richard Dowd
Michael Fixler
Morris Friedkin
Martin B. Friedman
Sol Gittleman
Edward Goldberg
Leon Gunther
Hilde Hein
Dennis V. Higgins
David F. Isles
William S. Jacobson
Ellsworth Keil
Melvin K. Ketchel
Norman I. Krinsky
Maxine Kumin
George F. Leger

Zena Luria
Bernard McCabe
James H. McIntosh
Samuel C. McLaughlin, Jr.
Charles E. Magraw
Lewis F. Manly
Kivie Moldave
Roy M. Moore
Daniel Onjian
James T. Park
John Oliver Perry
Wolf Prensky
Gene Reeves
Jesper Rosenmeier
Lura N. Roth
H. Ronald Rouse
Moselio Schaechter
Gerhardt Schmidt
Edwin M. Schur
Newlin R. Smith
W. Royal Stokes
Marcia Stubbs
Robert J. Taylor
Jack Tessman
Albert D. Ullman
Ann C. Watts
Robert H. Webb
Edmund M. Wise, Jr.
WELLESLEY
  COLLEGE
Sigmund Abeles
Lillian A. Anderson
Duncan Aswell
Grazia Avitabile
Sylvia Berkman
Paul A. Cohen
Alice B. Colburn
Ann Congleton
Helen Storm Corsa
Fred Denbeaux
Herbert Gale
Janet Z. Giele
Arthur Gold
Edward V. Gulick
Louis Hammer
Nancy L. Howell

Rosalind E. Krauss
Gabriele B. Jackson
Thomas H. Jackson
Owen Jander
Florence McCulloch
Eleanor C. McLaughlin
Robert J. McLaughlin
Edith Melcher
Barry Phillips
Ruth Anna Putnam
Suzanne Robinson
A. Santas
Paul Schwaber
Adele Spitzer
Kathryn Turner
W. W. Wagar
Richard W. Wallace
Marcia Wright
MICHIGAN
  ALBION COLLEGE
Bruce Borthwick
Maurice Branch
John Cheek
Keith J. Fennimore
Willard B. Frick
William Giltham, Jr.
Renato J. Gonzalez
Paul Loukides
John M. Mecartney
Laurence Meredith
Arthur W. Munk
Kent Christopher Owen
MICHIGAN STATE
  UNIVERSITY
Harold H. Anderson
Lawrence H. Battistini
Franklin D. Blatt
J. Bruce Burke
Nelson Edmondson
Donald Gochberg
Thomas Greer
Ronald P. Grossman
Roy T. Matthews
J. Wilson Myers
John H. Reimoehl
Karl F. Thompson

William A. Vincent
Karen West
UNIVERSITY OF
 MICHIGAN
Robert Audi
Frithjof H. Bergman
Albert Chammah
Norma Diamond
Gerald F. Else
Eugene Feingold
Irving Fritz
Madeline Fusco
William Gamson
Zelda Gamson
Julien Gendell
Edward Glaser
Alvin I. Goldman
Gerald Gurin
Donald Hall
Martin Hoffman
Joel Isaacson
Robert L. Kahn
Stanislav V. Kasl
Nicholas Kazarinoff
Chester R. Leech
Richard L. Malvin
Harold Orbach
James B. Ranck, Jr.
Harold Raush
Cyril Robinson
Marshall Sahlins
Harold S. Shapiro
Allen L. Shields
J. David Singer
Arthur J. Vander
Austin Warren
Leroy Waterman
Albert Weber
Thomas Winner
WAYNE STATE
 UNIVERSITY
David Asdourian
Janet Asdourian
Ernst Benjamin
Robert Broner
Robert Buckeye

David Burner
H. Warren Dunham
Otto Feinstein
Ronald Formisano
Eugenie Fox
Alan Gross
Herbert Haber
Harold Fromm
Adrienne James
Lawrence Jennings
James Keeney
Alexandra McCoy
Emerson R. Marks
Lynn Parsons
Geraldine Pittman
Richard Place
Richard Reinitz
Barry Rothaus
Murray Seidler
Stanley Shapiro
William F. Shuter
Leo Stoller
Paul Sporn
Ellen Stekert
Athan Theoharis
David Wineman
R. H. Wright
MINNESOTA
UNIVERSITY OF
 MINNESOTA
Henry E. Allen
Marvin Bacaner
Robert H. Beck
May Brodbeck
Edward Coen
Marc S. Cohen
H. Ted Davis
Mr. & Mrs. Lionel B.
 Davis
Lonnie J. Durham
Charles Edwards
David L. Eggenschwiler
Herbert Feigl
Avrom Fleishman
Mr. & Mrs. Clayton Giase
David Haley

Russell G. Hamilton
William H. Hanson
Allan B. Hooper
Charles W. Huver
B. L. Israel
Kenneth H. Keller
Norman S. Kerr
Maxine M. Klein
Robert E. Klein
Edward Landin
J. C. Levenson
Jerome Liebling
Victor Lorber
Peter Luykx
Robert L. Martin
Homer E. Mason
Gareth B. Matthews
Grover Maxwell
Toni McNaron
Jeffrie G. Murphy
Paul L. Murphy
Thomas E. Nelson
Herbert L. Pick, Jr.
A. W. Plumstead
Lewis J. Potlet
Karl H. Potter
Francis J. Raab
Murray D. Rosenberg
Martin Roth
Lanny D. Schmidt
James L. Scoggins
Mulford Q. Sibley
Allan H. Spear
G. Robert Stange
Henry L. Taylor
Romeyn Taylor
Burnham Terrell
Leonard Unger
Mr. & Mrs. Laurence
 Victor
Maurice B. Visscher
Elaine E. Vogt
Joseph L. Waldauer
Dennis W. Watson
Frank W. Whiting
F. M. Williams

MISSOURI
UNIVERSITY OF
  MISSOURI
Bruce J. Biddle
Allen F. Davis
Justin C. Huang
William R. Morrow
Lindon J. Murphy
John C. Schuder
Paul Wallace
Betty K. Wilson
H. Clyde Wilson
Harold D. Woodman
Leonora Woodman
David Wurfel
MONTANA
UNIVERSITY OF
  MONTANA
David Alt
William Ballard
Chester Beaty
Agnes Boner
Meyer Chessin
Merrel Clubb, Jr.
Philip Favero
Robert Fields
Clarence Gordon
Annette Gottfried
C. Rulon Jeppesen
Fred Kersten
Barclay Kuhn
John Lawry
Edwin Marvin
Rodney Mead
James Peterson
David Pevear
Ronald Plakke
Sherman Preece, Jr.
Howard Reinhardt
Dexter Roberts
Carlton Scott
Arnold Silverman
Arthur Wills
NEW JERSEY
  DREW UNIVERSITY
John W. Bicknell

A. Charles Brouse
Charles Courtney
Chickford Bobbie Darrell
Charles W. Estus
William Johnson
James S. Sessions
Calvin Skaggs
John T. Von der Heide, r.
John Warner
James Wilson
FAIRLEIGH
DICKINSON
UNIVERSITY
Joseph Bernstein
Robert S. Browne
Jean Christie
Frank G. Davis
Stephen Ettinger
Dorothea Hubin
Dolores Elaine Keller
Erwin Rosen
Willis Rudy
Unicio J. Violi
MONMOUTH
  COLLEGE
Bernard Aptekar
Stephen A. Black
Richard E. Brewer
Richard Damashek
Philip C. Donahue
Gilbert S. Fell
Burdett H. Gardner
John Illo
David S. Lifson
Charles R. Mayes
Rudolph Pasler II
William Bruce Pitt
Robert Rechnitz
Martin Ryan
Martin A. Watkins
Janet M. Wennik
Richard R. Wescott
NEWARK COLLEGE
  OF ENGINEERING
Martin Jay Beohner
Leonard Chabrowe

Warren H. Crater
Joel J. Epstein
Nicholas G. Evans
Herman A. Estrin
Leonard Fleischer
Hayden Goldberg
Warren Grover
Clarence Johnson
James J. Napier
Sverre Lyngstad
Abraham H. Steinberg
Stanley B. Winters
Robert L. Wacker
PRINCETON
  UNIVERSITY
Hans Aarsleff
Joel H. Baer
V. Bargmann
Edward F. Bauer
Paul F. Baum
Hugo Adam Bedau
G. E. Bentley
Enid Bierman
E. B. D. Borgerhoff
Gerald E. Brown
Victor Bruce
A. F. Buddington
Lamar Cecil, Jr.
Paul W. Conner
Bernard M. Dwork
Walter M. Elsasser
Donald Epstein
Robert Fogles
Joel Feinberg
John V. A. Fine
Charles S. Fisher
Allan Franklin
Sheldon Hackney
Richard F. Hamilton
Gilbert H. Harman
Carl G. Hempel
Leon-Francois Hoffman
Laurence B. Holland
Werner Hollmann
Maitland Jones, Jr.
Suzanne Keller

John Kuehl
Thomas S. Kuhn
Alexander Lande
Lewis Lockwood
Kenneth Love
Arno J. Mayer
James M. McPherson
Robert M. McKeon
Arthur Mendel
Kurt Mislow
William G. Moulton
Gary B. Nash
Edward Nelson
John Neubauer
Ronald B. deSousa Pernes
Colin S.Pittendrigh
Carroll C. Pratt
J. K. Randall
Michael Schlessinger
Paul Schleyen
Edward Schneier
John Schrecker
Leo Seidlitz
Jerrold E. Siegel
James M. Smith
Thomas G. Spiro
John H. Strange
Albert Sonnenfeld
Terry Tenner
Willard Thorp
Robert C. Tucker
Michael Walzer
RUTGERS
  UNIVERSITY
Bradford Abernathy
Elihu Abrahams
Emily Alman
Francisco Alvarado
Alexander Habib Arkon
Seymour Becker
Gerald A. Bertin
John H. Best
Eleanor Bishop
Barbara Breasted
Harry Bredemeirer
Alexander D. Brooks

Terence Butler
Julius Cohen
George Collier
Ronald M. Colvin
Joseph Contorti
Eileen M. Corey
Aldo Covelto
Roger E. Craig
Robert Crane
Dorothy Dinnerstein
Sidney Fiarman
Arthur Getis
Bert Garskof
David Gershator
I. Glopnik
Joseph N. Ginocchio
Richard Gundy
David Haber
Nelson Hanawatt
Richard Hawes
William Heckel
Sol Heckelman
Hovhaness Heukelekian
Edward M. Hoagland
Ralph Kaplan
Mary Ann Karpel
Arthur Kinoy
Solomon Leader
Daniel S. Lehrman
Alan Leshner
Hannah A. Levin
Peter Lindenfeld
William Lodding
Trueman MacHenry
Simon Marcson
Norman G. Martien
James D. McGowan
Loren Meeker
Marjorie Murphy
Edith Neimark
Paul Nelson
Samuel Neuschatz
Bruce Newling
Barry Pass
William B. Pavlik
Maurice P. Pelanne

Martin Picker
Richard Poirier
Sidney L. Posel
Carl A. Price
Jean Quandt
Mathew Radom
Glorianne Robbi
Amelie Rorty
Claire Rosenfield
Joel Sandak
Jane Cronin Scanlon
Barbara H. Schaeffer
Harvey Schiffman
Richard Schwartz
John A. Scott
Michael Seitz
Barry B. Seldes
Agnes B. Sherman
Lawrence Shulman
B. P. Sonenblick
Norman E. Spear
Hans Stoeckler
Cecile Stolbof
Benjamin Stout
Robert Sylvester
Paul Tillett
Roger Tishler
Charles Waldauer
Joyce Walstedt
Robert Watts
David R. Weimer
Anna Mary Wells
Myriam Yevick
Seymour T. Zenchelsky
E. Zimmerman
Robert Zimmerman
STEVENS INSTITUTE
  OF TECHNOLOGY
Frederick P. Bowes
Hugh Byfield
J. B. Crabtree
Thomas J. Dougherty
Peter Geismar
Jonathon Goldberg
Lawrence Goldman
Jim Harris

Maurice Kastern
Earl L. Koller
I. Richard Lapidus
Arthur G. Layzer
Joel Magid
Robin A. Motz
Robert Packard
Ralph Schiller
Snowden Taylor
Lawrence J. Wallen
George Yevick

UPSALA COLLEGE
Roger S. Boraas
Lewis W. Brandt
Kent C. Christensen
Delbert L. Earisman
Bernard G. Faris
Carl G. Fjellman
John Gallagher
Ralph O. Hjelm
Hugo Lutz
Carole G. Merrow
Gerald Robbins
Ammon C. Roth, Jr.
Jean E. Simmons
James H. Stam
John Wallhausser
Spencer Wilson

NEW YORK
  ADELPHI
  UNIVERSITY
Stuart Astor
Gloria Beckerman
Sydney Davis
Celia S. Deschin
Marion K. Forer
Beatrice Freeman
Tom Heffernan
Steve Klass
Tom Knight
Donald Koster
Stanley Millett
Theresa Nathanson
Catherine P. Papell
Rubin Starer
Marianne Welter

Cedric Winslow
Donald Wolf

ALBERT EINSTEIN
COLLEGE OF
MEDICINE

Francis Baker-Cohen
Sybel Barten
Ira Belmont
Lillian Belmont
Joseph Bethell
Boyce Bennett
Herbert B. Birch
Beverly Birns
Wagner Bridger
Everett Bovard
Betty C. Buchsbaum
Irving Bunkin
Alex Charlton
Joseph Cramer
David Crystal
Mark Daniel
J. E. Darnell, Jr.
Leo Davidoff
Ida Davidoff
Helen Deane
David Dubnan
Syblle Esoalong
Evelyn Firestone
Lewis M. Froad
Martin Gittelman
Mark Golden
Sidney Goldtischer
Leonard Graziani
George Green
Joan Gubin
Ida Hafner
Lee Hoffman
Leonard Hollander
Eric Holtzman
Edward Hornick
Eric Karp
Zelda S. Klapper
Robert A. Klein
George Kleiner

Howard Kremen
Arthur Lefford
Shirley London
Stella Lubetsky
Sasha Malamed
Irwin Mandel
Jerome Mangan
David Mann
Tina Moreau
Selig Neubart
Lillian Newton
Alex Novikoff
William Obrinsky
James O'Brien
Donald Overton
Jacques Padawer
Irwin Pesetsky
Maurice M. Rafford
Anna Rand
Isabelle Rapin
Joseph Richman
Melvin Roman
Seymour Romney
Ora Rosen
Samuel Rosen
Benjamin Rudner
Betta Scharrer
Sam Seifter
Issar Smith
Joseph Smith
Edna H. Sobel
Edward Sperling
David Stein
David Steinberg
Donald J. Summers
Herman Teitelbaum
Minoa Turkel
Gerald Turkewitz
Maurice H. Vaughan, Jr.
Jonathan R. Warner
Mary Weitzman
Herbert Winston
Natalie Yarow
Edward Yellin
Leon Yorburg
Roger Zeeman

BELFER GRADUATE
  SCHOOL OF
  SCIENCE
R. E. Behrends
David Finkelstein
Arthur Komar
Joel L. Lebowitz
Joseph Lewittes
Elliott Lieb
D. J. Newman
H. E. Rauch
William Spindel
Leonard Susskind
Marvin J. Stern
A. E. Woodruff
BROOKLYN
  COLLEGE
Michael Aita
Abraham Ascher
C. A. Beam
Melwin Belsky
Leonard Bernstein
John Boardman
Manuel Cynamon
Norman Eaton
A. S. Eisenstadt
G. Ezorsky
Robert Fanelli
Elizabeth Fehrer
William Forman
George Fried
Solomon Goldstein
Walter Goldstein
Brijen Gupta
Rita Guttman
Ann Haiberle
Lawrence Hyman
William Ittelson
Linda Keen
Vera R. Lechmann
Naphtali Lewis
Albert McQueen
Barten Meyers
Howard Moltz
Harold Proshansky
Leonard Radinsky

Evelyn Raskin
Karen Reichard
David M. Reimers
Rebecca Ruggles
S. Salthe
Carl Schafer
Melvin Selsky
Charlotte Sempell
Charles R. Sleeth
Michael Sobel
George Skorinko
Ruth Temple
Norman Weissberg
Carl B. Zukerman
CITY COLLEGE
Eric Adler
Leonard Alshan
Harry Applegate
Jane Aptekar
Paul B. Bachrach
Allan Ballard
Morton Bard
Philip Baumel
Bernard Bellush
Nathan Berall
Arthur Bierman
Frederick M. Binder
D. C. Brink
Mark Brunswick
Alice Chandler
Emanuel Chill
Herman J. Cohen
Kazuko Dailey
Allan Danzig
Walter Daum
Helen H. Davidson
Morton Davis
Roger Deakins
Otto Deri
Sidney Ditzion
Abraham Edel
Sophie L. Elam
J. A. Elias
Joseph A. Ellis
Sandra M. Epps
Bertram Epstein

Charles Evans
Irwin Feinberg
Lloyd Fields
Marlene Fisher
Jane P. Franck
Reuben Frodin
Graham Frye
Joan Gadol
David I. Gaines
Carol Galligan
Arthur Ganz
Alice Gaskell
Ronald Gaskell
Lois Gordon
Fred Hauptman
Samuel Hendel
Fred L. Israel
Matthew Grace
Daniel Greenberger
Theodore Gross
James Haddad
Leo Hamalian
James V. Hatch
Fritz Jahoda
Anthony Jansic
Crane Johnson
Florine Katz
Wallace Katz
Margaret Kenny
Samuel J. Klein
Yvonne M. Klein
Leonard Kriegel
Jeffrey W. Kurz
Dan Leary
Gerald Leinward
Sandra Levinson
Carol Lipkin
W. B. Long
Harry Lustig
Irving Malin
Marvin Markowitz
Samuel J. Meer
David J. Mervis
Alexander Mintz
Edith Nagel
Gladys Natchez

Herbert Nechia
P. L. Nesbeitt
Fred Newman
Aaron Noland
Hironori Onishi
Saul Ostrow
Melva Peterson
Donald Petty
George W. Phillips
Brayton Polka
Betty Popper
Edward M. Potoker
Edward Quinn
Virginia Red
Norma A. Roldan
Ruth V. Roseman
Viola D. Rosenheck
Irving Rothman
Deborah Schechtel
Conrad Schirokauer
Peggy M. Schwartz
Mimi C. Segal
Aurel M. Seifert
Norman P. Shapiro
James J. Shields, Jr.
Marietta Shore
Marvin Siegelman
Catherine Silverman
Erwin Singer
Richard Skolnik
Bernard Sohmer
Harry Soodak
Irwin Stark
Judith Stein
Fritz Steinnardt
Walter S. Struve
Harry Tartar
Peter Tea, Jr.
H. S. Thayer
John C. Thirwall
Martin Tiersten
Sheila Tobias
Sigmund Tobias
George F. Tully
Stuyvesant Van Veen
Edmund L. Volpe

Geoffrey Wagner
Barbara Watson
James F. Watts
Lureline Weinberg
Bert Weinstein
David Weissman
Martha Weisman
William Wernidi
Harold Wilensky
Suzanne Wolkenfeld
Miles Wolpin
Theresa Woodruff
Irwin H. Yellowitz
Philip Zacuto
Bernard Zelechow
Rose Zimbardo
Michael Zimmerman
COLGATE
UNIVERSITY
Jerome Balmuth
Lester Blum
Bruce M. Brown
Lloyd Chapin
Leo M. Elison
Marcus F. Franda
John M. Head
Clement L. Henshaw
Charles R. Naef
Arnold A. Sio
William Skelton
Robert V. Smith
Rosalind W. Smith
Linden D. Summers
Huntington Terrell
Clarence W. Young
COLUMBIA
UNIVERSITY
John W. Alexander
Alexander Alland
William G. Anderson
Robert Alter
Albert Auerbach
Herbert Barden
Hyman Bass
Paul Bauchatz
M. V. L. Bennett

Allen Bergson
Sacvan Berkovitch
Lipman Bers
Alan F. Blum
George Brager
Philip W. Brandt
Peter Brock
David Brown
Justus Buchler
Ruth Bunzel
Desmond Callan
John Cannon
David Caplovitz
Theodore Caplow
Leigh Cauman
Gerald Cavanaugh
Richard Christie
Richard D. Cloward
Stephen Cohen
Samuel Coleman
Arthur Collins
Francis Connolly
Robert Cumming
Arthur Danto
H. McParlin Davis
Istvan Deak
R. Della Cava
Leonard De Morelos
Herbert Deane
Stephen Denker
Vernon Dibble
Lee Dlugin
H. M. Edwards, Jr.
Dan Ehrlich
Samuel Eilenberg
Ainslee Embree
David Epstein
Bernard E. Erlanger
Alexander Erlich
David Fanshel
Samuel Finestone
George Fischer
Andrew Fitch
Anne Florant
Shepard Forman
Murray Frank

Rita V. Frankiel
Julian Franklin
Marcia K. Freedman
Alan R. Freeman
Morton Fried
Albert Friedlander
Patrick Gallagher
John Garraty
Peter Gay
Michael Goldman
M. M. Goldsmith
William J. Goods
Irving Goodman
Michael Goodman
Carington Goodrich
Frederic Grab
Robert Grab
Loren Graham
Richard Greeman
Andrew M. Gross
Nathan Gross
Hyman Grossbard
Robert Grossman
Victor Guillemin
James O. F. Hackshaw
Peter Haidu
Leopold Haimson
Robert Hanning
Ellen Hansen
Lincoln Hanson
Vilma S. Harrington
Jonathan Harris
Marvin Harris
Jacqueline Hellerman
Amelia Hess
Isidor Hoffman
Harland W.
Hoisington, Jr.
Terence K. Hopkins
Carl Hovde
Herbert H. Hyman
Hunter Ingalls
Jacob Jaffe
Jeffry Kaplow
George M. Katz
Peter Kenen

Ethan Kennel
Mark Kesselman
Peter Kivy
Morton Klass
Steven Kleiman
Morie Klopot
E. R. Kolchin
Richard Kuhns, Jr.
P. Kusch
Joan Landman
Edward Lanning
Alexander Lesser
Stanley Lieberfreund
Herbert Liebowitz
S. B. Littauer
Robert E. Lovelace
Raymond Lubitz
Clarence Lukes
Henry Malcolm
Andrew March
Thomas Marshall
Alan Mayer
Peter McHugh
Robert McShea
Seymour Meiman
Joan Mencher
Carol H. Meyer
Irving Miller
Jacob Millman
Esther Modell
Sidney Morgenbesser
Lloyd Motz
John Mundy
J. R. Munson
Robert Murphy
James Nakamura
David Naokes
Lionel Ovesey
George D. Pappas
Charles Parson
Anthony F. Philip
Harvey Pitkin
Howard W. Polsky
Andre Racz
John J. Randall, Jr.
Eugene Rice

David F. Ricks
Abraham Rosman
Samuel Ross
David Rothman
William Ryding
Edward Said
Phillips Salman
Mario Salvadori
Joseph Schachter
Alfred Schatz
Emanuel Schegloff
Claude Schoept
Rosalea A. Schonbar
William Schwartz
Ralph Schwarz
Morton D. Schweitzer
James Shenton
Mindel C. Sheps
R. J. Shofer
Allan Silver
Ernest Simon
Carl Singer
Simon Slavin
Michael Slote
Burton Slotnick
Willen Smit
Paul A. Smith
George Stade
William Starr
Robert Stigler
Bluma Swerdloff
Nettie Terestman
Michael Tobin
Stephen Unger
William Vickrey
Immanuel Wallerstein
Preston R. Wilcox
Bernice Wilson
Margaret Wilson
Omar Wing
Kenneth Winston
Robert Wolff
Milton Zerkin
David Zipser
COOPER UNION
Arnold Allentuch

Sholom Arzt
Alice Baldwin Beer
Richard S. Bowman
John Condon
Ferdinand De Vito
Raymond B. Dowden
Stephen M. Edelglass
W. D. Ellison
Wller B. Embler
Johnson E. Fairchild
Edward F. Ferrand
Thaddeus R. Gatza
Howard W. Gelman
Kingman N. Grover
Robert Gwathmey
Phyllis W. Humphrey
Edward J. Hundert
Edward Kallop
Leo S. Kaplan
Elizabeth Leonard
I. L. Lynn
Leo Manso
Walter J. Middleton
Paula K. Nelson
Bernard Pfriem
H. Christian Rohlfing
Charles Seide
David Sider
Bertram Silverman
Milton Stecher
Jack Stewart
Eleanor M. Townsend
Ruth Wiesmann
Matthew Wysocki
CORNELL
  UNIVERSITY
Eqbal Ahmad
A. R. Ammons
Robert L. Aronson
Douglas N. Archibald
Sylvester E. Berki
Jonathan P. Bishop
Nelson H. Bryant
Edwin A. Burtt
John V. Canfield
Melvin G. de Chazeau

Alice Cook
John W. Dewire
Donald P. Dietrich
Douglas F. Dows
Richard Epand
John Freccero
Harrop A. Freeman
Jack Peter Green
Robert Greenblatt
David I. Grossvogel
Baxter Hathaway
Neil H. Hertz
F. Jelinek
H. Peter Kahn
Steven R. Katz
T. M. Lodahl
Gordon M. Kirkwood
Henry A. Landsberger
David Lyons
J. McConky
Chandler Morse
Benjamin Nichols
David Novarr
M. Perlman
Pierro Pucci
Donald B. Scarl
Karl-Ludwig Selig
Sidney Shoemaker
Sidney Shoemaker
Seymour Smidt
Cushing Strout
William Foote White
FINCH COLLEGE
Christine Block
Rosa Trillo Clough
Mary Houston Davis
Daniel Dickerson
Robert Diffenderfer
Ruth Elson
Margaret Hall
Roslyn Hayes
George Holoch, Jr.
Margaret Maxwell
Iris Mueller
Marshall Mount
Luciana Pietrosi

William Post, Jr.
Jane Ross
Ray Senior
HOFSTRA
  UNIVERSITY
Adolph G. Anderson
Rubin Z. Baratz
Ethel S. Brook
David Christman
Harold E. Clearman
June M. Cooper
Lois M. Crews
Robert A. Davison
Michael N.
  D'Innocenzo, Jr.
Dorothy W. Douglas
Paul G. England
Hyman A. Enzer
Phillip Evans
Robert Friedman
Larry Goldberg
Robert S. Guttchen
Elizabeth Hogan
Paul J. Hutt
George D. Jackson
John R. Jeanneney
Shirley P. Langer
Harvey J. Levin
Mary G. Ligon
Broadus Mitchell
Anne Morgenstern
Arthur Niederhoffer
Burton W. Onstine
Sylvia F. Pines
Sabine Rapp
John L. Rawlinson
Morton Reitman
Jerry Rosenfeld
Gabrielle Savet
Wilbur S. Scott
David Shapiro
Evelyn U. Shirk
Elie Siegmeister
Esther Sparberg
E. Russell Stabler
Ruth M. Stauffer

Lawrence Stessin
Janice M. Studholme
Harold Tanyzer
Marcel Tenenbaum
Albert Tepper
Lynn Turgeon
John E. Ullmann
C. Roland Wagner
Azelle B. Waltcher
Alexander Weiner
Murray Yanowitch
June M. Zaccone
HUNTER COLLEGE
Jack Barschi
Mary Owen Cameron
Peter J. Caws
Enid Coel
Ralph A. Dale
Arthur Edelstein
Alice Feinberg
Mae V. Gamble
Elizabeth Gellert
Bernard Greenberg
Sandor Halebsky
Murray Hausknecht
Irvin Howe
Horst W. Hoyer
Elizabeth Hunter
Linda Keen
Sam J. Korn
Otto Krash
Selwyn Lederman
Bernard S. Miller
Dorothy Naiman
R. J. H. Neuwirth
Paul Oppenheimer
William Parsons
A. Pinkney
Diane Robinson
I. H. Rose
Marcia Rose
Barbara Siecherman
Robert M. Sikora
Norman Singer
John P. M. Somerville
G. H. Weightman

Ingrid Matson Wekerle
M. H. J. Wijnen
Roger R. Woock
LONG ISLAND
   UNIVERSITY
Miriam S. Aronow
Albert A. Berman
Kenneth Bernard
Kenneth Bridenthal
Naomi Cramer
Harry Fenson
Joseph Friedman
Esther F. Hyneman
John F. Lane
Elizabeth E. Malament
Jean Mundy
Edward Pomerantz
Suzanne Popper
Robert Prener
Jack Salzman
Edith Schor
Paul N. Siegel
Leon Sinder
Robert D. Spector
Martin Tucker
Donald Warren, Jr.
NEW YORK
   MEDICAL
   COLLEGE
Hiroshi Asanuma
Irving Bieber
Ann Birch
M. M. Black
Edmund Braun
Vernon Brooks
William Burke
Bernard Carol
Ruth Carol
Ada de Cnabon
Charles Cherubin
Stella Chess
Mary Clark
Harold Cole
Isidore Danishefsky
Albert Dinnerstein
Leonard Fisher

Morton Frank
Alfred Freedman
Sam Gelfan
Norman Gevirtz
Leonard Gold
Robert Goldstein
William Gutstein
David Haft
Ruth Heifetz
Stanley Kramer
Rema Lapouse
Ruth Lavietes
Barbara Levenson
Rachmiel Levine
Victor Lief
Martin Livenstien
Jo Leigh Luckett
Herbert Mark
David Maude
Alfred Moldovan
Jonas Muller
Carl McGahee
William Normand
Samuel Prigal
Irving Rappaport
Edward Reith
Alfred Rifkin
Fred Rosenthal
Sheldon Rothenberg
Samuel Rubin
Daniel Ruchkin
Clifford Sager
Miriam de Salegui
Sara Schiller
Irvin Schwartz
Joseph Seifter
George Shugart
Samuel Slipp
Jack Sobel
Bernard Straus
Robert Strobos
Gerald Tannenbaum
Milton Terris
Felix Wasserman
Marvin Weinberg
Herbert Weisberg

Martin Weitzner

STATE UNIVERSITY
OF NEW YORK,
ALBANY

Theodore S. Adams
Werner C. Baum
M. I. Berger
Elton A. Butler
Frances L. Colby
Gloria DeSole
De Witt Ellinwood
Morris E. Eson
Harry Hamilton, Jr.
David Hartley
William Hudson
J. Richard Johnston
Richard Jongedyk
W. E. Knotts
Violet Larney
Paul C. Lemon
William H. Leue
Arthur O. Long
J. C. Mancuso
Roland Minch
Erick Nussbaum
Daniel N. Odell
C. Odenkirchen
David C. Redding
John M. Reilly
Henry Rosenbaum
William E. Rowley
Paul Schaefer
Joan Schulz
Jon S. Scott
Susan E. Shafarzek
Fred Silva
Eunice Clark Smith
Theodore G. Standing
Margaret M. Stewart
Dona Strauss
Dante Thomas
Donald Van Cleve
Robert Wernick
Y. K. Wong

STATE UNIVERSITY
OF NEW YORK,
BINGHAMTON

George R. Adams
Paul Baumgartner
Morris Budin
Stanley Ferber
Michael Horowitz
Melvin Leiman
Bruce Lercher
William D. Lipe
Owen M. Lynch
Seymour Pitcher
Elias Schwartz
Melvin Seiden
Louise E. Sweet
Peter N. Vukasin
Eugene Vasilew

STATE UNIVERSITY
OF NEW YORK,
BUFFALO

John Anton
Erica Brook
Newton Garver
Bill J. Harrell
George G. Iggers
Arthur D. Kahn
Byron J. Koekkoek
Jane A. LaRue
Ann London
Donald C. Milulecky
John D. Milligan
Carl Moos
Joan Moos
Peter Nicholls
Edwin H. Powell
R. R. Rogers
Herman Schwartz
William Sylvester
Sidney M. Willhelm

STATE UNIVERSITY
OF NEW YORK,
STONY BROOK

Kenneth T. Abrams
W. T. Ampers
Francis T. Bonner

Hugh Cleland
Max Dresden
Alfred Ehrenfeld
Leonard Eisenbud
E. M. Eisenstein
Frank E. Meyers
Steven Obrebski
William Rose
Susan Schwartz
Peter Shaw
R. Sloan
Catherine Stodolsky
Margaret C. Wheeler

NEW YORK
UNIVERSITY

Raziel Abelson
Elaine Allen
Bernard Atshuler
Charles E. Ares
Michael E. Arons
John H. Atherton
Ralph A. Austen
John D. Barlow
Harold Bascowitz
Sabert Basescu
Barbara J. Bachman Beam
James F. Becker
Avrom Ben-Avi
Sidney Belman
Eugene Y. Berger
A. W. Bernheimer
Robert Bierstedt
Stanley Blumenthal
Phyllis Pray Bober
Roscoe C. Brown, Jr.
Robert D. Burrowes
Edwin S. Campbell
Robert D. Childres
T. G. S. Christenson
Jacob Cohen
Daniel G. Collins
James T. Crown
Jane S. Dahlberg
Ruth Dale
H. Clark Dalton
Martin Davis

Thomas W. Davis
Ashley T. Day
Daniel E. Diamond
S. Carlton Dickerman
Daniel A. Dubin
Jeanne Dubnau
Peter Eisbach
Arnold Eisen
Kenneth Eisold
Jack Famularo
Emmanuel Farber
Irwin Feigen
Robert S. Fine
Harry Fiss
Joan Fiss
Leopold Flatto
Thomas M. Franck
Eliot Friedson
David Gans
Bernard Garniez
Florence Geis
Leo Goldberger
Marvin Goldiner
Esther R. Goldman
Malcolm Goldman
Bernard Goldschmidt
Rosalind Gould
Howard Green
Hans Guggenheim
Walter Haines
James B. Harnson
Robert D. Hart
Melvin Hausner
William Haut
Michael Heidelberger
Jerome R. Hellerstein
Melvin Herman
Irving Hirshfield
Louis Hodes
Robert Hoppock
Pearl Horn
Murray Horwitz
Nathan Jaspan
Bernard Kalinkowitz
Irving Karp
Bernard Katz

Irwin Katz
Phyllis Katz
George Kaufer
Evelyn F. Keller
Joseph B. Keller
Charles L. Knapp
I. Kupferman
M. Daniel Lane
Cornelius W. Langley
Lillian Langseth
Herman Leon
Gerson T. Lesser
Harvey M. Levy
Robert M. Lewis
Hilbert Levitz
K. Brooks Low
Abraham Lurie
Mae Lee Maskit
Elizabeth McFall
Martin Mendelson
Herbert Mentzel
Edwin H. Miller
Nancy Modiano
Helene Moglen
Chandler Montgomery
Wheeler Mueller
Louis Nirmberg
R. A. Nixon
Maxwell Nurnberg
Ruth Ochroch
Leo Orris
Esther Ostroff
Martin T. Paul
Anthony Pearce
Blanche Persky
Mildred E. Phillips
Richard Pollack
Alice M. Pollin
Robert Pstofsky
Richard Quinney
Michael Rabins
Leo Rauch
Frederick L. Redefer
Yorke E. Rhodes
Elsa E. Robinson
H. Mark Roelofs

Hugh Lawrence Ross
Milton Salton
Irving Sarnoff
David I. Shuster
Jack Schwartz
James Schwartz
Milton Schwebel
Ellie Seeger
Barbara Sher
Burt Shacter
Jane Shipton
Eric Simon
Joseph Slade
Grace Smith
Herschel Snodgrass
W. A. Spenser
Larry Spruch
Linda Stampfli
Wendel M. Stanley
Milton Stern
Chandler A. Stetson
W. James Sullivan
Constance Sutton
Michael R. Swift
Angeo Taranta
Thelma Taub
Bernard Tieger
Herbert Tonne
Gilbert M. Trachtman
Walter Troll
William Vanderkloot
John Varney
Jacqueline Wendt
Robert Wolfe
David Wolitzky
Ann Yasuhara
Seymour Yellin
Irving Younger
Phillip Zimbardo
Pearl Zipser
Daniel Zwanziger
Martin Zuckerman
POLYTECHNIC
   INSTITUTE OF
   BROOKLYN
E. Banks

Judith S. Bellin
Judith Bregman
Edward S. Cassedy, Jr.
Kenneth K. Clarke
Irving Cohen
Frank C. Collins
Sid Deutsch
J. J. Dropkin
Marvin E. Gettleman
H. Juretschke
Ernest M. Loebe
Meir Menes
Irving F. Miller
B. Morawetz
Clifford Osborne
Gerald Oster
Donald Rapp
Kurt Salzinger
Paul E. Spoerri
Joseph Steigman
George Stell
Richard M. Stern
Leonard Strauss
Max Sucher
Rubin N. Summergrad
PRATT INSTITUTE
Leonard Bacich
William Broger
Michael Brill
Edward B. Carroll
Martin C. Davidson
Robert Dennis
Robert E. Disch
Rice Estes
Anita Feldman
Josef E. Garai
Daniel Gerzog
Jack B. Glickman
David Hack
Norton Juster
Richard D. Kaplan
Sidney L. Katz
Jacob Landau
Harold Leeds
Charles R. McCurdy
Josephine McSweeney

Jack Minkoff
Sibyl Moholy-Nagy
Rolf Myller
George M. Raymond
George Rozos
Stanley Salzman
Barry N. Schwartz
Arthur H. Seidman
Oscar H. Shaffel
Edward T. Shiffer
Ronald Shiffman
H. Irving Sigman
Pauline Tish
Christopher Wadsworth
QUEENS COLLEGE
Robert Ante
Arnold Bernstein
Anne Burchess
Joseph R. Catinella
Bell G. Chevigny
Michele F. Cooper
Louis Costa
George Dorris
Lloyd Delaney
Bernard Dukors
Margaret Eberbach
Robert Engler
Dora Fisher
Harvey Fried
Lewis Fried
Louis Geller
C. Lola Gersch
Sandra M. Gilbert
Richard Goldman
Myron Gordon
Toby Hobish
Lawrence Hochman
Evelyn Hoover
Samuel H. Hux
Robert Ilson
Dan Isaac
George Jochnowitz
Dorothy R. Jones
Lawrence Kaplan
Leonard Kaplan
Jacob H. Kirman

Michael Kowal
Keith R. Lampe
Esther Levine
Allan W. Low
Lila Lowenherz
John J. McDermott
Joseph McElroy
Richard Nonas
Elizabeth Nottingham
James O'Connell
Olaf Olsen
Nicholes Pastore
Allen Plantz
Murray Polner
Gerald Portner
Ronald Radosh
Melvin Reichler
Vera Reichler
Edmund O. Reiter
Walter Ritter
Eugene Rosenfeld
Anita N. Ross
Robert E. Savage
Edward Seltzer
Peter H. Shalus
John Shaffer
Sue Shanker
Eleanor M. Sickels
Babette Solon
John S. Stomm
Michael G. Sundell
Estelle Thaler
John Teitelbaum
Ruth M. Van de Kieft
Carey Wall
Frank A. Warren
Michael Wreszin
L. Steven Zwerling
RENSSELAER
   POLYTECHNIC
   INSTITUTE
Clifford O. Bloom
Eliot Deutsch
Edward A. Fox
J. Mayo Greenberg
Carl Hedman

Robert L. Hoffman
Roland M. Lichtenstein
William A. McKinley
Ashakant Nimbark
Charles Sanford
Paul Slepian
Isadore Traschen
Fredric Weiss
David Wieck

UNIVERSITY OF
ROCHESTER

William F. Bale
Ralph Barocas
Stephen D. Berger
Bruce Berlind
Emory L. Cowen
Jay Efran
Joseph Frank
Richard M. Gollin
Myron J. Gordon
E. M. Hafner
Norman I. Harway
Robert L. Holmes
John B. Hursh
David W. John
R. J. Kaufmann
William D. Lotspeich
Louis Martin
Arthur Mitzman
Vincent Nowlis
Bernard A. Weisberger
Hayden White

ROCKEFELLER
UNIVERSITY

Laurence Eisenberg
Harry Frankfurt
Jack Goldstein
Alexander Mauro
Paul Milvy
Morton Printz
Hans Rademacher
Paul Rosen
Robert Schoenfeld
Philip Siekevitz

STERN COLLEGE
FOR WOMEN

Mirella Afron
Gerald J. Blidstein
Robert Cowen
Doris S. Goldstein
Jules M. Greenstein
Edward Horowitz
Jo Lechary
Jules Levey
Howard I. Levine
Blanche Wiesen

SYRACUSE
UNIVERSITY

Norman Balabanian
Elias Balbinder
Evelyn Balbinder
Priscilla Barnum
Harvey H. Bates, Jr.
Seymour Bellin
Peter Bergmann
Randall Brune
Jesse Burkhead
Max Casper
Oliver E. Clubb, Jr.
Stanley Diamond
David Dobereiner
Warren W. Eason
James H. Elson
Marguerite Fisher
Andre Fontaine
Julian Friedman
Nathan Ginsburg
Joshua Goldberg
Sylvia Gourevitch
Robert Hardt
Erich Harth
Arnold Honig
Daniel F. Jackson
Joseph V. Julian
Harvey Kaplan
Gordon Kent
Lawrence Krader
Louis Krasner
Louis Kriesberg
Eric W. Lawson

Fred D. Levy, Jr.
H. Richard Levy
Jacques Lewin
Tekla Lewin
William Mangin
Sanford B. Meech
Allen Miller
Jerry Miner
Ephraim Mizruchi
Franklin Morris
Rajendra Nanavati
Robert E. Newman
David H. Owen
George Pappastravrou
A. W. Phillips
Betty Potash
Fritz Rohrlich
Robert Root
Helen Sata
Bernard Silverman
Harwood Simmons
Ralph A. Slepecky
Edward J. Stevens
Norman Stokle
Marcel Wellner
Waldo Whitney
Roland E. Wolseley

VASSAR COLLEGE

Noel L. Brann
Eugene Carroll
Bud Etherton
Robert Fortna
Patricia R. Johnson
Nancy Lindbloom
Ilse Lipschutz
L. Paul Metzger
Joan Elizabeth Murphy
Linda Nochlin
Ria Stavrides

NORTH CAROLINA
DUKE UNIVERSITY

Carl L. Anderson
Katharine M. Banhan
Waldo Beach
Frederick Bernheim
Mary L. C. Bernheim

J. L. Blum
Jack Botwinick
Nancy Bowers
Clifton Cherpack
Thomas H. Cordle
John S. Curtiss
Robert E. Cushman
Bernard J. Duffey
Donald E. Ginter
Norman Guttman
Frederic B. M. Hollyday
Bronislaw Jezierski
Gregory A. Kimble
Peter H. Klopfer
Frederick Krantz
Weston Labarre
Warren Lerner
Sidney D. Markman
Robert M. Marsh
Seymour H. Mauskopf
Ursula B. Perivier
Harold Schiffman
John R. Staude
Robert O. Swan
Charles R. Young
Mark J. Van Aken

OHIO

CASE INSTITUTE
   OF TECHNOLOGY
George C. Carrington
John W. Culver
Stanton L. Davis
Thomas G. Eck
Paul O. Fredricksen
Thomas De Gregori
Leslie L. Foldy
Melvin Henriksen
Martin J. Klein
Robert H. Klein
Peter Kovacic
Kenneth Kowalski
Gustav Kuerti
Harvey Leff
Henry Lesnick
Robert Lovejoy
Robert Welker

KENT STATE
   UNIVERSITY
D. L. Arnold
John B. Beacom
Bernard Benstock
Harold R. Collins
Lois H. Emmanuel
Danforth R. Hale
William H. Hidebrand
Clara Jackson
S. L. Jackson
K. R. Pringle
Bobby L. Smith
Barbara Tenner
Richard A. Toerne

WESTERN RESERVE
   UNIVERSITY
Robert P. Bolande
Allison L. Burnett
Phillip Burwasser
Charles C. Davis
Robert P. Davis
Leo A. Despres
Christopher Q. Dummond
Robert E. Eckel
Harriet Ephrussi-Taylor
Thomas Esper
Samuel Gorovitz
Peter E. Haiman
Edwin Haller
Lee Hyde
William Insull, Jr.
Robert K. Josephson
Robert R. Kohn
Rosi Kuerti
Irwin W. Lepon
Alice Martin
Hugh C. McCorcle
Lois McCorcle
Thomas McFarland
Myrna B. Miller
Richard D. Moore
Arthur J. Ness
Donald I. Payne
Sidney M. Peck
E. W. Pfeiffer

Richard O. Recknagel
Jonathan F. Reichert
Frank Rosengarten
Norman B. Rushforth
Howard Sachs
George Sayers
Howard A. Schneiderman
Leonard Share
Marcus Singer
John Chandler Smith
Arthur Steinberg
Peter Sterling
Theodore J. Voneida
Robert Wallace
Howard R. Webber
James A. Weston
Jess Yoder

PENNSYLVANIA

LASALLE COLLEGE
R. Almeder
M. Barth
J. F. Connors, III
J. S. Cziraky
G. J. DeFederico
P. Frank
A. L. Hennessy
A. S. Janik
R. C. Leonard
J. Lukacs
J. P. Mooney
E. R. Naughton
W. J. O'Toole
R. J. Pierzchalski
J. P. Rossi
B. Strieb
R. Tekel

LEHIGH UNIVERSITY
D. C. Amidon
J. R. Baker
R. S. Barnes, Jr.
Donald D. Barry
M. Broberg
A. L. Brody
A. F. Brown
H. E. Cole
Frank T. Colon

R. Cook
J. De Bellis
E. N. Dilworth
J. A. Dowling
G. J. Dullea
J. Elkus
W. M. Fleischman
R. T. Falk
J. R. Frakes
R. E. Fuessle
T. Hailperin
J. A. Hertz
J. C. Hirsh
S. S. Hook
E. A. James
R. L. Johnstone
R. G. Hones
G. R. Keiser
J. Kirk
G. Laison
Nancy Larrick
N. M. La Para
R. E. Layden
G. D. Marsh, Jr.
P. Marx
J. B. McFadden
N. Melchert
T. Moisiades
Marianne Platner
M. Schechter
J. Shahin
G. S. Stranch
D. H. Taylor
D. P. Updike
V. N. Valenzuela
John F. Vickrey
Scott W. Williams
R. C. Williamson
K. F. Winch
J. Z. Zwed

PENNSYLVANIA
STATE UNIVERSITY
R. G. Ayoub
P. H. Cutler
A. J. Engel
I. Feller

E. Hans Freund
J. Van Der Kar
W. H. Keddie
Charles Marsh
Hugo Ribiero
M. E. Rozen
Mark D. Shaw
A. Trachtenberg
W. Zelinsky

UNIVERSITY OF
PENNSYLVANIA
S. Bludman
W. D. Bonner
M. O. Bradley
D. Bodde
H. J. Bright
H. Brody
E. Burstein
H. E. Caspari
A. Cassels
S. S. Cohen
W. Curnow
H. Davies
W. E. Davies
A. R. Day
A. M. Delluva
F. R. Frankel
S. Frankel
E. S. Gersh
I. Gersh
H. S. Ginsberg
S. Goodgal
G. de la Haba
J. Halpern
B. F. Hammond
A. J. Heeger
E. S. Herman
H. Holtzer
Dorothea Jameson Hurvich
Leo M. Hurvich
Dell Hymes
M. M. Joullie
R. G. Kallen
N. Kallenbach
W. Klinman
A. Kowalsky

K. Lande
R. P. Lane
J. Lash
D. Lavin
P. S. Leboy
L. Levine
Harold Lewis
I. S. Lustig
M. Lustig
J. B. Marsh
G. Marzullo
M. K. Mass
A. S. Mildvan
J. Mirsky
A. M. Nemeth
R. J. Osborn
J. K. Parker
R. P. Peterson
S. H. Pitkin
A. R. Post
E. H. Postel
H. Primakoff
R. J. Rutman
B. Shostak
H. J. Spiro
E. Staple
D. Tredinnick
C. W. Ufford
L. Warren
A. F. Whereat
V. H. Whitney
S. C. Williams

SWARTHMORE
COLLEGE
Harriet S. Baguskas
Carl Barus
Monroe C. Beardsley
Thompson Bradley
Lewis R. Gaty, II
Arthur J. Komar
Olga Lang
Bernard Morrill
John A. Nevin
Harold E. Pagliaro
Jerome A. Shaffer
Peter van de Kamp

Alice S. Walker
Robert M. Walker
James F. Wanner
TEMPLE UNIVERSITY
Alice J. Anderson
Franklin R. Baruch
R. Bentman
S. Berg
H. Braun
R. Buttel
E. Caplan
Richard Clark
Allan H. Cristol
G. Deaux
C. A. Domenicali
Anne M. Edelmann
R. Edenbaum
G. Fiderer
Irwin Griggs
H. Francis Havas
Peter Havas
Martin E. Itzkowitz
Mabel Jessee
Robert J. Kleiner
W. T. Kulik
Mary Jane Lupton
Maxwell S. Luria
S. J. Marks
Herbert Needleman
J. D. Perry
Mark Sacharoff
R. J. Swenson
B. Tomsu
R. Tomsu
Victor C. Vaughn
M. P. Worthington
Morton Zivan

RHODE ISLAND
  BROWN
  UNIVERSITY
Edward J. Ahearn
Helen Biedermann
John Casparis
Herman B. Chase
William F. Church

William E. Feinberg
W. L. Fichter
Stanton Garner
John Gilbert
Michael S. Goldstein
Neil I. Gonsalves
John Hawkes
Herbert Heidelberger
William L. Hendrickson
Robert E. Hill
Werner Hoffmeister
Jeanette C. Honan
Paul Honan
Edwin Honig
Francois Hugot
R. R. Jojokian
Edward S. Kennedy
Michael Klein
Edward Koren
David Krause
John Ladd
Hugo Leckey
Barbara Lewalski
Stephen Lottridge
Eugene Luschei
William G. McLoughlin, Jr.
Harold Organic
Thaddeus Osmolski
John Patterson
Charles Philbrick
Beverly S. Ridgely
D. W. Schumann
Alene F. Silver
Einar Siqueland
D. Smith
Mark Spilka
David Stea
John L. Thomas
Vincent Tomas
Hugh Townley
Hyatt Waggoner
Karl S. Weimar
Leonard A. Weiss
Mark Whitney
Margaret Yarvin
Stanley Zimmering

UNIVERSITY OF
  RHODE ISLAND
Alan Bostrom
Elena Clough
Garret Clough
Joel A. Dain
William G. Gard
Charles G. Hoffman
Robert M. Gutchen
Melvin Lurie
Miels Madsen
Nelson Marshall
William D. Metz
Charles V. Mulholland
Richard Neuse
Jules Piccus
Elton Rayack
Myron S. Rosenbaum
Richard A. Roughton
Stanley Rubinsky
Richard A. Sabatino
Bernard Schurman
David Shilling
Alberta Smith
Robert F. Smith
Frederick Stern
Grace E. Stiles
A. Ralph Thompson
Harold A. Waters
VERMONT
  BENNINGTON
  COLLEGE
Frank Baker
Henry Brant
Louis Calabro
Louis Carini
Julian DeGray
Margaret DeGray
George Finckel
Claude Fredericks
Paul Gray
George Guy
Mary Hopkins
A. Norman Klein
Lionel Nowak
Orrea Pernel

R. Arnold Ricks
Leonard Rowe
Bert Salwen
Gunnar Schonbeck
Wallace Scott
William Sherman
Reinhoud van der Linde
GODDARD COLLEGE
Frank T. Adams, Jr.
C. George Benello
Joshua Berrett
Corinne Elliott
Vincent Erickson
Francis Fay
Nancy Fay
Barry Goldensohn
Wilfrid Hamlin
Richard O. Hathaway
W. Allan Last
Ray Lavallee
Albert Lopez-Escobar
Stephen Noren
William E. Osgood
Buryl Payne
William J. Reeves
Jerry Richard
Mark Ryder
John R. Salter, Jr.
Kehnroth Schramm

Robert Silverstein
Arthur H. Westing
Thomas R. Whitaker
David York
Charles Zerby
WASHINGTON
  UNIVERSITY OF
  WASHINGTON
Giovanni Costigan
John E. Crow
R. G. Fleable
Alex Gottfried
Gordon Griffiths
Mary Griffiths
Alfred Kogon
Arthur R. Kruckeberg
Linden A. Mander
L. K. Northwood
Laureen Nussbaum
Rudi H. Nussbaum
Hans Patnalski
Richard J. Reed
Mabel Turner
Robert W. Williams
WISCONSIN
  UNIVERSITY OF
  WISCONSIN
Bert N. Adams
Robert R. Alford
Neal Billings

Warner Bloomberg
Mendel F. Cohen
N. Jay Demerath, III
Eugene Eisman
Joseph W. Elder
Hugo Engelmann
Hans H. Gerth
Morgan Gibson
Manuel Gottlieb
Sidney Greenfeld
Phillip E. Hammond
Hugh H. Iltis
Arnold Kaufman
T. David Kemper
Edgar Litt
David R. Luce
Kenneth Lutterman
Thomas L. McFarland
Richard Poltz
Frederico Prehaska
Robert Ressler
Kenneth J. Reichstein
David R. Schmitt
William H. Sewell
George Sopkin
Aviva Sorkin
Leonard Sorkin
Gerald Stanick
Walter I. Trattner

An Open Letter to President Johnson on Vietnam

Each day we hear fresh news from Vietnam, news both strange and grim. We strike by air in reprisal against North Vietnam because our soldiers, sent as armed technicians and advisers to an army which cannot yet guard them well, have been attacked in their barracks in the very heart of South Vietnam. We have widened the war—how wide will it become?

Fear of escalation of this undeclared war against North Vietnam mounts with each sudden report of renewed violence. Unless the situation is very different from what it appears to be, we have lost the political initiative in Vietnam and are attempting to substitute military actions for political ones. We face grave risks in Vietnam. Americans have faced even graver risks for good and high cause, Mr. President, but we must first understand why we must take such risks. What are our goals in Vietnam? Are they just? Can they be accomplished? Are they truly worth what they are bound to cost in dollars and human lives?

With whom are we allied in Vietnam? Are our soldiers fighting side by side with troops of a representative and legitimate national government, or are we embroiled in defense of an unpopular minority in a fierce and costly civil war? Our representatives assure us that we and the Saigon government have the overwhelming support of the Vietnamese people. How can this be so? On the same day that Mr. McNamara said sneak attacks upon our soldiers cannot be prevented, an American officer on the scene in Vietnam declared that "any of the people in the hamlet over there could have warned us that the Vietcong were around, but they did not warn us." The weapons used against us are most often American weapons, captured from or surrendered by the South Vietnamese Army. Mr. President, we submit that weak field intelligence in South Vietnam and a steady loss of workable weapons to the enemy, are deep symptoms of an unpopular cause.

Why are we fighting in Vietnam? Mr. President, we think we understand why we went into Vietnam after the French withdrew. It was because this Nation hoped to encourage the development of a popular, stable, and democratic government which would help to lead all southeast Asia toward lasting peace. Historical, political, social, religious, and sectional factors have prevented this development. The original assumptions are no longer valid. We have become increasingly unwelcome everywhere in southeast Asia. Our presence seems to deepen, rather than to relieve, the bitterness and hostility of the people. It was only 10 years ago that the Vietnamese defeated a French Army of nearly half a million men. Will the same battles occur again?

Can we win in Vietnam? Mr. President, we know that our Nation has sufficient fire power to destroy the entire world. We also know that you do not wish to call upon this awesome power. How can we possibly win and yet prevent a widening of this conflict? How can we win in Vietnam with less than 30,000 advisers when the French could not win with an army of nearly half a million fighting both north and south of the present dividing frontier?

Is it worth the cost? The French defeat in Indochina cost them 172,000 casualties. Yet, before their final bloody defeat at Dienbienphu, the French generals and diplomats spoke with the same toughness and optimism, the same assurances we now hear from our leaders.

The French had overwhelming numbers and fire power but they lost in Vietnam because they lacked the support of the population. Do we face the same prospect, or are there facts which the public does not know which show our situation to be clearly different?

Mr. President, we are aware that you have secret information which cannot be shared with us. But could such information completely refute the picture of events and the political insights provided to us by serious newspapermen who have been in the area for years?

All we can see is a seemingly endless series of demonstrations and riots in Saigon and Hue, of military coups, of threats and challeges to the dignity of our Ambassador and our other representatives by the very men we seek to sustain in power.

We have lost the initiative in Vietnam. A few guerrillas can trigger American reactions that widen the war. The events of the past weeks are leading step by step along the path to war with China.

Would it not be both prudent and just to take the initiative toward peace in Vietnam? If we are not to widen the war beyond all conscience, as reasonable men we must initiate negotiations while there is still time.

Andover-Newton Theological School: Herbert Gezork, ethics (plus four signers, Feb. 16).

Boston University: Irwin E. Chase, psychiatry; William A. Hire, psychology; Francis Johnson, chemistry; Philip E. Kubzansky, psychology, Louis Lowy, social work; S. Joseph Nemetz, medical school; Irwin I. Portner, medical school; Henry N. Rosenberg, medical school (plus 24 signers, Feb. 16).

Brandeis University: Stanley Deser, physics; Harry Rand, psychiatry (plus 55 signers, Feb. 16)

Bryn Mawr College: Warner Berthoff, English; Paul R. Brass, political science;

T. R. S. Broughton, Latin; Fredericka de Laguna, anthropology; R. B. De Boff, economics; Mary Dunn, history; Alice F. Emerson, political science; Rosallie Hoyt, physics; Mabel Lang, Greek; Richard Lattimore, Greek; Gertrude Leighton, political science; A. K. Michels, Latin; Eleanor Pauker, Spanish; Robert Patten, English; Kyle Phillips, archaeology; Eugene Schneider, sociology; Laurence Stapleton, English.

Drexel Institute of Technology; Joel Balsham, English; William Hollis, English; David Holtz, English; Sol M. Kilpnes, chemistry; Samuel S. McNeary, mathematics; James A. Richards, Jr., physics; Eugene J. Rosenbaum, chemistry; Cecil O. Smith, Jr., history; J. W. Smith, sociology; John A. Taylor, physics; Stanley A. Wasson, history.

Haverford College: Edwin Bronner, history; Dean Burnham, political science; John Cary, German; Aldo Caselli, Italian; Thomas D'Andrea, psychology; William Davidson, physics; Paul Desjardins, philosophy; Alfred Diamant, political science; Irving Finger, biology; Lewis Green, astronomy; Elizabeth Green, biology; Theodore Hetzel engineering; Dietrich Kessler, biology; Lewis Kosman, philosophy; Wallace MacCaffrey, history; Sidney Perloe, psychology; Melvin Santer, biology; Ralph Sargent, English; Alfred Satterthwaite, English.

Harvard University: Sidney Alexander, medical school; Daniel S. Bernstein, medical school; Martin A. Berezin, medical school; Donnell W. Boardman, medical school; Louis S. Chase, medical school; Sidney Coleman, physics; Lincoln H. Day, public health; Daniel Deykin, medical school; Frank R. Ervin, medical school; Sanford Gifford, medical school; Lester Grinspoon, medical school; George Grosser, medical school; Calvin Leeman, medical school; Sidney Levin, medical school; John E. Mack, medical school; Jack H. Mendelson, medical school; David L. Rabin, public health; Peter Reich, medical school; Samuel Silverman, medical school; Harold J. Stein, medical school; Myron Stocking, medical school; Anna K. Wolff, medical school; Stephan Thernstrom, history; Norman E. Zinberg, medical school (plus 42 signers, February 16).

Institute for Advanced Study: Felix Gilbert, history; Harold Chernias, classics.

Massachusetts Institute of Technology: Nesmyth C. Ankeny, mathematics (plus 66 signers February 16).

Princeton University: Oakes Ames, physics; Carlos Baker, English; Elmer Beller, history; G. E. Bentley, English; David Berlinsky, philosophy; David Bien, history; Arthur L. Bigelow, engineering graphics; Jerome Blum, history; R. Bon de Sousa Pernes, philosophy; E. B. O. Borgerhoff, romance languages; Boruch Brody, philosophy; G. E. Brown, physics; Joseph Brown, school of architecture; Nicholas R. Clifford, history; W. R. Conner, classics; John I. Dalland, psychology; Willard Dalrymple, M.D., university health services; M. L. Diamond, religion; William S. Dix, librarian; Martin Dubermann, history; R. A. Faulkner, politics; Joel Feinberg, philosophy; George B. Field, astrophysical sciences; John V. A. Fine, classics; Charles K. Fish, English; Robert Freeman, music; Sam Glucksberg, psychology; F.R.B. Godolphin, classics; Ernest Gordon, dean, university chapel; M. B. Gottlieb, astrophysical sciences; Claudio Guillen, romance languages; Stirling Haig, romance languages; Richard F. Hamilton, sociology; W. F. Hanrieder, politics; John A. Hanson, classics; Frederick Harbison, economics; Gilbert H. Harman, philosophy; C. G. Hempel, philosophy; Laurence B. Holland, English; John B. Hughes, romance languages; Edmund Keeley, English; Earl Kim, music; Edmund L. King, romance langauges; Arthur C. Kirsch, English; Axel Kornfuehrer, history; Thomas Kuhn, history; Victor Lange, German; Donald R. Larson, romance languages; Sue Larson, philosophy; Rensselaer W. Lee, art and archaeology; Michael Lipsky, politics; A. Walton Litz, English; Duane Lockard, politics; L. H. Lockwood, music; John Rupert Martin, art and archaeology; Arno J. Mayer, history; Arthur Mendel, music; Dimitri Mihalas, astrophysical sciences; George Paul Mras, art and archaeology; R. Nozick, philosophy; A.B. Pardee, biology; George Pepe, classics; George Pitcher, philosophy; James K. Randall, music; L. I. Rebhun, biology; Thomas P. Roche, Jr., English; Remington E. Rose, II, English; Robert Rosenblum, art and archaeology; Israel Rosenfield, politics; G.S. Rousseau, English; Charles A. Ryskamp, English; Joseph Schraibman, romance languages; John Schrecker, history; Roger Sessions, music; J. E. Seigel, history; Steve M. Slaby, engineering graphics; Philip Solomon, astrophysical sciences; Kimberly Sparks, German; Stanley Stein, history; Stephen P. Stich, philosophy; John H. Strange, politics; Edward D. Sullivan, romance languages; George F. Thomas, religion; Lawrence R. Thompson, English; A. Richard Turner, art and archaeology; Jack A. Vernon, psychology; A. N. Wahl, politics; Peter S. Walch, art and archaeology; Michael Walzer, politics; Sam Willis, romance languages; Franklin W. Young, religion; P. R. Zilsel, physics.

Princeton Theological Seminary: George S. Hendry, theology; Cullen I. K. Story, Biblical studies; Charles C. West, Christian ethics.

Rutgers—The State University: Eliahu Abrahams, physics; Robert F. Allen, director, language laboratory; Samuel L. Baily, history; Howard Ball, political science; Saul Barshay, physics; John E. Bebout, director, urban studies center; F. Kenneth Berrien, psychology; Gerald Bertin, romance languages; Paul Bertram, English; Werner W. Boehm, dean, graduate school of social work; Harry C. Bredemeier, urban studies center; David J. Bredin, physics; Vernon Bryson, microbiology; John L. Cammett, history; Peter L. Carlton, psychology; Sandi E. Cliadakis, history; Bertram D. Cohen, psychology; George H. Collier, psychology; Michael R. Curtis, political science; Michael R. D'Amato, psychology; James E. Durkin, Jr., psychology; Thomas R. Edwards, Jr., English; Richard M. Fontera, political science; Paul Fussell, Jr., English; Ralph Garber, social work; Lloyd C. Gardner, history; Bertram E. Garskof, psychology; Joseph N. Ginocchio, physics; Bernard G. Guerney, psychology; Robert Gutman, sociology; Nelson G. Hanawalt, psychology; Don F. Heisel, urban studies center; David J. M. Higgins, English; Daniel F. Howard, English; Solomon Leader, mathematics; Hannah Levin, psychology; Donald J. Lewis, psychology; Peter Lindenfeld, physics; Ernest Lynton, physics; Martin Manosevitz, psychology; Simon Marcson, sociology; David Markowitz, physics; John O. McCormick, English; Donald C. Mell, Jr., English; William G. Miller, archivist, library; Carol Ann Millsom, psychology; Edith D. Neimark, psychology; Gerald Pomper, political science; David Popenoe, urban studies center; Donald H. Riddle, Eagleton Institute of Politics; Glorianne Robbi, Eagleton Institute of Politics; Allen B. Robbins, physics; Amelie O. Rorty, philosophy;

Claire Rosenfield, English; William A. Rust, Jr., political science; Anne Saxon, English; Frank R. Scarpitti, sociology; Norman E. Spear, psychology; Marshall Stalley, urban studies center; Charles H. Stember, sociology; Siegfried A. Streufert, psychology; Warren I. Susman, history; Frank Tachau, political science; Paul Tillett, Eagleton Institute of Politics; Jackson Toby, sociology; Jack Undank, romance languages; Rudolph J. Vecoli, history; David R. Weimer, English; Virginia P. Whitney, urban studies center; Seymour T. Zenchelsky, chemistry.

Rockefeller Institute: Lawrence Elsenberg, electronics; Rollin D. Hotchkiss, genetics; Dorothy Lane, Alexander Mauro, biophysics; Richard Novick, genetics; Priscilla J. Ortiz, genetics; Muriel Roger, genetics; Paul Rosen, electronics; Robert L. Schoenfeld, electronics; Norton D. Zinder, genetics.

Simmons College: Ina M. Granara, chemistry; Henry J. Halko, history; Edith F. Helman, Spanish; Lawrence L. Langer, English; Ruth S. Leonard, library science; Samuel T. Leverich, mathematics; Manfred Klein, German; William M. Manly, English; Carroll F. Miles, government; George W. Nitchie, English, John A. Timm, chemistry; Roy M. Tollefson, government; Wylie Sypher, English; Robert C. Vernon, physics; Marion I. Walter, mathematics (plus eight signers last week).

Swarthmore College: Monroe Beardsley, philosophy; Thompson Bradley, modern languages; Albert Poseberg, natural science;

Syracuse University: Norman Balabanian, electrical engineering; Elias Balbinder, microbiology; David H. Bennett, American studies; Peter G. and Margot Bergmann, physics; Joshua Goldberg physics; N. Horwitz, physics; Gordon Kent, electrical engineering; H. Richard Levy, biochemistry; Rajendra P. Nanavati, electrical engineering; Bernard Silverman, electrical engineering; Ralph Slepecky, microbiology; Edward P. Stabler, electrical engineering; Ralph Swalm, industrial engineering.

Tufts University: Louis Geller, medical school; Charles E. Magraw, medical school (plus 31 signers February 16).

University of Pennsylvania: Lee Benson, history; Derk Bodde, oriental studies; Walter Bonner, Johnson Foundation; Herbert Callen, physics; Max I. Caspari, physics; Alan Cassels, history; Hilary Conroy, history; Paul Davidoff, city planning; Allan R. Day, chemistry; Helen C. Davis, microbiology; Thomas J. Davy, Fels Institute; Elizabeth Flower, philosophy; Sherman Frankel, physics; Harold S. Ginsberg, microbiology; Sol H. Goodgal, microbiology; Joseph S. Gotz, microbiology; Britton Harris, city planning; Walter P. Hempfling, Johnson Foundation; Henry Hiz, linguistics; Arthur Kowalsky, Johnson Foundation; A. Klein, physics; Norman R. Kleinman, microbiology; Fred Karush, microbiology; J. S. Leigh, Jr., Johnson Foundation; Lawrence Levine, Fels Institute; Irma S. Lustig, English; Morton Lustig, Fels Institute; John Marshall, anatomy; Anshell Melamed, Fels Institute; Albert S. Mildvan, Johnson Foundation; Grace Milgram, Institute for Urban Studies; Dennis Palumbo, Fels Institute; Jean Platt, anatomy; Berton C. Pressman, Johnson Foundation; Charles C. Price, chemistry; Henry Primakoff, physics; W. A. Rickett, oriental studies; Robert Rutman, chemistry; Abraham M. Stein, chemistry; E. Dale Saunders, oriental studies; Franklin C. Southworth, South Asia regional studies; C. W. Ufford, physics; Walter D. Wales, physics; Roger H. Walmsley, physics; G. T. Wood, physics.

sociology; Barbara B. Green, political science; Eleanor L. McLaughlin, history; Annemarie Shimony, sociology; Owen S. Stratton, political science; Kathryn Turner, history; W. Warren Wagar, history (plus 4 signers February 16).

Others: Stringfellow Barr, writer and lecturer; Everett Gendler, Rabbi, Princeton; Eric Kahler, writer and lecturer; Richard Jeffrey, CCNY; Ashley Montagu, writer and lecturer; Carol C. B. Savage, Ben Shahn, artist; Ernest Young, Dartmouth.

(From the New York Times, Feb. 28, 1965)

Open Letter to President Johnson on Vietnam

We, as members of the academic community, feel impelled to raise publicly with you, Mr. President, the question of our Government's present policy toward South Vietnam. We ask you to reconsider our present course of action in view of the following facts:

We are intervening unilaterally in support of a succession of undemocratic regimes that are opposed by a majority of the South Vietnamese people.

We are waging an immoral and inhumane war that has brought untold suffering to the people of South Vietnam.

Our recent air attacks on North Vietnam intensify the danger that a local conflict will develop into a major war.

It is maintained that the United States is protecting a popularly supported government against foreign subversion. We maintain, Mr. President, that the evidence available to the Congress and to the public does not support this interpretation of the Vietnamese conflict.

The fact is that the United States is maintaining regimes which are not supported by the bulk of the rural population. How else explain a situation in which 35,000 Viet Cong regulars have been able to make increasing gains against a Government army of over 200,000 men together with 23,000 American "advisers"? The close-range attacks on Bienhoa and Pleiku indicate the lack of support by neighboring villagers for the Saigon government.

What has our policy meant for the people of South Vietnam? Only a small minority of the people profits from the $600 million in foreign aid we send annually to South Vietnam. The peasantry of

Vietnam has been terrorized. The country, once one of the most prosperous areas of southeast Asia, is being devastated by the napalm bombing of peasant villages, by the unbridled strafing of the countryside by American-supplied aircraft, by the detention and mass transfers of the South Vietnamese people. Prisoners are being tortured in South Vietnam. It does not seem likely that this could be done without the knowledge of American officials.

What effect has our policy had on U.S. prestige abroad? By supporting dictatorial military regimes in South Vietnam we have undermined confidence in our professed belief that nations should be allowed to develop their own destinies free from outside interference. Although we pledged to respect the Geneva accords of 1954, we have violated those agreements by supplying troops and weapons to South Vietnam. We have belied our adherence to international law by refusing to submit the dispute to an international conference, such as the parties to the Geneva accords or one of the bodies of the United Nations.

Our justification for intervention in South Vietnam has been that we are preventing the spread of communism in southeast Asia. The effect of our policy, however, has been to alienate both the neighboring countries and our allies.

As recent events have shown, the longer the war in South Vietnam continues, the greater are the chances of escalation. Our air and sea attacks upon North Vietnam have not appreciably altered the situation in the south, but they have succeeded in increasing the danger of a major conflagration on the continent of Asia and of nuclear war.

When 81 percent of the American people, according to a recent Gallup poll, indicated they were in favor of a conference with the leaders of southeast Asia and China in an effort to reach a peace agreement, must we continue any longer along this dangerous path?

Mr. President, we urge you to consider another course of action:

We ask that you bring an end to the investment of American men and money in the war in South Vietnam.

We ask you to seek a negotiated settlment by every possible means in order to create an independent, neutralized government and to bring about the withdrawal of U.S. troops.

We ask you to lay the problem immediately before an international body and to put an end to our unilateral and illegal actions.

We urge you, Mr. President, to take immediate action to end the war in South Vietnam. The longer we persist in our present policy, the fewer will be the alternatives open to us.

Adelphi University: Harold Allen, philosophy; Stuart Astor, English; Wesley Camp, history; Paul Crosser, economics; Sydney Davis, education; Robert Endleman, sociology; Robert Ernst, history; Beatrice Freeman, social work; David Gordon, sociology; Murray Greene, philosophy; Philip Greene, English; Harlon Joye, sociology; Stephen Klas, English; Donald Koster, English; Allen M. Krebs, sociology; David Levin, history; Jerry March, chemistry; Joan Martin, English; Ronald McHaffy, mathematics; Robert Pasotti, philosophy; Robert Payton, mathematics; Eugene Roth, English; Henry F. Smith, English; Virginia Terris, English; Alfred Vogel, chemistry; Argyrios Vourkas, sociology; Henry T. Wilt, Greek and Latin; Cedric Winslow, English; Donald Wolf, English; Stephen Yeh, sociology.

Albert Einstein College of Medicine: Beverly Birns, psychiatry; Everett W. Bovard, anatomy; Wagner H. Bridger, psychiatry; N. M. Buckley, physiology; Jean L. Cook, medicine; Lewis M. Fraad, pediatrics; Sidney Goldfischer, pathology; Eric Holtzman, pathology; Edward J. Hornick, psychiatry; William Obrinsky, pediatrics; Samuel M. Rosen, medicine; Bertram A. Lowy, biochemistry; Mary Weitzman, anatomy; N. Henry Williams, medicine.

Brooklyn College: Harry Gracey, sociology; Brijen Gupta, history; Paul Haberfield, chemistry; David Koulack, psychology; Barton Meyers, psychology; Myriam Miedzianogora, philosophy; Rose Mukerji, education; Herman E. Zieger, chemistry; Carl B. Zuckerman, psychology.

City College of New York: Bernard Bellush, history; Nathan Berall, English; Gustave Bischof, mechanical engineering; Daniel Bronstein, philosophy; M. Vertner Brown, physics; Mark Brunswick, music; Maurice Cohen, philosophy; Ephraim Cross, romance languages; Helen Davidson, education; Sidney Ditzion, history; Abraham Edel, philosophy; Sophie L. Elan, education; J. A. Elais, philosophy; Joseph A. Ellis, history; Ernest Ferguson, physical education; Dorothy H. Gampel, psychology; Geoffrey J. Gibson, philosophy; Daniel Greenberger, physics; Leo Hamalain, English; Fritz Jahoda, music; Florine Katz, education; Y. H. Kirkorian, emeritus, philosophy; Edward Mack, English; Irving Malin, English; Aaron Noland, history; Stanley W. Page, history; George W. Phillips, history; A. I. Rabin, psychology; Sidney M. Rosenblatt, education; Aurel M. Seifert, physics; Oscar Sherwin, English; Irwin Stark, English; Samuel Sumberg, Germanic and Slavic languages; Martin Tammy, philosophy; Harry Tarter, philosophy; H. S. Thayer, philosophy; Martin S. Tiersten, physics; Barbara Watson, English; Phillip Wiener, philosophy; Harold Wilensky, psychology; Bohdan Zawadski, psychology; Rose Zimbardo, English.

Columbia University: Alexander Alland, Jr., anthropology; Hugh Amory, English; E. Duncan Aswell, English; Bertram L. Bassuk, architecture; Sacvan Bercovitch, English; Lipman Bers, mathematics; Rudolph Binion, history; Robert brustein, English; Justus Buchler, philosophy; Sue Buckingham, medicine; Jack Budowsky, dentistry; Arthur C. Carr, medicine; Eloise E. Clark, zoology; Jonathan

H. Collett, English; Lambros Comitas, philosophy; Mason Cooley, English; Arnold Cooper, medicine; Stephen M. Corey, Teachers College; Robert Cross, history; Elizabeth Czoniczer, French; Leonardo C. De Morelos, Spanish; H. M. Edwards, mathematics; Alexander Erlich, economics; Amitai Etzioni, sociology; Samuel Finestone, social work; James M. Fitch, architecture; David Fitelson, English; Goodwin L. Foster, emeritus, biochemistry; Marie L. Franciscus, occupational therapy; Morton H. Fried, anthropology; Herbert Gans, Institute of Urban Studies; Willard Gaylin, medicine; Percival Goodman, architecture; Frederic Grab, English; Richard L. Greeman, French; E. I. Gumbel, industrial engineering; Robert W. Hanning, English; Marvin Harris, anthropology; Teru Hayashi, zoology; Amelia Hess, anthropology; Charles H. Hinnant, English; Terrence K. Hopkins, sociology; E. R. Kolchin, mathematics; Alexander Kouzmanoff, architecture; Corliss Lamont, philosophy; Serge Lang, mathematics; Robert F. Lynd, professor emeritus; William Martin, sociology; A. L. Mayer, mathematics; Peter McHugh, sociology; Fabrizio Melano, English; Seymour Melman, engineering; Solomon Miller, anthropology; Mary Mothersill, philosophy; John Mundy, history; Jay Neugeboren, English; George Pappas, medicine; Lawrence Pinkham, journalism; J. Herman Randall, Jr., philosophy; John D. Rosenberg, English; Leon S. Roudiez, French; Phillips Salman, English; Mario G. Salvadori, civil engineering; J. Schilt, astronomy; Paul Schwaber, English; Arthur Schwartz; mathematics; Jerome Schwartz, French; Morton D. Schweitzer, epidemiology; Peter Shaw, English; William Silverman, medicine; Ernest Simon, French; Susan Sontag, religion; Robert Spitzer, medicine; Harold Stahmer, religion; Michael Studdert-Kennedy, psychology; Samuel Sutton, medicine; Mark Van Doen, English; William Vickrey, economics; Frederick E. Warburton, zoology; Michael Wood, English; David Zipser, zoology.

Cornell University: Douglas F. Dowd, economics; Robert M. Durling, romance literature; Chandler Morse, economics; David E. Novack; economics; Taylor Stoehr, English literature; Harold Widom, mathematics.

Hofstra College: Adolf Anderson, New College; Ethel Brook, modern languages; Frances Z. Kalman, educational foundations; Shirley P. Langer, psychology; Harvey Levin, economics; Mary Gilbert Ligon, education; Broadus Mitchell, new college; Anne Morgenstern, education; Elie Siegmeister, music; E. R. Stabler, mathematics; Ruth Stauffer, English; Albert Tepper, music, Lynn Turgeon, economics; Murray Yanowitch, economics; June Zaccone, economics.

Long Island University: Kenneth Bernard, English; Kenneth Bridenthal, history; George Economou, English; Harry Fenson, English; Leonard Fleischer, English; Frederic Jaher, history; John McDermott, philosophy; Edward Pomerantz, English; Kenneth W. Scott, English; Paul N. Siegel, English; Robert Vas Dias, English.

New York University: Elaine Allen, medicine; Michael Arons, physics; Sabert Basescu, psychology; Marvin Belsky, medicine, Joy Gould Boyum, English; Robert Burrowes, government; Edwin Campbell, chemistry; James Tracy Crown,, government; Stanley Deutsch, medicine; Eugenie Dubnau, medicine; Dora Fisher, psychology; Emanuel Fisher, medicine; H. H. Giles, social studies; Mary A. Giles, education; Vinvent Glinsky, sculpture; Jacob Goodman, mathematics; Martin Hamburger, guidance; George Kaufer, spychology; Gerson T. Lesser, medicine; Leah Levinger, psychology; Harvey Levey, medicine; Evelyn Mauss, dentistry; L. Nirenberg, mathematics; Ruth Ochroch, psychology; Robert Perlman, medicine; Morris Perlmutter, medicine; Richard Pallack, mathematics; Frederick L. Redefer; education; Albert Romasco, history; Sanford Rosenzweig, dentistry; H. Laurence Ross, sociology; Irving Sarnoff, psychology; Ernest G. Schachtel, psychology; Milton Schwebel, guidance; Martin Spencer, sociology; Herbert A. Tonne, business education; Gilbert M. Trachtman, educational psychology; William G. Vander Kloot, medicine; Louis Wilker, sociology; Pearl Zipser, reading institute.

Polytechnic Institute of Brooklyn: E. Banks, chemistry; Judith S. Bellin, chemistry; Irving Cohen, chemistry; Sid Deutsch, electrical engineering; Owen Fleischman, physics; Marvin E. Gettleman, history; H. P. Gregor, chemistry; Helmut Gruber, history; Frederick C. Kreiling, history; Eleanor B. Leacock, history; David Mermelstein, economics; Carol Moodie, history; Gerald Oster, chemistry; R. F. Riley, chemistry; Paul E. Spoerri, chemistry; J. Steigman, chemistry.

Pratt Institute: Joseph L. Cobtiz, philosophy; Robert B. Dennis, architecture; Frances Esecover, architecture; Sibyl Moholy-Nagy, architecture, Sidney M. Shelov, architecture; Christopher D. Wadsworth, architecture; J. Sherwood Weber, English.

Queens College: Kenneth T. Abrams, English; Arnold Berstein, psychology; Ellen Bindman, mathematics; Bell Gale Chevigny, English; E. Richard Covert, student personnel; Jack Cypin, economics; M. Herbert Danzger, sociology; Herbert Fremont, education; Hilliard Gardiner, contemporary civilization; L. Terrell Gardner, mathematics; Louis Geller, economics; Ronald Glassman, sociology; Del Greenblatt, history; Alan Harwood, sociology; Mark A. Haskell, economics; L. Hochman, physics; Lawrence Kaplan, philosophy; Joel Kauffman, economics; Lawrence B. Kirschner, history; Benjamin Lapkin, education; Marvin Leiner, education; Thomas M. Mongar, political science; James R. O'Connell, history; Melvin Reichler, sociology; Vera Reichler, political science; Edmund Reiter, contemporary civilization; Sol Resnik, political science; Anita Ross, education; Selma Sapir, education; Robert E. Savage, biology; Edward Seltzer, philosophy; John B. P. Shaffer, psychology; Sidney B. Simon, education; Harvard Sitkoff, contemporary civilization; Harry Sitomer, mathematics; Julia Sutton, music; Frank A. Warren, III, history; Frank White, philosophy; Elizabeth Friar William, education; John S. Williams, sociology; Michael Wreszin, history; Martin Zelin, psychology; Burton Zwiebach, political science.

Rutgers University: John M. Cammett, history; Eugene D. Genovese, history; John Gorgol, management; Arnold M. Paul, history; B. P. Sonnenblick, zoology; Warren I. Susman, history.

Rockefeller Institute: Erwin Fleissner, biochemistry; Max Gottesman, biochemistry; Fritz Lipmann; David Mauzerall; Philip Siekevitz, cell biology.

Sarah Lawrence College: Robert Engler, political science; Ira Glasser, mathematics; Helen Merrell Lynd, prof. emeritus; Carl Resek, social science; Harvey Swados, literature.

Sloan-Kettering Institute for Cancer Research: Aaron Bendich, biological chemistry; Roland Finston, biophysics; Richard Lee, biophysics; Paul Milvy, biophysics; Allen C. Nadler, clinical investigation; Edmund O. Rothschild, clinical investigation; Martin Sonenberg, clinical investigation; Herbert Weiss, biophysics; Louis Zeitz, biophysics.

State University of New York at Stony Brook: Karl S. Bottigheimer, history; Hugh G. Cleland, history; Sallie S. Goldstein, English; Charles Hoffmann, economics; Norman Leer, English; Ruth Misheloff, English; Michael Parenti, political science; Joel Rosenthal, history.

Stevens Institute of Technology: James L. Anderson, physics; Hugh W. Byfield, physics; I. Richard Lapidus, physics; Arthur Layzer, physics; Kenneth C. Rogers, physics; George Schmidt, physics; Snowden Taylor, physics; George Yevick, physics.

Yeshiva University: R. E. Behrends, physics; Barbara Berger, educational psychology; William Block, psychology; Morris N. Eagle, psychology; Melvin Feffer, psychology; David Finkelstein, physics; Joshua Fishman, psychology; Gertrude Goldberg, educational psychology; Allan C. Goldstein, psychology; Herbert Goldstein, special education; Edmund W. Gordon, educational psychology; Norman Gordan, psychology; Aaron Hershkowitz, psychology; Adelaide Jablonsky, education; Shelly P. Koenigsberg, educational psychology; Arthur Komar, physics; Ruth Lesser, psychology; Boris Levinson, psychology; D. J. Newman, mathematics; Harry E. Rauch, mathematics; Irvin Rock, psychology; William Spindel, chemistry; Paul C. Whitworth, education; Doxey A. Wilkerson, educational psychology.

Other institutions: Carl R. Baldwin, Hunter College; Carl Barus, Swarthmore College; Herbert Bassow, Fieldston School; Walter Bonime, New York Medical College; Richard S. Bowman, Cooper Union; Lewis Brandt, Fairleigh Dickinson University; Emile Capouya, New School for Social Research; Neil A. Chassman, Fieldston School; Carla Drije, Bank Street College of Education; Stephen Edelglass, Cooper Union; Bernard Elevitch, Fairleigh Dickinson University; Hanna Faterson, Downstate Medical Center; Jules Feiffer, Hall Syndicates; Dorothy Ferguson, Long Island City High School; Doris Z. Fleischer, New York Institute of Technology; Burton Goodman, Queensborough Community College; Paul Goodman, Institute for Policy Studies; Robert Gwathmey, Cooper Union; Eleanor Hakim, New School for Social Research; Robert Hodes; Mount Sinai Hospital; Ralph Douglas Hyslop, Union Theological Seminary; Herbert C. Jackson, Union Theological Seminary; E. Roy John, New York Medical College; Marc Karson, Kingsborough Community College; Anatole Norman Klein, Bennington College; Eric Krystall, University of Michigan; Arnold Lieber, Hillside Hospital; Donah B. Litauer, Jewish Child Care Association; William Paul Livant, University of Michigan; Edward Margolies, Staten Island Community College; Arno J. Mayer, Princeton; June Nash, Yale University; John A. Nevin, Swarthmore College; K. H. Niebyl, New School for Social Research; Hans Rademacher, University of Pennsylvania; Ronald Radosh, Kingsborough Community College; Philip Rahv, Brandeis University; Richard M. Reinitz, Wayne State University; Alfred H. Rifkin, New York Medical College; Arthur J. Samuels, Hunter College; Jane C. Schneider, University of Michigan; Peter T. Schneider, University of Michigan; Jack Stuart, Hunter College; Paul M. Sweezy, Economist; Arthur Vidich, New School for Social Research; Andrews Wanning, Bard College, John Weiss, Wayne

State University: Ken Wibecan, Harper and Rowe; H. H. Wilson, Princeton: Robert Wolfe, Harvard: J. S. Wolkenfeld, Kingsborough Community College.

Mr. Ronald Glassman, Chairman: Dr. Myriam Miedzianogora, secretary: Dr. Stanley Deutsch, co-treasurer: Miss Del Greenblatt, co-treasurer.

NEW YORK TIMES, February 19, 1965
VIETNAM: America Must Decide Between a Full-Scale War and a Negotiated Truce

A spiraling exchange of blows and counter blows in Vietnam căn lead to a major war involving the United States and China—a war nobody wants and no one can win. The present tragic conflict can only be resolved by political, not military means. Join with us in asking negotiations to end the war in Vietnam. Help mobilize public opinion to—

Stop the widening of the war—Bombing North Vietnam will not stop the conflict in South Vietnam. Widening the war only serves to invite the intervention of the North Vietnamese regular army, the U.S.S.R., and China.

Seek a cease-fire—No issues will be decided by prolonging the bloody and fratricidal conflict in South Vietnam. The fighting must be brought to a halt so that the devastated nation may recover.

Negotiate an international settlement—Now, before the war escalates into a major disaster, means must be found and found urgently to take the issue from the field of battle to the conference table.

SPONSORS

Michael Amrine,
American Psychological Association
Stringfellow Barr,
author and lecturer
John C. Bennett,
theologian.
Robert S. Browne,
Fairleigh Dickinson University
Stuart Chase,
economist, author.

O. Edmund Clubb,
East Asian Institute.
Columbia University.
Alexander H. Cohen,
producer.
Benjamin V. Cohen,
former counselor,
U.S. State Department.
Edward U. Condon,
University of Colorado.
Charles D. Coryell,
Massachusetts Institute

of Technology.
Edwin T. Dahlberg,
Crozier Theological Seminary.
William C. Davidon,
Haverford College.
Mrs. Valerie Delacorte,
New York.
Rabbi Maurice N.
Eisendrath, president,
Union of American
Hebrew Congregations

James Farmer,
national director,
CORE.

Jules Feiffer,
cartoonist.

W. H. Ferry, Center for
the Study of
Democratic Institutions.

Rabbi Leon I. Feuer,
president, Central
Conference of American
Rabbis.

D. F. Fleming,
professor emeritus,
Vanderbilt University.

Harry Emerson Fosdick,
minister emeritus,
the Riverside Church.,
N.Y.

Jerome D. Frank, M.D.,
Johns-Hopkins Medical
School.

Erich Fromm,
psychoanalyst, author.

William Gibson,
playwright.

Rabbi Roland B.
Gittlesohn, Temple
Israel, Boston.

Nathan Glazer,
University of California.

Bishop Charles F. Golden,
chairman, division of
peace and world order,
Methodist Board of
Christian Social
Concerns.

Patrick E. Gorman,
secretary-treasurer,
Amalgamated Meat
Cutters.

Rev. Dana McLean
Greeley, D.D.,
president, Unitarian
Universalist Association

Nat Hentoff, writer.

William A. Higinbotham,
Brookhaven National
Laboratory.

Hudson Hoagland,
Worcester Foundation
for Experimental
Biology.

Herbert C. Kelman,
University of Michigan.

Jerome B. King,
Williams College.

Rabbi Edward E. Klein,
Stephen Wise Free
Synagogue.

Mrs. Robert Korn,
New York.

Mrs. Philip Langner,
New York.

Mrs. Albert D. Lasker,
New York.

Chauncey D. Leake,
University of California.

Abba P. Lerner,
Michigan State
University.

S. E. Luria,
Massachusetts
Institute of
Technology.

Rollo May, New York
University.

William H. Meyer, former
Congressman, Vermont.

Mr. and Mrs. Frederick
Morgan, New York.

Hans J. Morgenthau,
director, Center for
Study of American
Foreign and Military
Policy.

Stuart Mudd, M.D.,
microbiologic research.

Lewis Mumford, writer.

Gardner Murphy, director
of research, Menninger
Foundation.

James R. Newman, editor.

John H. Niemeyer,
president, Bank State
College, N. Y.

Robert Osborn, artist.

Hildy Parks, actress.

James G. Patton,
president, National
Farmers Union.

Eleanor Perry, writer.

Frank Perry, film director.

Josephine Pomerance,
U.N. Association of the
United States of
America.

Ralph Pomerance,
architect.

Darrell Randall,
American University.

Tony Randall, actor.

A. Philip Randolph,
president, Brotherhood
of Sleeping Car Porters.

Anatol Rapoport,
University of Michigan.

John P. Roche, national
chairman, Americans
for Democratic Action.

Bruno Rossi,
Massachusetts Institute
of Technology.

John Nevin Sayre, Nyack,
N. Y.

Dore Schary, writer,

James T. Shotwell,
president emeritus,
Carnegie Endowment
for International Peace.

Jack Schubert, radiation
chemist.

Theodore Shedlovsky,
Rockefeller Institute.

J. David Singer,
University of Michigan.

B. F. Skinner, Harvard
University.

Pitirim A. Sorokin, president, American Sociology Association.

Edward J. Sparling, president emeritus, Roosevelt University.

C. Maxwell Stanley, Stanley Engineering Co.

Albert Szent-Gyorgyl, M.D., Marine Biological Laboratory, Woods Hole, Mass.

Harold Taylor, educator, author.

Howard Thurman, minister at large, Boston University.

Louis Untermeyer, author.

Mark Van Doren, writer.

Maurice B. Visscher, University of Minnesota.

Jerry Voorhis, executive director, Cooperative League of the U.S.A.

Bryant Wedge, director, Institute for the Study of National Behavior.

Bernard S. Weiss, Jenkintown, Pa.

Paul Weiss, Yale University.

Quincy Wright, University of Virginia.

Morton Deutsch, Teachers College, Columbia University.

David R. Inglis, Argonne National Laboratory.

David Livingston, president, District 65, Retail Wholesale, Department Store Union, AFL-CIO.

A. H. Parker, chairman, Old Colony Trust Co.

Frank Rosenblum, secretary, Amalgamated Clothing Workers Union, AFL-CIO.

Board of directors

Co-chairmen: Benjamin Spock, M.D.;Prof. H. Stuart Hughes.

Vice chairmen: Steve Allen; Dr. M. Stanley Livingston.

Treasurer: Lawrence S. Mayers, Jr.

Counsel: William J. Butler.

Roy Bennett;
Norman Cousins;
Helen Grahagan Douglas;
Rabbi Isidor Hoffman;
Homer A. Jack;

Walter Lear, M.D.;
Lenore G. Marshall:
Stephanie May;
Prof. Seymour Melman:
Orlie Pell;
Victor Reuther;
Robert Ryan;
Robert J. Schwartz;
Norman Thomas;
H. B. Allinsmith, New Jersey;
Robert D. Bloom, New York;
Mrs. Jeanne Coggeshall, New York;
Norman Hunt, Connecticut;
Mort Junger, New York;
Dr. John A. Lindon, California;
Frank McCallister, Illinois;
Dr. Paul Olynyk, Ohio;
Gilbert Seldes, Pennsylvania;
Snowden Taylor, New York;
Samuel Tucker, New Jersey;
Clayton Wallace, District of Columbia.

Staff: Donald Keys, Marie Runyon, Sanford Gottlieb.

STOP THE WAR, MR. PRESIDENT

We business executives believe, on moral and practical grounds, that the war in Vietnam is not in our national or world interest
Over 300 business executives—more than half Presidents or Chairmen of their companies—signed the following open letter:

The President of the United States/Washington, D. C. 20025

Dear Mr. President,

We, the undersigned American business executives, most of whom have served at least once in the Armed Services of the United States, protest against escalation of the war in Vietnam. We believe this war is against our national interest and world interest. We feel this on moral and practical grounds.

Whatever may have been the reasons for past involvement, the United States is now in a situation in which the risks we are running and the price we are paying seem to us to be out of proportion to any possible benefit that can reasonably be foreseen for the South Vietnamese, for the United States, or for the Free World.

Secretary McNamara in his speech in Montreal on May 18, 1966, said:

"But neither conscience nor sanity, itself, suggests that the United States is, should, or could be the Global Gendarme . . .

"The United States has no mandate from on high to police the world, and no inclination to do so . . . Certainly we have no character to rescue floundering regimes who have brought violence ᵣ r themselves by deliberately refusing to meet the legitimate expectations of their citizenry."

We agree with the Secretary. We believe his words are applicable to the Vietnamese situation today.

We urge you, Mr. President, to follow the suggestions of Secretary-General U Thant, which seem to us to be reasonable and constructive. They were: — stop the bombing, de-escalate military activity in South Vietnam, negotiate with all parties which are now fighting. Our opponents are not likely to be impressed by our words of wishing a peaceful settlement until we suit our actions to our words. Such actions have risk, but are less dangerous than continuing along the present course.

Respectfully,

Signers signed as individuals and NOT in their official capacities. Affiliation is given for identification only.

THOMAS B. ADAMS,
President, Adams
Security Co., Boston,
Mass.

B. AISENBERG,
President, Rosedale
Engin. Co., Bronx,
N. Y.

B. L. ALDRICH, Owner,
A & A Remodeling Co.,
Denver, Colo.

BENEDICT S. ALPER,
Brookline, Mass.

HENRY ARIAN,
Owner, Henry Arian,
San Francisco, Calif.

RALPH B. ATKINSON,
President, Ferroprint
Corp., Monterey,
California 93940

BRADFORD
BACHRACH,
President, Bachrach,
Inc., Newton, Mass.

ERWIN H. BAKER,
Adv. Sales Mgr., R. R.
Bowker Co., New
York, N. Y.

LISLE BAKER, JR.,
Exec. Vice-Pres.
Courier-Journal &
Louisville Times,
Louisville, Ky.

LESLIE L. BALASSA,
President, Barrington
Industries, Inc.,
Providence, R. I.

S. MORGAN BARBER,
President, West Credit
Corp., Pasadena, Calif.

HAROLD J.
BARNHEAD,
President, Packease-
Servease Corp.,
Buchanan, N. Y.

LEWIS W. BARTON,

President, Lewis W.
Barton Co.,
Haddonfield, N. J.

CYRIL BATH,
President, Cyril Bath
Co., Solon, Ohio

GEORGE E. BEGGS,
JR., President, Leeds &
Northrup Co.,
Philadelphia, Pa.

HAROLD K. BELL,
President, Bell Realty &
Inves. Co., Yonkers,
N. Y.

NELSON BENGSTON,
President, Bengston &
Co., Inc., N. Y., N. Y.

J. MALVERN
BENJAMIN, President,
Bionic Instruments, Inc.
Bala Cynwyd, Pa.

RAYMOND L.
BENOIT, Manager,
Hollingshead Co.,
Moorestown, N. J.

CHASE H. BENSON,
Ret., (Formerly V.P.),
Pilot Life Ins. Co.,
Greensboro, N. C.

HENRY A. BERG,
President, Direct Mail
Envelope Co., N. Y.,
N. Y.

BERNARD H.
BERGER, President,
Phila. Pension
Planning Corp.,
Jenkintown, Pa.

EDMUND C.
BERKELEY,
President, Berkeley
Enterprises,
Newtonville, Mass.

HAROLD BERLINER,
President, Berliner &
McGinnis, Inc., Nevada

City, Calif.

WILLIAM L.
BERLINGHOF, JR.,
President, Woodmont
Products, Inc.,
Huntingdon Valley, Pa.

IRVING BERMAN,
Owner, Berman Realty,
Falls Church, Va.

NAT BERNARD, Sales
Mgr. Counsel,
Bernard Associates,
Roslyn, N. Y.

ROBERT L. BERNEY,
Treasurer,
Hamburger's,
Baltimore, Md.

KARL BERNHARD,
Partner, Bernhard
Studios, N. Y., N. Y.

DANIEL J.
BERNSTEIN,
Member, New York
Stock Exch., Scarsdale,
N. Y.

PETER L.
BERNSTEIN,
President, Berstein-
Macaulay, Inc., New
York, N. Y.

HAROLD BERRY,
Vice-President,
Fisher-New Center Co.,
Detroit, Mich.

PAUL H.
BERWALD, Vice-
President, Consolidated
Retail Stores, Inc.,
St. Louis, Mo.

MORELAND N.
BLAINE, President,
Blaine Drug Co.,
Mitchell, N. Y.

ALAN H. BLANK,
Executive, Central
States Theater Corp.

Des Moines, Iowa
MAX BOLLOCK,
Milbrae, Calif.
DON A. BRENNAN,
Director Market
Development,
Automatic Retailers
of Am., Inc.,
Philadelphia, Pa.
MOYLAN E. BROWN,
Vice-President, Pioneer
Hi-Bred Corn Co., Des
Moines, Iowa
STIMSON BULLITT,
President, King
Broadcasting Co.,
Seattle, Wash.
BENJAMIN J.
BUTTENWIESER,
New York, N. Y.
RICHARD E. BYE,
Vice-President, R. R.
Bowrer Co., N. Y.
HENRY B. CABOT,
Boston, Mass.
G. CHESTON CAREY,
Chairman of Board,
Carey Machinery &
Sup. Co., Baltimore,
Md.
CHESTER F.
CARLSON,
Consultant, Xerox
Corp., Pittsford, N. Y.
SAM CARSMAN,
President, Ferndale
Cooperative, Inc.,
Ferndale, Mich.
RALPH CARSON,
President, Carson/
Roberts/Inc., Los
Angeles, Calif.
MARTIN P. CARTER,
Partner, Irving Weber
Associates, Inc., New
York, N. Y.

P. M. CASADY,
President, Casady
Engineering Associates,
Gardena, Calif.
SIMON CASADY,
Secretary, Pioneer Hi-
Bred Co., Des Moines,
Iowa
NATHAN CHALNICK,
President, Chase
Cleaners, Birmingham,
Mich.
ERNEST R. CHANES,
President, Consolidated
Water Conditioning
Corp., N. Y.
ROBERT A.
CHILDERS,
President, Childers
Manufacturing Co.,
Houston, Texas
BRONSON CLARK,
Past VP, Gilford
Instrument Lab. Co.,
Oberlin, Ohio
W. F. CODY, President,
Cody's Books, Inc.,
Berkeley, Calif.
SYLVAN COHEN,
President, Cohen's
Quality Shop,
Alexandria, Va.
WALLACE T.
COLLETT, Vice-
President, Servomation
Corp., Cincinnati, Ohio
RANDOLPH P.
COMPTON,
Investment Banker,
Scarsdale, N. Y.
WILLIAM A. CROW,
President, W. A. Crow
& Associates, Houston,
Tex.
THOMAS B.
DARLINGTON,

President, J. J. White,
Inc., Browns Mills,
N. J.
LAURENCE DAWSON,
President, Larry
Dawson Productions,
San Francisco, Calif.
HERBERT A. DAVIS,
Partner, Chase &
Davis, Baltimore, Md.
DAVID E. DIENER,
President, Diener,
Hauser, Greenthal Co.,
Inc., N. Y.
DOUGLAS DOBSON,
President, The Dobson-
Evans Co., Columbus,
Ohio
LEO A. DREY, Owner,
Pioneer Forest, St.
Louis, Mo.
MELVIN DUBIN,
President, Slant/Fin
Corp., Greenvale,
N. Y.
MARRINER S.
ECCLES, Chairman
of Board, First Security
Corp., Salt Lake City,
Utah
WILBUR E.
ECKSTEIN, President,
American Commission
Paper Co., St. Louis,
Mo.
LEE EISEMAN, JR.,
General Manager,
Arundel Distributors,
Baltimore, Md.
HENRY W. WEISNER,
President, S. A. Levyne
Co., Baltimore, Md.
NORMAN EISNER,
President, Lincoln
Graphic Arts, Inc.,
New York, N. Y.

LYNN M. ELLING, C.L.U., Gene al Agent, Lincoln National Life Ins. Co., Minneapolis, Minn.

ARMIN ELMENDORF, President, Elmendorf Research, Inc., Palo Alto, Calif.

SANDY ELSTER, Presidnet, Elster's Sales, Los Angeles, Calif.

M. R. EMRICH, Chairman of Exec. Com., International Shops, Inc., Denver, Colo.

JACOB EPSTEIN, President, Cumberland Furniture Co., New York, N. Y.

JULIUS EPSTEIN, President, Worth Electric Supply Co., Houston, Texas

MICHAEL C. ERLANGER, Chairman of Board, Erlanger Mills, Inc., Redding, Conn.

J. MORRIS EVANS, Vice-President, Philadelphia Quartz Co., Wyncote, Pa.

GEORGE J. FEIGENBAUM, President, Fillmore, Inc., Arlington, Va.

B. A. FELDMAN, M. C. Feldman & Co., New York, N. Y.

JAMES E. FENN, Vice-President, Plymouth Rubber Co., Inc., Canton. Mass.

STANLEY FEUER, Vice President, Feuer Corp., Los Angeles, Calif.

WILLIAM F. FISCHER, JR., President, Fischer Machine Co., Phila., Pa.

JOSEPH FLORET, St. Louis, Mo.

RAYMOND L. President, Fontaine & Bean, Inc., Sacramento,

LOUIS J. FRANK, President, L. J. Frank Corp., San Francisco, Calif.

WILLIAM STIX FRIEDMAN, President, Burns, Stix Friedman Co., St. Louis, Mo.

ROBERT C. GARRETSON, New York, N. Y.

OTTO E. GEPPERT, Chicago, Ill.

GEORGE C. GIBSON, JR., Associate, VanZandt & Emrich, Inc., Louisville, Ky.

SAUL R. GILFORD, President, Gilford Instrument Lab. Co., Oberlin, Ohio

MORT GLANKOFF, New York, N. Y.

MORRIS GLEICHER, President, M. G. Advertising Co., Inc., Detroit, Mich.

DAVID A. GOLDBERG, Owner,

David A. Goldberg & Son, New Haven, Conn.

JACK GOMPERTS, President, Calagrex, Inc., San Francisco, Calif.

ARNOLD GOODMAN, Owner, Prop. Management-Insurance, Racine, Wisc.

JACK GORDON, President, Washington Fed. Savings & Loan Assoc., Miami Beach, Fla.

HARRY GORSKY, Vice-President, Manfred Hunter & Co., Inc., San Francisco, Calif.

S. NORMAN GOURSE, President, Gorsart Co., Inc., New York, N. Y.

HAROLD GREENE, President, Potomac Employment Agency, Inc., Arlington, Va.

MYRON J. GREENFIELD, President, Tom Fields, Ltd., Northvale, N. J.

JEROME GROSSMAN, President, Massachusetts Envelope Co., Boston, Mass.

G. STANLEY GRUMMAN, President, G. S. Grumman & Associates, Inc., Boston, Mass.

RICHARD HABER, Berkeley, Calif.

T. WALTER HARDY,

JR., President, The
Hardy Salt Co., St.
Louis, Mo.

WILLIAM H.
HARLAN, JR.,
President, Manchester
Bank, St. Louis, Mo.

SIDNEY HARMAN,
President, Jervis Corp.,
Hicksville, N. Y.

THOMAS B. HARVEY,
President, Thomas B.
Harvey Leather Co.,
Camden, N. J.

J. V. HAWLEY, JR.,
Vice-President, Katz
Newspaper Sales, San
Francisco, Calif.

TIMOTHY HAWORTH,
General Partner,
Edward N. Hay &
Associates,
Philadelphia, Pa.

CLARENCE E.
HELLER, Partner,
Schwabacher & Co.,
San Francisco, Calif.

AL HENSELYN, Vice-
President, Processed
Foods, Inc., San
Francisco, Calif.

DAVID B. HILL, JR.,
President, David B.
Hill & Assoc., Inc.,
Penndel, Pa.

EZRA HIMELFARB,
Partner, Himelfarb
Bros., Baltimore, Md.

IRA HIRSCHMANN,
President, Ira
Hirschmann Co., New
York, N. Y.

HAROLD K.
HOCHSCHILD, New
York, N. Y.

SIDNEY
HOLLANDER, SR.,
Past Pres., Md.
Pharmaceutical Co.,
Baltimore, Md.

SIDNEY
HOLLANDER, JR.,
Partner, Sidney
Hollander Associates,
Baltimore, Md.

IRVING
HOLLINGSHEAD,
Owner, Hollingshead
Co., Moorestown, N. J.

PROCTOR W.
HOUGHTON,
President, Philip A.
Houghton, Inc., Boston,
Mass.

RAYMOND W. ICKES,
President Lines, Ltd.,
San Francisco, Calif.

PHILIP ISELY,
Owner & Manager, The
Builders Foundation,
Denver, Colo.

EDWARD J. JAHODA,
President, Andrews
Paper & Chemical Co.,
Pt. Washington, N. Y.

FRANK JAROS,
President, Allied
Compositions
Company, Maspeth,
New York

THEODORE JONES,
President, WCRB-
WCRQ-WCRX,
Boston, Mass.

FREDERICK A.
KAUFMANN,
President, Certified
Business Forms, Inc.,
Newton, Mass.

HAROLD A.
KAUFMAN, Vice-

President, Kaufman
Luggage Co., Hartford,
Conn.

EDWARD M.
KEATING, President,
Ramparts Magazine,
Inc., San Francisco,
Calif.

PAUL J. KERMIET,
Owner, Square Dance
Record Roundup,
Denver, Colorado

NOLAN K.
KERSCHNER,
President, Kerschner
Construction Co.,
Norwalk, Conn.

SAMUEL KIPNIS,
Dupont Plaza Hotel,
Miami, Fla.

SAMUEL E. KIRK,
Retired Builder, West
Grove, Pa.

EDWARD E. KLEIN,
President, Edward E.
Klein, Assoc.,
Pleasantville, N. Y.

ALAN E.
KLIGERMAN,
Senior Partner, Sugar-
Lo Co., Atlantic City,
N. J.

ARTHUR S. KLING,
Chairman of Board,
Kling Co., Louisville,
Ky.

D. B. KRIMGOLD,
Bethesda, Md.

EDWARD KRISCHER,
President, Hospi-Video
Services, Inc., Los
Angeles, Calif.

SHEPARD KURNIT,
President, Delehanty,
Kurnit & Geller, Inc.,
N. Y.

EDWARD LAMB,
Chairman & President,
Lamb Enterprises, Inc.,
Toledo, Ohio

WILLIAM F.
LATHOM,
Washington, D. C.

IRVING F. LAUCKS,
Past President, I. F.
Laucks, Inc., Seattle,
Wash.

DONALD R.
LEFEVER,
Merchandiser,
Greenbelt Consumer
Serv. Co., Inc.,
Beltsville, Md.

GEORGE LEOPOLD,
President, Leopold
Homes, Incorporated,
Meadowbrook,
Pennsylvania

HERBERT M.
LEVENGARD,
Owner, District
Housing Co.,
Washington, D. C.

JACK L. LEVIN,
Partner, Shecter &
Levin Adv. Agency,
Baltimore, Md.

LESTER S. LEVY,
Chairman Exec. Com.
(Ret.), Men's Hats,
Inc., Baltimore, Md.

A. BARTON LEWIS,
President, A. Barton
Lewis Co., Inc.,
Philadelphia, Pa.

NORMAN S. LEZIN,
President, A. K. Salz
Tannery, Inc., Santa
Cruz, Calif.

ERNEST N. LONG,
Gen'l. Supt., DePue
Warehouse Co., San

Francisco, Calif.

WILLIAM A.
LONGSHORE,
Partner, I. Reifsnyder
Sons Co., Inc.,
Philadelphia, Pa.

GRAEME LORIMER,
Director, Girard Trust
Bank, Philadelphia,
Pa.

EMANUEL D.
LOWENSTEIN,
Philadelphia, Pa.

ALBERT LUTZKY,
President, Martha
Washington Laundry,
Inc., New York, N. Y.

PHILIP MACHT,
Construction Co.,
Baltimore, Md.

DAVID B.
MACKENZIE,
Manager, Geology
Dept., Denver
Reasearch Center,
Marathon Oil Co.,
Littleton, Colo.

MARVIN L.
MADESON,
Treasurer, I T T Aetna
Finance Co., St. Louis,
Mo.

HERBERT D.
MAGIDSON,
President, Metric
Products, Inc., Culver
City, Calif.

J. J. MALLON,
President, Midwest
Mutual Insurance Co.,
Des Moines, Iowa

LAFAYETTE MARSH,
Owner, John P. Marsh
Co., Chicago, Ill.

LOUIS R. MATLACK,
President, Geo. D.

Wetherill Co., Inc.,
Philadelphia, Pa.

WILLIAM MAZER,
President, Hudson Pulp
Paper Corp., New
York, N. Y.

JOSEPH E.
McDOWELL,
President, Servomation
Corp., New York,
N. Y.

GEORGE R. McCOY,
C.L.U., McCoy &
Harper, Chicago, Ill.

MALCOLM
McWHORTER,
Vice-President, Vidar
Corp., Mt. View, Calif.

PAUL M. MERNER,
President, Merner
Lumber Co., Palo Alto,
Calif.

SIDNEY S. METZNER,
Vice-President,
Maryland Metals, Inc.,
Hagerstown, Md.

SIDNEY MEYER,
President, Sidney
Meyer Advertising,
Los Angeles, Calif.

J. A. MIGEL,
Charlestown, Rhode
Island

MORRIS MILGRAM,
President, Planned
Communities, Inc.,
Philadelphia, Pa.

LEON MILLER,
President, United
Bindery, Inc., New
York, N. Y.

SIDNEY M. MILLER,
President, L. V.
Myles, Inc., New
York, N. Y.

SOL MILLMAN,

Owner, National Monogram Co., Detroit, Mich.

HARRY E. MILTON (Ret.), Former Pres., Milton Savex Co., St. Louis, Mo.

MAURICE F. MOGULESCU, President, Designs For Business, Inc., New York, N. Y.

IRWIN MOHR, Vice-President, Witte Hardware Co., St. Louis, Mo.

PETER B. MOORE, President, LDJ, Inc., Philadelphia, Pa.

DAVID A. MOREINES, President, Triplex Machine Tool Corp., Long Island City, N. Y.

ERNEST MORGAN, President, Antioch Book Plate Co., Yellow Springs, Ohio

MARLIN W. MORGAN, Vice-President, Baltimore Life Ins. Co., Baltimore, Md.

ELLIOTT MORGANSTERN, Secretary, Nor Jay Co., Cleveland, Ohio

WILLIAM MORRIS, Malibu, Calif.

JACOB M. MOSES, General Counsel, Sun Life Ins. Co., of Am., Baltimore, Md.

MORRIS J. MOSKOVITZ, President, Ched-MJM Supermarkets,

Inc., New York, N. Y.

HOWARD H. MURPHY, Bus. Mgr., Afro-American, Baltimore, Md.

HERBERT L. MYERS, Presidnet, Climax Dental Supply Co. Philadelphia, Pa.

JACK NADEL, President, Jack Nadel, Inc., Culver City, Calif.

L. MELVIN NELSON, Hotel Owner, North Shore Hotel Co., Evanston, Ill.

NAT NEWMARK, President, J. Newmark & Sons, Inc., New York, N. Y.

HENRY E. NILES, Chairman of Board, Baltimore Life Ins. Co., Baltimore, Md.

MARTIN ORAM, President, Cardwright, Inc., Rockville, Md.

EARL D. OSBORN, Business Exec., New York, N. Y.

R. WILSON OSTER, Financial Vice-Pres., U. S. Fidelity & Guaranty Co., Baltimore, Md.

SENIEL OSTROW President, Sealy Mattress Co. of S. Calif., Los Angeles, Calif.

JOHN B. PAINE, JR., Trustee, Boston, Mass.

STANLEY I. PANITZ, President, Stanley I. Panitz, Inc., Baltimore, Md.

AUGUSTIN H. PARKER, chairman of the Board, Old Colony Trust Co., Boston, Mass.

WILLIAM A. PASSANO, President, Williams & Wilkins Co., Baltimore, Md.

HARRY J. PATTON, Owner, Patton Photography, Baltimore, Md.

SEYMOUR PECARSKY, President, Decatur Drugs, Inc., Washington, D. C.

GEORGE T. PECK, New York, N. Y.

JOHN BRITTAIN PENDERGAST, JR., Vice-Pres., Southern Cross Industries, Inc., Atlanta, Ga.

MILES PENNYBACKER, President, Voltarc Tubes, Inc., Fairfield, Conn.

ROBERT B. PERRY, President, Washington Trust Co., Westerly, R. I.

GERARD PIEL, President, Scientific American, Inc., New York, N. Y.

STANLEY K. PLATT, President, Platt, Tschudy & Co., Minneapolis, Minn.

WILLIAM M. PLYMAT, President, Preferred Risk Mutual Insur. Co., Des

Moines, Iowa

FRANK POLLATSEK,
Exec. Director,
Neighborhood Cleaners
Assoc., New York,
N. Y.

DONALD S. PRATT,
Owner, Donald S. Pratt
Greenhouses,
Avondale, Pa.

ROLF QUARCK,
President, Chemtan
Co., Inc., Exeter, N. H.

WILLIAM G. RAOUL,
President, Cavalier
Corp., Chattanooga,
Tenn.

EARL S. RAPPAPORT,
C.L.U., The Rappaport
Agency, Chicago, Ill.

EUGENE
RAPPAPORT(C.L.U.,
The Rappaport Agency,
Chicago, Ill.

RODNEY REHFELD,
Baltimore, Md.

STUART REINER,
President, Teca Corp.,
White Plains, N. Y.

JOSEPH REMPELL,
President, Grace
Cleaners, Brooklyn,
N. Y.

DELBERT E.
REPLOGIE, Chairman
of Board, Molecular
Dielectrics, Inc.,
Clifton, N. J.

L. VICTOR RICHES,
President, Riches
Research, Inc., Los
Altos, Calif.

LEON P. RIED,
President, Ried Heat &
Home Improve. Co.,
Baltimore, Md.

JACK ROBERTS,
Exec. Vice-President,
Carson/Roberts/Inc.,
Los Angeles, Calif.

DUDLEY ROBINSON,
President, A. R. Barnes
& Co., Skokie, Ill.

RALPH A. ROSE,
Vice-President,
Turnpike Press,
Annandale, Va.

JAMES M.
ROSENBLUM,
Louisville, Ky.

ROBERT M.
ROTHAUSER,
President, East House
Enterprises, Inc., N. Y.

FLORENCE
ROTHAUSER,
Vice-President, East
House Enterprises,
Inc., N. Y.

JOEL ROTHMAN,
Secretary-Treasurer,
Advance Printing Co.,
Inc., N. Y.

JOSEPH ROUS,
President, R. J. Rous,
Inc., Chicago, Ill.

ROBERT H. ROWES,
Vice-President. League
Life Insurance Co.,
Detroit, Mich.

MEL RUBIN, Chairman
of Board Shaller-Rubin
Co., Inc., New York,
N. Y.

RICHARD A.
RUSSELL, President,
Northeast Leasing, Inc.,
Bostin, Mass.

R. D. RUSSELL, Assoc.
Research Dir.,
Marathon Oil Company,
Littleton, Colo.

ARNOLD SABAROFF,
Vice-President, Max
Sabaroff & Co., Inc.,
Detroit, Mich.

JOHN SAEMANN,
San Francisco, Calif.

ERWIN A. SALK,
President, Salk, Ward
& Salk, Inc., Chicago,
Ill.

F. PORTER SARGENT,
Owner, Porter Sargent
Pub., Boston, Mass.

HRAND SAXENIAN,
President, Hrand
Saxenian Associates,
Concord, Mass.

EZRA L. SCHACHT,
President, Lightguard
Elec. Manuf. Co.,
Houston, Texas

EDWARD J.
SCHADLER, Partner,
American Piano Supply
Co., Clifton, N. J.

PHILIP J. SCHARPER,
Vice-President, Sheed
& Ward, Inc., N. Y.,
N. Y.

JULIUS SCHATSKY,
President, J. S. Realty,
Inc., Baltimore, Md.

MARTIN L.
SCHEINER, President,
Electronics for
Medicine, Inc., White
Plains, N. Y.

JESS G.
SCHIFFMANN,
President, Atlantic
Furniture Products Co.
Baltimore, Md.

HARRY S. SCOTT,
JR., President, Harry
S. Scott, Inc.,
Baltimore, Md.

WILLIAM SEITZ,
Director, N. Y. School
of Drycleaning, N. Y.,
N. Y.
JOSEPH J. SELDIN,
President, Blythe-
Pennington, Ltd., New
York, N. Y.
JOHN W. SEYBOLD,
President, Rocappi,
Inc., Swarthmore, Pa.
MILTON G. SHALLER,
New York, N. Y.
JOS. R. SHANNON,
Chm. of Board,
Shannon & Co., Houston,
Texas
MYRON E. SHARPE,
President, International
Arts & Science Press,
White Plains, N. Y.
T. KITE SHARPLESS,
Vice-President,
Marketing, Technitrol,
Inc., Philadelphia, Pa.
JACK S. SHERMAN,
President, Allied
Trailers Sales, Inc.,
Brandywine, Md.
MALCOLM
SHERMAN, President,
Mal Sherman, Inc.,
Baltimore, Md.
ROBERT SIEGEL,
President, Arrow
Photo Service, Inc.,
New York, N. Y.
DR. B. A. SILARD, Dir.
& Ret. Pres., Photovolt
Corp., New York,
N. Y.
HAROLD
SILVERMAN,
President, Maid-Rite
Novelty Corp., N. Y.,
N. Y.

SOL SILVERMAN,
President, Silbro
Products Corp., Long
Island City, N. Y.
CHARLES G.
SIMPSON, Gen'l.
Mgr., Phila. Gas
Works, Phila, Pa.
SIDNEY SLAYTON,
President, Slayton
Cleaners, New York,
N. Y.
PETER SMITH, Owner,
Peter Smith, Publishers,
Magnolia, Mass.
N. L. SMOKLER,
Builder, Ferndale,
Mich.
ROBERT J. SNYDER,
Lyntex Corp., Rye,
N. Y.
MARTIN SOLOW,
President, Solow-
Wexton, Inc., N. Y.,
N. Y.
GEORGE C. SPARKS,
President, Sparks
Corp., Harleysville, Pa.
WILLIAM E.
SPAULDING, Former
Chm. of Board,
Houghton-Mifflin Co.,
Boston, Mass.
GEORGE SPENCER,
President, Observer
Publishing Co.,
Washington, D.C.
WALTER A. SPIRO,
President, Lavenson
Bureau of Adv.,
Philadelphia, Pa.
ARMAND C.
STALNAKER, St.
Louis, Mo.
C. MAXWELL
STANELY, President,

Stanley Consultants,
Inc., Muscatine, Iowa
DALE I. STEELE,
President, National
Instrument Lab., Inc.,
Rockville, Md.
ROBERT A.
STEINBERG,
Secretary-Treasurer,
Equip. Leasing Corp. of
Am., Inc., Baltimore,
Md.
ARTHUR L. STERN,
Owner, Arthur L. Stern
Co., South Orange, N. J.
ROBERT D. STERN,
Exec. Vice-Pres.,
U. S. Shoe Corp.,
Cincinnati, Ohio
D. IAN THIERMANN,
President, Johnson &
Thiermann, Inc., Los
Angeles, Calif.
LEE B. THOMAS, JR.,
President, Vermont
American Corp.,
Louisville, Ky.
DONALD A.
President, Arthur
Thompson & Co.,
Baltimore, Md.
SUSUMU TOGASAKI,
President, Mutual
Supply Co., San
Francisco, Calif.
SIDNEY H.
TOMLINSON, JR.,
Vice-Pres., Tomlinson
Furniture Co., High
Point, N.C.
RICHARD TRAVIS,
Partner, Travis Oil Co.,
Los Angeles, Calif.
HARDY W.
TROLANDER,
President, Yellow

Springs Instrument Co., Yellow Springs, Ohio

SIDNEY UNGER, President, Kord Manuf. Co., Bronx, N. Y.

A. J. UNION, Sec. & Vice-Pres., Union Bros., Inc., Baltimore, Md.

ROBERT VANDERBEEK, President, League Life Ins. Co., Detroit, Mich.

JOHN L. VOLLBRECHT, Owner, John L. Vollbrecht Co., Chicago, Ill.

J. H. VOORSANGER, San Francisco, Calif.

ROBERT B. WALLACE, President, Wallace By-Cross Hatcheries, Inc., Doylestown, Pa.

IRA D. WALLACH, President, Gottesman & Co., New York, N. Y.

ARTHUR W. WANG, President, Hill & Wang, New York, N. Y.

ROBERT M. WAY,

Owner-Manager, Robert M. Way Greenhouse, Kennett Sq., Pa.

IRVING WEBER, President, Irving Weber Associates, N.Y., N.Y.

R. WEHMEYER, General Agent, Lincoln Nat. Life Insur. Co., Denver, Colo.

HERMAN S. WEINSTEIN, Owner, Weinstein Educational Services, Washington, D.C.

EUGENE J. WEISBERG, Exec. Vice-Pres., Denver, Colo.

BERNARD S. WEISS, Controller, Gimbel Bros., Philadelphia, Pa.

MILTON M. WEISS, Executive, New Rochelle, N. Y.

MAX WENDER, President, Wetmore & Co., Houston, Tex.

BARCLAY WHITE, Chairman, Barclay White Co., Philadelphia, Pa.

THEODORE

WILENTZ, Treasurer, Corinth Brooks, Inc., New York, N. Y.

HAROLD WILLENS, President, Factory Equip. & Supply Co., Los Angeles, Calif.

HENRY J. WINEBERG, Evanston, Ill.

ELLIS A. WOHLNER, Staff Actuary, League Life Insur. Co., Detroit, Mich.

THOMAS YOSELOFF, President, A. S. Barnes & Co., Inc., Cranbury, N. J.

FLOYD YUDELSON, Los Angeles, Calif.

LOUIS ZEMEL, Treasurer, Powder Hill Ski Area Cabana Club, Middlefield, Conn.

ARTHUR L. ZIGAS, Partner, Wald & Zigas, New York, New York

WALLACE ZUCKERMANN, President, Zuckermann Harpsichords, Inc., New York, N. Y.

JOINT U.S.-SOUTH VIETNAM STATEMENT ON ATTACKS ON NORTH VIETNAM, SAIGON, FEBRUARY 11, 1965[1]

Since February 8, there have been continued acts of aggression by the Communist Viet Cong under the direction and with the support of the Hanoi regime against the Vietnamese people and installations in

---

[1]Department of State *Bulletin*, Mar. 1, 1965, p. 291.

South Vietnam and against their American advisers. For example, these aggressive acts have included the following:

The mining of 13 bridges and 7 separate acts of sabotage against the railroads resulting in death and injury to 18 Vietnamese civilians and 2 escort soldiers in addition to the material damage;

Attacks on hamlets and convoys resulting in death or injury to many Vietnamese civilians and the kidnapping of others in addition to substantial military casualties;

The vicious attack and related actions involving the American enlisted men's quarters at Qui Nhon by Viet Cong terrorist demolition teams resulting in 12 known Vietnamese and American dead, and including more than 40 others wounded and missing. Many of the latter must be supposed dead.

In response to these continued attacks by the Communists, South Vietnamese and American air elements today carried out air operations against selected military installations in the southern part of North Vietnam which have been used by the Hanoi regime for training and support of the Viet Cong personnel carrying out these acts.

AGGRESSION FROM THE NORTH: State Department Report, February 27, 1965[1]

INTRODUCTION

South Vietnam is fighting for its life against a brutal campaign of terror and armed attack inspired, directed, supplied, and controlled by the Communist regime in Hanoi. This flagrant aggression has been going on for years, but recently the pace has quickened and the threat has now become acute.

The war in Vietnam is a new kind of war, a fact as yet poorly understood in most parts of the world. Much of the confusion that prevails in the thinking of many people, and even many governments, stems from this basic misunderstanding. For in Vietnam a totally new brand of aggression has been loosed against an independent people who want to make their own way in peace and freedom.

---

[1]Department of State *Bulletin,* Mar. 22, 965, pp. 404-425. (Appendices, pictures, and maps omitted.)

Vietnam is *not* another Greece, where indigenous guerrilla forces used friendly neighboring territory as a sanctuary.

Vietnam is *not* another Malaya, where Communist guerrillas were, for the most part, physically distinguishable from the peaceful majority they sought to control.

Vietnam is *not* another Philippines, where Communist guerrillas were physically separated from the source of their moral and physical support.

Above all, the war in Vietnam is *not* a spontaneous and local rebellion against the established government.

There are elements in the Communist program of conquest directed against South Vietnam common to each of the previous areas of aggression and subversion. But there is one fundamental difference. In Vietnam a Communist government has set out deliberately to conquer a sovereign people in a neighboring state. And to achieve its end, it has used every resource of its own government to carry out its carefully planned program of concealed aggression. North Vietnam's commitment to seize control of the South is no less total than was the commitment of the regime in North Korea in 1950. But knowing the consequences of the latter's undisguised attack, the planners in Hanoi have tried desperately to conceal their hand. They have failed and their aggression is as real as that of an invading army.

This report is a summary of the massive evidence of North Vietnamese aggression obtained by the Government of South Vietnam. This evidence has been jointly analyzed by South Vietnamese and American experts.

The evidence shows that the hard core of the Communist forces attacking South Vietnam were trained in the North and ordered into the South by Hanoi. It shows that the key leadership of the Viet Cong (VC), the officers and much of the cadre, many of the technicians, political organizers, and propagandists have come from the North and operate under Hanoi's direction. It shows that the training of essential military personnel and their infiltration into the South is directed by the Military High Command in Hanoi. (See section I.)

The evidence shows that many of the weapons and much of the ammunition and other supplies used by the Viet Cong have been sent into South Vietnam from Hanoi. In recent months new types of weapons have been introduced in the VC army, for which all ammunition must come from outside sources. Communist China and other Communist states have been the prime suppliers of these weapons and ammunition, and they have been channeled primarily through North Vietnam. (See section II.)

The directing force behind the effort to conquer South Vietnam is the Communist Party in the North, the Lao Dong (Workers) Party. As in every Communist state, the party is an integral part of the regime itself. North Vietnamese officials have expressed their firm determination to absorb South Vietnam into the Communist world. (See section III.)

Through its Central Committee, which controls the government of the North, the Lao Dong Party directs the total political and military effort of the Viet Cong. The Military High Command in the North trains the military men and sends them into South Vietnam. The Central Research Agency, North Vietnam's central intelligence organization, directs the elaborate espionage and subversion effort. The extensive political-military organization in the North which directs the Viet Cong war effort is described in section IV.

Under Hanoi's overall direction the Communists have established an extensive machine for carrying on the war within South Vietnam. The focal point is the Central Office for South Vietnam with its political and military subsections and others specialized agencies. A subordinate part of this Central Office is the Liberation Front for South Vietnam. The front was formed at Hanoi's order in 1960. Its principal function is to influence opinion abroad and to create the false impression that the aggression in South Vietnam is an indigenous rebellion against the established government. (See section IV).

For more than 10 years the people and the Government of South Vietnam, exercising the inherent right of self-defense, have fought back against these efforts to extend Communist power south across the 17th parallel. The United States has responded to the appeals of the Government of the Republic of Vietnam for help in this defense of the freedom and independence of its land and its people.

In 1961 the Department of State issued a report called *A Threat to the Peace*. It described North Vietnam's program to seize South Vietnam. The evidence in that report had been presented by the Government of the Republic of Vietnam to the International Control Commission (I.C.C.). A special report by the I.C.C. in June 1962 upheld the validity of that evidence. The Commission held that there was "sufficient evidence to show beyond reasonable doubt" that North Vietnam had sent arms and men into South Vietnam to carry out subversion with the aim of overthrowing the legal Government there. The I.C.C. found the authorities in Hanoi in specific violation of four provisions of the Geneva accords of 1954.

Since then, new and even more impressive evidence of Hanoi's aggression has accumulated. The Government of the United States believes that evidence should be presented to its own citizens and to the world. It is important for free men to know what has been happening in Vietnam, and how, and why. That is the purpose of this report.

I.   HANOI SUPPLIES THE KEY PERSONNEL FOR THE ARMED AGGRESSION AGAINST SOUTH VIETNAM

The hard core of the Communist forces attacking South Vietnam are men trained in North Vietnam. They are ordered into the South and remain under the military discipline of the Military High Command in Hanoi. Special training camps operated by the North Vietnamese army give political and military training to the infiltrators. Increasingly the forces sent into the South are native North Vietnamese who have never seen South Vietnam. A special infiltration unit, the 70th Transportation Group, is responsible for moving men from North Vietnam into the South via infiltration trails through Laos. Another special unit, the maritime infiltration group, sends weapons and supplies and agents by sea into the South.

The infiltration rate has been increasing. From 1959 to 1960, when Hanoi was establishing its infiltration pipeline, at least 1,800 men, and possibly 2,700 more, moved into South Vietnam from the North. The flow increased to a minimum of 3,700 in 1961 and at least 5,400 in 1962. There was a modest decrease in 1963 to 4,200 confirmed infiltrators, though later evidence is likely to raise this figure.

For 1964 the evidence is still incomplete. However, it already shows that a minimum of 4,400 infiltrators entered the South, and it is estimated more than 3,000 others were sent in.

There is usually a time lag between the entry of infiltrating troops and the discovery of clear evidence they have entered. This fact, plus collateral evidence of increased use of the infiltration routes, suggests strongly that 1964 was probably the year of greatest infiltration so far.

Thus, since 1959, nearly 20,000 VC officers, soldiers, and technicians are known to have entered South Vietnam under orders from Hanoi. Additional information indicates that an estimated 17,000 more infiltrators were dispatched to the South by the regime in Hanoi during the past 6 years. It can reasonably be assumed that still other infiltration groups have entered the South for which there is no evidence yet available.

To some the level of infiltration from the North may seem modest in comparison with the total size of the Armed Forces of the Republic of Vietnam. But one-for-one calculations are totally misleading in the kind of warfare going on in Vietnam. First, a high proportion of infiltrators from the North are well-trained officers, cadres, and specialists. Second, it has long been realized that in guerrilla combat the burdens of defense are vastly heavier than those of attack. In Malaya, the Philippines, and elsewhere a ratio of at least 10-to-1 in favor of the forces of order was required to meet successfully the threat of the guerrillas' hit-and-run tactics.

In the calculus of guerrilla warfare the scale of North Vietnamese infitration into the South takes on a very different meaning. For the infiltration of 5,000 guerrilla fighters in a given year is the equivalent of marching perhaps 50,000 regular troops across the border, in terms of the burden placed on the defenders.

Above all, the number of proved and probable infiltrators from the North should be seen in relation to the size of VC forces. It is now estimated that the Viet Cong number approximately 35,000 so-called hard-core forces, and another 60,000-80,000 local forces. It is thus apparent that infiltrators from the North—allowing for casualties— make up the majority of the so-called hard-core Viet Cong. Personnel from the North, in short, are now and have always been the backbone of the entire VC operation.

It is true that many of the lower level elements of the VC forces are recruited within South Vietnam. However, the thousands of reported cases of VC kidnappings and terrorism make it abundantly clear that threats and other pressures by the Viet Cong play a major part in such recruitment.

A. THE INFILTRATION PROCESS

The infiltration routes supply hard-core units with most of their officers and noncommissioned personnel. This source helps fill the gaps left by battle casualties, illness, and defection and insures continued control by Hanoi. Also, as the nature of the conflict has changed, North Vietnam has supplied the Viet Cong with technical specialists via the infiltration routes. These have included men trained in armor and ordnance, antiaircraft, and communications as well as medical corpsmen and transport experts.

There is no single infiltration route from the North to South Vietnam. But by far the biggest percentage of infiltrators follow the same general course. The principal training center for North Vietnamese army men assigned to join the Viet Cong has been at Xuan Mai near Hanoi. Recently captured Viet Cong have also reported an infiltration training camp at Thanh Hoa. After completion of their training course—which involves political and propaganda work as well as military subjects—infiltrating units are moved to Vinh on the east coast. Many have made stopovers at a staging area in Dong Hoi where additional training is conducted. From there they go by truck to the Laos border.

Then, usually after several days' rest infiltrators move southward through Laos. Generally, they move along the Laos-South Vietnam border. Responsibility for infiltration from North Vietnam through Laos belongs to the 70th Transportation Group of the North Vietnamese army. After a time the infiltration groups turn eastward entering South Vietnam in Quang Nam, Quang Tri, Thua Thien, Kontum, or another of the border provinces.

The Communists have established regular lanes for infiltration with way-stations established about 1 day's march apart. The way-stations are equipped to quarter and feed the Viet Cong passing through. Infiltrators who suffer from malaria or other illnesses stay at the stations until they recover sufficiently to join another passing group moving south.

The map on page 409 shows the infiltration route from North Vietnam to the South followed by VC Sgt. Huynh Van Tay and a group of North Vietnamese army officers and men in September 1963. Tay was captured during an engagement in Chuong Thien Province in April 1964.

Local guides lead the infiltration groups along the secret trails. Generally they direct the infiltrators from halfway between two stations, through their own base station, and on halfway to the next supply base. Thus the guides are kept in ignorance of all but their own way-stations. Only group leaders are permitted to talk with the guides in order to preserve maximum security. The men are discouraged from asking where they are or where they are going.

The same system of trails and guides used along the Laos infiltration routes is used within South Vietnam itself. Viet Cong infiltrators may report directly to a reassignment center in the highlands as soon as they enter South Vietnam. But in the past year or more some groups have moved down trails in South Vietnam to provinces along the Cambodian border and near Saigon before receiving their unit assignment. Within South Vietnam infiltration and supplies are handled by VC units such as the Nam Son Transportation Group.

At the Laos border crossing point infiltrators are re-equipped. Their North Vietnamese army uniforms must be turned in. They must give up all personal papers, letters, notebooks, and photographs that might be incriminating. Document control over the infiltrators has been tightened considerably over the past 2 years. A number of Vietnamese infiltrators have told of being fitted out with Laos "neutralist" uniforms for their passage through Laos.

Infiltration groups are usually issued a set of black civilian pajama-like clothes, two unmarked uniforms, rubber sandals, a sweater, a hammock, mosquito netting, and waterproof sheeting. They carry a 3-5 day supply of food. A packet of medicines and bandages is usually provided.

The size of infiltration groups varies widely. Prisoners have mentioned units as small as 5 men and as large as 500. Generally the groups number 40-50. When they arrive in South Vietnam these groups are usually split up and assigned to various VC units as replacements, although some have remained intact . . .

C. INFILTRATION OF NATIVE NORTH VIETNAMESE

The Communist authorities in Hanoi are now assigning native North Vietnamese in increasing numbers to join the VC forces in South Vietnam. Heretofore, those in charge of the infiltration effort have sought to fill their quotas with soldiers and others born in the South. The 90,000 troops that moved from South Vietnam to the North when the Geneva accords ended the Indochina War have provided an invaluable reservoir for this purpose. Now, apparently, that source is running dry. The casualty rate has been high, and obviously many of those who were in fighting trim 10 years ago are no longer up to the rigors of guerrilla war.

In any case, reports of infiltration by native North Vietnamese in significant numbers have been received in Saigon for several months. It is estimated that as many as 75 percent of the more than 4,400 Viet Cong who are known to have entered the South in the first 8 months of 1964 were natives of North Vietnam . . .

D. INFILTRATION OF VIET CONG AGENTS

No effort to subvert another nation as elaborate as that being conducted by the Ho Chi Minh regime against South Vietnam can succeed without an intelligence-gathering organization. Recognizing this, the authorities in Hanoi have developed an extensive espionage effort. An essential part of that effort is the regular assignment of secret agents from the North to South Vietnam.

The heart of the VC intelligence organization is the Central Research Agency in Hanoi (see section IV, C). Communist agents are regularly dispatched from North Vietnam, sometimes for brief assignments but often for long periods. Many of these agents move into South Vietnam along the infiltration trails through Laos; others are carried by boats along the coasts and landed at pre-arranged sites. A special maritime infiltration group has been developed in North Vietnam, with its operations centered in Ha Tinh and Quang Binh Provinces just north of the 17th parallel . . .

II. HANOI SUPPLIES WEAPONS, AMMUNITION, AND OTHER WAR MATERIEL TO ITS FORCES IN THE SOUTH

When Hanoi launched the VC campaign of terror, violence, and subversion in earnest in 1959, the Communist forces relied mainly on stocks of weapons and ammunition left over from the war against the French. Supplies sent in from North Vietnam came largely from the same source. As the military campaign progressed, the Viet Cong depended heavily on weapons captured from the Armed Forces in South Vietnam. This remains an important source of weapons and ammunition for the Viet Cong. But as the pace of the war has quickened, requirements for up-to-date arms and special types of weapons have risen to a point where the Viet Cong cannot rely on captured stocks. Hanoi has undertaken a program to re-equip its forces in the South with Communist-produced weapons.

Large and increasing quantities of military supplies are entering South Vietnam from outside the country. The principal supply point is North Vietnam, which provides a convenient channel for materiel that originates in Communist China and other Communist countries.

An increasing number of weapons from external Communist sources have been seized in the South. These include such weapons as 57-mm. and 75-mm. recoilless rifles, dual-purpose machineguns, rocket launchers, large mortars, and antitank mines.

A new group of Chinese Communist-manufactured weapons has recently appeared in VC hands. These include the 7.62 semi-automatic carbine, 7.62 light machinegun, and the 7.62 assault rifle. These weapons and ammunition for them, manufactured in Communist China in 1962, were first captured in December 1964 in Chuong Thien Province. Similar weapons have since been seized in each of the four Corps areas of South Vietnam. Also captured have been Chinese Communist antitank grenade launchers and ammunition made in China in 1963.

One captured Viet Cong told his captors that his entire company had been supplied recently with modern Chinese weapons. The re-equipping of VC units with a type of weapons that require ammunition and parts from outside South Vietnam indicates the growing confidence of the authorities in Hanoi in the effectiveness of their supply lines into the South.

Incontrovertible evidence of Hanoi's elaborate program to supply its forces in the South with weapons, ammunition, and other supplies has accumulated over the years. Dramatic new proof was exposed just as this report was being completed.

On February 16, 1965, an American helicopter pilot flying along the South Vietnamese coast sighted a suspicious vessel. It was a cargo ship of an estimated 100-ton capacity, carefully camouflaged and moored just offshore along the coast of Phu Yen Province. Fighter planes that approached the vessel met machinegun fire from guns on the deck of the ship and from the shore as well. A Vietnamese Air Force strike was launched against the vessel, and Vietnamese Government troops moved into the area. They seized the ship after a bitter fight with the Viet Cong.

The ship, which had been sunk in shallow water, had discharged a huge cargo of arms, ammunition, and other supplies. Documents found on the ship and on the bodies of several Viet Cong aboard identified the vessel as having come from North Vietnam. A newspaper in the cabin was from Haiphong and was dated January 23, 1965. The supplies delivered by the ship—thousands of weapons and more than a million rounds of ammunition—were almost all of Communist origin, largely from Communist China and Czechoslovakia, as well as North Vietnam. At least 100 tons of military supplies were discovered near the ship.

A preliminary survey of the cache near the sunken vessel from Hanoi listed the following supplies and weapons:

—approximately 1 million rounds of small-arms ammunition;
—more than 1,000 stick grenades;
—500 pounds of TNT in prepared charges;
—2,000 rounds of 82-mm. mortar ammunition;
—500 antitank grenades;
—500 rounds of 57-mm. recoilless rifle ammunition;
—more than 1,000 rounds of 75-mm. recoilless rifle ammunition;
—one 57-mm. recoilless rifle;
—2 heavy machineguns;
—2,000 7.92 Mauser rifles;
—more than 100 7.62 carbines;
—1,000 submachineguns;
—15 light machineguns;
—500 rifles;
—500 pounds of medical supplies (with labels from North

Vietnam, Communist China, Czechoslovakia, East Germany, Soviet Union, and other sources).

The ship was fairly new and had been made in Communist China. Documents aboard the ship included three North Vietnamese nautical charts (one of the Haiphong area and one of Hong Gay, both in North Vietnam, and one of the Tra Vinh area of South Vietnam). The military health records of North Vietnamese soldiers were found. One man had a political history sheet showing he was a member of the 338th Division of the North Vietnamese army.

Also aboard the North Vietnamese ship were: an instruction book for a Chinese Communist navigational device; postcards and letters to addresses in North Vietnam; and snapshots, including one of a group of men in North Vietnamese army uniforms under a flag of the Hanoi government.

Members of the I.C.C. and representatives of the free press visited the sunken North Vietnamese ship and viewed its cargo. The incident itself underlined in the most dramatic form that Hanoi is behind the continuing campaign of aggression aimed at conquering South Vietnam. It made unmistakably clear that what is happening in South Vietnam is not an internal affair but part of a large scale carefully directed and supported program of armed attack on a sovereign state and a free people.

There have been previous seizures of large stocks of ammunition and weapons and other military supplies that could only have come from Communist sources outside South Vietnam. In December 1963 a Republic of Vietnam force attacked a VC stronghold in Dinh Tuong Province southwest of Saigon. A large cache of VC equipment was seized. Included in the captured stocks were the following weapons and ammunition, all of Chinese Communist manufacture:

—One 99-mm. rocket launcher;
—2 carbines (type 53);
—120 rounds of 75-mm. recoilless rifle ammunition;
—120 detonating fuses for recoilless rifle ammunition;
—14,000 rounds of 7.62 (type P) ammunition;
—160,000 rounds of 7.62 carbine ammunition;
—150 fuses for mortar shells;
—100,000 rounds of 7.92 Mauser-type ammunition;

—110 lbs. (approximate) of TNT;

—Two 60-mm. mortars.

These weapons and ammunition are the same as those used in the North Vietnamese army. Some of the 7.62-mm. ammunition was manufactured as recently as 1962.

Materiel is sent into South Vietnam from the North by a variety of methods—overland, by river and canal, and by sea. In one instance, Vietnamese troops discovered a cache in which the 75-mm. ammunition alone weighed approximately 1½ tons. It has been estimated that it would require more than 150 porters to carry this quantity of ammunition over rough terrain. However, a few sampans, each manned by a few men, could transport it with little difficulty. It is worth noting, in this connection, that the delta where the cache of materiel was seized has 460 miles of seacoast as well as 2,500 miles of canals navigable by large water craft and another 2,200 miles of canals over which sampans can move easily. Much of the transport of large stocks of ammunition is undoubtedly waterborne for at least much of its travel into South Vietnam.

Large quantities of chemical components for explosives have been sent into South Vietnam for the Viet Cong. During 1963 there were at least 15 incidents in which boats, junks, or sampans were seized with explosives aboard. More than 20 tons of potassium chlorate or nitrate were captured. All these cases were in the delta area, and the majority were on or near the Mekong River. Red phosphorus made in Communist China has been among the chemicals captured from the Viet Cong.

The Communists have shown extreme sensitivity to exposure of the fact that war materiel is going to the Viet Cong from North Vietnam, Communist China, and other Communist countries. A secret document captured from a VC agent last year reflected this sensitivity. The document was sent from VC military headquarters in Bien Hoa Province to subordinate units. It ordered them to "pay special attention to the removal of all the markings and letters on weapons of all types currently employed by units and agencies and manufactured by friendly East European democratic countries or by China." It said incriminating marking should be chiseled off "so that the enemy cannot use it as a propaganda theme every time he captures these weapons."

III. NORTH VIETNAM:
BASE FOR CONQUEST OF THE SOUTH

The Third Lao Dong Party Congress in Hanoi in September 1960 set forth two tasks for its members: "to carry out the socialist revolution in North Vietnam" and "to liberate South Vietnam."

The resolutions of the congress described the effort to destroy the legal Government in South Vietnam as follows: "The revolution in the South is a protracted, hard, and complex process of struggle, combining many forms of struggle of great activity and flexibility, ranging from lower to higher, and taking as its basis the building, consolidation, and development of the revolutionary power of the masses."

At the September meeting the Communist leaders in the North called for formation of "a broad national united front." Three months later Hanoi announced creation of the "Front for Liberation of the South." This is the organization that Communist propaganda now credits with guiding the forces of subversion in the South; it is pictured as an organization established and run by the people in the South themselves. At the 1960 Lao Dong Party Congress the tone was different. Then, even before the front existed, the Communist leaders were issuing orders for the group that was being organized behind the scenes in Hanoi. "This front must rally * * *"; "The aims of its struggle are * * *"; "The front must carry out * * *"—this is the way Hanoi and the Communist Party addressed the "Liberation Front" even before its founding.

The Liberation Front is Hanoi's creation; it is neither independent nor southern, and what it seeks is not liberation but subjugation of the South.

In his address to the Third Lao Dong Party Congress, party and government leader Ho Chi Minh spoke of the necessity "to step up the socialist revolution in the North and, at the same time, to step up the national democratic people's revolution in the South."

The year before, writing for *Red Flag,* the Communist Party newspaper of Belgium, Ho had said much the same thing:

> We are building socialism in Vietnam, but we are building it in only one part of the country, while in the other part we still have to *direct and bring to a close* the middle-class democratic and anti-imperialist *revolution.*

In the same vein, the commander-in-chief of the North Vietnamese armed forces, Vo Nguyen Giap, spoke at the 1960 party congress of the need to "*step up* the national democratic people's *revolution in the South.*" Earlier in the year, writing for the Communist Party journal *Hoc Tap* in Hanoi, General Giap described the North as "*the revolutionary base for the whole country.*"

Le Duan, a member of the politburo and first secretary of the Lao Dong Party, was even more explicit when he talked at the party congress about the struggle in the South and the party's role. After noting the difficulties involved in overthrowing the existing order in South Vietnam, Le Duan said:

Hence the southern people's revolutionary struggle will be long, drawn out, and arduous. It is not a simple process but a complicated one, combining many varied forms of struggle—from elementary to advanced, *legal and illegal*—and based on the building, consolidation, and development of the revolutionary force of the masses. In this process, *we must constantly intensify our solidarity and the organization* and education *of the people of the South* . . . .

Another high official of the Hanoi regime, Truong Chinh, writing in the party organ *Hoc Tap* in April 1961, expressed confidence in the success of the struggle to remove the legal Government in South Vietnam because: "North Vietnam is being rapidly consolidated and strengthened, *is providing good support to the South Vietnamese revolution, and is serving as a strong base for the struggle for national reunification.*"

He outlined the steps by which the Communists expect to achieve control over all Vietnam as follows: The "Liberation Front" would destroy the present Government in the South; a "Coalition Government" would be established; this government would agree with the North Vietnamese government in Hanoi regarding national reunification "under one form or another." It takes little imagination to understand the form that is intended.

"Thus," wrote Truong Chinh, "though *South Vietnam will be liberated by nonpeaceful means,* the party policy of achieving peaceful national reunification is still correct."

The official government radio in Hanoi is used both overtly and covertly to support the Viet Cong effort in South Vietnam. Captured agents have testified that the broadcasts are used sometimes to send instructions in veiled code to Viet Cong representatives in the South.

Hoc Tap stated frankly in March 1963: "They [the authorities in South Vietnam] are well aware that *North Vietnam is the firm base for the southern revolution* and the point on which it leans, and that *our party* is the steady and experienced vanguard unit of the working class and people and *is the brain and factor that decides all victories of the revolution."*

In April 1964 the Central Committee of the Lao Dong Party issued a directive to all party echelons. It stated: "When the forces of the enemy and the plots of the enemy are considered, it is realized that *the cadres, party members, and people in North Vietnam must * * * increase their sense of responsibility in regard to the South Vietnam revolution by giving positive and practical support to South Vietnam in every field."*

Nguyen Chi Thanh, writing a Hanoi newspaper in May 1963, underlined the importance of the role of the North Vietnamese army in Hanoi's plans to unify Vietnam under Communist rule:

"Our party set forth two strategic tasks to be carried out at the same time: to transform and build socialism in the North and to struggle to unify the country. *Our army is an instrument of the class struggle in carrying out these two strategic tasks."*

IV. ORGANIZATION, DIRECTION, COMMAND, AND CONTROL OF THE ATTACK OF SOUTH VIETNAM ARE CENTERED IN HANOI

The VC military and political apparatus in South Vietnam is an extension of an elaborate military and political structure in North Vietnam which directs and supplies it with the tools for conquest. The Ho Chi Minh regime has shown that it is ready to allocate every resource that can be spared—whether it be personnel, funds, or equipment—to the cause of overthrowing the legitimate Government of South Vietnam and of bringing all Vietnam under Communist rule.

A. POLITICAL ORGANIZATION

Political direction and control of the Viet Cong is supplied by the Lao Dong Party, i.e., the Communist Party, led by Ho Chi Minh.

Party agents are responsible for indoctrination, recruitment, political training, propaganda, anti-Government demonstrations, and other activities of a political nature. The considerable intelligence-gathering facilities of the party are also at the disposal of the Viet Cong.

Overall direction of the VC movement is the responsibility of the Central Committee of the Lao Dong Party. Within the Central Committee a special Reunification Department has been established. This has replaced the "Committee for Supervision of the South" mentioned in intelligence reports 2 years ago. It lays down broad strategy for the movement to conquer South Vietnam.

Until March 1962 there were two principal administrative divisions in the VC structure in the South. One was the Interzone of South-Central Vietnam (sometimes called Interzone 5); the other was the Nambo Region. In a 1962 reorganization these were merged into one, called the Central Office for South Vietnam. The Central Committee, through its Reunification Department, issues directives to the Central Office, which translates them into specific orders for the appropriate subordinate command.

Under the Central Office are six regional units, V through IX plus the special zone of Saigon/Cholon/Gia Dinh. A regional committee responsible to the Central Office directs VC activities in each region. Each regional committee has specialized units responsible for liaison ,propaganda, training personnel, subversive activities, espionage, military bases, and the like.

Below each regional committee are similarly structured units at the province and district levels. At the base of the Communist pyramid are the individual party cells, which may be organized on a geographic base or within social or occupational groups. The elaborateness of the party unit and the extent to which it operates openly or underground is determined mainly by the extent of VC control over the area concerned.

1. The "Liberation Front"

The National Front for the Liberation of South Vietnam is the screen behind which the Communists carry out their program of conquest. It is the creature of the Communist Government in Hanoi. As noted above, the Communist Party in the North demanded establishment of such a "front" three months before its formation was actually announced in December 1960. It was designed to create the illusion that the Viet Cong campaign of subversion was truly indigenous to South Vietnam rather than an externally directed Communist plan.

The front has won support primarily from the Communist world. Its radio faithfully repeats the propaganda themes of Hanoi and Peiping. When its representatives travel abroad, they do so with North Vietnamese passports and sponsorship. The front's program copies that of the Lao Dong Party in North Vietnam.

In late 1961, in still another effort to conceal the extent of Communist domination of the front, the Communists announced formation of a new Marxist political unit, the People's Revolutionary Party (PRP). This mechanism provided a way to explain the Communist presence in the front while at the same time making it appear that the Communist voice was only one of several affiliated organizations in the front. The PRP itself claimed direct descent from the original Indochinese Communist Party and from the North Vietnamese Communist Party in Hanoi.

B. MILITARY ORGANIZATION

Military affairs of the Viet Cong are the responsibility of the High Command of the People's Army of North Vietnam and the Ministry of Defense, under close supervision from the Lao Dong Party. These responsibilities include operational plans, assignments of individuals and regular units, training programs, infiltraton of military personnel and supplies, military communications, tactical intelligence, supplies, and the like. The six military regions are the same as those of the VC political organization.

The military structure of the Viet Cong is an integral part of the political machinery that controls every facet of VC activity in South Vietnam under Hanoi's overall direction. Each political headquarters from the Central Office down to the village has a military component which controls day-to-day military operations. Similarly, each military headquarters has a political element, an individual or a small staff. This meshing of political and military activity is designed to insure the closest cooperaton in support of the total Communist mission. It also gives assurance of political control over the military.

Associated with the Central Office, believed to be located in Tay Ninh Province, is a military headquarters. Through this headquarters, as well as through other channels, Hanoi maintains direct contact with its principal military units in the South.

In addition to its supervision of the general military effort of the VC, the military section of the Central Office is believed to have direct command of two regimental headquarters and a number of security companies.

The hard core of the VC military organization is the full-time regular unit usually based on a province or region. These are well-trained and highly disciplined guerrilla fighters. They follow a rigid training schedule that is roughly two-thirds military one-third political in content. This compares with the 50-50 proportion for district units and the 70 percent political and 30 percent military content of the village guerrilla's training.

The size of the Viet Cong regular forces has grown steadily in recent years. For example, the Viet Cong have five regimental headquarters compared with two in 1961. And the main VC force is composed of 50 battalions, 50 percent more than before. There are an estimated 139 VC companies. Hard-core VC strength now is estimated at about 35,000 where it was less than 20,000 in 1961.

The main force battalions are well armed with a variety of effective weapons including 75-mm. recoiless rifles and 81-82-mm. mortars. The companies and smaller units are equally well equipped and have 57-mm. recoilless rifles and 60-mm. mortars in their inventory. It is estimated that the Viet Cong have at least 130 81-mm. mortars and 300 66-mm. mortars. There is no precise estimate for the number of recoilless rifles in their hands, but it is believed that most main force units are equipped with them. In at least one recent action the Viet Cong employed a 75-mm. pack howitzer. This mobile weapon, which has a range of 8,500 yards, will increase the Viet Cong capabiliites to launch long-range attacks against many stationary targets in the country.

Supporting the main force units of the Viet Cong are an estimated 60,000-80,000 part-time guerrillas. They are generally organized at the district level where there are likely to be several companies of 50 or more men each. These troops receive only half pay, which means they must work at least part of the time to eke out a living.

Below the irregular guerrilla forces of the district are the part-time, village-based guerrillas. They are available for assignment by higher headquarters and are used for harassment and sabotage. They are expected to warn nearby VC units of the approach of any force of the legal government. They provide a pool for recruitment into the VC district forces.

The record shows that many of the village guerillas are dragooned into service with the Viet Cong. Some are kidnapped; others are threatened; still others join to prevent their families from being harmed. Once in the Viet Cong net, many are reluctant to leave for fear of punishment by the authorities or reprisal by the Communists.

Lam Van Chuoi is a typical example. He was a member of the Village Civil Defense force in his home village in Kien Giang Province. In March 1960, he was kidnapped by the Viet Cong and kept a prisoner in the highlands for one month. There he was subjected to intense propaganda and indoctrination. He was returned to his village but kept under close observation and steady pressure. Finally, he was convinced he must join the VC. Later, he was transferred to a Communist military unit in another province. After learning of the Government's "Open Arms" program, he decided to defect from the VC. In May 1964, he walked into a Government outpost and asked for protection.

Money to pay the regular VC units comes from a variety of sources. Funds are sent from Hanoi. "Taxes" are extorted from the local population. Landowners and plantation operators often must pay a tribute to the VC as the price for not having their lands devastated. Similarly, transportation companies have been forced to pay the VC or face the threat of having their buses or boats sabotaged. Officials and wealthy people have been kidnapped for ransom. The VC have often stopped buses and taken the money and valuables of all on board.

For the most part, the VC have concentrated their attention on individuals, isolated or poorly defended outposts, and small centers of population. They have mercilessly killed or kidnapped thousands of villiage chiefs and other local officials. But over the past year the VC have moved into larger unit operations. Their ability to operate on a battalion level or larger has substantially increased.

C. INTELLIGENCE ORGANIZATION

A key element in the Viet Cong effort is an elaborate organization in Hanoi called the Central Research Agency (C.R.A.) (Cua Nghien-Cuu Trung-Uong). Though it handles Hanoi's intelligence effort on a worldwide scale, the main focus of its operation is on South Vietnam. This agency is able to draw on the intelligence capabilities of both the Lao Dong Party and the North Vietnamese armed forces for information, personnel, and facilities.

The C.R.A. reportedly operates under the close personal scrutiny of Ho Chi Minh himself. Some of the top officials in the Hanoi government reportedly sit on its directing committee, including Premier Pham Van Dong, Deputy Premier Truong Chinh, and Defense Minister Vo Nguyen Giap.

Considerable information on the organization of the C.R.A. has become available from captured Viet Cong agents and from the work of intelligence agents of the Republic of Vietnam. Much of this information cannot be made public for security reasons, but it is possible to describe the C.R.A. organization and its operations in broad outline.

The headquarters of the C.R.A. in Hanoi is divided into six main sections, not including a special code unit. The six sections are responsible for administration, cadres, communications, espionage, research, and training. Each section has units to handle the specialized activities of its particular area of responsibility. The research section, for example, has subsections that handle political, economic, and military affairs, respectively.

C.R.A. headquarters directs a number of special centers for overseas operations. One such center maintains intelligence channels to overseas areas. It operates through special units at Haiphong and at Hongay.

A second special center is responsible for VC intelligence operations in Cambodia and Laos. A third center handles activities along the "demarcation line," the border with South Vietnam. This unit, based in Vinh Linh in southeast North Vietnam, is responsible for sending agents and supplies to the South by sea. It also cooperates with the North Vietnamese army in planning and carrying out infiltration. The C.R.A. maintains intelligence bases in Laos and other countries.

Inside South Vietnam the Viet Cong have a large intelligence network. Some of its units are responsible for receiving and sending on agents arriving from the North. They feed and give instructions to groups infiltrating into South Vietnam. They take delivery of equipment and supplies received from the North and relay them to Viet Cong units in the South.

Many Viet Cong agents have been captured in Saigon. They have exposed the extensive effort by the C.R.A. to penetrate all Republic of Vietnam Government agencies, foreign embassies, and other specialized organizations. Party and military intelligence units and agents work closely with the C.R.A.

Each of the main centers operating under C.R.A. headquarters has its own sections and units designed to carry out its main functions. The center at Vinh Linh, responsible for the main infiltration effort of the Viet Cong, has separate sections for radio communications, coding, documentation and training, and liaison. It also has specialized units for infiltration through the mountains, infiltration by sea, and "illegal action" in the mountain area.

The C.R.A. maintains a large and expanding radio communications network. Agents also are used to carry messages, usually in secret writing or memorized.

Taken as a whole, the North Vietnamese intelligence operation in support of the Viet Cong is one of the most extensive of its kind in the world.

V. A BRIEF HISTORY OF HANOI'S CAMPAIGN OF AGGRESSION AGAINST SOUTH VIETNAM

While negotiating an end to the Indochina War at Geneva in 1954, the Communists were making plans to take over all former French territory in Southeast Asia. When Vietnam was partitioned, thousands of carefully selected party members were ordered to remain in place in the South and keep their secret apparatus intact to help promote Hanoi's cause. Arms and ammunition were stored away for future use. Guerrilla fighters rejoined their families to await the party's call. Others withdrew to remote jungle and mountain hideouts.

The majority—an estimated 90,000—were moved to North Vietnam.

Hanoi's original calculation was that all of Vietnam would fall under its control without resort to force. For this purpose, Communist cadres were ordered to penetrate official and nonofficial agencies, to propagandize and sow confusion, and generally to use all means short of open violence to aggravate war-torn conditions and to weaken South Vietnam's Government and social fabric.

South Vietnam's refusal to fall in with Hanoi's scheme for peaceful takeover came as a heavy blow to the Communists. Meantime, the Government had stepped up efforts to blunt Viet Cong subversion and to expose Communist agents. Morale in the Communist organization in the South dropped sharply. Defections were numerous.

Among South Vietnamese, hope rose that their nation could have a peaceful and independent future, free of Communist domination. The country went to work. The years after 1955 were a period of steady progress and growing prosperity.

Food production levels of the pre-war years were reached and surpassed. While per capita food output was dropping 10 percent in the North from 1956 to 1960, it rose 20 percent in the South. By 1963, it had risen 30 percent—despite the disruption in the countryside caused by intensified Viet Cong military attacks and terrorism. The authorities in the North admitted openly to continuing annual failures to achieve food production goals.

Production of textiles increased in the South more than 20 percent in one year (1958). In the same year, South Vietnam's sugar crop increased more than 100 percent. Despite North Vietnam's vastly larger industrial complex, South Vietnam's per capita gross national product in 1960 was estimated at $110 a person while it was only $70 in the North.

More than 900,000 refugees who had fled from Communist rule in the North were successfully settled in South Vietnam. An agrarian reform program was instituted. The elementary school population nearly quadrupled between 1956 and 1960. And so it went—a record of steady improvement in the lives of the people. It was intolerable for the rulers in Hanoi; under peaceful conditions, the South was outstripping the North. They were losing the battle of peaceful competition and decided to use violence and terror to gain their ends.

After 1956 Hanoi rebuilt, reorganized, and expanded its covert political and military machinery in the South. Defectors were replaced by trained personnel from party ranks in the North. Military units and political cells were enlarged and were given new leaders, equipment, and intensified training. Recruitment was pushed. In short, Hanoi and its forces in the South prepared to take by force and violence what they had failed to achieve by other means.

By 1958 the use of terror by the Viet Cong increased appreciably. It was used both to win prestige and to back up demands for support from the people, support that political and propaganda appeals had failed to produce. It was also designed to embarrass the Government in Saigon and raise doubts about its ability to maintain internal order and to assure the personal security of its people. From 1959 through 1961, the pace of Viet Cong terrorism and armed attacks accelerated substantially.

The situation at the end of 1961 was so grave that the Government of the Republic of Vietnam asked the United States for increased military assistance. That request was met. Meantime, the program of strategic hamlets, designed to improve the peasant's livelihood and give him some protection against Viet Cong harassment and pressure, was pushed energetically.

But the Viet Cong did not stand still. To meet the changing situation, they tightened their organization and adopted new tactics, with increasing emphasis on terrorism, sabotage, and armed attacks by small groups. They also introduced from the North technicians in fields such as armor and anti-aircraft. Heavier weapons were sent in to the regular guerrilla forces.

The military and insurgency situation was complicated by a quite separate internal political struggle in South Vietnam, which led in November 1963 to the removal of the Diem government and it replacement with a new one. Effective power was placed in the hands of a Military Revolutionary Council. There have been a number of changes in the leadership and composition of the Government in Saigon in the ensuing period.

These internal developments and distractions gave the Viet Cong an invaluable opportunity, and they took advantage of it. Viet Cong agents did what they could to encourage disaffection and to exploit demonstrations in Saigon and elsewhere. In the countryside the Communists consolidated their hold over some areas and enlarged their military and political apparatus by increased infiltration. Increasingly they struck at remote outposts and the most vulnerable of the new strategic hamlets and expanded their campaign of aggressive attacks, sabotage, and terror.

Any official, worker, or establishment that represents a service to the people by the Government in Saigon is fair game for the Viet Cong. Schools have been among their favorite targets. Through harassment, the murder of teachers, and sabotage of buildings, the Viet Cong succeeded in closing hundreds of schools and interrupting the education of tens of thousands of youngsters.

Hospitals and medical clinics have often been attacked as part of the anti-Government campaign and also because such attacks provide the Viet Cong with needed medical supplies. The Communists have encouraged people in rural areas to oppose the Government's anti-malaria teams, and some of the workers have been killed. Village and town offices, police stations, and agricultural research stations are high on the list of preferred targets for the Viet Cong.

In 1964, 436 South Vietnamese hamlet chiefs and other Government officials were killed outright by the Viet Cong and 1,131 were kidnapped. More than 1,350 civilians were killed in bombings and other acts of sabotage. And at least 8,400 civilians were kidnapped by the Viet Cong.

Today the war in Vietnam has reached new levels of intensity. The elaborate effort by the Communist regime in North Vietnam to conquer the South has grown, not diminished. Military men, technicians, political organizers, propagandists, and secret agents have been infiltrating into the Republic of Vietnam from the North in growing numbers. The flow of Communist-supplied weapons, particularly those of large caliber, has increased. Communications links with Hanoi are extensive. Despite the heavy casualties of 3 years of fighting, the hard-core VC force is considerably larger now than it was at the end of 1961.

The Government in Saigon has undertaken vigorous action to meet the new threat. The United States and other free countries have increased their assistance to the Vietnamese Government and people. Secretary of State Dean Rusk visited Vietnam in 1964, and he promised the Vietnamese: "We shall remain at your side until the aggression from the North has been defeated, until it has been completely rooted out and this land enjoys the peace which it deserves."

President Johnson has repeatedly stressed that the United States' goal is to see peace secured in Southeast Asia. But he has noted that "that will come only when aggressors leave their neighbors in peace."

Though it has been apparent for years that the regime in Hanoi was conducting a campaign of conquest against South Vietnam, the Government in Saigon and the Government of the United States both hoped that the danger could be met within South Vietnam itself. The hope that any widening of the conflict might be avoided was stated frequently.

The leaders in Hanoi chose to respond with greater violence. They apparently interpreted restraint as indicating lack of will. Their efforts were pressed with greater vigor and armed attacks and incidents of terror multiplied.

Clearly the restraint of the past was not providing adequately for the defense of South Vietnam against Hanoi's open aggression. It was mutually agreed between the Governments of the Republic of Vietnam and the United States that further means for providing for South Vietnam's defense were required. Therefore, air strikes have been made against some of the military assembly points and supply bases from which North Vietnam is conducting its aggression against the South. These strikes constitute a limited response fitted to the aggression that produced them.

Until the regime in Hanoi decides to halt its intervention in the South, or until effective steps are taken to maintain peace and security in the area, the Governments of South Vietnam and the United States will continue necessary measures of defense against the Communist armed aggression coming from North Vietnam.

VI. CONCLUSION

The evidence presented in this report could be multiplied many times with similar examples of the drive of the Hanoi regime to extend its rule over South Vietnam.

The record is conclusive. It establishes beyond question that North Vietnam is carrying out a carefully conceived plan of aggression against the South. It shows that North Vietnam has intensified its efforts in the years since it was condemned by the International

Control Commission. It proves that Hanoi continues to press its systematic program of armed aggression into South Vietnam. This aggression violates the United Nations Charter. It is directly contrary to the Geneva accords of 1954 and of 1962 to which North Vietnam is a party. It shatters the peace of Southeast Asia. It is a fundamental threat to the freedom and security of South Vietnam.

The people of South Vietnam have chosen to resist this threat. At their request, the United States has taken its place beside them in their defensive struggle.

The United States seeks no territory, no military bases, no favored position. But we have learned the meaning of aggression elsewhere in the postwar world, and we have met it.

If peace can be restored in South Vietnam, the United States will be ready at once to reduce its military involvement. But it will not abandon friends who want to remain free. It will do what must be done to help them. The choice now between peace and continued and increasingly destructive conflict is one for the authorities in Hanoi to make.

A REPLY TO THE WHITE PAPER*

That North Vietnam supports the guerrillas in South Vietnam is no more a secret than that the United States supports the South Vietnamese government against them. The striking thing about the State Department's new White Paper is how little support it can prove. "Incontrovertible evidence of Hanoi's elaborate program to supply its forces in the South with weapons, ammunition and other supplies," the White Paper says, "has accumulated over the years." A detailed presentation of this evidence is in Appendix D; unfortunately few will see the appendices since even the *New York Times* did not reprint them, though these are more revealing than the report. Appendix D provides a list of weapons, ammunition and other supplies of Chinese Communist, Soviet, Czech and North Vietnamese manufacture, with the dates and place of capture from the Viet Cong guerrillas, over the 18-month period from June, 1962, to January 29 last year when it was presented to the International Control Commission. The Commission was set up by the Geneva agreement of 1954. This list provides a good point at which to begin an analysis of the White Paper.

The Pentagon's Figures

To put the figures in perspective, we called the Pentagon press office and obtained some figures the White Paper does not supply— the number of weapons captured from the guerrillas and the number lost to them in recent years:

	Captured From Guerrillas	Lost to Them
1962	4,800	5,200
1963	5,400	8,500
1964	4,900	13,700
3-Year Total	15,100	27,400

In three years, the guerrillas captured from our side 12,300 more weapons than they lost to us.

What interests us at the moment is not this favorable balance but the number of guerrilla weapons our side captured during the past

---

*From I. F. STONE'S WEEKLY, March 8, 1965. Reprinted with permission.

three years. The grand total was 15,100. If Hanoi has indeed engaged in an "elaborate program" to supply the Viet Cong, one would expect a substantial number of enemy-produced weapons to turn up. Here is the sum total of enemy-produced weapons and supplies in that 18-month tally to the Control Commission—

72 rifles (46 Soviet, 26 Czech)
64 submachine guns (40 Czech, 24 French but "modified" in North Vietnam)
15 carbines (Soviet)
 8 machine guns (6 Chinese, 2 North Vietnamese)
 5 pistols (4 Soviet, 1 Czech)
 4 mortars (Chinese)
 3 recoilless 75-mm. rifles (Chinese)
 3 recoilless 57-mm. guns (Chinese)
 2 bazookas (1 Chinese, 1 Czech)
 2 rocket launchers (Chinese)
 1 grenade launcher (Czech)
——
179 total

This is not a very impressive total. According to the Pentagon figures, we captured on the average 7500 weapons each 18-months in the past three years. If only 179 Communist-made weapons turned up in 18 months, that is less than 2½% of the total. Judging by these White Paper figures, our military are wrong in estimating, as they have in recent months, that 80% of the weapons used by the guerrillas are captured from us. It looks as if the proportion is considerably higher. The material of North Vietnamese origin included only those 24 French sub-machine guns "modified" in North Vietnam, 2 machine guns made in North Vietnam, 16 helmets, a uniform and and undisclosed number of mess kits, belts, sweaters and socks. Judging by this tally, the main retaliatory blow should be at North Vietnam's clothing factories.

Not Enough for a Battalion

There is another way to judge this tally of captured Communist weapons. A Communist battalion has about 450 men. It needs 500 rifles, four 80-mm. mortars, eight 60-mm. mortars and at least four recoilless rifles. The weapons of Communist origin captured in 18 months would not adequately outfit one battalion. The figures in the appendix on ammunition captured provides another index. We captured 183 (Chinese) shells for a 60-mm. mortar. This fires about 20 shells a minute, so that was hardly enough ammunition for 10 minutes of firing. There were 100,000 (Chinese) cartridges for 7.26 mm. machine guns. That looks impressive until one discovers on checking with knowledgeable military sources that these machine guns fire 600 rounds a minute. A machine gun platoon normally has four machine guns. This was enough ammunition for about 40 minutes of firing by one platoon. Indeed, if the ratio of Communist-made weapons captured is the same for weapons used, then only 12½ days of those 18 months were fought by the guerrillas on the basis of Communist made supplies.

If these figures were being presented in a court of law, they would run up against a further difficulty; one would have to prove the arms actually came from the Communist side. There is a world-wide market in second-hand weapons. One can buy Soviet, Czech and Chinese Communist weapons of all kinds only two miles from the Pentagon through Interarmco, Ltd., 10 Prince Street, Alexandria, Va. Interarmco, one of the world's foremost dealers, can provide more Communist weapons than we picked up in 18 months on Vietnamese battlefields. The supply of East European Communist weapons comes in large part from the huge stocks of Soviet and Czech arms captured by the Israelis in the Suez campaign. Many Chinese Communist weapons were captured by our side in the Korean war. There is also, of course, a wide selection of our own military surplus. This has turned up in strange places.

For example, a book on the Algerian war, *Les Algeriens en guerre,* by Dominique Darbois and Phillippe Vingneau, was published in Milan in 1960 by Feltrinelli. It shows pictures of NLF (National Liberation Front) Algerian rebels wearing U.S. Marine Corps uniforms from which the "USM" and the eagle and globe insignia have not even been removed. It shows Algerians carrying U.S. 80-mm. mortars and U.S. 50-calibre machine guns. Such photos could have been used by France to accuse the U.S. of supplying the Algerian rebels.

The State Department's White Paper says "dramatic new proof was exposed just as this report was being completed" in the discovery of a suspected Viet Cong arms cargo ship on Feb. 16. The *New York Times* commented astringently on this in an editorial Feb. 28—

> Apparently, the major new evidence of a need for escalating the war, with all the hazard that this entails, was provided by the sinking in a South Vietnamese cove earlier this month of a 100-ton cargo ship loaded with Communist-made small arms and ammunition. A ship of that size is not much above the Oriental junk class. The standard Liberty or Victory ship of World War II had a capacity of 7,150 to 7,650 tons.

The affair of the cargo ship is curious. Until now there has been little evidence of arms coming in by ship. A huge fleet of small vessels patrols the coast and there have been glowing stories in the past of its efficiency. "About 12,000 vessels," the AP reported from Saigon (*New York Times*, Feb. 22) "are searched each month by the South Vietnamese coastal junk patrol force but arrests are rare and no significant amounts of incriminating goods or weapons ever have been found." This lone case of a whole shipload of arms is puzzling.

Few Northern Infiltrees Cited

The White Paper's story on the influx of men from the North also deserves a closer analysis than the newspapers have given it. Appendix C provides an elaborate table from 1959-60 to 1964 inclusive, showing the number of "confirmed" military infiltrees per year from the North. The total is given as 19,550. One way to measure this number is against that of the military we have assigned to South Vietnam in the same years. These now total 23,500, or 25% more, and 1,000 are to be added in the near future. The number of North Vietnamese infiltrees is "based on information . . . from at least two independent sources." *Nowhere are we told how many men who infiltrated from the North have actually been captured.* There is reason to wonder whether the count of infiltrees may be as bloated as the count of Viet Cong dead; in both cases the numbers used are estimates rather than actual bodies.

The White Paper claims "that as many as 75% of the more than 7000 Viet Cong who are known to have entered the South in 1964 were natives of North Vietnam." But a careful reading of the text and the appendices turns up the names of only six North Vietnamese infiltrees. In Part I of the White Paper, Section B gives "individual case histories of North Vietnamese soldiers" sent South by Hanoi but all nine of these are of South Vietnamese origin. The next Section C, is headed "Infiltration of Native North Vietnamese." It names five infiltrees but one of these is also from the South. That leaves four North Vietnamese natives. Then, in Appendix C, we are given the case histories and photographs of nine other Viet Cong sent South by Hanoi. The report does not explain which ones were originally from the South but it does give the names of the provinces in which they were born. When these are checked, it turns out that only two of the nine were born in North Vietnam. This gives us a total of six Northern infiltrees. It is strange that after five years of fighting, the White Paper can cite so few.

None of this is discussed frankly in the White Paper. To do so would be to bring the war into focus as a rebellion in the South, which may owe some men and materiel to the North but is largely dependent on popular indigenous support for its manpower, as it is on captured U. S. weapons for its supply. The White Paper withholds all evidence which points to a civil war. It also fails to tell the full story of the July 1962 Special Report by the International Control Commission. Appendix A quotes that portion in which the Commission 2-to-1 (Poland dissenting) declared that the North had in specific instances sent men and materiel south in violation of the Geneva accords. But nowhere does the State Department mention that the same report also condemned South Vietnam and the U. S., declaring that they had entered into a military alliance in violation of the Geneva agreements. The U. S. was criticized because it then had about 5,000 military advisers in South Vietnam. The Geneva accords limited the U. S. military mission to the 684 in Vietnam at the time of the 1954 cease-fire. The U. S. and South Vietnam were also criticized by the ICC for hamstringing the Commission's efforts to check on imports of arms in violation of the Geneva accords.

The reader would never guess from the White Paper that the Geneva accords promised that elections would be held in 1956 to reunify the country. The 1961 Blue Book at least mentioned the elections, though somehow managing to make them seem a plot. "It was the Communists' calculation," the Blue Book put it, "that nationwide elections scheduled in the accords for 1956 would turn all of South Vietnam over to them . . . The authorities in South Vietnam refused to fall into this well-laid trap." The White Paper omits mention of the elections altogether and says, "South Vietnam's refusal to fall in with Hanoi's scheme for peaceful takeover came as a heavy blow to the Communists." This is not the most candid and objective presentation. From the Viet Minh point of view, the failure to hold the elections promised them when they laid down their arms was the second broken promise of the West. The earlier one was in 1946 when they made an agreement to accept limited autonomy within the French union, and welcomed the returning French troops as comrades of the liberation. Most of the French military did not want to recognize even this limited form of independence, and chose instead the road which led after eight years of war to Dienbienphu.*

That "Economic Miracle" Again

The most disingenuous part of the White Paper is that in which it discusses the origins of the present war. It pictures the war as an attack from the North, launched in desperation because the "economic miracle" in the South under Diem had destroyed Communist hopes of a peaceful takeover from within. Even the strategic hamlets are described as "designed to improve the peasant's livelihood" and we are asked to believe that for the first time in history a guerrilla war spread not because the people were discontented but because their lot was improving!

The true story is a story of lost opportunities. The Communist countries acquiesced in the failure to hold elections. Diem had a chance to make his part of the country a democratic show-case. The year 1956 was a bad one in the North. There was a peasant uprising and widespread resentment among the intellectuals over the Communist Party's heavy-handed thought control. But Diem on the other side of the 17th Parallel was busy erecting a dictatorship of his own. In 1956 he abolished elections even for village councils.

---

*See Jean Sainteny's Histoire d' une paix manquee (Paris 1953) and Ellen Hammer's The Struggle for Indochina (Stanford 1954).

In 1957 his mobs smashed the press of the one legal opposition party, the Democratic Bloc, when it dared criticize the government. That was the beginning of a campaign to wipe out every form of opposition. It was this campaign and the oppressive exactions imposed on the peasantry, the fake land reform and the concentration camps Diem set up for political opponents of all kinds, which stirred ever wider rebellion from 1958 onward in the grass roots *before* North Vietnam gave support.** It was this which drove oppositionists of all kinds into alliance with the Communists in the National Liberation Front.

Long before the North was accused of interference, its government was complaining to the Control Commission of "border and airspace violations by the south and infringements of the Geneva agreement by the introduction of arms and U.S. servicemen."***

For four years after Geneva, both North Vietnam and China followed the "peaceful co-existence" policy while the U.S. turned South Vietnam into a military base and a military dictatorship. It is in this story the White Paper does not tell, and the popular discontent it does not mention, that the rebellion and the aid from the North had their origins.

LEGAL BASIS FOR UNITED STATES ACTIONS AGAINST NORTH VIET-NAM: Department of State Memorandum, March 8, 1965

I—THE ISSUE

This memorandum considers the question whether United States-South Vietnamese actions against military targets in North Viet-Nam are justified in international law, particularly in light of the United Nations Charter and the 1954 Geneva Accords on Viet-Nam. It concludes that these actions are fully justified.

II—THE FACTS

On February 27, the Department of State issued "Aggression From the North," a report of North Viet-Nam's campaign to con-

---

**Philippee Devillers in the China Quarterly, Jan.-Mar. 1962.
***Survey of International Affairs 1956-58, by Geoffrey Barraclough, a publication of Britain's Royal Institute of International Affairs, p. 420.

quer South Viet-Nam. That Report establishes beyond question that North Viet-Nam is carrying out a carefully conceived plan of aggression against the South.

The evidence shows that the hard core of the Communist forces attacking South Viet-Nam were trained in the North and ordered into the South by Hanoi. It shows that the key leadership of the Viet Cong, the officers and much of the cadre, many of the technicians, political organizers, and propagandists have come from the North and operate under Hanoi's direction. It shows that the training of essential military personnel and their infiltration into the South is directed by the Military High Command in Hanoi. It shows that many of the weapons and much of the ammunition and other supplies used by the Viet Cong have been sent into South Viet-Nam from the North. The evidence plainly indicates that under Hanoi's overall direction the Communists have established an extensive machine, both political and military, for carrying on the war against South Viet-Nam.

The history of Hanoi's campaign to conquer South Viet-Nam is a long one. It was documented earlier in a report entitled "A Threat to the Peace" issued by the Department of State in December 1961. In a special report of June 1962, the International Control Commission in Viet-Nam concluded that there was "sufficient evidence to show beyond reasonable doubt" that North Viet-Nam was sending arms and men into South Viet-Nam to carry out subversion with the aim of overthrowing the legal government there, in violation of the 1954 Geneva Accords.

To meet the threat created by these violations of the Geneva Accords, and by North Viet-Nam's aggressive intervention contrary to general international law, the Government of the Republic of Viet-Nam requested United States assistance. We had been providing Viet-Nam since 1950-51 with both economic and military aid. This assistance was continued after the conclusion of the 1954 Geneva Accords, within the limitations prescribed by those agreements. It had become apparent, however, by 1961 that this limited assistance was not sufficient to meet the growing Communist threat. Consequently, in 1961, the Government of the Republic of Viet-Nam requested additional aid from the United States. The United States responded with increased supplies and with larger numbers of training and advisory personnel to assist the Vietnamese forces in prosecuting the war against the Viet Cong. This response was proportioned with the design of sustaining Viet-Nam in its defense against aggression without extending the conflict beyond the borders of the country.

The Communists, however, increased their intervention without regard to obligations under international law and international agreements by which they were bound. They stepped up the assistance from the North and increased the use of neighboring Laos as an infiltration route, in violation of the freshly concluded 1962 Geneva Agreement for the Settlement of the Laotian Question.

In more recent months North Viet-Nam has sharply increased the infiltration of men and equipment into the South, and virtually all personnel now coming in are natives of North Viet-Nam. Dramatically illustrative of Hanoi's role is the discovery along the South Vietnamese coast on February 16, 1965 of a huge cargo of arms, ammunition and other supplies, delivered by ship from North Viet-Nam. Major attacks by organized units are being launched against government forces. The North Vietnamese have even attacked United States vessels in international waters in the Gulf of Tonkin.

Thus, what began as covert and indirect aggression has become open armed aggression. This aggression has been carried out across the internationally agreed demarcation line of 1954 between North and South Viet-Nam, and across international frontiers between Viet-Nam and Laos.

III – INTERNATIONAL LAW – THE UN CHARTER

As has been seen, North Viet-Nam is engaged in a continuing armed aggression against South Viet-Nam in violation of international agreements and international law.

This being the case, what are the Republic of Viet-Nam and the United States entitled to do under international law by way of response?

Under international law, the victim of armed aggression is obviously permitted to defend itself and to organize a collective self-defense effort in which others who are willing may join. This right is recognized in Article 51 of the United Nations Charter. Article 51 states that —

Nothing in the present Charter shall impair the inherent right of individual or collective self-defense if an armed attack occurs against a member of the United Nations, until the Security Council has taken the measures necessary to maintain international peace and security. Measures taken by the members in the exercise of this right of self-defense shall be immediately reported to the Security Council and shall not in any way affect the authority and responsibility of the Security Council under the present Charter to take at any time such actions as it deems necessary in order to maintain or restore international peace and security.

As has been shown above, the whole course of conduct of North Viet-Nam, particularly as it has evolved in recent months, adds up to open armed attack within the meaning of Article 51. Indeed it is more than a single armed attack; it is a continuing program of armed aggression carried on across international frontiers and established demarcation lines. In these circumstances, South Viet-Nam has requested and received assistance from the United States and other nations in a collective defense effort.

Article 2, paragraph 4, of the Charter is also relevant to the Viet-Nam situation. Article 2, paragraph 4, provides that —

All members shall refrain in their international relations from the threat or use of force against the territorial integrity or political independence of any state, or in any other manner inconsistent with the purposes of the United Nations.

In the first place, it is plain that the use of force against territorial integrity and political independence has been initiated by North Viet-Nam and not by anyone else. Secondly, paragraph 4 of Article 2 of the Charter does not place an absolute prohibition on the use of force. It permits the use of force in a manner consistent with the purposes and principles of the Charter. Moreover, the Charter itself specifically provides for the use of force in certain circumstances — action through the United Nations itself, action through regional arrangements, and action in self-defense. The actions of the United States and the Republic of Viet-Nam, being defensive in character and designed to resist armed aggression, are wholly consistent with the purposes and principles of the Charter and specifically with Article 2, paragraph 4.

It was as a measure of self-defense under Article 51 that the United States responded in August 1964 to the North Vietnamese attack on our vessels in the Gulf of Tonkin. Those measures were immediately reported to the Security Council in accordance with Article 51. The Security Council did not see fit to take any action to maintain or restore international peace and security in the area. Indeed, North Viet-Nam refused to participate in the deliberations of the Security Council and explicitly denied the right of the Council to examine this question.

The attacks against South Viet-Nam have mounted in intensity since August. In these circumstances, it has been mutually agreed between the Government of South Viet-Nam and the United States Government that further means of providing for the collective defense of South Viet-Nam are required. Prompt defensive action has been decided upon, and airstrikes have been made against military installations and facilities in North Viet-Nam which support the aggression against the South. The actions taken constitute a limited and measured response, fitted to the situation that called for it. Again, these measures have been reported to the Security Council in accordance with Article 51 of the United Nations Charter. As yet, the Council has taken no action to maintain an effective peace in the area. Until the regime in Hanoi decides to cease its aggressive intervention in South Viet-Nam, or until effective steps are taken to maintain international peace and security in the area, the Governments of the United States and the Republic of Viet-Nam have every right to continue their individual and collective self-defense against the Communist armed aggression coming from North Viet-Nam.

IV – THE GENEVA ACCORDS

It has been demonstrated that the North Vietnamese have repeatedly violated the 1954 Geneva Accords in a most serious and flagrant manner. In so doing, of course, North Viet-Nam is ignoring an international Agreement which it signed and by which it is bound. In addition, by the continued presence in neighboring Laos of North Vietnamese forces and their use of Laotian territory for infiltration into South Viet-Nam, North Viet-Nam is violating solemn commitments which it undertook in the 1962 Geneva Agreements to refrain from such activities.

In these circumstances, international law recognizes the principle that a material breach of a treaty by one party entitles other parties at least to withhold compliance with an equivalent, corresponding or related provision until the other party is prepared to observe its obligations.

The actions of the Republic of Viet-Nam and the United States are fully consistent with this principle. North Vietnamese violations of the Geneva Agreements have created an immediate danger to the continued independence and integrity of the Republic of Viet-Nam. The response of South Viet-Nam and the United States is designed to meet this threat created by North Viet-Nam's disregard of the Accords. The extensive North Vietnamese violations certainly justify South Viet-Nam at least to withhold compliance with those provisions of the Accords which limit its ability to protect its very existence. Both South Viet-Nam and the United States have made clear that the actions which they have taken will no longer be necessary if North Viet-Nam would comply with the Accords.

[From the New York Times, Jan. 15, 1967]
LEADING AMERICAN AUTHORITIES ON INTERNATIONAL LAW REPLY TO THE PRESIDENT. — U.S. INTERVENTION IN VIETMAN IS ILLEGAL

The President, in his State of the Union Message, advanced as basic grounds for our involvement in Vietnam, our "commitment" under the SEATO Treaty, "aggression" by North Vietnam, and the Korean "precedent". These same grounds have been advanced by the Legal Adviser of the State Department in a detailed Memorandum, "The Legality of the U.S. Participation in the Defense of Vietnam", issued in March 1966 — and more recently in an address to the University of Pittsburgh Law School on December 13. Ten days ago our Committee submitted to the Secretary of State a comprehensive 45,000-word Analysis prepared by its Consultative

Council* demonstrating that the Administration's legal justification of U.S. involvement in Vietnam is based on misleading presentations of fact and unwarranted interpretations of law. Observance of the law would have spared the American people as well as the Vietnamese a cruel war. So that the American people may gauge the legality or illegality of our involvement in Vietnam, our Council's Analysis is summarized on this page in Points I to V — as briefly as is possible for a responsible understanding of the issues. Point III deals with the SEATO "commitment," Point I (1) deals with "aggression" by North Vietnam. Point I (5) deals with the Korean precedent. Other points deal with our commitments under the United Nations Charter, the 1954 Geneva Accords, and our own Constitution. At stake are not "legalisms".

At stake are the norms of behavior essential for world order. Therefore our government must, we plead, conduct its foreign relations in conformity with international law. We have requested the Senate Foreign Relations Committee to hold hearings on the legality of U.S. involvement in Vietnam. We urge your support.

Consonant with international law, and in support of Secretary General U Thant's peace plan, we urge the United States Government to take immediately the following specific steps:

1. *Unconditional* termination of bombings in North Vietnam.

2. Cooperate in replacing U.S. military forces with personnel of the International Control Commission which is legally responsible for supervising the execution of the 1954 Geneva Accords.

3. De-escalation of military operations in South Vietnam starting with the cessation of offensive operations.

---

*Consultative Council: Richard A. Falk, Chairman, Milbank Prof. International Law, Princeton University; John H. E. Fried, Rapporteur, Prof. Political Science, City University of New York; Richard J. Barnet, Co-Director, Institute for Policy Studies, Washington, D.C.; John H. Herz, Prof. International Relations, City University of New York; Stanley Hoffmann, Prof. International Law, Harvard University; Saul H. Mendlovitz, Prof. International Law, Rutgers University School of Law; Wallace McClure, Prof. International Law, World Rule of Law Center, Duke University; Richard S. Miller, Prof. International Law, Ohio State University College of Law; Hans J. Morgenthau, Michelson Distinguished Service Prof. Political Science and Modern History, University of Chicago; William G. Rice, Prof. International Law, University of Wisconsin Law School; Quincy Wright, Prof. International Law, University of Chicago; Rice University.

4. Recognition of the National Liberation Front as possessing belligerent status, and hence negotiating status, equal to that of the Saigon regime.

5. Commitment to negotiate on the basis of the 1954 Geneva accords, including the withdrawal of all foreign military forces and the elimination of all foreign bases in South and North Vietnam within a specified period of time.

United States intervention in Vietnam constitutes a series of violations of the United Nations Charter and of other fundamental rules of international law governing the use of force in international relations.

The United States has a duty—embodied in our Constitution— to abide by general international law and by the treaty obligations it has freely and sovereignly accepted.

In the nuclear age, the survival of the United States and the world requires that we become again a nation "of laws and not of men," as truly in international affairs as in domestic life.

Therefore, we, the undersigned, call upon the United States Government to cease its present conduct and to heed the counsels of restraint prudently built into international law as protection against the ever-worsening scourge of war; we call upon the United States Congress without delay to exercise its prerogatives toward these ends; and we call upon fellow Americans and men and women everywhere to support this effort to promote the cause of peace.

POINT I—THE UNILATERAL MILITARY INTERVEN-
TION OF THE UNITED STATES IN VIETNAM VIO-
LATES THE CHARTER OF THE UNITED NATIONS.
THE CHARTER'S EXCEPTIONAL AUTHORIZATION
OF INDIVIDUAL AND COLLECTIVE SELF-DEFENSE
"IF AN ARMED ATTACK OCCURS AGAINST A MEM-
BER OF THE UNITED NATIONS" DOES NOT APPLY
IN THE CASE OF VIETNAM

The Charter of the United States is a treaty that specifically obligates the United States (1) to refrain from the unilateras use or threat of force in international relations (Article 2(4)) and (2) to settle international disputes by peaceful means.

The Charter of the United Nations is a treaty that specifically obligates the United States (1) to refrain from the unilateral use the "inherent right of individual or collective self-defense if an *armed attack* occurs against *a Member of the United Nations. . . ."*

The Department Brief seizes upon the word "inherent" to argue that prior to the adoption of the United Nations Charter, states possessed a broad right of self-defense; that this right is not diminished by Article 51. Hence, it argues, the exercise of this right of "collective self-defense" by the United States on behalf of South Vietnam is not inconsistent with the Charter.

This contention is fallacious for several reasons:

1. *There has been no "armed attack" upon South Vietnam within the meaning of Article 51 of the Charter*

The question crucial for world order is — What kind of grievance permits a state to act in "self-defense"?

The right of self-defense under the Charter exists only if an "armed attack" has occurred. The language of Article 51 is unequivocal. The concrete term "armed attack" was deliberately introduced into the Charter to eliminate the discretion of states to determine for themselves the scope of permissible self-defense — that is, to wage war without *prior* U.N. authorization. A claim for self-defense is permissible only "when the necessity for action is instant, overwhelming, and leaving no choice of means, and no moment for deliberation." This definition of self-defense was stated in classic form by Secretary of State Daniel Webster in the *Caroline Case*, (VII Moore's Digest of International Law, 919) and was affirmed in the Nuremberg judgment and by unanimous vote of the U.N. General Assembly at its First Session. Res. 95(1).

The State Department Memorandum acknowledges that a *specific* form of aggression, namely, an *"armed attack"* is an essential condition precedent to the use of force in self-defense, and that a mere allegation of indirect aggression does not entitle a state to wage war by unilateral discretion. However, the Memorandum blurs the essential distinction between the broad and vague *general* concept of aggression and the narrow one of armed attack. Evidently endeavoring to justify the U.S.'s open combat actions against North Vietnam and in South Vietnam which started on February 7, 1965, the State Department merely alleges the occurrence of an armed attack by North Vietnam "before February 1965," without providing a convincing demonstration of why its allegations about the gradual infiltration of North Vietnamese guerrillas over a period of ten years in support of the Vietcong insurgency should be regarded as an armed attack.

The Department Brief quotes selectively from the reports of the International Control Commission to support its claims of subversion and infiltration over the "years." It fails, however, to acknowledge passages in the reports of the ICC that criticize the forbidden, and progressively increasing, military build-up of South Vietnam by the United States that commenced almost immediately after the Geneva Accords of 1954. It is in the context of this gradually increasing American military build-up of South Vietnam and American presence in South Vietnam that one must assess the contention that the infiltration of 40,000 North Vietnamese between 1954 and 1965 should be viewed as an armed attack.

The Department Brief itself provides the reasoning with which to reject its charge of "armed attack" by North Vietnam. The long-smoldering conditions of unrest, subversion and infiltration in South Vietnam that it describes is an example of the very opposite of an emergency demanding immediate response "leaving no choice of means, and no moment for deliberation" and justifying a claim of self-defense. The State Department's argument, if accepted, would broaden Article 51 far beyond either its intended or desirable meaning. Whereas the Charter limits the use of force, by uni-lateral decision to specific emergencies where there is no time to seek authorization from the Security Council, the State Department's doctrine would grant all states – and even "entities" which are not sovereign states – a dangerous and virtually unlimited discretion to decide when force shall be used. This is in clear contrast to the letter and spirit of the Charter.

The Department Brief does not even sustain its charge of indirect aggression, it indicates that prior to 1964 the "infiltrators" were South Vietnamese that had previously moved North after July 1954. Moreover, the lumping together of "40,000 armed and unarmed guerrillas" is not meaningful. How can an unarmed Vietnamese who moves from one zone of his country to another be classified as a "guerrilla" and "infiltrator", contributing to "armed attack"? Above all, the implication that by 1964 the Southern insurgents had been reinforced by 40,000 guerrillas from the North is altogether, misleading; for this figure, even if correct, fails to deduct all those who during a whole decade died, became incapacitated, were taken prisoners, deserted, or simply withdrew from or never participated in the insurgency.

The Mansfield Report shows that before 1965 infiltration from the North, "was confined primarily to political cadres and military leadership." On the other hand it notes that by 1962, "United States military advisers and service forces in South Vietnam totaled approximately 10,000 men. The Report makes plain that significant armed personnel were introduced from the North only *after* the United States had intervened when "total collapse of the Saigon government's authority appeared imminent in the early months of 1965." It states (at p. 1):

"United States combat troops in strength arrived at that point in response to the appeal of the Saigon authorities. The Viet-cong *counter-response* was to increase their military activity with forces strengthened by intensified local recruitment and infiltration of regular North Vietnamese troops. With the change in the composition of the opposing forces the character of the war also changed sharply." The Report (p. 3) underscores that significant forces from the North followed and did not precede the direct involvement of the United States.

To summarize this crucial point—self-defense is legally permissible only in response to a particularly grave, immediate emergency—described in international law and the Charter as "armed attack." The kind of force allegedly employed by North Vietnam in South Vietnam cannot appropriately be regarded as an "armed attack" within the meaning of Article 51. Therefore a claim to act in self-defense is unavailable to South Vietnam; and, *a fortiori,* unavailable to the United States as an ally acting in collective self-defense.

2. The United States failed to fulfill its charter obligation to seek a peaceful solution in Vietnam

The State Department also ignores the obligation under the Charter to seek *first of all* a peaceful solution by any method of the disputant's own choice, within or outside the machinery of the United Nations. This legal requirement is elaborated in Article 33(1): "The parties to any dispute, the continuance of which is likely to endanger the maintenance of international peace and security, shall *first of all*, seek a solution by negotiation, enquiry, mediation, conciliation, arbitration, judicial settlement, resort to regional agencies or arrangements, or other peaceful means of their own choice."

The United States has had many years within which to seek a peaceful solution of the Vietnam situation. Indeed, a report prepared for the American Friends Service Committee — "Peace in Vietnam" — discussing "The Negotiation Puzzle", points out that "a careful reading of the *New York Times* shows that the United States has rejected no fewer than seven efforts to negotiate an end to the war" (p. 51), citing efforts by U Thant, President de Gaulle, Hanoi and others, made long before the United States embarked upon an active combat role in February, 1965.

Ever since the mid-1950's the reports of the International Control Commission contain many complaints about South Vietnam's deliberate and systematic sabotage of the machinery created by the Geneva Accords to prevent dangerous developments. The United States has done little to dispel the belief that it has favored a "military solution" to the conflict in Vietnam.

3. *The doctrine of "collective self-defense" cannot justify the United States military intervention in the civil war in South Vietnam*

If the conflict in South Vietnam is a civil war the intervention of the United States is a violation of the undertaking, fundamental in international law, that one state has no right to intervene in the internal affairs of other countries.

It seems most correct to regard the present conflict in South Vietnam as essentially a civil war among, what James Reston has described a "tangle of competing individuals, regions, religions and sects ... [among] a people who have been torn apart by war and dominated and exploited by Saigon for generations." (*New York Times,* April 3, 1966.)

The Charter of the United Nations is silent on the subject of civil war. It has been generally assumed, however, that a civil war is a matter essentially within the domestic jurisdiction of a state (Article 2(7)), and that therefore even the United Nations is obliged to refrain from intervening unless the civil war is identified by a competent organ of the U.N. as a threat to international peace. Certainly if the United Nations must stay aloof from civil wars, then it is even clearer that individual states are likewise obliged to refrain from interfering in civil wars. The weight of opinion among international lawyers lays stress upon a duty of non-intervention in ongoing civil wars.

Even if North Vietnam and South Vietnam are accorded the status of separate entities in international law, approximating the status of independent countries, rather than being "temporary zones" of a single country as decreed by the Geneva Accords, the United States may not respond to the intervention of North Vietnam in the civil war in the South by bombing the North. There is no legal basis for an outside state to respond to an intervention by another state in a civil war with a military attack on the territory of the intervening state. Neither Germany under Hitler nor Italy under Mussolini claimed that their intervention in behalf of Franco during the Spanish Civil War would have vindicated their use of military force upon the territory of the Soviet Union, a state intervening in behalf of the Loyalists. Correspondingly, the Soviet Union, intervening in behalf of Spain's legitimate government, did not claim any right to use military force against Germany or Italy. It is sobering to realize that if the United States was lawfully entitled to bomb North Vietnam in response to North Vietnam's intervention in the Southern civil war, then North Vietnam or any of its allies would have been lawfully entitled to bomb the United States in response to the United States' much more massive intervention in that civil war.

4. *The "request" of the "Government" of South Vietnam does not provide a legal basis for "collective self-defense"*

The evidence shows that in many respects the present Saigon regime, just as its predecessors since 1954, is a client government of the United States. These governments seem to have been incapable of independent action, as regards either inviting American assistance or requesting modification or termination of American assistance. Furthermore, these regimes have been unable to act on behalf of their people or even to rule effectively the territory under their control.

The present government has no constitutional basis, and is incapable of even achieving stability on its own side in the face of the emergency represented by the ongoing civil war, a factor that normally postpones protest movement until the civil war is settled. The recurring protests of Buddhists, Catholics, business leaders, students, intellectuals, and other civilian groups in South Vietnam are dramatic evidence of the tenuous existence and the repressive quality of Premier Ky's regime.

If the United States were to withdraw from South Vietnam the Ky government would collapse. In what sense, then, is such a regime sufficiently constituted as a government to authorize military intervention of the United States on its own behalf? It is hardly comforting to rely upon the Soviet suppression of the Nagy uprising of 1956 in Hungary as a useful precedent to support what the United States is doing in Vietnam on a far larger and sustained scale.

5. The Korean precedent does not justify the unilateral intervention of the United States in Vietnam

The State Department's reliance upon the Korean precedent to sustain "the right to organize collective defense" is inadequate to establish a legal basis for the unilateral U.S. military intervention in Vietnam. General Ridgway, among others, has pointed to some of the important differences between Korea and Vietnam (Look Magazine, April 5, 1966, p. 82):

"In South Korea, we had a workable government . . . We acted in concert with many nations and had been deputized by the United Nations to repel the aggressor in its name."

In Korea, a massive invasion (armed attack) from the North had occurred, as attested to by United Nations observers; nevertheless the United States did not claim a right of "collective self-defense" on behalf of the South but brought the case before the United Nations Security Council, and thereafter acted in the name of the United Nations.

POINT II—THE MILITARY PRESENCE OF THE UNITED
    STATES IN VIETNAM VIOLATES THE GENEVA
    ACCORDS OF 1954

The State Department claims that the U.S. military intervention in Vietnam is compatible with the Geneva Accords of 1954 and, in fact, is based on U.S. assurances made at the time of their signing.

The Geneva Conference dealt with the situation created by the defeat of the French in their 8-year war against the Viet Minh for control over the whole of Vietnam. After the battle at Dien Bien Phu in June 1954, the Viet Minh occupied the major part of the country north of the thirteenth parallel. However, Ho Chi Minh agreed to withdraw his forces to the north of the seventeenth parallel in exchange for two central commitments: (1) the unconditional promise that all foreign military forces in Vietnam would be removed, and (2) that within two years elections would be held under international supervision to unify the country, so that the temporary division of Vietnam into a northern and southern zone would end by July 1956.

The United States pledged on July 21, 1954 not "to disturb" the Geneva Accords. Article 6 of the Final Declaration of the Geneva Conference explicitly stated that the military demarcation line is provisional and shall not in any way be interpreted as constituting a political or territorial boundary.

It is generally acknowledged that Hanoi initially carried out the central provisions of the Accords and eschewed violence south of the seventeenth parallel because it expected to win the elections and did not wish to alienate those whose electoral support it sought. (See, e.g., Fourth Interim Report of the International Control Commission, Vietnam No. 3, Command Paper 9654 [1954]). Nevertheless, on July 16, 1955, the Diem regime, with United States backing, announced that it would not participate in the prescribed nation-wide elections and would not even negotiate with Hanoi, as also prescribed in the Accords, about their modalities. The fact that the Accords granted Diem a full year (July 1955 – July 1956) to demand any safeguards for fair elections refutes the State Department's assertion that Diem's obstruction of the central provision of the Geneva Settlement – reunification – was justified because the elections would not have been fair in the North.

As late as September 18, 1961, the International Control Commission (ICC) insisted upon compliance with the obligation to hold elections for reunification. In a Special Report of June 2, 1962, the ICC declared that the United States "increased military aid" to South Vietnam and that the United States' "factual military alliance" with South Vietnam violated the Geneva Agreement.

POINT III – THE UNITED STATES IS NOT COMMITTED BY THE SEATO TREATY OR OTHERWISE TO INTERVENE IN VIETNAM

The State Department's claim that the United States military involvement in Vietnam is in fulfillment of its obligation under the Southeast Asia Collective Defense Treaty is untenable. The argument is a late discovery. SEATO was not mentioned in the official U.S. announcements in February 1965, when the bombing of North Vietnam commenced. In March 1965, the State Department, in a Memorandum entitled "Legal Basis for the United States Actions Against North Vietnam," did not refer to SEATO. Neither Secretary of State Rusk, in an address on Vietnam before the American Society of International Law in April 1965, nor President Johnson, in a statement on July 28, 1965 explaining, "Why We Are in Vietnam," made any reference to SEATO.

In fact, the SEATO Treaty does not enlarge the legal basis for the use of force contained in the U.N. Charter. The State Department misleadingly asserts that the Treaty's Article 4(1) creates an "*obligation* . . . to meet the common danger in the event of *armed aggression*". The term "*armed aggression*" is not contained in the Treaty. Repeating the language of the U.N. Charter, Article 4(1), speaks of "aggression by means of *armed attack*." Since an armed attack has not occurred; SEATO does not authorize defensive action; if an armed attack *had* occurred, SEATO would be redundant, as the use of force would be permissible under Article 51 of the Charter.

In the event of an "armed attack" the United States would have had, at most, the legal *right*, but certainly not an *obligation*, to assist South Vietnam. None of the other SEATO parties regard military intervention in Vietnam as legally required by SEATO. On the contrary, two leading members of SEATO — Pakistan and France — have publicly denounced the United States' role in the Vietnam war.

Article 4 (2) of the SEATO Treaty makes clear that if South Vietnam were threatened "in any way *other* than by armed attack," the (SEATO) parties "shall consult immediately in order to agree on the measures which should be taken for the common defense." And Article 2 of the Treaty makes clear that "subversive activities directed from without" does *not* constitute "an armed attack," but call for consultation by the treaty members. *Consultation* is not unilateral military assistance. Indeed, the Treaty presupposes unanimous *agreement* among the other seven partners before any SEATO power would be authorized to offer military support. In 1964, the unanimity requirement was reinterpreted by the United States to mean that "measures" could be taken in the absence of a dissenting vote among the SEATO partners.

As regards "commitments" of former Presidents, the Department Brief fails to point out that President Eisenhower initially offered limited *economic* aid to the Diem regime if it would be "prepared to give assurances as to the standards of performance it would be able to maintain in the event such aid were supplied," and only on condition that the American "aid will be met by performance on the part of the Government of Vietnam in undertaking needed reforms." (Department of State Bulletin XXXI, November 15, 1954, pp. 735-736). President Eisenhower has stated categorically that his Administration had made no commitment to South Vietnam "in terms of military support or programs whatsoever."

President Kennedy insisted that the war in Vietnam was "their war" and promised only equipment and military advisers. His view of the United States involvement in Vietnam was summed up in the statement he made in September 1963:

"In the final analyses, it's their war. They're the ones who have to win or lose it. We can help them, we can give them equipment, we can send our men out there as advisers, but they have to win it, the people of Vietnam."

It is strange legal logic retrospectively to construe these carefully guarded offers of limited assistance as commitments for military invervention.

POINT IV—THE INTENSITY AND DESTRUCTIVENESS OF UNITED STATES WARFARE IN VIETNAM IS CONTRARY TO INTERNATIONAL LAW

The intensity, indiscriminateness, and destructiveness of United States war actions in Vietnam violate basic rules of warfare that have been part of international law at least since the formulation of the Hague Conventions in 1907.

These actions are particularly reprehensible so far as North Vietnam is concerned. It has never been denied that the United States military presence vastly exceeds that of the North in South Vietnam. Under the Geneva Accords, the United States is not entitled to introduce military personnel and equipment anywhere in Vietnam (except man-for-man and piece-for-piece replacements as of the status of July 1954) and much less to participate in active fighting in that country. Even if, as the Department Brief contends, reprisal or response to violations of the Geneva Accords by North Vietnam were justified, the United States would be entitled to disregard these Accords only in proportion to their disregard by North Vietnam.

Long before the advent of the United Nations, it was a basic rule of international law that force used in reprisal must be proportional to the illegal provocation. In the leading case of the pre-United Nations era on the subject (the *Naulilaa Incident*, involving the shelling of Portuguese forts by Germany in 1914), a German-Portuguese Mixed Tribunal emphasized that reprisals "are limited by considerations of humanity and good faith"; and more generally, that, "One should certainly consider as excessive, and therefore illegal, reprisals out of all proportion with the act which motivated them." Bombing North Vietnam, as of February, 1965, in alleged reprisal for Vietcong attacks on two American airbases in South Vietnam, certainly seems to flaunt this rule of proportionality.

POINT V – UNITED STATES ACTIONS IN VIETNAM VIOLATE TREATIES WHICH ARE PART OF THE SUPREME LAW OF THE LAND, AND HENCE VIOLATE THE UNITED STATES CONSTITUTION

Since United States actions in South Vietnam and North Vietnam violate treaties to which the United States has become a party by ratification pursuant to the Constitution, they violate the Supreme Law of the Land. No branch of the Government, alone or together, may, under the Constitution, authorize actions in violation of treaties or delegate power to do so. There is no Constitutional authority to violate the Charter of the United Nations, a treaty of which the United States was a principal architect, which embodies the conscience of mankind, and which is legally binding on all its members.

The reliance of the Department Brief upon alleged past precedents as applicable to the Vietnam situation is wholly unfounded, and the assertion that, since 1789, Presidents have at least 125 times ordered "armed forces to take action or maintain positions without prior Congressional authorization" is misleading. None of these incidents, except possibly the Korean conflict, involved U.S. war actions comparable in magnitude to those in Vietnam. None involved the dispatch of military forces for combat to a territory from which, by solemn international compact, foreign military personnel, foreign equipment, and foreign bases were to be excluded. Moreover, most of these instances were the product of "gunboat diplomacy" undertaken before the United Nations Charter limited the permissible use of force under international law to self-defense against an armed attack.

The Korean precedent is especially inapposite, as President Truman's actions were authorized by a Security Council Resolution, and were not unilaterally undertaken as are the actions in Vietnam.

We petition the Congress to adopt the council's 5 point program and thus, by adhering to the precepts of international law, help to bring peace to our country and to Vietnam.

The signers of this statement agree with its general tenor and conclusions, although not necessarily with every formulation that it contains. Names of institutions are listed for identification only.

LAWYERS COMMITTEE ON AMERICAN POLICY
TOWARDS VIETNAM,
WILLIAM L. STANDARD, *Chairman*
CAREY McWILLIAMS, *Vice Chairman,*
JOSEPH H. CROWN, *Secretary-Treasurer.*

PATTERN FOR PEACE IN SOUTHEAST ASIA: Address by President Johnson, Johns Hopkins University, April 17, 1965[1]

Last week 17 nations sent their views to some two dozen countries having an interest in Southeast Asia. We are joining those 17 countries and stating our American policy tonight, which we believe will contribute toward peace in this area of the world.

I have come here to review once again with my own people the views of the American Government.

Tonight Americans and Asians are dying for a world where each people may choose its own path to change. This is the principle for which our ancestors fought in the valleys of Pennsylvania. It is a principle for which our sons fight tonight in the jungles of Vietnam.

[1]Department of State *Bulletin,* Apr. 26, 1965, pp. 606-610.

Vietnam is far away from this quiet campus. We have no territory there, nor do we seek any. The war is dirty and brutal and difficult. And some 400 young men, born into an America that is bursting with opportunity and promise, have ended their lives on VietNam's steaming soil.

Why must we take this painful road? Why must this nation hazard its ease, its interest, and its power for the sake of a people so far away?

We fight because we must fight if we are to live in a world where every country can shape its own destiny, and only in such a world will our own freedom be finally secure.

This kind of world will never be built by bombs or bullets. Yet the infirmities of man are such that force must often precede reason and the waste of war, the works of peace. We wish that this were not so. But we must deal with the world as it is, if it is ever to be as we wish.

The world as it is in Asia is not a serene or peaceful place.

The first reality is that North Vietnam has attacked the independent nation of South Vietnam. Its object is total conquest. Of course, some of the people of South Vietnam are participating in attack on their own government. But trained men and supplies, orders and arms, flow in a constant stream from North to South.

This support is the heartbeat of the war.

And it is a war of unparalleled brutality. Simple farmers are the targets of assassination and kidnapping. Women and children are strangled in the night because their men are loyal to their government. And helpless villages are ravaged by sneak attacks. Large-scale raids are conducted on towns, and terror strikes in the heart of cities.

The confused nature of this conflict cannot mask the fact that it is the new face of an old enemy.

Over this war—and all Asia—is another reality; the deepening shadow of Communist China. The rulers in Hanoi are urged on by Peiping. This is a regime which has destroyed freedom in Tibet, which has attacked India, and has been condemned by the United Nations for aggression in Korea. It is a nation which is helping the forces of violence in almost every continent. The contest in Vietnam is part of a wider pattern of aggressive purposes.

their own way. We will do everything necessary to reach that objective, and we will do only what is absolutely necessary.

In recent months attacks on South Vietnam were stepped up. Thus, it became necessary for us to increase our response and to make attacks by air. This is not a change of purpose. It is a change in what we believe that purpose requires.

We do this in order to slow down aggression.

We do this to increase the confidence of the brave people of South Vietnam who have bravely borne this brutal battle for so many years with so many casualties.

And we do this to convince the leaders of North Vietnam — and all who seek to share their conquest — of a simple fact:

We will not be defeated.

We will not grow tired.

We will not withdraw, either openly or under the cloak of a meaningless agreement.

We know that air attacks alone will not accomplish all of these purposes. But it is our best and prayerful judgment that they are a necessary part of the surest road to peace.

We hope that peace will come swiftly. But that is in the hands of others besides ourselves. And we must be prepared for a long continued conflict. It will require patience as well as bravery — the will to endure as well as the will to resist.

I wish it were possible to convince others with words of what we now find it necessary to say with guns and planes: armed hostility is futile — our resources are equal to any challenge — because we fight for values and we fight for principle, rather than territory or colonies, our patience and our determination are unending.

Once this is clear, then is should also be clear that the only path for reasonable men is the path of peaceful settlement. Such peace demands an independent South Vietnam — securely guaranteed and able to shape its own relationships to all others — free from outside interference — tied to no alliance — a military base for no other country.

These are the essentials of any final settlement.

We will never be second in the search for such a peaceful settlement in Vietnam.

There may be many ways to this kind of peace: in discussion or negotiation with the governments concerned; in large groups or in

small ones; in the reaffirmation of old agreements or their strengthening with new ones.

We have stated this position over and over again 50 times and
more to friend and foe alike. And we remain ready with this purpose
for unconditional discussions.

And until that bright and necessary day of peace we will try to
keep conflict from spreading. We have no desire to see thousands
die in battle — Asians or Americans. We have no desire to devastate
that which the people of North Vietnam have built with toil and
sacrifice. We will use our power with restraint and with all the
wisdom that we can command.

But we will use it.

This war, like most wars, is filled with terrible irony. For what do
the people of North Vietnam want? They want what their neighbors also desire — food for their hunger, health for their bodies, a
chance to learn, progress for their country, and an end to the bond-
age of material misery. And they would find all these things far
more readily in peaceful association with others than in the endless
course of battle.

These countries of Southeast Asia are homes for millions of impoverished people. Each day these people rise at dawn and struggle
through until the night to wrest existence from the soil. They are
often wracked by diseases, plagued by hunger, and death comes at
the early age of 40.

Stability and peace do not come easily in such a land. Neither
independence nor human dignity will ever be won, though, by arms
alone. It also requires the works of peace. The American people
have helped generously in times past in these works, and now there
must be a much more massive effort to improve the life of man in
that conflict-torn corner of our world.

The first step is for the countries of Southeast Asia to associate
themselves in a greatly expanded cooperative effort for development. We would hope that North Vietnam would take its place in
the common effort just as soon as peaceful cooperation is possible.

The United Nations is already actively engaged in development
in this area, and as far back in 1961 I conferred with our authorities
in Vietnam in connection with their work there. And I would hope
tonight that the Secretary-General of the United Nations could use
the prestige of his great office and his deep knowledge of Asia to

initiate, as soon as possible, with the countries of that area, a plan for cooperation in increased development.

For our part I will ask the Congress to join in a billion-dollar American investment in this effort as soon as it is underway. And I would hope that all other industrialized countries, including the Soviet Union, will join in this effort to replace despair with hope and terror with progress.

The task is nothing less than to enrich the hopes and existence of more than a hundred million people. And there is much to be done.

The vast Mekong River can provide food and water and power on a scale to dwarf even our own TVA. The wonders of modern medicine can be spread through villages where thousands die every year from lack of care. Schools can be established to train people in the skills needed to manage the process of development. And these objectives, and more, are within the reach of a cooperative and determined effort.

I also intend to expand and speed up a program to make available our farm surpluses to assist in feeding and clothing the needy in Asia. We should not allow people to go hungry and wear rags while our own warehouses overflow with an abundance of wheat and corn and rice and cotton.

So I will very shortly name a special team of outstanding patriotic, and distinguished Americans to inaugurate our participation in these programs. This team will be headed by Mr. Eugene Black, the very able former President of the World Bank.

This will be a disorderly planet for a long time. In Asia, and elsewhere, the forces of the modern world are shaking old ways and uprooting ancient civilizations. There will be turbulence and struggle and even violence. Great social change—as we see in our own country—does not always come without conflict.

We must also expect that nations will on occasion be in dispute with us. It may be because we are rich, or powerful, or because we have made some mistakes, or because they honestly fear our intentions. However, no nation need ever fear that we desire their land, or to impose our will, or to dictate their institutions.

But we will always oppose the effort of one nation to conquer another nation.

We will do this because our own security is at stake.

But there is more to it than that. For our generation has a dream. It is a very old dream. But we have the power, and now we have the opportunity to make that dream come true.

For centuries nations have struggled among each other. But we dream of a world where disputes are settled by law and reason. And we will try to make it so.

For most of history men have hated and killed one another in battle. But we dream of an end to war. And we will try to make it so.

For all existence most men have lived in poverty, threatened by hunger. But we dream of a world where all are fed and charged with hope. And we will help to make it so.

The ordinary men and women of North Vietnam and South Vietnam, of China and India, of Russia and America, are brave people. They are filled with the same proportions of hate and fear, of love and hope. Most of them want the same things for themselves and their families. Most of them do not want their sons to ever die in battle, or to see their homes, or the homes of others destroyed.

Well, this can be their world yet. Man now has the knowledge— always before denied—to make this planet serve the real needs of the people who live on it.

I know this will not be easy. I know how difficult it is for reason to guide passion, and love to master hate. The complexities of this world do not bow easily to pure and consistent answers.

But the simple truths are there just the same. We must all try to follow them as best we can.

We often say how impressive power is. But I do not find it impressive at all. The guns and the bombs, the rockets and the warships, are all symbols of human failure. They are necessary symbols. They protect what we cherish. But they are witness to human folly.

A dam built across a great river is impressive.

In the countryside where I was born, and where I live, I have seen the night illuminated, and the kitchen warmed, and the home heated, where once the cheerless night and the ceaseless cold held sway. And all this happened because electricity came to our area along the humming wires of the REA. Electrification of the countryside—yes, that, too, is impressive.

A rich harvest in a hungry land is impressive.

The sight of healthy children in a classroom is impressive. These—not mighty arms—are the achievements which the American nation believes to be impressive. And if we are steadfast, the time may come when all other nations will also find it so.

Every night before I turn out the lights to sleep I ask myself this question: Have I done everything that I can do to unite this country? Have I done everything I can to help unite the world, to try to bring peace and hope to all the peoples of the world? Have I done enough?

Ask yourselves that question in your homes—and in this hall tonight. Have we, each of us, all done all we can do? Have we done enough?

We may well be living in the time foretold many years ago when it was said: "I call heaven and earth to record this day against you, that I have set before you life and death, blessing and cursing: therefore choose life, that both thou and thy seed may live."

This generation of the world must choose: destroy or build, kill or aid, hate or understand. We can do all these things on a scale that has never been dreamed of before.

Well, we will choose life. And so doing, we will prevail over the enemies within man, and over the natural enemies of all mankind.

ADDITIONAL APPROPRIATIONS TO MEET MOUNTING MILITARY REQUIREMENTS IN VIETNAM: Message From the President of the United States, May 4, 1965[1]

To the Congress of the United States of America:

I ask the Congress to appropriate at the earliest possible moment an additional $700 million to meet mounting military requirements in Vietnam.

This is not a routine appropriation. For each Member of Congress who supports this request is also voting to persist in our effort to halt Communist aggression in South Vietnam. Each is saying that the Congress and the President stand united before the world in joint determination that the independence of South Vietnam shall be preserved and Communist attack will not succeed.

---

[1]H. Doc. 157, 89th Cong., 1st sess.

I have reviewed the situation in Vietnam many times with the Congress, the American people and the world. South Vietnam has been attacked by North Vietnam. It has asked our help. We are giving that help because our commitments, our principles, and our national interest demand it.

This is not the same kind of aggression with which the world has been long familiar. Instead of the sweep of invading armies, there is the steady, deadly stream of men and supplies. Instead of open battle between major opposing forces, there is murder in the night, assassination, and terror. Instead of dramatic confrontation and sharp division between nationals of different lands, some citizens of South Vietnam have been recruited in the effort to conquer their own country.

All of this shrouds battle in confusion. But this is the face of war in the 1960's. This is the "war of liberation." Kept from direct attack by American power, unable to win a free election in any country, those who seek to expand communism by force now use subversion and terror. In this effort they often enlist nationals of the countries they wish to conquer. But it is not civil war. It is sustained by power and resources from without. The very object of this tactic is to create the appearance of an internal revolt and to mask aggression. In this way, they hope to avoid confrontation with American resolution.

But we will not be fooled or deceived, in Vietnam or any place in the world where we have a commitment. This kind of war is war against the independence of nations. And we will meet it, as we have met other shifting dangers for more than a generation.

Our commitment to South Vietnam is nourished by a quarter century of history. It rests on solemn treaties, the demands of principle, and the necessities of American security.

A quarter century ago it became apparent that the United States stood between those who wished to dominate an entire continent and the peoples they sought to conquer.

It was our determined purpose to help protect the independence of the Asian peoples.

The consequence of our determination was a vast war which took the lives of hundreds of thousands of Americans. Surely this generation will not lightly yield to new aggressors what the last generation paid for in blood and towering sacrifice.

When the war was over, we supported the effort of Asian peoples to win their freedom from colonial rule. In the Philippines, Korea, Indonesia, and elsewhere we were on the side of national independence. For this was also consistent with our belief in the right of all people to shape their own destinies.

That principle soon received another test in the fire of war. And we fought in Korea, so that South Korea might remain free.

Now, in Vietnam, we pursue the same principle which has infused American action in the Far East for a quarter of a century.

There are those who ask why this responsibility should be ours. The answer is simple. There is no one else who can do the job. Our power is essential, in the final test, if the nations of Asia are to be secure from expanding communism. Thus, when India was attacked, it looked to us for help, and we gave it gladly. We believe that Asia should be directed by Asians. But that means each Asian people must have the right to find its own way, not that one group or nation should overrun all the others.

Make no mistake about it. The aim in Vietnam is not simply the conquest of the South, tragic as that would be. It is to show that American commitment is worthless. Once that is done, the gates are down and the road is open to expansion and endless conquest. That is why Communist China opposes discussions, even though such discussions are clearly in the interest of North Vietnam.

Moreover, we are directly committed to the defense of South Vietnam. In 1954 we signed the Southeast Asia Collective Defense Treaty. That treaty committed us to act to meet aggression against South Vietnam. The U.S. Senate ratified that treaty and that obligation by a vote of 82 to 1.

Less than a year ago the Congress, by an almost unanimous vote, said that the United States was ready to take all necessary steps to meet its obligations under that treaty.

That resolution of the Congress expressed support for the policies of the administration to help the people of South Vietnam against attack—a policy established by two previous Presidents.

Thus we cannot, and will not, withdraw or be defeated. The stakes are too high, the commitment too deep, the lessons of history too plain.

At every turning point in the last 30 years, there have been those who opposed a firm stand against aggression. They have always been wrong. And when we heeded their cries, when we gave in, the consequence has been more bloodshed and wider war.

We will not repeat that mistake. Nor will we heed those who urge us to use our great power in a reckless or casual manner. We have no desire to expand the conflict. We will do what must be done. And we will do only what must be done.

For, in the long run, there can be no military solution to the problems of Vietnam. We must find the path to peaceful settlement. Time and time again we have worked to open that path. We are still ready to talk, without conditions, to any government. We will go anywhere, discuss any subject, listen to any point of view in the interests of a peaceful solution.

I also deeply regret the necessity of bombing North Vietnam.

But we began those bombings only when patience had been transformed from a virtue into a blunder—the mistaken judgment of the attackers. Time and time again men, women, and children—American and Vietnamese—were bombed in their villages and homes while we did not reply.

There was the November 1 attack on the Bien Hoa airfield. There was the Christmas Eve bombing of the Brinks Hotel in Saigon. There was the February 7 attack on the Pleiku base. In these attacks 15 Americans were killed and 245 were injured. And they are only a few examples of a steady campaign of terror and attack.

We then decided we could no longer stand by and see men and women murdered and crippled while the bases of the aggressors were immune from reply.

But we have no desire to destroy human life. Our attacks have all been aimed at strictly military targets—not hotels and movie theaters and embassy buildings.

We destroy bridges, so it is harder to convey the instruments of war from north to south. We destroy radar stations to keep our planes from being shot down. We destroy military depots for the infiltration of men and arms to the south. We patrol routes of communications to halt the invaders. We destroy ammunition dumps to prevent the use of explosives against our men and our allies.

Resistance to aggression, moderation in the use of power, and a constant search for peace. Nothing will do more to strengthen your country in the world than the proof of national unity which an overwhelming vote for this appropriation will clearly show. To deny and delay this means to deny and delay the fullest support of the American people and the American Congress to those brave men who are risking their lives for freedom in Vietnam.

LYNDON B. JOHNSON.

THE WHITE HOUSE, *May 4, 1965*.

EXCERPT FROM LETTER FROM ASSISTANT SECRETARY MACARTHUR TO SENATOR FULBRIGHT, AUGUST 2, 1965, TRANSMITTING A PAPER ENTITLED: THE U.S. COMMITMENT TO ASSIST SOUTH VIETNAM

THE U.S. COMMITMENT TO ASSIST SOUTH VIETNAM

1. December 23, 1950: Realizing that the Communist-led Vietminh drive against the French in Indochina was part of the general Communist offensive in the Far East whose northern front was in Korea, the United States, under the Truman administration, signed the Mutual Defense Assistance Agreement (Pentalateral Agreement) with France, Vietnam, Cambodia, and Laos. This agreement, authorized by Public Law 329, 81st Congress, provided for indirect U.S. military aid through France to Vietnam, Cambodia, and Laos.

2. September 7, 1951: The United States signed an agreement authorized by Public Law 535, 81st Congress, with Premier Tran Van Huu's government providing for direct U.S. economic aid to Vietnam.

3. July 21, 1954: During the concluding plenary session of the Geneva conference, the head of the U.S. delegation, Under Secretary of State Walter Bedell Smith, made a unilateral U.S. declaration. The main points of this declaration were as follows:

---

[1]Page references are to the committee print dated June 16, 1965, of the Senate Foreign Relations Committee entitled "Background Information Relating to Southeast Asia and Vietnam."

(*a*) The United States "will refrain from the threat or the use of force to disturb" the Geneva agreements.

(*b*) The United States "would view any renewal of the aggression in violation of the aforesaid agreements with grave concern and as seriously threatening international peace and security."

(*c*) The United States "shall continue to seek to achieve unity through free elections, supervised by the United Nations to insure that they are conducted fairly" (p. 61).[1]

4. October 23, 1954: President Eisenhower sent a letter to Prime Minister Ngo Dinh Diem pledging U.S. aid and support to South Vietnam (p. 67).

5. January 1, 1955: On the basis of the existing Pentalateral Agreement, the United States began sending direct supporting assistance to the Vietnamese armed forces.

6. February 19, 1955: The Southeast Asia Collective Defense Treaty (SEATO Treaty) came into force. In a protocol to the treaty, the "SEATO umbrella" was extended to cover Vietnam, Cambodia, and Laos should these countries request SEATO assistance in resisting Communist aggression. The U.S. Senate ratified the treaty on February 1, 1955, by a vote of 82 to 1 (p. 62).

7. March 7, 1955: The United States, under the Eisenhower administration, and the government of Premier Ngo Dinh Diem signed an agreement which supplemented the agreement mentioned in (2) above.

8. July 6, 1956: Vice President Richard Nixon visited Vietnam and delivered a letter from President Eisenhower to President Diem stating that President Eisenhower looked forward to many years of cooperation between the two countries.

9. May 11, 1957: A joint communique of President Eisenhower and President Diem was issued in Washington. President Eisenhower assured President Diem of the willingness of the United States to continue to offer effective assistance within the constitutional processes of the United States to promote political stability and economic welfare in the Republic of Vietnam (p. 73).

10. October 26, 1960: In a letter of good wishes on South Vietnam's fifth anniversary, President Eisenhower assured President Diem that "for so long as our strength can be useful, the United

States will continue to assist Vietnam in the difficult yet hopeful struggle ahead."

11. May 13, 1961: At the close of Vice President Johnson's visit to Vietnam, a joint Vietnamese-United States communique was issued stating that:

(a) Both Governemnts will extend and build upon existing programs of military and economic aid.

(b) Vietnam's regular armed forces will be increased with U.S. assistance.

(c) The United States will provide assistance for the entire Vietnamese Civil Guard.

(d) U.S. military experts will be used to assist Vietnam's armed forces in health, welfare, and public works activities at the village level.

(e) A special group of U.S. economic and fiscal experts will be sent to Vietnam to work out a financial plan as the basis for joint efforts (p. 77).

12. August 2, 1961: President Kennedy declared that the United States would do all it could to save South Vietnam from Communism.

13. October 26, 1961: In a letter to President Diem, President Kennedy reaffirmed U.S. determination "to help Vietnam preserve its independence, protect its people against Communist assassins, and build a better life through economic growth."

14. December 7 and 14, 1961: An exchange of messages between President Diem and President Kennedy resulted in President Kennedy's stating that the United States, in response to the Vietnamese Government's request, was prepared to help the Republic of Vietnam to protect its people and preserve its independence. President Kennedy went on to promise that the United States would promptly increase its assistance to Vietnam's defense efforts against Communist aggression (p. 84).

15. January 4, 1962: The United States and Vietnamese Governments issued a joint communique on the expansion of economic development programs which called for both Governments to do "their utmost to improve the protection and prosperity of the Vietnamese in the face of Communist guerrilla aggression and depredations directed and supported by the Communist regime in Hanoi" (p. 86).

16. November 24, 1963: President Johnson affirmed the U.S. intention to continue its military and economic support of South Vietnam's struggle against the Communist Vietcong.

17. December 31, 1963: In a New Year message to Gen. Duong Van Minh, President Johnson pledged that the "United States will continue to furnish you and your people with the fullest measure of support in this bitter fight. We shall maintain in Vietnam American personnel and material as needed to assist you in achieving victory" (p. 106).

18. April 20, 1964: President Johnson stated that no one should "doubt that we are in this battle as long as South Vietnam wants our support and needs our assistance to protect its freedom."

19. August 7, 1964: The Congress approved the southeast Asia resolution by a vote of 88 to 2 in the Senate and 416 to 0 in the House of Representatives. The resolution stated that "the Congress approves and supports the determination of the President, as Commander in Chief, to take all necessary measures to repel any armed attack against the forces of the United States and to prevent further aggression." It also declared that the United States was prepared "as the President determines, to take all necessary steps, including the use of armed force, to assist any member or protocol state of the Southeast Asia Collective Defense Treaty requesting assistance in defense of its freedom" (p. 128).

20. April 7, 1965: In his speech at Johns Hopkins University, President Johnson stated that he intended to keep the promise repeated since 1954 to help South Vietnam. "To dishonor that pledge, to abandon this small and brave nation to its enemies, and to the terror that must follow, would be an unforgivable wrong" (p. 197).

21. May 4, 1965: In his message to the Congress accompanying a request for an additional $700 million to meet mounting military requirements in Vietnam, President Johnson stated: "This is not a routine appropriation. For each Member of Congress who supports this request is also voting to persist in our efforts to halt Communist aggression in South Vietnam. Each is saying that the Congress and the President stand united before the world in joint determination that the independence of South Vietnam shall be preserved and Communist attack will not succeed." The House approved the appropriation by a vote of 408 to 7 and the Senate by a vote of 88 to 3 (p. 219).

22. July 28, 1965: President Johnson told his press conference that "We are in Vietnam to fulfill one of the most solemn pledges of the American Nation. Three Presidents — President Eisenhower, President Kennedy, and your present President — over 11 years, have committed themselves and have promised to help defend this small and valiant nation."

EXCERPT FROM "THE VIETNAM CONFLICT: THE SUBSTANCE AND THE SHADOW" - REPORT TO SENATE COMMITTEE ON FOREIGN RELATIONS - JANUARY 6, 1966.

E. CONCLUDING COMMENTS

A rapid solution to the conflict in Vietnam is not an immediate prospect. This would appear to be the case whether military victory is pursued or negotiations do, in fact, materialize.

Insofar as the military situation is concerned, the large-scale introduction of U.S. forces and their entry into combat has blunted but not turned back the drive of the Vietcong. The latter have responded to the increased American role with a further strengthening of their forces by local recruitment in the south and reinforcements from the north and a general stepping up of military activity. As a result the lines remain drawn in South Vietnam in substantially the same pattern as they were at the outset of the increased U.S. commitment. What has changed basically is the scope and intensity of the struggle and the part which is being played by the forces of the United States and those of North Vietnam.

Despite the great increase in American military commitment, it is doubtful in view of the acceleration of Vietcong efforts that the constricted position now held in Vietnam by the Saigon government can continue to be held for the indefinite future, let alone extended, without a further augmentation of American forces on the ground. Indeed, if present trends continue, there is no assurance as to what ultimate increase in American military commitment will be required before the conflict is terminated. For the fact is that under present terms of reference and as the war has evolved, the question is not one of applying increased U.S. pressure to a defined military situation but rather of pressing against a military situation which is, in effect, open-ended. How open is dependent on the extent to which North Vietnam and its supporters are willing and able to meet increased force by increased force. All of mainland southeast Asia, at least, cannot be ruled out as a potential battlefield. As noted, the war has already expanded significantly into Laos and is beginning to lap over the Cambodian border while pressures increase in the northeast of Thailand.

Even if the war remains substantially within its present limits, there is little foundation for the expectation that the government of Vietnam in Saigon will be able, in the near future, to carry a much greater burden than it is now carrying. This is in no sense a reflection on the caliber of the current leaders of Vietnam. But the fact is that they are, as other Vietnamese Governments have been over the past decade, at the beginning of a beginning in dealing with the problems of popular mobilization in support of the Government. They are starting, moreover, from a point considerably behind that which prevailed at the time of President Diem's assassination. Under present concepts and plans, then, what lies ahead is, literally, a vast and continuing undertaking in social engineering in the wake of such military progress as may be registered. And for many years to come this task will be very heavily dependent on U.S. foreign aid.

The basic concept of present American policy with respect to Vietnam casts the United States in the role of support of the Vietnamese Government and people. This concept becomes more difficult to maintain as the military participation of the United States undergoes rapid increase. Yet a change in the basic concept could have a most unfortunate impact upon the Vietnamese people and the world at large. What is involved here is the necessity for the greatest restraint in word and action, lest the concept be eroded and the war drained of a purpose with meaning to the people of Vietnam.

This danger is great, not only because of the military realities of the situation but also because, with a few exceptions, assistance has not been and is not likely to be forthcoming for the war effort in South Vietnam from nations other than the United States. On the contrary, as it now appears, the longer the war continues in its present pattern and the more it expands in scope, the greater will become the strain placed upon the relations of the United States with allies both in the Far East and in Europe.

Many nations are deeply desirous of an end to this conflict as quickly as possible. Few are specific as to the manner in which this end can be brought about or the shape it is likely to take. In any event, even though other nations, in certain circumstances, may be willing to play a third-party role in bringing about neogtiations, any prospects for effective negotiations at this time (and they are slim) are likely to be largely dependent on the initiatives and efforts of the combatants.

Negotiations at this time, moreover, if they do come about, and if they are accompanied by a cease-fire and standfast, would serve to stabilize a situation in which the majority of the population remains under nominal government control but in which dominance of the countryside rests largely in the hands of the Vietcong. What might eventually materialize through negotiations from this situation cannot be foreseen at this time with any degree of certainty.

That is not, to say the least, a very satisfactory prospect. What needs also to be borne in mind, however, is that the visible alternative at this time and under present terms of reference is the indefinite expansion and intensification of the war which will require the continuous introduction of additional U.S. forces. The end of that course cannot be foreseen, either, and there are no grounds for optimism that the end is likely to be reached within the confines of South Vietnam or within the very near future.

In short, such choices as may be open are not simple choices. They are difficult and painful choices and they are beset with many imponderables. The situation, as it now appears, offers only the very slim prospect of a just settlement by negotiations of the alternative prospect of a continuance of the conflict in the direction of a general war on the Asian mainland.

REMARKS OF THE PRESIDENT ON THE SUBMITTAL TO CONGRESS OF THE SUPPLEMENTAL APPROPRIATION FOR 1966, JANURAY 19, 1966[2]

In the last 2 years, in repeated acts of authorization and appropriation, the Congress has provided continuing support for our national decision "to prevent further aggression" in southeast Asia.

---

[1]Department of State press release No. 12 dated Jan. 17, 1966.
[2]White House press release dated Jan. 19, 1966.

The quoted words come from the joint resolution of the Congress that was approved on August 10, 1964. It is in the letter and the spirit of the resolution the I request this supplementary appropriation. While that resolution remains in force, and until its obligations are discharged, we must persevere. I believe the resolution is right, and I believe that the course we follow is necessary. I intend that those who must face danger and death as we follow that course shall be supported. I am confident that the Congress will agree.

This is an opportunity for us to demonstrate once again—to friend and to foe alike—that there is no difference between one party and another, or between the Congress and the executive branch when it comes to effective and sustained support of our fighting men and their allies. Whatever differences there are on other issues, we are as one in support of our men in Vietnam. As I said just 1 week ago, "Until peace comes, or if it does not come, we will give our fighting men what they must have: every gun, every dollar, and every decision—whatever the cost or whatever the challenge." And we will continue to help the people of South Vietnam and our allies in resisting aggression and in protecting the independence of that beleaguered country.

DECLARATION OF HONOLULU, FEBRUARY 8, 1966[1]

Part I

The Republic of Vietnam and the United States of America jointly declare:
   their determination in defense against aggression,
   their dedication to the hopes of all the people of South Vietnam,
   and their commitment to the search for just and stable peace.
In pursuit of these objectives the leaders of their governments have agreed upon this declaration, which sets forth—
   the purposes of the Government of Vietnam,
   the purposes of the Government of the United States,
   and the common commitment of both Governments.

---

[1]White House press release dated Feb. 8, 1966.

Part II

THE PURPOSES OF THE GOVERNMENT OF VIETNAM

Here in the mid-Pacific, halfway between Asia and North America, we take the opportunity to state again the aims of our government.

We are a government—indeed a generation—of revolutionary transformation. Our people are caught up in a mortal struggle. This struggle has four sides.

1. *We must defeat the Viet Cong and those illegally fighting with them on our soil.*—We are the victims of an aggression directed and supported from Hanoi. That aggression—that so-called "War of National Liberation"—is part of the communist plan for the conquest of all of Southeast Asia. The defeat of that aggression is vital for the future of our people of South Vietnam.

2. *We are dedicated to the eradication of social injustice among our people.*—We must bring about a true social revolution and construct a modern society in which every man can know that he has a future; that he has respect and dignity; that he has the opportunity for himself and for his children to live in an environment where all is not disappointment, despair and dejection; that the opportunities exist for the full expression of his talents and his hopes.

3. *We must establish and maintain a stable, viable economy and build a better material life for our people.*—In spite of the war, which creates many unusual and unpredictable economic situations, we are determined to continue with a policy of austerity; to make the best possible use of the assistance granted us from abroad; and to help our people achieve regular economic growth and improved material welfare.

4. *We must build true democracy for our land and for our people.*—In this effort we shall continue to imbue the people with a sense of national unity, a stronger commitment to civic responsibility. We shall encourage a widened and more active participation in and contribution to the building of a free, independent, strong and peaceful Vietnam. In particular, we pledge again—

to formulate a democratic constitution in the months ahead, including an electoral law;

to take that constitution to our people for discussion and modification;

to seek its ratification by secret ballot;

to create, on the basis of elections rooted in that constitution, an elected government.

These things shall be accomplished mainly with the blood; intelligence, and dedication of the Vietnamese people themselves. But in this interdependent world we shall need the help of others—to win the war of independence; to build while we fight; to reconstruct and develop our nation when terror ceases.

To those future citizens of a free, democratic South Vietnam now fighting with the Vietcong, we take this occastion to say come and join in this national revolutionary adventure:

Come safely to join us through the open arms program;

Stop killing your brothers, sisters, their elders and their children;

Come and work through constitutional democracy to build together that life of dignity, freedom, and peace those in the north would deny the people of Vietnam.

Thus, we are fighting this war. It is a military war, a war for the hearts of our people. We cannot win one without winning the other. But the war for the hearts of the people is more than a military tactic. It is a moral principle. For this we shall strive as we fight to bring about a true social revolution.

Part III

THE PURPOSES OF THE GOVERNMENT OF THE UNITED STATES

(1) The United States of America is joined with the people and Government of Vietnam to prevent aggression. This is the purpose of the determined effort of the American Armed Forces now engaged in Vietnam. The United States seeks no bases. It seeks no colonial presence. It seeks to impose no alliance of alinement. It seeks only to prevent aggression, and its pledge to that purpose is firm. It aims simply to help a people and government who are determined to help themselves.

(2) The United States is pledged to the principles of the self-determination of peoples and of government by the consent of the governed. It, therefore, gives its full support to the purpose of free elections proclaimed by the Government of South Vietnam and to the principle of open arms and amnesty for all who turn from terror toward peace and rural construction. The United States will give its full support to measures of social revolution including land reform based upon the principle of building upward from the hopes and purposes of all the people of Vietnam.

(3) Just as the United States is pledged to play its full part in the worldwide attack upon hunger, ignorance, and disease, so in Vietnam it will give special support to the work of the people of that country to build even while they fight. We have helped and we will help them—to stabilize the economy—to increase the production of food—to spread the light of education—to stamp out disease.

(4) The purpose of the United States remains a purpose of peace. The U.S. Government and the Government of Vietnam will continue in the future, as they have in the past, to press the quest for a peaceful settlement in every forum. The world knows the harsh and negative response these efforts have thus far received. But the world should know, too, that the U.S. Government and the Government of Vietnam remain determined that no path to peace shall be unexplored. Within the framework of their international commitments, the United States and Vietnam aim to create with others a stable peace in southeast Asia which will permit the governments and peoples of the region to devote themselves to lifting the condition of man. With the understanding and support of the Government of Vietnam the peace offensive of the U.S. Government and the Government of South Vietnam will contine until peace is secured.

Part IV

THE COMMON COMMITMENT

The President of the United States and the Chief of State and Prime Minister of the Republic of Vietnam are thus pledged again:

To defense against aggression;
To the work of social revolution;
To the goal of free self-government;
To the attack on hunger, ignorance, and disease; and
To the unending quest for peace.

EXCERPTS FROM THE REPORTS OF THE INTERNATIONAL
COMMISSION FOR SUPERVISION AND CONTROL IN
VIETNAM RELATING TO ARTICLES 16-20 BANNING
THE INTRODUCTION OF FRESH TROOPS, MILITARY
PERSONNEL, ARMS AND MUNITIONS – MILITARY
BASES IN VIETNAM

FIRST REPORT—AUGUST 11, 1954 to DECEMBER 10,
1954 (Cmnd. 9461, May, 1955)

100. To date, the Commission has received two specific complaints from the Democratic Republic authorities alleging violations
of Article 17:—
  (a) a report that on the 8th of August, 1954, the ship *Esperanzat*
      was alleged to have unloaded war material at Tourane.
  (b) A report that on the 5th of October, 1954, the ship *Vietnam*
      was alleged to have arrived with a load of aircraft engines
      and two thousand persons.
With regard to the first specific allegation . . . The matter is being
investigated . . . With regard to the second specific allegation, details
have been asked for from the Democratic Republic Liaison Mission
and the Commission is conducting investigation.

101. . . . one general complaint was received . . . from General
Giap, Commander-in-Chief of the People's Army of Vietnam, re-
garding violations under various Articles of the Agreement including
Article 19. The complaint is being considered by the Commisson.

102. The Commission also received a complaint from the
French Liaison Mission . . . alleging that important quantities of
war material had been imported by the High Command of the
People's Army of Vietnam since the coming into force of the
Geneva Agreement . . . The Commission has requested the French
authorities to furnish further details . . .

THIRD REPORT—FEBRUARY 11, 1955 to APRIL 10, 1955
(Cmnd. 9499-June, 1955)

14. The reports of Mobile Teams sent to . . . the North and . . .
the South and the report of the control operations at Dong Dang . . .
have been reviewed. No violations of Articles 16 or 17 were noticed
by these teams.

16. Reference was made . . . to the want of co-operation between the parties to the Agreement, to the failure by the parties to carry out their obligations under the Agreement due to intransigence of local civil or/and military authorities and the general warning given by the Commission to both High Commands regarding need for specific action . . . During the period under report, the Commission has had several occasions to recommend to the High Commands that specific action be taken by them . . . against particular local authorities concerned . . . regarding grant of all facilities required by the team from local civil and military authorities. Four cases of this type in the Vinh region have been referred to the High Command of the P.A.V.N. and two in the Nha Trang region to the High Command of the French Union Forces . . .

FOURTH REPORT—APRIL 11, 1955 to AUGUST 10, 1955
(Cmnd. 9654—December, 1955)

37. The Commission completed investigations of the complaints made by the P.A.V.N. High Command referred to in paragraph 100 of the First Interim Report and found that no real violation of Article 16 or 17 had occurred, though the failure of the French High Command to notify the entry and exist of unserviceable aircraft engines which were sent to Japan during the hostilities for repairs but were returned without the necessary repairs and re-exported by the French High Command from Vietnam was inconsistent with Article 17. The Commission received two more complaints from the P.A.V.N. High Command . . . regarding import of seven helicopters and nine military liaison planes and . . . regarding import of thirty L-19 reconnaissance aircraft. Both these complaints are being investigated.

38. The P.A.V.N. High Command has sent another complaint regarding the failure of the French High Command to send necessary notification . . . regarding the arrivals or departures of units or of war material, arms, etc., in or from Vietnam to the Joint Commission. This has been referred to the French High Command.

FIFTH REPORT—AUGUST 11, 1955 to DECEMBER 10, 1955 (Cmnd. 9706—March, 1956)

26. The Commission completed the investigation of the two complaints made by the P.A.V.N. High Command referred to in

paragraph 37 of the Fourth Interim Report. As regards the first complaint it found that six liaison airplanes and seven helicopters were landed at Saigon in March 1955 for the use of the International Commission and that a team of the International Commission had controlled their import and the Commission was satisfied that no illegal entry had taken place. As regards the second complaint the Commission found from the evidence produced before it that the French Union Forces High Command had imported a number of L-19 aircraft before the cease-fire and that they transferred twenty-seven of them to the Vietnamese Air Force on June 17, 1955, and considered that this transfer was an internal one and not contrary to the Articles of the Agreement.

27.   The Commission received four more complaints from the P.A.V.N. High Command, one regarding visits of foreign military missions to South Vietnam and of South Vietnam military missions to other countries, two about introduction of arms and ammunitions by two ships and the fourth about the building at Nha Ban of an airfield which it was alleged could be utilized for introduction of war material. As a result of the first complaint the Commission has stated that notifications should be given by both parties regarding visits of foreign military missions. The Commission investigated the two complaints about the introduction of arms and ammunition and found that in one case the ship had only carried fodder and in the other case no such ship had come to the port in question and hence no violation of Articles 16 or 17 had taken place in either case. With regard to the fourth complaint the Commission decided to carry out a reconnaissance of the airfield before coming to a final decision.

28.   The Saigon Fixed Team reported to the Commission that military aircraft including United States Navy planes were visiting the Saigon airport regularly. No advance notification of these movements was being received by the Team. The Commission informed the French Liaison Mission that these planes should have been included in the aircraft forecast normally given to the Team and that it should take necessary steps in the future to see that the forecasts submitted to the Team are full and accurate.

29.   The Commission also received one complaint from the French High Command about the introduction of war material into
The charter creates a very narrow exception to the broad prohi-

bition of unilateral force. This exception (Article 51) affirms North Vietnam. The complaint was that in October 1955, fourteen railway wagons had come to Hanoi from Moscow via Peking with armament and other articles, and that after unloading the freight the wagons were not going back to Moscow. On investigation the Commission found that the complaint was not supported by any evidence.

30. The P.A.V.N. High Command has sent in two more complaints regarding the failure of the French High Command to send necessary notifications under Articles 16 (f) and 17 (e) about the introduction of war materials, etc., into South Vietnam. The French Liaison Mission informed the Commission that they were providing the information to the Joint Commission during its meeting but were not obliged under protocol 23 to give those documents to the P.A.V.N. Delegation. The Commission has recommended that notifications should be given in written form . . .

35. Difficulties were also encountered about the control of the Saigon airport, as in August the team's movements came to be restricted to the V.I.P. stand and the parking area. The Commission deputed a team of its Military Advisers to report to the Commission whether these restrictions interfered with the exercise of adequate control. On its recommendation the Commission has informed the French High Command, among other things, that the team must have access to the V.I.P. enclosure and to the customs building and that it must be permitted to go to the loading and unloading area whether it be in the civil or military section of the aerodrome.

SIXTH REPORT—DECEMBER 11, 1955 to JULY 31, 1956
(Cmnd. 31, January, 1957)

47. The Commission . . . ordered reconnaissance of all offshore islands both in North and South Vietnam in view of complaints made by the parties about lightening of ships and in view of a case which came to the notice of the Commission. The French High Command in a letter to the Commission on the 16th December, 1955, alleged that there were a great number of places in the area of Haiphong, where lightening of ships could be effected. In January 1956 the Haiphong Fixed Team brought to the notice of the Commission an instance where a ship was lightened in the Baie D'Along before entering Haiphong. The Captain of the ship freely gave the informa-

tion to the team that his ship had anchored in the Baie D'Along for some time for off-loading into barges approximately 1,000 tons of cargo there in order that the ship might be sufficiently light to enter Haiphong harbour. The team checked the cargo of the ship and the lightened material in Haiphong port and found them to be general merchandise. On the 4th February, 1956, the P.A.V.N. High Command alleged in a letter to the Commission that numerous ships were anchoring off the Mekong estuary at night time and unloading war material into barges which brought them to the shore.

49. However, the Commission's teams have not so far been able to carry out any reconnaissance of the offshore islands in North Vietnam. The Commission has been pressing the P.A.V.N. High Command since March 1956 to provide necessary transport to the teams concerned, but the High Command has not done so . . . . In South Vietnam this task of reconnaissance was partially done. However, further reconnaissance was held up as the Government of the Republic of Vietnam in reply to the Commission's requests to provide suitable sea transport to the teams concerned informed the Commission that it would not oppose the continuance of the reconnaissance of he coastal islands south of the 17th Parallel provided similar reconnaissance was carried out of all the islands north of the 17th Parallel. The Commission refused to accept such conditional co-operation and informed the French High Command that it took decisions in each zone on merits. It was also informed that the P.A.V.N. High Command had been requested to make available suitable transport to carry out reconnaissance of the offshore islands in the North. The Government of the Republic of Vietnam has now given its concurrence for the continuance of the reconnaissance of the offshore islands and the reconnaissance has been resumed.

50. The Commission's teams both in South and North Vietnam have been encountering difficulties in the performance of their normal duties . . . .

51. The difficulties in respect of South Vietnam are: (a) time notice restrictions on team movements to certain areas and delays in certain cases in the provision of necessary sea and air transport; (b) lack of notifications due under Articles 16 (f) and 17 (e) of the Agreement; (c) restrictions on the exercise of spot-checks on ships and aircraft and failure in certain cases to make available the

required documents . . . . According to the Instructions to the Fixed Teams and their Mobile Elements prescribed by the Commission, the fixed teams are required to give half an hour's notice before moving to any part of their zones of action and their mobile elements to give two hours' notice. Though this has been accepted by the two High Commands, the Government of the Republic of Vietnam has been demanding on grounds of insecurity and other reasons 24 hours' notice and in some cases even 48 hours, thus restricting the movements of the majority of teams . . .

53. The second problem faced by some of the Commission's teams in South Vietnam is with regard to notifications to be given under Article 16 (f) and 17 (e) before the introduction of military personnel and war material. Under Article 16, military personnel can be introduced into Vietnam only by way of rotation, notification for which is required to be given to the Joint Commission and to the International Commission at least two days in advance of the arrivals or departures of such personnel. Under Protocol 23 signed by the two High Commands, within 72 hours of arrivals or departures of military personnel a report is to be submitted to the Joint Commission and to the International Commission. A reference was made in paragraph 28 of the Fifth Interim Report to the visits of military aircraft including United States Navy planes to Saigon, without advance notification of these movements to the Commission's team. The Commission had informed the French High Command that advance notifications must be given in respect of all civil and military aircraft carrying military personnel and war material in accordance with the provisions of Articles 16 (f) and 17 (e). However, according to the reports received from some of the teams, especially the Saigon Fixed Team, United States Naval and Military planes continued to enter and leave Vietnam without notification during the period under review. In a number of these cases these planes were seen bringing in and taking out United States and Vietnamese military personnel. In reply to the Commission's inquiry, the French High Command has stated that the United States personnel are either in transit or replacements for the MAAG (Miliary Aid Advisory Group) and that Vietnamese personnel are returning after attending training courses outside the country. In most cases notifications under Articles 16 (f) and 17 (e) were not given.

As regards the military transport aircraft as distinguished from their cargoes, the Commission decided on July 26, 1956, that these aircraft in themselves constituted war material in terms of Article 17 (*a*) and Protocol 23. The Commission has communicated the above decision to the French High Command and has informed it that the Commission will require advance notifications about the arrivals and departures of these planes in order to ensure that they do not remain in the country and that they do not unload any war material. The Commission has indicated that it was preparing detailed modalities for the control of transit operations. In the last six weeks there has been an improvement in respect of notifications and in the majority of cases such notifications are being received by the team concerned.

54. In paragraph 35 of the Fifth Interim Report, mention was made of the difficulties encountered by the Commission's Fixed Team at Saigon with regard to the control of Saigon airport and of the suggestions made by the Commission to the French High Command in this connexion. As the situation did not show any improvement, the Commission reviewed the position and made certain recommendations to the party in April 1956. In spite of this, the team continues to encounter difficulties in the exercise of its control duties. It has not been permitted to go to the loading and unloading area and in a number of cases, in spite of the team's request, foreign incoming aircraft were not brought to the parking area for the purpose of spot checking of their cargo. These aircraft taxied directly to the military section of the airport to which the team is not given access.

55. Manifests and other relevant documents of the aircraft were also not made available to the Saigon Fixed Team on numerous occasions on the ground that the local customs and other authorities had not received instructions to show them to the team.

56. In the harbour, the Saigon Fixed Team noticed instances where war material was brought in without notification; neither were manifests made available. There were also instances where war material was shipped out and notification was given either after the loading or after the departure of the ship. The team could not check the cargo. The team was also not allowed in some cases to carry out spot checks on ships in the harbour. The Liaison Officer told the team that the ships over which the team wanted to exercise control did not carry any war material and that there was therefore no need

for the team to do its spot checking and that its request for manifests would be communicated to the higher authorities.

59. In paragraph 27 of the Fifth Interim Report reference was made to complaints received from the P.A.V.N. High Command regarding alleged violations of Articles 16 and 17 of the Geneva Agreement. The Commission has not been able to carry out its investigation mentioned in that paragraph regarding the alleged construction of a new airfield at Nha Ban in South Vietnam, the reasons being alleged insecurity conditions in the area and the stand of the Government of the Republic of Vietnam, mentioned in paragraph 44 above. The P.A.V.N. High Command has also alleged the construction of two other airfields in South Vietnam. This is under investigation.

60. During the period under report, the Commission has received a total of twenty-four complaints alleging seventy-six specific instances of violations of Articles 16 and 17 in South Vietnam. In two cases where United States and Vietnamese Military personnel were introduced into South Vietnam without any notification under Article 16 (*f*), the Operations Committee of the Commission came to the conclusion that there had been a violation of Article 16. In one case where a United States military plane brought to Saigon a consignment of aircraft wheel tyres the Committee concluded that there had been a technical violation of Article 17. In the first two cases, mentioned above, the Commission asked the French High Command to show cause why a finding of violation of Article 16 should not be given, and in the third case why a finding of violation of Article 17 should not be given. The French Liaison Mission in its reply dated the 21st July has not denied the facts but has stated that due to lack of co-ordination between the various Vietnamese services, notifications were not given. The matter is under the consideration of the Commission. In another case the Commission decided that there had been no violation as on the date mentioned by the P.A.V.N. High Command in its complaint, no United States plane had landed at Tourane and, in one more case, that the allegation had not ben proved. In two cases the Commission declined to undertake any investigation as the allegations were too general. For the same reason the Commission just noted two complaints from the P.A.V.N. High Command. The other complaints are under en-

quiry. In some cases it has been found that team reports bear out the allegations made by the P.A.V.N. High Command of violations of Articles 16 and 17. In such cases the party has been asked to explain why notifications as required under the Agreement have not been given and why the procedure laid down in Protocol 23 for the introduction of war material and military personnel has not been followed.

61. During the period under review the Commission considered the question of introduction into South Vietnam of a number of Landing Ships (Tank) mentioned in the team reports. The Commission decided that LSTs were war material. It has asked the French Liaison Mission to explain why they were introduced without notification under Article 17 and without following the procedure under Protocol 23.

62. With reference to paragraph 30 of the Fifth Interim Report regarding necessary notification under Articles 16 (f) and 17 (e) to the Central Joint Commission, the situation remains unchanged. The French High Command has not implemented the recommendations. In fact, the position has become more complicated due to the non-functioning of the Central Joint Commission after the disappearance of the French High Command on 28th April, 1956.

63. One major case of a foreign military mission in South Vietnam came up during the period under report. On 25th April, 1956, the Commission received a request from the French Liaison Mission and the Republic of Vietnam for grant of permission for the entry of 350 military personnel of the United States Army Service Corps into South Vietnam. It was stated that these persons would constitute a mission called "TERM"—Temporary Equipment Recovery Mission—whose duties would be to examine war material and military equipment lying in South Vietnam which was the property of the United States Government for the purpose of selecting material to be exported from Vietnam and to protect and preserve this material. The Commission was informed that the members of "TERM" would start entering South Vietnam by the last week of May 1956. The Commission informed the French Liaison Mission that the matter was under consideration and that pending the decision of the Commission no entry should be effected. In spite of this, 290 United States military personnel belonging to the "TERM"

have been introduced into South Vietnam, thus facing the Commission with a *fait accompli*. The Commission takes exception to this method of procedure adopted by the French Liaison Mission and the Government of the Republic of Vietnam. The Commission gave due consideration to the request of the Republic of Vietnam and communicated its decision on the 29th May, 1956. In this letter the Commission asked for assurances that the functions of "TERM" would be solely the selection of material for export from the country and that it would not be used for any other purpose. The Commission further asked for details regarding the mission, number and names of personnel, their postings in the country and the tasks assigned to each one of them. Lastly, the Commission proposed certain conditions on acceptance of which the Commission would be prepared to agree to the entry of the "TERM" personnel. These conditions include submission of fortnightly progress reports on the work of "TERM," submission of notifications regarding entry and exit of "TERM" personnel, right of the Commission and its fixed teams to control entry and exit, and the right of the Commission to conduct spot checks at any place where "TERM" personnel were functioning. The matter is being pursued with the authorities of the Republic of Vietnam, whose final acceptance of the Commission's conditions has not yet been received. The Commission has also received complaints from the P.A.V.N. High Command regarding alleged activities of certain United States military missions in South Vietnam as constituting violations of Articles 16, 17, 18 and 19 of the Agreement.

64. The difficulty that is being experienced by the Commission's teams in the North is with regard to obtaining suitable and modern means of sea or air transport for control purposes. Since June 1955 the Commission has been making efforts to get the P.A.V.N. High Command to provide a suitable sea-worthy boat for Fixed Team Haiphong for controlling the coast between Do Son and Sam Son. It had informd the High Command that in its view control could best be exercised by means of an amphibian aircraft. The High Command informed the Commission, in reply, that a naval craft could serve the purpose equally well and that it was negotiating with the French for obtaining two LSTs. However, when the French High Command informed the P.A.V.N. High Command that it was willing to send four boats to Haiphong harbour in one

of its naval vessels, the latter did not accept the offer on the ground that it could not allow the French vessel to enter its waters. The French High Command, in a letter to the Commission dated 16th December, 1955, requested the Commission's assurance that there was really effective control in the areas of Haiphong, Hong Gay, Cam Pha Port and Pho Cac Ba, particularly with reference to the means of transport available to the Team. This was examined by the Operations Committee of the Commission, and on its recommendation the Commission informed the French High Command that up to that time the control in the area in question had been as effective as possible with the transport facilities available to the team. The facilities consisted of vehicles only. The Fixed Team Haiphong did not have a boat to control part of its zone of action along the coast from Do Son to Sam Son once a week as prescribed by the Commission. Except for this, the control of the other areas within the zone of action of the team has been carried out by road as prescribed by the Commission in the Instructions to Fixed Teams and their Mobile Elements. In the last week of July, Fixed Team Haiphong was provided with a boat and did two short trips within its zone of action. But the team has reported that in its opinion the boat does not fulfill all the requirements of the team for the purpose of its control duties. The matter is under the consideration of the Commission. The Tien Yen and Vinh Teams have not been provided with the required sea transport.

SEVENTH REPORT—AUGUST 1, 1956 to APRIL 30, 1957
(Cmnd. 335-July, 1957)

50. In paragraph 60 of the Sixth Interim Report reference was made to the recommendations of the Operations Committee to record the violations of Articles 16 and 17 in 1955, in South Vietnam. During the period under report, the Commission, after considering the reply of the French High Command in these cases, decided, Canadian Delegation dissociating itself, that there was violation of Article 16 in two cases and of Article 17 in one. The Commission further decided that there was violation of Article 16 in three cases and, Canadian Delegation dissociating itself, of Article 17 in two cases, of which three pertain to 1955 and two to July-August, 1956. Details

of these decided cases are shown in Appendix G. In 18 cases the Government of the Republic of Vietnam was requested to explain why the procedure under Articles 16 and/or 17, as the case may be, and Protocol 23 was not followed. During the period under review the Commission, after examining team reports, notifications from the Government of the Republic of Vietnam, where received, and complaints from the P.A.V.N. High Command, concerning Articles 16 and 17, was seized with 96 cases which may violate Article 16 and 114 cases which may violate Article 17 in South Vietnam. The reply of the Government of the Republic of Vietnam denying many allegations of the P.A.V.N. High Command is under consideration. In four cases, the Commission, after considering the reply given by the Government of the Republic of Vietnam, asked it to show cause why a finding of violation of Article 17 should not be recorded.

During the period under review, the Commission did not consider any violation of Articles 16 or 17 by the P.A.V.N. High Command as there was no team report, notification or complaint, warranting such consideration.

51. Many instances of arrival of military personnel and war materials in South Vietnam were reported by the Commission's teams and were stated by the Government of the Republic of Vietnam to be in transit. Some of the arrivals took place without advance notification. In some instances, during the period under report, the Commission was not notified about the exit, if any, of these war materials and military personnel and it was not in a position to say whether or not they left the country. The matter is being pursued.

52. During the period under report the Commission's fixed teams at Nha Trang and Tourane in South Vietnam reported that they were not allowed to control American military and other planes stated by the Government of the Republic of Vietnam to be United States Embassy planes . . . .

55. In paragraph 63 of the Sixth Interim Report reference was made to the entry of an American Military Mission, called "TERM" (Temporary Equipment Recovery Mission), into South Vietnam in May, 1956. The Commission could not review the question after a lapse of three months, as originally decided, or carry out spot checks as no reply was received from the Government of the Republic of Vietnam until December, 1956. In this reply it was stated that

TERM was expected to complete its task of cataloguing United States war material for eventual re-export from South Vietnam in a limited time and that before its withdrawal due intimation would be given, so that the Commission might exercise appropriate control. The Government of the Republic of Vietnam also agreed that the Commission might visit the installations where TERM personnel were carrying on their activities. The strength of the Mission was stated not to exceed 350. The said Government did not comply with the Commission's request to furnish fortnightly reports regarding the activities of the Mission. The Commission informed the Government of the Republic of Vietnam in February, 1957, that it regarded this lapse with concern and asked for a report concerning the activities of TERM up to the end of January, 1957, and thereafter fortnightly reports to be sent expeditiously and without fail. It further asked to be informed when TERM would be completing its task and where TERM's activities were going on so that the Commission may decide where to send a mobile team for the purpose of ascertaining the activities of TERM. No reply has been received so far.

56. In paragraph 63 of the Sixth Interim Report a reference was made to the complaints of the P.A.V.N. High Command with regard to certain United States Military Missions in South Vietnam. During the period under review the Commission received a few more complaints and considered some of these. In one of these it was alleged that the existence of "MAAG" (Military Aid Advisory Group) and the introduction of United States military personnel were in effect a factual realization of a military alliance between the Governments of the Republic of Vietnam and of the United States of America in contravention of Articles 16 and 19 and paragraphs 4 and 5 of the Final Declaration. In November, 1956, the Government of the Republic of Vietnam was asked to offer its specific comments on the allegations and also on certain enclosures to the letter of the P.A.V.N. High Command, in which it was stated that a military agreement had been concluded between the above two countries in February, 1955, and to furnish certain information regarding the status, purpose, original and present strength and the present activities of "MAAG." In February, 1957, the Commission received a letter from the Government of the Republic of Vietnam denying that the presence of "MAAG" constituted a violation

of Articles 16 and 19 and stating that "MAAG" had started its activities in 1950 and that there had been no change in its activities, statute or structure and it had never exceeded its original strength and that there did not exist a formal or factual military alliance between the Governments of the Republic of Vietnam and of the United States of America. The matter is under consideration.

The P.A.V.N. High Command also alleged that two United States Military Missions—"TRIM" (Training Reorganization Inspection Mission) and "CATO" (Combat Arms Training Organization) founded in March, 1955, and in May, 1956, respectively, had come into existence in South Vietnam. The Commission asked in January, 1957, for the comments of the Government of the Republic of Vietnam. The reply is awaited.

In one of its complaints the P.A.V.N. High Command alleged a factual materialization of a military alliance between the Government of the Republic of Vietnam and the member countries of "SEATO" (South-East Asia Treaty Organization) as military personnel, warships and jet planes of the said member countries participated in the National Day celebrations of South Vietnam on October 26, 1956. The Government of the Republic of Vietnam denied the factual materialization of a military alliance with the "SEATO" Powers. The Commission viewed with concern the omission of the Government of the Republic of Vietnam to follow the procedures laid down by the Commission for the introduction of military missions and consequently concluded that it was not in a position to state whether and, if so, how far the provisions of Article 16 had been observed by the Government of the Republic of Vietnam and, whether or not, all or any of the war material in question had left South Vietnam. The Commission also concluded that the participation of foreign military personnel and war material in public celebrations of a ceremonial character did not necessarily prove the existence of a military alliance. The Commission has closed the case.

57.　The Commission has not been able to exercise the prescribed control of Nha Be harbour, near Saigon, since the end of August, 1956. The Commission did not accept the contention of the Government of the Republic of Vietnam that this harbour was not in the zone of action of Saigon Fixed Team and reaffirmed that it should be controlled. As no reply was received, the Commission converted its request into a recommendation on December 28, 1956. The Government of the Republic of Vietnam did not implement the recommendation and the Commission decided that it would take action under Article 43 to inform the Members of the Geneva Conference if its recommendation was not implemented immediately. The Commission was informed on February 20, 1957, that Nha Be was a military base and could not be subjected to regular control; however, its Team would be authorized to go to Nha Be every time notice was given about the loading and unloading of war material on the spot. The matter is under the Commission's consideration.

60. As the Government of the Republic of Vietnam did not afford the necessary assistance and co-operation to the Commission in cases under Article 14 (c) and, in particular, decided not to send any more replies to the Commission's communications and not to permit the deployment of any mobile teams for investigation of complaints under this Article in South Vietnam, the Commission addressed a special letter to the Co-Chairmen on April 11, 1957, (vide Appendix C) and expressed its grave concern to the Government of the Republic of Vietnam.

Particulars of Cases of Violations of Articles 16 and 17
in South Vietnam

Serial No	A.—Cases referred to in paragraph 60 of the Sixth Interim Report	Article of the Agreement violated
1	On November 24, 1955, a plane of the United States Navy landed at Tan Son Nhut airfield with some Vietnamese and American military personnel	16
2	On November 27, 1955, a plane of the United States Navy landed at Tan Son Nhut with 10 American military personnel	16
3	On November 8, 1955, a plane of the United States Navy brought into South Vietnam aircraft wheel tyres	17
4	On November 10, 1955, a United States Navy plane brought into South Vietnam, one American Major-General and some other military personnel	16
5	On November 12, 1955, a United States Navy plane brought into South Vietnam several military personnel	16
6	On December 2, 1955, a United States Air Force plane brought into South Vietnam several military personnel	16

Serial No.	B.—Cases during the period under report	Article of the Agreement violated
1	On July 20, 1956, S.S. *Marit Maersk* brought to Saigon 21 cases containing 1,000 revolvers	17
2	On August 15, 1956, S.S. *Alice Brown* brought to Saigon 610 cases of munitions for revolvers	17

Serial No.	1 Subject	2 Article involved	3 Date of incident
	A.—Instances in which the Government of the Republic of Vietnam was asked by the Commission to show cause why a violation of Article 17 should not be recorded—		
1	Introduction of aircraft parts	17	January, 1956
2	Introduction of war material on S.S. *Steel Seafarer*	17	August, 1956
	B.—Instances in which the Government of the Republic of Vietnam was asked by the Commission to take up the matter with the French authorities to explain why war materials were imported without following the prescribed procedure and to show cause why a violation of Article 17 should not be recorded (as the Government of the Republic of Vietnam had explained that the responsible services were at this time under the control of the French High Command)—		
1	Introduction of aircraft parts	17	January, 1956
2	Introduction of 14 armoured boats	17	April, 1956

EIGHTH REPORT—MAY 1, 1957 to APRIL 30, 1958 (Cmnd. 509—August, 1958)

32. The Government of the Republic of Vietnam submitted a report on TERM personnel up to September 30, 1957, and a statement of damaged or worn-out material of American origin shipped out of Vietnam up to May 31, 1957. Monthly reports asked for by the Commission have been submitted thereafter, though not on time, and no change in TERM personnel has been reported. The Government of the Republic of Vietnam furnished information about eight places where TERM is working, and the Commission decided to carry out spot checks in four of the eight places, and has carried out these spot checks in three places. The reports of the Teams are under consideration. Regarding the question when this Mission, which is claimed to be temporary, would be completing its task and leaving Vietnam, the Government of the Republic of Vietnam has replied that it is impossible to forecast when TERM will cease its activities. The matter is under consideration.

As regards MAAG and other organizations referred to above, the Government of the Republic of Vietnam did not supply information on all the points requested by the Commission and the Commission expressed grave concern that all assistance and co-operation in this matter had not been offered in terms of Article 25 and asked the Mission in charge of relations with the Commission to supply the necessary information. The Canadian Delegation dissented from this decision citing Article 25 because it held that the essential information had already been supplied. Indian and Polish Delegations would like to point out that the Commission had unanimously decided earlier that the information furnished was inadequate and unsatisfactory and had expressed its concern over the non-receipt of a reply within the specified period and only then was Article 25 cited. A reply has since been received enclosing a copy of the Agreement of December 23, 1950, under which, according to the Party, MAAG operates and the reply is under consideration.

33. During the period under review, the Commission considered the case of introduction of 22 armoured launches into South Vietnam by the French High Command in 1956 and held, Canadian Delegation dissenting, that this introduction was in violation of Article

17 and Protocol 23. The introduction had taken place before any credit under Article 17 had been established. The Commission has, however, adjusted this introduction against a credit given subsequently. In another case of introduction of 11 boxes of field artillery parts into South Vietnam, the Commission held that as no prior permission of the Commission was obtained and the introduction of the items was not notified, the introduction of artillery parts was a violation of Article 17 of the Geneva Agreement. The Commission also held in a case of introduction of guns and machine-gun parts into South Vietnam that there was a violation of Article 17 (e) and Protocol 23.

The Commission further recorded procedural contraventions of Article 16(f) in 11 cases and of Article 17 (e) in six cases. In four cases under Articles 16 and 17, it decided that all possible assistance and co-operation under Article 25 of the Agreement were not afforded to it by the Government of the Republic of Vietnam.

During the period under report, the Commission received a few notifications under Articles 16 and 17 from the P.A.V.N. High Command. The Commission did not record any violation under these Articles against the P.A.V.N. High Command.

During the period under review, the Commission received from the P.A.V.N. High Command 31 and 45 complaints alleging violations of Articles 16 and 17 respectively by the Government of the Republic of Vietnam.

34. As regards the question of physical control of the cargo of the incoming aircraft at Saigon airport, referred to in paragraph 54 of the Seventh Interim Report, the Government of the Republic of Vietnam informed the Commission that military planes transporting military personnel or war material would stop at the civilian parking area in order to allow physical control after unloading, but not of the material inside the planes. Since the receipt of this letter there have, however, been some instances where incoming planes have proceeded directly to the military parking area to which the Commission's Team has no access and in some cases no manifest concerning personnel or cargo were produced. The Commission has asked the Secretary-General to discuss the difficulties of the Saigon Fixed Team with the Mission in charge of relations with the Commission in an effort to solve them. The matter is being pursued.

35. The Commission's teams have been experiencing difficulties in the matter of having access to the control tower registers at airfields and registers at sea ports. The P.A.V.N. High Command has, "as an exception," agreed to make available for inspection these registers, when required by the Commission's teams, where the control is not daily. Since November, 1957 the teams in the North have access to control tower registers at Gia Lam airport and to port registers at Campha, the only two places where the Commission has asked for these registers. The Government of the Republic of Vietnam has not so far acceded to the Commission's request. The Commission has directed its Senior Military Advisers to explain to the Party the Commission's point of view and the necessity and requirements of the teams having access to these registers and recommend what action should be taken to meet the requirements of the Commission. Their report is under consideration.

36. The Commission has been receiving claims for credit for the replacement of war material under Article 17(b) from the Government of the Republic of Vietnam and also of war material exported by the French High Command from the cease-fire up to June 30, 1956.

The Commission has worked out and accepted the principles and procedures under which such claims for credit are to be granted, the Polish Delegation dissenting to granting of credit for war material taken out of Vietnam by the withdrawing French Union Forces in Vietnam. . . .

NINTH REPORT—MAY 1, 1958 to JANUARY 31, 1959
(Cmnd. 726—May, 1959)

31. In paragraph 32 of the Eighth Interim Report a reference was made to the American Military Mission called TERM (Temporary Equipment Recovery Mission). The Commission considered all relevant reports and documents connected with TERM and informed the Government of the Republic of Vietnam that the Commission was of the view that TERM should be able to complete its remaining work by the end of June, 1959, and that, the status of TERM being temporary, TERM should cease to exist thereafter and its personnel should leave the Republic of Vietnam.

32. The situation in regard to MAAG, referred to in paragraph 32 of the Eighth Interim Report, remained unchanged.

33. During the period under report, the Commission recorded procedural contravention by the Government of the Republic of Vietnam under Article 16 (f) in 27 cases and under Article 17 (e) in six cases. In four cases where no notification was given and the Team was not allowed to carry out physical control, the Commission decided that all possible assistance and co-operation under Article 25 of the Geneva Agreement was not afforded to it by the Government of the Republic of Vietnam. These cases pertain to a period prior to the period covered by this report.

During the period under report, the Commission received a few notifications under Articles 16 and 17 from the P.A.V.N. High Command. The Commission did not record any violation under these Articles against the P.A.V.N. High Command.

During the period under report, the Commission received from the P.A.V.N. High Command 16 and 26 complaints alleging violation of Article 16 and 17 respectively by the Government of the Republic of Vietnam.

34. The Commission has been receiving complaints from the P.A.V.N. High Command alleging increase in the strength of American military personnel in South Vietnam. The Commission examined the Team reports for the period 7th January, 1956, to 28th December, 1957, with regard to the arrivals and departures of military personnel in the Republic of Vietnam. On the basis of information available to it, it was seen during this period that 2,002 American military personnel arrived in South Vietnam and 1,243 left this country and thus the arrivals exceeded the departures by 759 persons. The Government of the Republic of Vietnam was informed that the Commission was holding in abeyance for further consideration the implications to be drawn under Article 16 of the Cease-Fire Agreement and requested its comments. The Government of the Republic of Vietnam informed the Commission that checking of these figures was under way and they would communicate the result thereof to the Commission. Their further communication is awaited.

35. During the period under report a few instances of the difficulties experienced by the Fixed Team Saigon referred to in paragraph 34 of the Eighth Interim Report were reported . . .

During the period under review, there were a number of cases where no notifications of airplane movements were given, and/or where manifests were not produced before the Fixed Team Saigon on the ground that the planes in question were in transit or landed for refuelling only. The Commission called for corrective action.

36. In paragraph 35 of the Eighth Interim Report a reference was made to the Report of the Senior Military Advisers on the question of the Commission's teams having access to control tower registers and registers at sea ports in South Vietnam. The Commission held that in case of airports where the control was daily or any other airport which may be subject to daily control in the future, the Government of the Republic of Vietnam would be required to show the registers only to verify "a specific case" or to investigate "a specific complaint" as and when such contingency arose. It was further decided, Polish Delegation dissenting, that the Commission's teams be allowed access to registers showing external traffic only at the other airports. In the case of one airport where the Government of the Republic of Vietnam stated that there was no manned control tower in existence, the Commission instructed its Fixed Team to verify. Regarding the Commission's teams not having similar access to registers maintained at sea ports, the Commission expressed its concern and recommended to the Government of the Republic of Vietnam to make necessary arrangements as soon as possible. The Government of the Republic of Vietnam has informed that control tower registers at airports and registers at sea ports where the control is daily, cannot be shown to the Commission's team as they contain information concerning both internal and external movement. Regarding access to registers at sea ports where the control is not daily, the Government of the Republic of Vietnam has informed that no register is maintained as these sea ports are not open to international movement. The matter is under consideration. The Commission's teams have been given access to control tower registers in South Vietnam showing external traffic at other airports where the control is not daily.

42. The Commission has continued and will continue to discharge its duties of supervision and control under the Geneva Agreement but unless the Commission receives a larger measure of cooperation from the Parties and the difficulties hindering the Com-

mission's activities are removed, the Commission cannot function effectively in carrying out satisfactorily its tasks in regard to the Agreement for the Cessation of Hostilities in Vietnam.

TENTH REPORT - FEBRUARY 1, 1959 to JANUARY 31, 1960
(Cmnd. 1040 - June, 1960)

40. During the period under review, the Commission received a letter from the P.A.V.N. High Command alleging an increase from 6 to 46 in the number of airfields in South Vietnam, utilizable as military airfields. This is under consideration.

41. The P.A.V.N. High Command in its reply regarding the reconnaissance of the Bach Mai airfield, referred to in paragraph 27 of the Ninth Interim Report, reiterated the information furnished previously by it to the Commission that Bach Mai airfield was inoperative and was used as a cantonment for troops and that this situation had been ascertained by the Commission's Mobile Teams and by the Operations Committee in March 1957. The P.A.V.N. High Command further stated that it would inform the Commission when the Bach Mai airfield was put into use again so as to enable control of this airfield. The Commission, having considered the Party's reply, drew the attention of the P.A.V.N. High Command to the fact that the Commission's request was first conveyed to it in July 1957 and requested it to extend to the Commission all possible assistance and co-operation in the matter. Since the attitude of the Party remained unchanged, the Commission converted its request into a recommendation. While the Party, in reply, repeated its previous stand, it did suggest that should the Commission maintain its desire for such a reconnaissance they might reconsider the matter. The Commission then once again recommended that arrangements be made for the reconnaissance of the Bach Mai airfield. Since the Party still maintained its stand, the Commission, Polish Delegation dissenting, informed the P.A.V.N. High Command that it had not afforded all possible assistance and co-operation to the Commission in terms of Article 25 and that the Commission would take action under Article 43 of the Geneva Agreement.

48. In regard to the American Military Mission called the Military Assistance Advisory Group (MAAG), referred to in paragraph

32 of the Ninth Interim Report, the Commission, having considered the reply received from the Government of the Republic of Vietnam, reiterated its concern and informed the Party that it had not furnished full information and specific answers to the queries raised by the Commission and, to this extent, therefore, had still not afforded all possible assistance and co-operation in terms of Article 25 of the Geneva Agreement. The Commission recommended that full information and specific replies to the Commission's queries be furnished. The reply of the Government of the Republic of Vietnam has been received and is under consideration.

During the period under report, the Commission considered the question of import of war material by MAAG. The Commission also considered the alleged setting-up of the organisation called the United States Air Force Detachment and the alleged creation of the organisations called the Controller Division and the Direct Aid Division, all claimed by the Government of the Republic of Vietnam to be sections of MAAG.

49. During the period under report, the Commission recorded 12 procedural contraventions by the Government of the Republic of Vietnam under Article 16(f) and 20 procedural contraventions under Article 17(e) of the Geneva Agreement.

...the Commission also received a few notifications under Articles 16 and 17 from the P.A.V.N. High Command. The Commission did not record any violation under these Articles against the P.A.V.N. High Command.

50. The Commission continued to receive complaints from the P.A.V.N. High Command, during the period under report, in regard to the alleged increase in the strength of American military personnel in the Republic of Vietnam. The Government of the Republic of Vietnam furnished its explanation for the excess figure of 759 of arrivals over departures of American military personnel in the Republic of Vietnam for the period 7th January, 1956, to 28th December, 1957, referred to in paragraph 34 of the Ninth Interim Report. The Commission, having considered this reply, informed the Party that is had not shown cause why violation of Article 16 of the Geneva Agreement should not be recorded. The Commission also informed the Party that it had not furnished documentary proof that the figures arrived at by the Commission did not correspond to the

facts. In regard to the Party's contention that the Commission's teams did not carry out control continuously for 24 hours and that most American military personnel attached to MAAG and TERM enter Vietnam in military planes and after one year's duty leave Vietnam in civilian clothes by commercial planes which are not controlled by the Commission's teams, The Commission pointed out that Article 16(*f*) of the Geneva Agreement imposes upon the Party the responsibility to notify to the Commission all entries and exits of military personnel into and out of Vietnam irrespective of whether such personnel travel by commercial aircraft or wear civilian clothes. In support of its claim the Government of the Republic of Vietnam forwarded to the Commission photostat copies of slips of reservation of seats (U.S.A. Transportation Requests) and extracts of commercial airlines manifests in respects of movement of a certain number of American military personnel who, the Party maintained, had departed by commercial aircraft from Saigon and were not controlled by the Commission's teams. These documents are under consideration.

The Government of the Republic of Vietnam was also informed that the Commission was making similar investigations in regard to the movement of American military personnel into and out of South Vietnam for the period subsequent to 28th December, 1957.

51. During the period under report, a few instances of the difficulties experienced by the Fixed Team Saigon, referred to in paragraph 35 of the Ninth Interim Report, were reported. The Commission is pursuing the matter.

There were 86 cases in the Republic of Vietnam wherein aircraft either arrived without prior notification or in respect of which manifests or other documents were not produced by the Party during the period under report. The Commission is examing these cases and will take appropriate action in the matter.

52. In regard to the question of control tower registers and registers at sea ports, referred to in paragraph 36 of the Ninth Interim Report, the Commission considered the reply received from the Government of the Republic of Vietnam and reaffirmed its stand in the matter. During the period under review, there were a few instances in South Vietnam in which the Commission's teams were not allowed access to control tower registers and port registers even

to verify "a specific case" or entry to docks and warehouses while carrying out their control duties. The Commission has taken corrective action in these cases.

...some cases occurred in South Vietnam when the teams were not supplied with manifests or were not permitted to carry out a spot-check when asked for by them. The Party has been requested to comply with the existing procedure in this regard.

...the Commission considered a case which occurred in North Vietnam of a Liaison Officer refusing to approach the Captain of a ship for permission for the Commission's team to board the ship when requested by the team. This incident occurred prior to the period under review. The Party has been requested to issue suitable instructions to its liaison staff to avoid a recurrence of such incidents.

57.   A complaint was received from the Government of the Republic of Vietnam regarding the alleged introduction of war material into North Vietnam at Haiphong by *s.s. Lidice*. The Commission informed the Party that this ship visited the port of Haiphong in June 1959 and was controlled by the Commission's Team which did not report the introduction of any war material. The case was, therefore, closed.

59.   In paragraph 33 of the Eighth Interim Report reference was made to the violation of Article 17 recorded in the case of 22 armoured launches introduced into South Vietnam by the French High Command in 1956. During the period under report, the Government of the Republic of Vietnam furnished further information and requested the Commission to review its decision in this regard. This is under consideration.

ELEVENTH REPORT – FEBRUARY 1, 1960 to FEBRUARY 28, 1961 (Cmnd. November, 1961)

38.   In reply to the Commission's recommendation concerning the reconnaissance of the seven airfields, the Government of the Republic of Vietnam reiterated its stand referred to in paragraph 37 of the Tenth Interim Report. The Commission, after due consideration, informed the Government of the Republic of Vietnam, Canadian Delegation abstaining, that as it had not afforded all possible assistance and co-operation to the Commission in terms of Article

25, the Commission would take action under Article 43 of the Geneva Agreement.

40. Further to the subject referred to in paragraph 40 of the Tenth Interim Report, the Commission requested the Government of the Republic of Vietnam in September 1960 to offer its comments on the allegations made by the P.A.V.N. High Command that four of the alleged 46 newly built airfields at Ban Don, Madrak, Gia Vuc and Choudron in South Vietnam had been used for the landing of a great number of American military planes bringing military advisers and war material to South Vietnam. The reply of the Party has since been recieved and is under consideration.

With regard to the airfield at Na San, the Government of the Republic of Vietnam alleged that this airfield, which was completely destroyed after the Dien Bien Phu battle, had been reconditioned and equipped with radio and radar equipment and was capable of receiving four-engined planes. In April 1960 the Commission requested the P.A.V.N. High Command to offer its comments in this regard. The reply from the Party is under consideration.

42. In addition to the two airfields referred to in the paragraph above, the Government of the Republic of Vietnam, in a subsequent note, alleged that the airfield of Thai Nguyen in North Vietnam had been repaired and put into service again and that the planes, forming part of the Peoples' Republic of China's aid, were hidden in the workshops of the Corps of Engineers of this area. In October 1960, the Commission requested the P.A.V.N. High Command to offer its comments. The Party in reply stated that this airfield has remained unserviceable to date and that the allegations of the Republic of Vietnam are unfounded. The case is under consideration by the Commission.

46. With regard to the air reconnaissance of the off-shore islands in the Haiphong-Tien Yen Zone, referred to in paragraph 44 of the Tenth Interim Report, the Party did not comply with the Commission's recommendation and the Commission, Polish Delegation dissenting, informed the P.A.V.N. High Command that as it had not afforded all possible assistance and co-operation to the Commission in terms of Article 25, the Commission would take action under Article 43 of the Geneva Agreement.

49. In paragraph 47 of the Tenth Interim Report, it was stated that the Commission recommended to the Government of the Re-

public of Vietnam that the Temporary Equipment Recovery Mission (TERM) complete its work and all its personnel be withdrawn from Vietnam by 31st December, 1960. During December 1960 and January/February 1961 the Commission received three communications from the P.A.V.N. High Command alleging that TERM has not ceased to exist in South Vietnam and instead was extending the scope of its activity under the assumed name of the Logistics Section of the Military Assistance Advisory Group (MAAG). Meanwhile, the Government of the Republic of Vietnam informed the Commission in January 1961 that TERM had ceased its activities and was disbanded on 31st December, 1960. The Party further stated that out of the total strength of 350 personnel, 261 had left South Vietnam during the course of 1960 and the remaining 89 were transferred on the spot to MAAG on account of their technical ability. They also stated that this transfer of 89 personnel to MAAG was within the authorized quota of MAAG. The Commission considered the communications from the Government of the Republic of Vietnam and the P.A.V.N. Liaison Mission and asked the Government of the Republic of Vietnam to furnish more detailed information regarding the evacuation of TERM personnel from Vietnam and distribution by numbers of officers and enlisted men within MAAG; the Party's reply is awaited. . .

The Polish Delegation holds the view that the communication of the Government of the Republic of Vietnam dated 11th January, 1961, informing the Commission, among other things, that 89 personnel of TERM have been transferred on the spot to MAAG amounts to non-implementation of the Commission's decision under which this Mission had to cease its activities and its entire personnel had to leave Vietnam by 31st December, 1960.

The concern of the Polish Delegation is all the stronger in the light of an allegation made by the P.A.V.N. High Command that not 89 but — in fact — the whole TERM continues to operate in the Republic of Vietnam incorporated into MAAG Mission under an assumed name of the Logistics Section of MAAG. In this connection the Polish Delegation holds the view that this fact amounts to a violation of Articles 16 and 25 of the Geneva Agreement.

With regard to the above sub-paragraph the Indian and Canadian Delegations consider that as this matter is still under consideration and no decision has been taken, any conclusions are not justified.

50.   A reference was made in paragraph 48 of the Tenth Interim Report to the activities of MAAG. During the period under report, the Government of the Republic of Vietnam informed the Commission that it had made aproaches to the Government of the United States of America with a view to bringing the strength of United States military instructors of MAAG from the figure as it then stood, 342, to 685. The Party further pointed out that this increase in strength would still be well below the combined strength of 888 MAAG and French instructors present in Vietnam at the time of the Armistice. The Commission considered this matter and, Polish Delegation dissenting, informed the Government of the Republic of Vietnam that the Commission had noted the contents of the Party's letter pertaining to the subject and that the Commission understood that additional United States military instructors will not be introduced except in conformity with the procedure stipulated in Article 16(f) and (g) of the Geneva Agreement.

A communication was received from General Vo Nguyen Giap, Commander-in-Chief of the P.A.V.N. High Command, emphasizing the seriousness of the position and also alleging that the Republic of Vietnam had "requested the Commission to let the United States of America introduce United States armaments and military personnel into South Vietnam to replace the French Expeditionary Corps which had invaded Vietnam." The Commission informed General Giap that the Republic of Vietnam had made no such request.

Several communications were received from the Democratic Republic of Vietnam on this subject. In his communication of May 1960 General Giap alleged that the decision of the Commission in respect of MAAG was in complete contradiction with the spirit and letter of the Geneva Agreement and requested the Commission to cancel it. In June 1960 His Excellency Mr. Pham Van Dong, Prime Minister of the Democratic Republic of Vietnam, sent to the Commission a copy of his letter addressed to the Co-Chairmen of the Geneva Conference requesting them to issue instructions to the International Commission to reconsider and repeal the decision authorizing the American military personnel from entering South Vietnam in replacement of French military personnel. The Commission informed the P.A.V.N. High Command that their views had been considered and re-affirmed that the decision taken was fully within its competence. The Commission also reiterated once again that while any communication may be addressed to the Co-Chairmen by any Party, it found no provision in the Agreement for an appeal by the Parties to the Co-Chairman against its decision. The Polish Delegation dissented from sending this communication to the Party.

During the period under report, the Commission received communications from the P.A.V.N. High Command alleging increase in the activities of MAAG, and in November 1960 the Commission requested the Government of the Republic of Vietnam to furnish details regarding the composition and activities of the organizations called United States Air Force Detachment, the Controller Division and the Direct Aid Division, which were all stated by the Republic of Vietnam to be sections of MAAG. The reply of the Party has been received and is under consideration. Further, as mentioned in paragraph 49 above, the Party has been asked to intimate the distribution of the number of officers and enlisted men within MAAG.

During the period under report, the Commission considered the question of war materials imported by MAAG between June 1956 and April 1960 such as heavy artillery equipment, modern radar equipment, aircraft and other kinds of armaments, and requested the Government of the Republic of Vietnam to offer clarification as to whether this equipment has been brough in legally or otherwise. Its reply is awaited. In reply to an earlier query concerning the importation of war material in the name of MAAG, the Government of the Republic of Vietnam informed the Commission that all war materials though imported in the name of MAAG and which were subject to Proforma "B" forwarded to the International Commission, were actually destined for the Army of the Republic of Vietnam. This letter is under consideration.

The MAAG Mission, whose activites have never been subjected to the Commission's control despite the Commission's efforts, should have been withdrawn from this country along with the French Expeditionary Corps.

In the opinion of the Polish Delegation the Commission's decision allowing the Party to double the strength of the personnel of

MAAG is contradictory with the letter and spirit of the Geneva Agreement and particularly with its Article 16 and paragraph 4 of the Final Declaration. For these reasons the Polish Delegation voted against this decision.

In this light the request of the South Vietnamese authorities to increase the personnel of MAAG cannot be construed otherwise than as an attempt at taking advantage of the Commission's authority in order to attain certain definite targets of internal policy which have nothing to do either with the Geneva Agreement or with the tasks entrusted under this Agreement to the Commission.

The Indian and Canadian Delegations point out that the question of the numbers of MAAG military personnel, the composition and activities of certain organizations within MAAG, as outlined above, are still under consideration by the Commission and no decision has been taken. Therefore the views expressed by the Polish Delegation are not justified.

52. Reference paragraph 51 of the Tenth Interim Report, six cases out of the 86 cases mentioned in that Report wherein aircraft either arrived in the Republic of Vietnam without prior notification or in respect of which manifests or other documents were not produced, have been referred to the Party and included in the figure of 225 mentioned in the sub-paragraph below. There has been no progress in the remaining 80 cases.

In November 1960, the Commission requested the Government of the Republic of Vietnam to explain why a procedural contravention of Article 17(e) and Protocol 23 should not be recorded in regard to 225 foreign military aircraft which landed at the airfield of Tan Son Nhut in Saigon during the period from 1st January, 1956, to 31st March, 1959, without prior notification and for which no documents were produced when requested by the Team. The reply from the Party has been received in December 1960 and is under consideration.

59. During the period under report, the Commission's Fixed Teams Haiphong, Vinh and Dong Hoi reported the presence in their Zones of Action of naval craft flying the flag of North Vietnam manned by crews in naval uniform and in some cases described as being new in appearance. The Commission also received a complaint from the Government of the Republic of Vietnam alleging acquisition and operation of naval vessels by the P.A.V.N. On con-

sidering this matter the Commission found that it has no records of war material in possession of the Party at the time of the cease-fire, and no records of any import of naval craft by the P.A.V.N. since the time of the cease-fire. The Commission, therefore, asked the P.A.V.N. High Command to offer their comments in this respect. The Party's reply is awaited.

60. During the period under report the Commission considered the matter of transfer of three mine-sweepers to the Navy of the Republic of Vietnam by the United States Navy effected during 1960 and controlled and reported by the Commission's Fixed Team. The Commission has decided that its Secretariat check and report whether credit existed in favor of the Party for these minesweepers. The matter is being pursued by the Commission.

61. During the period under report the Commission received complaints from the Government of the Republic of Vietnam accusing the Government of the Democratic Republic of Vietnam of open and direct aggression in Kontum and Pleiku provinces during October 1960 from North Vietnam through the territory of Laos. The Commission received three communications from the Government of the Republic of Vietnam in this regard, two in November 1960 and one in December 1960. The Commission considered this matter twice, once in December 1960 and again in January 1961. The Commission at the latter meeting decided to forward these allegations made by the Government of the Republic of Vietnam to the Government of the Democratic Republic of Vietnam for their comments, with the Polish Delegation not participating in the vote. The reply from the Party is awaited.

The Polish Delegation did not participate in the voting since, in its view, the South Vietnamese complaint did not constitute a *prima facie* case. The Polish Delegation considered that this complaint could not be entertained by the Commission as it is entirely groundless.

The Indian and Canadian Delegations believe it is the responsibility of the Commission to investigate if necessary all allegations covered by the Geneva Agreement made by either Party, including those of aggression, without attempting to prejudge the merits of the case. As this complaint is still under investigation the Indian and Canadian Delegations are of the view that to pronounce an advance judgment on it is inappropriate.

62. During the period under review the Commission has received and considered complaints from the P.A.V.N. High Command alleging that the Government of the Republic of Vietnam was using Road No. 9 for transit of arms and equipment to Laos . . .

63. The Commission considered an allegation by the Republic of Vietnam about the transit of military personnel and war material through Hanoi to Laos. The Commission decided to forward the relevant extracts from the allegations to the P.A.V.N. High Command for their comments...

64. During the latter part of the period under review, complaints were received from the P.A.V.N. High Command alleging, among other things, that the Government of the Republic of Vietnam was mobilizing additional forces, including artillery, and that their troops have been concentrated in the area South of the Demilitarized Zone and had been placed in a state of emergency, and that these actions and the introduction of large quantities of war material into south Vietnam amounting to large scale militarization of the country in violation of Articles 17 and 19 of the Geneva Agreement as well as paragraphs 4 and 5 of the Final Declaration and Protocol 23 were jeopardizing peace in Indo-China, allegedly preparing for a war of aggression against the D.R.V.N. The subject matter of these complaints has been sent to the Government of the Republic of Vietnam for their comments.

During the same period, the Commission received communications from the Government of the Republic of Vietnam concerning the activities of the P.A.V.N. which, they alleged, were endangering peace in Indo-China, in that, they have increased their war potential in violation of Articles 16, 17 and 18 by the introduction of an enormous quantity of equipment and the calling up of their reserves. They further alleged that the P.A.V.N. have effected large concentration of Armed Forces immediately to the North of the Demilitarized Zone and have also developed the Con Co Island (Ile de Tigre) which lies immediately north of the seaward extension of the Demilitarized Zone, into a new military base, including building of barracks, with a view to aggression and that, therefore, the P.A.V.N. were preparing military action against South Vietnam. The Commission forwarded these communications to the P.A.V.N. High Command for their comments...

65. During the latter part of the period covered by the Report communications were received from the P.A.V.N. High Command alleging introduction into South Vietnam of considerable quantities of war material from the Federation of Malaya in violation of Article 17 of the Geneva Agreement. A communication was received from the Government of the Republic of Vietnam stating that they were receiving certain consignments of arms and vehicles from the Federation of Malaya for use by the security forces. They further stated that they would notify the arrivals of this equipment as required under the Geneva Agreement. The Commission has communicated the allegations of the P.A.V.N. High Command to the Government of the Republic of Vietnam for their comments as early as possible...

During the same period, the Commission received from the Government of the Republic of Vietnam six complaints alleging violations of Article 17 by the P.A.V.N. and from the P.A.V.N. High Command against the Republic of Vietnam 122 and 132 complaints alleging violation of Articles 16 and 17 respectively.

SPECIAL REPORT TO THE CO-CHAIRMEN OF THE GENEVA CONFERENCE ON INDOCHINA - June 2, 1962 (Cmnd. 1755 - June, 1962)

4. Since the presentation of the 11th Interim Report, the situation in Vietnam has show signs of rapid deterioration. The Commission is obliged to make this Special Report to the Co-Chairmen with regard to the serious allegations of aggression and subversion on the part of the Democratic Republic of Vietnam against the Republic of V etnam and the serious charges of violation of Articles 16, 17 and 19 of the Geneva Agreement by the Republic of Vietnam, in receiving military aid from the United States of America.

The Polish Delegation dissents from the views expressed in this Special Report. The Statement of the Polish Delegation if forwarded herewith.

5. Reference is invited to paragraph 24 of the 10th Interim Report and paragraph 32 of the 11th Interim Report, in which mention was made of the concern which the Republic of Viet-Nam has been expressing over the problem of subversion in South Viet-Nam.

atmosphere, a communication was received on 9th September, 1961, from the Liaison Mission of the Republic of Vietnam, alleging the the PAVN forces had launched another action in the Kontum region on 1st September, 1961. The letter containing these allegations was forwarded to the Liaison Mission of the PAVN High Command for its comments. In its reply under its letter No. 492/CT/I/B dated 11th December, 1961, the Mission stated that "the PAVN High Command will resolutely reject all decisions taken by the International Commission relating to the so-called 'subversive activities' in South Vietnam, a question which has no relevance to the Geneva Agreement". It further informed the Commission that "henceforth the Mission would find itself contrained to resolutely reject all possible requests for comments of this kind".

6. The Commission also received several complaints from the High Command of the People's Army of Vietnam (PAVN) making serious allegations with regard to the increased introduction of U.S. military personnel into South Vietnam, along with substantial quantities of war material, in contravention of Articles 16 and 17. All these allegations were forwarded to the South Vietnamese Mission for comments. The Party in most cases denied these allegations. But the Commission was not in a positttion to make a precise assessment as to the correctness or otherwise of these allegations, as the Commission's Teams at most points of entry have not been able to carry out effective inspections and controls. However, the South Vietnamese Mission did state in July, 1961, that whatever American aid its Government was receiving was meant to fight Communist subversion in South Vietnam, and in support of this contention it had also referred to the text of the communiqué published after the visit of the U.S. Vice-President Johnson to Saigon, in May, 1961.

7. While the Commission continued to function in this difficult

9.   The Legal Committee has made a careful examination of the
various allegations and the evidence produced to support them, in
the form of documents and other material evidence, and has made
the following report, with the Polish Member dissenting:

"We have studied the Agreement on the Cessation of Hostilities in Vietnam, the South Vietnamese Mission's letter No.
4660/PDVN/CT/TD/2 dated the 24th October, 1961, and
No. 5078/PDVN/CT/TD/2 dated the 16th November, 1961,
and related references from the Commission together with the
evidentiary material made available by the South Vietnamese
Mission in connection therewith, and reached the following conclusions:

(1)   The Agreement on the Cessation of Hostilities in Vietnam
proceeds on the principle of the complete cessation of all
hostilities in Vietnam, respect by either Party of the Zone
assigned to the other, and the inescapable responsibility of
the Parties for the fulfilment of the obligations resulting
therefrom.

Article 10 of the Agreement states expressly the obligation of the two Parties to order and *enforce* the *complete*
cessation of all hostilities in Vietnam.

Article 19 of the Agreement casts the obligation on the
two Parties to ensure that the Zones assigned to them are
not used for the resumption of hostilities or to further
an aggressive policy.

Article 24 of the Agreement proceeds on the principle of
the inviolability of the Demilitarized Zone and the territories
assigned to the two Parties and states expressly that the
armed forces of each Party shall respect the territory under
the military control of the other Party and shall commit
no act and undertake no operation against the other Party.

Article 27 of the Agreement affirms expressly the responsibility of the Commanders of the Forces of the two
Parties of ensuring full compliance with all the provisions
of the Agreemnt by *all elements* and military personnel
under their Command.

It follows that the using of one Zone for the organisation
or the carrying out of any hostile activities in the other

Zone, violations by members of the Armed Forces of one Party of the territory of the other Party, or the commission by any element under the control of one Party of any act directed against the other Party, would be contrary to the fundamental provisions of the Agreement which enjoin mutual respect for the territories assigned to the two Parties.

(2) Having examined the complaints and the supporting material sent by the South Vietnamese Mission, the Committee has come to the conclusion that in specific instances there is evidence to show that armed and unarmed personnel, arms, munitions and other supplies have been sent from the Zone in the North to the Zone in the South with the object of supporting, organising and carrying out hostile activities, including armed attacks, directed against the Armed Forces and the Administraton of the Zone in the South. These acts are in violation of Articles 10, 19, 24 and 27 of the Agreement on the Cessation of Hostilities in Vietnam.

(3) In examining the complaints and the supporting material, in particular documentary material sent by the South Vietnamese Mission, the Committee has come to the further conclusion that there is evidence to show that the PAVN has allowed the Zone in the North to be used for inciting, encouraging and supporting hostile activities in the Zone in the South, aimed at the overthrow of the Administration in the South. The use of the Zone in the North for such activities is in violation of Articles 19, 24 and 27 of the Agreement on the Cessation of Hostilities in Vietnam.

(4) The Committee considers that further investigation is necessary to reach a final conclusion as to whether the kidnapping and murder of Colonel Nam, late Chief of the South Vietnamese Mission, was a part of the activities referred to in sub-paragraphs (2) and (3) above and the prohibited under Articles 19, 24 and 27 of the Agreement. The South Vietnamese Mission has furnished *prima facio* evidence to warrant such a full investigation of the case by the Commission.

2. We shall submit in due course a full report setting out in detail the complaints made by the South Vietnamese Mission, the evidence forwarded in relation to these complaints, and our specific observations thereon."

10. The Commission accepts the conclusions reached by the Legal Committee that there is sufficient evidence to show beyond reasonable doubt that the PAVN has violated Articles 10, 19, 24 and 27 in specific instances. The Polish Delegation dissents from these conclusions. On the basis of the fuller report, that is being prepared by the Legal Committee covering all the allegations and incidents, the Commission will take action as appropriate in each individual case.

11. Concurrently with the developments referred to in paragraphs 7 and 8 above, and subsequently, the Commission received communications from the PAVN High Command and its Liaison Mission alleging direct military intervention in South Vietnam by the Government of the United States of America, and ever-increasing import of war material and introduction of military personnel in violation of the Geneva Agreement. The allegations, amongst others, were:

(a) the conclusion of a bilateral military Agreement between President Ngo Dinh Diem and United States Ambassador Nolting;

(b) the gradual introduction of about 5,000 United States military personnel into South Vietnam, "which will soon be increased to 8,000";

(c) the arrival of 4 aircraft carriers—*Core, Breton, Princeton* and *Croaton*—on different occasions, bringing in helicopters, other aircraft, military equipment and military personnel:

(d) the introduction by the United States of America of approximately four companies of helicopters, many jet fighters, fighters/fighter bombers and transport planes, along with military vehicles and other stores;

(e) the visits of a large number of high United States military experts and dignitaries to Saigon for inspection and guidance, particularly those of General Maxwell Taylor, Admiral H. Felt and General Lemnitzer;

(f) the establishment of a United States Military Assistance Command, with a four-star General, Paul D. Harkins, as its Chief.

12. Since December 1961 the Commission's Teams in South Vietnam have been persistently denied the right to control and inspect, which are part of their mandatory tasks. Thus, these Teams, though they were able to observe the steady and continuous arrival of war material, including aircraft carriers with helicopters on board. were unable, in view of the denial of controls, to determine precisely the quantum and nature of war material unloaded and introduced into South Vietnam.

13. On the other hand, the Commission received a communication from Liaison Mission of the Republic of Vietnam dated 9th December, 1961, stating that: "In the face of the aggression, directed by the so-called 'Democratic Republic of Vietnam' against the Republic of Vietnam, in flagrant violation of the Geneva Agreement, the Government of the Republic of Vietnam has requested the Government of the United States of America to intensify the aid in personnel and material which the latter was already granting to Vienam. The right of 'self-defence' being a legitimate and inherent attribute of sovereignty, the Government of the Republic of Vietnam found itself constrained to exercise this right and request for increased aid, since North Vietnam continues to violate the Geneva Agreement and to do injury to life and property of the free people of Vietnam.

"These measures can end as soon as the North Vietnam authorities will have ceased the acts of aggression and will have begun to respect the Geneva Agreement."

14. The Commission considered this communication from the Government of the Republic of Vietnam and drew the attention of the South Vietnamese Mission to the provisions of Articles 16 and 17 of the Geneva Agreement and the procedures laid down thereunder by the International Commission for the import of war material and the introduction of military personnel, and to the obligations resulting therefrom. The Commission also informed the Mission that its complaints regarding allegations of subversion and aggression by the North were under active examination of the Commission separately.

15. In the light of the stand of the Commission as stated in paragraph 14 above, the numerous allegations received from the

PAVN High Command have been receiving the attention of the Commission with a view to the strict implementation of Articles 16 and 17 of the Agreement and the procedures laid down thereunder.

16. A summary of the allegations made by the PAVN High Command, from December, 1961, up to 5th May, 1962, would place the number of military personnel and the quantum of important war materials introduced into South Vietnam at approximately 5,000 personnel ("which are likely to increase to 8,000 shortly"), 157 helicopters, 10 reconnaissance aircraft, 34 jet aircraft, 34 fighters/fighter bombers, 21 transport aircraft, 35 unspecified aircraft, 40 armoured and 20 scout cars, "numerous" armoured boats and amphibious craft, 3,000 tons and 1,350 cases of war material, and 7 warships (exclusive of 5 destroyers of the United States Seventh Fleet alleged to have come for training). Most of the letters containing the allegations, referred to in this paragraph and paragraph 11 above, were sent to the Liaison Mission of the Republic of Vietnam for its early comments: but no satisfactory replies have been received. Also, in some cases the Southern Party has been asked to state reasons, if any, why violations of Article 17 (e) relating to prior notification, as well as violations of Articles 16 and 17 governing the introduction of military personnel and war material themselves, should not be recorded against it.

17. As the Commission has been denied mandatory controls, as pointed out earlier in paragraph 12 above, it has not been able to make a precise assessment of the number of military personnel and the quantum of war material brought in. However, from 3rd December, 1961, up to 5th May, 1962, the Commission's Teams have controlled the entry of 72 military personnel, and observed but not controlled 173 military personnel, 62 helicopters, 6 reconnaissance aircraft, 5 jet aircraft, 57 fighters/fighter bombers, 25 transport aircraft, 26 unspecified types of aircraft, 102 jeeps, 8 tractors, 8 105-mm. howitzers, 3 armoured carriers (tracked), 29 armoured fighting vehicle trailers, 404 other trailers, and radar equipment and crates, 5 warships, 9 LSTs (including 4 visiting LSTs), 3 LCTs, 5 visiting aircraft carriers and spares of various kinds. In respect of some of the instances of import of war materials between 3rd December, 1961, and 16th January, 1962, violations under Article 17 (e) as well as violation of Article 25, have been recorded against the Republic of Viet-

nam for its failure to notify arrivals and imports as required by the Geneva Agreement, and for not affording all possible assistance to the Commission's Teams in the performance of their tasks.

18. In regard to claims for credits made by the Southern Party in justification of certain imports, the Commission wishes to point out that in so far as major items of war material are concerned, except in a limited number of cases, there is no established credit in favour of the Republic of Vietnam. On the other hand, for some of these items, there is already a debit against it. In this context, it must be borne in mind that, even where credit exists, according to Article 17 (*b*) of the Agreement, the Party can only import war material "piece-for-piece of the same type and with similar characteristics." However, controls not having been permitted, the Commission is not in a position to satisfy itself whether this essential requirement has in fact been fulfilled even in cases where credit exists.

20. Taking all the facts into consideration, and basing itself on its own observations and authorised statements made in the United States of America and the Republic of Vietnam, the Commission concludes that the Republic of Vietnam has violated Articles 16 and 17 of the Geneva Agreement in receiving the increased military aid from the United States of America in the absence of any established credit in its favour. The Commission is also of the view that, though there may not be any formal military alliance between the Governments of the United States of America and the Republic of Vietnam, the establishment of a U. S. Military Assistance Command in South Vietnam, as well as the introduition of a large number of U.S. military personnel beyond the stated strength of the MAAG (Military Assistance Advisory Group), amounts to a factual military alliance, which is prohibited under Article 19 of the Geneva Agreement.

21. The Commission would also like to bring to the notice of the Co-Chairmen a recent and deliberate tendency on the part of both the Parties to deny and refuse controls to the Commission's Teams, thereby completely immobilising their activities and hindering the Commission in the proper discharge of its obligations to supervise the implementation of Articles 16 and 17 of the Geneva Agreement. During the last few months, there has been a near-complete

breakdown so far as this important function of the Commission is concerned. The Commission considered the situation and addressed detailed communications to the two Parties recommending the resumption of normal controls immediately. (Copies of the letters sent to the two Parties are attached as Annexure I to this Report.) The Commission, however, regrets to inform the Co-Chairmen that there has been no improvement in this regard.

22. The International Commission wishes to draw the serious and earnest attention of the Co-Chairmen to the gravity of the situation that has developed in Vietnam in the last few months. Fundamental provisions of the Geneva Agreement have been violated by both Parties, resulting in ever-increasing tension and threat of resumption of open hostilities. In this situation, the role of the Commission for the maintenance of peace in Vietnam is being greatly hampered because of denial of co-operation by both the Parties.

SELECTED BIBLIOGRAPHY

Bator, Victor, *Vietnam: A Diplomatic Tragedy*. Dobbs Ferry, New York, Oceana Publications, 1965.

Browne, Malcom W., *The New Face of War*. Bobbs-Merrill, New York, 1965.

Burchett, Wilfred ,*Vietnam: Inside Story of the Guerrilla War*, New York, International Publishers, 1965.

Burchett, Wilfred, *Vietnam North*. New York, International Publishers, 1966.

Cady, John F., *The Roots of French Imperialism in Eastern Asia*, Cornell University Press, 1954.

Clark, Bronson P. et al., *Peace in Vietnam*. New York, Hill and Wang, 1966.

Considine, Bob, *It's All News To Me*. New York, Meredith Press, 1967.

Eden, Anthony, *Full Circle*. Boston, Houghton Mifflin, 1960.

Eden, Anthony, *Toward Peace in Indochina*. Boston, Houghton Mifflin Company, 1966.

Eisenhower, General Dwight D., *Mandate For Change*. New York, Doubleday & Company, 1963.

Evans, Rowland and Novak, Robert, *Lyndon B. Johnson: The Exercise Of Power*. New York, The New American Library, 1966.

Fall, Bernard B., *Street Without Joy*, Harrisburg, The Stackpole Company, 1964.

Fall, Bernard B., *The Two Vietnams*. New York, Praeger, 1965.

Fall, Bernard B., *The Vietminh Regime*. New York, Institute of Pacific Relations, 1956.

Fulbright, Senator J. William, *The Arrogance of Power*. New York, Vintage House, 1967.

Fulbright, Senator J. William, *The Vietnam Hearings*. New York, Random House, 1966.

Gettlemen, Marvin E., *Vietnam: History, Documents and Opinions On A Major World Crisis*. New York, Fawcett World Library, 1965.

Halberstam, David, *The Making Of A Quagmire*. New York, Random House, 1965.

Hammer, Ellen J., *The Struggle For Indochina*. Stanford, Stanford University Press, 1954.

Hanh, Thich Nhat, *Vietnam: Lotus In A Sea Of Fire*. New York, New York. Hill and Wang, 1967.

Herman, Edward S. and Du Boff, Richard B., *America's Vietnam Policy*. Washington, D.C., Public Affairs Press, 1966.

Hickey, Gerald C., *Village In Vietnam*. New Haven, Random House, 1965.

Hilsman, Roger, *To Move A Nation*. New York, New York, Doubleday & Company, 1967.

Honey, P. J., *North Vietnam Today*. New York, Praeger, 1962.

Kahin, George McT., *Governments and Politics of Southeast Asia*. Ithaca, Cornell University Press, 1964.

Kahin, George McTurnan and Lewis, John W., *The United States in Vietnam*. New York, Dial Press, 1967.

Lacouture, Jean, *Vietnam Between Two Truces*. New York, Random House, 1966.

Lancaster, Donald, *The Emancipation of French Indochina*. London and New York, Oxford University Press, 1961.

Lucas, Jim G., *Dateline: Vietnam*. New York, New York, E. W. Scripps Co., 1966.

Lynd, Staughton and Hayden, Thomas, *The Other Side*. New York, The New American Library, 1966.

Mecklin, John, *Mission in Torment*. New York, Doubleday, 1965.

Murti, B. S. N., *Vietnam Divided*. New York, Asia Publishing House, 1964.

Osborne, Milton E., *Strategic Hamlets in South Vietnam*. Ithaca, New York, Cornell University, 1965.

Pickerell, James H., *Vietnam in the Mud*. Indianapolis, Indiana. The Bobbs-Merrill Company, 1966.

Pike, Douglas, *Viet Cong*. Cambridge, The M.I.T. Press, 1966.

Raskin, Marcus G and Fall, Bernard B., *The Vietnam Reader*. New York, Random House, 1965.

Ridgway, Mathew B., *Soldier*. New York, Harper & Bros. 1956.

Roberts, Charles, *L. B. J. Inner Circle*. New York, Delacrete Press, 1965.

Schlesinger, Arthur M., Jr., *A Thousand Days*. Boston, Houghton Mifflin, 1965.

Schlesinger, Arthur M., Jr., *The Bitter Heritage*. Boston, Houghton Mifflin, 1967.

Schurman, F., Scott, P., and Zelnik, R., *The Politics of Escalation in Vietnam*. Greenwich, Connecticut, Fawcett Publications, 1966.

Scigliano, Robert, *South Vietnam: Nation Under Stress*. Boston, Houghton Mifflin Company, 1963.

Shaplen, Robert, *The Lost Revolution*. New York, Harper and Row, 1966.

Sorensen, Theodore C., *Kennedy*. New York, Harper & Row, 1965.

Trager, Frank N. *Why Vietnam?* New York, Frederick A. Praeger, 1966.

Warbey, William, *Vietnam: The Truth*. London, Merlin Press, 1965.

Warner, Denis, *The Last Confucian*. London, Penguin Books, 1964.

Weinstein, Franklin B., *Vietnam's Unheld Elections*. Ithaca, New York, Cornell University, 1966.

Roy, Jules, *The Battle of Dienbienphu*. New York, Harper & Row, 1965.

White, Theodore H., *The Making Of The President 1964*. New York, Signet Press, 1965.

Zinn, Howard, *Vietnam: The Logic of Withdrawal*. Boston, Beacon Press, 1967.

INDEX

Acheson, Dean: 67, 69
Adams, Brock: 304
Addabbo, Joseph: 304
Adelphi University: 336
Adran, Bishop of: 39
Adriatic: 58
Advisers: 205
Afghanistan: 26
Africa, North: 76
Agency for International Development: 226, 275, 346, 350, 353
Aggression, Communist: 95, 191, 205, 210, 284, 382
"Aggression from the North," State Dept. paper: 155, 204, 205, 209, 243, 276, 282, 293, 295; see also White Paper, 1965
Agreement, Cessation of Hostilities in Vietnam; cease-fire provision: 127
Agriculture; Under Chinese in Vietnam: 33
Agroville; fortified village: 217
Aiken, George: 24, 306, 315, 316
Akron University: 254
Alamogordo, New Mexico: 57
Alexander of Rhodes; Inspired Catholic missionaries: 38
Algeria: 383
Alperovitz, Gar: 57
Alsop, Joseph: 182
Alsop, Stewart: 347
American Civil Liberties Union: 343
American Friends Committee: 341
American Influence; resentment: 88
American Legion; Illinois First Department resolution against sending GIs to Indochina: 105
Americanization of the War: 357
Anderson, Clinton P.: 92
Anderson, William: 322
Annam: 39, 42, 43, 72, 73, 38
Anphu: 351
Appeasement; Policy against appeasing Soviet Union: 58
Apple, R. W., Jr.: 360, 361, 364
Area: North Vietnam: 30
Argenlieu, Thierry d' (Admiral): 73, 76
Armed attack; under SEATO: 130
Ashley, Thomas: 304
Asia: 273, 291, 342
Assassinations: 184
Associated Press; commodity import program: 354-355
Associated States; see Indochina
Atlantic Charter: 47
Atomic bomb; Changed Truman's policies: 57
Australia: 14, 22, 23, 26, 97, 101, 129, 367

Baldwin, Hanson W.: 274, 275, 276
  Dulles over optimistic, 94
Bao Dai: 6, 60, 135, 138, 139, 151
  abdicates, 52
  appointed Diem, 116
  appointed Supreme Advisor by Viet Minh, 52
  arrangements re gambling and prostitution, 147
  asked to intervene with Diem, 150
  Diem moves against, 152
  Ho Chi Minh more popular, 158
  loses election, 164
  opposes partition, 111
  peace proposals, 114, 115
  power derived from French, 146
  proclaims independent Vietnam, 52
  recalled General Hinh, 148
  recognized by France, 61
  regime recognized by US and GB, 77
  turns over legal powers to Ho Chi Minh, 73
  would lose election, 114
Barnet, Richard J.: 339
Bartlett, Sen. E. L. (Bob): 306
Batista Y Zaldivar: 199
Bay of Pigs: 27, 199, 200
Bay of Tonkin: see Tonkin, Gulf of
Belgium: 4, 60
Berlin: 84
Berlin airlift: 60
Berlin blockade: 65

Bidault: 88, 98, 99, 106, 107
  confers with Eden and Dulles, 107, 108
  opposed independence for Indochina, 76
  wanted Indochina included in agenda, 84
Bigart, Homer: 222
Bingham, Jonathan: 22, 304, 322, 324
Binh Xuyen: 147, 151, 153, 171, 181
Black, Eugene: 282
Black market: 355, 376
Blatnik, John: 304, 322
Boggs, J. Caleb: 24, 262
Boland, Edward P.: 305
Bollaert, Emile: 76
Bombing: 373
Bombing in South Vietnam: 377
Bombing of North Vietnam: 377
Bonnet, Henri: 87
Brademas, John: 304, 322
Brazil: 26
Brelis, Dean: 12
Bribery: 369
Bridges, Styles: 106
Brink, Francis G. (Brigadier General): 89
Brooklyn College: 336
Brown, George E., Jr. (D-Calif.): 21, 22, 287, 304, 324
Browne, Malcolm: 18, 221, 224
  "advisers" fighting, 214
  civil war in South Vietnam, 12
  credibility gap, 197, 222, 223
  immolation picture, 225
  Pleiku incident small, 20, 268
Buchwald, Art: 257
Buddhists: 225, 259, 260
Bulgaria: 59, 307
Bundy, William P.: 263, 268, 368
Burdick, Quentin: 306
Bunker, Ellsworth: 363
Bureau of the Budget: 333
Burma: 26, 93
Burton, Philip: 21, 22, 287, 324
Buttinger, J.: 36
Byrne, James, 304, 322
Byrnes, James F.: 58

Cadbury, Dr. Henry J.: 337
Cairo agreement: 60
Cairo Conference: 47
Cameron, Ronald B.: 304, 322
Cambodia: 4, 5, 6, 30, 43, 71, 76, 92, 106, 109, 144, 244, 370
  cease fire for, 113
  cessation of hostilities in, 121, 125
  charges against U.S. in V.N., 233
  covered by SEATO protocol, 130, 190
  disproves "domino theory," 375
  France calls for its neutrality, 235, 256
  French announcement on future status, 78
  French conquest of, 38
  Geneva Accords, 118
  Independence, 83
  invited to Dalat meeting, 54
  lack of independence deplored, 99
  occupied by Vietnamese, 35
  Pigneau de Behaine in, 39
  to remain independent, 117
  treaty with France, 41
  U.S. aid to, 140
Canada: 123, 279
  member International Control Commission, 13, 119
  member, U.N. Temporary Commission on Korea, 61, 62
  signs North Atlantic Treaty, 60
Cao Dai: 147
Carney, Robert B. (Admiral): 86
Casablanca Conference: 46
Castain, Sam: 139, 221
Catholics: 40, 259
Catholic intellectuals: 381
Catholic missionaries: 38
Catroux, Georges (General): 45

Cease-fire: 170, 172, 378
Celler, Emanuel: 322
Censorship: 359, 360
Central Intelligence Agency: 27, 200, 208
Ceylon: 101, 279
Champs: 34, 35
Chiang Kai-shek: 48, 51, 66, 68
  chances of winning hopeless, 59
  "China Lobby," 70
  encourages resistance movement, 49
  friend of Syngman Rhee, 68
  takes over Kuomintang Party, 44
  troubles with Mao Tse Tang, 53
  with Roosevelt at Ciaro Conference, 47
Childs, Marquis: 112
China: 30, 47, 56, 370
  attempt to assimilate Vietnamese, 32
  attempts to sinicize Vietnamese, 33
  conquest in Vietnam, 43
  conquest of Vietnam, 32, 33
  driven out of Vietnam, 31
  French and British in, 41
  Great Britain asserts privileges in, 40
  Han dynesty, 32
  influence on Vietnam, 32
  Japan's attempts to conquer, 45, 49
  repression of Vietnamese, 33
  rule of Vietnam overthrown, 34
  rule of Vietnam thrown off, 33
  split between Kuomintang–2nd Communist Parties, 44
  tribute exacted from Vietnamese, 34
China, Communist: see China, Mainland
China Lobby: 67, 70
China, Mainland: 66, 69, 70, 81, 116, 188, 264, 279, 317, 335
  affected by war, 24, 375
  aid to Indochina, 83
  charged with supplying arms to North Vietnam, 143
  Geneva Accords, violations of, 233
  Geneva, at, 5, 113
  Geneva Declaration, insisted on U.S. signing, 117, 127
  Ho, aid to, 182
  Ho, did not back, 203
  Ho, ships arms to, 77
  Ho's appeal on elections supported, 162, 163
  Ho's appeal to, 167, 183
  Ho's regime, recognizes, 77
  in danger, 67
  no evidence of participation in Vietnam according to Eisenhower, 85
  note from non-aligned countries, 279
  objected to not holding election, 159
  price for acceptance of partition of Indochina, 110
  strategy with respect to, 108
  threat to Formosa, 69
  time to consolidate in 1954, 136
  to occupy northern Korea, 60
  U Thant proposed meeting with, 278
  viewed by Dulles as running war, 82
  warning not given to, 96
  would sit on sidelines, 106
China, Nationalist: 68, 69
  American equipment shipped to Viet Minh from, 51
  announces loss of Manchuria, 60
  enters northern Vietnam, 52
  favored "united action," 88
  fled to Formosa, 60
  forces enter Vietnam, 51
  in U.N., 65
  Kuomintang split with Moscow, 44
  member, U.N. Temporary Commission on Korea, 61, 63
  no invitation to Geneva, 98
  sponsors common front, 50
  surrendered Peiping, 60
  troops leave northern Vietnam, 53
China, Red: see China, Mainland
China Sea, South: 30, 31, 34, 236
Chinese Association: 218
Chinese Communists: 218
  in Malaya, 218
China Theater: 51.

Chou En Lai: 126
  forced Ho Chi Minh to compromise, 135, 137
  meets with Mendes-France, 117
  suggests reconvening Geneva Conference, 163
Church, Sen. Frank: 273, 306, 361
Churchill, Sir Winston: 47, 57, 107, 108, 110, 136, 209
  agrees to seven point peace proposal, 117
  British being used to deceive Congress, 108
  Iron Curtain speech, 58
  support of French recolonialization, 48
  "united action," on, 86
City College of New York: 336
Civil war in South Vietnam: 180, 188, 204, 224, 243, 283, 347, 372
  Browne, according to, 12
  Eisenhower, according to, 113
  Kennedy, according to, 11
  Lacouture, according to, 188
  Lawyer's brief, according to, 338
  medieval Vietnam, in, 35, 36
  Osborne, according to, 219
  people started fighting back in South Vietnam, 179
  Schlesinger, according to, 205
  The Australian, according to, 26
  Young, Senator Stephen, according to, 11
Clark, Joseph S.: 289, 290, 306, 321, 326, 361
Clergy: French, struggle with Portugese clergy, 38
Cochinchina: 39, 41, 43, 72, 73, 79
  invited to Dalat meeting, 54
  recognized by France, 54
Cohelan, Jeffery: 304, 322, 323
Cohen, Benjamin V.: 336
Columbia Broadcasting System: 378
Columbia University: 336, 341
Collins, J. Lawton (General): 8, 143, 144, 148, 150, 151, 191
Colonialization; of Vietnam by Vietnamese: 31, 34
Comintern: 44
Command, South China, U.S.: 51
Commercial import program: 353
Committee for European Economic Cooperation: 60
Communists: 70, 175, 277, 289; see also China, Mainland
Communist Party Congress: 186
Concentration Camps: 172, 174, 212, 221
Congress, United States: 28, 243
  Truman Doctrine announced to, 58
  Truman message to implement Marshall plan, 60
  see also specific chapters on
"Congress, The Sapless Branch": 326
Congo: 199, 200
Connally, Tom: 68
Considine, Bob: 278
Constellation: 237
Constituent Assembly: 358, 360, 364
Constitution of United States: 134, 373
Conyers, John J. (D-Mich.): 21, 22, 287, 324
Coplon, Judith: 71
Cooper, John Sherman: 247, 361
"CORE," U.S.S.: 197
Corman, James: 304, 322
Cornell University: 336
Corruption: 172, 208, 209, 212, 372, 374
Corson, William (Lt. Col.): 351
Cost of War: 373
Council of Foreign Ministers: 58
Credibility gap:
  Browne on, 197, 222, 223
  Kennedy, John F., on, 80, 90, 327, 330
  managed views, 220, 224
  McNamara's reports, 228, 229
  Schlesinger on, 222
  whitepaper of 1961, 212
Crimea Agreement: 57
Cromley, Ray: 346
Cronkite, Walter: 9, 226
Cuba: 199, 247, 384
Cyprus: 279
Czechoslovakia: 22, 60

Dahlberg, Dr. Edwin T.: 337
Dalat: 54, 73
Danang: 369
Daniels, Dominick: 322

Dawson, William: 322
Dayan, Moishe (General): 349
Declaration of Honolulu: 358
Declaration of Independence: issued by Viet Minh, 52
Declaration of Former Resistance Fighters: 175, 177, 179, 186, 188, 201, 208, 212
Decoux, Jean (Admiral): 45
De Gaulle, Charles: 46, 274, 296
  calls for ending foreign intervention in South Vietnam, 233
  regime recognized, 48
  should neutralize Indochina, 263
  urges return to Geneva Accords, 256
De Lattre, de Tassigny (General): 89, 91
Denmark: 25, 60
Denton, Winfield: 304
Demilitarized Zone: 170
Desertions: 79, 81, 374
Devillers, Philippe: 185, 186
Diem: see Ngho Dinh Diem
Dien Bien Phu: 5, 6, 54, 74, 75, 78, 80, 84, 86, 99, 109, 110, 135
  fall of, 112
  U.S. air strike requested for, 107
  U.S. airlift of French troops to, 106
Diggs, Charles, Jr.: 22, 322
Dinh, Tran Van: 357, 358
Dirksen, Everett: 92
Dissent:
  by Congress, 19, 22, 241, 250, 285, 292, 302, 326
  by the public, 233, 344
Dominican Republic: 4, 288
Domino theory: 115, 206, 230, 375
  explained by Eisenhower, 93
  modified by Dulles, 116
Dong: see Pham Van Dong
Dong Hoi: 329
Dong Minh Hoi: Kuomintang sponsored party, 72
Douglas, William O.: 139
Dow, John G.: 21, 287, 304, 322
Draftees: 318, 320
Drummond, Roscoe: 363, 364
Dulles, John Foster: 14, 79, 86, 88, 90, 96, 105, 110, 128, 159
  agrees to seven point peace proposal, 117
  analysis of 1954 situation, 82
  at Berlin meeting, 84
  attempts to create "united front," 81
  backs Diem's stand not to hold elections, 162, 165
  Berlin meeting, report on, 84
  bows to Congress, 93
  circumvented Geneva restrictions on rearming South Vietnam, 190
  concept of how SEATO would work, 129
  conditions for dispatch of naval vessels, 109
  confers with Eden and Bidault, 107, 108
  Congressional leaders, 1954 meeting with, 87
  continued support for Diem, 149
  decision to replace Diem, 151
  describes Navarre Plan, 78, 85
  did not want NATO type treaty for Southeast Asia, 130
  Eden "repudiates" agreement, 101-102
  Geneva Accords, changes election terms of, 160
  Geneva Conference, leaves, 115, 126
  Geneva Conference, proposal for joint declaration in advance of, 108
  Geneva Conference, strategy for, 87
  Geneva Declaration, refuses to sign, 127
  Geneva, leaves, 126
  Geneva, prospects at, 106
  message from Navarre for air strike, 107
  "Mission for Peace through Strength," 93
  modifies "domino theory," 115, 116
  need for Indochina independence, 94
  picked Diem, 139
  propose S.E. defense organization, 97
  proposes restricted meeting on Far East, 84
  report to Eisenhower on Eden meeting, 98, 100
  tries to restrict SEATO to Communist aggression, 130, 204
  under SEATO, Congress would have to approve U.S. participation, 129
  U.S. would not let self be nibbled to death, 106

Dulles, John Foster (continued)
  views on Indochina, 83
Duncan, Donald: 302
Duong Van (Big) Minh (General): 257
Dutch: 56
  granted independence to Indonesia, 59
  resistance to French East India Company, 39
Dyal, Ken: 304, 322

Economic assistance: 353
Ecuador: 25
Eden, Sir Anthony: 99, 109, 136
  agrees to seven point peace proposal, 117
  British could hold Malaya if Indochina fell, 97
  conference with Dulles and Bidault, 107
  confers with Dulles and Bidault, 108
  continued hostilities will not help France, 126
  insists countries invited not be named before SEATO Conference, 98
  message to Churchill re air strike, 107
  talks with Dulles, 96
  tells Churchill air strikes without ground troops ineffective, 108
Edwards, Don: 21, 22, 287, 304, 322, 323
Egypt: 65
Einstein, Albert; College of Medicine: 336
Eisenhower, Dwight D.: 128, 206, 316, 371
  agrees to seven point peace proposal, 117
  approves "united front," 81
  civil war in Vietnam, 113
  comments on French proposals at Geneva, 113
  conditions on U.S. intervention in Vietnam, 85
  credibility gap, 327
  declined to send troops to Indochina, 5
  Dulles on Berlin meeting, report to from, 84
  Dulles report on Eden meeting, 98
  Dulles reports to, 99, 100
  Dulles's misunderstanding with Eden, 102
  explains domino theory, 93
  French reaction to Korean armistice, 77
  Independence for Indochina, 93
  letter to Diem, 141, 142
  limited commitment, 207
  meeting with Churchill and Eden, 117
  message to Churchill on "united action," 86
  no evidence of "Red Chinese" participation in Vietnam, 85
  no intervention without allies, 109
  no national pledge, 10
  no war without congressional action, 85
  objections to French plan, 114
  O.K.'d Diem, 139
  partion, on, 113
  pledge to go to Korea, 24, 106
  proffer of aid to Diem, 7, 9, 211, 215
  promised to support Gen. Collins re Diem, 151
  promises on mechanics to Vietnam, 81
  receives Navarre request for air strikes, 109
  Southeast Asia pact possible without Great Britain, 136
  support for mutual security program for France in Indochina, 90
  supported intervention, 115
  team of experts to study Vietnam terrain, 86
  Vietnam elections, 114
  would refrain from disturbing Geneva Accords, 6, 15, 125, 126
Elections:
  Diem's "rigged" elections, 164
  fradulent 1967 elections, 359, 365
  term perverted, 374
  Viet Minh proposals, 116
  why reunification elections were not held, 158, 168, 182, 201, 371, 372
Elementary and Secondary Education Act: 334
Ellender, Allen J.: 247
Ely, Paul (General): 86, 150
England: see Great Britain
El Salvador:
  member, U.N. Temporary Commission on Korea, 61, 63
Escalation: 17, 21, 189, 197, 204, 211, 229 235, 262, 283
Esthonia: 22

Ethiopia: 279
Eufaula Dam: 253
Europe: 57, 60
Evans, Rowland: 269, 292, 298, 307, 310, 332, 342
Exploitation; of Indochina by France: 42

Falk, Richard A.: 339
Fall, Bernard: 54, 73, 77, 152, 182, 216, 222
Fanfani, Amintore: 296, 297
Far East: 45, 84
Farbstein, Leonard: 22, 304, 322
Farming, tenant: 42
Federal Bureau of Investigation: 343
Feiffer, Jules: 336
Fellon, George H.: 322
Fellowship of Reconciliation: 341
Felt, Harry D. (Admiral): 223, 225
Fino, Paul A.: 323
Flanders, Ralph E.: 102
Foisie, Jack: 12
Fontainebleau: 54, 73, 76
Ford, Gerald R.: 235, 255
Former Resistance Fighters: see Resistance Fighters
Formosa: 60, 65, 68, 70, 88, 101, 130
    under domino theory, 93
Fortified hamlet: 217, 218
France: 56, 72, 82, 83, 94, 95, 99, 101, 109, 110, 122,
    136, 138, 144, 146, 155, 158, 181, 185, 193, 194,
    201, 202, 210, 274, 278, 279, 370, 371, 385
    abstains in U.N., 307
    agreement for MAAG, 190
    aid to U.S. in Vietnam, 367
    announcement on future status of Indochina, 78
    assistance from United States, 54, 69, 93, 139, 141
    attempt to wipe out Vietnamese history, 42
    at Berlin meeting, 84
    calls for neutrality of Indochina, 235
    captures Saigon, 40
    colonial agrarian policies, 42
    colonial ruler, 4, 41, 42
    completes conquest of Indochina, 34, 38, 41
    continues colonial policies, 73
    controls Mekong Delta, 41
    disrupts village life, 42
    exploitation of Indochina, 42
    forces begin fighting Republican Government forces, 53
    Ho appealed to, to uphold Geneva Accords, 162
    Ho Chi Minh asks independence from, 76
    if, stopped fighting, 102
    Indochina war, 75, 80
    installs puppet government, 74
    legal status in Vietnam, 71
    lip service to self-determination, 78
    member, U.N. Temporary Commision on Korea,
        61, 62, 63
    mutual security programs for proposed, 90
    no aid to U.S., 25
    objected to failure to hold reunification elections, 158
    peace feelers from Ho, 77
    peace proposals, 114
    position deteriorates, 112
    proposal at Geneva, 113
    reaction to Korean armistice, 77
    reasons for French-Indochina war, 55
    recognized Vietnam, 61
    recognizes Republic of Cochinchina, 54
    refugees, 173
    rejects social and economic reforms, 42
    represented at Geneva, 5
    signatory of Geneva cease fire, 117
    signed Southeast Asia Treaty, 14
    signs agreement with Ho Chi Minh, 54
    signs North Atlantic Treaty, 60
    signs SEATO treaty, 128
    soldiers attacked by Japanese, 46
    to accelerate independence as condition to interven-
        tion, 87
    treaty with Cambodia, 41
    troop strength in Indochina, 80
    troops arrive in South Vietnam, 54
    troops in China, 41
    under Geneva cease fire, 189
    unwilling to grant Indochina independence, 92

France (continued):
    urged Diem to consult with Ho, 161
    Vichy government agreement with Japan, 45
    wanted end to fighting, 170
    weapons seized by Vietcong, 18, 52
    why, signed Geneva cease fire, 119
    withdrawal from Algeria, 383
    would not join "united action," 94
Frankel, Max: 364
Fraser, Rep. Donald: 304, 322
Fraser, Robert: 22
Freedom on religion: 379
Freedom of press: 368, 374, 379
Freedom of speech: 368, 374, 379
French: see France
French East India Company: 39
French Expeditionary Corps: 143
French Popular Front: 44
French Socialist Party: 52
French Union: 54, 60, 76, 94, 111, 144
Fried, John H.E.: 339
Friedel, Samuel: 304, 322
Fritchey, Clayton: 11, 12, 216
Fuchs, Klaus; found guilty of espionage: 71
Fulbright, Sen. William: 321, 361
    agrees to Sen. Nelson's interpretation of Tonkin Gulf
        resolution, 249, 280
    hearings, 307, 310
    justifies U.S. action at Gulf of Tonkin, 245
    no increase in aid from Allies, 25
    opposes resumption of bombing, 306
    power given President by Tonkin Gulf resolution, 247
    regret role in adoption of Tonkin Gulf resolution, 250
    Vietnam not vital to U.S. security, 317
    votes to repeal Gulf of Tonkin resolution, 310, 326
Fulton, Richard: 304, 322
Furfey, Paul Hanly (Monsignor): 338

Galbraith, John K.: 341, 344
Gallagher, Philip E. (Major General): 51
Gallup Poll: 264
Gannett, Frank E.: 103
Garmatz, Joseph: 322
Gavin, James M. (General): 309, 311, 314, 376
General Assembly, Vietnam: 1946 election: 53
Geneva Accords: 5, 6, 118, 127
Geneva Conference: 111, 116
    preliminaries, 82, 110
George, Walter; need for Cong. action under SEATO: 132
Germany: 4, 45, 48
Ghana: 274
Gia Long, Emperor: 39
Giaimo, Robert N.; signed letter to President on bombing
    pause: 304, 322
No Nguyen Giap: 53, 158
Gilbert, Jacob: 304, 322
Gilligan, Rep. John: 304, 322
Goldberg, Arthur: 292, 297, 305, 307
Goldwater, Barry: 1, 2, 232, 251, 256, 261, 263, 342
Gonzales, Henry: 304
Goodwin, Richard: 330
Gore, Sen.: 314, 316, 317
Grabowski, Bernard: 304
Graft: 373, 374
Great Britain: 56, 57, 71, 76, 78, 95, 109, 110, 278, 371,
    372, 383
    actions in Malaya, 219
    at Berlin meeting, 84
    at Dunkirk, 45
    at Geneva, 5, 113
    colonial policies, 42
    colonial ruler, 4
    eight point directive for Geneva Conference, 108
    favored partition, 112
    grants independence to India, 59
    helps French troops get to southern Vietnam, 54
    Ho appeals to, on elections, 167
    intervention but to include, 87
    jails Ho Chi Minh, 44
    need for Congressional action under SEATO, 129
    no aid to U.S. in Vietnam, 25
    not needed as U.S. ally, 136

Great Britain (continued):
  objected to postponement of reunification election's, 159
  policy toward India, 76
  protest to, by I.C.C., 196
  received letter from non-aligned countries, 279
  received Soviet note on reconvening Geneva conference, 163
  recognized de Gaulle regime, 48
  recognized Vietnam under Bao Dai, 73, 77
  signed SEATO treaty, 14
  signs North Atlantic Treaty, 60
  signs SEATO treaty, 128
  to occupy Vietnam South of 17th parallel, 48
  troops in China, 41
  turns down U.S. proposal, 109
  U.S. aid, 371
  urged Diem to hold reunification election consultations, 161
  wanted Diem replaced, 162
Great Society: 330, 334, 350
Greece: 25, 59, 92, 143
Greeley, Dana McLean: 337
Green, Edith: 21, 22, 287
Greene, Wallace M., Jr. (General): 345
Grider, George W.: 304
Griffiths, Martha: 304, 322
Grose, Peter: 260
Gruening, Ernest: 307, 361
  amendment against sending draftees to Vietnam involuntarily unless Congress acted, 318
  calls for U.N. cease fire, 233
  calls requested Vietnam appropriation "a blank check," 290
  comments on repression of Buddhists, 226
  conversation with President Johnson on draftee amendment, 319
  defends televised hearings, 313
  draftee amendment, 319
  March 10, 1964 that urges U.S. withdraw, 230
  notes Johns Hopkins contained "pre-condition," 283
  paired against supplemental military authorization bill, 21
  questions increased aid requested by McNamara, 229
  resistance to war, 363
  speaks repeatedly against Vietnam war, 231
  Tonkin Gulf incident result of U.S. escalation, 248
  urges bombing pause, 306
  urges "hawks" not be followed, 274
  voted against Vietnam appropriation, 21
  votes against Tonkin Gulf resolution, 19, 250
  votes against Vietnam appropriation, 291
Guatemala: 25
Gubicher, Valentin: 71
Guinea: 279
Gulf of Tonkin: see Tonkin, Gulf of
"Gunboat diplomacy": 4

Hagan, Harlan: 304
Haiphong: 111, 120, 298
Hainah: 70
Haiti: 4
Halberstam, David: 17, 215, 223, 224
Han dynesty: 32
Hanna, Richard: 322
Hanoi: 11, 53, 54, 155, 300, 373
  "aggression from the North," 180, 201, 202, 260
  and dissent, 342, 343
  as one of three capitals, 43
  attacked formation of NLF, 186
  bombing of, 297, 298
  four points, 299
  Hanoi's aggression after Pleiku, 266, 268
  held by French, 111
  Ho established Provisional Government at, 52
  Kosygin in, 264, 265, 271
  not same as Vietcong, 273, 283, 293, 358
  peace feeler from, 296
  reveals secret note on bombing pause, 294, 295
  U.S. insistence on unconditional surrender, 375
  under Geneva cease fire, 120
Hansen, Julia Butler: 322
Harkins, Paul (General): 221, 222, 225

Harriman, Averell, 224, 300
Hartke, Sen. Vance: 306, 307, 314
Harvard Institute of Politics: 57
Harvard, University of: 59
Harwood, Richard: 351
Hassler, Alfred: 338
Hathaway, William: 304, 322
Hawaii: 22, 275, 276
Hawkins, Augustus: 304, 322
Hechler, Ken: 304, 322
Helstoski, Henry: 22, 322
Herz, John H.: 339
Heschel, Abraham J. Rabbi: 338
Hessian: 383
Hickenlooper, Bourke B.: 102
Hickey, Gerald: 180, 181, 184
Hicks, Floyd: 304, 322
Hilsman, Roger: 217, 270, 271, 328
Hiroshima: 57
Hitler, Adolf: 18, 48
Ho Chi Minh: 5, 50, 61, 65, 69, 82, 115, 123, 137, 139, 153, 154, 156, 158, 163, 166, 168, 170, 171, 172, 173, 181, 188, 201, 202, 205, 211, 264, 269, 370, 372
  abandons Vietnam People's Liberation Comm., 52
  aid from Soviet Union and Mainland China, 182
  anxious to send envoy to Rangoon, 263
  appeals to big powers, 201
  begins to lose control, 53
  campaigns in South, 159
  capitalizes on no self-determination, 78
  complains against Law 10/59, 174
  consolidates Viet Minh hold, 53
  continues to hope for Geneva elections, 162
  controls General Assembly, 53
  desertions to, 81
  difficulties in "communizing" North Vietnam, 182
  Fontainebleau Conference, at, 76
  forms Indochinese Communist Party, 44
  four peace points, 297
  great popularity, 116
  in Paris, 54
  jailed by British, 45
  jailed by Nationalist Chinese, 50
  liquidates other parties, 53
  ministerial post in Provisional Revolutionary Government, 50
  opposes partition, 111
  peace feeler, 256, 296
  peace feelers, 77
  placed in charge of Viet Minh, 50
  proposes opening borders, 184
  regime recognized by Mainland China and Soviet Union, 77
  reorganize Party, 75
  seizes French and Japanese weapons, 52
  signed agreement with France, 72, 73
  signs agreement with Sainteny, 54
  statement that reunification would have to wait, 183
  takes no direct action, 185
  tones down Communist doctrines, 77
  troop strength, 80
  unable to obtain international support for elections, 164
  why accepted Geneva decision, 135
  would win election, 114
Hoa Hao: 147, 148, 150, 151
Hoffman, Isidor B.: 337
Hoffman, Stanley: 339
Hofstra College: 336
Holifield, Chet: 304, 322
Holland, Elmer: 304
Honduras: 25
Honey, P. J.: 174
Hong Kong: 44, 88
Honolulu Conference: 309, 310, 350
Honolulu, Declaration of: 309
Hornig, Donald R.: 344
Howard, James: 322
Hue: 34, 39, 41, 43, 52, 111, 138, 225, 369
Hughes, H. Stuart: 336
Humphrey, Hubert: 103
Hungary: 22, 136

Huot, J. Oliva: 322

Iceland: 60
ICP: see Indochinese Communist Party
Impounded funds: 333
Independence of Indochina: see Indochinese Independence
India: 26, 98, 101, 123, 159, 162, 167, 265, 274
    abstained from voting on Korean Resolution, 65
    British colonial policies in, 42
    forbids U.S. to overfly, 106
    granted independence by Great Britain, 59
    Great Britain policy toward, 76
    influence on Vietnam, 32
    member, International Control Commission, 13, 119
    member, U.N. Temporary Commission on Korea, 61, 63
    statement of protest, 269
Indochinese Communist Party:
    attends 1941 Congress, 50
    dissolved, 53
    dominates Vietnam People's Liberation Committee, 52
    formed, 44
    went underground, 49
Indochinese Federation: 54
Indochinese Independence: 83, 84, 92, 93
    condition of intervention, 87
    Eisenhower and Dulles see need for, 94
    John F. Kennedy on, 92
Indonesia: 101, 375
    granted independence by Dutch, 59
    under domino theory, 93
Inefficiency of South Vietnam Government: 374
Inflation: 373
Inouye, Daniel K.; open ended war: 24, 262
Intellectuals: 42
International Communism: 199, 205, 210, 375
International Control Commission: 143, 297
    Diem inspires demonstrations against, 161
    Ho protests to, 185
    investigates arms dumps in South Vietnam, 156
    lack of cooperation with, 163, 174
    membership, 119
    North Vietnam sending arms and men to South Vietnam, 276
    notification to, 120
    restrictions on investigating power, 192
    tasks of, 119, 169
    U.S. arms to Vietnam, 13, 191, 197, 211, 276
Iran: 26
Iraq: 279
Ireland: 25
Iron Curtain speech: 58
Israel: 25
Italy: 4, 60

Jackson, Henry: 92
Jacobs, Andrew, Jr.: 305
Japan: 4, 26, 31, 98, 102, 370, 385
    agreement with Vichy Government, 45
    attack on French, 46
    demands control of Chinese border, 45
    occupation of Korea, 60
    surrender, 48
    under domino theory, 93
    War with China, 49
    weapons seized by Ho Chi Minh, 52
Javits, Jacob: 361
Jefferson-Jackson Day: 318
Joelson, Charles: 322
Johns Hopkins speech: 7, 269, 281, 282
Johnson, Charles: 322
Johnson, Harold: 304
Johnson, Lyndon B.: 142, 198, 230, 235, 239, 240, 243, 256, 261, 263, 272, 278, 279, 280, 289, 299, 303, 312, 316, 325, 350, 352, 364, 368, 372, 375
    agrees to limited escalation, 270
    agrees to Rusk refusal to appear before Foreign Relations Committee, 309
    appoints election observer teams, 363
    announces beginning of bombing North Vietnam, 276
    attacks sending GI's to Indochina, 105
    Christmas, 1965, peace efforts, 298
    credibility gap, 328, 330

Johnson, Lyndon, B. (continued):
    did not recommend sending troops to Vietnam, 209
    Diem's promises to, of reforms, 211
    election of, 1
    escalate to 125,000 troops, 291
    guns and butter, 332, 333
    Johns Hopkins speech, 281, 282
    letter to, from Fanfani, 296
    letter to U Thant, 292
    nationwide broadcast on Tonkin Gulf incident, 236
    1961 trip to reassure Diem, 208
    "plays down" escalation, 342, 343
    reasons for being in Vietnam, 6, 13
    relies on SEATO, 133
    reply to Congressional requests for bombing pause, 305
    reply to nonaligned nations, 283
    requested special Vietnam appropriation, 21
    requests additional funds, 284
    requests Tonkin Gulf resolution, 237
    seeks Congressional approval through appropriation act, 286, 288, 290
    signs Tonkin Gulf resolution, 251
    State of Union message, 1966, 303
    sworn in, 4, 257
    Tonkin Gulf resolution drafted before incident, 250
    would not send U.S. troops to Asia, 252, 253, 254, 255
Johnson, U. Alexis: 165, 166
Joint Chiefs of Staff: 205
Judd, Walter H.; 1954 Report on Associated States: 91
Just, Ward: 348, 350, 357

Karnow, Stanley: 270
Karth, Joseph E.: 305
Kastenmeier, Robert: 22
Kay, Keith: 365
Kee, James: 304, 322
Kefauver, Estes: 102
Kennan, George F.: 65, 310
    genesis of policy of containment, 58
Kennedy, John F.: 202, 203, 228-229, 316, 352
    admin. views on Vietnam, 201
    against ground war in Indochina, 199
    Bay of Pigs, 27
    calls it civil war in South Vietnam, 11
    Conference on Laos, 200
    credibility gap, 89-90, 221, 327-328
    debate with Nixon, 198
    futility of sending American men into internecine struggle, 92
    incident with Halberstam, 223
    increased MAAG and arms in South Vietnam, 196-197
    increases troops, 210
    issues 1961 White paper, 204
    letter to Diem, 211, 213, 214
    military situation when sworn in, 195
    need for independence in Indochina, 92
    1951 Report in Indochina, 91
    no amt. American assistance can win in Vietnam, 91
    no pledge, 7, 9, 10
    staff divided, 224
    support for Vietnam Government, 91
    television interview, 226-227
    tripled advisers—changed their duties, 205
    U.S. aid, 372
    why escalated, 206-208
Kennedy, Joseph P.: Diem's friend, 139
Kennedy, Robert F.: 290, 361
Kenya: 279
Khanh Hau: 181, 184
King, Cecil: 322
King, Martin Luther: 338
Knight, John S.: 231
Knowland, William: 92, 106
    assurances against U.S. ground forces to Indochina, 81
Korea: 136, 144, 191, 201, 233, 339, 22, 66, 77, 79, 84, 88, 102-103, 111
    as viewed by Truman, 69-71
    different than Vietnam, 24-25, 82-83
    establishment of United Nations Temporary Commision, 61
    impasse at Geneva, 112
    occupation by Japan, 60
    outbreak of hostilities, 74

Korea (continued):
  post-war status, 47
  Soviets would not agree to international super. of elections, 116
  U.N. General Assembly for unification of, 61
  under Cairo agreement to be occupied by China and U.S., 60
Korea, North: 64-66, 68
  invaded South Korea, 61, 62
  People's Republic established, 61
  organized by Soviet Union, 61
Korea, South: 63-68, 71
  invaded by North Korea, 61, 62
  Republic of Korea declared, 61
  U.N. supervised elections, 61
Kosygin, Alexksei N.: 264-265, 271
Kraft, Joseph: 264, 273
Krebs, Paul: 304, 322
Krock, Arthur: 100
Kuomintang Party: 44
Ky: see Nguyen Cao Ky

Lacouture, Jean: 153, 185, 188
Land reform: 216, 352
Landlords, absentee: 42, 82, 222, 352, 369, 373
Laniel, Joseph: 100, 116
Lao Dong (Communist) Party: 202
Laos: 4, 6, 30, 106, 111-127
  attempt to obliterate the past, 43
  bombing trails questioned, 263
  covered under SEATO protocol, 130, 190
  de Gaulle proposal, 256
  Dulles' desire for joint statement, 108
  French announcement on future status, 78
  French claim to legal status in, 71
  French conquest of, 38, 41
  Ho Chi Minh trail, 267
  hostilities renewed, 99
  independence, 83
  independence of, condition of U.S. entry into conflict, 92
  invited to Dalat meeting, 54, 73
  loss of U.S. planes over, 235
  neutralization vs "domino theory," 230
  proposals for independent status, 76
  represented at Geneva, 5
  status when Kennedy became President, 199-200
  to remain independent, 117
  "troika" arrangement for, 207, 224
  U.S. aid to, 140
  under Tonkin Gulf resolution, 244
  visit by Mansfield, 144
Latvia: 22
Laurence, Jack: 365
Lausche, Frank J.: 102, 311
Law 10/59: 174, 177, 181, 185
Leahy, William D. (Admiral): 57
Leggett, Robert: 304, 322
Lehman, Herbert H.: 103
Library and Services Construction Act: 334
Lincoln, Abraham; against Mexican War: 313, 318
Lindsay, John V.: 287
Lippman, Walter: 232, 271, 273
Lithuania: 22
Lodge, Henry Cabot: 8, 198, 258, 259, 363
Long, Clarence D.: 304, 322
Long Island University: 336
Long, Russell B.: 313, 314
Lord, John Wesley (Bishop): 337
Love, Rodney: 304
Luxembourg: 25, 60

MacArthur, Douglas, Gen.: 1, 28, 314
McCarthy, Eugene: 306, 307
  voted to rescind Tonkin Gulf Resolution, 320, 326
McCarthy, Joseph R.: 71, 106
  speech at Wheeling, W. Virginia, 70
McCarthy, Richard D.: 304
McCarthyism: 344
McClure, Wallace: 339
McCormick, Joseph: 103
McDowell, Rep. Harris B., Jr.: 304, 322
McGarry, Mrs. Barbara D.: 334

McGovern, George:
  against bombing North Vietnam, 277
  decides not to propose amendment limiting commitment, 317
  objects to haste in appropriating funds, 317
  possibility of war with China, 313
  questions Tonkin Gulf incident, 246
  Tonkin Gulf incident may have been manufactured, 329
  urges bombing pause, 306
  urges changed Vietnam policy, 361
  urges negotiations, 274
  warns against major war in Asia, 314
McKinley, William: 384
McNamara, Robert:
  account of Pleiku incident, 266
  account of Tonkin Gulf incident, 238, 239
  adviser to Kennedy on Bay of Pigs, 27
  Browne: "he misled American public opinion," 12
  credibility gap, 328
  first inspection trip to Vietnam; backs Diem, 222
  it will be a "long war," 301
  Kennedy's confidence in, 224
  major military task could be completed by end of 1965, 223, 229
  opposed talks with Ho's emissary, 257
  optimistic statements on Vietnam, 27, 28
  persuaded Kennedy to escalate, 9
  press conference on Tonkin Gulf incident, 237, 238
  reason for bombing North Vietnam, 285
  refused to appear publicly before Foreign Relations Committee, 309
  responsibility for shortsighted military policies, 259
  reveals additional military buildup, 240, 241
  testifies before Congress on Tonkin Gulf incident, 242
  "tremendously encouraged," 229
  urges further aid, 229
  White House briefings, 280
McVicker, Roy H.: 322
MacDonald, Torbert H.: 322
Mackay, James A.: 304, 322
Mackie, John: 305, 322
Madagascar: 76
Madden, Ray J. 305
Maddox: 236, 238, 239, 246
Magnuson, Warren G.: 92
Mahon, George H.: 287
Mainland China: see China, Mainland
Makins, Sir Roger: 100, 101
Malacca, Straits of: 39
Malaya: 25, 97
  pacification, 216, 220
Mali, 307
Management of the news: 213, 220, 330 see also Credibility gap
Manchuria: 60
Manifesto of the Eighteen Notables of Saigon: 208, 212
Manila Conference: see SEATO Treaty
Mansfield, Mike:
  asked for reassessment of war, 230
  assesses 1954 situation, 80
  comments on Geneva Accords, 146
  corruption in Saigon, 148
  delegate to Manila (SEATO) Conf., 130
  endorsed Diem, 140
  friend of Diem, 139
  joins debate on South Vietnamese elections, 360
  1953 report on Indochina, 79
  no consultation, 88, 89
  only 400 North Vietnamese in South Vietnam, 20
  open ended war, 262, 302, 303
  report of 1954, 144, 145
  report of 1966, 24
  SEATO not like NATO, 133
  tells Johnson he opposes war, 292
  urges indefinite suspensions of bombings, 306
  warning on Indochina war, 80
  warns on Indochina war, 79
Mao Tse Tang: 53, 65, 66
  breaks with Comintern, 44
  defeats Chiang Kai-shek, 44
Marine Combined Action Committee: 351
Marshall, George C.: 60, 70
  announces Marshall Plan, 59

Marshall Plan:
  announced for Western Europe, 59
  implementing message to Congress, 60
Maryknoll Seminary: 139
Matsunaga, Spark M.: 322
Mayer, Arno J.: 337
Mecklin, John: 257, 259
Meeds, Lloyd: 305, 322
Mekong Delta: 11, 31, 112, 151, 181, 182, 184, 202
  under control of French, 41
Mendes-France, Pierre: 126, 143
  meets with Chou En Lai, 117
  pledges end to fighting, 116
Mendlovitz, Sol H.: 339
Metcalf, Lee: 306
Mexico: 2, 4
Michigan, State of: 340
Michigan State University: 181, 341
Michigan, University of: 280, 340
Middleton, Drew; partition of Indochina under discussion, 110
Military assistance: 353
Military Assistance Advisory Group (MAAG): 143, 190, 191, 194, 195, 197
Military Junta: 361
Miller, George P.: 305
Miller, Richard S.: 339
Milwaukee Journal: 274
Mink, Patsy: 22, 322
Minority groups; driven into mountains: 31
"Mission of Peace through Strength": 94, 96, 104
Missionaries; persecutions—increased activities: 40
Moeller, Walter H.: 322
Mohr, Charles: 12, 267, 268
Molotov, Vyacheslav Mikhailovich: 117, 126, 135, 137
  agrees to neutral election supervision, 116
Monroe Doctrine: 4
Moore, Robert L., Jr.: 234
Moorhead, William S.: 305, 322
Moral degeneration: 357
Morgan, Thomas E.: 244, 245
Morgenthau, Hans J.: 339
Morse, Sen. Wayne (D-Ore.):
  amendment repealing Tonkin Gulf resolution, 318, 319
  criticizes Johns Hopkins speech, 282
  escalation policies, 321
  Great Society cut backs, 334
  in Committee, voted against Tonkin Gulf resolution, 242, 326
  Morse version of Tonkin Gulf confirmed, 248
  new version of Gulf of Tonkin, 247
  one of two original opponents in Senate of Vietnam policies, 307
  Pentagon and White House recognize only votes, 292
  signed letter to President on bombing pause, 306
  South Vietnam beyond American defense perimeter, 230
  spoke and voted against Vietnam appropriations, 291, 292
  U.S. going to U.N., 308
  urged U.N. cease fire, 233
  urged U.S. military withdrawal, 231
  voted against supplemental military authorization bill, 21, 322
  voted against supplemental Vietnam appropriation, 21
  voted against Tonkin Gulf resolution, 19, 250
  voted to repeal Tonkin Gulf resolution, 320
Moscow: 255, 260
  and Korean war, 65, 66, 69
  influence in South Vietnam, 202
  influence on Ho Chi Minh, 201
  Yugoslavia broke with, 23
Moss, John E.: 305, 322
Murti, B. S. N.: 161, 197
Muskie, Edmund S.: 24, 262
Mussolini, Benito: death, 48

Napoleon, Bonapart: 39
Napoleon, Louis: 40
"The Nation": credibility gap, 330
National Assembly: 164
The National Com. for a SANE Nuclear Pol.: 341

The National Liberation Front for South Vietnam: 201, 279, 297, 377
  announced from South Vietnam, 187
  announced in Hanoi, 186
  Hickey's observations of rise, 181
  not considered government by U.S., 282
  not 100 percent communist, 381
  official U.S. version, 180, 212
  origins and character, 179-188
  peace negotiations with, 299-300, 375
  real adversaries, 383
  southerners in, 358
  ten point program, 187
  troop strength, desertions, 374
National United Front: 149
National Security Council: 265
Nationalist movement: 44
  of Vietnamese under Chinese, 33
  predominant factor in Communist movement in Southeast Asia, 88
NATO Council: 106
NATO Treaty: 67, 128-131, 133
  signed, 60
  type treaty compared to SEATO type, 132
Navarre, Henri (General):
  message to Dulles for air strike, 107
  Navarre Plan, 78
Nedzi, Lucian: 305, 322
Nehru, Jawaharlal: 159, 190
Nelson, Gaylord:
  contemplates amd. to Tonkin Gulf resolution, 280-281, 307
  haste in passing appropriation resolution, 289
  risking U.S. ships in Tonkin Gulf, 247
  should negotiate, 274
  urges bombing pause, 306
  voted against supplemental military authorization bill, 21
  voted against Vietnam appropriation, 21
  votes against Vietnam app., 291
Nepal: 279
Netherlands: 4, 60
Neuberger, Maurine: 306
Neutrality: 188
The "New Republic," 231, 263, 268, 276, 348
The New York Times: 88, 94, 232, 279, 288, 361
  course to be pursued by Diem, 137
  SEATO treaty only requires consultation, 129
New York State University: 336
New York University: 336
New Zealand: 14, 22-23, 95, 97, 101, 129, 367
  signs SEATO treaty, 128
  under domino theory, 93
"Newsweek" banned: 365
Ngo Dinh Cah: 153
Ngo Dinh Diem: 310, 350, 360, 371, 372, 179, 181, 185, 186, 213, 224, 264, 9, 18, 122, 143, 150, 156, 162, 166, 176, 177
  aid from U.S., 183
  alienates non-Communist groups, 167
  attacked pagodas, 226
  background, 138-139
  bribes generals, 151
  Buddhist difficulties in Hue, 225
  compared to Laos government, 207
  controlled General Assembly elections, 164
  corruption, 221
  deprived countryside of autonomy, 154
  did not carry out promised reforms, 214-220
  did not control police, 147
  disarmed plantations, 222
  Eisenhower letter to, 7, 8
  establishes police state, 153
  faced chaos, 146
  increasing favoritism and personalism, 212, 234
  invites sects to meet, 149
  Johnson calls him Winston Churchill of Asia, 209
  Kennedy letter to, 208
  letter from Eisenhower, 141-142
  letter to Kennedy, 210
  Mendes-France asks Smith to prevent, from obstructing Geneva Accords, 116
  military coup fails, 186-187

Ngo Dinh Diem (continued):
  no freedoms in South Vietnam, 160
  oppression of his people, 25, 171-174
  overthrown and killed, 10
  prisoner, 148, 170
  propaganda against Geneva Accords and ICC, 161
  received letter from Ho asking for consultation on
    reunification elections, 164
  refused Ho's offer to open border to trade, 184
  refused to hold reunification elections, 157-159,
    165, 182
  repression campaign against "communists" and former
    resistance fighters, 175, 188, 201-202
  southerners fighting southerners, 203
  speaks of reunification, 144
  takes over in South Vietnam, 135-145
  U.S. backing for not holding reunification elections,
    162-168
  U.S. cuts back aid to, 227
  U.S. installs, as Vietnamese President, 6, 138
  weapons captured from, forces, 204
  why chosen, 140
  wins rigged election against Bao Dai, 152
Ngo Dinh Nhu: 153
Ngo Dinh Nhu (Madam): 153, 259
Ngo family: 154
Nguyen Ai Quoc: see Ho Chi Minh
Nguyen, Anh: 39
Nguyen Cao Ky:
  Declaration of Honolulu, 358
  discussions with Johnson at Honolulu, 309
  elections, 359-361 (216, 357, 368)
  his hero: Adolph Hitler, 18
  peace overtures cause uneasiness, 300
  plea to Vietcong, 309
Nguyen dynasty: 43
  rule in south, 36
Nguyen Hai: 50
Nguyen Than Phuong (General): 181
Nguyen Van Hinh (General): 148
Nguyen, Khanh (General): 229, 233, 257-259, 264
Nicaragua: 4
Nigeria: 308
Nix, Robert: 322
Nixon, Richard M.: 103, 198
  approved of Diem, 140
  criticized by President Johnson for urging invasion of
    North Vietnam, 253
  "risk taker," 198
  urged sending troops to Vietnam, 5, 102
"Nixon War": 105
Nolting, Frederick: 221-222, 226
Norodom, Sihanouk; Treaty with France: 41
Nosavan, Phoumi (General): 200
North Atlantic Treaty Organization: see NATO
North Vietnamese Communist Party: 179
Norway: 25, 60
Novak, Robert: 269, 292, 298, 307, 310, 332, 342

O'Daniel, John W. (General): 90
Office of Strategic Services: 51, 54
O'Hara, Barratt: 305
O'Hara, James: 322
O'Hara, James G.: 305
Olsen, Arnold: 322
Olson, Alec G.: 305
Open letter by eighteen: 175-176, 179
open-ended: 375
Organizations, underground; formation: 44
Osborne, Milton E.: 217, 219, 220

Pakistan: 14, 25, 101, 129-131
Paris, University of: 38
Partition: 111, 115
Pastore, John O.: 361-363
Pathet Lao: 200
Patten, Edward J.: 322
Peace; 1954 desire for, in Saigon: 88
Peace and neutrality: 368
Peace feelers; from Ho Chi Minh to France: 77
Pearson, Drew: 268, 277, 308
Peasants: 42

Peking: 64-65, 69, 201, 202, 260, 273, 358
Pham Van Dong: 159, 161-162
Phan Huy Quat: 151
Philippines: 15, 25, 22, 65, 69, 71, 87, 95, 101, 109,
    129-130, 269, 367, 384
Phu Loi, Camp: 174, 176, 195
Pigneau de Behaine: 39
Plantations, rubber: 42
Pleiku: 293
  credibility gap, 328
  decision to bomb North made before incident, 270
  initial limitation of targets, 373
  less than 400 North Vietnamese in South Vietnam at
    time, 373
  Pearson account, 268
  Pleiku, to divert public attention, 269
  public reaction, 342
  Stevenson account, 267
  U.S. needed an incident, 270
Poland: 22, 57, 123, 136, 279
Polish Delegation; on ICC: 195-196
"The Politics of Escalation": 296
Polytechnic Institute of Brooklyn: 336
Pope Paul VI: 274, 296
Popular Front: 49
Population; Vietnam: 31
Population; Vietnam, North: 31
Population; Vietnam, South: 31
Portugal: 4, 60
Potsdam Agreement: 52, 72
Potsdam Conference: 48, 57
Pratt Institute: 336
Price, Melvin: 322
Profiteering: 373, 376
"The Progressive": 274
Protocol to SEATO Treaty: 190
Provisional Government of the Democratic Republic of
    Vietnam; formed: 52
Provisional Republican Government; dropped: 52
Provisional Revolutionary Government; formed: 50
Proxmire, William: 306
Public Protests: 327, 335
Puerto Rico: 384

Queens College: 336
Quinhon: 270, 271
Quint, Bert: 365

Race, John A.: 305
Radest, Howard B.: 338
Radford, Arthur B. (Admiral): 5, 107
  advocated air strikes against Viet Minh, 86
  1954—French would win, 90
  1954 meeting with Congressional leaders, 87
Rapoport, Anatol: 340
Raymond, Jack: 229
Red River Delta: 31
Redlin, Rolland: 305, 322
Reed, Thomas Brackett: 384, 385
Rees, Thomas M.: 22, 305, 322
Reforms: 373
  rejected by France, 43
Refugees: 171, 348, 350, 378
Regroupment: 170, 171
Reinhardt, G. Frederick: 152
Repression: 171, 183, 374, 379
Resistance fighters: 49, 173, 174, 176, 181, 185
Resnick, Joseph Y.: 322
Reston, James: 100, 272, 273
Reunification elections: 176, 188
Reuss, Henry S.: 305, 322
Revolts; against French: 43
Revolts; in Vietnam: 33, 34, 36
Revolts; stirred up by Indochinese Communist Party, 44
Revolution, French: 39
Revolutionary Development teams: 350, 352
Rhee, Syngman: 68, 71
  forced to flee from Seoul, 64
Rhodes, George M.: 305, 322
Rice, William G.: 340
Ridgway, Matthew B. (General): 1, 5, 28, 311, 314
  against committing land forces to Vietnam, 86
Riga, Father Peter: 337

Rivers, L. Mendel: 343
Roberts, Charles: 328, 329
Roberts, Chalmers M.: 231
Robertson, Walter S.: 126, 165, 173
Roche, Prof. John P.: 336
Rockefeller Institute: 336
Rockefeller, Nelson: 253
Roosevelt, Elliott: 46
Roosevelt, Franklin D.: 47, 48, 56, 57
    death, 48
    views on post-war colonies, 46
Rosenthal, Benjamin S.: 22, 305, 322, 323
Rostow, Walt: 199, 209, 214
Roybal, Edward R.: 22, 305, 322, 323
Rural pacification: 217-218
Rusk, Dean: 11, 279, 308
    advisor on Bay of Pigs, 27
    "Aggression from the North," 209
    announces increase in military assistance, 208
    answered U Thant peace proposal, 272
    briefings, 280
    communique with Ky, 300
    could not compete with Pentagon, 214
    credibility gap, 328
    did not reply to Fanfani peace statement, 296
    during Truman Administration, 201
    reply to Ho four points, 297
    SEATO basic to U.S. involvement, 15
    sent note to Ho on bombing pause, 294
    testified on Tonkin Gulf incident, 242
    yielded to military, 224
Russell, Richard B.: 285, 314, 317, 321, 325
Rutgers University: 336
Ryan, William Fitts: 21, 22, 287, 323, 324

Saigon: 39, 43, 111, 270, 301, 303, 328, 350, 351,
        369, 376
    conquered by Vietnamese, 35
    corruption, 352-357
    early small MAAG, 6
    local personnel appointed by, 152
    mutual hostage to Hanoi, 302
    news policies in, 12
    police force in, in 1954, 147
    taken by French, 40
    treaty of, 41
    troop increase announced from, 276
    weakness in Saigon's, 273
Sainteny, Jean: 72, 73
    impeded by U.S. in getting to Hanoi, 54
    signs agreement with Ho Chi Minh, 54
Saltonstall, Leverett: 102
San Francisco Conference: 57
Sarah Lawrence College: 336
Scheuer, James H.: 22, 305, 322
Schlesinger, Arthur M., Jr.:
    bombings increased U.S. deaths, 20-21
    credibility gap, 222
    dissenters in White House, 224
    Kennedy against escalation, 210
    Kennedy had to escalate, 206
    more attention to military side, 214
    no alternative to confining 1954 policy, 207
    Saigon censored Kennedy criticism of Diem regime,
        226
    South Vietnamese government needs support of
        people, 352
    war in South Vietnam "civil war," 205
Schomer, Howard: 338
School milk program: 334
Schurman, Franz: 296
Scigliano, Richard G.: 139, 152
Scott, Peter Dale: 296
Search and destroy: 357, 374, 378
SEATO: 115, 149, 371, 373
    allies give little support to war, 25
    area covered, 130
    as applied to Tonkin Gulf incident, 244
    cannot be implemented without Cong. approval, 132
    circumscribed for U.S., 204-205
    protocol to evade Geneva accords, 190
    referenced to by Eisenhower, 142
    type treaty comp. to NATO type, 132

SEATO (continued):
    umbrella over South Vietnam, 167
    violations by U.S. of, 15-17
    what it really means, 128-134
Secure and hold: 357
Self-determination; Ho Chi Minh capitalizes on French
        lip service to: 78
Sevareid, Eric: 256, 296
Seventeenth parallel: 120, 156
Seventh Fleet: 17
Shaplen, Robert: 202
    Diem believed division of Vietnam permanent, 144
Sheehan, Niel: 348-349, 352, 357
Shoup, David M. (General): 28, 231, 374
Sickles, Carlton: 322
Sisk, B. F.: 305
Sloan-Kettering Institute for Cancer Research: 336
Smith, Desmond: 347, 368
Smith, H. Alexander: 130, 132-133
Smith, Hedrick: 229
Smith, Walter Bedell:
    assurances not to disturb Geneva Accords, 6, 10, 15,
        125, 159, 166
    favorable military situation in Indochina, 80
    message from Eisenhower, 126
    met with Mendes France, 116
    no intervention without allies, 109
    sent to Geneva by Dulles, 117
Société des Missions Estrangères; organized in Paris: 38-40
Sorensen, Theodore C.: 199-200, 205, 208-209, 214, 224
Southeast Asia Resolution: see Tonkin Gulf resolution, 243
Southeast Asia Treaty: see SEATO
Southeast Asia Treaty Organization: see SEATO
Souvanna Phouma: 200
Soviet Union: 22, 74, 81, 97, 183, 196, 203, 278, 279
    absent from 1950 Security Council vote, 65
    aid to Indochina, 83
    aid to North Vietnam, 182
    asked for reconvening of Geneva conference, 163
    at Berlin meeting, 84
    Cambodia accepts, aid, 235
    did not war with U.S., 68
    Dulles—"calling the shots," 82
    establishes People's Republic in Korea, 61
    exploded atomic bomb, 1949, 70
    favored reunification elections, 159
    Geneva, at, 113
    Ho's appeal to on Diem's refusal to hold reunification
        election, 162
    military and political situation in Vietnam should be
        settled, 116
    organizes northern portion of Korea, 61
    possibility of major war, 136
    price for acceptance of partition of Indochina, 110
    recognized de Gaulle regime, 48
    recognized Viet Minh, 61
    recognizes Ho's regime, 77
    refused access to U.N. Commission to North Korea, 63
    represented at Geneva, 5
    seeking to dominate nations on its borders, 56-57
    situation on invasion of Korea, 66
    strategy with respect to, 108
    turned Ho down on reunification elections, 167
    vetoes in United Nations, 58
    view of U.S. involvement in Vietnam, 24
    would sit on sidelines, 106
Spain: 4, 25-26
Special Forces: 210
Spellman, Francis Cardinal: 139-140
Spheres of influence: 56
Spock, Dr. Benjamin: 336
St. Germain, Fernand: 322
St. Louis (Mo.) Post Dispatch: 233
St. Onge, William: 305
Stalin, Joseph: 48
    becomes intransigent, 56
    death of, 136
    feud with Tito, 65-66
    Potsdam meeting, at, 57
    Teheran Conference, at, 47
    seizes countries surrounding Soviet Union, 22
State, Department of: 63
    briefing paper for Formosa, 56

State Department of (continued):
 1949 White Paper, 67
 1961 White Paper, 211-212
 1965 White Paper, 204, 211
 1965 White Paper, basis for Johns Hopkins speech, 281
 1965 White Paper; Hilsman critical of, 271
 1965 White Paper; I. F. Stone critical of, 276
Stennis, Sen.: 290, 315-316
 Congress would never agree to go into Indochina
  militarily, 92
 warns on Indochina war, 79
Stettin, 58
Stevens Institute of Technology: 336
Stevenson, Adlai:
 answers Cambodia's charges, 233
 called "cynical" by St. Louis Post-Dispatch, 233
 peace feeler, 256
 report on Tonkin Gulf incident, 16, 237-238, 246
 reports to Security Council after Pleiku raid, 267
Stillwell, Joseph (General): 11
Stimson, Henry L.: 57
Stone, I. F.: 260, 276, 294
Strategic hamlet: 216-217, 219-221, 350, 378
Subversion: 180
 under SEATO treaty, 131
Sulzberger, C. L.: need of Congressional action under
  SEATO, 129
Sulzberger, Arthur Ochs: 223
Sun Yat Sen: 44
Sweeney, Robert: 322
Switzerland: 25
Symington, Stuart: 361
Syria: 61-62, 279

Ta-Quang Buu: 119
Task Force, 1961; report to Kennedy on Vietnam: 205
Taylor, Maxwell (General): 214, 329
 decision to bomb made before Pleiku, 270, 271
 disagreed with Gavin on enclave concept, 311
 military intervention would end by end of 1965, 223, 229
 mission to Vietnam, 209
 recommended escalation, 263
 recommended retaliating raids, 268
 replaced Lodge as Ambassador, 259
Tay-son rebellion: 43
Teach-ins: 280, 293, 295, 325, 327, 341
Teheran Conference: 47
Term: 193, 194
Tenzer, Rep. Herbert: 322
Thailand: 131, 360
 aid to U. S. in Vietnam, 367
 American equipment shipped to Viet Minh from, 51
 bombers moved to after Tonkin Gulf, 241
 meeting before Geneva Conference, 101
 "next Vietnam," 29
 pleas rejected for NATO type treaty, 129, 130
 Post-war status, 47
 signatory of SEATO treaty, 14
 signs SEATO treaty, 128
 U. S. troops in 17
 under domino theory, 93
 wanted NATO type treaty, 128
Thant, U: 263, 272, 279, 296
Theft; commodity import program: 354
Thich Nhat Hanh: 377, 378, 381
Thich Tri Quang: 360, 365
Thieu-Ky regime: 18
Thieu-Tri, King: 40
Thieu-Ky: 360, 361, 364
Thieu, General Nguyen Van: 357, 359
"Third alternative": 29, 375, 383
Thirty-eight parallel: 64, 65, 67
Thompson, Frank, Jr.: 305, 322
Thompson, R.G.K., (Brigadier): 217
Ticonderoga: 237, 239
Times, The (London): 180
Tito, Marshal: 23
Todd, Paul, Jr.: 305, 322
Tongking: 39, 42, 43
Tonkin, Gulf of; incident and resolution: 16, 30, 31, 134,
  228, 235, 236, 250, 251, 254, 285, 292, 303, 304,
  316, 321, 329, 372
 amendment to repeal resolution, 314, 319, 320

Tonkin, Gulf of; incident and resolution (continued):
 analysis of resolution, 243, 244
 comparison of Tonkin response to Pleiku response,
  265, 269
 debates in House of Representatives, 244, 245
 debates in Senate, 245, 250
 effect of air strikes on Saigon regime, 259
 facts questionable, 19
 Gruening, inevitable result of U. S. action, 248
 Johnson announcement of incident, 236, 237
 Johnson announcement that resolution had been
  prepared in May 1964, 250
 Johnson asks reaffirmation, 315
 McNamara description of incidents, 238, 239
 Morse version of incident, 247, 248
 Nelson proposed amendment, 247, 249
 Senator McGovern questions incident, 246
 Sen. Morse on interpretation of resolution, 291
 U. S. escalation, 241
 why Congress agreed, 325, 326
Topping; Seymour: 264, 321
Tourane: 40, 41
Tran Van Huong: 264, 364
Trieste: 58
Trinh dynasty; rule in North: 36, 43
Truman Doctrine: see Truman, Harry S.
Truman, Harry S.: 67, 332
 adopted Kennan's containment policy, 311
 announces Truman Doctrine, 58
 belief atomic bomb gave U. S. strength, 57
 changed views on Russia, 57
 changes in Roosevelt's policies, 56
 doctrine, 58-59
 message to Congress to implement Marshall Plan, 60
 orders assistance to Indochina, 64, 191
 Potsdam meeting, at, 57
 recognizes Rep. of Korea, 63
 Rusk, advisor on Korea and Vietnam, 201
 view of Korean invasion, 62, 65, 70, 71
Tu-Doc, King: 40, 41
Tunisia; statement of protest: 279
Tunney, John V.: 305
Turkey: 25, 145
 aid from the United States, 59
Turnerjoy: 239
Tuylon: 351
Twinning, Nathan F. (General); effectiveness of air strikes,
  86

Udall, Morris: 305, 322
Uganda: 279, 308
Ukranian Soviet Socialist Republic: 61, 62
UNESCO: 184
United action: 190
 French Cabinet refuses to join, 94
 Monroe Doctrine for Asia, as, 88
 policy announced by Dulles, 85-87
United Arab Republic: 279
United Front: 81
United Kingdom: see Great Britain
United National Front: 151
United Nations: 24, 233, 244, 273
 admission of Mainland China, 110
 assumed jurisdiction over Korea, 74
 had not assumed jurisdiction over Vietnam, 74
 Johnson reference to, 332
 suggestions by members of Congress, 304
 supervised Korean elections, 71
 to supervise elections, 114
 U. S. as signatory, 14
United Nations; Charter of: 99, 373
 discussed in Lawyers Brief, 338-339
 ratification by Senate, 57
 SEATO, and, 133-134
 South Korea under, 71
 Tonkin Gulf resolution, and, 242, 244
 U. S. under, 14
 violation of by U. S., 15
United Nations Commission on Korea: 61-62, 67
 certified elections in southern Korea, 63
 established by U. N., 62
United Nations forces: 66

United Nations; General Assembly:
consideration of Korean question, 62
Dulles speech before, 83
Pope Paul VI Address to, 296
recognized government of South Korea, 63
resolution for unification of Korea, 61
U. N. Security Council:
first meeting, 58
passed resolution to aid Korea, 64, 65
Pleiku incident reported to, 267
referral of disputes to, 15, 16
SEATO, and, 133-134
Tonkin Gulf incident reported to, 237, 238
U. S. actions in Korea under resolution of, 71
U. S. answer to, on Cambodia, 233
voted to consider Vietnam war, 308
U. S. Constitution: 16, 19, 244, 343
Lawyers brief, 339
United States Information Office: 197
U. S. Military Advisory Group to the Republic of Korea, 63
U. S. Military aid: 9
United States Military Aid mission: 148
U. S. News and World Report: 233
U. S. Seventh Fleet: 18
United States-Soviet Joint Commission for Korea: 60
Uong Bi: 298
Uruguay: 25

VAFA: see Vietnam-American Friendship Association
VJ Day: 72
VNQDD: see Vietnamese Nationalist Party
Van Deerlin, Lionel: 322
Versailles: 39
Vetoes; Soviet; in United Nations: 58
Vichy Government: see France
Vietcong: 11, 19, 184, 207, 215, 220, 221, 225, 234, 257,
260, 275, 293, 300, 302, 373, 376, 377, 378, 383
asked to surrender unconditionally, 283
called Viet Minh by villagers, 181
commodity import program, 353-354
indigenous to South, 347, 358
infiltration, 328
instability of Saigon government, and, 258
levy tribute, 222
live off jungle, 219
mostly southerners, 11, 205
negotiations, at, 299, 309
not same as Hanoi, 273
pacification program, 345, 351
plea to, by Ky, 309-310
Pleiku, at, 266, 271
Siagon, no peace talks with, 321-322
snipers, 235
tactics, 75
terrorist tactics, 263, 264
troop strength—desertions, 374
using captured French or U. S. weapons, 18, 204
violate Geneva Accords, 233
weapons from North Vietnam, 277

Viet Minh; Vietcong called: 55, 75, 117, 135, 146, 170,
172, 186, 190
advances by, unimportant, 80
backed by Molotov, 116
begin to lose control, 53
beginning of movement, 49, 50
built popular base, 76
charged with increasing forces, 143
China to stop aiding, 110
consolidate hold, 53
control of countryside, 182
Diem, and, 139
Diem refused to join, 138
Dien Bien Phu, at, 84
extent of control at time of Geneva, 158
families of, 164
French agreement to train, 72
gain control of Northern Vietnam, 51
General Gallagher sings over radio, 51
Geneva, at, 113
hoped to win, 112
increase mass support, 51

Viet Minh; Vietcong called (continued):
issue declaration of Independence, 52
local Vietnamese forces, 5
minority in Provisional Revolutionary Government,
50-51
Nationalist Chinese place Ho in charge, 50
1956 elections, and, 165, 166-167
no aid from French, 53
not invited to Dalat, 73
not invited to Dalat meeting, 54
oppose partition, 111
peace feelers, 77
peace proposal, 114
receives American military equipment 51
receives U. S. supplies, 54
recognized by Soviet Union, 61
regroupment, 120
resettlement in North, 155, 157
Rusk's view of, 201
signed cease fire agreement, 118-119
situation when Korea invaded, 74
training of Southerners joining them, 203
Vietcong called, 181
Vietnamese desertions to, 79
would be beaten by 1955, 90
Vietnam; American Friendship Association: 51
Viet Nam Doc Lap Dong Minh Hoi: See Viet Minh
Vietnam elections: see elections
Vietnam People's Liberation Committee; abandoned: 52
Vietnam People's Liberation Committee; formed: 52
Vietnam; Republican Government of; begins fighting
French: 53
Vietnam; Republic of; recognized by France: 54
Vietnam Revolutionary League; formation: 50
Vietnamese Communist: 264
Vietnamese National Assembly: 350
Vietnamese Nationalist Party (VNQDD): 44, 52, 53, 72
Village life; disrupted by French: 43
Vinson, Fred M. Jr.: 343
Vivian, Weston: 305, 322

Waggoner, William H.: 115-116
War of National Liberation: 383
Washington Post: 333
SEATO Treaty and war powers of Congress, 129
Washington Post and Times Herald; editorial against
comparing Korea and Indochina: 105-106
Weapons; shipped to Ho from Korea: 77
Wedemeyer, Albert C. (General): 48, 51
Weiss, Peter: 297
Weltner, Charles: 305
Western Reserve: 341
Westmoreland, William C. (General): 11, 303, 343
Wheeler, Earle G. (General): 242
White Papers: see State, Department of
White, Theodore H.: 254
White, William S.: 88, 363
Whiting, Kenneth L.; commodity import program: 354
Williams, Harrison A., Jr.: 306
Wilson, Charles: 90
Wilson, Harold: 308
Wisconsin; University of: 344
Wolff, Lester L.: 305, 322
World War II: 72
Wright, Quincy: 340

Yates, Sidney R.: 22
Yeshiva University: 336
Young, Sen. Stephen: 361
civil war in South Vietnam, 11
urges bombing pause, 306
urges negotiations, 273-274
votes to rescind Tonkin Gulf resolution, 320
Yugoslavia: 23, 279
Abstains from voting on aiding South Korea in
Security Council, 64
Yunnan: 46

Zambia: 279
Zelnick, Reginald: 296
Zinn, Howard: 380